State and Nation Making in Latin America and Spain

In 1960, Latin America and Spain had the same level of economic and social development, but, in just twenty years, Spain raced ahead. This book provides an in-depth analysis of the design and implementation of developmental state policies in both regions and examines the significant variance in success between Latin America and Spain. The second volume in a trilogy, this collection of studies on state institutions in Latin America and Spain covers the period 1930–1990 and focuses on the successes and failures of the developmental states. This book assumes a wide social science perspective on the phenomenon of the developmental state, focusing on the design, creation and management of public institutions, as well as the creation of national projects and political identities related to development strategies.

Agustin E. Ferraro has worked in diverse public policy fields for governments, NGO's and international organizations. As a Humboldt scholar 2001–2003, he did postdoctoral research at the Institute for Latin American Studies in Hamburg, and at the London School of Economics and Political Science (LSE). In 2009, he won a prestigious national award in Spain (INAP) for original research on state institutions in Latin America.

Miguel A. Centeno is Professor of Sociology and International Affairs at Princeton University. He is well known for his work on Latin America, state capacity, war, and globalization.

State and Nation Making in Latin America and Spain

The Rise and Fall of the Developmental State

Edited by

AGUSTIN E. FERRARO
University of Salamanca

MIGUEL A. CENTENO
Princeton University, New Jersey

CAMBRIDGE
UNIVERSITY PRESS

CAMBRIDGE
UNIVERSITY PRESS

University Printing House, Cambridge CB2 8BS, United Kingdom

One Liberty Plaza, 20th Floor, New York, NY 10006, USA

477 Williamstown Road, Port Melbourne, VIC 3207, Australia

314–321, 3rd Floor, Plot 3, Splendor Forum, Jasola District Centre,
New Delhi – 110025, India

79 Anson Road, #06–04/06, Singapore 079906

Cambridge University Press is part of the University of Cambridge.

It furthers the University's mission by disseminating knowledge in the pursuit of
education, learning, and research at the highest international levels of excellence.

www.cambridge.org
Information on this title: www.cambridge.org/9781107189829
DOI: 10.1017/9781316995785

First published 2019

Printed and bound in Great Britain by Clays Ltd, Elcograf S.p.A.

A catalogue record for this publication is available from the British Library.

Library of Congress Cataloging-in-Publication Data
NAMES: Centeno, Miguel Angel, 1957– editor. | Ferraro, Agustin E., editor.
TITLE: State and nation making in Latin America and Spain : the rise and fall of the
developmental state / edited by Miguel A. Centeno and Agustin E. Ferraro.
DESCRIPTION: Cambridge, United Kingdom ; New York, NY : Cambridge University
Press, [2018]
IDENTIFIERS: LCCN 2018007412 | ISBN 9781107189829
SUBJECTS: LCSH: Latin America – Economic conditions – 20th century. | Latin America –
Economic policy. | Economic development – Political aspects – Latin America. | Spain –
Economic conditions – 20th century. | Spain – Economic policy. | Economic development –
Political aspects – Spain.
CLASSIFICATION: LCC HC125 .S745 2018 | DDC 851/.1–dc23
LC record available at https://lccn.loc.gov/2018007412

ISBN 978-1-107-18982-9 Hardback

In memory of Juan J. Linz

Contents

Figures

Tables

Contributors

Jordi Catalan, Universitat de Barcelona

Eduardo Dargent, Pontificia Universidad Católica del Perú

Marshall C. Eakin, Vanderbilt University

Margarita Fajardo, Sarah Lawrence College

Tomàs Fernández-de-Sevilla, Université Libre de Bruxelles

Brodwyn Fischer, University of Chicago

Matthias vom Hau, Institut Barcelona d'Estudis Internacionals

Robert Karl, Princeton University

Alan Knight, Oxford University

Joseph Love, University of Illinois

Vivekananda Nemana, Princeton University

José Carlos Orihuela, Pontificia Universidad Católica del Perú

Yovanna Pineda, University of Central Florida

Juan José Rastrollo, Universidad de Salamanca

Patricio Silva, Leiden University

Luciana de Souza Leão, Columbia University

Preface

This book represents the next stage of a long friendship and scholarly collaboration. Published in 2013, the first volume of our project on state and nation making in Latin America and Spain examined states and nations during the long "liberal era" from 1810 to 1930. [1] The present, second volume of the collection, continues the story of state building in the Hispanic–American world through 1990, focusing on state institutions and economic and social development. We hope to spend the next five years completing the collection with a third volume on the neoliberal state, from 1990 to the present.

The fundamental inspiration for the comparison between Spain and Latin America came from one of the co-editors' teachers, Juan Linz. His commitment to scholarship and his fruitful comparative perspectives still motivate many, and we only hope that he would approve of this book.

We were very lucky to find such an outstanding group of collaborators. Anyone who has ever planned a series of conferences knows how difficult it can be to identify attendees and then count on them to produce solid scholarship and generous discussion. We received some "nos" to our initial queries, but mostly "yesses" and were delighted when practically everyone showed up at Princeton in the fall of 2015. By this time, the papers were already well developed and the meeting began to progress as much more of a bottom-up enterprise than we had hoped. The result was a much better conference than we could have imagined and much enthusiasm for a second meeting at Princeton in 2017. The contributors once again demonstrated great patience as we asked for further and further revisions and additions to the chapters and tried to find a publisher for a book that was quite long by today's standards.

It was again our extraordinary good luck to find Robert Dreesen and Robert Judkins at Cambridge University Press. Both have been wonderful partners: supportive and insightful, firm and clear about the work that had to be done. The staff at Cambridge University Press and the associated indexing and copy-

---

[1] Centeno and Ferraro, 2013.

editing teams have been outstanding and we could not have asked for more. In preparing the conferences at Princeton we had the very able and kind support of Jayne Bialkowski and Nikki Woolward. Vivekananda Nemana and David Reineke assisted with the final preparation of the manuscript.

We would like to offer special thanks for the cover image of this book to the Museu Arqueològic de l'Esquerda (Roda de Ter, Barcelona) and to the museum's Director, María Ocaña i Subirana. The image shows three workers next to textile machinery in a factory in Salou, Roda de Ter, c.1960. This and other images were collected by Director Ocaña i Subirana for a museum's exhibit, and for publication by María Ocaña i Subirana and Nuria Cabañas Anguita, *La dona i la fàbrica a Roda de Ter. De la filosa a la contínua (s. XVIII-XX)*, Roda de Ter: Ajuntament de Roda de Ter, 2006.

Our home institutions have served as wonderful and generous hosts and deserve our heartfelt thanks. Financial support for the project came from Princeton University's Program in Latin American Studies, from the Princeton Institute for International and Regional Studies, and from central University funds.

As always, our families deserve our ever-larger thanks for allowing us the luxury of spending so much time on an era so long ago and a place so far away. Deborah Kaple, Maya Centeno, and Alex Centeno amazingly keep putting up with one of the editors. The fascinating Rachel Straus, ideal intellectual companion and partner of the other editor, receives his thanks for constant support and encouragement. Sarah L. Ferraro and Ana V. Ferraro were extremely patient and understanding while having to bear long absences from their father.

PART I

INTRODUCTION

Those Were the Days: The Latin American Economic and Cultural Boom vs. the Spanish Miracle

Miguel A. Centeno, Agustin E. Ferraro, and Vivekananda Nemana

More than three decades ago, Albert Hirschman wondered why not enough attention had been paid to Latin America's post-war economic boom, certainly not while it happened.[1] Only in retrospect, from the "lost decade" of the 1980s, did the accomplishments of the developmental era become relatively clear. But even then, the comparison with East Asia that began during the 1980s diminished the region's achievements.[2] If anything, the period from 1945 to 1975 came to be seen as a lost opportunity, when Latin America supposedly took the wrong direction while East Asia cleared the path to its economic success. This perspective could not be more different than the attention paid to the "Spanish Miracle" – with its own Wikipedia entry! Spain's developmental achievements were seen as a victory for the Franco regime, whose replacement by a vigorous democracy made those achievements even better.

Much of the criticism of the Latin American cases was directed at the supposed failure of the developmental state in the continent. Developmental policies came to be seen as obstacles to the economic progress of the region, leading finally to the debt crisis of the early 1980s, and the subsequent collapse of the Latin American economic model.

In the present volume, we will examine both the achievements and failures of developmental states in Latin America and Spain. We will seek to clarify how developmental state institutions were conceived in the context of far-reaching visions for national affirmation and progress, and how they were designed and established since the early 1930s. We will analyze what the developmental states tried to do, and why they succeeded or failed at their many diverse tasks. We intend to use the contrasting views of the national cases under discussion as a source to continue our long-term investigation, begun with *Republics of the Possible*.[3] That previous volume discussed the politics and techniques of state and nation making in Latin America and Spain during the long "liberal era"

---

[1] Hirschman, 1987: 8. [2] For example, see Gereffi *et al.*, 1990. [3] Centeno and Ferraro, 2013.

from 1810 to 1930. The first volume on the liberal state, and the second or present volume on the developmental state, can be read separately without any loss of content or perspective, since they represent complete units by themselves. Nevertheless, the editors and the authors have followed some key issues, and employed some common categories of research, which we will briefly describe further below. At the conclusion of the first volume, we realized that while we could find significant variances between the countries under examination, a similar narrative could be told of the creation of a liberal order founded on domestic privilege and international dependence across the Hispanic-American world.

The Great Depression shattered that status quo. In the case of Spain, the subsequent Civil War, 1936–1939, left an economy much smaller and less vibrant than before, and a devastated society. The Spanish state after the Civil War, while not particularly strong, did enjoy a monopoly over political power, and it played a central role in defining economic policy. While Franco remained head of state until 1975, Francoism can be divided into two periods. During the first two decades of the regime, the government was dominated by Falangist and corporatist military officers and politicians, who favored an autarchic economy. Economic difficulties and the need to reach out to the rest of the world required a shift in power to a new generation of technocrats, especially after 1959. It was only in the 1960s that Spain became "different" from its own Black Legend, and began to acquire a new reputation as a dynamic society.

While Latin America largely avoided military conflicts – with the most prominent exception of the Chaco War, 1932–1935 – the collapse of commodity markets in the 1930s led to broad economic decline, and produced new social and political tensions. The post-depression era, however, also witnessed a growth in state capacity and the completion of the process of institutionalization initiated during the nineteenth century. Interestingly, Latin America began its return to prosperity much earlier than Spain. It was only in the late 1950s that the Spanish economy returned to 1929 levels, after spending almost three decades poorer than most of the continent across the Atlantic. It was not until the 1960s that Spain's national income per capita began to outpace the major Latin American economies.

Even during that decade, the cultural dynamism of Latin America could contrast with the conservative repression of Franco's Spain. The 1960s represented the zenith of the Latin American (almost uniformly white) middle class. Internationally, the continent was in the midst of economic expansion. Just as importantly, the region was a cultural and intellectual powerhouse as represented by the literary "boom" and the high regard in which Latin American artists, thinkers, and lifestyles came to be held. Yet, the global centrality of Latin America was temporary. Consider that in 1968, when Mexico hosted the summer Olympics, its economy was roughly the same size as Spain's. Twenty years later, the Olympics were held in Seoul, and Mexico was poorer than both Korea and Spain. By 1992, when the Olympics were held in Spain, the gap had grown even larger. By 2014, when the Olympics returned to Latin America, Spain and Korea's per capita income was more than double that of Mexico and Brazil. While the latter two's economies had largely flatlined, Spain and Korea had grown exponentially.

Why? There is not a student of Latin America who on visiting Madrid or Seoul does not ask themself the same question. The too-often heard explanation of "Confucian" discipline as opposed to "Latin" self-indulgence does not survive the inclusion of Spain in the comparison. What was it about the developmental state in Latin America that slowed growth, beginning in the late 1960s?

THE DEVELOPMENTAL STATE CONCEPT

Before we address in detail the issue of the consistent deceleration of economic growth since the late 1960s in Latin America, and its marked contrast to increasing growth in Spain, we will introduce the general concept of a developmental state. We will also describe, in this section, the dimensions or categories of state capacity that we employ as analytical tools in the book.

According to Woo-Cumings, the developmental state is a "seamless web of political, bureaucratic, and moneyed interests that structures economic life."[4] The term was originally used to describe the Asian "Tigers" and primarily Japan, followed by Korea and Taiwan. Intended as an argument against those who attributed Northeast Asian success to following market-centered economic policies, the concept involves a national commitment to development guided by career bureaucrats controlling state finances allied with private industry. The Latin American equivalent can be seen as sharing several characteristics: investment decisions made by the state, a "developmental discourse," and the partial exclusion of the popular sector (depending on regime type). Importantly, and as we will see, significantly, it does not include in a consistent way the Weberian, professional bureaucracy common to Northeast Asian countries.

For the study of the developmental state, we employ in the present volume four categories of research, which we define as dimensions of state capacity or strength: infrastructural, territorial, economic, and symbolic. The different parts of the book, as shown in the table of contents, are organized in relation to their focus on one or more of those categories. We employed the same pattern of analysis, based on four dimensions of state strength, for the first book on state and nation making in Latin America and Spain, published by the same editors a few years ago.[5] As mentioned above, the earlier volume discussed the politics and techniques of state building during the long liberal era from 1810 to 1930. The two volumes represent complete units by themselves, but the editors and authors have followed some central issues, and applied conceptual categories that connect both projects.

---

[4] Woo-Cumings, 1999: 1.   [5] Centeno and Ferraro, 2013: 15.

Sociology and political science frequently employ the concept of state capacity and related terminology and ideas, such as strength, power, and influence. However, the notion of state capacity became a regular part of developmental literature only in the 1980s. Ideas such as strength and power are deceptively simple: the problem comes from attempting to use them in a systematic manner across a variety of cases. What is it that states do, and how can we trace the transformation of their various capacities across time in Latin America and Spain? Combining a variety of typologies, from Weber to Bourdieu and Mann, we propose four different categories or dimensions of state strength.

The first category of state capacity that we employ is based on the notion of *infrastructural* power, as originally introduced by Michael Mann.[6] According to Mann, infrastructural power refers to the capacity of the state to coordinate society by means of the diffusion of law and administration in many areas of social life, which had remained outside the scope of state concern before the vast expansion of this state capacity during the second half of the nineteenth century. Infrastructural power involves organizational and technical skills to collect and process information, build organizational structures, and maintain communication and interaction networks. Infrastructural power is a key dimension, because this is what makes modern states exceptionally strong.[7]

The expansion and diversification of bureaucratic organizations increases the penetration of the state in terms of infrastructural power. However, according to Mann, such increase of infrastructural power does not imply, as Weber mistakenly assumed, more vertical concentration of power in a central authority. Infrastructural capacity does not involve centralization of power; rather, the contrary is the case. First of all, modern state administration "almost never forms a single, bureaucratic whole."[8] The infrastructure of the modern state is formed by an array of bureaucratic organizations variously linked to power networks in civil society. Secondly, the expansion of infrastructural penetration predictably goes both ways: as a result of the embeddedness of relatively autonomous bureaucratic organizations, civil society's capacity to bring influence to bear on the state also increases. The expansion of infrastructural power occurs simultaneously with the widespread politicization of civil society.[9]

The second dimension of state strength we call *territorial power*, and it involves the classic Weberian notion of monopoly over the means of violence. Note that we explicitly do not specify the legitimate use of that violence as we wish to distinguish between a simple capacity to coerce from the much more complex notion of justifying such coercion. Mann also called this category of power *despotic*, and it represents the influence that state elites are able to exert over the population of a certain area, without having to enter into routine negotiations with other actors. The concept of despotic power captures the

[6] Mann, 1993.   [7] Mann, 1993: 60, 66.   [8] Mann, 1993: 68.   [9] Mann, 1993: 56.

conventional perception of power as the capacity to issue and impose commands. This form of state power or capacity is the simplest to wield, as it merely requires the acquisition and utilization of enough relative coercive force to impose order on a certain territory. This is the state as disciplinary institution, and it takes place on two fronts: first, in relation to other states defining sovereignty; and secondly, against internal or domestic rival claimants and subjugated groups.

Before we consider the next two dimensions of state strength, economic, and symbolic, we will briefly examine the close interconnection of the first two categories during the developmental era. In the context of national development strategies, infrastructural and territorial power were thoroughly articulated by long-term institutional projects. In contrast, during the previous period of state building, the liberal era both in Latin America and Spain, territorial power in itself was a predominant concern of state elites, and they attempted to consolidate this capacity by creating and deploying military and police forces, including custom guards, in areas close to national borders and in rural spaces – the prominent and controversial Spanish *Guardia Civil* was created for this purpose in 1844. However, during the developmental era, the states focused instead on increasing their dominion over peripheral territories by creating new bureaucratic organizations, which took the form, on the one hand, of many regional developmental agencies created in Latin America since the 1940s. As unitary states, on the other hand, Chile and Spain avoided the creation of regional developmental agencies. However, the promotion of economic development by central agencies, in both countries, was deliberately targeted on peripheral regions, as shown by the case of Catalonia, for example, where substantial projects of state-led industrialization under Francoism were located.

Developmental strategies included from the beginning plans to achieve the modernization and professionalization of public bureaucracies, that is to say, plans to increase the overall infrastructural strength of the state. Almost in every case, moreover, the professionalization of the central civil service was carried out together with the creation of semi-autonomous developmental agencies. Those semi-autonomous developmental agencies were conceived and designed as institutions of superior bureaucratic quality, compared to the rest of the public administration. The concept of "islands of development" was created by Thurber to define precisely those "nuclei of strength, especially organizational strength" that developmental agencies represented.[10] In sum, the many regional development agencies created in Latin America, or the central autonomous development agencies created by Chile and Spain, were designed with the goal of increasing infrastructural power or bureaucratic capacity and, at the same time, improving the territorial – regional – reach of the state, its territorial strength. Since infrastructural and territorial power were so closely

[10] Thurber, 1973: 45.

intertwined during the developmental era, the corresponding part of the book – chapters five to eight – examine those two dimensions of state strength in combination.

We define the third category of state capacity as *economic power*, and this involves diverse connected processes. First, economic power is about the state promoting the general prosperity of a society. Prior to the Keynesian revolution, states mostly contributed to prosperity in the course of the unification of an economic space through the creation of a national market. Of greater relevance for our cases, the states may also increase prosperity by creating the physical and legal infrastructure supporting the insertion of their domestic economy into a global system of exchange. A second aspect of economic power involves the control over and appropriation of resources through the establishment of an efficient tax system. The third and perhaps most extensive aspect of economic power, during the developmental era, concerns the formulation and implementation of long-term economic policies, particularly industrial promotion, welfare and labour services and regulations, public credit, trade strategies, and others.

The fourth dimension of state capacity is what Bourdieu calls *symbolic power* or what Weber discussed as legitimacy. As Bourdieu notes, "what appears to us today as self-evident, as beneath consciousness and choice, has quite often been the stake of struggles and instituted only as the result of dogged confrontations."[11] The study of the state's symbolic power is the history of how it attempts to construct its own sense of inevitability. Symbolic strength is the quality that should – ideally – place the authority of the state out of the bounds of contention. Regarding this symbolic dimension, Joseph Strayer assigns a central role to what he calls "loyalty" during the consolidation of state power, a "shift in the scale of loyalties" from earlier societies, and a new "priority of obligation" towards public institutions, or what he later calls a "cult of the state."[12]

During the developmental era, new and powerful narratives of the national community emerged, and redefinitions of citizens' political and ethnic identities were attempted in several national cases. States were eager, of course, to take control of national narratives, and to position public institutions and official practices as stages for the performance of citizens' political identities, in order to expand and strengthen mass loyalties. Developmental projects were heavily invested with the symbolism of national destiny, while at the same time they were often conceived and carried out by new social and political actors that demanded to enter the public scene. States and public agencies tried to appropriate the symbolic potential emerging from those social and cultural transformations, by their own self-presentation as agents of change, with more or less success in the diverse national cases.

---

[11] Bourdieu, 1994: 15.   [12] Strayer, 1973: 47.

DEVELOPMENTAL SUCCESS COMPARED

Why did some developmental states succeed, occasionally beyond all expectations, while others did not? The most popular explanations examine Latin America and Northeast Asia, arguing for instance that the geopolitical situation in Asia provided significant political will, as well as ample funding, resulting from the West's grand strategy during the Cold War. One aspect that has also drawn attention is the extent of policy continuity. For many, the consistency of the Northeast Asian model is critical. Others, however, point out that Latin America adhered for too long to the model of import-substitution industrialization (ISI). There was also a long debate about the extent to which democracies could not solve the collective action problems of rapid development, but this relationship was found to be generally weak.[13] Another interesting approach comes from Fajnzylber's critique of the "showcase modernity" in Latin America, which he argues was too focused on providing a middle-class lifestyle to urban professionals, as opposed to more effective policies of capital accumulation.[14]

The case of Spain provides a significant empirical comparison in this whole discussion. As mentioned above, the Spanish economy lagged behind several major Latin American countries at the middle of the twentieth century. The association of the developmental state with authoritarian policies was a feature of both the Latin American and Spanish cases during the 1960s, and the divergent fortunes of Spain and its former colonies were actually less predetermined than intuition suggests. In 1960, it was not obvious which country of the Iberian world would be better off by 1990. In the pages that follow, we will begin to address this question by comparing the Latin American and Spanish cases across diverse empirical measures.

ECONOMIES AND SOCIETIES

We begin with a well-known tale of economic history. In 1995, Spain's real gross domestic product (GDP) per capita was $12,860, almost $5,000 more than Argentina's and over double that of Mexico and Brazil, an apparently clear reflection of the global North–South divide.[15] But at the middle of the twentieth century, Spain's economic performance compared to that of Latin America seemed mediocre at best. Even before the Civil War ravaged its economy, Spain was far behind Argentina in terms of real GDP per capita. In 1925, Argentina's output was nearly $4,000 per capita (in 1990 dollars), compared to under $2,500 for Spain. Latin American economies would develop more rapidly for years to come. Between 1925 and 1960, real output per capita grew

---

[13] Centeno, 1994.   [14] Fajnzylber, 1990.
[15] Source for GDP data: Maddison, 1995, 2001. Real GDP figures are in 1990 GK dollars.

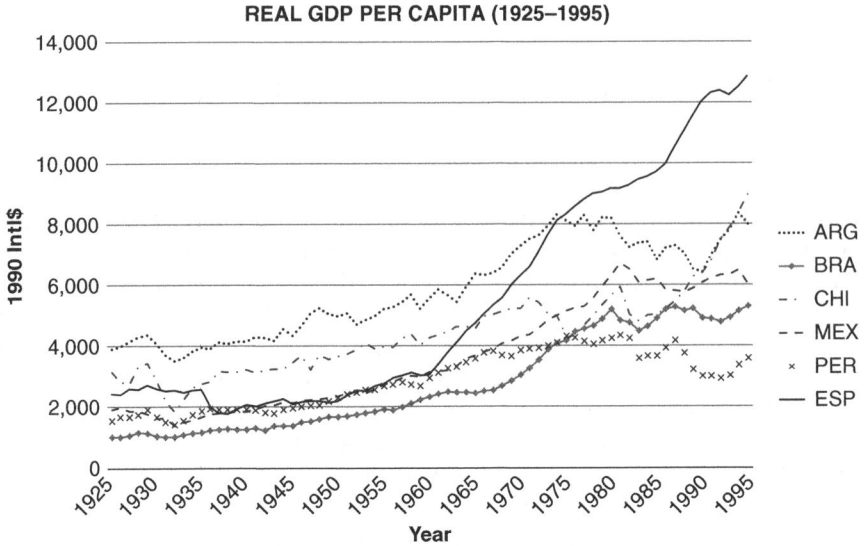

FIGURE 1.1 Real GDP per Capita, 1925–1995, for Spain and Select Latin American Countries, in 1990 Geary-Khamis (GK) dollars[16]

by 40 percent in Argentina, 65 percent in Mexico, and 133 percent in Brazil. Spain's output, meanwhile, increased just 25 percent during the same period.

It was only afterwards that the familiar North–South divide took shape. Figure 1.1 illustrates how, after decades of mediocre growth, Spain's real GDP per capita accelerated at an average rate of 9.1 percent *every year* between 1960 and 1995. By contrast, the Latin American economies – particularly Argentina's – floundered, in many cases actually losing ground.

The solid black line representing Spain sticks out on the chart. The drastic reversal of fortunes holds even when comparing Spain and Mexico to their highly developed neighbors. Despite high economic growth in Mexico between 1925 and 1960, the economy of the United States consistently remained twenty times as large. Events in the second half of the century, including industrialization, and the 1994 signing of the North American Free Trade Agreement (NAFTA), had a relatively modest impact: by the 2000s, the Mexican economy had settled at 9 percent the size of its American counterpart. As for Spain, when the Civil War ended in 1939, its economy was less than half the size of the Western European average, a ratio that only modestly improved by 1960. If Spain's growth could be explained by the post-war European boom, then we would expect this ratio to remain fairly stable. Instead, when the European Union formed in 1988, Spain's economy reached

[16] Maddison, 1995, 2001.

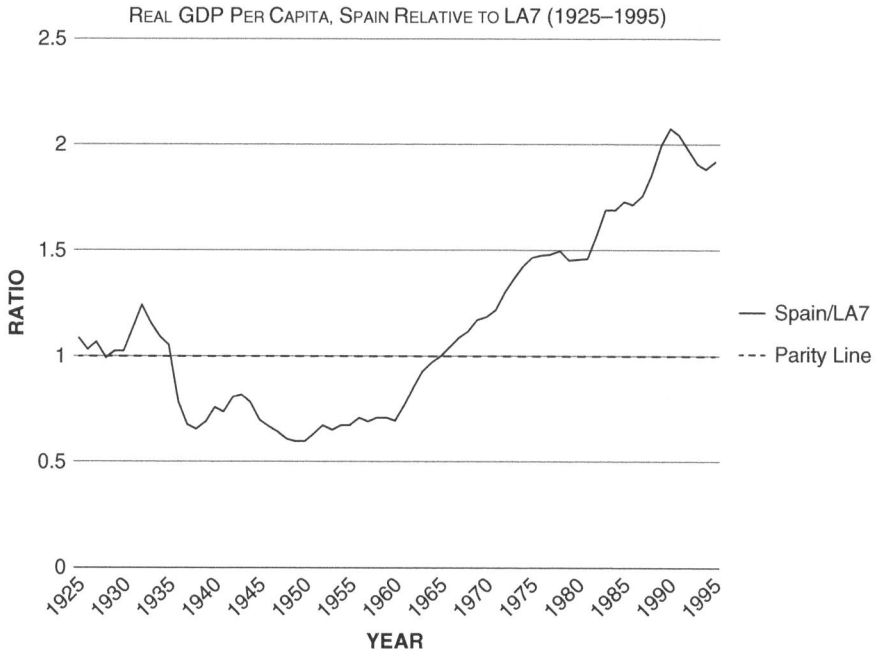

REAL GDP PER CAPITA, SPAIN RELATIVE TO LA7 (1925–1995)

FIGURE 1.2 Spain's Real GDP per Capita, Relative to Seven Latin American Economies (LA7), 1925–1995
The dashed line marks parity. Excluding oil-rich and economically turbulent Venezuela from the comparison shifts the curve further left but doesn't change the underlying trend.[17]

parity with the continental average; by the early 2000s, it surpassed the Western European mean by a third.

Clearly, some profound transformation occurred in Spain during the 1960s. The economic boom has been associated with the authoritarian government's decision to replace, in leading public policy positions, old Falangists with young, highly influential technocrats.[18] Afterwards, the Spanish developmental state was very successful at promoting industrial production and export growth. Why similar Latin American attempts ended in disaster is less obvious. As we have seen, not only did the continent enjoy high levels of economic development in the first half of the twentieth century, but Latin American rulers emulated Spain's developmental model without delay. As early as the mid 1960s, the military dictatorships of Argentina and Brazil were eager to hire expert managers from Opus Dei, the same right-wing Catholic organization that trained Spanish technocrats.[19] And yet when these

---

[17] Maddison, 1995, 2001.   [18] Casanova, 1983: 27.
[19] Jaguaribe, 1973: 532–533; Casanova, 1983: 29.

nations eventually emerged from military rule, only Spain could claim to have witnessed substantial developmental achievements.

Figure 1.2 plots Spain's GDP per capita as a ratio of the Latin American mean. Average Spanish citizens were earning just 60 cents to the dollar of their counterparts across seven Latin American countries (LA7: Argentina, Brazil, Chile, Colombia, Mexico, Peru, and Venezuela) between 1935 and 1960. One generation later, they were making double. In other words, the Spanish developmental success is made more remarkable by the conspicuous absence of any Latin American equivalent.

Later chapters and the conclusion of this volume examine in detail why the developmental state did not reach any extraordinary results in Latin America, as it did in Spain. Before discussing the issue, however, let us define here the heart of this comparison: the inflection point circa 1960, when the Spanish and Latin American growth trajectories diverged. In the rest of this section we compare historic trends in Spain and Latin America across further empirical measures associated with developmental results. The broad period of analysis, from 1925 to 1995, provides thirty-five years of observations on either side of the inflection point. We examine economic, demographic, social, and political trends for peculiar historical circumstances that may help explain Spain's very fast economic growth. Our aim is to examine common explanations of developmental success (or failure) while understanding the inflection point in more detail. Two patterns stand out in particular: one, that for most of the twentieth century, Spain tracks closely with the Latin American average across a wide range of developmental measures; and two, the inflection point appears in the data with surprising frequency, albeit at different periods across measures.

MANUFACTURING AND TRADE

One plausible explanation for Spain's fast industrial growth during the 1960s is that Spain was simply more industrialized to begin with. The data, however, suggest otherwise. As late as 1970, Spain lagged behind Argentina, Chile, and Venezuela in its share of GDP per capita originating in industrial activity, a measure on which it historically resembled the Latin American average.[20] Over the next decade, however, Spain experienced a near-exponential rate of industrialization that dwarfed the linear growth paths of Latin American economies. By 1981, Spain's industrial GDP per capita had risen *eightfold* to more than double the level in Argentina, and two and a half times as large as the Latin American mean.

Crucially, Latin American nations did not "fail" to industrialize – they simply did so at linear rates that were no match for Spain's exponential pace. An identical trend occurs in the per capita production of steel and cement, a historic industrial activity easy to compare over time and space.[21] Spanish

[20] Maddison, 1995, 2001. Industrial GDP data from Databanks International, 2017.
[21] Sources for steel and cement production: Databanks International, 2017.

production levels were essentially flat between 1925 and 1955, lagging behind Chile and Venezuela. They began skyrocketing soon afterward, reaching a peak in the 1980s, when Spain annually produced 2.2 megatons of steel and cement per capita, *thrice* as much as the largest producers in Latin America, Brazil, and Mexico. Although these states significantly increased their output during this period, it remained a fraction of Spain's.

If Spain wasn't historically more industrialized, was it at least more integrated into world markets? After all, Spain was an imperial power that conducted vast military and economic operations for centuries. Perhaps trade linkages helped to "unlock" the growth potential of the Spanish economy. In fact, between 1925 and 1962, the average annual share of world trade among Argentina, Brazil, and Mexico (LA3) was 56 percent larger than Spain's.[22] This difference was especially pronounced during wartime: in 1937, Spanish trade was worth just 14 percent of Argentina's share and less than half of Mexico's (and it stayed that way until the 1950s). Here the data reveal another inflection point: Spanish international commerce surpassed LA3 in 1963, accounting for an even larger share of global trade throughout the rest of the twentieth century.

Spain's trade boom occurred in the early years of the Spanish period of intensive growth, suggesting that trade policy (along with steel and cement production) was central to the development strategies implemented by the technocrats. For example, absolute levels of Spanish exports often lagged behind two major commodity-rich Latin American economies – Brazil and Mexico – until at least the late 1980s. Behind the scenes, however, Spain transformed from a commodity-exports to a manufacturing-exports regime. The manufacturing share of Spanish exports (as a percentage of all exports) grew from just under 30 percent in 1962 to 73 percent in 1988. By contrast, value-added manufactured goods accounted for only 57 percent of all 1988 exports from Brazil and 49 percent of exports from Mexico. The changing nature of Spanish exports is thus an important qualitative distinction that can be directly linked to developmental strategies.

One critical aspect of trade provided Spain with a key source of foreign currency. The Net Travel and Tourism Balance (NTTB) calculates a country's revenues from travel and tourism after deduction of the money its nationals spend on travel abroad.[23] In 1995, Spain's NTTB was $20.8 billion, ten times greater than Mexico. But in 1960, Mexico's travel balance, at $260 million, was actually higher than Spain's. While tourism to Mexico suffered during the peso crisis of the 1980s, it expanded eighty-fold in Spain. Like other forms of trade, Spain's travel balance did not begin at high levels but rather hit an inflection point in the early 1960s.

---

[22] Databanks International, 2017.
[23] Source for NTTB data: Mitchell and Palgrave Macmillan, 2013.

DEVELOPMENT FOR WHOM?

If Spain had no clear initial advantage over Latin America in growth, industrialization, or trade prior to 1960, then we might want to narrow our scope and look at aspects of human development. For instance, developmental states (especially in East Asia) are associated with relatively low inequality. Did Spain start off more highly equal than Latin America, possibly impacting on the relative success of developmental strategies? The twentieth-century tale of inequality in Latin America is a turbulent one with no clear narrative – for most of the second half of the century, the Gini coefficients of the major Latin American countries oscillated wildly between 40 and 60, although the continent as a whole ended the century with greater income inequality than it had mid century.[24] Surely Spain was more egalitarian? In fact, available data shows that Spain was slightly more *unequal* than Latin America until the 1960s! By the 1970s, however, Spain's Gini coefficient dropped dramatically relative to the LA7 median (a more sensible measure than the mean due to nation-wide differences in Gini calculation). In 1973, for instance, median income inequality in Latin America was 30 percent higher than in Spain. And by 1980, Spanish inequality dropped to half of the LA7 median (although the gap later narrowed). Surprisingly, this relative performance was driven largely by rising *equality* in Spain rather than increasing *inequality* in Latin America.

We can still imagine that Spain enjoyed an early comparative advantage in other essential developmental factors, like education. Perhaps Spain started off with a more highly educated population than Latin America, resulting in a high stock of human capital, which enabled the Spanish developmental state to reach the extraordinary economic success that remained missing in the Latin American cases. Yet again, the data reveal a post-1960s inflection point: relative to Latin America, education levels in Spain grew only *after* this time. In 1970, Argentina, Peru, and Chile each had significantly more university students per 10,000 population than Spain.[25] Through most of the 1960s, Argentina had a higher rate of tertiary education than Spain, Brazil, and Mexico combined. And while university attendance in Spain grew rapidly after 1970, increasing sevenfold by century's end, it expanded at impressive rates across Latin America as well. Tertiary education rates in Argentina and Peru, particularly, tracked closely with Spain until the 1990s. We can be fairly confident that the shortcomings of the developmental state in Latin America were not caused by lack of higher education.

Spain had no initial advantage over Latin America in secondary schooling either, but these trends provide more nuanced evidence: we find here differences in general developmental strategies. By 1965, when its university attendance still lagged far behind Argentina's and Chile's, Spain became the leader in

---

[24] Source for Gini data: UNU-WIDER, 2017.
[25] Source for education enrollment data: Databanks International, 2017.

secondary school attendance, and continued to grow at a rate outpacing any country in Latin America, where enrollment tended to grow in quick bursts before suddenly leveling off. As of 1990, secondary school attendance in Spain was one and a half times more than that of Mexico and Peru, nearly twice the levels of Argentina and Chile, and nearly five times as much as Brazil – a puzzling development considering that university attendance in Argentina and Peru more or less equaled Spain that year. This suggests that while Spain emphasized democratizing education early on, it remained largely a middle-class domain in Latin America. Expanding access to secondary schooling had important consequences for the creation of Spain's skilled workforce. But as we shall see in a later section, while this may have been a concerted effort on behalf of Spanish authorities, they also benefited from demographic advantages beyond the reach of any Latin American state.

To be fair, Spain certainly had *some* early-stage developmental advantages over Latin America, particularly in two important arenas: infant mortality and access to health care. Spain lagged only behind Argentina on both measures in the 1920s. Moreover, Spain's progress on infant mortality *preceded* the Spanish period of fast economic growth, for once. During the war, infant mortality rates in Spain spiked to higher levels than most LA7 countries, but recovered quickly under the old Falangist guard (a period, we might recall, of otherwise sluggish development). By the mid 1940s, infant mortality in Spain dropped from about 145 to roughly 60 deaths per 1,000 live births – lower even than Argentina.[26] Latin American states made commendable progress on infant mortality in their own right. By 1995, Chile's infant mortality rate dropped to 12 deaths per 1,000 live births from a high of over 250 earlier in the century; Mexico's rate dropped to 16 from a height of over 200. Nevertheless, Spain's rate by then dropped to below 6 deaths per 1,000. Ironically, the least progress on mortality was made by the former leader, Argentina, which by 1995 ranked next to last (after Peru), with a rate of 23 deaths per 1,000.

Argentina's relatively poor performance was not equivalent to lack of access to health care. The number of physicians per capita is frequently used by the World Health Organization (WHO) and other organizations as a measure of health care availability.[27] In the mid 1940s, both Spain and Argentina had one doctor per 1,000 residents, nearly twice as many as Chile and Mexico. While Latin America's access to health care improved slowly and steadily between 1946 (the first year this measure is available for most countries) and 1995, Spain's ratio virtually flatlined at one doctor per 1,000 between 1946 and 1960. The reader will not be surprised to learn that the logic of the inflection point also applies to doctors in Spain, whose numbers rose dramatically shortly after 1960. By 1994, Spain had four doctors per 1,000 residents – thrice as many as

---

[26] Source for infant mortality data: Mitchell and Palgrave Macmillan, 2013.
[27] Source for physicians per capita data: Databanks International, 2017.

the Latin American average, four times the level of Mexico, and much higher than Argentina's rate of 2.63.

MIDDLE-CLASS CREATION

In sum, overall comparison with Spain shows that Latin American states were by no means developmental failures. Rather, it demonstrates steady progress on important measures of manufacturing, trade and human development throughout most of the twentieth century. On some measures, like higher education, Latin American states made very significant progress on the whole. What the inflection point tells us, though, is that Spain somehow pivoted from mediocre to exponential progress on all of these measures *after* 1960 (with the notable exception of infant mortality).

From our vantage point, the period of fast economic growth in Spain looks like a developmentally self-reinforcing cycle, with substantial improvements in health, human capital stock, and industrial infrastructure, which all served to supercharge each other, and the economy as a whole. But Spain was a dark horse lacking any obvious comparative advantage. If anything, Argentina was the clear favorite in the developmental race, maintaining a wide lead on most measures for most of the twentieth century. But when the Argentine bureaucratic-authoritarian state tried to copy Spain's technocratic model, it faltered. So did other Latin American states that closely resembled Spain prior to the 1960s.

What happened? Now may be a good time to revisit Fajnzylber's "show-case modernity" critique of Latin America. Did the continent squander its potential on middle-class urban professionals? If that were indeed the case, then we would expect not to see the Spanish inflection point in measures of middle-class lifestyle. We begin by analyzing the consumption patterns of air traffic, phones, and automobiles. We selected these as they can be used as comparative levels of middle-class consumption. Yet here again we see the same patterns as before. From 1929 to 1959, Spain and LA7 had roughly comparable levels of commercial air traffic with the exception of Mexico, where air travel was much more common.[28] But by the early 1960s, commercial air travel began to grow exponentially in Spain. By the late 1960s, air traffic in Spain pulled ahead of Mexico, and far ahead of the LA7 average, which proceeded to rise at a more or less linear rate. Similarly, in the 1920s, Spain had fewer phones per capita than the Latin American average – 10.5 connections per 1,000 population for Spain in 1927, compared to LA7's mean of 11.92.[29] But by 1967, Spain had well over *three* times as much landline penetration, and more than 4.5 times as many per capita landlines by 1977. Between 1948 and 1984 phone penetration in Spain grew by 2,027 percent – averaging 50 percent per year.

[28] Source for air traffic data: Mitchell and Palgrave Macmillan, 2013.
[29] Source for phones per capita data: Databanks International, 2017.

Given that these empirical trends closely follow cross-national patterns in more "productive" measures, perhaps we should re-examine the "showcase modernity" conclusion. A closer look at the case of automobiles, however, does lend credence to Fajnzylber and the import-substitution hypothesis. Until 1960, Argentina, Mexico, and Brazil together boasted higher rates of car ownership than Spain. There were 2.8 cars for every 1,000 people in Spain in 1960, and 5 per 1,000 on average in LA3 (2.85 for LA7).[30] But by the mid 1990s, Spain and Brazil had nearly twice as many cars per capita as Mexico, and 3–4 times as many as Argentina. If in Mexico and Brazil the Volkswagen Beetle was the automotive symbol of development, the home-grown SEAT 600 was the vehicle of Spain. Most importantly, while most Latin American auto industries (with the exception of Mexico) produced largely for the domestic market, and all were owned by multinationals, Spain's auto industry included a significant share of national capital and public ownership, and it was able to expand substantially into export markets.

DEMOGRAPHY

We haven't yet mentioned a critical structure component that sets Spain apart from Latin America independently of any inflection points: people. Population growth in Latin America far outstripped Spain in the twentieth century. Even the LA7 country with the least rate of population increase, Argentina, grew nearly *three times as much as Spain* between 1925 and 1995.[31] Not only was Brazil always the most populous country among LA7 and Spain, but it also experienced a high population growth rate relative to all other countries under comparison, growing especially rapidly post-1960. This is also true of Venezuela, Colombia, and Mexico, which unseated Spain as the second-most populous country in 1954.

Where the population concentrated was also markedly different. Among LA7 and Spain, Argentina and Chile had the highest percentage living in their major city. Over 30 percent of the Argentinian population lived in Buenos Aires as early as 1960, a trend that continues until at least 1990; in Chile, nearly 38 percent of the population had moved to Santiago by 1970, an aggressive rate of capitalization that crossed *40 percent* by 1990. Peru too saw a rapid rate of capitalization, with Lima accounting for 3.3 percent of the national population in 1920, and 30.2 percent by 1990. On the other hand, only 3.5 percent of the Spanish population lived in Madrid in 1920, and this figure rose modestly to 7.6 percent by 1990. Migration is another interesting comparison. The big picture is that Spain made a dramatic transformation in the second half of the century from being a major *sending* country in Europe to, by 1990s, a net

---

[30] Source for car ownership data: Databanks International, 2017.
[31] Source for demographic data: Databanks International, 2017.

recipient country of global migration flow. LA7, meanwhile, moved from a net *receiving* region to a net *sender* of the Global South.

POLITICAL AND ECONOMIC STABILITY

For diverse reasons, Latin American dictators could not maintain the kind of stability that the Franco regime was able to impose. During the years leading up to and during the Spanish Civil War, the country was highly politically fragmented. During the period 1925–1939, Latin America was significantly less fragmented than Spain, with a fragmentation score averaging 44.4/100 for the period.[32] In other words, through the Second Spanish Republic and until the moment Franco assumed power, Spain was substantially *more* politically fractionalized than LA7.

A turning point occurred in 1939, and continued until 1976, the year after Franco's death. During this period Spain witnessed preternatural political stability resulting from Franco's authoritarian rule. Latin America, meanwhile, oscillated between the low 30s and high 60s on the political fractionalization index (although Brazil remained relatively stable and other countries, specifically Mexico, Peru, and Venezuela, are missing data) until the 1980s.

Until 1972–1973, Spain and LA3 (Argentina, Brazil, Mexico) had a current budget deficit per capita that hovered around zero (in current US dollars).[33] But then Spain began a period of intense deficit spending, causing the annual per capita deficit to grow prodigiously. By 1980, Spain's budget deficit per capita had risen to $203.80. By 1990, it was $689.04, and almost $1,500 by 1995. In comparison, LA3's budget deficit per capita averaged $78.05 in 1980, $96.52 in 1990, and $97.94 in 1995. In other words, Spain's annual budget deficit per capita was *fifteen times higher* than the average for the three largest Latin American economies.

It's clear that the Spanish economy enjoyed a price stability throughout the second half of the twentieth century that was rare in Latin America.[34] Price levels were relatively stable for both Spain and the three major Latin American economies in the years prior to 1950. Runaway inflation began affecting South America soon after, but Spain and Mexico continued to have nearly identical rates of inflation until 1980 – when the value of a basket of consumer goods in Mexico was 990 percent of its 1953 price level, and in Spain 1,151 percent. Then began the Mexican peso crisis. By 1985, the Mexican consumer price index (CPI) shot up to 10,609. Just five years after that, it mushroomed to 149,200 and kept growing, peaking at 230,834 in 1993! The Mexican experience pales still in comparison to the runaway inflation of

---

[32] Source for political fractionalization data: Databanks International, 2017.
[33] Source for budget deficits per capita: Databanks International, 2017.
[34] Source for price level data: Mitchell and Palgrave Macmillan, 2013.

Brazil and Argentina. As early as 1970, Brazil's CPI hit 14,895 percent of 1953 values, while Argentina's reached 3,774 percent. By 1980, the index values were 275,934 and 986,282 for Brazil and Argentina respectively; by 1985 they were 19.8 *million* for Brazil and 1.33 *billion* for Argentina. Only five years later, in 1990, Brazil's price level was 422.8 *billion* percent of its 1953 value, and Argentina's 18.45 *trillion* percent. In Spain, by comparison, the CPI relative to 1953 was just 2,033.7 in 1985, 2,770.9 in 1990, and 3,249 in 1993.

The differences in financial stability are also reflected in the premiums the countries had to pay for their debt. Between 1978 and 2000 (the years for which data is available), the average Mexican Treasury bill rate was 35.15 percent.[35] For Spain, it was 11.17 percent. This means that relative to Latin America, Spain had access to far cheaper external debt servicing, an important consideration in light of Spain's high deficit spending noted above. The rate on Mexican T-Bills also fluctuated dramatically during this period, with a standard deviation of 23.25 compared with a standard deviation of 4.40 for Spain. After joining the European Union, Spain's T-Bill rates dropped to single digits: 8.1 percent in 1994, 9.79 percent in 1995, and a low of 3.01 percent in 1999. Mexican rates also came down from their crisis-level highs, but continued to fluctuate: 14.09 percent in 1994, 48.4 percent in 1995 (a year of high global interest rates), and 21.4 percent in 1999.

Spain also had very low lending interest rates relative to Latin America as a whole, although this too fluctuated over time. On average, between 1977 and 2002 (and including the tumultuous 1980s), mean annual lending interest rates in LA7 were 112.53 percent – ten times higher than Spain's average of 11.77 percent. The *median* Latin American rate, discounting outliers, was 42.91 percent – significantly lower, but still four times as high as Spain's.

What about exchange rates? Compared with LA7, Spain did not always have the best exchange rates against the dollar, but even the most cursory historical analysis shows how much more stable Spanish currency was relative to Latin America. Between 1960 and 1980, Spain enjoyed remarkable currency stability averaging 64.58 against the dollar, with a range of just 19.10 and a single-digit standard deviation of 6.04. Among LA7 countries, only oil-rich Venezuela had a currency stability that came anywhere close to Spain's. Mexico enjoyed the next most stable currency, although it too faced a sudden spike during the 1982 Mexican crisis, and in general did not come close to Spanish numbers. The Latin American economies also suffered sweeping currency swings in very short time frames, particularly during the turbulent 1980s.

SUMMARY

The comparison between the largest Latin American economies and Spain suggests several possible observations. First, it confirms that the

---

[35] Source for interest and exchange rates data: World Bank, 2017; IMF, 2008.

developmental state did *not* fail in Latin America; on the contrary, it produced impressive results well into the 1970s. This is especially true of measures of human development. The region did this while dealing with massive demographic change and political and economic instability. But Spain's progress was certainly astounding, and it represented a profound social transformation. Why the difference in outcomes? We suspect two critical factors, which will be further analyzed in the book: greater institutional stability through the consolidation of professional state bureaucracies, and much easier access to foreign capital, permitting much greater deficit spending. To this we may add the geopolitical context which encouraged both Western Europe and the United States to provide as many opportunities and support as possible to Spain, in contrast with often counterproductive policies followed in Latin America.

All in all, the questions and puzzles presented in this introduction will be analyzed and discussed throughout the chapters of the book, and they will be re-examined in the book's overall conclusion. For this purpose, we intent to follow a general plan of research, based on the four dimensions of state strength already defined above, which we will also consider in the next section, together with short summaries of each chapter.

PARTS AND CHAPTERS OF THE VOLUME

The present volume begins, after this introductory chapter by the editors and Vivekananda Nemana, with a first part on Visions and Politics of Development, including Chapters 2, 3, and 4. Those three chapters of the first part do not focus –yet – on one or more of the dimensions of state strength in any particular national case. The developmental era was characterized by the circumstance, especially in Latin America, that relatively detailed strategies and "visions" for development were conceived and formulated by international organizations such as the UN commission CEPAL,[36] the World Bank, the Organization of American States, and others. The international organizations, foremost among them CEPAL, generated considerable resources, such as public policy programs, trained experts and their networks, and economic data, which national states could employ to support their own economic and infrastructural capacities. Moreover, economic policies and development experts gained national and international legitimacy – symbolic strength – as a result of being publicly endorsed by international organizations such as CEPAL, the Tennessee Valley Authority (TVA), the Alliance for Progress, and others. But the work and resources of international organizations did not form, at first, part of the capacities of any particular national state, until the state authorities decided to employ them – which they often did.

---

[36] Created in 1948, the UN Economic Commission for Latin America and the Caribbean, ECLAC, is best known by its Spanish acronym, CEPAL, and generally we follow this use in the book.

Chapter 2 by Joseph Love discusses the origins, intellectual history, and political influence of CEPAL on Latin American countries, and also on Spain and Portugal, between 1950 and 1990. The chapter focuses on "Structuralism" as a school of thought that was central for CEPAL's economic analysis and public policy proposals. The chapter considers other contributions of CEPAL that are very rarely discussed in the literature, such as blueprints for institutional design of developmental agencies, and programs for training of public policy experts and high-ranking civil servants. Love also describes briefly the attempt by Celso Furtado, who was trained at CEPAL, to implement some of the ideas of the commission, acting as a leading public policy expert and politician during the early 1960s in Brazil. Finally, the chapter discusses how CEPAL reacted to the challenge represented by the ascent of the neoliberal consensus in the 1990s.

Margarita Fajardo in Chapter 3 takes further the analysis of the difficult – and sometimes dangerous – political implementation of CEPAL's vision and strategies for development "on the ground," considering again in particular the case of Brazil. The chapter focuses on sociologists and economists, and their academic and political engagement to promote development as a long-term national project. The chapter shows that intellectuals, academics, and public policy experts were initially enthusiastic and optimistic as regards their potential for creating and leading state institutions that were going to advance social and economic development. However, the initial optimism turned relatively soon to political disorientation, and theoretical bafflement. Since the middle of the 1960s, intellectuals and experts realized – sometimes already in exile – that it was necessary to think again about the sociological foundations of state power, and about how to reconcile capitalism with democracy in Latin America and Spain.

Chapter 4 by Robert Karl discusses another key source for developmental visions and strategies in Latin America, particularly in the case of Colombia: the TVA. Created in 1933, TVA was regarded not only as a blueprint for institutional design as a public agency, but also as a model for the public policy strategies it applied – with great success – to promote the economic and social development of a vast geographical area in the United States. After World War II, the TVA model was studied and applied by several national governments in Latin America, it was promoted by the World Bank, and it became influential on the development vision championed by the Alliance for Progress. The author describes the fact that Colombia was an early "showcase" for US American development agencies and experts. However, due to a series of difficulties and setbacks, the country found itself relatively soon considered as a "failure," even by many – or most – Colombian sociologists and economists. Development programs seemed never to fulfill the high expectations that surrounded them at the beginning.

José Carlos Orihuela, in Chapter 5, begins the part of the book that focuses on the study of infrastructural and territorial power. The volume has been similarly organized for each part: the initial chapter compares several national cases, and the rest of the chapters present each one national case study. Orihuela's chapter compares three developmental agencies in Chile, Colombia, and Peru. The blueprint for the three national agencies was the TVA, the flagship developmental agency of the New Deal, which is also discussed in the previous chapter – as well as in several others, and again particularly in the conclusions of the volume. This same institutional blueprint was "translated" in very different ways by the political and institutional actors of the three countries. The chapter examines the reasons or factors that explain the bureaucratic strength of each of the agencies thus created, considering not only their autonomy and professionalism, but also other significant factors such as political legitimacy and embeddedness.

Chapter 6 by Eduardo Dargent examines a key developmental agency in Peru, the Instituto Nacional de Planificación (INP). The INP was created in 1962 following blueprints suggested by the Organization of American States (OAS) and CEPAL. The author evaluates the institutional project of INP as failed, but the case is very revealing nonetheless, and the author examines on its basis diverse theoretical models that have tried to explain the emergence and endurance of state capacity in Latin America. The initial phase of INP was already very problematic, because evidence points out to the fact that the organization was originally conceived as a "Potemkin institution." This interesting characterization of certain institutional projects in developing countries was first formulated in Russia, of course. The chapter pays special attention to informal political practices as the foundation for bureaucratic autonomy, as suggested by Carpenter's theory of agency reputation, among other relatively recent contributions.

Luciana de Souza Leão, in Chapter 7, analyzes the many efforts and projects that aimed at strengthening and expanding both the infrastructural power and the territorial reach of the federal state in Brazil from 1930 to 1985. The chapter begins with the creation of a career civil service during the era of President Vargas, in the late 1930s, and goes on to consider other projects of institutional modernization in the following decades, including the creation of independent developmental agencies. The author discusses the fact that bureaucratic autonomy, in Brazil, was never understood to mean real political independence for public agencies, but rather their direct subordination to the president. This institutional design facilitated frequent political interference on public policy decisions, and their erratic character as a result. The chapter examines also the diverse projects of bureaucratic modernization that involved expanding the territorial reach of the Brazilian state with the creation of regional development agencies.

Chapter 8 by Agustin E. Ferraro and Juan José Rastrollo discusses the correlation between professional bureaucracies and economic development, first postulated by Weber, and the development of the Spanish industry as an instance of this correlation during the developmental era. First of all, the authors consider the reasons that explain the curious lack of attention to the Spanish case in the literature on economic development, even among studies of development in Latin America. Secondly, the study of a specific economic area, the automobile industry, shows that state-led industrial promotion was very effective during the period 1950–1990 in Spain, and that the effectiveness of industrial policy was substantially increased after the modernization and professionalization of the central state bureaucracy in the early 1960s. The chapter argues, finally, that the legal and institutional blueprints for civil service reform in Spain, implemented during the period of state modernization and (controlled) transition to democracy between 1960 and 1978, had been originally established during the era of profound social and political modernization of the country from 1914 to 1936.

In Chapter 9, Jordi Catalan and Tomàs Fernández-de-Sevilla begin the part of the book focused on the state's economic power. The chapters in this part consider also bureaucratic structures and the territorial reach of states, certainly, but they pay particular attention to the economic public policy framework, including labor, welfare, and fiscal policies, and their impact on diverse areas and variables, such as industry, trade, growth, public debt, and others. As mentioned above, the first chapter in each part adopts a comparative perspective, and discusses several national cases. In Chapter 9, the authors examine and compare the sometimes fluctuating developmental strategies, and the macroeconomic evolution for three countries: Argentina, Brazil, and Spain. The chapter examines the often conflictive political context for economic decisions, the long-term consistency – or lack thereof – in the implementation of developmental programs, and their impact on the main economic variables during the period under study.

Chapter 10 by Alan Knight examines the general political context, the economic policies, and the state building programs during five periods of Mexican history, from before the Revolution to the end of the developmental era. The first period, the Porfiriato, witnessed a deterioration in welfare, fall in real wages, and rising inequality. The revolutionary generation of the 1920s and 1930s began building a stronger state, with enhanced powers in areas such as commercial and labor regulation. However, the most successful growth model was reached during the period from 1945 to 1972, under the semi-authoritarian regime of the Revolutionary Institutional Party (PRI). This period included effective long-term, state-led industrialization policies. During the late 1970s, the PRI regime tended to overreach in terms of statism, nationalism, and economic populism, leading to the debacle of the early 1980s.

Yovanna Pineda, in Chapter 11, analyzes import-substitution policies in Argentina, from the early 1940s until the end of the developmental era in the country. Across different periods and political regimes, the chapter focuses on a particular area of production, the farm machinery industry, in order to evaluate the economic impact of the – frequently – shifting public policy frameworks. Based on deep interviews with key informants, associated directly or indirectly to a traditional harvester manufacturing firm in the Province of Santa Fe, the chapter also explores the sociocultural impact of developmental initiatives. The interviews provide crucial insights into the experiences and beliefs of firm owners, engineers, farmers, and their family members, including their perceptions of public officialdom, and of distant government decisions. Finally, the author considers a relatively recent attempt to reestablish industrial developmental programs in Argentina, and the sudden protagonism that the agriculture machinery industry came to assume in one of the episodes of this failed political project.

Chapter 12 by Patricio Silva presents a study of the Chilean developmental state that begins by considering the country's nitrate-based economy during the late nineteenth century, and its political correlation, the Aristocratic Republic. The decline of the aristocratic regime, and the comparatively early establishment of developmental institutions and strategies during the second half of the 1920s, resulted from three main factors: the decadence of the nitrate industry after World War I, the increasing discontent with the aloof ruling elite, and the eruption of the middle class on the political scene. Already in the second half of the 1920s, new specialized state agencies were created to manage policies of wide credit support for central areas of national production, including mining, agriculture, and industry. Nevertheless, the Chilean development state consolidated as a national project only in the late 1930s, with the establishment of Corporación de Fomento de la Producción (CORFO). The Chilean developmental state became one of the most successful in Latin America but, as the author shows, the stability of economic policies depended on political compromises between the main political coalitions of the left and right. The increasing political polarization since the early 1960s, and the loss of the willingness to reach stable political compromises among political actors, had catastrophic consequences not only for the developmental project, but also for Chilean democracy.

Matthias vom Hau in Chapter 13 begins the part of the book focused on symbolic state power, including discussions of national and civic identities, their relationship to the developmental state, and their transformations during the developmental era. As the first chapter in this part, the study presents a comparative analysis of popular nationalism and the developmental state in three national cases: Mexico, Argentina, and Peru. Nevertheless, as the author indicates, the chapter's main theoretical claim can be applied to other national cases, as shown by brief references to Brazil and Bolivia. Vom Hau argues that popular nationalism was neither a mere legitimation tool of the developmental state, nor completely unrelated to it. Instead, he suggests that the concept of "selective affinity" works better to describe the relationship. Originally employed by the writer and statesman Johann Wolfgang von Goethe to analyze human relationships, the concept of selective affinities was first applied in the social sciences by Max Weber, who famously postulated a selective affinity between Protestantism and capitalism. The chapter shows that, far from being a mere legitimation tool of the developmental state, Latin American nationalism had sometimes a conflictive relationship with it.

Chapter 14 by Marshall C. Eakin examines the powerful Brazilian narrative of cultural and racial *mestiçagem* (miscegenation) that was promoted by diverse social and political actors since the 1930s in the country. The author argues that the developmental state in Brazil, after 1930, played a central (but not determinant) role in the construction and success of this narrative, that the narrative played a critical role in the gradual emergence of Brazil as a robust nation state by the 1970s, and that the power of the narrative spanned political parties, social movements, classes, and regimes. The narrative of *mestiçagem* was at the core of cultural nationalism in Brazil, and also helped foster a dynamic civic nationalism by the 1980s and 1990s. Finally, the author claims that the appeal of the narrative continues, but that its potency has eroded over the past two decades. At the end of the chapter, the Brazilian narrative of *mestiçagem* is briefly compared with dominant narratives of race and nation in other Latin American countries.

Brodwyn Fischer in Chapter 15 discusses urban informality, and the paradoxes of its relationship to economic development and political citizenship during the twentieth century in Brazil. Often described as development's negation, the author claims that urban residential informality has played a much more complex role than such simplistic analysis would suggest. On the one hand, urban informality has been a vital escape hatch from a long series of developmentalist dilemmas: in economic, legal, and political terms, it has facilitated the adoption of ambitious policies that far outstrip available resources and capacities. On the other hand, urban informality has served to reinforce deep economic and civic inequalities, perpetuating historical forms of marginalization, and facilitating the creation of layered, contradictory, and often destabilizing economic and citizenship regimes. Urban informality has shown the capacity of the developmental state to redefine citizenship, but at the same time it has put in evidence its limitations.

Chapter 16 by the editors summarizes the results of the volume, and includes a concluding discussion, as well as attempted answers, for two related issues or questions raised in this introduction, and further examined throughout the book: first of all, the reasons for the relative lack of success of development programs under technocratic-authoritarian regimes during the 1960s and 1970s in Brazil, Argentina, and other Latin American countries, compared with their remarkable achievements in Spain; and secondly, the institutional design, modes of operation, and political practices adopted by developmental agencies under democratic regimes, which we can, in retrospect, evaluate as contributing factors to their effectiveness in promoting economic growth and social progress during the developmental era.

REFERENCES

Bourdieu, Pierre. "Rethinking the State: On the Genesis and Structure of the Bureaucratic Field." *Sociological Theory* 12, 1, 1994: 1–19.
Casanova, José V. "The Opus Dei Ethic, the Technocrats, and the Modernization of Spain." *Social Science Information* 22, 11, 1983: 27–50.
Centeno, Miguel A. *Democracy Within Reason: Technocratic Revolution in Mexico.* University Park: Pennsylvania State University Press, 1994.
Centeno, Miguel A. and Agustin E. Ferraro, eds. *State and Nation Making in Latin America and Spain. Republics of the Possible.* Cambridge and New York: Cambridge University Press, 2013.
Databanks International. *Cross-National Time-Series Data Archive,* by Kenneth A. Wilson, 2017, www.cntsdata.com.
Fajnzylber, Fernando. *Unavoidable Industrial Restructuring in Latin America.* Durham and London: Duke University Press, 1990.
Gereffi, Gary, and Donald L. Wyman, eds. *Manufacturing Miracles: Paths of Industrialization in Latin America and East Asia.* Princeton University Press, 1990.
Hirschman, Albert. "The Political Economy of Latin American Development: Seven Exercises in Retrospection." *Latin American Research Review* 22, 3, 1987: 7–36.
International Monetary Fund (IMF). *International Financial Statistics (IFS) Online,* 2008, www.imf.org/external/pubs/cat/longres.aspx?sk=20095.
Jaguaribe, Helio. *Political Development. A General Theory and a Latin American Case Study.* New York: Harper & Row, 1973.
Maddison, Angus. *Monitoring the World Economy 1820–1992.* Paris: OECD, 1995. *The World Economy. A Millennial Perspective.* Paris: OECD, 2001.
Mann, Michael. *The Sources of Social Power. Vol. 2: The Rise of Classes and Nation-States, 1760–1914.* Cambridge University Press, 1993.
Mitchell, Brian and Palgrave Macmillan. *International Historical Statistics.* Basingstoke: Palgrave Macmillan, 2013, www.eui.eu/Research/Library/ResearchGuides/Economics/Statistics/DataPortal/IHS.
Strayer, Joseph. *On the Medieval Origins of the Modern State.* Princeton University Press, 1973.
Thurber, Clarence E. "Islands of Development." In *Development Administration in Latin America,* eds. Clarence E. Thurber and Lawrence S. Graham, Durham: Duke University Press, 1973: 15–46.
United Nations University World Institute for Development Economics Research (UNU-WIDER). *World Income Inequality Database (WIID) 3.4,* 2017, www.wider.unu.edu/project/wiid-world-income-inequality-database.
Woo-Cumings, Meredith. "Introduction: Chalmers Johnson and the Politics of Nationalism and Development." In *The Developmental State,* ed. Meredith Woo-Cumings. Ithaca: Cornell University Press, 1999: 1–31.
World Bank. *World Bank Open Data,* 2017, https://data.worldbank.org.

PART II

VISIONS AND POLITICS OF DEVELOPMENT

2

CEPAL as Idea Factory for Latin American Development: Intellectual and Political Influence, 1950–1990

Joseph L. Love

This chapter traces the evolution of the major concerns of the UN Economic Commission for Latin America and the Caribbean (best known by its Spanish acronym, CEPAL) from 1949 to 1990, a period in which the organization passed from an emphasis on industrialization led by national states to one stressing greater income equality among the citizens of those states, based on growth of foreign trade and the incorporation of new technology. The structuralist analysis of CEPAL fitted easily into the aspirations of the economic nationalism of the early post-war era. Structuralism was a school of thought – one might even say movement – that in its early years focused on industrialization and greater independence of national states from the international trading system, in which Latin America at the time was largely producing agricultural and mineral goods to exchange on the world market for industrial imports.[1] Economic nationalism had made an appearance in the inter-war years with assertions of state control of mineral resources, along with protection and subsidization of manufacturing industry – timid at first – as Latin American states reacted to protectionist trends in the United States and Western Europe. Before World War I, however, tariff protection in Latin America had been higher than that of elsewhere, although this fact was not widely appreciated at the time.[2]

In the inter-war years, with the breakdown of the international trading system following the Smoot-Hawley Tariff (1930) and the failure of the world trade conference in London (1933), independent Third World states – notably

---

[1] "Structuralism" means a variety of things in economics, as in other disciplines, and my definition is a broad and simple one. Structuralism refers to theoretical efforts to specify, analyze, and correct economic structures that impede or block the "normal," implicitly unproblematic, development and functioning allegedly characteristic of Western economies. Because of these impediments and blockages, standard classical or neoclassical prescriptions were rejected by structuralists as inappropriate, inapplicable. Some structuralist theory, in fact, was designed to move the economy to the point where neoclassical economics *would* be applicable.

[2] Coatsworth and Williamson, 2004: 210, 212.

those in East-Central Europe – moved more resolutely to state-sponsored industrialization as a response to the breakdown of the international trading system.[3] For the new and enlarged states stretching from the Baltic Sea to the Black Sea, the development of manufacturing industries was seen as both a means of creating new wealth and the economic basis of a strategic guarantee of the post-war order. Jan Kofman, in Henrik Szlajfer's collection *Economic Nationalism in East-Central Europe and South America: 1918–1939*, holds that "protectionism, autarky and industrialism … along with the dislike of foreign capital" were "the basic ingredients of economic nationalism." A "holistic" economic nationalism for Kofman placed a state-sponsored industrialization program at the center of the development process. "Holistic nationalism" had integrative aspirations, seeking to place a whole society behind the development objective, as opposed to a "particular nationalism only serving a fraction of the local bourgeoisie."[4]

In Latin America, industry's strategic role in national defense was far less salient. One reason was that no states there, unlike those of East-Central Europe, had been born recently, nor had existing borders of the large majority of states been changed for a century.[5] This, because of the existence of an informal Pax Americana, under which no state in Latin America posed a threat to existing borders, the only exception being the conflict between Bolivia and Paraguay over the Chaco region in 1932–1935.

A more aggressive wave of Latin American nationalism arrived in the 1950s, following the fifteen years of disruption in the international trading system from 1930 to 1945. This movement coincided and interacted with the Cold War; with the early professionalization of economics as a discipline in Latin America; and with the arrival of the new subdiscipline of development economics.[6] Economic nationalism benefited from more effective "stateness," achieved through greater revenue extraction and enhanced Weberian rationalization of the state.

In Laurence Whitehead's opinion, "stateness," in terms of government income, outlay, and efficiency in Latin America rose markedly between the late 1920s and the late 1950s, so that "modernizing" states had replaced "oligarchic" states by the end of the period. Gains were especially notable in direct taxation, as Argentina, Brazil, Chile, and Venezuela, among others, introduced taxes on income. On the outlay side, governments had acquired new obligations in social spending; Brazil, Chile, and Uruguay put social security systems in place before the War, and Argentina and Mexico followed in the 1940s.[7]

---

[3] See for example, David, 2009; Love, 1996.   [4] Kofman in Szlajfer, 1990: 53.
[5] Exceptions: Panama's separation from Colombia (with US backing), and Chile's incorporation of part of Peru's Pacific coastline and all of Bolivia's.
[6] For an elaboration, see Love, 2005.   [7] Whitehead, 1994: 76.

Concurrently, a new populism arose, based on rising urbanization, the extension of suffrage, the expansion of mass media, and newly created or expanded state-sponsored welfare systems. A phenomenon at times confused with CEPAL-derived structuralism was *desarrollismo* ("developmentalism"), a form of populist nationalism that sometimes borrowed arguments for industrialization from CEPAL.

The structuralist school of thought was associated with the UN Economic Commission for Latin America, created in 1948 and directed in its early years by the Argentinian Raúl Prebisch, who assumed leadership of the organization the following year as Executive Secretary.[8] His prestige in Latin American economic and financial circles was already of fifteen years' standing. Prebisch had organized Argentina's Central Bank in 1935, and he had advised the governments of other countries on the establishment of central banks while lecturing at the Banco de Mexico in the mid 1940s. Prebisch was also Latin America's leading authority on John Maynard Keynes, whose theories were regnant in the early post-war era; his *Introducción a Keynes* (1947) is a classic work still in print in the twenty-first century.

In *The Economic Development of Latin America and its Principal Problems* (1949) – the "CEPAL manifesto" as Albert Hirschman dubbed it – Prebisch described the international economy as a set of relations between a "center" exporting industrial goods in exchange for foodstuffs and raw materials produced by the "periphery". The center emanated the signals that moved the whole system. Focusing on the problems of the periphery, CEPAL emphasized structural unemployment owing to the inability of traditional export industries to grow and therefore to absorb excess rural population. Persistent external disequilibrium – that is, balance-of-payments problems because of Latin America's greater propensity to import industrial goods than to export traditional agricultural and mineral goods, and deteriorating terms of trade – could be eliminated by a properly implemented policy of industrialization.

In the early 1970s CEPAL formalized another basic feature of its doctrine, implicit in Prebisch's early writings: the characterization of underdevelopment as "structural heterogeneity," in which economic processes of vastly different productivities coexisted in the same economy.[9] This became the very definition of economic backwardness for CEPAL: underdevelopment was conceived of not as characterizing a low-productivity, largely agricultural subsistence economy (as in Arthur Lewis' conception), but rather a situation in which the periphery was characterized by *heterogeneous* productivities of economic activities existing side by side in both urban and rural areas. Nor was there any spontaneous tendency for the modern sector to absorb those of lesser

---

[8] Later renamed the Economic Commission for Latin America and the Caribbean (ECLAC). I will use "CEPAL" throughout. The Spanish acronym did not change to reflect the inclusion of the Caribbean area.

[9] Pinto, 1970.

productivity.[10] In the early post-war years CEPAL economists viewed Latin America as more heterogeneous than other underdeveloped regions, because of its nascent industrial activities and its resulting mix of modern and traditional technologies, a pattern deepened by the "invasion" of transnational corporations in the 1960s. The informal sector of the Latin American economies, which, by one estimate, included more than half of Latin America's economically active population as late as the 1990s, was especially heterogeneous.[11]

Latin American structuralism thus used standard economic analysis in combination with the historical examination of a continually evolving center–periphery system.[12] This scheme was quite at odds with standard economics. It was not a paradigm in Thomas Kuhn's sense, but a school that sought to analyze the problems of a particular world region in a specific era. Surprisingly, perhaps, CEPAL was not dominated by the United States, though it was a member state. CEPAL was funded by the United Nations, not directly by constituent governments. This arrangement differed from that of both the Organization of American States and the World Bank, in both of which the US has been dominant as a funding source and policy maker.[13]

CEPAL offered an explanation of Latin American economic backwardness and presented measures that would allegedly quicken the pace of growth and enhance national sovereignty. This occurred against an international background of sustained state interventionism during the Depression and World War II. By the end of the war, economic planning had become respectable in both Europe and the United States. As early as 1947, the UN Department of Economic Affairs produced a list of dozens of state agencies involved in economic planning and development in four large Latin American countries – Argentina, Mexico, Brazil, and Venezuela.[14]

As a constituent unit of the United Nations, CEPAL could only recommend its measures directly to sovereign governments, but it did provide a rationale for state action to stimulate industry and, by implication, for developing a powerful social group of industrial entrepreneurs. They in turn could compete with dominant agricultural and commercial interests domestically, and, in the longer term, with First World industrial firms in the international market.

CEPAL was the chief "idea factory" of Latin American structuralism, but the school extended well beyond it. Structuralist economists associated with CEPAL also moved in and out of national governments – e.g., Celso Furtado, Jorge Ahumada, and Victor Urquidi in their respective national governments of

---

[10] Pinto, 1970: 88.   [11] Thorp, 1998: 221.

[12] Cf. Armando di Filippo, "Center-Periphery is 'a structural totality'" in Filippo 1981: 117.

[13] Two-thirds of the OAS budget is supplied by the United States, and the US is the leading source of finance for the World Bank and the IMF, where its political policies are dominant. On the IMF and World Bank, see Woods, 2006.

[14] United Nations, 1947.

Brazil, Chile, and Mexico. One former researcher for CEPAL, Fernando Henrique Cardoso, even became a two-term president of Brazil.

Other means by which CEPAL affected the debate on development were the frequent publication of structuralist social scientists in leading journals and publishing houses – *Trimestre Económico* (Mexico), usually regarded as the leading Latin American economics journal, *Revista Brasileira de Economia*, and *Desarrollo Económico* (an interdisciplinary journal in Argentina). Mexico's Fondo de Cultura Económica, Latin America's leading publishing house in the social sciences, brought out the works of many structuralist economists, though the Fondo, like *Trimestre Económico*, was open to many schools of thought.

Some universities welcomed structuralist viewpoints. Among the most sympathetic was the Universidad de Chile; similarly, structuralists were represented along with other schools in the pluralist faculties of the National University of Mexico (UNAM) and the University of Sao Paulo (USP), though neoclassical theory tended to predominate at USP in the latter years of the twentieth century.[15] While neoclassical economics was winning out in most Brazilian universities, the State University of Sao Paulo at Campinas (UNICAMP) became (and remains today) a stronghold of structuralist thought.[16]

Structuralism also made an appearance at the global level of economic policy. If deteriorating terms of trade for primary goods made raw materials specialization in world trade a raw deal, Prebisch reasoned, why not try to raise and stabilize their volatile prices on the international market? But such a project would require a global solution. So Prebisch brought CEPAL's theses to the world stage in 1964, when he became Secretary General of the UN Conference on Trade and Development.[17]

He envisioned UNCTAD as a Third World counterpart and counterweight to the developed countries' "club," the General Agreement on Tariffs and Trade (GATT), predecessor to the World Trade Organization (WTO). Prebisch's *Reports* on the two UNCTAD conferences that he organized, those of 1964 and 1968, contained some of the theses familiar to all those acquainted with CEPAL structuralism. First of all, the world was divided into "centers" and "peripheries."[18] Secondly, the secular deterioration of the terms of trade was asserted *as fact* despite the objection of First World countries' representatives, who doubted or denied the existence of secular deterioration.[19] But the huge

---

[15] Prado, 2001: 14–18.

[16] On the development of the Instituto de Economia at UNICAMP, see Cano, 2007.

[17] His title was the same as that of U Thant, the chief of the United Nations itself.

[18] Prebisch, 1964: 20–26; 1968: 27–28.

[19] Prebisch, 1964: 14–17. Prebisch's views on trade – beginning with the terms-of-trade thesis – and his experience in CEPAL had taught him that commodity policy, such as buffer stocking, however necessary, was not sufficient to advance the growth and development of the world's agrarian nations. Industrialization was still necessary, and Third World countries needed as part

conferences that UNCTAD organized produced few concrete results, and the political scientist Joseph Nye reported that for its critics UNCTAD was an acronym for "Under No Circumstances, Take Any Decisions."[20,21] Disillusioned, Prebisch returned to CEPAL after presiding over the second UNCTAD gathering in New Delhi in 1968, though UNCTAD lives on.[22]

Structuralism also overlapped with other international agencies and movements. The International Labor Office (ILO) collaborated with CEPAL in setting up the Programa Regional del Empleo para América Latina y el Caribe (PREALC), a regional agency to study the informal sector of the Latin American economy with structuralism-infused methods of analysis and interpretation.[23] For many social scientists in the sixties and seventies, structuralism was firmly bracketed with the dependency movement, and the two related schools affected development theory and policy in North Africa and social science theory in the United States academy.[24] These two related schools also had an impact in three countries in "peripheral Europe" – Spain, Portugal, and Romania – as I have tried to establish in past papers.[25]

Finally, a European venue for CEPAL was the Madrid-based journal *Pensamiento Iberoamericano*, published by the Spanish government's Instituto de Cooperación Iberoamericano with the support of CEPAL. Beginning in 1982, *Pensamiento Iberoamericano* published articles in Portuguese and Spanish, and its first editor was Aníbal Pinto; the board of editors was largely composed of well-known structuralists. Prebisch and the Spanish economist Juan Velarde Fuertes introduced the first number, in which Furtado wrote the lead article. Osvaldo Sunkel later replaced Pinto as editor, remaining in that post until the journal ceased publication in 1998.

Further afield, at the ideological level, the structuralist thesis on deteriorating terms-of-trade; the use of a center–periphery framework; and reference to "the economic dependence of our countries," were all incorporated into the foundational document of Liberation Theology, the final declaration of the Medellin Conference of Latin American Bishops in 1968.[26]

As for Latin American national governments, to which CEPAL directly reported, there are many ways to judge the effectiveness of the CEPAL message, addressed to governments, but implicitly seeking the cooperation of industrial leaders. One such method is to look at official endorsements of

---

of their intermediate and long-term industrialization policies to move from exporting raw materials to exporting manufactures.

[20] At New Delhi, 137 countries and 44 international organizations had representatives during the eight weeks of the meeting.

[21] Nye, 1973: 334.   [22] For more on Prebisch at UNCTAD see Love, 2010.

[23] Thirion, 1993: 18.

[24] On Africa, see Amin, 1974, where the author describes Raúl Prebisch as the founder of the theory of unequal exchange. Amin was president of the African Institute for Economic Development in Dakar. On dependency's impact in the United States, see Packenham, 1992.

[25] Love, 2004: 114–139; 2006.   [26] See CELAM, 2017: 8–9.

CEPAL tenets by heads of national states. Surveying this material involves trolling the annual presidential "State of the Union" messages to congress, along with reports from state banks. I have done this for the 1950s and 1960s for five countries – Argentina, Brazil, Chile, Mexico, and Venezuela. Looking at certain concepts and propositions put forth by CEPAL, I found that some items were an easy sell – the recognition of the process of "import-substitution industrialization," which began long before the "CEPAL manifesto" of 1949, but was now proclaimed as a policy, for example, by Romulo Betancourt, in his 1962 report to the Venezuelan congress. The thesis of the deterioration of the terms of trade was endorsed by presidents Betancourt in Venezuela (1962), his successor Raul Leoni (1964), and Adolfo Ruiz Cortines in Mexico (1953). The demand for more "just" prices for primary goods by Leoni (1964) was followed by his support the following year for the new UNCTAD. The CEPAL objective of "inward-directed development" was picked up by Carlos Ibanez of Chile (1954) and Leoni of Venezuela (1965). And even the objective of exporting manufactures was endorsed by at least two chief executives – Venezuela's Betancourt (1962) and Gustavo Diaz Ordaz of Mexico (1968). Regional integration in the form of the Latin American Free Trade Association (LAFTA, or in Spanish, ALALC), a CEPAL initiative, was specifically mentioned by three heads of state – Betancourt (1960), Arturo Frondizi of Argentina (1961), and Diaz Ordaz (1965), in their annual reports. Likewise, the principle of state planning, in the modest form advanced by CEPAL called "programming," was welcomed by Chilean President Eduardo Frei (1970).

The most enthusiastic proponent of CEPAL recommendations was probably Brazilian President Juscelino Kubitschek (1956–1961). With his slogan "fifty years of progress in five," Kubitschek announced in his 1956 presidential address that CEPAL and the Brazilian National Development Bank (BNDE) had devised a five-year development plan. In carrying out the plan the Structuralist Celso Furtado figured prominently as head of the new regional development commission for Northeast Brazil (SUDENE).[27] Kubitschek endorsed CEPAL's analysis of deteriorating terms of trade and its interpretation of the persistent disequilibrium in Brazil's balance of payments. The Brazilian president asserted the need for industrialization to absorb surplus labor in agriculture, and embraced CEPAL's programming techniques.[28] Furtado, for instance, used them in SUDENE.

Should we associate dependency theory with CEPAL itself in this brief look at presidential messages? Dependency was not an official ideology of CEPAL, but dependency analysis was a set of propositions growing out of structuralism and was famously propagated by three leading CEPAL-associated structuralists, Osvaldo Sunkel, Celso Furtado, and Fernando Henrique

[27] In the government of President Joao Goulart (1961–1964), Furtado became Minister of Planning.
[28] Kubitschek, 1956: 47–48, 54, 275, 278, 362.

Cardoso.[29] Dependency, like structuralism, posited a center–periphery system developing historically, characterized by unequal exchange and a dependence of the periphery on the center. But dependency went beyond structuralism in asserting that the national bourgeoisie was incapable of developing modern capitalism in Latin America.

If any government ever tried to put dependency theory into effect, it was that of Salvador Allende of Chile (president, 1970–1973), tragically overthrown by a bloody military coup. In his 1971 report to the Chilean Congress, he referred to Chile's century and a half of "dependent and capitalist development" and wanted to break out of the center–periphery system by securing structural changes.[30] His government sought to use the economic "surplus" to advance far-reaching structural change in the economy and a radical redistribution of income. These measures would help Chile break out of its peripheral status, in which a chronic lack of foreign exchange was linked to the consumption habits of the top income-receiving classes. Several former CEPAL researchers were members of his government.[31] Allende's minister of economics, Pedro Vuscovic, called for "drastic modifications in the concentration of property and in the distribution of income ... [while] reorienting production toward the basic needs of the population."[32] But a careful study of the objectives and achievements of the Allende government by Alejandro Foxley and Oscar Muñoz shows that the growth-with-redistribution targets were unrealistic.[33]

And what impact did structuralism have on industrialists' associations? I only have data on Brazil, where industrialists were generally enthusiastic about CEPAL doctrines. Furtado and Prebisch courted Brazilian industrialists, participating in the debates of the National Confederation of Industries (CNI) in 1950. The organization and many individual manufacturers received Prebisch's thesis warmly. In the same year *Estudos Econômicos* (Economic Studies), the CNI journal, ran an article explaining and implicitly endorsing CEPAL's position, and in 1953 the Industrialists' Confederation financially supported a regular CEPAL session in Brazil. A later CNI review, *Desenvolvimento e Conjuntura* (Development and the Business Cycle), founded in 1957, endorsed CEPAL's interpretations and proposals in its first editorial. In general, industrial leaders in Furtado's Brazil accepted state intervention and structuralist doctrines in the 1950s much more readily than did their counterparts in Prebisch's Argentina,[34] though Brazil may have been an outlier in its industrialists' enthusiasm for CEPAL's theses.

Of the several CEPAL theses, deteriorating terms-of-trade generated the most scholarly debate. The controversy continues, with a sophisticated

---

[29] Love, 1990.   [30] Allende, 1971: 637.

[31] Pedro Vuskovic as Minister of Economics and Development; Gonzalo Martner as Director of the Office of Planning; and Carlos Matus in several lesser positions.

[32] Vuskovic, 1974: 71.   [33] Foxley and Muñoz, 1973.

[34] For documentation on material in this paragraph, see Love, 1996: 155.

examination and defense of the deterioration thesis for most of the twentieth century by José Antonio Ocampo, former Executive Secretary of CEPAL, and María Angela Parra. They hold that "there was an improvement in the barter terms of trade for non-fuel commodities vs. manufactures in the late nineteenth and early twentieth centuries, followed by significant deterioration over the rest of the twentieth century."[35] Contrary to Prebisch, they suggest the possibility that real commodity prices might rise again in a long-term swing in the twenty-first century. There is also a revisionist view that argues the terms of trade are less important than other factors in certain respects. Jeffrey Williamson believes that market *volatility* was more important than declining terms of trade in discouraging new investment in peripheral countries.[36] But the terms of trade thesis remains important for CEPAL because it undergirds the thesis of the structural tendency toward external disequilibrium.

Lest it be thought that CEPAL was only interested in propagating its often controversial propositions, it should be noted that much of the day-to-day activity of the CEPAL staff was gathering, ordering, revising, and publishing economic and social data on Latin America and CEPAL's member states. Such data were organized according to categories and definitions supplied by United Nations statistical agencies. These included long historical series that did not exist in the early post-war years for most Latin American countries. Interpretative essays accompanied the data, but the data for a given country stood alone and could be compared with those of other countries in Latin America and elsewhere.

Perhaps the most effective means of diffusing the structuralist doctrine was by teaching it in short but formal courses. CEPAL had organized courses in basic economic concepts and techniques, along with structuralist doctrine, as early as 1952 (when Jorge Ahumada directed the teaching program). It also influenced the international master's program ESCOLATINA at the University of Chile later in that decade. These two institutions, often in collaboration with others outside Chile, trained and indoctrinated middle-ranking Latin American personnel in central banks, development and finance ministries, and university faculties. Scores of such men and women studied at CEPAL itself in courses varying from several months' duration to a year's length before the creation of the Instituto Latinoamericano de Planificación Económica y Social (ILPES) in 1962. Instructors in the 1960s included such leading structuralist economists as Aníbal Pinto, Jorge Ahumada, Antônio Barros de Castro, Maria da Conceição Tavares, Carlos Lessa, Leopoldo Solís, and Osvaldo Sunkel, himself a graduate of the ILPES program. In sociology and political science, Fernando Henrique Cardoso, Torcuato di Tella, Rodolfo Stavenhagen, Aldo Solari, and Francisco

---

[35] Ocampo and Parra, 2003: 56.

[36] He also argues that improving terms of trade in the nineteenth century up to 1870 in some cases – notably India – resulted in a serious deindustrialization, but that Latin America – notably Mexico, Brazil, and Chile – resisted this trend. Williamson, 2013.

Weffort offered courses.[37] ILPES and CEPAL "played a significant role in developing ... schools of public administration and planning ministries."[38] If one takes into account the seminars of a few weeks' duration and the other courses lasting up to a year, between 1962 and 1992 ILPES offered over three hundred courses, registering over twelve thousand participants.[39]

On the matter of the design of an effective central bank, Prebisch himself led the way. Growing out of his long experience in government by the time he took over CEPAL, Prebisch was aware of the importance of designing effective fiscal and monetary institutions. Sir Otto Niemeyer had been invited to provide a plan for governing Argentina's Central Bank, one which would be free of interference by the political executive, but one with limited powers beyond controlling the money supply. Prebisch modified Niemeyer's plan, adding the functions of the treasury, exchange control, and a conversion fund, bringing together 1,000 employees. The new bank could adjust the exchange rate, and remained off the gold standard, which, like the United States, Argentina had abandoned at the outset of the Great Depression. The new Banco Central of Argentina took over bankrupt commercial banks incorporating their frozen assets in exchange for cash and bonds. Unlike the Niemeyer model, Prebisch's Banco Central could conduct open market operations to smooth the effects of the international business cycle "absorbing excess financial flows in the upswing and releasing them in the downturn." It furthermore was charged with oversight of private banks. The Banco Central was further made responsible for trying to manage the business cycle and control inflation – all these attributes making it more independent of the executive than Niemeyer's model would have. Only one of the twelve governors was appointed by the government of the president, General Jose Uriburu. Prebisch served as president of the Bank until 1943, when, under the dictatorship of General Edelmiro Farrell (with Juan Perón as power broker), Prebisch was dismissed.[40]

Returning to the story of CEPAL's reformist endeavors, we should note that the agency addressed the operational concerns of Latin American governments by offering assistance in setting up public administration schools, in developing the many technical training programs in CEPAL and ILPES, and in creating planning agencies. The last-named activity included a methodology for economic "programming," that is, calculating required savings and inputs to meet government-specified development targets. An unpublished history of ILPES shows that CEPAL and ILPES did consider the practical details of reforming bureaucracy.

Many or most of the studies on Latin American bureaucracies are pessimistic about the degree to which they conform to the rational Weberian model. Jack Hopkins writes that bureaucrats tend to have long careers, but their loyalty to current power holders counts for much more than efficiency and effectiveness.

---

[37] ILPES, 1969.   [38] Cárdenas *et al.*, 2000: "Introduction," 12 (referring to CEPAL as a whole).
[39] Montecinos, 1996: 296.   [40] Dosman, 2008: 95, 99, 109.

"The bureaucracies appear to have deeply absorbed and internalized certain characteristics of colonial administration as well as cardinal features of the [colonial] culture." The ability to impartially formulate and implement policy tends to be overwhelmed by "the myriad pressing tasks of economic growth, distribution, and development." Other problems include low wage levels, absenteeism, lack of a merit system, and slowly moving administrative procedure. Roberto Oliveira de Campos, a former finance minister of Brazil, cites traditions of state paternalism, overcentralization in decision-making, and the absence of "a realistic theory of the role and limits of government intervention" as outstanding problems. The political scientist Clarence Thurber believes reformers must choose their battles carefully, and locate "islands of development," that is, "nuclei of organizational strength" that can be built upon.[41]

CEPAL's interest in the details of planning and rational administration was evident by 1965, when ILPES held an international seminar on the complexities of the several processes. Participants made the obvious but important points that effective planning depends on the grade of development of public administration, the existence of technically qualified personnel, and good statistics. But the ILPES seminar also noted the proliferation of centers of decision-making and control; it further called for both long- and short-term planning as well as flexibility, because of continuous changes in the economy. A consensus formed around the need for an effective merit system and full-time employees, as well as the importance of equal pay for equal work.[42]

A history of ILPES still in manuscript shows that it was a serious and flexible institution. Created in 1962 by Prebisch, ILPES was funded by the UN Development Program and the Inter-American Development Bank, but Prebisch criticized it in 1973 for its increasing politicization, when a number of left-wing Chilean planners left ILPES to work for their country's president, Salvador Allende. Planning was considered less relevant by the "Chicago Boys" under Chilean dictator Augusto Pinochet. The ILPES staff was reduced from twenty-eight to twelve in 1976, and its annual budget fell from $840,000 to $400,000, rising again to $3.4 million in 1982.[43]

In judging the degree to which governments adopted outside agencies' recommendations for reform, we need more studies like that of Beatriz Wahrlich and Lawrence Graham on Brazil.[44] Reform includes the expansion of state responsibilities over time. A relevant and ongoing multivolume project is *Saberes del Estado*, organized by Mariano Plotkin and Eduardo

---

[41] Hopkins, 1991: 711; Hopkins, 1974: 125; Clarence E. Thurber, "Islands of Development," in Thurber et al. 1973: 45.

[42] ILPES, 1965: 15, 34, 118, 119. [43] Franco, 2015: 179, 194, 202, 243, 275.

[44] See Wahrlich, 1983 and Graham, 1968. Graham concluded that Getulio Vargas' sweeping reform of 1938 was on balance a failure. A comic opera product of the fight against featherbedding bureaucracies in Brazil was the military dictatorship's Ministry of Debureaucratization (*Desburocratização*) in 1979; it turned out to be just another agency in the bloated civil service, and was abolished by a civilian government in 1986.

Zimmermann, showing how various Argentine state agencies recruited well-trained specialists – for example, psychiatrists in mental hospitals – and trained experts in urban planning, highway construction, statistical services, and labor relations.

One of the most enthusiastic proponents of planning was the Brazilian Celso Furtado, who was after Prebisch perhaps the most innovative and influential member of the CEPAL team. Furtado's passion for planning partly grew out of his academic training in Brazil. But in a letter to the author in 1996 he pointed to the importance of planning in the United States under Franklin Roosevelt as a source of inspiration, further noting that "the modernization of Brazil's federal administration was effected with the US technical assistance ... Many high-level *técnicos* came to the US and did internships while working in the Civil Service Commission and the Bureau of the Budget, while studying at the American University."[45]

Furtado was the chief author of Brazil's Plano Trienal, set up to revive the long run of economic growth over which President Juscelino Kubitschek presided in the late 1950s. But the political crisis following the sudden resignation of newly empowered President Quadros in 1961, combined with a sluggish economy, resulted in political instability that drove Joao Goulart and his government from office in March 1964. Furtado's Three-Year Plan (1962) had called for fiscal and agrarian reform, the latter being a sharply divisive issue. Furtado called for increased competences for regional governments over public health, while at the same time seeking to integrate all government development activities at a central planning office. In this way, the federal government was strengthened as a planning authority, or infrastructural power, while at the same time public health and other competences could be devolved to regional governments, increasing the territorial reach of the state. In Furtado's view it was important to separate (central) planning from (regional) execution.[46] In a memoir Furtado discusses his experience as the first director of the Superintendency of the Development of the Northeast (SUDENE), the Northeast of Brazil being the most backward and impoverished region of the country. SUDENE, like the Plano Trienal later, had been established by Kubitschek in an atmosphere of crisis to respond to a (perceived) radicalization of the peasantry in the Northeast. Data were lacking for adequate planning, but Furtado was able to limit congressional participation to setting an overall budget, leaving to him the distribution of funds among the subagencies.[47] It was here that Furtado encountered the power of local bosses entrenched in their fiefs and eager to accuse him of communism.[48] His memoir

---

[45] Furtado to author, August 8, 1996.   [46] Presidencia da Republica, 1962: 190.
[47] Furtado, 1989: 148.
[48] Albert Hirschman emphasizes that federal authorities, including Furtado, were able to limit graft by bringing state governors into the SUDENE board, but offers no substantiation for this assertion. Hirschman, 1963: 83.

emphasizes the highly politicized resistance to his reformism. He may have been relieved to move to a ministerial post in charge of planning that produced the Plano Trienal, although its implementation too was blocked by the 1964 military coup.

At the international level, state-led economic change lost ground in the 1970s, when Keynesian economics failed to eliminate "stagflation." In the following decade, Margaret Thatcher and Ronald Reagan launched successful attacks on the perceived excesses of the welfare state. They also made income taxes much more regressive, an action complemented by Thatcher's strong preference for a regressive value-added tax.[49] Therefore, "neoliberalism" – a return to the values of nineteenth-century economic liberalism – made its appearance on the international scene, and its prestige grew as the Soviet Union collapsed and capitalist globalization intensified. With it came greater competition in world markets.

The Latin America of the 1970s witnessed the exhaustion of import substitution for the region's most industrialized nations, runaway inflation in a variety of countries, oil price shocks in 1973 and 1979, and a move from cheap international credit to a sudden and sharp rise of interest rates by the US Federal Reserve at the end of the decade. And despite Prebisch's denunciation of rapidly rising protectionism to insulate hothouse industries in 1963, CEPAL's justification of industrialization in the 1940s and 1950s had become a Pandora's box by the 1960s, allowing Latin American executives and legislatures to read whatever they wanted into rationales for "inward-directed growth," a CEPAL slogan.[50]

In the face of economic and financial turmoil at the international level, Latin American governments moved abruptly from one fiscal policy to another, resulting in what Cardenas, Ocampo, and Thorp call "the macro mess."[51] Latin American countries in the 1980s were facing a debt crisis of greater proportions than that of the Great Depression, and there were conflicting signals from Wall Street and the US government. Whereas the Latin American debt crisis of the Depression had ended by 1937, full recovery from the debt crisis of the 1980s didn't come until 1994, a decade and a half after it began![52] Furthermore, the 1980s was a period in which not only Japan, but also the newly industrialized East Asian Tigers, advanced enormously in world trade while Latin America regressed, as both the region's composite product and its share of international trade fell over the decade.

---

[49] Bourguignon, 2015: 91–92.
[50] Prebisch (1963: 71) had written that Latin America had, on average, the highest tariffs in the world, depriving it of economies of scale and opportunities to specialize for export.
[51] Cárdenas et al., 2000: 28. For detailed studies of macro mismanagement in Argentina, Brazil, and Mexico in the years 1970–1985, see Larrain and Selowsky, 1991.
[52] Bertola and Ocampo, 2012: 208.

The "Washington Consensus" of officials in the International Monetary Fund (IMF), World Bank, and State Department, along with members of Washington think tanks, was drawn in 1989 by John Williamson of the Institute for International Economics. He composed a ten-point agenda for pursuing economic growth through liberalization and privatization. It was "prescribed" to Latin America in 1989, and was applied quickly thereafter to Eastern Europe, now freed from Soviet-directed socialism.[53]

CEPAL answered this challenge in several studies and programs, culminating in 1990. The chief articulator of CEPAL's new theoretical and programmatic thrust was a Chilean economist named Fernando Fajnzylber. He had been head of the foreign trade department in the Allende government and had held posts in several UN agencies, notably the UN Industrial Development Organization (UNIDO) in Vienna. In *The Incomplete Industrialization of Latin America* (1983) Fajnzylber had compared Latin American industrialization with that of the newly industrialized East Asian Tigers, but had focused on Japan.[54] He had done a study tour there as a Chilean engineering student in 1962, just as Japan was moving into its leading position in industrial exports. In *Incomplete Industrialization*, Fajnzylber described Japan's export-driven industrialization, a model that other East Asian countries were following. It called for selective import-substitution industrialization, focusing on industries that could open up export markets using advanced technologies. Japan and its followers, Fajnzylber wrote, especially Korea, had learned to adapt, innovate, and compete. In Latin America, he argued that protection should be provided for industries that required apprenticeship in new technologies for both workers and managers – this was in contrast to the region's historical pattern of protection, an ad hoc affair that Fajnzylber termed "frivolous protection."[55]

In Japan the state was heavily involved in development through the Ministry of International Trade and Industry (MITI), and the government offered subsidies and protection for groups with cutting-edge technologies that could penetrate foreign markets. Fajnzylber wanted Latin American governments and firms to emulate Japan, combining planning and market-based export strategies. This would require alliances of Latin America's still relatively weak industrial bourgeoisie with other actors.[56]

In 1990 CEPAL regrouped under the banner of "Neostructuralism," articulated by Fernando Fajnzylber in 1990 and enthusiastically endorsed by *cepalinos* Osvaldo Sunkel and Gustavo Zuleta in the same year.[57] Like the neoliberals, Fajnzylber condemned the excesses of protectionism in *Changing Production Patterns with Social Equity* – a complaint that Prebisch, as noted

---

[53] See essays by Brada and Kochanowicz in Baer and Love, 2000.   [54] Fajnzylber, 1983.
[55] Fajnzylber, 1984: 183.
[56] On the weak industrial bourgeoisie, see Cardoso, 1964 and his other studies of that group in Brazil and Argentina cited in Love, 1996: 287–288.
[57] ECLAC, 1990; Sunkel and Zuleta, 1990: 35–52.

above, had made as early as 1963 in *Towards a Dynamic Development Policy* – but Fajnzylber further argued that growth could only be sustained by progressively introducing high-technology, high-productivity goods for the international market. The goal was to endogenize technological innovation by establishing research and development traditions in Latin America. But he also called for a greater degree of equity in the distribution of income, consistent with rising levels of productivity in agriculture as well as industry. The two goals of new forms of production and equity

... must be achieved within the context of greater international competitiveness, based more on the deliberate and systematic absorption of technical progress by the production process (with corresponding rises in productivity) than on the maintenance of low real wages ... Emphasis must be placed on the systemic nature of competitiveness. Sustained growth based on competitiveness is incompatible with the continued existence of lags as regards equity.[58]

Thus for Fajnzylber, competitiveness resulting from the acceptance of lower salaries was a "spurious" competitiveness. An "authentic" form would be based on apprenticeship in the use of more advanced technology, which, in turn, results in higher wages. Policies that simultaneously promote competitiveness, apprenticeship, and a more equal distribution of income, he contended, are often complementary.[59]

New technology, of course, is not entirely a public good, because of patent rights and royalties; moreover, the introduction of new technologies – almost by definition focusing on saving labor – also results in job losses. Therefore the state, as in Europe and the United States, should subsidize technological research, including the introduction of new technologies in agriculture as well as industry, to lessen technological heterogeneity throughout the economy. But the state must also participate in "human capital" formation through education and basic scientific research; both will have positive externalities, that is, spillover effects. Because this is a long-term project, private firms are much less likely to make these investments.[60] Following the publication of *Changing Production Patterns*, still in 1990, CEPAL and the regional office of UNESCO issued a statement calling for "educational reform as the foundation for economic competitiveness with equity." Soon after, the governments of Chile, Argentina, Mexico, and Uruguay "launched policies to improve the quality of the schools attended by marginalized children," in the wake of the deterioration of elementary education during the 1980s.[61]

Changing Patterns called attention to the fact that Latin American growth in the 1980s was a negative 8.3 percent – thus the phrase "the lost decade." Accompanying this shrinking product were persistent macroeconomic

---

[58] ECLAC, 1990: 14.   [59] For support of this claim, see Porcile, 2011: 43, 61.
[60] Rodriguez, 2006: 377–398.
[61] Fernando Reimers, "Education and Social Progress" in Bulmer-Thomas *et al.*, 2006: 477–478.

imbalances, a regressive adjustment in income distribution, a weakening of the public sector, and a decline of capital formation. In addition, Latin America's share of world exports fell from 7.7 percent in 1960 to 3.9 percent in 1988. One of the few bright spots of the period was the rapid growth of exports of manufactures based on research and development over the years 1962 to 1985 at an annual average of 8.1 percent.[62] In Neostructuralism the state was to serve as regulator, and structural heterogeneity would be replaced by "inclusive growth," as opposed to relying on cheap labor and currency devaluations to advance in international markets. Unfortunately, Fajnzylber did not live to see the maturation of Neostructuralism, dying in 1991 at the age of 51.

But CEPAL's serious interest in greater equity among the citizenry of the Latin American states doesn't date from the late 1980s, but from 1963, when Prebisch authored *Towards a Dynamic Development Policy for Latin America*. In this document he wrote, "The test of a system's dynamic strength lies in its ability to accelerate the rate of development and progressively improve the distribution of income."[63] He estimated that 50 percent of the Latin American population accounted for 20 percent of total personal consumption, while 5 percent consumed 30 percent of the total. The top 5 percent of the population consumed 15 times as much as the lower 50 percent, and if the ratio were reduced to 11 to 1, annual economic growth could be raised from 1 percent per annum to 3 percent.[64] Prebisch argued that Latin American industrialization was based on the technology appropriate to the labor-saving needs of the developed countries, and that the consumption patterns of Latin America's upper strata exacerbated the problem through their preferences for capital-intensive consumer goods.

A decade later CEPAL economists Anibal Pinto and Armando di Filippo put forward a more concrete proposal for income redistribution, calling for agrarian reform, including the transfer of rural property to the peasantry with technical and marketing advice. These measures would be accompanied by opportunities for political organization by peasant farmers. Presumably, this program would be introduced on a gradual basis in which productivity in agriculture would rise. This, in contrast to the "populist" solution of immediate redistribution (implicitly that of the Allende government).[65] Other CEPAL researchers also made contributions to the study of income distribution and possibilities for redistribution in the 1970s – for example, Ricardo Ffrench-Davis and Victor Tokman.[66]

---

[62] ECLAC, 1990: 20, 21, 40. An outstanding success in this area was the Brazilian firm EMBRAER, which eventually became a world leader in producing jet airplanes for short-term hauls. See Baer and Love, 2017.

[63] Prebisch, 1963: 4.   [64] Prebisch, 1963: 6.

[65] Anibal Pinto and Armando di Filippo. "Notas sobre la estrategia de la distribucion y la redis-tribucion del ingreso en America Latina" in Pinto, 1991: 546–547.

[66] See Ffrench-Davis, "Mecanismos y objetivos de la redistribucion del ingreso," 320–358, and Tokman, "Distribucion del ingreso, tecnologia y empleo en el sector industrial de Venezuela," 415–447 in Foxley,1974.

Neostructuralism, the official CEPAL doctrine from 1990, made significant concessions to the Washington Consensus, or more properly, formalized a program that had been implicitly accepted in a more piecemeal manner. Growth was to be pursued in the international market, just as growth before 1930 had been led by exports, but this time those goods would have a high-tech component designed to put them on a footing with products from the East Asian "Tigers." Inward-directed development, the watchword of the halcyon days of import-substitution industrialization, was long gone.[67] And the form of bargaining that labor and management had used in the past, including confrontation, would implicitly be abandoned in a more collaborative approach requiring a social pact.[68] This is a dramatically different understanding of labor relations from Celso Furtado's description of capitalist development in 1964, in which the system advances through labor's attack, by organizing, and capital's counterattack, by introducing new technology to eliminate jobs.[69]

Among the enthusiastic contributors to Neostructuralism was Osvaldo Sunkel, one of the early members of Prebisch's team. Sunkel had been one of the theorists of "structural inflation," and in 2011 admitted he had been wrong not to give more weight to monetary policy in controlling inflation in those South American countries where it had been so rampant in the 1970s and 1980s. Economic theory would have been better served, he thought, if there had been a real dialog between those who called for state intervention and those who saw the market as the key to all problems. "Inward-directed development" should be replaced by what Sunkel called "development *from within*" but directed both inward and outward. Technology had to be upgraded in industry, but also in agriculture, as Fajnzylber had argued.[70] Sunkel thought that state development agencies like Chile's Corporación de Fomento (CORFO), established in 1939, still had a major role to play in technological advance, especially in small firms where Chile's modest investments in research and development might make significant contributions.[71]

In the 1990s, however, Latin American governments generally pursued policies recommended in the Washington Consensus and tended to ignore CEPAL's economic doctrines, if not its data sets and studies and conferences on such matters as the environment, schooling, migration, and aging populations. For more than a decade after 1990, the rate of growth of the Latin American countries, whose governments generally

---

[67] Stephen Haber points out that import-substitution industrialization is a misnomer, because most "substitution" was really the expansion of the domestic market rather than the satisfaction of preexisting demand for manufactured imports. Haber, "The Political Economy of Industrialization," in Bulmer-Thomas *et al.*, 2006: 578.

[68] Fajnzylber, 1990.

[69] Celso Furtado, "The Dialectic of Capitalist Development," in Furtado 1965: 47–62.

[70] Fajnzylber, 1990.   [71] Fernandez, 2011.

implemented neoliberal policies, fell far behind the growth of the region in the years 1950 to 1980. Orthodoxy's prescription had resulted in a much worse performance than that of the period of CEPAL's greatest influence, although the performance of the Latin American economy in both periods was linked to, and dependent on, the performance of the world economy.

Recent (standard) economic theory supports the neostructuralist position that further development, as well as political stability, depends on greater equity, replacing the implicit assumption that growth is associated with the consumption of durable goods, which in turn depends on the consumption habits of middle- and high-income recipients.[72] And inequality of wealth, even more than inequality of income, results in inequality in access to credit, and is a source of economic inefficiency.

In the new millenium, center–periphery dialogue again began to feature more prominently in CEPAL's theoretical discourse.[73] This phenomenon was surely helped by the appearance of the terms core (or center) and periphery in the global economic histories of neoclassically-trained economists such as Jeffrey Williamson (Harvard), Michael Bordo (Rutgers), John Coatsworth (Columbia), and Alan Taylor and Peter Lindert (University of California, Davis).[74] Several prominent neoclassically trained economists who studied Latin America – Rosemary Thorp, José Antonio Ocampo, Enrique Cárdenas, and Valpy Fitzgerald – were already using the terms.

And in fact, it is remarkable that CEPAL retained its basic theses across the whole second half of the twentieth century: structural heterogeneity as the definition of economic backwardness, the balance of payments as a crucial bottleneck producing external disequilibrium, and deteriorating terms of trade, although the last-named thesis lost support in the new millennium. Addressing these issues required an active state. The "adaptive continuity" of CEPAL doctrine is probably attributable not only to the imagination and ingenuity of Fajnzylber, but also to the resistance to neoliberal pressures by CEPAL's Executive Secretary in 1990, Gert Rosenthal.

---

[72] Stiglitz, 2013: 114, 146. With more qualifications, Elhanan Helpman supports the conclusion that more rapid growth is dependent on less inequality in Helpman,2004: 91–93.

[73] I strongly disagree with Fernando Ignacio Leiva, who believes that Neostructuralism has "jettisoned" the center–periphery framework. In making this claim, he misreads the article he cites by Filippo, 1998. See Leiva, 2008: 31. Leiva offers a post-modernist analysis of Neostructuralism employing literary theory with little heuristic effect.

[74] In addition, the economic historian Ivan Berend (UCLA) has used a core–periphery framework in his numerous books about East-Central Europe and its relations with the developed West. ("Core," rather than "Center," was the innovation of the historical sociologist Immanuel Wallerstein.)

REFERENCES

Allende, Salvador. *Mensaje al Congreso Nacional.* Santiago, Chile, 1971.

Amin, Samir. *Accumulation on a World Scale: A Critique of the Theory of Underdevelopment.* Translated by Brian Pearce. New York: Monthly Review Press, 1974.

Baer, Werner and Joseph L. Love, "Brazil's EMBRAER: Institutional Entrepreneurship." In *Brazil's Economy: An Institutional and Sectoral Approach*, eds. Werner Bauer et al., London: Routledge, 2017: 119–135.

Baer, Werner and Joseph L. Love, eds. *Liberalization and its Consequences: A Comparative Perspective on Latin America and Eastern Europe.* Cheltenham, UK: Edward Elgar, 2000.

Bértola, Luis and José Antonio Ocampo. *The Economic Development of Latin America since Independence.* New York: Oxford University Press, 2012.

Bourguignon, François. *The Globalization of Inequality.* Translated by Thomas Scott Railton. Princeton University Press, 2015.

Bulmer-Thomas, Victor, John Coatsworth, and Roberto Cortes-Conde, eds. *Cambridge History of Latin America. Vol. 2: The Long Twentieth Century.* New York: Cambridge University Press, 2006.

Cano, Wilson. "Instituto de Economia da Unicamp: Notas Sobre sua Origem e Linhas Gerais de sua Evolução." In *Ensaios de História do Pensamento Econômico no Brasil Contemporâneo*, eds. Tamás Szmrecsányi and Francisco Da Silva Coelho, São Paulo: Atlas, 2007: 199–209.

Cárdenas, Enrique, José Antonio Ocampo, and Rosemary Thorp, eds. *An Economic History of Twentieth-Century Latin America. Vol. 3: Industrialization and the State in Latin America: The Postwar Years.* New York: Palgrave, 2000.

Cardoso, Fernando Henrique. *Empresário Industrial e Desenvolvimento Econômico no Brasil.* São Paulo: Difusão Européia do Livro, 1964.

CELAM. "II Conferencia General del Episcopado Latinoamericano. Documentos Finales de Medellin." 2017 www.celam.org/doc_conferencias/ Documento_Conclusivo_Medellin.pdf (accessed December 2, 2017).

Coatsworth, John H. and Jeffrey G. Williamson. "Always Protectionist? Latin American Tariffs from Independence to the Great Depression." *Journal of Latin American Studies*, May , 2014: 205–232.

David, Thomas. *Nationalisme économique et industrialization: L'expérience des pays de l'Est (1789–1939).* Genève: Librairie Droz, 2009.

Dosman, Edgar J. *The Life and Times of Raúl Prebisch.* Montreal: McGill-Queens University Press, 2008.

Economic Commission for Latin America and the Caribbean (ECLAC; Fernando Fajnzylber, principal author). *Changing Production Patterns with Social Equity.* Santiago, Chile: United Nations, 1990.

Fajnzylber, Fernando. *La industrialización trunca de América Latina.* México, DF: Nueva Imagen, 1983.

"Industrialización en América Latina: De la 'caja negra' al 'casillero vacío.' Comparación de patrones contemporáneos de industrialización." Cuadernos de la CEPAL No. 60. Santiago de Chile: Naciones Unidas – CEPAL, 1990. https:// repositorio.cepal.org/handle/11362/27955 (accessed April 25, 2018).

Fernandez, Joaquin. "Neoestructuralismo y política económica: Entrevista a Osvaldo Sunkel." *Revista de Actualidad Política, Social y Cultural.* 2011. www.redseca.cl/? p=2015 (accessed December 3, 2017).

Filippo, Armando di. *Desarrollo y desigualdad social en la América Latina.* México, DF: Fondo de Cultura Económica, 1981.

"La visión centro-periferia hoy." *Revista de la CEPAL,* número extraordinario, October 1998: 175–185.

Foxley, Alejandro. *Distribución del Ingreso.* México, DF: Fondo de Cultura Económica, 1974.

Foxley, Alejandro and Óscar Muñoz. "Redistribución del Ingreso, Crecimiento Económico y Estructura Social (El caso chileno)." *El Trimestre Económico* 40, 160(4): 905–936, Octubre–Diciembre 1973.

Franco, Rolando. "História del ILPES (1962–2012)." Unpublished manuscript. 2015.

Furtado, Celso. *Diagnosis of the Brazilian Crisis.* Berkeley, University of California Press, 1965. [Portuguese original: *Dialéctica do desenvolvimento,* 1964.]

  A Fantasia Desfeita. Rio de Janeiro: Paz e Terra, 1989.

  Letter to Joseph L. Love. Author's possession, Rio de Janeiro. August 8, 1996.

Graham, Lawrence. *Civil Service Reform in Brazil: Principles versus Practice.* Austin: University of Texas Press, 1968.

Helpman, Elhanan. *The Mystery of Economic Growth.* Harvard: Belknap, 2004.

Hirschman, Albert O. *Journeys Toward Progress: Studies of Economic Policy-making in Latin America.* New York: Twentieth Century Fund, 1963.

Hopkins, Jack W. "Evolution and Revolution: Enduring Patterns and the Transformation of Latin American Bureaucracy." In *Handbook of Comparative and Development Public Administration,* ed. Ali Farazmand, New York: Marcel Dekker, 1991: 705–706.

  "Contemporary Research on Public Administration and Bureaucracies in Latin America." *LARR* (IX, 1), Spring 1974.

Instituto Latinoamericano de Planificación Económica y Social (ILPES), "Programa de Capacitación 1963 [through 1969]." ILPES Archive, CEPAL, 1969.

  Discusiones sobre Planificación: Informe de un seminario. Santiago, 6–14 de Julio de 1965. México: Siglo XXI, 1990 (1st edn. 1976).

Kubitschek, Juscelino. *Mensagem ao Congresso Nacional: 1956.* Rio de Janeiro: Imprensa Nacional, 1956.

Larrain, Felipe and Marcelo Selowsky, eds. *The Public Sector and the Latin American Crisis.* San Francisco, CA: ICS Press, 1991.

Leiva, Fernando Ignacio. *Latin American Neostructuralism: The Contradictions of Post-Neoliberal Development.* Minneapolis: University of Minnesota Press, 2008.

Love, Joseph L. "The Origins of Dependency Analysis." *Journal of Latin American Studies* 22, 1: 143–168, February 1990.

  Crafting the Third World: Theorizing Development in Romania and Brazil. Stanford University Press, 1996.

  "Structuralism and Dependency in Peripheral Europe: Latin American Ideas in Spain and Portugal." *Latin American Research Review* 39, 2, June 2004: 114–139.

  "Institutional Foundations of Economic Ideas in Latin America, 1914–1950." In *Economic Doctrines in Latin America: Origins, Embedding and Evolution,* eds. Rosemary Thorp and Valpy Fitzgerald, Houndmills, UK: Palgrave, 2005: 142–156.

"Flux and Reflux: Interwar and Postwar Structuralist Theories of Development in Romania and Latin America." In *History and Culture of Economic Nationalism in East-Central Europe,* eds. Helga Schultz and Eduard Kubu, Berlin: Berliner Wissenschafts-Verlag, 2006: 71–86.

"Latin America, UNCTAD, and the Postwar Trading System." In *Economic Development in Latin America: Essays in Honor of Werner Baer,* eds. Hadi Salehi Esfahani, Giovanni Facchini, and Geoffrey Hewings, New York: Palgrave Macmillan, 2010: 22–33.

Montecinos, Veronica. "Economists in Political and Policy Elites in Latin America." In *The Post-1945 Internationalization of Economics,* ed. A. W. Coats. Durham: Duke University Press, 1996.

Nye, Joseph S. "UNCTAD: Poor Nations' Pressure Group." In *The Anatomy of Influence: Decision Making in International Organizations,* eds. Robert W. Cox and Jacobson Harold Karan, New Haven, Connecticut, 1973: 334.

Ocampo, José Antonio and María Ángela Parra. "Returning to An Eternal Debate: The Terms of Trade for Commodities in the Twentieth Century." CEPAL, series *Informes y estudios especiales* 5, 2003: 1–56.

Packenham, Robert A. *The Dependency Movement: Scholarship and Politics in Development Studies.* Cambridge, MA: Harvard University Press, 1992.

Pinto, Aníbal. "Naturaleza e implicaciones de la 'heterogeneidad estructural' de la América Latina." *El Trimestre Económico* 37, 1, 145, 1970: 83–100.

América Latina: una visión estructuralista. México, DF: UNAM, 1991 [1974].

Porcile, Gabriel. "La teoría estructuralista del desarrollo." In *El desarrollo inclusivo en América Latina y el Caribe: Ensayos sobre políticas de convergencia productiva para la igualdad,* ed. Ricardo Infante, Santiago: CEPAL, 2011: 31–64.

Prado, Eleuterio F. S. "A ortodoxia neoclássica." *USP: Estudos Avançados* 15, 41, January/April 2001.

Prebisch, Raúl. *Towards a Dynamic Development Policy for Latin America.* New York: United Nations, 1963.

Towards a New Trade Policy for Development. New York: UNCTAD, 1964.

Towards a Global Strategy of Development. New York: UNCTAD, 1968.

Presidência da República [Celso Furtado, principal author]. *Plano trienal de desenvolvimento econômico e social: 1963–1965 (Síntese).* Rio: n. pub, December 1962.

Rodriguez, Octavio. *El Estructuralismo latinoamericano.* México, DF: Siglo XXI and CEPAL, 2006.

Stiglitz, Joseph E. *The Price of Inequality: How Today's Divided Society Endangers Our Future.* New York: Norton, 2013.

Sunkel, Osvaldo and Gustavo Zuleta. "Neostructuralism vs. Neoliberalism in the 1990s." *CEPAL Review* 42: 35–52, 1990.

Szlajfer, Henryk. *Economic Nationalism in East-Central Europe and South America (1918–1939).* Genève: Librairie Droz, 1990.

Thirion, Gerard. "The Birth of PREALC (1968–1973)." In *PREALC: 25 Years.* Santiago: International Labour Organization, 1993.

Thorp, Rosemary. *Progress, Poverty, and Exclusion: An Economic History of Latin America in the Twentieth Century.* Washington, DC: Inter-American Development Bank, 1998.

Thurber, Clarence E., Edgardo Boeninger and Lawrence S. Graham, eds. *Development Administration in Latin America*. Durham, NC: Duke University Press, 1973.
United Nations. *Economic Development in Selected Countries: Plans, Programmes and Agencies*. Lake Success, NY: UN Department of Economic Affairs, 1947.
Vuskovic Bravo, Pedro. "Distribucion del ingreso y opciones del desarrollo." In *Desarrollo latinoamericano: Ensayos críticos*, ed. José Serra. Mexico, DF: Fondo de Cultura Económica, 1974: 51–74.
Wahrlich, Beatriz M. de Souza. *Reforma administrativa na era de Vargas*. Rio de Janeiro: Fundação Getúlio Vargas, 1983.
Whitehead, Laurence. "State Organization in Latin America since 1930." In *Cambridge History of Latin America*, Vol. VI, Part 2, ed. Leslie Bethell, Cambridge University Press, 1994: 1–96.
Williamson, Jeffrey G. *Trade and Poverty: When the Third World Fell Behind*. Cambridge, MA: MIT Press, 2013.
Woods, Ngaire. *The Globalizers: The IMF, the World Bank, and their Borrowers*. Ithaca, NY: Cornell University Press, 2006.

ADDITIONAL READING

Bielschowsky, Ricardo. "Cincuenta años del pensamiento de la CEPAL: una reseña." In *Cincuenta años del pensamiento de la CEPAL: textos seleccionados*. Vol. I, eds. Comisión Económica para América Latina y el Caribe / Naciones Unidas, Santiago: CEPAL and Fondo de Cultura Economica, 1998: 9–61.
  "Sesenta Años de la CEPAL y el pensamiento reciente." In *Sesenta años de la CEPAL: Textos seleccionados del decenio 1998–2008*, ed. Ricardo Bielschowsky, Buenos Aires: Siglo Veintiuno/CEPAL, 2010: 15–89.
Brown, Jonathan C. "Introduction, From Structuralism to the New Institutional Economics: A Half-Century of Latin American Economic Historiography." *Latin American Research Review* 40:3, 2005: 97–99.
Coatsworth, John H. "Structures, Endowments, and Institutions in the Economic History of Latin America." *Latin American Research Review* 40, 3, 2005, 126–144.
Kuntz Ficker, Sandra. "From Structuralism to the New Institutional Economics: The Impact of Theory on the Study of Foreign Trade in Latin America." *Latin American Research Review* 40, 3, 2005: 145–162.
Love, Joseph L. "The Rise and Decline of Economic Structuralism in Latin America: New Dimensions." *Latin American Research Review* 40, 3, 2005: 100–125.
  "Brazilian Structuralism." In Edmund Amann, Carlos Azzoni, and Werner Bauer, *The Oxford Handbook of the Brazilian Economy*. Oxford University Press, forthcoming.

3

The Arc of Development: Economists' and Sociologists' Quest for the State

Margarita Fajardo

INTRODUCTION

The notion of the state, and the underlying question of power structures, both drove and baffled Latin American development experts. As advisers and ministers, observers and interpreters, these social scientists made state power and public institutions the main instruments in the economic and social transformation that development entailed. The increasing state intervention in the economy spurred by the Great Depression, and reinforced during the Second World War, created an institutional infrastructure on which development experts came to rely for their own purposes. Central planning institutions, investment banks, public policy councils, and professional bureaucracies situated the state at the center of national development projects in the postwar era. The looming presence of the state nurtured hopes of transformation and fears of accommodation, yet at times it also appeared to be disappointingly ineffective. For development experts, especially those whose nexus was the United Nations Economic Commission for Latin America (ECLA in English and CEPAL in Spanish and Portuguese), the developmental state was not merely an instrument but an object of deep theoretical concern.[1]

Entrusted with an institutional mandate to understand and transform the relationship between Latin America and the world, the social scientists at CEPAL conceptualized the obstacles and challenges to development coming from the international economic order emerging after the Second World War. By routinely assessing and portraying Latin America in surveys and conferences as well as advocating for economic policies for

---

[1] We will employ the acronym formed from Spanish, CEPAL (Comisión Económica para América Latina), following common usage in recent development literature. On intellectuals in this period, see: Miller, 1999; Gilman, 2003; Iber, 2015; Chilcote, 2014.

industrialization and international cooperation, these social scientists engaged in a sustained effort to think and rethink the historical trajectory of development in the region. In the pursuit of development, they created significant intellectual contributions for the study of global political economy, encapsulated in concepts like center-periphery and dependency. Embedded in the ideas and theories to bring about economic development and to explain social change was a constant preoccupation with the public and political role of social scientific knowledge. This chapter turns to the efforts of these social scientists not to strengthen but to conceptualize the development state, and to understand their own role in the process of development.[2]

From the vantage point of the political and social crisis that culminated with the 1964 military coup in Brazil, and inaugurated a series of authoritarian regimes in the region, this chapter explores the notions about the state that flourished within the CEPAL network. It draws particular attention to disciplinary contributions of economists and sociologists and the conjuncture that made social scientists of the Universidade de São Paulo (USP), such as Fernando Henrique Cardoso and Octavio Ianni, part of the CEPAL network. More than just observers and interpreters, social scientists were active participants of the process they were trying to understand. The discussion about the state that here began had important repercussions in the literature about the state, and it could well have merited the assertion that they were already "bringing the state back in."[3]

Through a series of snapshots of their intellectual elaborations about the state, the chapter shows how these social scientists drew the arc of development in Latin America, from the Great Depression to the military dictatorships that engulfed the region, beginning with the 1964 coup in Brazil, and including their creation of a whole new reading of the region's history, that accompanies us to this day. With their contributions, they established the contours of a historical era that they shaped as much as it shaped them. Moreover, by conceptualizing the onset and denouement of the developmental state, social scientists realized the potential and limits of the state, and of their own expertise, as mechanisms of social transformation. In the process, they transformed global institutions such as CEPAL, they redefined the emerging social scientific disciplines, and they reinvented the political options and career-paths open for development experts in the future.

---

[2] On what is known as Latin American "structuralism" and the trajectory of CEPAL, see: Love's chapter in this volume; Fajardo (2015); Boianovsky and Solis, 2014; Kay, 1989; Rodríguez, 1980. With a keen eye to institutional dynamics but less interested in ideas, Dosman has focused on one leading expert of the network: Dosman, 2008.

[3] Evans, Skocpol, and Rueschmeyer, 1985.

THE WORLD OF ECONOMISTS: STRUCTURES AND THE ONSET OF THE
ARC OF DEVELOPMENT

The resignation of the President of Brazil, Jânio Quadros, in August 1961, and
the ascent of Labour Party leader and Vice-President João Goulart, triggered
a process of reform as well as of social and political mobilization that outpaced
the capacity of the existing institutions in the country. It also outpaced the ability
of social scientists to grapple with the problem of the political implications of
development. The mobilization of party leaders, industrial and professional
associations, labor unions, student groups, and low-level sectors of the military
had thwarted an imminent military coup. Politically united under the name of
Campaign for Legality (Campanha da Legalidade), these multiple actors
defended Goulart's right to the presidency. As a result, he was able to continue
in office with the compromise of introducing some elements of parliamentary
design into the political system and a constitutional reform a few years later.[4]
The across-the-board mobilization guaranteed the continuation of the
democratic regime but dwarfed the strength of the executive power, and it
made Goulart accountable to a myriad of contending forces. Roberto Schwarz,
a young political scientist from USP, and future member of the *Centro Brasileiro
de Análise e Planejamento* (CEBRAP), a think tank that emerged in opposition to
the military dictatorship, declared in view of the political infighting and the social
mobilization that surrounded the presidency of Goulart that "we were seeing the
structures crumbling before our eyes."[5]

To rally the support of a divided left and reinforce presidential powers, Goulart
made *Reformas de Base,* or structural reforms, his signature program and the
mechanism to transform those crumbling structures. Increasing taxation for
the wealthy, additional control over foreign investments, land redistribution, and
the granting of the right to vote to the illiterate population were some of the most
contested initiatives of the Goulart program. The Brazilian *Reformas de Base* were
not unique in the Latin American political landscape of the early 1960s. Aside from
the social reforms advocated by the Catholic Church and the Alliance for Progress,
the economists in Santiago had also advanced a notion of "structural reforms,"
one that a few years later was also adopted by the Christian Democrat Eduardo
Frei in his campaign to bring about a *Revolution in Liberty* in Chile.[6]

Structural reforms seemed to be required to tackle structural problems.
The CEPAL network had identified the constant scarcity of foreign
exchange – captured by measures such as international terms of trade and
capacity to import – and the limited size of the market given by the large rural
population as some of those structural problems.[7] Therefore, they had insisted

---

[4] Ferreira and Gomes, 2014: 41–42; Skidmore, 1967: 211–214.   [5] Moura and Montero, 2009.
[6] Gazmurri, 2000.
[7] The importance of access to foreign exchange and international cooperation in both trade and
investment appears prominently in CEPAL reports and meetings and reverberates throughout the
region in the language adopted by policymakers. For some crucial examples, see: CEPAL, 1950,

on the push for industrialization to save on scarce foreign exchange as well as diverse mechanisms of international cooperation including foreign aid, price agreements, and free-trade areas to increase the availability of hard currency and overcome a key obstacle for development. The implementation of those reforms would establish the foundations for economic and social transformation.

Formerly bound together by the conviction that Latin America was defined by its relation to the global economy, as well as by its path to development, social scientists and policymakers of the CEPAL network became divided in the late 1950s by the debates about inflation in Chile and Brazil.[8] Whether inflation was an obstacle to, or a consequence of, the process of development created a breach among CEPAL experts. Given contradictory experiences of inflation and development, these economists began to question the notion of Latin America – the regional economic structure – they had helped cement. As a result of these debates, many social scientists in the 1960s adopted the label of "structuralists" to identify themselves in a changing political environment in the region. In addition to the global character of Latin America's economic problems, these social scientists now rallied under the motto of "structural reforms."

One of those "structural reformers" was economist Celso Furtado. Born in the Northeastern state of Paraíba, trained in Law in Rio de Janeiro, and then in Economics in Paris, Celso Furtado had given extensive thought to Brazil's economic development mainly through his position at CEPAL in Santiago. Having joined this international commission since its inaugural year, Furtado became an active member: leading technical country missions, contributing to the consolidation of ties between national development institutions and the global body in Santiago, and delineating the Commission's research agenda. In defining the theoretical scope of the institution, Furtado was perhaps only second to Argentine economist Raúl Prebisch. After a politically contentious but ingenious policy trajectory in the Ministry of Finance, and then as architect and head of the Central Bank in his country, Prebisch joined CEPAL a few months after Furtado.[9] Never far removed from Brazil, Furtado established an academic journal in Rio and wrote extensively – with a striking rate of almost a book a year – about the Brazilian economy, with the aim not only of understanding economic processes, but also of trying to promote and rekindle the development trajectory at every turn of events. After CEPAL, and a brief intellectual sojourn at Oxford, Furtado was ready to return to Brazil,

---

1951. 1954. E/CN.12/359. On the turn towards social or institutional "structural reforms," see: Comisión Económica para América Latina, 1964; Ahumada, 1958.

[8] The labels of "monetarists" and "structuralists" were first advanced at a conference organized by Albert Hirschman. See: Hirschman, 1961. For some interpretations about this debate, see: Hirschman, 1963: 213–220; Boianovsky, 2012: 278–330; Love, 1995; Fajardo, 2015.

[9] For some additional references on Prebisch, see: Dosman, 2008; Pérez Caldentey and Vernengo, 2012: 7–22.

where he directed the national investment bank, tackled the problems of his native Northeast as architect and head of the Superintendência para o Desenvolvimento do Nordeste (SUDENE), and became Minister of Finance of the troubled Goulart government.[10] By the time of the military coup in Brazil that shook the intellectual and political ground of the development experts, Furtado had traversed multiple layers of academia, international research and consultancy, politics, and policymaking for the global enterprise of development.

A large part of the postwar policy and intellectual agenda of development was based on the role given to the Great Depression. Economists conceptualized the notion that a fundamental, structural change in the system of production had occurred in the region as a result of the 1930s global shock. Furtado and other postwar social scientists argued there had been a major shift from old patterns and orientations, and they thus established the onset of a new development path. Until 1914, Furtado claimed, "a colonial economy prevailed in Brazil."[11] Such an economy, based on coffee exports, was characterized by the "inability to grow without the impulse of another system, or better yet, [an economy] incapable of generating its own growth impetus."[12] The early signs of exhaustion of the coffee industry would come into full swing with the Great Depression, leading Furtado to claim that "1929 could be considered the end of an evolutionary phase of the Brazilian economy." The global economic shock had given the final blow to the colonial coffee system.[13]

The exhaustion of the colonial coffee economy that became evident with the Depression created an unexpected stimulus for domestic production. But the new favorable conditions for national producers were not merely the result of impersonal economic forces. Behind the new conditions, Furtado explained, was "a true program for stimulating national income." At the core of the program were the coffee policies of the federal state. The state of São Paulo had attempted to maintain the income of agricultural exporters through *valorização* schemes in which coffee was removed from the global market – at times even by physical destruction – to keep prices high. The state of São Paulo used the international financial system to buy and stockpile coffee. With the crisis, the federal government adopted the *paulista* policy but incorporated a pivotal innovation, Furtado claimed. Instead of financing the coffee purchases with external credit – unavailable due to the global contraction – the federal state financed it with internal credit expansion. The result of the policy was a rapid recovery from the crisis. "Unconsciously," Furtado remarked, the Brazilian state had "anticipated Keynesian anti-cyclical

---

[10] For a history and analysis of SUDENE, including the influence of TVA projects, see the chapter on Brazil in: Hirschman, 1963.

[11] Original in Portuguese. Translations here and thereafter are my own. Furtado, 1950: 8.

[12] Furtado, 1954: 15. [13] Furtado, 1950: 23.

policies."[14] Furthermore, the Brazilian state had created an "unprecedented situation" as "the sector linked to the internal market became predominant in the process of capital formation."[15] The state, not just economic forces, had been pivotal in the structural transformation that unraveled with the Great Depression. Yet, Furtado was adamant at emphasizing that this had been an "unconscious" or unintended process.

The uncovering of a powerful role of state institutions went hand-in-hand with sustained efforts at creating a space for economists in the policymaking world. If "structural change" after the Great Depression had commenced without any rational and concerted effort from any of the economic and political actors, the potential for planned efforts and directed policies seemed full of promise. The transition from mere anti-cyclical policy towards the "establishment of objectives to be reached by the different economic sectors in a specific period of time" with the "consequent private and public investment goals" was an opportunity for the economy, as well as a new career path for economists as planners and leaders.[16]

It was through the role of development experts such as those gathered around CEPAL that development became a dominating social and political project. Through regional economic surveys, training courses, and programming techniques, Furtado and other *cepalino* economists were mobilizing an idea that had been embedded in the fabric of the institution since its inauguration in 1948. The notion that Latin America was defined by its relationship to the global economy and that development entailed the transformation of that relationship was at the core of the project. These endeavors led Furtado to conclude that "only today" had "development become a problem."[17]

These economists imagined their role as intermediaries between global norms and national goals, and thus defined the field of development expertise. Only by acknowledging the cyclical character of capitalism and attempting to control its pendulous movement did economic development became an actual "problem." Paradoxically, the study of cycles had given economists the chance to assess secular tendencies and thus tackle the problem of long-term development. The end of what Furtado called the "colonial economy" was also the beginning of a space for economists, social science experts, and intellectuals who could bring about the desired "autonomy" of state institutions.

The character of the relationship between the region and the world, the so-called "external vulnerability," manifested itself in international monetary indicators such as terms of trade, balance of payments, and foreign-capital flows. The first of those factors was, according to Furtado and other economists at CEPAL, the fundamental source of economic disequilibria. Since industrialization of countries like Brazil demanded

---

[14] Furtado, 1954: 131.   [15] Furtado, 1954: 137.   [16] Furtado, 1954: 192.
[17] Furtado, 1954: 191.

large amounts of imported capital goods and raw materials, paid for with sharply fluctuating exports proceeds, the key to development lay in the management of scarce foreign exchange. The establishment of goals and the necessary investments to reach them required the allocation of both national currency and international reserves. That was precisely the area in which economic planning and the capacities of economists had to be mobilized.

During his second administration (1951–1954), and based on the work of the US-Joint Brazilian Economic Commission, President Getúlio Vargas established the Banco Nacional de Desenvolvimento Económico (BNDE) to provide credit for entrepreneurial activities in multiple sectors and to allocate the local counterpart to the funds that were expected from the Export–Import Bank and the International Bank for Reconstruction and Development (IBRD).[18] When the Eisenhower administration failed to deliver the expected resources, Roberto Campos, chief economist of BNDE, summoned the CEPAL economists to put into practice the planning or programming techniques generated in Santiago.[19] Furtado became the liaison figure between CEPAL in Santiago and BNDE in Rio as the latter incorporated planning to fulfill its original financial mission. Without a guaranteed flow of loans in foreign currency, and given highly fluctuating export proceeds, planning the allocation of foreign resources was a critical aspect in the minds of the CEPAL network economists. Both Furtado and Campos identified the chronic scarcity of foreign exchange as the main source of disequilibrium and major obstacle for development. The resulting CEPAL–BNDE working group provided the foundation for Juscelino Kubitschek's *Plano de Metas* and, in Furtado's words, "endowed the state with the technical resources to formulate and implement a broad development policy."[20] In doing so, social scientists like Furtado had become a constitutive part of the development institutional landscape.

The project of development was as much about transforming the relationship between Latin America and the world as of creating a social and public role for the region's experts and intellectuals. Furtado recalls Campos' "almost obsessive concern to curtail the 'irrationality' of politics."[21] Furtado was, at that moment, not too far from that interpretation. While he participated in the CEPAL–BNDE experiment, Furtado insisted on the need for "centralized organizations to influence the economic sphere," and on the idea of "men of thought" guiding these organizations. Furtado was equally enticed with the idea that policymaking implied the maneuvering of the state and the control of politics. Yet, Furtado's personal and intellectual stance with regards to politics as the struggle for the control of the state would change dramatically

---

[18] Tavares, Melo, and Caputo, 2010: 13–44. See also Furtado, 1989: 126. For the frustrations of Roberto Campos, with the extinct CMBEU and the IBRD, see: Campos, 1952.

[19] Campos, 1952.   [20] Furtado, 1989: 132.   [21] Furtado, 1989: 134.

from his years in the Brazil of Vargas to his participation in the arrested Goulart government. Only then would the structure and apparatus of the state itself grab completely his attention and that of younger Latin American intellectuals.

In their efforts to find the key to accelerate the development process, social scientists at the CEPAL network insisted on something more than the need to surpass the "export-led" or "outward-oriented growth." They advocated for the overcoming of the "stage of spontaneous growth" in which policies were circumstantial and state intervention reactive.[22] Along the lines of Furtado, Prebisch, Executive Secretary of CEPAL, better known for his thesis about the secular decline in the terms of trade, and for his leading role in advocating for industrialization and international cooperation as pillars for development, claimed, "in Latin America, the increasing state intervention in the economy has not been the result of ideology but of special circumstances: first, the Great Depression, then, the Second World War, and finally, inflation."[23] Just as the global shocks had inadvertently stimulated the production of manufactures for the internal market, as Furtado explained, the state gained pre-eminence during the Great Depression of the 1930s, Prebisch added.

This circumstantial involvement of the state in the economic sphere, observed since the 1930s, had to be superseded by a "form of intervention that creates or helps create conditions that indirectly influence the actions of the entrepreneurs," Prebisch claimed. Therefore, the state should "resort to monetary and fiscal policy and basic investments' policy, both of which stimulate private entrepreneurs without orienting their individual decisions."[24] In addition, Prebisch observed, "since external markets cannot absorb the region's exports ... in order to meet the demand for imports, economic development forces the substitution of import for internal production." That process, he explained, "requires protection and promotion policies" which so far "have not met rational efficiency criteria nor have they anticipated the investment needs that [development] requires."[25]

The problem of accelerating development was a matter of better policies, and therefore, a task for economists. Prebisch advocated for policies that connected investment, planning, and the transformation of the region's relation to the global economy. Given the constant scarcity of foreign exchange and the recurrent external payments crises, Latin American countries would benefit, Prebisch argued, from larger availability of foreign capital in the form of public loans, export earnings, and private investment. Therefore, the CEPAL proposal for financing development – presented at the Inter-American conference of Ministers of Economy and Finance held in a resort-town near Rio de Janeiro in November 1954 – aimed at providing foreign exchange for private entrepreneurs whose activities had been hindered by the inability to buy

[22] CEPAL, 1954: 3.   [23] CEPAL, 1954: 7.   [24] CEPAL, 1954: 9.   [25] CEPAL, 1954: 11.

imported capital goods and raw materials. In an astute political balancing act, Prebisch wanted to convince potential donors that international public finance wouldn't hinder private initiative, on the one hand, and his fellow Latin Americans that "vigorous stimulation of private activity did not entail the economic abstention of the state," on the other.

State intervention, especially in regards to international financial constraints, was not under scrutiny; Prebisch and Furtado were beginning to focus instead on the tools and mechanisms to perform such intervention. Their insistence on the "spontaneity" or "empirical character" of the past experiences of state intervention was their own contribution in an effort to legitimize a new political sphere of action for economists more broadly, and for CEPAL specifically. Prebisch's proposal was driven precisely by the considerations about the role that economists had to play in the management of state institutions. Therefore, by establishing investment goals and then "continuing with the analysis and forecasts of economic development carried out by CEPAL," the state could engage in a serious development policy that systematically allocated resources in national and foreign currency.[26]

If the global shock of the 1930s had provided the impulse for a change in the economic system, economists and social scientists believed that another global shock, the Second World War, had given them the chance to seize control of the process through the formulation and implementation of public policies. The war economy had fostered the creation of national planning and industrial promotion institutions such as the Conselho Nacional do Café, Comissão Siderurgica Nacional, and the Conselho Nacional do Petróleo, in the case of Brazil.[27] Chile and Colombia created similar agricultural and industrial promotion institutions, discussed in José Orihuela's chapter 5 in this volume.[28] The war had also resulted in the use of exchange controls and multiple exchange rates, as well as the stockpiling of coffee beans, and the increasing rate of industrial output. Yet, the postwar moment and its inclination towards open, freer trade and global integration, forced the economists to reconsider national and international institutional frameworks, in the pursuit of the reconstruction of the global economic order.

This was precisely the context in which CEPAL emerged and became a significant international actor. As leading members of a key international institution, Prebisch and Furtado contributed to a new kind of discourse on public policy and political issues. They touched upon the daily challenges of

---

[26] CEPAL, 1954: 22 and 24.

[27] For more on the economics and political economy of the Vargas era, see: Araujo, 1999; Bastos and Fonseca, 2011; and chapter 7 by Luciana de Souza Leão in the present volume.

[28] The connection of planning with regional development has been noticed, particularly in relation to the model of TVA, which was very influential in Latin America. See Lilienthal, 1944, and Orihuela's chapter in this volume.

handling monetary and fiscal policies while meeting industrialization demands that policymakers in the region were trying to come to terms with. But they also pointed towards the role of global capital markets and institutions. The fusing of the objectives of autonomy and integration in the regional commission, and in the profession of the economist, would help consolidate a program for development in the region, one that would become the object of vast discussions in the next decade. For Furtado and Prebisch, the "developmental state" was defined by public policy programs under the purview of the economists, but also by new institutional designs, and innovative political practices.

SÃO PAULO INTELLECTUALS AND THE "STATE QUESTION"

Emerging side-by-side and feeding off each other, development was woven into the intellectual, institutional, and political fabric of the Latin American social sciences. From the mid 1930s to the early 1960s, university departments and schools, professional associations, and academic journals in sociology, economics, and political science were established.[29] Not without contestation, new international institutions such as the United Nations Education, Scientific, and Cultural Organization (UNESCO) and later on non-governmental groups like the Ford Foundation further reinforced the trend towards the organization of the production of knowledge in specific disciplines around the world.[30] However, the relation between the Latin American social sciences and the national and international, public and private apparatus of development went beyond patronage or ideology. At the moment of the internationalization of the social sciences, CEPAL became the nexus for a network of economists and social scientists whose project was to produce situated knowledge for the overarching project of economic development. With the end of the war and through the endeavors of the new institution, development or modernization increasingly became the main theoretical and research problem for the emerging academic disciplines.

Sociologists took up the intellectual quest for the state, which had begun as policymakers and economists made 1930 the genesis of the development arc. It was amidst the upsurge in political activity and social mobilization of the Goulart years that a group of social scientists at Universidade de São Paulo initiated a research program to provide a "sociological examination of underdevelopment." Given the political mobilization of the Goulart years, the research project entitled "Economy and Society in Brazil," identified three main

---

[29] For an institutional approach to the history of social sciences in the region, see: Trindade, Garretón, Murmis, and Sierra, 2007. For additional literature on the relationship between the social sciences and development, see: Miceli, 1995; Babb, 2004; Montecinos, 1998. Devés, 2003. See also the articles by Blanco, Jackson, and Adelman in Altamirano, 2010.

[30] See articles by Ross and Barshay in: Ross and Porter, 2008. See also: Coats, 1995.

social and political actors as agents of social change: the industrial entrepreneurs, the state, and the labor force. Florestan Fernandes, the so-called "architect of Brazilian academic sociology" spearheaded the collective effort to apply the social sciences to this new field of study.[31] Fernandes wanted to surpass the prevailing humanist tradition and implement quantitative and qualitative research methods to "understand the collapse of the order based on masters and slaves and the formation of a class society in Brazil."[32] To do so, he rallied the financial support of the Confederação Nacional da Industria, the São Paulo industrialists, and the Fundação da Amparo a Pesquisa do Estado de São Paulo. Far from an exclusive academic pursuit, "in underdeveloped countries," Fernandes argued, "the selection of a research topic is not a completely free intellectual initiative." Rather, he explained, the researcher is compelled to study "those aspects that have real implications for the renovation of the cultural horizon and offer a rational solution for the ongoing process of development."[33] Among those aspects was the question of the role of state and its institutions.

Fernandes believed the key question for Brazil was not whether or not state intervention in the economy was necessary. Nor was it whether that intervention served to protect certain groups and interests with the purpose of fostering economic growth. After all, he argued, "ever since the imperial government," the intervention in the economy and the protection of economic interests had been vital components of the Brazilian state. Instead, the current and pressing challenge, Fernandes claimed, was the question of the "democratization of political authority" and "the modernization of the state apparatus." As the conflict of interests and the competition over the state clouded the Brazilian political climate, social scientists set out in the quest for a state that buttressed developmentalism while consolidating democracy. "Developmentalism," Fernandes argued, "could easily become a corrupt version of a republican regime veering towards a plutocracy."[34] Only by democratizing the state, had developmentalism the chance of becoming a truly collective project.

Simultaneously at Santiago, a growing concern about the politics of development was taking hold. Under the leadership of Spanish sociologist José Medina Echavarría, and of Prebisch and Furtado, a new intellectual endeavour was in the making, based on the restless desire to come up with an interpretation of reality so accurate that it could dovetail the historical trajectory, and thus alter it. Trying to supersede narrow definitions of the "social" as unintended effects of the focus on economic development, Medina Echavarría, along with other leading sociologists, strived to comprehend the social and political conditions that made development possible.[35] This intellectual project would create a space

---

[31] Arruda, 1995. See also: Jackson, 2010.   [32] Fernandes, 1976: 300.
[33] Fernandes, 1976: 309.   [34] Fernandes, 1976: 317–318.   [35] Medina Echavarría, 1963.

for the São Paulo sociologists within the Commission in Santiago and culminate in the production of a concept that would revolutionize Latin American social sciences and politics in the following decade: dependency.

The sociological approach to development unfolding in São Paulo was driven by the questions of power, politics, and the role of the state. Francisco Weffort, Octavio Ianni, and Fernando Henrique Cardoso were prominent figures in this quest. Octavio Ianni was born, raised and educated in the state of São Paulo. Ianni, who believed in the use of literature to understand sociological problems, paired the analysis of industrial capitalism in Brazil with the "incorporation of new functions and redefinition of old ones that led to the transformation of the structure of the state itself after 1930."[36] Contesting Furtado's assertion that the growing role of the state after 1930 had been circumstantial and spontaneous, Ianni explained that such a claim entailed "charging the Revolution of 1930 with a high level of irrationality and confusion." Far from it, Ianni implied. Though the economists had walked a long way in understanding Brazil's economic development, Ianni argued, they had characterized the process as a "blind force," "occurring behind the back of men . . . as if the structural forces did not have the ability to produce, in different degree, a consciousness of the situation."[37] By taking Getúlio Vargas from the borderland state of *Rio Grande do Sul* to the center of national politics, the Revolution of 1930 captured the shifting tendency in the structure of production and thus, it constituted "a turning point for Brazil in which the power structure [was] deeply transformed."[38] The movement that took the most influential political figure in twentieth-century Brazil to power could not be the product of a coincidence. Therefore, the Revolution and the crisis of 1930 became a marker of the arc of development in which structures and conjunctures aligned.

The social scientists at CEPAL had made 1930 a trope. The significance of 1930 signaled a shared conviction of the global character of Latin American development. It was a global shock that had shifted the orientation from the external to the internal market. Furthermore, the Great Depression and its rippling effects over the economic structure were constantly reiterated in the reports made by CEPAL and in the academic articles of its members. In doing so, the *cepalinos* marked the beginning of an era defined by import-substitution industrialization or the so-called "inward-looking development" that still prevails. The global shocks of the postwar era were interpreted in that light. The recurrent balance-of-payments crises, for instance, threatened a model of development that hinged on both the expansion of the internal market and the supply of imported goods for such an expansion. Thus, every crisis forced the CEPAL network economists to rethink the development arc that had commenced in 1930.

---

[36] Ianni, 1964: 551.   [37] Ianni, 1964: 554.   [38] Ianni, 1964: 568.

In drawing the development arc, sociologists made Furtado and CEPAL active participants in the process. The power structure that emerged in the 1930s included the national bourgeoisie, and to a lesser extent the working and the middle classes, but it also included the intellectuals and experts. The "renovating movement" that began in the 1930s and started to "sweep industrialists, managers, experts, and politicians along the way ... was reinvigorated at the end of the Second World War with institutions like CEPAL," Ianni explained.[39] In the mind of the sociologist, Furtado was a participant of development, trying to direct the countervailing forces, as much as Vargas or the national entrepreneurs could have been.

If 1930 had veered the structure of production and altered the organization of the state, what role did entrepreneurs, the alleged drivers of capitalism, have in the process? Were state and class interests aligned? Fernando Henrique Cardoso tackled the problem of power from the perspective of the entrepreneurs as "agents of social change." He established a research agenda on the class-consciousness and political ambition of the Brazilian industrial entrepreneurs. Illustrating the difficulties of getting to the crux of the problem in the convoluted Goulart years, Cardoso described the industrialists' relation to the state as a conflict of opposing impulses. At first, he characterized the industrialists as "lacking the necessary process of socialization to perform their duties within a bourgeois, democratic republic." Instead of acting according to their class interests, "industrialists confronted the state," Cardoso argued, "as part of the electoral mass, adhering to general grievances such as the rising cost of living, inflation, or simply in opposition to the government."[40] Cardoso had expected to find a dominant bourgeoisie behind the state endeavors to promote development. Instead, surveys of attitudes of the Brazilian entrepreneurs revealed an intimidated and vacillating bourgeoisie, one that accommodated to traditional values and agricultural interests at times, sided with the emerging working class in others, and more often than not sympathized with foreign industrialists, their competitors in many respects.

Despite the industrial bourgeoisie "missing its chance to exercise total class domination," Cardoso perceived some tendencies that pointed in that direction. Industrialists had in the past opted for the favors and the protection of the government, which for Cardoso implied a penetration of patrimonial relationships into the state. Changing course, however, in recent pronouncements, the industrialists' position towards "state intervention was full of reservations and conditions."[41] This could reveal, Cardoso argued, that "industrial leaders are reorganizing themselves in ways that reveal a new form of self-consciousness," one in which "political action is aligned with their own interests." But the consequences of the political action of the industrialists were yet to be seen.

[39] Ianni, 1964; 564–565. [40] Cardoso, 1964: 163, 165. [41] Cardoso, 1964: 173.

To a certain extent, the pace of events was going faster than the analytical abilities of the social scientists. Actors were behaving in puzzling and chaotic ways. In the eyes of perplexed intellectuals, the multiplication of forces contending for political domination, and for control of the state, would result in several diverse explanations about what made Latin American states suddenly prone to renewed forms of military intervention. Coming to terms with the economists' arc of development, the sociologists had turned towards an intellectual quest for the state.

WHEN ECONOMISTS AND SOCIOLOGISTS MET

The widespread support rallied to guarantee Goulart's ascendancy when threatened by military intervention in 1961 was short-lived. Social groups and political parties, of both the right and the left, organized and mobilized to push through their own particular version of the proposed public policy programs.[42] By 1962, inflation had reached 52 percent while GDP growth only amounted to 1 percent. In addition, almost 45 percent of the country's foreign debt matured in the following three years, increasing the urgency of renewed foreign capital flows.[43] To resolve the impasse, Goulart turned to economist Celso Furtado, then at SUDENE, who in turn produced the *Plano Trienal*. The *Plano* combined a monetary stabilization program that included credit control, wage freezes, and budget cuts with a development plan to carry *reformas de base* forward. It was his legitimacy as a planner and his association with the "positive" or moderate left in Brazil that made Furtado the perfect candidate to accompany Minister of Finance San Tiago Dantas in the pursuit of growth and monetary stability.[44] The *Plano* would give Goulart a road map to maintain governability and appease foreign investors.

In April 1963, the *Plano* confronted increasing resistance. Goulart received initial support from the large labor unions and industrial associations until the deterioration of the economic situation became too hard to endure. In the meantime, San Tiago Dantas managed to renegotiate the existing debts but not to secure additional resources. The International Monetary Fund mission, whose approval of the plan would send a positive signal for private banks, arrived in Brazil just as the pressure for wage readjustment was mounting. Goulart ceded to the pressure for raising wages and easing credit, resulting in another cabinet reshuffling. What Minister San Tiago Dantas had called the negative left quickly seized the chance to denounce the foreign intervention in Brazilian politics. As Jorge Ferreira and Angela Gomez describe the situation, the plan simply imploded.[45]

---

[42] Ferreira and Gomes, 2014. For more description and analysis of the mobilization of both the left and the right, see chapters 4 and 5.

[43] San Tiago Dantas, 1963.   [44] Skidmore, 1967: 217–218.

[45] Ferreira and Gomes, 2014: 158–159.

The ministerial endeavors of Furtado and San Tiago Dantas were Goulart's last efforts to generate a broader national consensus. After the abandonment of the *Plano*, the president's collaboration with the "positive left" ended and the reliance on an uncompromising radical left began. The experience of being at the frontline of the debate about controlling inflation while stimulating growth dramatically altered the perspective of economist and policymaker Celso Furtado. The fall of Goulart, and the subsequent establishment of, in the words of Furtado, "a military state," triggered a long-lasting interrogation about the politics, and the political economy of development.

Shunned from national politics and the front stage of policymaking, Furtado returned to SUDENE, if only briefly. The implosion of the *Plano Trienal* was followed by a series of events and struggles that until today defy in part the understanding of social scientists and historians. On the night of March 31, 1964, and after both the left and right had courted their intervention, military forces were deployed in all major cities of the country. A week later, the first of multiple Institutional Acts limiting the rights guaranteed by the Constitution was issued, dissolving the expectations about a contained military intervention.

Given the initial restriction of political rights to politicians, journalists, and intellectuals, among which was Celso Furtado, social scientists found refuge within an already familiar intellectual community. At Santiago, both Weffort and Cardoso became part of a group that was to establish the "political conditions of economic planning." It was the same group that had, under the leadership of Medina Echavarría, set out to include the "social aspects of development" and broadened both the understanding and the area of competence of the Santiago-based institution. In the midst of the political turmoil, Furtado had urged for reconsideration of "the conditions on which power rests, that is, the conditions that uphold these structures." From a place of deep disappointment with policy making, Furtado was impatient to come to terms with power. In early 1964, he had explained to the members of the board of the new institute at Santiago: "Given a specific socio-economic structure, one that is reflected in a particular equilibrium of power, economic planning is fruitless." His experience had forced him to realize that the "instruments of the economists," such as the agrarian, fiscal, and administrative reforms, "do not change the existing structures."[46] Coming from the author of the *Plano Trienal* and long-term advocate of planning, the statement must have shocked the board of the recently created Instituto de Planificación Económica y Social (ILPES) in Santiago. Nevertheless, Furtado was not giving up on the power of social scientific knowledge and expertise. Politics, not policies, had hindered the possibility of development. Therefore, the new task for social scientists was to comprehend the national power structures. As Cardoso and Weffort moved to Santiago, Furtado's call catalyzed a process that would have long-term implications for the social sciences in Latin America. In the case of Cardoso,

---

[46] ILPES, 1964.

for instance, the intellectual endeavor to come to terms with a tumultuous political scenario and theorize about the state would culminate in a career in politics, and the presidency of Brazil 1995–2002.

Since it raised questions about the failure of developmental policies, and the denouement of the arc of development, explaining the fall of Goulart and the advent of military rule captured the minds of social scientists for years to come. Policies that seemed necessary for promoting the development process had created or exacerbated political conflicts, and destroyed long-term planning efforts. On the one hand, the push for agrarian reform and redistribution of property, as well as granting the vote to the illiterate population, seemed to antagonize traditional landed interests and made them support radical anti-democratic interventions. On the other hand, the attempts to control foreign investment by imposing limits to remittances abroad and promote local capital seemed to antagonize the interests of industrialists who had increasingly built partnerships with foreign companies. To complicate the scenario even further, the radical left had fragmented the strength of Goulart's traditional constituency, the labor unions. Even the military itself was divided between nationalists and conservative modernizers.

It was hard to establish which structures were shifting when society as a whole seemed in turmoil. But solving that question was key to understanding what was originally perceived as the demise of development. Did the military state represent a rupture or a continuation of the state that assumed the task of development? The collapse of the democratic regime, Furtado initially argued, entailed the triumph of the traditional landed interests. The stalemate between the executive and congress lay at the root of political instability, and the inability to carry out the project of national development. According to Furtado, those power branches were responding to two very different constituencies. "In the postwar period, the pact with the masses, represented the necessary condition to reach Executive power," Furtado explained. Nonetheless, "given the power of those who control Congress and large part of the state apparatus," "the goals of the President are always incompatible with the limits imposed by Congress."[47] The confrontation with Congress resonated strongly in the mind of former Minister Furtado. Nonetheless, his view, though authoritative, was charged with the immediacy of politics and the failure of intellectuals whose ability to transform society had imploded the closest they got to power.

Nevertheless, the ultimate contradiction within the state that had assumed the task of development was not to be found in the political conjuncture of the moment. Francisco Weffort, a political scientist and a friend of Cardoso, explained that the contradiction lay with the political regime established with the Revolution of 1930. The latter led to "the elimination of the oligarchic state based on the large, export-oriented landholdings and the establishment of

[47] Furtado, 1965: 384.

a democratic state buttressed on the popular urban mass and the sectors associated with industrialization."[48] But the transition had been incomplete. Populism had not solved but just absorbed the contradictions of a developmental state that only seemed to be democratic and not subject to the interests of the landed and for that matter, other elites.

By situating the origins of the "military state" in the Revolution of 1930 instead of with the triumph of reactionary forces, Weffort's analysis was therefore providing a response to Furtado, both as an intellectual and a policymaker. It was also closing down the arc of development. Furtado had highlighted the importance of the global economic crisis in shaking the economic structure of Brazil. But he had also suggested that the state itself, even if unknowingly, had transcended old patterns of politics and policies. Yet, according to Ianni and Weffort, the political structure and the shape of the state had only changed so much. Given the inability of the landed interests, the rising industrialists, or the professional middle sectors to "offer a solid foundation for the state," "the urban masses became the only source of legitimacy for the Brazilian state." In turn, "based on his personal prestige with the urban masses, Getúlio Vargas inaugurated the state's power as an institution."[49] The political interplay between the contending groups "fostered the image of a sovereign state." Acting as an arbiter, the "sovereign state" appeared autonomous from economic interests, Weffort argued. The quest to come to terms with the state, the one underpinning development and in which Furtado had participated, resulted in a profound examination of the part played by development experts as well, of which the notion of dependency was the most salient result, as I argue elsewhere.

The national "developmental state" was denounced as a fiction created by populist politics. In the words of Weffort, the crisis that unfolded with the resignation of Jânio Quadros, continued with the fall of Goulart, and resulted in the ascent of the military revealed the lack of autonomy, or sovereignty of the state. The state could not "set itself above vested interests and, in the name of national interests, reform the structures," as economists like Furtado had expected.[50] The process of democratization of the state was never fully consolidated and had run into an impasse. To consolidate its power, the state had to reform itself. In the words of Furtado, the democratization had to continue by expanding political citizenship in order to carry out the necessary structural reforms to foster growth.[51] Nonetheless, for Furtado, the developmental state was an unfinished project, and its continuation required better policies, and a widening of citizens' participation in political decisions.

Amidst the turmoil before the coup, social scientists had been unable to precisely locate the economic interests behind dominant structures. The multiplicity of contending interests and social groups, running

---

[48] Weffort, 1965: 53.   [49] Weffort, 1965: 57.   [50] Weffort, 1965: 68.
[51] Furtado, 1965: 379, 387.

continuously into a stalemate, contrasted with the image of an autonomous state. Because it carried out the transition from underdevelopment to development without the hegemony of one group, the state gave the impression of autonomy, Cardoso argued. It favored industrial interests but it was not a bourgeois democracy. It favored the interests of a landed elite but it was not an oligarchic state. The same was true of the urban popular sectors, whose interests were mediated by populism. Yet, the military coup struck a blow on that scheme and the economic interests emerged more clearly. Notions such as dependency and dependent development that would emerge a few years later reveal these social scientists' increased sense of confidence in their assessment. The alliance of foreign and national industrialists became the key factor in the new understanding of the state. Suddenly, a class-based state appeared before their eyes, leading Cardoso to deem the regime a "bourgeois hegemony."[52]

Weffort had situated the irruption of the military as the end of an era, and thus closed the arc of development.[53] The democratization of the state through populism was over and with it, the idea of an autonomous, developmental state. In his earlier work during the CEPAL years, Furtado had sounded, prematurely perhaps, the death knell of the power of the oligarchy, and thus of the oligarchic state, and the beginning of the developmental state. Later on, Cardoso had exposed the lack of political aspirations and will to achieve domination of the Brazilian bourgeoisie. Then, in an effort to explain the political crisis, Weffort condemned both the right and the left for believing in the autonomy of the state and ascribing to it the power of arbitrage that development entailed. Ianni had described the increasing role of the state as entrepreneur and central-planner, driven by economists, engineers, and white-collar civil servants. Social scientists, among other experts, had helped foster what for the observers of the coup seemed in retrospect an illusion of autonomy. Cardoso held intellectuals and experts like Furtado accountable for the aspirations deposited on the developmental state. Referring to CEPAL, the "possibility of self-propelling development," Cardoso claimed, "found theoretical ground in the most conspicuous writings ever produced on the 'economic development' in Latin America."[54] The São Paulo social scientists were coming full circle in an analysis that through the quest of the state drew the arc of development, but most importantly, found the social and political role of intellectuals and experts in creating the idea of the developmental state. The search for the roots of the political instability and military intervention had this time, unlike during the fall of Vargas, promoted a renewed search for the theory and practice of the politics of the development state in Brazil and Latin America.

---

[52] Cardoso, 1968. For some North American ramifications of the São Paulo sociological tradition, see: Evans, 1979; Wirth, 1970.
[53] Weffort, 1965.   [54] Cardoso, 1965: 1.

CONCLUSIONS

The concept of bureaucratic-authoritarianism (BA), originally developed by Guillermo O'Donnell, represents one of the most influential efforts to theorize the state in Latin America.[55] Beginning with Brazil in 1964, followed by Argentina in 1966, Peru in 1968, and finally Uruguay and Chile in 1973, the establishment of military regimes led to multiple and original attempts at grappling with the specificity of the emerging power configurations. Yet, for historically minded, analytically structuralist economists, sociologists, and political scientists, the end of electoral politics and the new focus on authoritarianism represented the culmination of a long-winded quest to come to terms with the political economy of development. As this chapter has shown, the quest for the state began with the economists' need to legitimize their own position in the development process, and passed by the sociologists' critique on the political, economic, but also the intellectual elites of development. O'Donnell's work was the culmination of this process.

Development not only underpinned the modernization of the state but also the professionalization of the social sciences. It gave Latin American social scientists a position in the political economy of development but also prompted a quest for theorizing the state. Development legitimized research agendas, inspired policies, and mobilized social scientists towards leading positions in state institutions. At first, economists aimed at maneuvering the state through monetary and fiscal policies and planning institutions, and thus they conceived the state as an object of development. With the end of the Second World War and the prospects of reconstruction of the global order, economists began to recast the development arc. They conceptualized the global shock of the 1930s as the final blow to the "colonial economy" and the onset of a new state apparatus for development. But the spontaneous policies that emerged in response to the crisis had to be transformed into effective planning, a task conceptualized by the economists.

Yet, the global order in which the state bureaucracies had found strength was not the same as the one unfolding after the Second World War. The pre-war world of restricted trade, controlled currencies, and remnants of British leadership gave way to a world of less restricted trade, more global integration, and the enduring dominance of the American dollar. The economists conceptualized their role and that of the state, as mediating between national and international domains, reconciling national autonomy and global integration. Their focus on the scarcity of

---

[55] The literature on authoritarian regimes in Latin America boomed in the 1970s after Guillermo O'Donnell's initial formulation: O'Donnell, 1973. O'Donnell underscores the extent to which his formulation was based on the Brazilian experience and the intellectual production it had sparked. Years later, an edited volume consolidated the main contributions of the period, see: Collier, 1979. For an analysis of the social sciences in the 1970s, see: Adelman and Fajardo, 2016: 3–22.

foreign exchange or external vulnerability aimed to offer national states the possibility of navigating in the American-led global order without sacrificing the gains in industrialization. Thus, the economists had privileged the global sphere as their scope of intervention, and state intervention as the tool for the transformation of the region's relation to the global economy.

When the sociologists embraced the problem of the political economy of development, the political and intellectual discourse about development was already filled with references to the negative effects of the terms of trade, the chronic balance-of-payments crisis, and the vocabulary of center and peripheries. At the same time, CEPAL economists in both Chile and Brazil were coming closer to power. The time had come to make the state the actor of development and understand the political forces that underpinned those initiatives. Therefore, they turned to the analysis of the elites and classes that strengthened or weakened the state. This renewed quest for the state was marked by political turmoil and the advent of military rule, clouding the ability of social scientists to identify changing structures. The advent of what appeared to be a new form of state prompted an effort to theorize the developmental state under authoritarian regimes. Whereas some perceived the military state as a rupture, others identified continuities that pointed to the fiction of an autonomous state, or of a state that could bestow the promised autonomous development. In the process of searching for the state and for agents of social change, the social scientists discovered themselves as part of the Latin American political economy of development, giving rise to Fernando Henrique Cardoso's notion of dependency. Then, in the mid to late 1960s, Latin American social sciences would find new possibilities of politics as an arena for intellectuals. For some, this process entailed a new path to violent revolution; for those who remained loyal to CEPAL tenets, electoral politics remained the instrument for development, but they had first to think again how to reconcile capitalism with democracy in the region.

REFERENCES

Adelman, Jeremy and Margarita Fajardo. "Between Capitalism and Democracy: A Study in the Political Economy of Ideas in Latin America, 1968–1980." *Latin American Research Review*, 51, 3 (2016): 3–22.
Ahumada, Jorge. *En vez de la miseria*. Santiago: Editorial del Pacífico, 1958.
  ed. *Historia de los intelectuales en América Latina: Los avatares de la "ciudad letrada" en el siglo XX*. 2 vols., vol. II. Buenos Aires: Katz Editores, 2010.
Arruda, Maria Arminda. "A Sociologia no Brasil: Florestan Fernandes e a 'escola paulista.'" In *História das Ciências Sociais no Brasil*, ed. Sergio Miceli. São Paulo: Editora Sumaré; IDESP, 1995.
Babb, Sarah. *Managing Mexico: Economists from Nationalism to Neoliberalism*. Princeton University Press, 2004.
Boianovsky, Mauro. "Celso Furtado and the Structuralist-Monetarist Debate on Economic Stabilization in Latin America." *History of Political Economy*, 44, 2 (2012): 277–329.

Boianovsky, Mauro and Ricardo Solís. "The Origins and Development of the Latin American Structuralist Approach to the Balance of Payments (1944–1964)." *Review of Political Economy*, 26, 1 (2014): 23–59.

Campos, Roberto de Oliveira. "Projeto de acôrdo sobre coordenação de pesquisas entre o Banco Nacional do Desenvolvimento Economico e a Comissão Econômica da America Latina." Roberto de Oliveira Campos to Dr. J.S. Maciel Filho, Rio de Janeiro, 29 de Setembro, 1952. Roberto Campos, Rio de Janeiro, Centro de Pesquisa e Documentação de História Contemporânea do Brasil, Fundação Getulio Vargas, RC e bnde 1952.09.29, pasta I, doc. 1, 1952.

Cardoso, Fernando Henrique. *Empresariado industrial e desenvolvimento no Brasil.* São Paulo: Difusão Europeia do Livro, 1964.

"Hegemonia Burguesa e Independência Econômica: Raízes Estruturais da Crise Política Brasileira." In *O Brasil: Tempos Modernos*, ed. Celso Furtado. São Paulo: Paz e Terra, 1968.

CEPAL. "Estudio Económico de América Latina, 1949." New York, 1950.

"Estudio Económico de América Latina, 1950." New York, 1951.

"La cooperación internacional en la política de desarrollo latinoamericana." New York, 1954. E/CN.12/359.

Chilcote, Ronald. *Intellectuals and the Search for National Identity in Twentieth-Century Brazil.* Cambridge University Press, 2014.

Collier, David, ed. *The New Authoritarianism in Latin America.* Princeton University Press, 1979.

Devés, Eduardo. *El pensamiento latinoamericano en el siglo XX: de la CEPAL al neoliberalismo.* Buenos Aires: Biblos, 2003.

Evans, Peter. *Dependent Development: The Alliance of Multinational, State, and Local Capital in Brazil.* Princeton University Press, 1979.

Evans, Peter, Theda Skocpol, and Dietrich Rueschmeyer, eds. *Bringing the State Back In.* Cambridge University Press, 1985.

Fajardo, Margarita. *The Latin American Development Experience: Social Sciences, Economic Policies, and the Making of a Global Order, 1944–1971.* PhD Dissertation, Princeton University, 2015.

Fernandes, Florestan. "Economia e Sociedade no Brasil: análise sociológica do subdesenvolvimento." In: *A Sociologia numa Era de Revolução Social*, ed. Florestan Fernandes. Rio de Janeiro: Zahar Editores, 1976.

Ferreira, Jorge. *João Goulart: uma biografia.* Rio de Janeiro: Civilização Brasileira, 2011.

O populismo e sua história: debate e crítica. Rio de Janeiro: Civilização Brasileira, 2011.

Ferreira, Jorge and Angela de C. Gomes. *1964: O golpe que derrubou um presidente, pôs fim ao regime democrático e instituiu a ditadura no Brasil.* Rio de Janeiro: Civilização Brasileira, 2014.

Furtado, Celso. "Características da economia brasileira." *Revista Brasileira de Economia*, 4, 1, 1950: 7–38.

A Economia Brasileira: contribuição a análise do seu desenvolvimento. Rio de Janeiro: Editora A Noite, 1954.

"Obstáculos políticos para el desarrollo económico." *Desarrollo Económico*, 4, 16, 1965: 373–389.

La Fantasía Organizada. Bogotá: Tercer Mundo Editores, 1989.

Garretón, Manuel Antonio, Miguel Murmis, Geronimo Sierra, and Hélgio Trindade. "Social Sciences in Latin America: A Comparative Perspective –Argentina, Brazil, Chile, Mexico, and Uruguay." *Social Science Information*, 5 57, 2005: 557–593.

Gilman, Claudia. *Entre la pluma y el fusil: Debates y dilemas del escritor revolucionario en América Latina.* Buenos Aires: Siglo XXI, 2003.

Hirschman, Albert, ed. *Latin American Issues.* New York: Twentieth Century Fund, 1961.

Journeys Toward Progress: Studies of Economic Policy-Making in Latin America. New York: The Twentieth Century Fund, 1963.

Ianni, Octavio. "El Estado y el desarrollo económico del Brasil." *Desarrollo Económico*, 2, 4, 1964: 551–572.

ILPES (Instituto Latinoamericano y del Caribe de Planificación Económica y Social). "Actas Resumidas de la Cuarta Reunión del Consejo Directivo." Santiago January 13–14. INST/32/Rev.1, 1964.

Jackson, Luiz Carlos. "Generaciones pioneras de las ciencias sociales en Brasil." In *Historia de los intelectuales en América Latina*, ed. Carlos Altamirano. Buenos Aires: Katz Editores, 2010.

Kay, Cristóbal. *Latin American Theories of Development and Underdevelopment.* London: Routledge, 1989.

Love, Joseph. "Economic Ideas and Ideologies in Latin America since 1930." In *The Cambridge History of Latin America*, ed. Leslie Bethell. Cambridge University Press, 1995.

Medina Echavarría, José. "Sección de Sociología del Desarrollo." Santiago: ILPES, 1963, https://repositorio.cepal.org/handle/11362/32938 (accessed October 17, 2017).

Miller, Nicola. *In the Shadow of the State: Intellectuals and the Quest for National Identity in Twentieth-Century Spanish America.* London: Verso, 1999.

Montecinos, Verónica. *Economists, Politics and the State: Chile, 1958–94.* Amsterdam: CEDLA, 1998.

Moura, Flavio and Paula Montero. *Retrato de grupo.* São Paulo: Cosac y Naify, 2009.

O'Donnell, Guillermo. *Modernization and Bureaucratic Authoritarianism: Studies in South American Politics.* Berkeley: Institute of International Studies, University of California, 1973.

Oliveira, Lúcia Lippi de "As Ciências Sociais no Rio de Janeiro." In *História das Ciências Sociais no Brasil*, ed. Sergio Miceli. São Paulo: Editora Sumaré: FABESP, 1995.

Ross, Dorothy and Theodore Porter, *The Cambridge History of Science, Vol. 7: The Modern Social Sciences.* Cambridge University Press, 2008.

San Tiago Dantas, Francisco Clementino de. Plano Restituição Dívida Externa, March 25. Rio de Janeiro, Arquivo Nacional, AP. 47 No. 41: 2, 1963.

Skidmore, Thomas. *Politics in Brazil, 1930–64: An Experiment in Democracy.* Oxford University Press, 1967.

Tavares, Maria Conceição, Hildete Melo, and Ana Caputo, "As origens do Banco Nacional Econômico (BNDE) 1952–1955." *Memórias do Desenvolvimento*, 4, 4, 2010: 13–44.

Trindade, Helio, Manuel Antonio Garretón, Miguel Murmis, and Gerónimo Sierra, *As Ciências Socias na América Latina em Pespective Comparada, 1930–2005.* Porto Alegre: Editora UFRGS, 2007.

Weffort, Francisco. "Estado y masas en el Brasil." *Revista Latinoamericana de Sociología*, 1, 1965: 53–71.

4

From "Showcase" to "Failure": Democracy and the Colombian Developmental State in the 1960s

Robert Karl

"Political Philosophy is today inseparable from Technical Philosophy," Colombia's leading constitutional lawyer, Carlos Restrepo Piedrahita, observed in 1963, "because relations of intimacy and reciprocity have been established between one and the other."[1] Even before the United Nations declared the 1960s the "decade of development," Colombia seemed to provide global observers with verification of the mutually constitutive linkages between democracy and development.[2] Colombia's government counted among the first in Latin America to advance an ambitious new reform agenda in the countryside and other national sectors, and thus to open a route considered crucial to deepening political stability. Moreover, Colombian and US policymakers maintained that the democratic political transition of the late 1950s had created the conditions necessary for the very formation of Colombia's incipient developmental state.

Colombia in the 1960s may seem an unlikely choice for inclusion in an analysis of the Latin American developmental state in the half-century after the Great Depression. The country never matched the degree of import-substitution industrialization seen in Mexico, Argentina, Chile, or Brazil; and institution-building in the name of development occurred over a decades-long timescale. Colombia in the 1960s is nevertheless a compelling case for understanding the various meanings of development in mid-century Latin America, as well as the intentionality that lay at the heart of the developmental state. Colombia had one of the region's highest rates of manufacturing growth from the 1930s through the 1990s.[3] More significantly, Colombian conceptualizations of "development" encompassed fields well beyond industrialization, from agrarian redistribution to community involvement in setting local policy priorities. Giving rise to these efforts, and drawing energy from them, was a sense that development could be made quickly. To varying degrees of explicitness, the Rostovian motif of

---

[1] Restrepo Piedrahita, 1963: 4.   [2] UNICEF, n.d.   [3] Thorp, 1998: 119, 162, 322.

"takeoff," originally applied to industrialization, enjoyed currency across various corners of Colombian national life.[4]

However, Colombia's status as a "showcase" of development would dissipate just as quickly as it had been constructed. Amidst an extended, hemisphere-wide economic crisis, the Colombian state found itself unable to carry through on the commitments of the early part of the 1960s, in no small part because of those political institutions and coalition politics previously hailed for their contributions to development. Institutional arrangements intended to defuse hostilities between Colombia's two major parties gradually limited Bogotá's management of foreign and domestic elements of the development process. At the same time, enduring partisan pressures helped to sharply curtail the capacities of developmental agencies into the mid 1960s. The connection between democracy and development was not the virtuous cycle that had once been imagined.

Restrepo Piedrahita's 1963 piece on the postwar fusion of politics and science was itself intended as a caution, albeit of a different sort. Restrepo Piedrahita counseled that contemporary science enabled a "modern Leviathan," which could "squash" "a [citizen's] life and liberty."[5] Other Colombian intellectuals shared this critique, but saw in community development a salutary corrective to the potential antidemocratic dangers of the age.[6] Restrepo Piedrahita's commentary thus hints at a crucial distinction within the Colombian developmental state. In the conceptualization of the reformist social scientists who devised them, community development and agrarian reform programs were inherently participatory, a means to consolidate democracy at the local level. By contrast, the economists who oversaw government industrial policy and other forms of economic planning demonstrated a style with little connection to democratic ideals.[7]

The divide between these two camps, capped off by the ascendancy of the planners in the last years of the 1960s, had lasting consequences for the ways in which we conceptualize Colombia's historical processes of development. The timing of reform cycles – specifically when particular officials enter and depart the developmental state – can determine how experiments with development are later understood. The divergent experiences of the various social-science sectors that staffed the developmental state substantially shaped

---

[4] See specifically Departamento Administrativo de Planeación y Servicios Técnicos (hereafter DAP), Sección de Programación del Desarrollo Social, "Introduccion a los aspectos sociales del Plan General de Desarrollo Economico y Social de Colombia," July 1962: 6, Archivo General de la Nación [Bogotá], Colección Camilo Torres Restrepo (hereafter CTR), Caja 8, Carpeta 1, Folio 64 (hereafter AGN.CTR.8.1.64); and more broadly, Karl, 2017: chapter 5.

[5] Restrepo Piedrahita,1963: 30.   [6] Fals Borda, 1961: 20; Guillén Martínez, 1961: 3.

[7] This chapter does not employ the term "technocrat," because of the negative associations mentioned in Agustin E. Ferraro and Miguel A. Centeno's last chapter ('Conclusions') in this volume. However, the term did sometimes also circulate in domestic and foreign discourse as an affirmative signifier. Karl, 2017: 130.

the narrative dualism that marks much of the scholarly production on Colombia – a contrast between portrayals of a state unable to transform a backwards rural sector or to respond to popular demands, and upbeat accounts of the national economy.[8] The story of the Colombian developmental state in the 1960s is therefore also the story of the making of modern social science in Colombia and of those disciplines' role in constructing narratives of the developmental state's success versus failure.

"THE BRILLIANT PROLOGUE:" DEMOCRACY AND ECONOMIC PLANNING, 1957–1961

The restoration of democratic rule in 1957–1958 marked Colombia's return to its previously privileged position in the evolution of post-1945 global developmental thought and policy. The political crises that wracked Colombia throughout the initial postwar period were not necessarily an impediment to international economic cooperation. For instance, figures ranging from economist Albert O. Hirschman to the social Catholic pioneer Louis-Joseph Lebret carried out formative research in the country during the successive civilian and military dictatorships of the 1950s.[9] The World Bank had similarly selected Colombia as the site of its first extensive survey mission in 1949, the year in which the Conservative Party government closed national democratic institutions and tens of thousands of people died in the countryside, most at the hands of local Conservative forces.[10] It was only under the subsequent military government (1953–1957) that foreign advisors withdrew and the World Bank suspended its cooperation on account of the dictatorship's refusal to alter increasingly untenable trade and monetary policies.[11]

The toppling of the dictatorship in mid 1957 brought about a new political order and the prospect of renewed attention to development. The democratic opening allowed Liberal and Conservative party leaders to finalize a series of power-sharing mechanisms meant to resolve the crises of the 1940s and to put an end to partisan fighting in the provinces. The better-known elements of this National Front (Frente Nacional) pact centered on politics, namely the practices of parity (wherein the parties each received half of elected and appointed government posts) and presidential alternation. Less recognized are the National Front's developmental priorities. In the short term, these consisted of "readjustment" and "stabilization" to right the economy. In the long term, National Front leaders turned their eyes toward "development" (*desarrollo*).[12]

---

[8] An illustrative example of the latter is Urrutia, 1991: 369.
[9] For Hirschman, see Adelman, 2013: 295–334. For Lebret, see Puel, 2001.
[10] Palacios, 2006: 142–146; Sáenz Rovner, 2001: 248.
[11] Sáenz Rovner, 2002: 188, 200–204; Hartlyn, 1984: 276–277 n.9.
[12] "Año del ejecutivo," 1960: 23, for quotes; Karl, 2017: 123. See also Gutiérrez Sanín, 2007: 100, for a similar but less detailed argument.

"This National Front ... cannot simply be a static armistice between two armies," the minister of agriculture told the Chamber of Representatives in April 1959. "It must be a holy truce in the hatreds of the parties so that these can come to agreement on definitive solutions for the economic and social problems of the Republic."[13] The early democratic transition set important precedents for the Colombian state's approaches to these problems.

Tackling the economic legacies of the dictatorship was Bogotá's top priority as the democratic transition got underway. The country's commercial debt stood at $400 million, the result of free-falling world prices for Latin American commodities and the military government's fixation on importing luxury goods in spite of the precipitous drop in coffee exports – Colombia's major source of revenue – after 1954.[14] In September 1957, four months after the dictatorship's fall, the National Planning Committee (Comité Nacional de Planeación) detailed the scale of the challenge: the continued slide in coffee prices meant that the government had to reduce national imports to $20 million per month, a nearly 50 percent reduction from the year's average levels. The Committee warned that "this is barely sufficient to supply the country with either only indispensable primary goods, or only the machinery, equipment, and spare parts it ought to purchase if it wishes to survive."[15] Faced with such a dilemma, the interim military junta (May 1957–August 1958) carried out two devaluations of the peso, which brought Colombia back under the good auspices of international lenders. World Bank assistance to Colombia in 1958, for instance, amounted to twice the level seen in any single year under the dictatorship.[16] Through such help and strict import restrictions, the Colombian state reduced its commercial debt by half by the end of 1958. Budget cuts brought down the government's own deficits as well. US diplomats later praised the administration's "sustained performance in maintaining the unpopular ... stabilization program," calling the effort "outstanding, and possibly without equal in any other Latin American country faced with similar problems."[17]

---

[13] *Anales del Congreso* (hereafter *Anales*), 2, no. 101, May 6, 1959: 1197.
[14] Consejo de Ministros (hereafter CM), Acta No. 145, May 22, 1957: 3–4 AGN. Presidencia de la República (hereafter PR), CM, 147.14.140–141; "The Mess in Bogota," 1956: 45.
[15] Comité Nacional de Planeación, "Plan Económico de Urgencia," n.d. [September 1959]: 1, AGN.PR.Junta Militar de Gobierno (hereafter JMG),1.24.12.
[16] Acta No. 151, June 18, 1957, 1, AGN.PR.CM.147.14.248.
[17] "1958," 1960: 224; Despatch 129, "First Year of the Lleras Administration," September 22, 1959, 6, 721.00/9–2259, National Archives and Record Administration II [College Park, Md.], Record Group 59, Central Decimal File 1955–1959, Box 2998, Folder 721.00/9–859 (hereafter NARA.59.CDF.2998.721.00/9–859), for quote. See also Karl, 2017: 36; Díaz-Alejandro, 1976: 21. Though it paled in comparison to later Latin American economic crises, the anxiety generated throughout 1957 should not be underestimated. Compare Eduardo Dargent's comment that "Colombian technocrats emerged in the late 1950s when there was ... [no] severe hyperinflationary crisis." Dargent, 2015: 11.

A crucial ingredient in Colombia's restored economic reputation was the installation of a generation of technically trained experts, freshly returned from graduate programs in the United States and Europe. Expertise and planning enjoyed a newfound relevance within the first months of the democratic transition, a change Albert Hirschman encountered when he returned to Colombia in late 1957. Hirschman recorded in his diary that under the military government, "appointments were capricious and investment decisions were taken exclusively on the basis of 'deals.' Now studies are again requested."[18] The unofficial leader of this new cohort of economists would later explain to a foreign journalist how his selection was "a technical, not a political appointment." "We feel," he added, "that we are modifying the [political] terms in which Congress discusses projects."[19]

By the end of the 1950s, this technical orientation applied to a broad array of economic activities. Import controls substantially expanded capital goods' share of national imports, as the central state sought to foster import-substitution industrialization.[20] Import-substitution agriculture received even more attention. While Colombia's industrial sector had grown 10 percent annually in the decade before the National Front, agriculture achieved scarcely a quarter of that rate. So marked was the discrepancy that the United Nations Economic Commission for Latin America (CEPAL) calculated that Colombia's agricultural machine imports for 1955 totaled less than the machinery brought into the country that year by a single Bogotá brewery. Even the National Association of Industrialists (ANDI; Asociación Nacional de Industriales), Colombia's most powerful economic interest group, "allowed [at the end of 1957] that a pause by industry in favor of agriculture must be accepted."[21]

---

[18] Albert O. Hirschman, "Diary: Brazil and Colombia. August 12–September 11, 1957," n.p. [1–2], Public Policy Papers, Princeton University Library [Princeton, NJ], Department of Rare Books and Special Collections, Public Policy Papers, Albert O. Hirschman Papers, Box 57, Folder 10 (hereafter PUL.AOH.57.10). Elsewhere, Hirschman humorously recounts the reaction of one of the dictatorship's finance ministers after Hirschman suggested that the minister be less "impulsive" in issuing decrees. The minister explained that he lacked the budget to hire sufficient researchers, and therefore relied on the data presented by the groups that would be affected by his rulings. "[I]f they convince me," he concluded, "I will issue another decree!" Hirschman, 1977: vii.

[19] "Youth Points Way for Colombia to Return to a Stable Economy," 1960: 83.

[20] "Instalación del Congreso," 1960: 473–474.

[21] Speech by Finance Minister Antonio Alvarez Restrepo, n.d. [1958]: 127, AGN.PR. JMG,2.38.58; speech by Finance Minister Jesús María Marulanda, n.d. [1958]: 28, AGN.PR. Despacho Señor Presidente (hereafter DSP), 110.45.48; Despatch 512, "Economic Summary for November, 1957," December 11, 1957: 9, 821.00/12–1157, NARA.59.CDF, 4241.821.00/ 6–757, for quote.

For individual commodities, the results of state policy could be dramatic. In one example that was much discussed at the time, government-facilitated labor-recruitment schemes and legally mandated bank loans promoted a two-fold increase in the acreage dedicated to cotton cultivation, and a slightly higher rise in production, between 1958 and 1959. Arriving at self-sufficiency allowed Colombia to fulfill the growing textile sector's demand for raw materials without reliance on imports and to substitute additional imports through the production of cottonseed oil.[22] Other food oils – notably that derived from African palm – would receive attention from state agencies in the 1960s as a means for enhancing the income of small farmers living on agricultural frontiers.[23]

Such shifts within agrarian promotion suggest the evolution of Colombian economic policy from "stabilization" to a broader, more ambitious agenda. When the 1958–1959 Congress debated elevating to law a junta-era tax decree meant to boost land usage, the national Catholic labor federation admonished against construing "the problem of production" as "agrarian reform." "A stimulus in production is a consequence and not an end [unto itself]," a federation representative told Congress. "The goal [of agrarian reform] is elevating rural [*campesino*] living conditions through a change to the medieval agrarian structure in which we live."[24] Calls for a comprehensive solution to the agrarian problem became increasingly prevalent by 1960, when the government began to draft a new land reform law with input from nonstate national institutions.[25] Social justice could be an end unto itself for advocates of reform, but the agrarian law had no shortage of technical merits as well. Justifying agrarian reform as a way to raise incomes and thus provide a larger market for national industry – an argument associated with CEPAL – was already a tactic in Colombia in the late 1950s. Its influence on planning nonetheless became more marked by the early 1960s.[26]

[22] República de Colombia, 1960: 200; República de Colombia, 1959: 80; Morales Benítez, 1962: 317; letter, Julio José Fajardo, Interventor de Rehabilitación, to Gonzalo Samper, Federación de Algodoneros, June 3, 1959, 1–2, AGN. PR.Oficina del Consejero.1.6.38–9; "Informe que presenta el Consejero de la Presidencia de la Republica a la Comision Especial de Rehabilitacion," July 8, 1959, 27, AGN.PR.Oficina de Rehabilitación.1.2.31; report, Finance Minister Antonio Alvarez Restrepo, n.d. [1958], AGN.PR.JMG.2.38.58; "1958," 1960: 224.

[23] Morales Benítez, 1962: 297–305; Instituto Colombiano de la Reforma Agraria, 1965: 23–24, 30, 44, 47–48, 72, 77; "Enorme incremento," 1965: 2.

[24] Speech, Unión de Trabajadores de Colombia representative to Congress, n.d. [1959], AGN.PR. Secretaría General (hereafter SG) 303.21.191. For the decree's origins and effects, which included increased cotton production, see Hirschman, 1965: 172–178.

[25] The best account remains Hirschman, 1965: 192–205.

[26] See, respectively, "Informe al Congreso," 1960: I, 500; DAP, "Resumen para el Señor Presidente de la Republica de los principales aspectos del Programa General de Desarrollo," March 27, 1962: 18–19, Archivo de la Presidencia de la República [Bogotá], Despacho Señor Presidente, 1962, Caja 4, Carpeta Planeación (hereafter APR.DSP.1962.4.Planeacion).

Trade balances, industrial modernization, and human welfare were fundamentally linked for Colombians of the late 1950s and early 1960s.[27] To understand the history of developmentalism in mid-century Colombia therefore requires examining "development" in the fullness of its contemporary implications. To be certain, as Rafael Ioris has shown in the case of postwar Brazil, Colombians expressed considerable disagreement on which elements of development deserved attention and on how those efforts should be achieved. [28] The ANDI, for instance, advocated a limited role for the Colombian state in industrial development.[29] By contrast, government officials interested in social reform came to define "development ... [as] fundamentally a responsibility of the State, on whose execution the total result of the effort realized by the country depends."[30]

Yet in comparison to subsequent periods, Colombia's initial postauthoritarian politics encouraged relative consensus between collective actors. The late 1950s represented a moment of possibility for both democracy and development. "The praiseworthy last three years are nothing but the closure of acrimonious vicissitudes and the brilliant prologue of the [new] decade," Colombia's newspaper of record announced at the start of 1960.[31] However hyperbolic, the statement conveys a sentiment that permeated Colombian policymaking circles. Within weeks of the Kennedy administration's 1961 unveiling of the Alliance for Progress, its massive aid program for Latin American development, the head of the Planning Department proudly declared that Colombia's post-1957 record of austerity and the advanced state of its planning uniquely positioned the country to participate in the Alliance.[32] Colombia would become the first nation to submit a long-term General Economic and Social Development Plan (Plan General de Desarrollo Económico y Social) to hemispheric experts – so rapidly, in fact, that an ad-hoc assessment team had to be convened because the institutional architecture of the Alliance was not yet in place.[33]

By most indications, Colombia's democratic opening of 1957–1958 had given the country a head start on a developmental path that, if fulfilled, could deepen political stability as well as prove the wisdom of government planning. "In its own peculiar, introverted and egocentric way," US officials later explained, "Colombia, barring a breakdown of the [National Front pact],

---

[27] This analysis is informed by Fajardo, 2015: 89.   [28] Ioris, 2014.

[29] Lleras Camargo, 1957: 6; Sáenz Rovner, 2002.

[30] DAP, "Introduccion a los aspectos sociales del Plan General de Desarrollo," July 1962, 6: 55.

[31] "De una década a otra," 1960: 4.

[32] Speech by Edgar Gutiérrez Castro, Jefe, DAP, May 27, 1961: 10, AGN.Departamento Nacional de Planeación (hereafter DNP),58.17.10.

[33] Comité de los Nueve, Alianza para el Progreso, "Evaluación del Programa General de Desarrollo Económico y Social de Colombia," July 1962: 1, AGN.DNP, 59.33.10.

appears to have time to allow processes of peaceful change to take effect. Here lies a special challenge for the Alliance for Progress."[34]

DEMOCRATS AND DEVELOPMENT, 1960–1962

The godfather of Colombia's postauthoritarian developmental state was also the father of the National Front pact and its first president (1958–1962). Though far from a technical specialist himself, Alberto Lleras Camargo – Liberal journalist, government minister, acting president of Colombia (1945–1946), international diplomat – held an abiding interest in overcoming the rural–urban gap widened by the modernization process. One of his administration's earliest legislative accomplishments, Law 19 of 1958, established the fundamental institutional infrastructure of a new developmental state, through an expansion of the civil service; the creation of additional planning agencies, including the National Planning Department (Departamento Administrativo de Planeación y Servicios Técnicos); and a reform of governance structures to allow for community participation in local development projects. Lleras Camargo also occasionally took a personal interest in the management of the growing developmentalist bureaucracy, intervening to ensure that officials like Orlando Fals Borda – a young, academically trained sociologist who ran the Ministry of Agriculture during the preparation of the agrarian reform bill – remained within the government apparatus.[35]

Such continuity in personnel seems to have been a crucial ingredient in the Lleras Camargo administration's early developmental achievements, including the land reform's passage in late 1960. International acclaim accrued not simply to economic planning, but to these efforts as well. Fals Borda in particular constructed meaningful "pockets of efficiency" across state and parastate institutions.[36] At the same time that he served as the only apolitical appointee atop the Ministry of Agriculture, and a competent one at that, Fals worked to create a sociology program at the National University (Universidad Nacional) in Bogotá. Fals never intended his intellectual project to stay confined within the halls of academia. As he wrote in 1961, "[we] sociologists have ... the grave responsibility to study the transformations that surround us, to search for the alleviation of the inevitable conflicts of this transition [toward modernity] or to reduce institutional dysfunction." Once spun off from its original home under economics, Fals' Faculty of Sociology (Facultad de Sociología) won

---

[34] "Strategy for the Aid Program in Colombia," March 17, 1962: 1, John Fitzgerald Kennedy Library [Boston, Mass.], National Security Files, Box 392, Folder Colombia 12/61–3/63 (hereafter JFKL.NSF.392.Colombia 12/61–3/63).

[35] Karl, 2017: 19, 41, 81, 127, 133, 134. The text of Law 19 can be found at www.alcaldiabogota.gov.co/sisjur/normas/Norma1.jsp?i=8271.

[36] Evans, 1992: 168–169.

a government contract to train specialists who would coach communities on how to establish local development councils (*juntas de acción comunal*), bodies created by Law 19 of 1958. The very premise of this government community-development policy could also be traced back to Fals and his colleagues, who derived insights from Fals' graduate field research during the 1950s. National University social scientists would go on to direct the research arms of the Colombian Institute of Agrarian Reform (INCORA; Instituto Colombiano de Reforma Agraria), and to head the Advanced School for Public Administration (Escuela Superior de Administración Pública), a Law 19 product dedicated to training development experts. Fals' Sociology Faculty became a magnet for US foundation funding, as well as for praise from across Latin America.[37]

Reformist social scientists such as Fals claimed an expertise on development that was no less technical than that of their economist counterparts, but was nonetheless more grounded in democratic precepts. Echoing Carlos Restrepo Piedrahita, Fals described communal action as a buffer against the formation of a totalitarian state, a means for the people to retain "rational liberty with collective responsibility."[38] For other intellectuals, empowering Colombia's local communities represented both the consolidation of the country's best political traditions and its surest path to a secure future. National University social scientist Fernando Guillén Martínez, for example, perceived communal action as an updated form of the Hispanic municipal tradition that had "enabled the realization of Independence."[39] This democratic vision of development was the antidote to purely technical concerns, argued a reformer in the Planning Department, as it would permit the creation of "solid foundations for self-sufficiency in welfare and security," and thus enable Colombia as a whole to break free of the underdevelopment trap of low demand and slow industrialization.[40]

In this environment, older development plans could be reconfigured for greater democratic content. During the military dictatorship of the 1950s, Tennessee Valley Authority (TVA) founder David Lilienthal oversaw the creation of a TVA for Colombia's southwestern Cauca River valley. As Hirschman would later remark, the Corporación Autónoma Regional del Valle del Cauca (Autonomous Regional Corporation of Valle del Cauca; CVC) "was presented to a reassured public as a true copy [of the TVA] ... certified expressly by David Lilienthal [himself]."[41] The diffusion of the TVA model likewise helped to cement Colombia's image as a "showcase" for development strategies in the eyes of US policymakers. Yet it was only during the Lleras

---

[37] Fals Borda, 1961: 21, for quote: Karl, 2017: 132–136.   [38] Fals Borda, 1961: 20.
[39] Guillén Martínez, 1961: 3.
[40] DAP, "Introduccion a los aspectos sociales del Plan General de Desarrollo."
[41] Hirschman, 1967: 21. See also José Carlos Orihuela's chapter in this volume.

Camargo administration that the CVC adopted the TVA's "grass roots" policy of public policy implementation, through a reorganization that included emphasis on the establishment of community-development councils.[42] As José Carlos Orihuela indicates in this volume, "global policy paradigms and organizational models end up 'nationalized,' translated to national practice" – in this case, through the institutional frame of Law 19 and the influence of Orlando Fals Borda.

Be they economic planners or, more especially, reformist social scientists, Colombian developmentalists operated in an environment of self-described mystique (*mística*) as the end of Lleras Camargo's term approached in 1962. Lleras' presidency had offered a second chance at state-led reform for many Liberal politicians and social scientists who had been involved in the reformist projects of Colombia's so-called Liberal Republic (1930–1946).[43] The reconstitution of these earlier networks at the National University and elsewhere contributed to a social embeddedness that enhanced the autonomy developmental bureaucrats enjoyed under Lleras Camargo's patronage.

Global processes also contributed ideas and ideals that augmented embeddedness beyond the "concrete set of social ties" suggested by Peter Evans' definition of the term.[44] Only weeks after Washington's announcement of the Alliance for Progress, Pope John XXIII issued a new encyclical instructing Catholics to recommit themselves to "social progress," reiterating the social function of property, and asserting that "the civil power must also have a hand in the economy. It has to promote production in a way best calculated to achieve social progress and the well-being of all citizens." These were not insubstantial contributions as Latin American states began debating agrarian reform in the 1960s, and complemented perfectly Colombians' revival of 1930s reformism.[45] The intellectual and moral environment of the early 1960s drove social scientists' pursuits, connected them to broader segments of society, and shielded them from outside pressures.

DEVELOPMENT AND POLITICS, 1962

Through this autonomy, Colombian social scientists made the key institutions of the developmental state in the 1960s, to an extent perhaps unmatched elsewhere in Latin America. Nevertheless, hemispheric economic conditions and a national political transition soon altered the trajectory – and, some might have argued, the very existence – of the Colombian developmental

---

[42] Posada and Posada, 1966: 12; Lilienthal, 1944: 77 ("grass roots"); Decreto 1707, July 18, 1960, www.suin-juriscol.gov.co/viewDocument.asp?id=1334996.

[43] Karl, 2017: 124, 130, 134.   [44] Evans, 1992: 163–164.

[45] Karl, 2017: 124–125; "Mater et Magistra," 1961: par. 52, for quote.

state. In other words, this story of development is necessarily one of both structure and individual agency – and in regards to the latter, the substantial influence that presidential personalities had on Colombia's development politics during the first three National Front administrations.

Structural challenges foreign and domestic loomed ever larger as Lleras Camargo moved deeper into his term. Observers calculated that coffee prices, which bottomed out in Lleras' first months in office, cost Colombia $500 million in lost revenue over his four-year presidency. Given these conditions, and the continued need to import capital-intensive goods to advance industrialization, the administration's decision to ease the import controls of 1957–1958 opened a fresh gap in the balance of payments (Figure 4.1).[46] The potential disruptions to the pace of development were magnified by fiscal imbalances that had been introduced by the administration's reform agenda. Because of the combination of the state's low extractive capacity and steps by Colombian elites to avoid their new tax burdens, a Harvard-advised 1960 tax reform – once held as an early developmental victory – ultimately failed to deliver $45 million in anticipated revenues. The ensuing drop in state investment rippled across the economy at the start of 1962, just months ahead of Colombia's first presidential transition under the National Front system.[47]

Lleras Camargo's choices at this conjuncture molded possibilities for democracy and development. Not wanting to grant the political opposition a major issue it could exploit in the March 1962 congressional elections, Lleras hoped to delay new import regulations, as well as to avoid entirely a devaluation of the peso and the rise in prices that would follow. When he met with US diplomats to discuss international aid to relieve Colombia's position, Lleras virtually dared Washington to do nothing. "If [the] U.S. [government was] not prepared to provide assistance," he told the US ambassador, it "would be best [for Lleras to] take the problem to [the] nation, devaluate, take [the] severest monetary and fiscal measures, forget economic growth and [the] development plan, and let political chips fall

---

[46] "Strategic Study of Colombia," April 4, 1963: 14, JFKL.NSF.392. Colombia Draft – Strategic Study 4/4/63; "Colombia Strategy Statement": 1; Telegram 442, Henry Dearborn to Rusk, November 13, 1962: 1, JFKL.NSF.27.Colombia General 10/62–2/63; Columbia University School of Law, Report No. 6, "Public International Development Financing in Colombia," June 1963: 124, JFKL.NSF.392.Colombia Public International Development Financing 6/63; "Scope Paper," June 20, 1962: 2, JFKL.NSF.26A.Colombia General 1/62–6/62. See also the discussion in Karl, 2017: 137–138.

[47] "Strategy for the Aid Program in Colombia," March 17, 1962: 1–2; Airgram A-144, "Joint WeekA No. 36," September 5, 1962: 5, 721.00(W)/9–562, Records of the US Department of State Relating to Internal Affairs of Colombia 1960–1963 (hereafter Internal Affairs), Scholarly Resources microfilm, reel 2; Consejo Nacional de Política Económica y Planeación, Acta No. 91, September 20, 1962: 3–4, APR.SG.1962.1.Consejo Nal de Politica Economica y Planeación Actas. Colombia dropped from ninth in Latin American per capita tax revenues in 1961 to fifteenth in 1965. Gonzalez, 1969: 92.

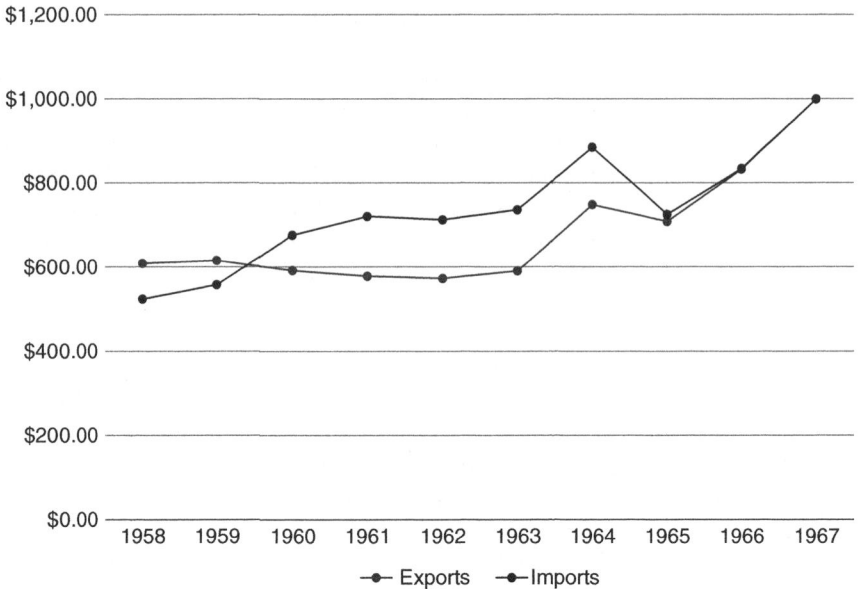

FIGURE 4.1 Colombia's Annual Exports and Imports, 1958–1967[48]

where they might."[49] US officials took seriously the threat economic conditions posed to the continuity of the National Front, but remained divided on the proper course. While a team from Washington hoped that Lleras would devalue between the May presidential election and the August presidential inauguration, Embassy staff rejected the idea as politically unwise and instead pushed Bogotá to modify Colombia's exchange rate.[50] In the end, however, Lleras pursued neither option.

The structure of the National Front agreements made this a fateful decision. Presidential alternation, enshrined in the constitution during the democratic transition, stipulated that a Conservative preside over the National Front's second administration. Guillermo León Valencia, the coalition's compromise choice to meet this requirement, inspired little confidence. "[Valencia] does not indicate that he has ever sat down and seriously thought about Colombia's problems and how he is to solve them," the US Embassy

[48] Based on data from Departamento Administrativo Nacional de Estadística, (hereafter DANE), 1964: 486–487; DANE, 1969: 579; DANE, n.d.: 532.
[49] Telegram 493 (Section 2 of 2), January 13, 1962: 3, JFKL.NSF. 26A.Colombia General 1/62–6/62; memorandum of conversation, "Varied Topics (Political, Economic, Social and Religious)," March 12, 1962: 4–5, JFKL.NSF.26A.Colombia General 1/62–6/62; Telegram 552 (Section 1 of 2), January 31, 1962: 1, JFKL.NSF.26A.Colombia General 1/62–6/62, for quote.
[50] "Strategy for the Aid Program in Colombia," March 17, 1962: 5.

reported in mid 1962. "Basically his administration remains a big question mark. Few have an inkling of what he will do, and Valencia himself probably does not know precisely what he will do or how he will do it."[51] As understandable as his prioritization of a coalition victory was from a political perspective, Lleras Camargo's subsequent inaction left the management of economic adjustment to the questionable skills of his successor. Any change to monetary policy during the lame-duck phase of Lleras Camargo's presidency would certainly have continued to echo politically and socially into Valencia's term. However, Lleras Camargo's political aptitude could have helped to ameliorate the ramifications.

What might have happened if the Liberal and Conservative parties had decided to modify the rules of the National Front in 1962 or if presidential alternation had not otherwise been an issue? The counterfactual case is not difficult to imagine, because the Liberal likely to have been his party's candidate in 1962 was Carlos Lleras Restrepo, Colombia's vice president (*designado*) from 1960 to 1962, the executor of the 1961 agrarian reform's ratification, and the National Front's eventual winning candidate in the 1966 election. As will be discussed below, Lleras Restrepo was a developmentalist par excellence.[52] Even in the case that an alternative Liberal administration had not been able to transcend Colombia's structural economic challenges between 1962 and 1966, the history of the developmental state would have looked very different.

The onset of Conservative control of the executive branch had particular meaning for social scientists. During his 1957 tour of Colombia, Hirschman had noted that economists were more often than not Liberals, an observation that would have held true for specialists from other social science disciplines as well. [53] If authoritarianism had possessed a silver lining for Colombia's burgeoning class of postwar experts, it was this: the Conservative stranglehold on the state bureaucracy (and the physical threats that sometimes enforced it) compelled Liberals to go abroad for further education. Those credentials would bolster social scientists' claims to expertise when they could finally repatriate.[54] However, the 1962 transfer of power meant that Fals Borda's Faculty of Sociology and other pockets of efficiency would no longer enjoy the blessing of a supportive president. As Evans notes in the case of the Brazilian developmental state, so long as autonomous expertise remains fragmentarily dispersed throughout the state, it is "dependent on the personal protection of individual presidents."[55]

---

[51] Despatch 670, "Guillermo León Valencia – His Views and Goals," June 18, 1962: 11, 721.00/6–1862, Internal Affairs, reel 2, for quote. See also Karl, 2017: 137–138.

[52] Lleras Restrepo's opposition to devaluation in the early 1960s was a major reason that his cousin Lleras Camargo did not pursue the policy. Díaz-Alejandro, 1976: 190.

[53] Arocha and de Friedemann, 1984: 8.   [54] Arocha, 1984.   [55] Evans, 1992: 169.

Such concerns were magnified by the fact that National Front-era Colombia was far from possessing a rational state. Indeed, only in 1958 had the state recommenced a decades-old push toward a full civil service system. Colombia possessed what Lleras Camargo termed "the feudal State," marked by a reliance on political criteria and outmoded forms of public administration.[56] For instance, civil servants made up only 4 percent of the central government's more than 37,500 employees in 1950 – scarce progress since a first round of civil service reform under the Liberal Republic.[57] Party operatives hence counted on access to a huge swath of the state employment sector. Moreover, the increasingly polarized politics of the 1940s raised the stakes of these clientelist politics, prompting Fernando Guillén Martínez to remark in 1963 that "the history of Colombian society" could be distilled down to the tale of "[a] mass of employees who confront a mass of aspirants to those jobs, all with arms in hand."[58]

Civil service reform was accordingly a major emphasis of the democratic transition. The interim military junta cited the lack of an impartial civil service as the cause of both the "war to the death between the parties" during the 1940s and 1950s, as well as the shortcomings of state programs.[59] Without a civil service, Lleras Camargo warned in his inaugural address, Colombians risked their state remaining little more than a fount of "remunerated sectarianism."[60] It was no wonder, then, that 35 percent of the statutes in the December 1957 constitutional plebiscite that formalized the National Front dealt with "the depoliticization of the bureaucracy."[61]

Sociologists would look to the consequent implementation of civil service rules as an essential piece of their discipline's future success. The profession won a place on the list of civil-service-eligible occupations in 1961, three years after Law 19 of 1958 brought an expanded civil service into being. Fals Borda estimated that the government alone could hire a hundred sociologists – a tremendous opportunity at a time when his faculty was admitting between twenty and twenty-five students a year.[62] To ensure continuity in employment

[56] Lleras Camargo, 1957: 71–74.
[57] 1,518 civil servants out of 37,545 total employees. Schmidt, 1974: 435f22. For the 1938 reform, see Molina, 1999: 294–295.
[58] Guillén Martínez, 1963: 148, quoted in part in Steffen W. Schmidt, 1974: 103f18. The best account of partisan politicking is Roldán, 2002.
[59] Speech by Admiral Rubén Piedrahita, May 10, 1957, 11, AGN.PR.JMG.2.38.7.
[60] "Discurso de posesión,"1960: I, 61.   [61] Schmidt, 1974: 433.
[62] "Program for the Development of the Faculty of Sociology of the National University of Colombia (1962–1965)," September 5, 1961: 4, RAC.RG 1–2.SS 311.SS 311-S.73.693; Rockefeller Archive Center [Sleepy Hollow, NY], Record Group 1.2: Rockefeller Foundation Projects, Series 311: Colombia, Subseries 311.R: Colombia – Social Sciences, Box 72, Folder 693 (hereafter RAC.SS 311-S.73.693); Orlando Fals Borda, interviewed by Erskine McKinley, Assistant Director, Social Sciences, Rockefeller Foundation, November 21, 1959: 1, RAC.RG 1–2.SS 311-S.72.692; letter, Fals Borda to McKinley, February 5, 1960: 5, RAC.RG 1–2.SS 311. SS 311-S.72.692.

and in the larger task of transformation, Fals and his colleagues began to arrange contingency plans as far out as a year ahead of the 1962 election. By accepting posts with Bogotá-based development projects of international agencies like the Organization of American States, or by lining up externally funded research projects and training programs for community development promoters, social scientists hoped to "arrive at a position ... in which [they would] be invulnerable" to political pressures.[63]

Valencia's administration ultimately frustrated developmentalists' designs on two main fronts. First, the new president's style deflated the anticipatory atmosphere of the early National Front. *New York Times* reporter Richard Eder, who grasped Colombian politics better than most, later described Valencia as "a proud man from a backwater province whose warfare with the twentieth century ... aroused his countrymen's derision."[64] Development experts counted among those to note how Valencia seemed out of step with the times: before taking office, Valencia announced that "his Government will not be one of the cold technician, but the Government of a burning heart." He could not imagine technical expertise overshadowing an old style of politics.[65]

This rhetorical challenge became a second and very real concern soon after Valencia's August 1962 inauguration. The plight of the National University's sociologists stemmed from Fals Borda's recent publication of a coauthored study on "violence in Colombia." The book pinned blame on the Conservative Party for the partisan violence of the 1940s and 1950s, which Fals and a co-author estimated to have had killed nearly 200,000 people. Conservatives responded with a merciless counter-campaign that extended from Congress to the editorial pages of national newspapers. Conservative critics denounced the sociologists as partisan hacks, thus explicitly dismissing any social-scientific claims to objective knowledge. The Faculty of Sociology would survive the confrontation unscathed, while the sociologists themselves continued to work alongside and within the bureaucracy. The episode nonetheless marked a signal moment in the sociologists' gradual alienation from the state and their creation of narratives about development.[66]

Economists caught the brunt of the political fallout from the 1962 presidential transition. Conservatives set their sights on the Planning Department as a potential well of clientelist favors. Valencia proved unwilling to halt the injection of political considerations into the technical realm, leading

---

[63] "Program for the Development of the Faculty of Sociology of the National University of Colombia (1962–1965)," September 5, 1961: 4, RAC.RG 1–2.SS 311.SS 311-S.73.693; Fals Borda, interviewed by McKinley: 1; letter, Fals Borda to McKinley, February 5, 1960: 5; Fals Borda *et al.*, interviewed by Charles M. Harden, Program Director, Rockefeller Foundation, October 20, 1961: 2, RAC.SS 311-S.72.693, for quote.

[64] Eder,1965: 36.

[65] Despatch 670, "Guillermo León Valencia – His Views and Goals," June 18, 1962: 11, 721.00/6–1862: 7.

[66] Karl, 2017: chapter 6.

80 percent of professional employees at the Planning Department and the Planning Council (Consejo Nacional de Política Económica y Planeación) to quit in the administration's first hundred days. Numerous foreign observers commented that Colombia's planning capacity "all but disintegrated."[67] Pockets of efficiency within the economic planning apparatus collapsed during the first months of the Valencia administration and would scarcely recover over the ensuing four years.

FROM "SHOWCASE" TO "FAILURE," 1962–1966

International praise for the Colombian developmental state lasted for a remarkably short span. Around the Alliance for Progress' first anniversary in March 1962, as World Bank experts reviewed Colombia's Development Plan and White House officials hailed Colombia's headway, sectors of the US Congress and press sensed that the Alliance's moment had already passed. "Anniversaries are always used for stock-taking; but it is a bit unfair to pick this one," offered a sympathetic *New York Times* editorial.[68] The ad hoc treatment received by Colombia's Development Plan epitomized the *Times'* viewpoint: the agencies that were to comprise the Alliance barely existed and aid disbursements had scarcely begun. However, this was an age of maximalism. The banalities of building bureaucratic capacity paled alongside the pace of revolutionary transformation in Cuba or the spectacle of the space race – an inescapable metaphor for development, as Walt Rostow's term "take-off" makes clear. The disconnect between "the sense of [euphoria] ... awakened" by the Alliance and the situation even a year later soon led US policymakers to urge caution, lest "building unrealistic expectations for short-term material gains ... only lead to widespread disillusionment with the Alliance."[69] From the perspective of others in Washington, however, that genie had already escaped the bottle.

The notion of the "Alliance without Progress," and its accompanying malaise, soon appeared in Colombia.[70] "A phrase describing Colombia as 'the showcase of the Alliance for Progress' is haunting those who devised it," wrote the *Times'* Richard Eder.[71] The initial triumph of the Development Plan

---

[67] Airgram A-284, "Joint WeekA No. 45," November 7, 1962: 5–6, 721.00(W)/11–762, Internal Affairs, reel 2; Eder, 1962: 42, for quote; Eder, 1963a: 13. See also Mares, 1993: 463.

[68] "The Alliance's Anniversary," 1962: 34. Representative examples from the opposing camp include Allen, 1962: 5; "Alianza Sí, Progreso No," 1962: 35.

[69] Despatch 579, "Joint WeekA No. 18," May 2, 1962: 3, 721.00(W)/5–262, Internal Affairs of Colombia 1960–1963, reel 2 ("the sense"); "IAL Guidelines for Agency Programming to Latin America," September 26, 1963: 5, JFKL.Richard Goodwin Papers.8. Latin American Policy (Folder 1 of 2) ("building").

[70] "Alianza Sí, Progreso No"; Airgram A-98, "Joint WeekA No. 35," August 29, 1965: 8, NARA.59. Subject-Numeric File 1964–1966 (hereafter SNF 1964–66) 2043. Joint WeekAs 7/1/65 1/2, for quote.

[71] Eder, 1963b: 8.

rang hollow by the end of 1962, as personnel shortages and the lack of leadership within the planning bureaucracy brought sector-specific studies to a standstill.[72] For his part, Valencia continued to wage his war on experts. In closed meetings with US diplomats and at public press conferences, the president denounced the pace of reform.[73]

The next two years would be decisive for not only Valencia's administration, but also the entire National Front project. Colombia's trade situation would remain virtually unchanged between 1961 and 1964 (Figure 4.1), as low coffee prices offset any move to minimize imports. The country had reached "an immediate critical financial juncture," Valencia's choice for finance minister, Carlos Sanz de Santamaría, concluded in October 1962. Sanz found himself struggling against the apparent apathy of both his fellow cabinet members as well as Valencia, who declared his commitment to directing state resources away from development and toward the elimination of an outbreak of rural violence. Only in December 1962, with the balance-of-payments problem "approaching critical proportions," did Sanz push through a comprehensive economic reform package, which avoided devaluation in favor of an exchange rate surcharge on imports. Though international lenders had pushed for devaluation, they consented to releasing tens of millions of dollars of aid crucial to resolving the balance-of-payments deficit. Ahead of Sanz's hard-fought victory within the administration, the US Embassy termed his plan "the most impressive tax reform program seen in Latin America during the past fifteen years."[74]

What followed was far removed from the 1967 devaluation later lauded in the scholarly literature.[75] Unable to hold the line on wage-price policy, Valencia conceded to wage increases demanded by Colombia's two major labor confederations. The ensuing bout of inflation reached 12 percent in the first two months of 1963, "close to the top whole-year figure for the last decade."[76] Confidence in the national situation – and the government's capacity to right

---

[72] Memorandum of conversation, October 4, 1962: 2, JFKL. 27. Colombia General 10/62–2/63; Eder, 1963a: 13; *Cincuenta años: Departamento Nacional de Planeación* 2009: 32.

[73] Memorandum of conversation, December 5, 1962: 4, JFKL.NSF.27.Colombia General 10/62–2/63; Airgram A-651, "President's Press Conference," April 2, 1963: 3, JFKL.NSF.27. Colombia General 3/63–11/63.

[74] Airgram A-209, "Joint WeekA No. 40," October 3, 1962: 5, 721.00(W)/10–362, Internal Affairs, reel 2 ("immediate"); Airgram A-368, "Joint WeekA No. 50," December 12, 1962: 721.00(W)/12–1262, 5, Internal Affairs, reel 2; Karl, 2017: 162; Karl, 2009: 506–508; "Joint WeekA No. 45": 5 ("the most"). Sanz had previously been Colombia's ambassador to Washington. In a surprising display of administrative inaction, that post went unfilled for the next eight months, from August 1962 until May 1963. For a critique, see "El embajador en Washington," 1963e: 5.

[75] Dargent, 2015: 68–70; Thorp, 1991: chapter 7.

[76] Eder, 1963d: 6, for quote; Airgram A-460, "Joint WeekA No. 3," January 16, 1963: 2–4, 721.00 (W)1–1663, Internal Affairs, reel 3.

it – sank accordingly. "We live in a country in such turmoil that we do not know what surprise will face us each morning, a new deficit or debt, an official measure correcting one adopted the evening before, a new problem that surpasses in gravity those we know," lamented one of Bogotá's Liberal newspapers.[77] For economists seasoned enough to remember the end of the dictatorship, the administration's style must have evoked the improvisational tendencies of the 1950s. Washington concurred, cutting off loans to its one-time Alliance showcase for a period of 17 months.[78]

For other Colombians, the economic dislocations of 1963 initiated a questioning of the relationship between science and politics. Carlos Lleras Restrepo had linked the Alliance for Progress and the National Front in the latter's 1962 election platform, but development was increasingly becoming a rhetorical tool that Colombians outside the coalition could deploy to question the political system.[79] The Liberal opposition in Congress cited the Valencia administration's deviation from the original, Lleras Camargo-era Development Plan to batter the National Front. The bipartisan pact, one congressman stated, reached "its achievement in the pacification of the country, but from the point of view of … its intention to promote economic development and social welfare, it has absolutely been a failure."[80] According to this line of reasoning, Colombia deserved a political system that could meet the people's needs; democracy and development had moved out of sync.

Many Colombian voters expressed this sentiment in the elections of 1964 and 1966. Levels of electoral abstention surged on the basis of popular dissatisfaction with Colombia's economic performance. Explaining his decision not to vote in the 1964 congressional contest, a salesman in the central provincial capital of Ibagué (Tolima) remarked that, "I don't see a single politician capable of managing public administration, let alone coming up with adequate responses to large and complex national problems." "The harsh blow suffered by the economy is proof of that," a white-collar employee confirmed.[81] Discontent with Colombia's economic performance – and not the National Front's negotiated limits on political opposition, as is commonly supposed – accounted for the bulk of the National Front's loss of support at the ballot box.[82]

[77] "Joint WeekA No. 3," January 16, 1963: 1, 721.00(W)1–1663, Internal Affairs, reel 3.

[78] "Colombia Credit Restored," 1966.

[79] "El programa del Frente Nacional. Orientaciones generales por la paz, el derecho, el progreso económico, y la transformación social. Programa del Frente Nacional, 1962–1966," n.d. [1962]: 13–14, Biblioteca Luis Angel Arango [Bogotá], Sala de Libros Raros y Manuscritos, Archivo Carlos Lleras Restrepo, Partido Liberal, Caja 2, Carpeta 13, Folios 955–956 (hereafter BLAA. CLR.PL.2.13.955–56).

[80] *Anales* 7, no. 103, November 2, 1964: 1715, for quote; *Anales* 7, no. 114, November 19, 1964: 1900.

[81] "Opiniones divididas sobre el voto el domingo pasado," 1964: 3.

[82] This traditional historiographical perspective is reviewed in Bejarano and Pizarro Leongómez, 2005.

Sociologists obtained a first-hand view of this popular frustration toward developmental reform and the state. In a letter to Albert Hirschman during the inflationary days of February 1963, Richard Eder advised that, "I have never seen morale and confidence as low as it is now."[83] His travels through Colombia moreover exposed him to anxiety far from Bogotá. In the dusty ranching town of Yopal, Eder surveyed the work of INCORA employees as they went about setting up a technical center whose very existence had been a concession hard won from partisan Conservatives in the administration. Though Eder did not record whether he met any sociologists among the INCORA staffers, he had contacts at the National University and these were precisely the kinds of jobs that the Faculty of Sociology was preparing its graduates to fill.[84] "The young men who run Colombia's land reform ... are trying to give the peasants forms of organization that can help make an effective peaceful change," Eder wrote in the *Times* roughly a month after his letter to Hirschman. "But "deal[ing] with vast rural agony and wordless rebelliousness" exacted its costs on the reformers: "in bad moments, in frustration over their lack of progress, they half hope it will fail."[85] In rural villages and urban shantytowns throughout the country, a generation of social scientists – including foundational figures like Orlando Fals Borda – experienced similar alienation from the developmental state. It was at once of a piece and distinct from the disillusionment that Colombian communities felt toward the process of development. Through their work designing and implementing reform, Fals and other social scientists moved toward a "clarification of commitment": a distancing from "pure," objective science in favor of solidarity with *campesinos* and workers.[86] This was a very different form of social embeddedness, one that would moreover unfold in opposition to, rather than inside, the state.

The trials of Colombia's developmental state after 1962 were not simply the outcome of a presidential transition. Beyond alternation, additional political rules established during the democratic transition compounded the difficulties of planning and reform. The 1957 plebiscite that enacted the National Front mandated a two-thirds congressional majority for legislation, a rule intended to prevent a single party from dominating Congress. Though it has long been derided as an undemocratic means by which political elites maintained their grip on power, Conservatives from Valencia's faction began to argue the reverse in 1962, saying that the rule was instead "a minority veto right" and "an undemocratic filibuster."[87] As the log-jam in Congress grew in subsequent

---

[83] Letter, Richard Eder to Hirschman, February 26, 1963: 2, PUL.AOH.68.13.

[84] Letter, Eder to Camilo Torres Restrepo, April 20, 1963: AGN.CTR.10.4.607.

[85] Eder, 1963c: 79.

[86] Karl, 2017: chapters 5–7 and epilogue; Fals Borda, interview, in Cubides, 2010: 101–102, for quotes.

[87] See, for instance, letter, Antonio García [Santiago de Chile] to junta, 1957: 4, AGN.PR. JMG.4.69; Henry Patiño Murillo, interviewed by the author, August 2, 2012.

years, so too would the chorus observing the flaws in the institutional design of Colombia's coalition agreement.[88]

The system did contain a solution: a clause in the plebiscite established that Congress could, again by two-thirds agreement, suspend the requirement for certain kinds of legislation for a two-year period. The National Front's first Congress had pursued this measure, which eventually made possible the passage of the 1961 agrarian reform law just weeks before the special powers' expiration.[89] It was no mistake that this would be the last major piece of reform legislation passed under Lleras Camargo or Valencia; by 1964, Congress considered reestablishing a simple majority for reform projects in order to "facilitate the functioning of the democratic system."[90]

Institutions intersected with policymaking and politics to inhibit effective state action in two additional ways. One contemporary analysis faulted the plebiscite's parity requirement for creating a bureaucratic hiring boom that would absorb the largest single share of state spending by the middle of the 1960s. On top of this came the rise of the developmental state, which largely took the form of decentralized, autonomous agencies whose hiring, by all accounts, exceeded the number of regular government employees (excluding soldiers and primary-school teachers). Colombia's bureaucracy more than doubled in size over the first seven years of National Front rule, far outstripping the expansion of the civil service, as decentralized agencies largely escaped the civil service controls established under Law 19 of 1958. This costly developmental showcase was made worse by a lack of central coordination and consequent duplication of effort in planning. Planning also became a political liability in itself, as Colombians witnessed ministries and agencies that drew up plans that never yielded policy. "Everything here is reduced to lectures by young economists, which do not solve anything," griped one congressman, summing up a broader critique.[91] Bureaucratic autonomy was accordingly difficult, given that so few arms of the developmental state enjoyed good organizational reputations by the middle of the decade.[92]

Second, coalition politics added a further extra wrinkle to the parity formula. As the parties underwent marked fragmentation, emboldened intra-party factions pressed Valencia to divide bureaucratic appointments among more than just the Liberal and Conservative parties and instead to calibrate his selections to the exact factional balance of power achieved in the previous

---

[88] Gómez Valderrama, 1966: 9 ("minority"); Acosta Polo, 1962: 4 ("an undemocratic"); Vieira, 1966: 5.

[89] Hirschman, 1965: 143–144.   [90] *Anales* 8, no. 14, May 6, 1965: 179–182.

[91] *Anales* 8, no. 43, July 7, 1965: 584–585; *Anales* 8, no. 83, September 21, 1965: 1190–1191, for quote.

[92] Carpenter, 2001.

election. This policy of "millimetric parity," complained one provincial newspaper, violated the sundry needs of Colombia's regions, for it substituted a proper "diversity of treatment" with "a petty administrative equality [*igualismo administrativo*] that paralyzes."[93]

Elsewhere in Latin America, the apparent inability of democratic institutions to advance industrialization helped to prompt a wave of military coups in the most industrialized economies after 1964.[94] This new hemispheric backdrop pushed Colombians to rearticulate their own stances on the relationship between development and democracy. As ongoing limits on imports threatened to shutter small manufacturers during the early months of 1965, the sector's representatives rushed to deny any interest in using force to compel the government to adopt more beneficial policies. Not by coincidence had President Valencia recently moved to depose the minister of war, a vocal advocate for change to Colombia's existing "structures," only days after the failure of a proposed nationwide general strike against the rising cost of living.[95] Brazil's 1964 military coup suggested that higher levels of industrialization might not translate into more robust democracies, as social-science models had previously held. Colombia showed by early 1965 that although the breakdown of development might not lead to authoritarianism, the consequences for democracy remained grim.

DEMOCRACY AND DEVELOPMENT REVISITED, 1966–1970

Could politicians return Colombia's political institutions to being a force for scientific development? Later in 1965, Carlos Lleras Restrepo, by then the National Front's Liberal candidate for the 1966 presidential election, laid out an agenda to achieve a rebalancing of democracy and development. In a series of lectures delivered in Cali, Lleras Restrepo hailed the original spirit of the National Front but critiqued its evolution into an "anachronism under which it [was] impossible to govern." Changes to parity and most especially the two-thirds rule, Lleras argued, would strengthen the executive branch and allow Colombia to move past the Valencia administration's misguided application of millimetric parity and its deviation from economic planning. US diplomats noted that the speeches seemed intended to undercut the opposition, which had been advocating the abandonment of the National Front structure for

---

[93] Gutiérrez Quintero, 1964: 4. A 1960 court ruling determined that parity did not apply to the civil service. Colombians henceforth thought that the expansion of the professional bureaucracy would naturally phase out parity. Acosta Polo, 1962: 4.

[94] See Collier, 1979.

[95] *El Clarín*, March 4, 1965, midday broadcast, Archivo Histórico de Medellín, Radioperiódico El Clarín transcripts, Tomo 213, Folio 210 (hereafter AHM.Clarín.213.210); *El Clarín*, April 30, 1965, evening broadcast, AHM.Clarín.218.556; Telegram 854, January 28, 1965: 2, NARA.59. SNF 1964–66.2046.POL 15-1 1/1/65 (3 of 3).

years. The US Embassy furthermore concurred that Colombia's democratic system had become an impediment to development.[96]

The developmental state – as both planning and reformism – would experience a rebirth of sorts after 1966. Lleras Restrepo "has put together the best Government Colombia has had in years," a US official opined in early 1967, six months into the administration. "Lleras Restrepo is a genuine developmentalist."[97] That praise might have sounded familiar, but in a change from the enthusiasm of the young days of the Alliance for Progress, observers tended to retain their high opinion.[98] Economists, many of them with recent degrees from foreign graduate programs and too young to have participated in the crushing reversals of the Valencia years, revived the state's planning apparatus and assisted in diversifying exports (Figure 4.1) while simultaneously limiting inflation.[99]

Subsequent presidents would pursue different policy lines, but economists who fell out of favor frequently reintegrated back into the state.[100] The most high-profile example is Lauchlin Currie, the Canadian-born economist who had first come to Colombia with the World Bank mission of 1949. Although he operated as a peripheral (if influential) government advisor during the Lleras Camargo and Valencia presidencies, and indeed left the country between 1967 and 1971 because of differences with Lleras Restrepo, Currie acquired a significant following among Colombia's new generation of economists during the mid 1960s. Moreover, upon Currie's return to Colombia in 1971, Lleras Restrepo's successor adopted Currie's development strategies to an unprecedented degree.[101] With their emphasis on regional and national planning, Currie and the economists around him exemplified a style of development thinking distinct from the community-centered approach of Fals Borda's school of sociologists. Beginning with the Lleras Restrepo administration, the Colombian state thus established a higher baseline of a certain kind of technical involvement in development; with it came a triumphalist story from those economists about the state, the nation, and their role in both. It is these economists whose accounts have dominated recent scholarly work on the Colombian developmental state, a process that has elided the disappointments and setbacks of the early and mid 1960s.[102]

[96] Telegram 191, August 6, 1965: 1, NARA.59.SNF 1964–66.2046.POL 15–1 1/1/65, for quote; "Lleras critica a grupos de presión," 1965: 1; "Trascendentales tesis políticas de Lleras," 1965: 20; attachment to Airgram A-372, "Appraisal of Extra-Legal Change Possibilities in Colombia," January 19, 1966: 9, NARA.59.SNF 1964–66.2047.POL 23 Internal Security Counter-Insurgency COL 1/1/64.

[97] de Onis, 1967: 18.   [98] de Onis, 1969: 4.

[99] Dargent, 2015: 69–71, 78–81, 86–89; Thorp, 1991: chapter 7.

[100] Carlos Caballero Argáez, interviewed by A. Ricardo López, Amy Offner, and the author, August 17, 2010; Dargent, 2015: 70, 83–84.

[101] Sandilands, 1990: 182–219, 240–273.   [102] Dargent, 2015; Vélez Álvarez, 2013: 233–239.

In addition to planning, a pair of complementary measures further strengthened Lleras Restrepo's developmental state. The first entailed a far-reaching constitutional reform that followed through on the proposals of Lleras Restrepo's 1965 Cali addresses by broadening and concentrating the state's administrative authority while also loosening parity in the legislative branch. "We are not proposing to destroy republican institutions but rather to reinvigorate them and make them vigorously and efficiently functional," Lleras told Congress.[103] Advocates celebrated the state's new capacities to intervene in private wages and salaries as the culmination of Liberal-led constitutional amendments from 1936 and 1945, which had set reform and development as possible political and legal horizons.[104] Colombia had reached "a new era in which, under the shadow of the partisan accord ... [it] will naturally have to confront very difficult problems of economic and social development," Lleras Restrepo remarked upon the passage of the constitutional reform. "But to fight that battle it will have the indispensable juridical and constitutional frameworks that will allow it to do so through democratic cooperation."[105] With the reform, Lleras gave institutional shape to more than half a decade of critiques against how Colombia's formal political structures constrained the work of development.

Lleras Restrepo's second initiative outside of the realm of planning looked to recover the lost *mística* of the early 1960s and thus break through the informal political structures which had helped to block reform in the countryside. His administration's creation of a popular base of "*campesino* associations" represents an alternative form of embeddedness; as Centeno and Ferraro have suggested, Evans' concept can be read as a statement on the need for engagement with civil society in order to further the implementation of development programs.[106] Beyond the bureaucracy, this could be achieved through civic participation – an approach the Colombian state attempted through the community-development provisions of Law 19 of 1958, but then substantially expanded through Lleras Restrepo's agrarian reform of the late 1960s. Although the state soon withdrew its backing, these *campesino* associations succeeded in carrying out popular mobilizations that greatly increased the pace of land redistribution.[107]

---

[103] Zuluaga Gil, 2016.
[104] Uribe Vargas, 1996: 229–246. For the 1945 reform, see also Andrade Melgarejo, 2018: chapter 1.
[105] Vidal Perdomo, 1970: 64, for quote.   [106] Centeno and Ferraro, 2017: 65–89.
[107] For community development, see Karl, 2017: chapter 5; for Lleras' agrarian reform, Zamosc, 1986: 34–65. Lleras' reforms may have limited the reach of the developmental state in the long term. Passage of the 1968 constitutional amendments entailed concessions to legislators that have been seen as worsening clientelist capture of state resources and decentering political authority (Gutiérrez Sanín, 2014: 113, 119). The pace of agrarian reform meanwhile provoked a backlash from large landowners that culminated with the curtailment of all government land redistribution under Lleras Restrepo's successor.

Lleras Restrepo's program of "national transformation" took place without the reformist social scientists who had participated in the developmentalism of the early 1960s. When the president-elect commenced discussions on his *campesino* organizing program in mid 1966, the organizing committee – which would once have included a figure like Orlando Fals Borda – lacked representation from his discipline.[108] The National University's Faculty of Sociology entered the late 1960s fragmented, its ranks segmented by generational politics and the trauma of its members' earlier breaks with the state.[109]

Fals Borda and his intellectual successors nonetheless retained a common critical stance toward state power. Their field and faculty divided, their access to the state severed by choice and by official fiat, National University sociologists could still fashion their own narrative about development. By the start of the 1970s, the generation of students-turned-professors who had inherited the Faculty of Sociology from Fals Borda widened the ambit of their sociological inquiry, scaling up from their previous monographic studies to broader critiques of politics and development.[110] Their transnational source base varied widely; drawing in part on the burgeoning hemispheric perspective of dependency, the authors further sustained their arguments by borrowing from North American discussions of development's past. So it was that a reflection on the National Front and development cited a 1969 US Senate report on the "failure" of the Alliance for Progress.[111] The sort of transnational exchange that had characterized optimistic dialogue about development a decade earlier now reinscribed claims about the failure of that development.

There are hints that the intellectual legacy of such frustration with the developmental state continues to inform our basic approach to the topic of development. The terms "developmental" or "developmentalism" do not seem to have appeared in Fals Borda's intellectual production from the showcase era of the Colombian developmental state. "Developmentalism" appeared long afterward, when Fals, near the end of his life, described to an interviewer how research and the work of reform had gradually exposed the "limitations" of

---

[108] Memorandum, "Comite operativo sobre asociaciones campesinas," July 4, 1966: 1, BLAA. CLR.Sección IV.1.2.1.

[109] Letter, Tomás Ducay to Fals Borda and María Cristina Salazar, April 28, 1968: 1–2, Archivo Central e Histórico, Fondo Documental Orlando Fals Borda, Caja 33, Carpeta 4, Folios 33–4; Karl, 2017: epilogue. See also Restrepo, 1981: 23.

[110] Parra Sandoval, 1970. Cataño, 1986: 67–70, provides a general summary of sociological production in the 1970s.

[111] Rojas Ruiz, 1970: 122. The original report is US Senate Committee on Foreign Relations and Comptroller General, "Survey of the Alliance for Progress: Colombia – A Case Study of U.S. Aid," February 1, 1969.

Around the same time, opponents of Lleras Restrepo's agrarian reform program also began publishing works that took "failure" as their central motif. Molina Ossa, 1970; Emiliani Román, 1971.

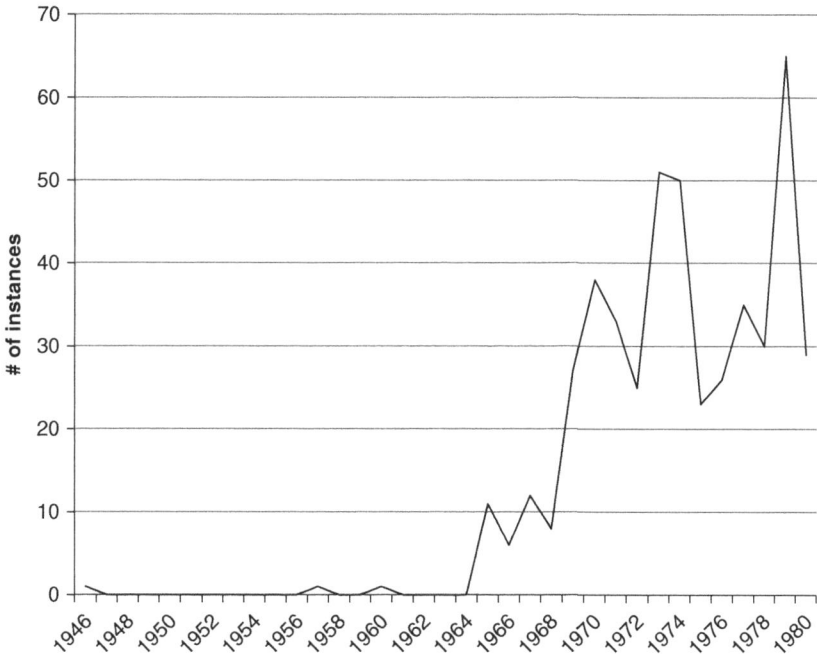

FIGURE 4.2 Instances of *"Desarrollismo"* in Spanish-Language Texts on Google NGram Viewer, 1946–1980[112]

"developmentalism," which he deemed the "dominant ideology" of the 1960s. "[W]e were evolving toward a critique ... a comprehensive critique [of developmentalism]," Fals recalled.[113] The idea of "developmentalism" may be a term that only became popular in Spanish–American social science subsequent to the heyday of the Alliance for Progress, a means for participants to process their experience with the "failures" of the decade of development.[114] An n-gram of *desarrollismo* offers suggestive evidence on this point, showing very few instances of the word before 1965 (Figure 4.2).

CONCLUSION: THE LEGACIES OF THE 1960S

By what means can we judge Colombia's development efforts in the 1960s? Land equality, one of the National Front's key targets, actually fell between 1960 and 1970, with "peasant farms ... decreas[ing] both in total number and

---

[112] Data taken from https://books.google.com/ngrams. Unfortunately, no similar data set exists for Portuguese.
[113] Fals Borda, interview, in Cubides, 2010: 101–102.
[114] I make a similar argument for the term "La Violencia," which Fals Borda also coined in the mid 1960s. Karl, 2017.

in area."[115] By contrast, World Bank statistics indicate that the bottom 20 percent of Colombia's population grew its share of national income between 1960 and 1970. If this increase was only from 3 to eq 4 percent, it must be kept in mind that inequality rose during the same period in every other Latin American country for which we have data.[116] This record takes on a different cast too if we consider the 1960s against the backdrop of the ensuing half century. As Francisco Gutiérrez Sanín has recently observed, the National Front was "one of the few periods in Colombian history in which we observe ... a systematic lessening – albeit too slow – in inequality."[117]

The case of Colombian social scientists' fraught relationship with the state – influenced in part by the politics of postauthoritarian power-sharing – is suggestive for historians of Latin American developmentalism more generally. Even if development experts (re)gain autonomy, and presidential administrations accelerate developmental efforts, social scientists' involvement with earlier periods of reform can determine how the state is subsequently portrayed in the public sphere. Therefore, as we contemplate the reach and effectiveness of National Front-era reform, we should pinpoint when certain narratives arrive and moreover remember that the term "failure" has accompanied the developmentalism of the early 1960s nearly from its inception. Developmental programs certainly never lived up to the high expectations that surrounded them at the start of the decade of development. Accounts from that period may express frustrations with Colombia's democratic system more than they do disappointment with the developmental state. At the same time, however, Colombia's experience in the decade after 1957 illustrates that the two strands are difficult to disentangle, given the profound and frequently contradictory relationship between democracy and development in postwar Latin America.

REFERENCES

"1958 [alocución de año nuevo]." Speech by Alberto Lleras Camargo, December 31, 1958. In *El primer gobierno del Frente Nacional*, vol. I, *Mayo de 1958–agosto de 1959*. Bogotá: Imprenta Nacional, 1960: 224.
Acosta Polo, Benigno. "Bondades y fallas del plebiscito." *La República*, September 29, 1962.
Adelman, Jeremy. *Worldly Philosopher: The Odyssey of Albert O. Hirschman.* Princeton University Press, 2013.
"Alianza Sí, Progreso No." *Time*, March 16, 1962.
Allen, Robert S. "Senators Ring Alarm on Latin Plan." *Los Angeles Times*, March 1, 1962.

---

[115] de Janvry, 1981: 134.   [116] Cuba would be the obvious exception. De Janvry, 1981: 36.
[117] Gutiérrez Sanín, 2014: 100–101.

Andrade Melgarejo, Diana. "'We Left Legality to Enter the Rule of Law:' The Constitutional Struggle for Congress in Colombia, 1945–1962," PhD dissertation, Princeton University, 2018.

"Año del ejecutivo." *Semana*, January 14, 1960.

Arocha, Jaime. "Antropología en Colombia: Una visión." In Un siglo de investigación social: Antropologia en Colombia, eds. Jaime Arocha and Nina S. de Friedemann. Bogotá: Etno, 1984.

Arocha, Jaime, and Nina S. de Friedemann. "Prólogo." In *Un siglo de investigación social: Antropología en Colombia*, eds. Jaime Arocha and Nina S. de Friedemann. Bogotá: Etno, 1984.

Bejarano, Ana María, and Eduardo Pizarro Leongómez. "From 'Restricted' to 'Besieged:' The Changing Nature of the Limits to Democracy in Colombia." In *The Third Wave of Democratization in Latin America: Advances and Setbacks*, eds. Frances Hagopian and Scott P. Mainwaring. Cambridge and New York: Cambridge University Press, 2005.

Carpenter, Daniel P. *The Forging of Bureaucratic Autonomy: Reputations, Networks, and Policy Innovation in Executive Agencies, 1862–1928*. Princeton University Press, 2001.

Cataño, Gonzalo. *La sociología en Colombia: Balance crítico*. Bogotá: Plaza & Janés, 1986.

Centeno, Miguel A. and Agustin E. Ferraro. "With the Best of Intentions. Types of Developmental Failure in Latin America." In *Why Latin American Nations Fail. Development Strategies in the Twenty-First Century*, eds. Esteban Pérez Caldentey and Matías Vernengo, Oakland: University of California Press, 2017.

Cincuenta años: Departamento Nacional de Planeación. Bogotá: Departamento Nacional de Planeación, 2009.

Collier, David, ed. *The New Authoritarianism in Latin America*. Princeton University Press, 1979.

"Colombia Credit Restored." *Washington Star*, December 3, 1966.

Cubides, Fernando. *Camilo Torres: Testimonios sobre su figura y su época*. Medellín: La Carreta Editores and Universidad Nacional de Colombia, 2010.

Dargent, Eduardo. *Technocracy and Democracy in Latin America: The Experts Running Government*. New York, NY: Cambridge University Press, 2015.

Departamento Administrativo Nacional de Estadística. *Anuario general de estadística. Colombia – 1962*. Bogotá: Imprenta Nacional, 1964.

Estadística fiscal, administrativa y financiera. 1963–1964–1965. Bogotá: Imprenta Nacional, 1969.

Estadística fiscal, administrativa y financiera, 1966–1967. Bogotá: Talleres del Departamento Nacional de Estadística, n.d.

Díaz-Alejandro, Carlos F. *Colombia. Vol. 9: Foreign Trade Regimes and Economic Development*. New York: National Bureau of Economic Research, 1976.

"De una década a otra." *El Tiempo*, January 2, 1960. https://news.google.com/newspapers?id=_QodAAAAIBAJ&sjid=K34EAAAAIBAJ&pg=2926,20812&hl=en.

"Discurso de posesión." Speech by Lleras Camargo, August 7, 1958, in *El primer gobierno del Frente Nacional, vol. I, Mayo de 1958–agosto de 1959*, Bogotá: Imprenta Nacional, 1960: I,61.

Eder, Richard. "2 Factors Peril Aid to Colombia." *New York Times*, November 11, 1962.

"Bogota Prepares for Aid Program." *New York Times*, December 29, 1963a.

"Colombia Lagging on Economic Plan." *New York Times*, October 3, 1963b.

"Colombia Works for Land Reform." *New York Times*, April 8, 1963c.

"Colombia's Dangerous Doldrums." *The Reporter*, October 7, 1965.

"Economic Dilemma in Colombia." *New York Times*, March 28, 1963d.

"El embajador en Washington." *El Tiempo*, May 17, 1963, http://news.google.com/newspapers?id=2RwhAAAAIBAJ&sjid=yWMEAAAAIBAJ&pg=7098%2C2559472.

Emiliani Román, Raimundo. *El fracaso ruinoso de la reforma agraria*. Bogotá: Editorial Revista Colombiana, 1971.

"Enorme incremento de los cultivos de palma africana." *El Tiempo*, March 20, 1965: 24, https://news.google.com/newspapers?id=MnQcAAAAIBAJ&sjid=wWMEAAAAIBAJ&pg=7290%2C3232988.

Evans, Peter. "The State as Problem and Solution: Predation, Embedded Autonomy, and Structural Change." In *The Politics of Economic Adjustment: International Constraints, Distributive Conflicts, and the State*, eds. Stephan Haggard and Robert R. Kaufman. Princeton University Press, 1992.

Fajardo, Margarita. "The Latin American Experience with Development: Social Sciences, Economic Policies, and the Making of a Global Order, 1944–1971." PhD diss., Princeton University, 2015.

Fals Borda, Orlando. *La transformación de la América Latina y sus implicaciones sociales y económicas*. Monografías sociológicas, no. 10. Bogotá: Universidad Nacional de Colombia, Facultad de Sociología, 1961.

Gómez Valderrama, Pedro. *Memoria del Ministro de Gobierno al Congreso de 1966*. Bogotá: Imprenta Nacional, 1966.

Gonzalez, Heliodoro. "The Failure of the Alliance for Progress in Colombia." *Inter-American Economic Affairs* 23, no.1, Summer 1969: 87–96.

Guillén Martínez, Fernando. "Notas sobre la vida social en Colombia." *El Tiempo*, June 4, 1961, sec. Lecturas Dominicales.

Raíz y futuro de la revolución. Bogotá: Ediciones Tercer Mundo, 1963.

Gutiérrez Quintero, Armando. "La violencia." *El Cronista*, January 3, 1964.

Gutiérrez Sanín, Francisco. *¿Lo que el viento se llevó? Los partidos políticos y la democracia en Colombia, 1958–2002*. Bogotá: Grupo Editorial Norma, 2007.

El orangutan con sacoleva: Cien años de democracia y represión en Colombia (1910–2010). Bogotá: IEPRI, 2014.

Hartlyn, Jonathan. "Military Governments and the Transition to Civilian Rule: The Colombian Experience of 1957–1958." *Journal of Interamerican Studies and World Affairs* 26, 2, May 1984: 245–281.

Hirschman, Albert O. *Journeys Toward Progress: Studies of Economic Policy-Making in Latin America*. Garden City, NY: Anchor Books, 1965.

Development Projects Observed. Washington: Brookings Institution, 1967.

The Passions and the Interests: Political Arguments for Capitalism Before Its Triumph. Princeton University Press, 1977.

"Informe al Congreso." Speech by Alberto Lleras Camargo, July 20, 1959, in *El primer gobierno: del Frente Nacional*, vol. II, *Agosto de 1959–julio de 1960*, Bogotá: Imprenta Nacional, 1960: I, 500.

"Instalación del Congreso." Speech by Alberto Lleras Camargo, July 20, 1960, in *El primer gobierno del Frente Nacional*, vol. II, *Agosto de 1959–julio de 1960*, Bogotá: Imprenta Nacional, 1960: 473–474.

Instituto Colombiano de la Reforma Agraria. *Informe de actividades, 1964: Tercer año de reforma agraria*. Bogotá: Imprenta Nacional, 1965.

Ioris, Rafael Rossotto. *Transforming Brazil: A History of National Development in the Postwar Era*. New York and London: Routledge, 2014.

Janvry, Alain de. *The Agrarian Question and Reformism in Latin America*. Baltimore and London: Johns Hopkins University Press, 1981.

Karl, Robert A. "State Formation, Violence, and Cold War in Colombia, 1957–1966." Unpublished PhD thesis, Harvard University, 2009.

   Forgotten Peace: Reform, Violence, and the Making of Contemporary Colombia. Oakland: University of California Press, 2017.

Lilienthal, David E. *TVA: Democracy on the March*. New York and London: Harper & Brothers, 1944.

Lleras Camargo, Alberto. *Nuestra revolución industrial*. Bogotá: Aedita Editores, 1957.

"Lleras critica a grupos de presión." *El Tiempo*, August 3, 1965: 12, https://news.google.com/newspapers?id=u30cAAAAIBAJ&sjid=3WMEAAAAIBAJ&pg=820%2C416024.

Mares, David R. "State Leadership in Economic Policy: A Collective Action Framework with a Colombian Case." *Comparative Politics* 25, no.4, July 1993: 455–473.

"Mater et Magistra." Encyclical letter of Pope John XXIII, May 15, 1961.

Molina, Adriana. "El servicio civil en Colombia." In *Hacia el rediseño del Estado: Análisis institucional, reformas y resultados económicos*, eds. Miguel Gandour Pordominsky and Luis Bernardo Mejía Guinand. Bogotá: TM Editores & Departamento Nacional de Planeación, 1999.

Molina Ossa, Camilo. *La reforma agraria colombiana*. Cali: Imprenta Departmental, 1970.

Morales Benítez, Otto. *Memoria del Ministro de Agricultura al Congreso de 1961, Parte General*. Bogotá:Imprenta Nacional, 1962.

Onis, Juan de. "Opiniones divididas sobre el voto el domingo pasado." *El Cronista*, March 19, 1964.

   "Bogota Development Plan Awaits I.M.F. Decision." *New York Times*, February 5, 1967.

   "Problems Mount in Colombia, a Model of Latin Reform." *New York Times*, June 16, 1969.

Palacios, Marco. *Between Legitimacy and Violence: A History of Colombia, 1875–2002*. Translated by Richard Stoller. Durham and London: Duke University Press, 2006.

Parra Sandoval, Rodrigo, ed. *Dependencia externa y desarrollo político en Colombia*. Bogotá: Imprenta Nacional, 1970.

Posada, Antonio J., and Jeanne Anderson Posada. *The CVC: Challenge to Underdevelopment and Traditionalism*. Colección Aventura Del Desarrollo 9. Bogotá: Ediciones Tercer Mundo, 1966.

Puel, Hugues. "Catholicism and Politics in France in the 20th Century." *Oikonomia: Rivista Di Etica e Scienze Sociali*, February 2001.

República de Colombia. *Memoria del Ministerio de Agricultura al Congreso Nacional – 1959*. Bogotá: Imprenta Nacional, 1959.

Memoria del Ministerio de Agricultura al Congreso Nacional – 1960. Bogotá: Imprenta Nacional, 1960.

Restrepo, Gabriel. "El Departamento de Sociologia de la Universidad Nacional y la tradicion sociologica colombiana." In *La sociología en Colombia: Balance y perspectivas. Memoria del III Congreso Nacional de Sociología, Bogotá, agosto 20–22 de 1980.* Bogotá: Asociación Colombiana de Sociología, 1981.

Restrepo Piedrahita, Carlos. "El moderno Leviatán: La ciencia y la política." *El Tiempo*, November 2. 1963, https://news.google.com/newspapers?id=YdkbAAAAIBAJ&sjid= 7mMEAAAAIBAJ&pg=5714%2C172620.

Rojas Ruiz, Humberto. "El Frente Nacional: ¿Solución política a un problema de desarrollo?" In *Dependencia externa y desarrollo político en Colombia*, ed. Rodrigo Parra Sandoval. Bogotá: Imprenta Nacional, 1970.

Roldán, Mary. *Blood and Fire: La Violencia in Antioquia, Colombia, 1946–1953.* Durham and London: Duke University Press, 2002.

Sáenz Rovner, Eduardo. "La Misión del Banco Mundial en Colombia, el Gobierno de Laureano Gómez (1950–1951) y la Asociación Nacional de Industriales (ANDI)." *Cuadernos de Economía* 20, 35, December 2001: 245–265.

Colombia años 50: Industriales, política y diplomacia. Bogotá: Universidad Nacional de Colombia, Sede Bogotá, 2002.

Sandilands, Roger J. *The Life and Political Economy of Lauchlin Currie: New Dealer, Presidential Adviser, and Development Economist.* Durham: Duke University Press, 1990.

Schmidt, Steffen W. "The Alliance's Anniversary." *New York Times*, March 13, 1962.

"Bureaucrats as Modernizing Brokers? Clientelism in Colombia." *Comparative Politics* 6, 3, April 1974: 425–450.

"La Violencia Revisited: The Clientelist Bases of Political Violence in Colombia." *Journal of Latin American Studies* 6, 1, May 1974: 97–111.

"The Mess in Bogota." *Time*, October 22, 1956.

Thorp, Rosemary. *Economic Management and Economic Development in Peru and Colombia.* University of Pittsburgh Press, 1991.

Progress, Poverty and Exclusion: An Economic History of Latin America in the 20th Century. Washington, D.C.: Inter-American Development Bank, 1998.

"Trascendentales tesis políticas de Lleras." *El Tiempo*, August 6, 1965: 20, https://news .google.com/newspapers?id=vnocAAAAIBAJ&sjid=3WMEAAAAIBAJ&pg=672% 2C853160.

UNICEF, "The 1960s: Decade of Development." N.d., www.unicef.org/sowc96/1960s .htm.

Uribe Vargas, Diego. *Evolución política y constitucional de Colombia.* Madrid: Instituto de Derecho Comparado, Universidad Complutense de Madrid, 1996.

Urrutia, Miguel. "On the Absence of Economic Populism in Colombia." In *The Macroeconomics of Populism in Latin America*, eds. Rudiger Dornbusch and Sebastian Edwards. University of Chicago Press, 1991.

US Senate Committee on Foreign Relations, and Comptroller General. "Survey of the Alliance for Progress: Colombia – A Case Study of U.S. Aid," February 1, 1969.

Vélez Álvarez, Luis Guillermo. "Lauchlin Currie: El maestro de los economistas colombianos." *Lecturas de Economía*, 79, December 2013: 233–239.

Vidal Perdomo, Jaime. *La reforma constitucional de 1968 y sus alcances jurídicos.* Bogotá: Universidad Externado de Colombia, 1970.

Vieira, Gilberto. "Los diez años de 'Documentos Políticos' y sus nuevas tareas teórico-políticas." *Documentos Políticos*, December 1966.

"Youth Points Way for Colombia to Return to a Stable Economy." *New York Times*, January 13, 1960.

Zamosc, León. *The Agrarian Question and the Peasant Movement in Colombia: Struggles of the National Peasant Association, 1967–1981.* Cambridge and New York: Cambridge University Press, 1986.

Zuluaga Gil, Ricardo. "Reforma constitucional de 1968. La última gran reforma." *Crónica Constitucional* (blog), April 29, 2016. http://ricardozuluagagil.blogspot.com/2016/04/reforma-constitucional-de-1968-la-ultima.html?q=colombia+1968.

PART III

INSTITUTIONAL DESIGN: INFRASTRUCTURAL AND TERRITORIAL POWER

5

One Blueprint, Three Translations: Development Corporations in Chile, Colombia, and Peru

José Carlos Orihuela

As neoliberalism, developmentalism was once portrayed as a homogenous phenomenon that spread all over Latin America. Once upon a time, the conventional narrative went, the Great Depression produced import-substitution industrialization (ISI) and overwhelming state interventionism as a reaction, until "the model" could not sustain its underpinning macroeconomic imbalances.[1] Myths always build upon fears and half-truths; although very real and significant for decision-making of individuals and collectivities, myths do not replace truth. Instead of the sketched tale, historically oriented scholarship portrays diverse developmentalisms within Latin America. In particular, (i) industrialization, industrial policies and state interventionism in general were not creations of critical junctures shaped by the 1929 or 1914 crises, but rather preceded them; and (ii) state interventionism took diverse national forms.[2] In short, the developmental state did not take the same route everywhere south of Río Grande.

Building on this line of historical political economy research, this chapter shows that the diffusion of "autonomous development corporations" in Latin America entailed quite different country-specific experiences. In those produced by Chile, Colombia, and Peru, the threat or plain reality of political party intervention, patronage, capture by vested industrial interests, or blunt corruption was always present. Yet, the degree to which each of these phenomena materialized varied markedly, as can be observed in the cases of Chile's Corporación de Fomento (CORFO, est. 1939), Colombia's Corporación del Valle del Cauca (CVC, est. 1954), and Peru's Corporación Peruana del Santa (CPS, est. 1944).

None of the cases in our country set produced a developmental state, say, half as strong as that of Korea, as not even Brazil actually did. Granted, they were

---

[1] Fishlow, 1990: 61–74; Thorp, 1998.
[2] Thorp, 1998; Cárdenas Ocampo, and Thorp, 2000; Coatsworth and Williamson, 2004: 205–232; Ocampo and Ros, 2011.

not all hyper-autonomous à la East Asian Miracle: under the "Latin American developmental state" umbrella one actually finds distinct national experiences. Autonomous development corporations varied markedly. In our sample, first, two relatively politically stable countries, Chile and Colombia, with traditions of institutional continuity and more solid processes of post-colonial state development, produced relatively autonomous development corporations, while politically unstable Peru gave birth to the kind of weak and short-lived state organization that is all too common to its national history. Secondly, while the Chilean political society generated a ruled-from-Santiago and massive nation-level state organization, those of Colombia and Peru established valley/region-based entities. Finally, while corporations survived the fall of the era of "state-led industrialization" in Chile and Colombia, those of Peru died prematurely in the early 1970s.[3] The claim is that development corporations are good case studies of more general national patterns of the politics of bureaucratic autonomy and economic development.

Developmental state diffusion unfolded in national variation and we want to shed light on this phenomenon. In policy proposals and domestic debates, Latin American state crafters claimed to be adopting what advanced nations had already been doing. In particular, the fostering of national economic development was seen as a standard state practice of advanced capitalist economies. On top, the Tennessee Valley Authority (TVA), established in 1933 by the USA government as a reaction to the Great Depression, emerged as a global model of bureaucratic autonomy and science-based state action to foster economic development. Yet, translating the institutional blueprint varied markedly. No matter that, as in Colombia, development corporation-mongers brought TVA's champion David E. Lilienthal to present the project as a "true copy" of TVA, as was also done elsewhere in Brazil, Mexico, Iran, and India.[4] Global policy paradigms and organizational models end up "nationalized," translated to national practice, depending on institutional mechanisms of diffusion and power dynamics.[5]

This chapter is organized as follows. Section 1 sketches the institutionalist theory frame underpinning the comparative study. The empirical analysis comes next, with a focus on success or failure in "the forging of bureaucratic autonomy".[6] Section 2 presents the case of Chile's CORFO, an extreme case of centralized state developmentalism. Section 3 details the development of CVC, which served as a model for another seventeen regional autonomous corporations that diffused in Colombia after World War II and before the reformist Constitution of 1991 – which was to increase the number of corporations to thirty-four (one per department). Section 4 presents the rise and fall of CPS, the first development corporation in Peru. Valley-based or

---

[3] Cárdenas, Ocampo, and Thorp, 2000: 3.   [4] Hirschman, 1967: 21.
[5] Orihuela, 2014: 242–265; Dargent, Orihuela, Paredes, and Ulfe, 2017.   [6] Carpenter, 2001.

regional development corporations in Peru grew to seventeen, one per department, by 1968, but unlike their Colombian cousins (only five corporations by the same year) they were seriously underfunded and did not survive the end of state-led industrialization. Section 5 concludes this article by highlighting the differences and similarities of developmental bureaucratic autonomy.

A BASIC FRAMEWORK TO UNDERSTAND DEVELOPMENTAL STATE VARIATION RESULTING FROM DIFFUSION

Why did Latin American political economies not converge to one model of developmental state?[7] An analytical toolkit to understand this and other processes of globalization and variegated institutional change is provided by bridging new institutionalisms proposed by the social sciences. There is no space here to discuss the points in common and areas of dispute among the three schools, namely sociological, historical, and rational-choice institutionalisms. Hall and Taylor (1996),[8] Campbell (2004 and 2010),[9] and Scott (2008)[10] offer authoritative reviews. In setting bridges between institutionalism traditions, I will present a simplified "theory frame"[11] to establish a dialogue with gathered evidence on developmental state formation.

New institutionalism in organizational sociology talks about isomorphism. Organizations embedded in historically constructed fields and social structures converge due to institutional mechanisms, namely normative, mimetic, and coercive.[12] The "world society" view on the homogenizing role of institutional environments on organizations has been put under review, however, so that there is more attention to the "interpretation, manipulation, revision and elaboration" performed by involved agents.[13] Ultimately, there is always some exercise of translation.

Such a perspective provides powerful hypotheses for the phenomena that concern us in this book. Why did Latin American societies all adopt a developmental state? It could be the norms guiding the decision making of Latin American political elites, given that around 1914, 1929, 1945, and before Thatcher and Reagan, global conventional wisdom favored active state interventionism in general, and state-led industrialization, in particular. However, it could also be imitation: when uncertain about which route to take, it is better to follow what everybody else is doing, like establishing the TVA model, a technical, science-based, autonomous corporation to foster domestic economic activities in the twentieth century. Uncertainty being

---

[7] This section draws on Orihuela, 2014.   [8] Hall and Taylor, 1996: 936–957.
[9] Campbell, 2004, 2010.   [10] Scott, 2008: 427–442.   [11] Rueschemeyer, 2009.
[12] DiMaggio and Powell, 1983: 147–160; Meyer *et al.*, 1997: 623–651; Schneiberg and Clemens, 2005; Dobbin, Simmons, and Garret, 2007: 449–472.
[13] Scott, 2008: 430.

a defining feature of the politics of development, state reformers love to borrow internationally acclaimed models to counteract skepticism and internal opposition to policy innovation. Albert Hirschman made sharp observations on such phenomena pervading both macroeconomic and microeconomic policymaking in Latin America.[14] Finally, adoption can also result out of coercion, as when the Alliance for Progress demanded a national development plan and a specialized economic planning bureau in order to begin channeling millions of USA dollars.

While sociological institutionalism helps us to understand half of the big picture, that is the account of institutional forces pulling towards convergence, historical institutionalism helps us with the other half. Divergence results from convergence fundamentally because of path-dependence phenomena: history conditions translation. Countries are particular, context-specific political-economic systems. Economic geography structures, colonial legacies of factor endowments and their distribution among social groups, early modern economic activities, and nineteenth-century post-colonial state formation have all greatly influenced country-specific political economy trajectories in Latin America.[15] The diffusing developmental state was not built on the void, but on material and cultural legacies of nation state building. Moreover, junctures, timing and sequence, produced by contingent shaping processes and events (such as a fall in commodity prices, change of government, and natural disasters) are also very significant in the unfolding of state action and institutional change.[16] Therefore, for those who believe that history matters, be it the legacy or the contingency, it is reasonable to expect diverging national paths. State formation is world-society-shaped, but also path-dependent.

Institutions are continuity, but also change. And by institutions I do not mean the narrow canonical view of North,[17] "the rules of the game," but the wide perspective of institutional regimens composed of formal rules, habits, strong beliefs and socially legitimated organizations.[18] How do institutions evolve for historical institutionalism? There are two basic views, which I do not take as exclusive. First, institutions change radically at critical junctures, and secondly, they evolve in piecemeal manner on an everyday basis.[19] One way or the other, one needs to look at processes and events contingent to the course of institutional change to make sense of the latter. Institutional analysis has to consider what the contentious politics literature calls "political opportunity structure."[20]

---

[14] Hirschman, 1963, 1967.
[15] Engerman and Sokoloff, 1994; John Coatsworth, 2005: 126–144; Mahoney; 2010; Soifer, 2015.
[16] Collier and Collier, 1991; Pierson, 1944; 213.   [17] North, 1990.
[18] Polanyi, 1944; Selznick, 1966; Greif, 2006.
[19] Collier and Collier,1991; Streeck and Thelen, 2005; Mahoney and Thelen, 2010.
[20] McAdam, Tarrow and Tilly, 2001; Tarrow, 1994.

The bridging of the new institutionalisms of the social sciences allows for a better conceptualization of the rationality and behavior of agents forging states, the developmental state in particular. In my reading of history, developmental state crafters were all "strategic" agents, but not of the ultra-selfish and ultra-rational ideal type all too commonly found in rational choice and new institutional economics literatures. Rationality is subject to social construction. The transnational structures and networks diffusing norms and knowledge, on the one hand, and the national institutional environment rooting domestic tradition, on the other one, embed the rationality and agency of the individuals who compose state and society. Developmentalist or not, real-world rationality is bounded, but also embedded in social relations: innovative policy agency – including the translation of global blueprints of state action – is situated in a concrete social, historically constructed context. *Situated in* rather than determined by. Passions and interests, and therefore human action, are shaped by particular institutional environments.

Finally, how autonomous were the resulting varieties of developmental state? In *The Forging of Bureaucratic Autonomy*, Daniel P. Carpenter insightfully argues that bureaucratic autonomy emerges only upon the historical achievement of three conditions: (i) political differentiation from the actors who seek to control state formation, (ii) unique organizational capacities, and (iii) political legitimacy or organizational reputations embedded in an independent power base. By calling to pay attention to the transnational diffusion of paradigms and models of state action, on the one hand, and to the specificities of historical domestic processes, on the other, I will show that the sketched theory frame contributes to better understanding of the forging of bureaucratic autonomy. Table 5.1 summarizes the assessment of our cases on these three conditions for bureaucratic autonomy, which will be explained in detail afterwards.

CORFO IN CHILE: NATIONAL AND STATE ENGINEER-DRIVEN

The first thing that strikes the observer about CORFO is its early creation within the Latin American context, in 1939. Under structuralist lenses, this was the result of early domestic industrialization, which generated a pro-industry political base and led policy elites to examine and imagine institutional innovations in industrialized nations. Historians and historically oriented social scientists have amply documented the strong development of the manufacturing economy and state apparatus in nineteenth-century Chile.[21] In *Instead of Misery*,[22] the developmentalist manifesto of an influential economist of the time, Jorge Ahumada stated that Chile had to use the mirror of Europe and the US: "... we Chileans have always had the pretension of being a people marching at the head of progress, imitating very closely the material

---

[21] Muñoz, 1986; Ortega, 2005; Soifer, 2015.   [22] Ahumada, 1970.

TABLE 5.1 *Assessing Bureaucratic Autonomy of Development Corporations with Carpenter (2001)'s Lenses*

Bureaucratic Autonomy Conditions	CORFO	CVC	CPS
Political differentiation	High	Low / Medium	Low
Organizational capacity	High	High	Medium
Political legitimacy	High	High	Low / Medium

and spiritual advances of Europe and the US ... We like to think that we are the British of brown America. To judge ourselves we cannot, therefore, use patterns that do not correspond to our most intimate aspirations."

Then and now, ideas mattered a great deal. To foster the national economy was a must for a critical mass of policy elites. With nitrates representing 80 percent of exports, Chile repetitively suffered the consequences of peripheral *mono*-dependence. War pushed the German state to produce synthetic nitrates, or weaponry capacity, which meant the end of a resource. Thus, political conditions in the core created an unstable political period for peripheral Chile. The 1929 crack made things worse. A League of Nations study reported Chile to be the worst hit economy of the Great Depression. Copper was to replace nitrates, but would not the story of "frustrated development" repeat again, given that national progress depended on basically the price of one mineral export?[23]

The critical juncture that brought CORFO took full shape with the 1939 Concepción Earthquake. Thirty thousand people died when the center-to-left Popular Front government (1936–1942), led by the Radical Party, held office. President Aguirre Cerda shared the view that the state had to be more active in promoting the national economy. Finance Minister Roberto Wachholdtz maintained that national industrial development needed "a vast, rational, scientifically elaborated plan, to be put into practice methodically and over a long period of time."[24] An industrialist elite had also emerged, establishing a *Confederación de la Producción y el Comercio* in 1934. The then five-decades-old *Sociedad de Fomento Fabril* (SOFOFA) was a leading organization within the *Confederación*. The *Confederación* and the SOFOFA promoted the establishment of a National Economic Council, for business leaders to advise national government on economic policy. Since the 1920s, leading politicians had proposed the idea of a corporatist National Economic Council as "the technical voice that informs governmental action."[25] A "modern state" was the collective dream of new political elites. Fears of traditional agricultural elites impeded this developmental agenda from advancing. Given the process, the earthquake made a large window of opportunity for pro-industrial institutional

---

[23] Orihuela, 2013: 138–148.   [24] Muñoz, 1986: 77.   [25] Ibañez, 1983: 49.

change. A form of state action that had never been seen before, the autonomous development corporation, was born.[26]

The SOFOFA was neither the only player nor, most significantly to our story, the most important one: the tracing of the CORFO bill leads us to consider state engineers. For two decades, civil engineers had been articulating a scientific discourse on the need for greater and improved state planning. They configured a network of domestic expertise that endowed bureaucratic entrepreneurship with vast political legitimacy. Most importantly, engineers' relationship with the state did not begin with the drafting of the CORFO bill. They gained prestige with the Empresa de los Ferrocarriles del Estado de Chile (FFCC), established in 1884 to centralize state-owned enterprises operating since the 1850s. FFCC was a national pride, and was widely believed to be managed in an efficient, business-like, and apolitical manner.[27] The engineers of FFCC continued their professional careers at CORFO, bringing their culture of public service and professionalism.[28] CORFO technical personnel enjoyed a paramount professional reputation among both colleagues in the public sector and business organizations.[29]

The significance of state engineers for state formation marks a central difference between Chile and the Colombian and Peruvian experiences. As I will explain below, CVC in Colombia was brought by local economic elites, while Santa in Peru was fundamentally a project of an industrialist president. Thus, in all the studied cases we find industrialists, politicians and *técnicos*. But the political weight of the last group was more significant in the Chilean one.

The professional bureaucracy constituted a powerful political actor, which had been progressively displacing the traditional elites from state control in Chile, since the nineteenth century.[30] In the hectic 1920s, key state modernizer Colonel Carlos Ibañez, president from 1927–1931 and the incarnation of Chilean populism against the traditional party system, opened the state doors for the entry of young engineers, the *"rotos* of Ibañez". A new policy elite was incorporated into the power system; in the words of Ibañez, they were "young, independent and mostly middle class men … little known in the political and social circles of Santiago".[31] Recruited from the Instituto de Ingenieros, the *técnicos* were called to run the Ministry of Finance and key organizations of the state, such as the Contraloría General de la República, the Office of Budget, the Superintendence of Customs, and so on.[32] A decade later, most of the engineers who headed CORFO were neither owners of firms, nor had been permanently employed by the private sector, although there were some with links with the industrial business association SOFOFA.[33]

---

[26] Muñoz, 2003.   [27] Ibañez, 1983.   [28] Ibañez, 1924–1960: 142.
[29] Cavarozzi, 1975: 129–130.   [30] Silva, 2008; Iván Jaksić, 2013.   [31] Ibañez, 1983: 49–50.
[32] Ibañez, 1983: 50.   [33] Cavarozzi, 1975: 128–129.

A regional corporation instead of a national model was unlikely in Chile during 1939. First, the political tradition favored a politically centralized state. After a short period of federalism and civil war, the early "conservative settlement" (1830s) shaped the political ethos of Chile, with a centralized state and a strong presidential figure, "the Portalian state". Secondly, and unlike the case of CVC in Colombia, CORFO was not primarily the project of regional economic but national policy elites. Both the state engineers who championed the initiative and the industrialists that supported it were based in Santiago. In that sense, CORFO can be seen as a product of strong and professional central government and the early industrialization that took place in the Central Valley. In other words, the Chilean state had an early development of "infrastructural capacity"; it was politically centralized but bureaucratically deconcentrated.[34]

A further yet important note on nineteenth-century state formation and its objective and subjective legacies for twentieth-century state making follows. In my encounters with Chilean economists and political figures over the years, I have recurrently heard the narrative that Diego Portales was the most important crafter of the Chilean modern state. That the Chilean state has managed to build more political legitimacy and organizational capacity than neighboring countries to date is commonly attributed to the actions of Portales. Yet Portales (1793–1837) died young and was survived for three decades by his contemporary Andrés Bello (1781–1865), the Venezuelan humanist who moved to Chile in 1829, recruited by Portales. If Portales was a fundamental political advisor and war strategist, Bello incarnated as no other man than the nonpartisan expert involved in Latin America state craft. The legacy of Universidad de Chile rector, Finance and Interior and Foreign Relations official, senator, drafter of the Civil Code, Andrés Bello, for Chilean state formation is arguably at least as important as the one of Diego Portales,[35] but this fact may be more agreed among historians than contemporary state actors.

The high level of political legitimacy regarding CORFO was also the result of its congressional origin and its governance structure, based on a state–business partnership. Unlike other starting points of developmental state organizations seen elsewhere, say CVC in Colombia and CPS in Peru, or Peru's National Planning Institute (see Chapter 6, by Eduardo Dargent, in this volume), Congress established CORFO, not a short-term dictator. It took a harsh debate among parliamentarians, but the fact that it was created by Congress and had received the approval of business unions provided it with extra political capital for its infant development. The autonomy of CORFO technicians was set to be supervised by business representatives and state ministries dealing with the productive economy. If the much-desired National Economic Council had failed to operate effectively, CORFO's board materialized a version of the same

[34] Mann, 1984: 185–213; Centeno and Ferraro, 2013.
[35] Jaksić, 2001, 2013: 105–125; Dunkerley, 2014.

corporatist policy paradigm: business and state leaders should get together to decide over long-term, nation-state policies. This was one of the central mechanisms of how Peter Evans' "embedded autonomy" worked in the case of Chile.[36]

Bureaucratic autonomy was also the result of a special organizational status set for CORFO. It had bureaucratic autonomy to operate as a private organization, autonomy for the management of its assets, and an endowment that resulted from a special tax on copper. To counterbalance so much autonomy, in addition to its high-level business-state management council, the Contraloría General de la República – then and now a well-respected institution – was set to oversee its bureaucratic practice, to minimize the possibility of short-sighted political intervention, patronage, and corruption.[37]

Over the years, political continuity favored technocratic continuity: Radical Party members were voted presidents of Chile for a decade and a half, until 1952. It is well established that the autonomy of CORFO was made possible because Radical Party leadership believed in isolating technical policymaking from "political" pressures, "their own at least".[38] The return of populist President Carlos Ibáñez (1952–1958) did not mean the reduction of autonomy for CORFO. Thus, for almost two decades the institution operated at will. The board of directors did not even exercise much of its budgetary control function.[39] But things ended up changing after Ibáñez's come-back. 1950s inflation and high economic uncertainty, the consequence of poor macroeconomic management in the face of adverse international economic conditions, brought the famous Klein-Saks Mission to advise stabilization measures.[40]

Political differentiation of CORFO was significant, but subtle. Indeed, its *técnicos* did not belong to business elites and did not respond to partisan mandate; however, many or most of these middle-class men (women joined later) were either affiliated to or voters of the Radical Party.[41] And so CORFO's high managerial ranks would end up replaced due to political dynamics. The 1950s economic crisis meant opportunity for institutional change: the policy pendulum moved towards the right, with the election of Jorge Alessandri (1958–1964). Pro-business Alessandri's administration had no problem with changing the policy tradition of bureaucratic continuity and autonomy, as it had promised precisely to end the Radical Party–Ibañez era, which had brought crisis according to the winning discourse. Alessandri broke with the autonomy of the Central Bank and of CORFO, bringing both institutions under the control of Finance Minister Roberto Vergara. The pattern was to replace the top *técnicos* with "owners and managers of the country's largest corporations".[42] Businessmen wanted to run the government themselves, again.

[36] Muñoz and Arriagada, 1977; Ibañez, 1924–1960; Orihuela, 2012.
[37] Reynolds, 1965; Ortega *et al.*, 1989.   [38] Cavarozzi, 1975: 125–126.
[39] Cavarozzi, 1975: 123–124.   [40] Hirschman, 1965.   [41] Cavarozzi, "The Government".
[42] Cavarozzi, 1975: 356.

Nonetheless, unable to end the economic crisis, the government of Alessandri was to be followed by a new pendulum switch, to the left, with the election of Christian Democrat Eduardo Frei Montalva (1964–1970), followed in turn by Socialist Salvador Allende. The Frei administration established the planning bureau (Oficina de Planificación Nacional, or ODEPLAN) within CORFO, which is symbolic of the progressive growth of importance of economists within the government. ODEPLAN later became an independent institution which advised the presidency directly on economic planning.[43]

CORFO was the pinnacle of organizational capacity in the Chilean state. It was so big and effective that it has been defined as the single most important organization of the state between the Great Depression and the Debt Crisis. From electricity and steel, it went on to foster the development of pine plantations, salmon, wine and almost every single new export. CORFO represented the Chilean developmental state's spirit as no other agency did. For sure, some (but not all!) of the radical free-market economists of Pinochet (1973–1990) wanted to close it, but they lacked the political coalition to maneuver the finale of such a politically legitimized state organization. Following Carpenter (2001), CORFO's political reputation, the widely held belief that it was capable of providing solutions for national problems of production and diversification, was seated in multiple networks. Downscaled and re-engineered, CORFO survived the bloody and virulent end of the developmental state era in Chile.[44]

CVC IN COLOMBIA: REGIONAL AND CITIZEN-BUSINESSMEN-DRIVEN

The Regional Autonomous Corporation of the Cauca Valley (Corporación Autónoma Regional del Cauca, CVC) was born fifteen years after CORFO, in 1954. CVC resulted from a remarkably different political-economic process. A decentralized scheme of regional development was a novelty, but a feasible one because Colombia was not Chile. At the turn of the twentieth century, the Colombian territory was composed of various "secondary peripheries," poorly articulated and limited in domestic markets. Colombia's export economy, moreover, was much less developed than those of comparable Latin American countries[45]. A small and changing commodity basket characterized the period 1850–1910; coffee dominated the export economy later – but was not too significant in the Cauca Valley.[46] As in Chile or Peru, political elites wanted more integration with international markets and more state formation. However, unlike these other Andean countries, Colombia did not experience a nineteenth-century commodity boom as big as that of copper, nitrates, or guano to speed up trade integration and state building. In short, structural

[43] Orihuela, 2012.   [44] Muñoz, 2009; Orihuela, 2012.   [45] Ocampo, 1984.
[46] Jackson, 1972: 85–86.

economic conditions were not conducive to an early, CORFO-type national corporation.

Also unlike CORFO, CVC was championed by a wealthy regional elite. Cauca Valley's promoters of CVC presented it as a version of the TVA prototype.[47] However, while TVA was a project designed by national political elites to bring development to a poor local economy, local industrial elites designed CVC for a region with income per capita about 30 percent above the national average, according to a 1951 census.[48] In addition, wealth was skewed in relatively wealthy Cauca. By the 1950s, 2 percent of landowners possessed about 40 percent of land.[49]

Unlike CORFO, there was not high political differentiation in this project of bureaucratic autonomy – but it was not a case of state capture either. In this nuanced case of state formation, the institutional entrepreneurs were members of traditional, yet modernizing Cauca Valley families, as well as new sugar industrialists, including the descendants of nineteenth-century American immigrant James Eder, who is considered to be the father of Colombia's sugar industry. Eder brought railroads from the Pacific Ocean seaport Buenaventura to Cali (the region's largest city) and established the Cali Electric Utility. The key actor behind the birth of CVC was Diego Garcés Giraldo, a merchant, farmer, and governor of the Department of Cauca Valley.[50] Cali-based industrialists made up the local chapter of Asociación Nacional de Empresarios de Colombia (ANDI), the Colombian Manufacturers Association.[51]

CVC's mission was to govern water with electricity as its first priority; flood-control, drainage, and irrigation came next. Programmed complimentary activities were agricultural extension and general infrastructure provision.[52] Rising electricity rates had become a salient regional political problem, with big public protests in 1932–1942 and 1944–1947. The government in response established the Anchicayá Power Company and its World-Bank-funded dam project. Large-scale planning identified five hydroelectric projects: Calima I, Alto Anchicayá, Salvajina, Timba, and Cauca Pacific Diversion.[53]

The other political base came from agriculture interests demanding irrigation and flood-control. Frequent flooding impeded new cattle and agriculture development: while on an average flood year, about 87,000 ha or 25 per cent of the flat area of the Cauca Valley was inundated, the season 1949–1950 had been extremely wet, in particular.[54] Water-resource development was to give all the answers to the industrialists' problems.[55]

[47] Garcés, 1962.　　[48] Jackson, 1972: 98.
[49] Posada and Posada, 1966; Sánchez Triana, 1998: 61–62.
[50] Sánchez Triana, 1998: 62–66, 75–84.　　[51] Jackson, 1972; World Bank, 1955.
[52] CVC, 1954.　　[53] Sánchez Triana, 1998: 84.　　[54] World Bank, 1955: 25–26.
[55] Sánchez Triana, 1998: 64–70.

The interests of industrialist regional elites for water-resource making and associated state formation pre-dated late 1940s Anchicayá. In 1928, the Cauca Valley's government contracted Puerto Rican experts for advice. In turn, CVC's jewel Salvajina Dam project, which had to wait until 1978 for national government approval, was first studied in 1942. Years later, in 1949, the regional government, with another member of the Garcés family playing the policy-entrepreneur role, contracted the local engineering firm Olarte, Ospina, Arias, and Payan (OLAP) to develop comprehensive electrification and irrigation plans.[56]

In its report, OLAP proposed the establishment of a valley-development corporation. OLAP was simply putting ink on what was already believed by Cali elites. However, convincing the national government to approve and fund a decentralized, valley-based scheme was a different matter. In 1953, upon the advice of the local ANDI chapter, the Government of the Valley formed a Departmental Committee of Planning (the national government had a National Committee of Planning), which became in 1954 the Provisional Board of newborn CVC. ANDI, moreover, was being used as a resource to lobby the national government, although with little success.[57]

It is in this idiosyncratic context that policy diffusion took place. The Cauca Valley industrialist elite thought that prestigious TVA champion David E. Lilienthal could persuade the national government about the soundness of CVC, a "true copy" of TVA.[58] Lilienthal had become a global doctor prescribing TVA medicine.[59] The window of opportunity to get the legal approval of a never seen "regional autonomous corporation" was the dictatorship of General Rojas Pinilla, who interrupted democracy between 1953 and 1957. The Colombian Ambassador to the United States ended up convincing Rojas Pinilla to invite Lilienthal in 1954.[60] The visit was successful; the dictator had found a development project that could increase the government's political capital.[61] At the request of the national government, in 1955, the International Bank for Reconstruction and Development sent a mission that produced a most favorable report entitled "The Autonomous Regional Corporation of the Cauca and the Development of the Upper Cauca Valley."[62]

Regional business goals were thus translated into a national public interest, with a TVA stamp certifying international technical legitimacy. For its champions, not only was CVC a technical/apolitical solution, but also a "demonstration project" for "rapidly advancing the agricultural, industrial, and educational welfare of the entire Colombian people."[63] The policy narrative became that CVC was "created as a result of recommendations

---

[56] Jackson, 1972: 95–102; Sánchez Triana, 1998: 64 and 85–86.
[57] Jackson, 1972: 95–102; Sánchez Triana, 1998: 85–86.   [58] Hirschman, 1965.
[59] Neuse, 1996.   [60] Jackson, 1972: 97.   [61] Jackson, 1972: 100.   [62] World Bank, 1955.
[63] Neuse, 1996: 261.

made by Mr. David E. Lilienthal, in his report of June 25, 1954 to President Gustavo Rojas Pinilla."[64] The law that created CVC proclaimed that the new state venture was to follow "the practices and methods of TVA." Moreover, a central legal argument for the establishment of regional autonomous bodies was that they "had been recommended by eminent public men such as Dr. David E. Lilienthal."[65] CVC propaganda stated it was straightforward to find inspiration and orientation in TVA, given that Brazil, Haiti, India, Afghanistan, and Italy had already adopted such a model.[66] CVC rented of TVA's myth: how effective TVA really was did not matter as much as the beliefs held by the globalized expert community.

In short, a clique of families belonging to the industrialist regional elite were directly involved in Cauca Valley politics of development and ended up using TVA and Lilienthal to legitimize their state formation project. Water resources and region-based developmental state action were ideas which had matured since the 1920s amongst the elite Cauca Valley families who ran the department's government. These "citizen-businessmen of Cali" dreamed and originally carried out decentralized, developmental state formation.[67]

Once more, unlike CORFO, CVC had a difficult early infancy: its first years of legal existence were full of uncertainty on the actual scope, income sources, and scheme's continuity – bureaucratic autonomy in particular. Thus, the corporation's experience resembles the case of Brazil more than that of Chile. Contingency mattered a great deal. Once supportive of CVC and its hydro ventures, the World Bank lost confidence in the Colombian government and, in turn, the Rojas Pinilla administration became suspicious of granting regional autonomy to Cali elites. Military men were put in place to manage the Anchicayá hydroelectric project.[68] The end of Rojas Pinilla under a new junta meant a new political opportunity structure. Opponents attacked CVC, attaching it to the falling regime.[69] A similar phenomenon took place in Peru with CPS, as we will see. However, in search of a supportive regional power base, the military junta ended up appointing CVC champion Harold Eder as minister of development. Political conditions for CVC formation changed. The World Bank did not pull out, CVC gained degrees of bureaucratic autonomy as Eder had Anchicayá transferred to CVC and the military left desks to the engineers.[70]

Most interestingly, given the unwillingness of the national government to finance the whole scheme, self-taxation was implemented to pay for the public venture. The very same Cali businessmen who were running CVC arranged an

---

[64] Letter of the engineering consortium made up by the Cali firm OLAP and the New York City firms G&H and KTAM to present the engineering report "The Unified Development of Power and Water Resources in the Cauca Valley" (1956).
[65] Decreto Ley 3110 (October 22, 1954), Considerando Segundo.　　[66] CVC, 1954: 7.
[67] Hirschman, 1963: 164.　　[68] Posada and Posada, 1996; Sánchez Triana, 1998.
[69] Jackson, 1972: 94.
[70] Hirschman, 1965; Lilienthal, 1969; Jackson, 1972; Sánchez Triana, 1998.

increase in land property tax, in order to finance CVC operations.[71] However, both the governors of Caldas and Cauca eventually withdrew from CVC, largely because of self-taxation.

Opposition to CVC also arose because land was more important than electricity for the relevant political economy actors. Traditional landowners and cattle ranchers, through their associations with Sociedad de Agricultores and Sociedad de Ganaderos, opposed the project. The opposition not only rejected paying taxes but found that land-making via flood control, drainage, and irrigation rather than electricity was the priority. However, the political base favoring CVC had expanded beyond the industrialists: networks of support now included the Church, labor groups, and the general public.

The solution to opposition was that CVC champions gave seats on the CVC's board to opposing ranchers and farmers. From 1954 on, CVC's board included regional representatives of sugar, cattle, agriculture, and manufacturing industries, as well as the owner of Cali's newspaper.[72] In turn, the tax was decreed in 1956, but the fall of Rojas Pinilla a year later provided a good chance to eliminate it; in 1959, it was reduced and partially redefined as a compulsory bond issue.[73]

How technical was the management of CVC? The three executive directors of CVC from 1954–1990 all boasted that party leaders never approached them seeking employment for their members. In its first twenty-two years, CVC was run by two economic elite members. The first executive director, from 1954 to 1968, was the farm owner and industrialist Bernardo Garcés Córdoba. He held an economics degree from a UK university. Garcés thought that a key lesson of CVC for much needed decentralization was the importance of incorporating "citizens of the greatest experience and highest standing" into public service.[74]

From 1968 to 1976, Henry Eder replaced Garcés. Eder's main economic interests were in the sugar industry. Oscar Mazuera, who had been Eder's lieutenant, came next. Unlike the previous two CVC chiefs, Mazuera did not come from an elite family, but held a PhD in economics from a US university. He headed CVC until 1991, the time when the regional development corporations system was being subject to a major policy reform. By the time of the constitutional reform that changed the corporations system, the pride of CVC was its "apolitical" stance.[75] According to its chiefs, CVC followed TVA in having a corporation "clothed with the power of government, but possessed of the flexibility and initiative of a private enterprise".[76]

Recruitment policy at CVC was meritocratic for top managerial positions. For the base, the policy was to hire inexperienced, freshly graduated *valleucanos*, who would be trained by CVC. Part of the developmental

---

[71] Hirschman, 1963: 184–187.   [72] Posada and Posada, 1996; Sánchez Triana, 1998.
[73] Hirschman, 1965: 186.   [74] Jackson, 1972: 113.
[75] Garcés, 1962; Jackson, 1972: 118–125 [interview with Mazuera].
[76] A CVC spokesperson quoted in Jackson, 1972: 124.

dreams of the first Executive Director Garcés was to help form local human capital.[77] For their experience, in turn, foreign engineers were much valued at the start point, making up twenty-one of the seventy-two professional staff in 1956.[78] Human capital came from the Universidad del Valle's departments of civil engineering, electrical engineering, agricultural economics, and administration. Thus, working at CVC became a source of professional prestige among Cali-educated professionals, a new middle class and new political actor.[79]

Organizational capacity developed remarkably well for the national bureaucratic yardstick. Having begun with a focus on electricity, CVC evolved to run a variety of agricultural development and resource management and conservation programs. Its scope of action, moreover, expanded spatially. CVC undertook development projects in the Pacific port of Buenaventura, strongly articulated to the Cauca Valley international economy. In the late 1970s, the Inter-American Development Bank helped to finance infrastructure projects from sanitation to roads executed by CVC. The 1979 earthquake that affected the southern Pacific Coast brought another round of rehabilitation and development programs funded by the national government, Inter-American Development Bank (IADB), and UNICEF, which were to be administered by CVC. These developments reflect the organizational capacity and policy legitimacy that CVC had vis-à-vis the national government. Reflecting its unique status as an autonomous regional corporation, CVC charged the national government an overhead for running the Buenaventura and Pacific Coast development programs.[80]

The "technical and apolitical" management of CVC, of course, needs to be qualified. It was apolitical in the sense that it did not engage in or get captured by shortsighted party politics and clientelistic practices. However, there is nothing more political than a state organization which promotes industrial development by supplying subsidized electricity. Regional elites not only ended up not paying the bill for building dams, but also CVC's electricity rates were systematically below production costs and so the national government covered the difference.[81]

Moreover, CVC was so deeply political that it became the technical pivot to oppose land reform in the Cauca Valley in the mid 1970s. The technopolitical discourse was that land in the valley was "properly managed." The Salvajina multipurpose project of power generation and land reclamation, through drainage, flood control, and water pollution control, was used to counteract land reform measures. Big farming was to pay a third of Salvajina's cost by giving up land that would became agrarian reform land[82]. In 1980, a DNP

[77] Jackson, 1972: 294.   [78] Jackson, 1972: 298.
[79] Jackson, 1972; Posada and Posada, 1996; Sánchez Triana, 1998.
[80] Sánchez Triana, 1998: 93–94.   [81] Sánchez Triana, 1998: 87.
[82] Sánchez Triana, 1998: 113–118.

deputy director born in the Cauca Valley and graduate of the Universidad del Valle reduced the required funding from farmers to 8% of Salvajina's cost, and ended up paying about half of that. Over the years, a large part of CVC's work was to lobby the national government, congressional representatives, and party leaders to get funding approval[83].

In the introductory section, I made the argument that the *relative* political stability in Chile and Colombia helped developmental state formation, while instability hindered equivalent Peruvian attempts. As has been seen, however, CVC was born in the hectic times of military coups, and CORFO came out after a period of major political convulsion – and survived Pinochet – in Chile. Thus, political stability should not be overplayed. However, it is also a fact that after the half decade of military rule in Colombia, the National Front government agreed to presidential alternation between liberals and conservatives between 1958 and 1974, which was followed by democratic governments with liberal hegemony. Despite *la violencia*, and the bloody violence that came next, relative macro-political continuity favored the continuity of autonomous development corporations in Colombia, just as it did in Chile, but not in Peru.

In particular, macro-political continuity helped the consolidation of the Departamento de Planeación Nacional (DNP), established in 1958. The economists of DNP had to supervise CVC's planning and approve the projects that the World Bank and Inter-American Development Bank were always ready to finance. Before DNP became such, there was a National Committee of Planning. At its time of creation, CVC statutes established that its plans would be subject to approval by the National Committee of Planning.[84] Thus, by design, the bureaucratic autonomy of DNP was to feed back the bureaucratic autonomy of CVC. In 1968, CVC was formally made a dependency of the Ministry of Agriculture, but that did not change its autonomous character.[85]

In a nutshell, CVC succeeded in constructing high political legitimacy. Which is why the young technocratic cadre of President Gaviria (1990–1994), running liberalizing reforms from DNP, would not think of closing CVC and the other seventeen autonomous regional corporations that came after it. Instead, corporations were expanded, from eighteen to thirty-three, and re-engineered to carry out sustainable development and environmental regulation with Law 99 of 1993.[86] The case of Peru comes next.

CPS IN START-FROM-SCRATCH PERU: REGIONAL AND PRESIDENT-DRIVEN

The Santa Peruvian Corporation (Corporación Peruana del Santa, CPS) was established in 1943, just four years after CORFO and a decade prior to CVC.

---

[83] Sánchez Triana, 1998: 121–122; Posada and Posada, 1996: 198.   [84] CVC, 1954: 12.
[85] Sánchez Triana, 1998: 81.   [86] Canal and Becerra, 2008: 303–390.

Without a strong embeddedness in either networks of state engineers or regional business elites, it is a complex development corporation to typify. As state organizations commonly rise – and fall – in Peru, CPS was above all the project of a transformative statesman with no party affiliation, the two-times president, Manuel Prado (1939–1945 and 1956–1962). Part of a wealthy family which owned the Banco Popular del Perú and had interests in textiles, real estate, and manufactures, Prado established CPS in his first administration and gave priority and inaugurated CPS' steel plant during his second one. "The era of steel began," euphorically celebrated newspapers in April of 1958. A decade later, and during the decline of the economic significance and political influence of the "Prado Empire",[87] CPS was to be divided and its units absorbed into new-era state organizations and enterprises, to virtually disappear from national memory, both metaphorically and in reality: unlike numerous secondary sources available on CORFO and CVC, neither a dissertation nor book has ever been written on CPS.

Established to "develop and exploit the riches coming directly or indirectly from the regions of the Santa River and tributaries . . . and all the mineral and industrial riches that use the port of Chimbote . . .", CPS was granted the legal capacity to embark into development projects in other regions of Peru, if there was any linkage with its ventures. CPS was conceived to produce hydro energy (with the Pato Canyon Dam), and steel (iron coming from Marcona, Ica, and the steel complex in Chimbote), in addition to coal (Chuquicara), and irrigation (Chao and Virú, the seeds of the nowadays major Chavimochic export agriculture). The corporation was legally established a year after the Corporación Peruana del Amazonas, the latter set up to promote the US-funded revival of rubber. As Prado's first mandate coincided with the Second World War, Peru became a close partner of the USA.[88]

The political economy of development in Peru had a mix of features observed in Chile and Colombia, as well as key particularities. A resource-based economy, with a deconcentrated economic geography, the era of guano (1840s–1870s) consolidated the power of Lima, in the coast, located next to the major port of Callao. From decades as a mono-export thanks to guano, à la Chile, Peru became a less exuberant export economy with a varying basket of commodities, à la Colombia. That in the early twentieth century Peru was not a relatively wealthy, mono-export peripheral economy meant that the Great Depression did not produce the kind of mega-crisis that impacted its southern neighbor. Compared to Chile, also, there was not such an advanced industrial development by the turn of the twentieth century, given a less integrated domestic economy, with smaller and dispersed urban centers and a higher size of indigenous population collectively owning land along the Andes. Unlike Colombia, African slavery was not as significant, because the colonizers found less plantation-friendly tropical ecologies and plenty of indigenous

[87] Portocarrero, 1995.   [88] CPS, 1955; Thorp and Bertram, 1978.

labor to exploit for mining. To summarize, both economically and politically, early twentieth-century Peru was neither as centralized as Chile, nor as decentralized as Colombia. The problem of land was the problem of "the *indio*" and the grievances of centralism and exclusion (Lima and the coast against "the real Peru" of the Andes, the Amazon not being part of the political imagination of elites) were to shape the politics of development for the next hundred years.

Caudillo-based politics within an unstable political system typifies Peru. Again and again, the nation-state "re-constitutes itself". First, there were some ten constitutions during Peru's first half-century as an independent republic. Later, between the 1879–1883 resource war with Chile and the 1982 Debt Crisis, Peru went through four constitutions (1879, 1920, 1933 and 1979), compared to two in Chile (one during the turbulent 1920s, the other with Pinochet) and one in Colombia (1886). Rather than a relatively solid party system, as in Chile (with Conservatives, Liberals and Radicals) or Colombia (with Liberals and Conservatives), the political arena that shaped developmental state formation was accustomed to the succession of "independent" strong men. The historical pattern of presidential succession has swung back and forth between military men and civilians. Chile, Colombia and all Latin America for that matter might be presidentialist, and even prone to messianic enchantment, but Peru has historically built very little of a party system to structure charismatic political agency. Outsiders have ruled; the call to end the "traditional party system" and to start again from scratch, has been a venerated republican tradition. With so many recurrent crises and such high-level bribery, "unbound graft,"[89] at some early point of post-colonial history it became national narrative that elites were a failure and the state corrupt.[90] Having made at the beginning of the chapter the theoretical argument that national history situates policy choice, the general hypothesis is that any project of bureaucratic autonomy formation is likely to face more cultural resistance in Peru than in its Andean neighbors, because of strongly held beliefs on state failure. There is no "Portalian state" myth to make use of and caudillos are prone to call for new beginnings.

The first government of Manuel Prado (1939–1945) was quite developmentalist, expanding export taxes and government expenditure. The Second World War meant imports scarcity, setting the incentives for import substitution and political demand for industrial policy. The economic interests of the Prado family, moreover, were in modernizing sectors rather than concentrated in staples. In addition to the international context and the family business interests, Prado happened also to be a *técnico* who studied sciences and civil engineering. In the turbulent 1930s, President General Benavides (1933–1939) appointed wealthy *técnico* Prado as Central Bank governor and later chose him as successor.

---

[89] Quiroz, 2008.   [90] Basadre, 1958, 1961.

In the land of caudillos, the most important part of the explanation on why CPS had a go is that President Prado wanted to. Unlike CORFO in Chile, CPS did not go through a long congressional debate and did not have a solid network of state engineers behind the project. The corporation was to be governed by a board of five directors appointed by the president and funded with new taxes to imports, oil exports, insurance companies and others.[91] Unlike CVS in Colombia, CPS did not have a local elite behind the project, the Santa valley not being economically advanced. CPS quickly fell victim of negative changes in the international economy, and therefore became embroiled in a public finance scenario. Additionally, the fact, that the corporation was the project of the ruling caudillo was the source of both its strength and its weakness. With such little political legitimacy at birth and not having been financially autonomous, once the caudillo was gone, CPS received low government transfers.[92]

Moreover, unlike CORFO and CVC, CPS was involved in a high-profile corruption controversy. Less than two years after its birth, a new elected Congress ran an investigation. The discontent pointed to irrational spending, an absence of planning and an authoritarian and cliquish corporation culture; thus, the parliamentary commission demanded the establishment of a Directive Council to constrain the autonomy of CPS' presidency.[93] CPS Chairman David Dasso (finance minister under Prado) and Congressman Pardo responded, accusing the report of being "baseless", pointing out that an auditor who conducted a central part of the investigation was an accountant with US Steel Corporation and that "autonomy" was precisely the number one lesson behind the success of TVA.[94]

CPS was defended as a science-based policy innovation modeled on TVA. According to Congressman Colonel César Pardo, CPS' guidelines followed those of the Tennessee Valley Authority, "a grand state corporation of the government of the United States that has successfully set the basis for the development of the same name valley."[95] Not only was CPS modeled on TVA, but TVA engineers and US government-recommended missions of engineers came to Peru to provide technical advice, including a program of swamp-draining and malaria eradication in Chimbote, while the Export Import Bank was also involved in the operation.[96]

CPS champions also made the case that the corporation was the right medicine to cure the redistributive cleavage between Lima and the rest of Peru. Thus, given that TVA exemplified how to achieve the dream of decentralizing development through regional corporations, Peru was an ideal case for adopting such a model given the length of backward regions and the significance of "a regionalist sentiment, more rooted in Peru than in most countries."[97]

---

[91] CPS, 1951.   [92] Thorp and Bertram, 1978: 186 and 216.
[93] Comisión Mixta Parlamentaria, 1945.   [94] Dasso, 1945; Pardo, 1946.   [95] Pardo, 1946.
[96] Pardo, 1946; CPS, 1955; 1958.   [97] Pardo, 1946: 7.

There were key Peruvian engineers behind the project, and President Prado was an engineer himself, but engineers had not been extensively incorporated into the state apparatus. An important technical adviser of CPS was the physicist and engineer Santiago Antúnez de Mayolo. Born in a small Andean town of the Santa river basin, and having undertaken graduate studies in France and the USA, Antúnez de Mayolo significantly contributed with science to the establishment of hydro energy in Peru, including the Pato Canyon Hydroelectric, which he had championed since the 1910s.[98] However, the less extended network of technical experts was society-based, with few nodes in the state, following the historical pattern. Jorge Basadre's dictum was that republican Peru had constructed an "empirical state", rather than a Weberian one, as political turmoil went hand-in-hand with the lack of expert professionals in government.[99]

State corporations and industrial policy experienced incongruous policy measures under the eight years long military coup of General Manuel Odría (1948–1956). Odría moved the Peruvian pendulum to the laissez-faire corner, while most of Latin America was actively experimenting with state interventionism.[100] With a liberal mining code and in the positive international context of the Korean War, which brought a surge of mineral prices, Marcona Mining Company was exploiting the iron ores that CPS had been called to extract a decade before. The Marcona was dominated by Utah Construction Company and had the Prado family as a minority shareholder.[101] Odría paid attention to CPS only at the end of his mandate because of the 1953–1954 export recession.[102]

In a characteristic episode of Peruvian politics, the fall of a caudillo, Odría, brought back the old one, Prado. The policy pendulum moved towards active state interventionism. In Prado's second mandate, with the establishment of first a National Fund for Economic Development, which was broadly supported in Congress, and later five new regional development corporations, the *juntas departamentales*, were legally established. Given the pendulum switch towards state developmentalism, the opportunity for new regional corporations was brought by catastrophic earthquakes: Cusco in 1957, Arequipa in 1958 and Madre de Dios in 1960. Then, the rest of the *departamentos*, which had not suffered natural disasters, demanded attention, so that the 1956 National Fund for Economic Development Law ruled that there was to be one junta *departamental* per department, which emerged as *corporaciones departamentales* in 1961–1968.[103] These were fundamentally paper corporations, financially poor and dependent on a number of earmarked taxes. Presidente Belaúnde (1962–1968) of the new Acción Popular Party was

---

[98] CPS, 1951; Ramírez, 1980.   [99] Basadre, 1961.
[100] Thorp and Bertram, 1978; Thorp, 1998.   [101] Thorp and Bertram, 1978: 212.
[102] Thorp and Bertram, 1978: 261.
[103] Instituto Nacional de Planificación 1980; Schmidt, 1984.

also a developmentalist, coming from the revolutionary and industrialist south. That the congressional coalition of Odriísta National Union and the APRA – the latter once persecuted by the former – made a bitter and senseless opposition to Belaúnde in Congress was of little help for his developmental state trials.

And so the final chapter of CPS history took place during the critical juncture of the Revolutionary Government of the Armed Forces (1968–1980), which found Belaúnde's reformism too soft and too pro-foreign oil interests. Under General Velasco Alvarado, who only ruled until 1975 as his economic experiment met with the oil crisis, the revolutionary army wanted a new beginning for what they saw as an oligarchy-dominated social system. This new radical military elite had been studying sociology and were frightened of the new waves of land conflict and the rise of Cuba-inspired guerillas. Thus, land reform was a central measure, a matter of social justice and political wisdom, and the communities of *indios*, which had been legally recognized in the 1920s, were to be re-baptized as communities of peasants. Nationalization of oil and part of mining – including Marcona's iron – was important too (in Chile, the Christian Democrats had already done it and Allende's Popular Front was radicalizing the process; plus some military chiefs wanted to go to war to recover the now-copper-rich north of Chile). Industrial policy had to catch up with the rest of Latin America – which actually had been moving from ISI to export-oriented state interventionism.[104]

Given such a transformative national political process, Prado and his legacy was to be remembered for its oligarchic rather than its developmental features. The all-powerful National System of Mobilization (SINAMOS), created to foster grass-roots support to the army's revolution, ended up absorbing all the system of regional development corporations.[105] CPS' steel plant became SIDERPERU, while a new narrative of resource regionalism took full shape with the rise of oil and mining *canon*, the right of producing regions to seize resource rents for autonomous regional development.[106] The closing of CPS took place during a time of radical institutional change, when it had gained comparatively little organizational reputation.

A radical translation of neoliberalism would take place in Peru years later. The return to democracy brought back President Belaúnde (1980–1985), who as a candidate politicized the cleavage of centralism. Later, APRA was finally voted to office, but the irrational state interventionism of a young President García (1985–1990), who redefined the Latin American caudillo, gave all the reasons for the incubation of strong neoliberal counter-reform under the new caudillo-outsider Fujimori (1990–2000), with the 1992 *autogolpe* (self-coup) and the 1993 Constitution. In the late 1980s, with state-owned enterprises and state institutions filled with patronage hires and countless cases of state corruption, under hyperinflation and with the

---

[104] Lowenthal, 1976; Cabieses *et al.*, 1982.   [105] Schmidt, 1984.
[106] Gruber and Orihuela, 2017.

Shining Path moving from the Andes to Lima, it became conventional wisdom among the powerful that the Peruvian state was a failure and so "it was time for the market"; the powerless just wanted the nightmare to stop, no matter what the cost. Another transformative juncture took full shape. And so most of the interventionist state – which according to the triumphing discourse was the creation of Velasco Alvarado and García – was either privatized or erased from Earth.

CONCLUSIONS

The forging of development corporations in Latin America was shaped by the transnational diffusion of developmental state ideas and the TVA myth, on the one hand, and national history, on the other. Chile, Colombia, and Peru gave birth to development corporations that exemplify more general features of national state formation processes: an early established, national-level, state engineers-driven, centralized but deconcentrated mega corporation in Chile, CORFO; a valley-level, local elites-driven, regional development corporation of high organizational reputation in Colombia, CVC; and an early established but poorly funded, valley-level but with the board of directors meeting based in Lima, caudillo-driven and therefore a corporation with comparatively low bureaucratic autonomy development in Peru, CPS.

Following Carpenter's "test," there was high bureaucratic autonomy in CORFO, low bureaucratic autonomy but high rational bureaucratic capacity in CVC, and bureaucratic autonomy miscarriage in CPS. On the failure case, there was ultimately success in delivering electricity, irrigated land and steel, but little accomplishment in gaining political legitimacy for the organization. CPS and the Peruvian developmental state gained so little political legitimacy, unlike CORFO or CVC and the Colombian corporations, that there are comparatively few secondary and primary sources to write a proper case-study on CPS. The Corporación Peruana del Santa is a forgotten chapter of national history, and development corporations – unlike in Chile and Colombia – were erased from national policy imagination, given the radical "structural reform" programs of Velasco Alvarado, and Fujimori.

The proposed theory frame bridging new sociological and historical institutionalisms provides a comprehensive toolkit to read and problematize the politics of bureaucratic autonomy. The argument is that national political processes contingent to developmental state formation mattered a great deal for the translation of the developmental state policy paradigm and TVA organizational model into national practice. National political processes, in turn, were highly dependent on national structural features and already undertaken institutional pathways.

Thus, development corporation mongers in Chile had more domestic institutional resources to build on, from the myth of the strong and capable "Portalian state" to well-developed networks of professional statesmen and state engineers in particular, which were the result of comparatively long periods of political stability, resource wars won, and early industrialization; instead, institutional entrepreneurs behind CVC and CPS had to borrow policy legitimacy from TVA entrepreneur David Lilienthal, TVA engineers, and the technical and financial support of the World Bank, the Export–Import Bank, and the USA government. But past state action was not all that mattered. The forging of developmental bureaucratic autonomy was shaped by contingency, in which earthquakes and other (water-management-related) natural disasters, as well as changes in political regimen and international economic conditions, opened different-size windows of opportunity for developmental state innovation.

REFERENCES

Ahumada, Jorge. *En vez de la miseria*. Santiago: Editorial del Pacifico S.A., 1970 [1958].
Basadre, Jorge. *La promesa de la vida peruana y otros ensayos*. Lima: Editorial Juan Mejía Baca, 1958 [1945].
    Historia de la República del Perú. Lima: Ediciones Historia, 1961 [1933].
Cabieses, Hugo *et al*. Industrialization and Regional Development in Peru. Incidintele Publicaties 23. Amsterdam: CEDLA, 1982.
Campbell, John. Institutional Change and Globalization. Princeton University Press, 2004.
    "Institutional Reproduction and Change." *In Oxford Handbook of Comparative Institutional Analysis*, eds. Glenn Morgan, John L. Campbell, Colin Crouch, Ove K. Pedersen, and Richard Whitley, New York, NY: Oxford University Press, 2007.
Canal, Francisco and Manuel Rodríguez Becerra. Las Corporaciones Autónomas Regionales, quince años después de la creación del SINA. Con Francisco Canal, Gobernabilidad, instituciones y medio ambiente en Colombia. Bogotá: Foro Nacional Ambiental, 2008: 303–390.
Cárdenas, Enrique, José Antonio Ocampo, and Rosemary Thorp. *Industrialization and the State in Latin America: the Postwar Years, An Economic History of the Twentieth Century Latin America*, III, Houndmills: Palgrave Press and St. Martins, 2000.
Carpenter, Daniel. *The Forging of Bureaucratic Autonomy: Reputations, Networks, and Policy Innovation in Executive Agencies, 1862–1928*. Princeton University Press, 2001.
Cavarozzi, Marcelo. "The Government and the Industrial Bourgeoisie in Chile: 1938–1964." Unpublished PhD thesis, University of California, Berkeley, 1975.
Centeno, Miguel Ángel and Agustin Ferraro. "Paper Leviathans. Historical Legacies and State Strength in Contemporary Latin America and Spain." In *State and Nation Making in Latin America and Spain: Republics of the Possible*, eds. Miguel A. Centeno, and Agustin E. Ferraro, New York City: Cambridge University Press, 2013.
Coatsworth, John. "Structures, Endowments, and Institutions in the Economic History of Latin America." *Latin American Research Review*, 4, 3, 2005: 126–144.

Coatsworth, John and Jeffrey Williamson. "Always Protectionist? Latin American Tariffs from Independence to Great Depression." *Journal of Latin American Studies*, 36, 2004: 205–232.

Collier, Ruth and David Collier. *Shaping the Political Arena: Critical Junctures, the Labor Movement, and Regime Dynamics in Latin America.* Princeton University Press, 1991.

Collier, Simon and William Sater. *A History of Chile, 1808–2002.* New York City, NY: Cambridge University Press, 2004.

Comisión Mixta Parlamentaria. "Informe sobre las actividades de la Corporación Peruana del Santa," Lima, 1945.

CPS. "Estatutos," 1951.

"La Corporación Peruana del Santa y el desarrollo industrial del país," 1955.

"Planta siderúrgica, central hidroeléctrica," 1958.

"Credit Valley Conservation Report. Department of Planning and Development. Toronto," 1954 [1956].

Dargent, Eduardo, José Carlos Orihuela, Maritza Paredes and María Eugenia Ulfe, eds. *Resource Booms and Institutional Pathways: The Case of Peru.* New York City: Palgrave Macmillan, 2017.

Dasso, David. "Observaciones al informe presentado por los auditores a la comisión parlamentaria investigadora de Corporación Peruana del Santa," Lima, 1945.

DiMaggio, Paul and Walter Powell. "The Iron Cage Revisited": Institutional Isomorphism and Collective Rationality in Organizational Fields." *American Sociological Review*, 48, 2, 1983: 147–160.

Dobbin Frank, Beth Simmons, and Geoffrey Garret. "The Global Diffusion of Public Policies: Social Construction, Coercion, Competition, or Learning?" *Annual Review of Sociology*, 32, 2007: 449–472.

Dunkerley, James. "Andrés Bello and the Challenge of Spanish American Liberalism." *Transactions of the Royal Historical Society*, 24, 2014: 105–125.

Engerman, Stanley and Kenneth Sokoloff. *Factor Endowments: Institutions, and Differential Paths of Growth among New World Economies: A View from Economic Historians of the United States.* NBER Historical Working Paper No. 66, 1994.

Evans, Peter. *Embedded Autonomy. States and Industrial Transformation.* Princeton University Press, 1995.

Fishlow, Albert. "The Latin American State." *The Journal of Economic Perspectives*, 4, 3, summer 1990: 61–74.

Garcés, Bernardo. "Las Corporaciones Regionales." In *La CVC en Colombia.* CVC, 1962.

Gootenberg, Paul. *Between Silver and Guano: Commercial Policy and the State in Post-Independence Peru.* Princeton University Press, 1989.

Greif, Avner. *Institutions and the Path to the Modern Economy: Lessons from Medieval Trade.* New York: Cambridge University Press, 2006.

Gruber, Stephan and José Carlos Orihuela. "Deeply Rooted Grievance, Varying Meaning: The Institution of the Mining Canon." In *Resource Booms and Institutional Pathways: The Case of Peru*, eds., Eduardo Dargent, José Carlos Orihuela, Maritza Paredes, and María Eugenia Ulfe, New York City: Palgrave Macmillan, 2017.

Hall, Peter and Rosemary Taylor. "Political Science and the Three New Institutionalisms." *Political Studies*, 44, 5, 1996: 936–957.

Hirschman, Albert. *Journeys Toward Progress. Studies of Economic Policy-Making in Latin America*. New York: Twentieth Century Fund, 1963.

"Brazil's Northeast." In Albert O. Hirschman, *Journeys Toward Progress, Studies of Economic Policy-Making in Latin America*. Anchor Books, 1965.

Journeys Toward Progress, Studies of Economic Policy-Making in Latin America. Anchor Books, 1965.

"The Principle of the Hiding Hand." *Public Interest*, 2. Washington, DC, National Affairs, winter 1967.

Development Projects Observed. Washington, DC: The Brookings Institution, 1995 [1967].

Hunt, Shane. "Growth and Guano in the Nineteenth-Century." In *The Latin American Economies: Growth and the Export Sector, 1880–1930*, eds., Roberto Cortes Conde and Shane Hunt, New York: Holmes & Meier, 1985.

Ibáñez, Adolfo. "Los Ingenieros, el Estado y la Política en Chile: Del Ministerio de Fomento a la Corporación de Fomento, 1927–1939." *Historia 18*, 1983: 45–102.

Herido en el Ala: Estado, Oligarquías y Subdesarrollo, Chile 1924–1960. Santiago: Universidad Andrés Bello, 2003.

Instituto Nacional de Planificación. *Análisis Comparativo entre Corporaciones y Juntas Departamentales de Desarrollo y Organismos de Desarrollo*. Lima, 1980.

Jackson, W. *The Basis of a Development Program for Colombia*. International Bank of Reconstruction and Development. Washington DC, 1972.

Jaksić, Iván. *Andrés Bello: Scholarship and Nation-Building in Nineteenth-Century Latin America*. New York: Cambridge University Press, 2001.

"Ideological Pragmatism and Non-Partisan Expertise in Nineteenth-Century Chile: Andrés Bello's Contribution to State and Nation Building." In *State and Nation Making in Latin America and Spain: Republics of the Possible*, eds. Miguel A. Centeno and Agustin E. Ferraro. New York City: Cambridge University Press, 2013.

Lilienthal, David. *The Journals of David E. Lilienthal, Volume 4: The Road to Change, 1955–1959*. New York City: Harper, 1969.

Lowenthal, Abraham. *The Peruvian Experiment: Continuity and Change Under Military Rule*. Princeton University Press, 1976.

Mahoney, James. *Colonialism and Postcolonial Development: Spanish America in Comparative Perspective*. Cambridge University Press, 2010.

Mahoney, James and Kathleen Thelen. *Explaining Institutional Change: Ambiguity, Agency, and Power*. New York: Cambridge University Press, 2010.

Mann, Michael. "The Autonomous Power of the State: Its Origins, Mechanisms and Results." *European Journal of Sociology*, 25, 2, 1984: 185–213.

McAdam, Doug, Sidney Tarrow, and Charles Tilly. *Dynamics of Contention*. New York: Cambridge University Press, 2001.

Meyer, John, David John Frank, Ann Hironaka, Evan Schofer, and Nancy Brandon Tuma. "The Structuring of a World Environmental Regime, 1870–1990." *International Organization*, 51, autumn 1997: 623–651.

Muñoz, Óscar. *Chile y su Industrialización. Pasado, Crisis y Opciones*. Santiago: CIEPLAN, 1986.

"El Desarrollo Institucional de CORFO y sus Estrategias desde 1990." In Óscar Muñoz, ed., *Desarrollo Productivo en Chile: La Experiencia de CORFO entre 1990 y 2009*. Santiago: Catalonia, 2009.

Muñoz, Óscar and Ana María Arriagada. *Orígenes Políticos y Económicos del Estado Empresarial en Chile*. CIEPLAN, 1977.

Neuse, Steven. *David E. Lilienthal: The Journey of an American Liberal*. Knoxville: The University of Tennessee Press, 1996.

North, Douglass. *Institutions, Institutional Change and Economic Performance*, Cambridge University Press, 1990.

Ocampo, José Antonio, *Colombia y la Economía Mundial*. Bogotá: Siglo Veintiuno, 1984.

Ocampo, Jose Antonio and Jaime Ros. "Shifting Paradigms in Latin America's Economic Development." Eds. José Antonio Ocampo and y Jaime Ros, *The Oxford Handbook of Latin American Economics*, 2011.

Orihuela, José Carlos. "Building and Re-engineering 'Good Governance' in Chile." In Rosemary Thorp, Stefania Batistelli, Yvan Guichauoa, José Carlos Orihuela, and Maritza Paredes. *The Developmental Challenges of Mining and Oil: Lessons from Africa and Latin America*. London: Palgrave Macmillan, 2012.

"How do 'Mineral-States' Learn? Path-Dependence, Networks and Policy Change in the Development of Economic Institutions." *World Development*, 43, 3, 2013: 138–148.

"Converging Divergence: The Diffusion of the Green State in Latin America." *Studies in Comparative International Development*, 49, 2, 2014: 242–265.

Ortega, Luis. *Chile en Ruta al Capitalismo: Cambio, Euforia y Depresión: 1850–1880*. Santiago: LOM Ediciones, 2005.

Ortega, Luis, Carmen Norambuera, Julio Pinto, and Guillermo Bravo. *Corporación de Fomento de la Producción: 50 Años de Realizaciones*. Santiago: CORFO, 1989.

Pardo, C. E. *Observaciones sobre el informe del Senador Coronel C. E. Pardo, al presidente de la Cámara de Senadores, relacionado con la Corporación Peruana del Santa* (pamphlet), 1946.

Pierson, Paul. *Dismantling the Welfare state? Reagan, Thatcher and the Politics of Retrenchment*. Cambridge University Press, 1994: 213.

Politics in Time: History, Institutions and Social Analysis. Princeton University Press, 2004.

Polanyi, Karl. *The Great Transformation*. New York: Rinehart & Co., Inc., 1944.

Portocarrero, Gonzalo. *El Perú frente al siglo XXI*. Lima: Pontificia Universidad Católica del Perú, 1995.

Posada, Antonio and Jeanne Posada. *The CVC: Challenge to Underdevelopment and Traditionalism*. Bogotá: Ediciones Tercer Mundo, 1966.

Quiroz, Alfonso. *Corrupt Circles: A History of Unbound Graft in Peru*. Washington: Johns Hopkins University Press, 2008.

Ramírez, Claudio. *Santiago Antúnez de Mayolo: vida y obra*. Lima: TIS, 1980.

Reynolds, Clark. "Development Problems of an Export Economy: The Case of Chile and Copper." In *Essays on the Chilean Economy*, eds. Markos Mamalakis and Clark Reynolds. Homewood: Richard D. Irwin, 1965.

Rueschemeyer, Dietrich. *Analytic Tools for Social and Political Research*. Princeton University Press, 2009.

Sánchez Triana, Ernesto. "How Rent Seeking, Learning and Path Dependence Shape Environmental Institutions: The Case of the Cauca Valley Corporation in Colombia." Unpublished PhD thesis, Stanford University, 1998.

Schmidt, Gregory. "State, Society, and the Policy Process: Planning, Decentralization, and Public Investment in Peru, 1956–1980." Unpublished PhD dissertation, Cornell University, 1984.

Schneiberg, Marc and Elizabeth Clemens. "The Typical Tools for the Job: Research Strategies in Institutional Analysis." In *How Institutions Change*, eds. Walter Powell and Dan Jones, University of Chicago Press, 2005.

Scott, Richard. "Approaching Adulthood: The Maturing of Institutional Theory." *Theory and Society*, 37, 2008: 427–442.

Selznick, Philip. *TVA and the Grass Roots: A Study in the Sociology of Formal Organization*. New York: Harper, 1966.

Silva, Patricio. *In The Name of Reason: Technocrats and Politics in Chile*. University Park: Pennsylvania State University Press, 2008.

Soifer, Hillel. *State Building in Latin America*. New York City: Cambridge University Press, 2015.

Streeck, Wolfgang and Kathleen Thelen. *Beyond Continuity: Institutional Change in Advanced Political Economies*. New York: Oxford University Press, 2005.

Tarrow, Sidney. *Power in Movement*. New York: Cambridge University Press, 1994.

Thelen Kathleen. "How Institutions Evolve: Insights from Comparative-Historical Analysis." In *Comparative Historical Analysis in the Social Sciences,* eds. James Mahoney and Dietrich Rueschemeyer, New York: Cambridge University Press, 2003.

Thorp, Rosemary. *Progress, Poverty and Exclusion: An Economic History of Latin America In The 20th Century*. Washington: IADB, 1998.

Thorp, Rosemary and Geoffrey Bertram. *Perú 1890–1977: Growth and Policy in an Open Economy*. New York. Columbia University Press, 1978.

World Bank. *The Autonomous Regional Corporation of the Cauca and the Development of the Upper Cauca Valley*. Washington DC, November 1955.

6

The Rise and Fall of the Instituto Nacional de Planificación in Peru, 1962–1992: Exploring the Limits of State Capacity Building in Weak States

Eduardo Dargent

INTRODUCTION

This chapter presents and discusses the rise and fall of the National Planning Institute (Instituto Nacional de Planificación, INP) in Peru from 1962–1992. Inspired by the developmental prescriptions of the Organization of American States (OAS) and the Economic Commission for Latin America (ECLA), this agency was initially created by a reformist military junta in 1962 to launch development planning in Peru. After a troublesome start, the INP gained institutional strength in 1968 during Juan Velasco's (1968–1975) revolution from above. This reformist military government relied heavily on the INP to design and advance its ISI developmental plans. Nonetheless, once the administration ended, the office lost its saliency and struggled to fulfill its goals. After a brief resurgence in the late1980s, it was finally closed in 1992 amid radical neoliberal reforms. In open contrast to other planning agencies in Latin America that remained influential during and after market reforms, neoliberal reformers in Peru closed what they considered an inefficient agency committed to inadequate developmental goals.[1]

What can we learn from this unsuccessful case of institution building in Peru? Through interviews, secondary sources, and archival research, I put the institutional trajectory of the INP in dialogue with diverse theories that aim at explaining the emergence and endurance of state capacity in Latin America. I present how these theories help us to understand the creation and institutional trajectory of the INP and discuss four topics that provide insights into why the INP failed to gain capacity and endurance: (1) the previous low level of state capacity in the Peruvian state; (2) the magnitude of the challenge of a complex ISI development plan that largely overpassed the agency's capacity; (3) a negative socio-political context and the INP's isolationist strategy from social interests that did not allow the office to build social support and

---

[1] Mejia 2014, 2015.

reputation; and (4) how the INP's strong commitment to ISI programs impeded its adaptation to neoliberal times.

Each of these topics informs theoretical and policy-oriented debates on the likelihood of successful agency capacity building in Latin America. The variation of factors associated in the literature with variation in state capacity across time allows me to highlight the relevance of factors that could have contributed to a more positive outcome in the case of the INP. In doing so, I aim to contribute to the ongoing discussion about more likely and less likely instances of capacity building in Latin American states.

One conceptual point before starting. Studies of the state utilize a myriad of concepts to denote different (although frequently fairly similar) qualities of state strength: state autonomy, state infrastructural power, state capacity, among others.[2] These studies usually portray the state as a unitary actor and focus in assessing its capacity to: achieve some goals, affect the interests of social actors, extract revenues, or effectively control its territory.[3] Trying not to contribute to the above-noted Tower of Babel of definitions, in this article I adopt the concept of state capacity as defined by Bersch, Praca and Taylor:[4] "the ability of a professional bureaucracy to implement policy without undue external influence"; "agency capacity" means state capacity in a particular agency. The concept combines autonomy and effectiveness, two characteristics associated with strong state agencies.

The article proceeds as follows. First I describe the institutional trajectory of the INP and provide evidence about its varying levels of capacity across time. Then, I discuss how diverse theories that explore why agencies gain and maintain capacity contribute to explain the institutional trajectory of the INP. In the last section, I discuss how the four issues mentioned above affected the potential of the INP to develop its capacity. I conclude with some theoretical and practical implications of these findings.

THE INSTITUTIONAL TRAJECTORY OF THE INP

The INP was created in 1962. In its more than thirty years of existence the office followed an irregular trajectory in which periods of high and low capacity alternated. After a slow start in which the office failed to achieve relevance (1962–1968), the INP gained prestige and power during the first phase (1968–1975) of the Revolutionary Government of the Armed Forces. During the second phase (1975–1980) the INP lost its influence and some of its competences. In Fernando Belaúnde's (1980–1985) democratic government the office did not achieve strong saliency and although it gained some vitality during the first years of Alan García's Government (1985–1990), it was

---

[2] Skocpol, 1985; Mann, 1986; Geddes, 1990: 217–235.; Soifer, and Vom Hau, 2008: 219–230.
[3] Kurtz, 2013; Skocpol, 1985; Mann, 1984: 185–213; Tilly, 1975.
[4] Bersch, Praca, and Taylor, 2016.

engulfed by the hyperinflationary crisis of the country. Ignored by market reformers in the Ministry of Economics and Finance (MEF) appointed during Alberto Fujimori's first government (1990–1995), the office was finally deactivated in 1992. In what follows I describe this institutional trajectory, with special emphasis on the level of state capacity achieved in each period. In the second and third sections I discuss what explains these abrupt changes in capacity levels and how other courses of action may have given the agency a better opportunity of maintaining capacity.

The adoption of a National Planning System in Peru was part of a broader set of international agreements and recommendations that favored state planning in the region. International organizations, such as the ECLA and the OAS, recommended as part of their development recipes the creation or reinforcement of planning offices. The Punta del Este Act, signed by OAS members in Uruguay in 1961, compromised member states to adopt a Planning System. Furthermore, the creation of strong planning offices was a necessary requirement to access funds offered by the US government as part of the Alliance for Progress initiative.[5]

As a result of these international incentives and pressures, Manuel Prado's (1956–1962) government created in 1961 the Oficina Central de Estudios y Programas within the Finance Ministry. Curiously, Prado's government had until then opposed the idea of planning and supported more laissez-faire policies. Nonetheless, the adoption of a formally strong planning system occurred during the brief government of the Junta Militar de gobierno (1962–1963).[6] A group of military officials with reformist ideas ousted Prado from office only weeks before the end of his term. During its brief government the junta created the institutions of a comprehensive planning system: the INP, the Consejo Nacional de Desarrollo Económico y Social, a Planning Advisory Council, and sectorial and regional planning offices. The INP was the technical and coordinating body of the system. Its director had ministerial rank, although no vote in the Council of Ministers, and chaired the Advisory Council.

The duties of the INP included preparing short-, medium-, and long-term development plans; supervising and coordinating sectorial and regional plans; producing reports about the economic situation in the country; coordinating the country's international technical assistance; and, in general, advising the president in political decisions linked to national development. The short term of the military junta did not allow for a proper implementation of these regulations.[7]

This implementation started during Fernando Belaúnde's government (1963–1968), although quite weakly. The planning system lost its saliency within the government's priorities, as a series of internal and external problems limited the interest in the system. To begin with, the agency lacked

---

[5] Saberbein, 1984; CIEPA, 1984; Mejía, 2014.   [6] Leceta, 2003: 155–179.
[7] ILPES, ECLA and ONU, 2012.

basic statistical information, there was a serious deficit of planning professionals in the country and, according to one of its first advisors, the foreign technical assistance it received was insufficient and defective.[8] At the same time, the office was under strong pressure from international agencies which conditioned external loans to the approval of development plans. These external pressures demanded from the INP premature results that it was in no way capable of producing.[9] As a result, the agency produced a first development plan that was never properly implemented.[10] On top of that, the government was trapped in an internal conflict with the political opposition in Congress that limited its attention to planning reforms. Furthermore, the economic crisis that started in the last years of the government led to the departure of several of the few technical cadres that had arrived in the INP.

This situation radically changed with the arrival of the Revolutionary Government of the Armed Forces (1968–1980), whose first phase was led by General Juan Velasco Alvarado (1968–1975). In contrast with other military governments of the region leaning to the right, the Peruvian government was highly reformist and conducted significant redistributive reforms (e.g. a radical land reform) and nationalizations. During these years the INP gained strength and achieved a leading role. President Velasco's military advisors found in the INP a crucial ally to provide technical assistance for the advancement of their reform plans and to counterbalance the more orthodox opinions of the Ministry of Economics and Finance.[11] The agency was to advance a complex and ambitious industrialization process in an, until then, export-led economy.

As part of their project of state modernization, the military government approved the Decree-Law N° 17289 that ordered the agency's reorganization. The purpose of the decree was to strengthen the INP with a technical bureaucracy. The office started an ambitious process of meritocratic recruitment, adopted competitive salaries, and provided good incentives to build a professional bureaucracy within the office. By 1971 the INP already had a team of highly qualified individuals, known as the "golden bureaucrats."[12] Furthermore, the office adopted formal and informal rules to strengthen their personnel, such as providing scholarships to officials for postgraduate studies abroad and organizing intensive courses in planning in the recently created Escuela Superior de Administración Pública.[13]

This reform process also implied some new competences for the INP. The most important was to be in charge of the Peruvian civil service reform. Another relevant competence was to include the INP Director in the group of top executive officials in charge of the formulation of the country's national

---

[8] De Las Casas, 1964.   [9] ILPES, ECLA and ONU, 2012: 85.   [10] Leceta, 2003: 10.
[11] Interview with Velasco 2015 and Guiulfo 2016. See also: Velasco, 1974.
[12] Malpic and Alayza, 1971.   [13] Interview with Velasco, 2015.

budget. Finally, a newly created Research Office had the responsibility of promoting research and academic networks with local and foreign experts and producing reports and analyses.[14]

The INP's previous functions remained the same. Its activities focused on preparing comprehensive global, sectorial, and regional development plans. The office produced a new national plan: Plan Nacional de Desarrollo 1971–1975. Given its new budgetary competences, the agency could now guarantee that yearly budgets matched these national plans. And being in charge of foreign technical aid allowed the INP to seek external loans for projects related to the National Development Plan.[15] In clear contrast to its previous trajectory, all these reforms allowed the INP to become an effective and influential agency.[16] About these golden years and the contrast with the previous ones, Cleaves and Pease mention that:

the influence of the National Planning Institute (INP) rose significantly. Before 1968, the INP was politically crippled in the cross fire between Belaúnde and the National Congress. Belaúnde had considerable confidence in his own grand design for the country; the Congress, unable to censure the INP director because he was not a cabinet member, chose instead to reduce the INP's powers and budget. In 1966, many professional planners, completely demoralized, left the institute and were replaced by non-specialists. With the military government, however, the situation turned around dramatically and the INP became one of the most important agencies in the Peruvian public sector. From 1969 to 1971, its budget increased by a quarter in real terms. It hired staff members with new technical skills, and it established sectorial planning offices in all the large investment ministries.[17]

This process was interrupted during the second phase of the military government under General Moráles Bermúdez (1975–1980), a more conservative and economically orthodox administration. Good economic conditions in the country favored the previous process of institution building by enhancing investments in state reform, but starting in 1975 economic problems mounted, which added fuel to already increasing political conflicts caused by divisions within the ruling coalition and a mounting social opposition in the streets. The INP declined in its capacity, losing, due to salary reductions, several cadres who sought better conditions in public enterprises or in the private sector.[18]

These negative economic conditions continued and worsened after the democratic transition, during Fernando Belaúnde's second government (1980–1985). The INP lost considerable influence, and planning in general received less attention from the Executive.[19] In 1981 the system was reorganized, abolishing the Consejo Nacional de Desarrollo Económico y Social and creating an area of Regional Planning.[20] During this period the

[14] Malpica and Alayza, 1971.   [15] Leiva, 2010.   [16] Leceta, 2003; Velasco, 1974; Leiva, 2012.
[17] Cleaves and Pease, 1983: 232–233.   [18] Leiva, 2012: 147.
[19] Interview with Velasco, 2015.   [20] Leiva, 2012: 148.

INP functions were more oriented towards the formulation and advising of regional development plans, rather than national ones.

During Alan García's government (1985–1990), it is possible to find a new (but brief) effort to reinforce the INP in the context of a pretty radical heterodox development plan. According to Leceta, García and APRA sought to bring back "golden bureaucrats" to the INP, a goal the president achieved due to the availability of resources during the first two years of his administration.[21] The INP was used by the young president to legitimize in open forums with political, business, and union leaders some of his radical heterodox policies. The agency hired back qualified experts and increased its personnel, although this action was also a sign of politicization: many were political cadres linked to APRA with little planning experience.[22] Also, the INP produced a new middle-term developmental plan (1986–1990).

Nonetheless, and partly as a result of the government's ambitious heterodox plan, in 1987 economic conditions strongly worsened and a hyperinflationary crisis erupted. This crisis caused a new reversal in the INP's institutional development, causing it to lose technical personnel and influence.[23] The INP lost legitimacy and the "golden bureaucrats" were strongly criticized for the calamitous results of García's government. And given the magnitude of the crisis, the National Development Plan was not worth the paper it was written on: resources were insufficient to invest in its implementation, making it completely irrelevant for policy making. As a result, the planning system strongly weakened and lost legitimacy.

Neoliberal reformers took control over economic policy and state reform after the election of Alberto Fujimori in 1990. These reformers, ideologically opposed to planning in general, were responsible for the adoption of a quite radical process of market reform that included the shrinking of the state. In 1992 the INP was deactivated, some of its competences transferred to the MEF, and the ones related to foreign technical cooperation, to the new Ministry of the Presidency. Neoliberal reformers saw these changes in the planning system as one of the main achievements of the reform process.[24] Other competences simply lost relevance in the state. Consequently, the INP and the National Planning System disappeared.

What can current theories about the determinants of state capacity tell us about this case of failed institution building? And what other factors, if favorable, could have contributed to its institutionalization and continuity? I turn to these questions in the next two sections.

---

[21] Leceta, 2003.   [22] Interview with Velasco, 2015.   [23] Leiva, 2012: 148.
[24] Interview with Dubois, 2007.

WHAT DOES EXPLAIN AND WHAT FAILS TO EXPLAIN THE INP'S
INSTITUTIONAL TRAJECTORY?

An analysis of a state agency, such as the INP, can inform current debates about the determinants of state capacity in Latin America. Diverse academics have highlighted the theoretical relevance of treating states as non-unitary actors, composed of different sub-parts with varying levels of capacity.[25] Within-country studies allow variation in capacity across state agencies to be explored in the same agency across time, and even between offices of the same agency. And comparative studies enable us to understand what lies behind cross-national patterns of agency capacity and weakness in the region.[26]

Two questions about agency capacity are especially relevant: (i) under what conditions do agencies gain capacity? And, more importantly, (ii) why do some agencies maintain such capacity? In developed countries with strong states it would be less relevant to discuss why agencies gain and maintain capacity. Agencies in these countries emerge with resources, qualified personnel, and legitimacy to carry out their institutional duties. State agencies are usually strong from the outset, capable of protecting themselves and advancing their duties. Citizens expect them to fulfill their duties. But in a region in which state capacity is far from given, in which many agencies never achieve strength, and others have just episodic instances of power, we need to explore the mechanisms behind these processes. Capacity is better understood as an outcome rather than a given.

Several theories point to different causal mechanisms leading to the emergence of strong agencies and their continuity.[27] Some of these

---

[25] Skocpol, 1985; Migdal, Kohli, and Shue, 1994; Geddes, 1990; Ziblatt, 2008: 273–289; Soifer, 2009: 158–180; Bersch, Praca, and Taylor, 2016.

[26] Dargent, 2015.

[27] I only discuss those theories I can relate with the institutional trajectory of the INP, so some important theories of capacity building are left out. Hegemonic preservation theories, for example, find in powerful actors fearful of democratic and participatory times the cause for the constitutional adoption, institutional reinforcement, and endurance of agencies that could provide counter-majoritarian insurance to these actors. Boylan (1998) uses such a theory to explain the creation of Chile's Central Bank. There are no hegemonic interests in the INP's story. "Insurance" theories, on the other hand, find in political pluralism an incentive for political actors to create and maintain strong agencies. Strong agencies can be born out of political engagement and pacts. Competing actors will act as check and balances on each other, protecting the agencies from political backlash, thus providing enough space for the agency to act autonomously and maintain its capacity. Geddes, "Building 'State' Autonomy in Brazil," for example, explains bureaucratic reforms aiming for higher professionalism in Colombia, Uruguay, and Venezuela in the past century by the similar power of two political parties competing against each other. And more recently, Ríos Figueroa finds in political pluralism the reason why courts were given considerable power in some Latin American countries in recent years (Ríos Figueroa 2007). The main problem with this perspective is that it is simply not true that political competition by itself always leads to professional agencies. The theory seems better fit to explain independence in horizontal accountability institutions that can affect other political players if

perspectives speak directly to the case of the INP. In this section, I focus on some of these theories (international diffusion, political incentives, and formal-institutional theories) and in the following section, when discussing why the INP failed to build social support and reputation, I discuss how other theories that link social actors to state capacity building inform the case at hand.

Some authors highlight the importance of the diffusion of foreign models and international demands for institutional creation.[28] The creation of a planning agency in Peru in 1961 was clearly driven by processes of external diffusion and incentives (loans, technical assistance) to adopt planning offices in the region. This external source would explain the wave-like pattern of adoption of planning offices in Latin America in the 1960s; in fact, by 1967 all countries in the region had a planning agency.[29] ECLA's and OAS' development recipes, the Alliance for Progress and the substantial funds it promised to deliver were conditional on the existence of such agencies and the elaboration of the first development plans, were all powerful external incentives that led to their creation.

Nonetheless, these perspectives do not fully explain why agencies gain and maintain capacity: as we know well, states in Latin America frequently adopt what scholars call "Potemkin institutions."[30] These are institutions adopted to respond to external demands which governments are never really committed to implementing. The creation of the first planning institutions in 1961 by a laissez-faire government that opposed state planning seem to follow precisely such a pattern: no commitment was made for a proper implementation. This was a general trend in Latin America since, as Mejía argues, the development plans elaborated by the agencies "were infrequently used as a basis for economic policy making and appeared to constitute a diplomatic maneuver for attracting foreign capital."[31] The first planning office was never strongly supported by the government. The office only gained some strength when in 1962 the reformist military junta that governed the country that year created the INP and adopted a comprehensive planning system.

Political incentives' theories, which focus on politicians' interests, expect agencies to gain capacity when politicians use them to advance their political goals or to face challenges that could affect their interests.[32] These theories capture well an observable trend in Latin America, quite relevant for the case at

controlled by one of the competing parties. In other cases, competing political forces often share the spoils of clientelism or simply pay little attention to agencies that do not affect their material interests. In the particular case of the INP, the political pluralism that existed in the eighties through two presidential terms made little difference as a source of capacity of the office. On the contrary, the office gained capacity during Velasco's authoritarian government.

[28] Weyland, 2006; Dargent, 2014: 9–40. [29] Mejía, 2014: 7.
[30] Grzymala-Busse, 2006:1–30. And for the application of the concept in Latin America see Blass, A. and Brinks, D., 2011.
[31] Mejía, 2014: 12. [32] Geddes, 1990, 1994.

hand: there are several instances of agencies gaining power to advance incumbents' goals or being reinforced to respond to an external or internal problem that threatens politicians. Indirectly, these theories are also good at explaining why agencies weaken when new incumbents do not share their predecessors' preferences, also a common pattern in the region. Agencies lack the resources and personnel to remain strong in the absence of political support; they fade away when their political sponsors lose power.

In fact, in a comparative study of planning offices in Latin America (Argentina, Ecuador, Chile, and Colombia), Mejía precisely links the relevance gained by these institutions with the incentives faced by incumbents.[33] The author argues that these agencies tend to gain power when incumbents see in them useful tools for the advancement of their preferred policies and interests, namely to mobilize external resources, exercise veto power over other competing state agencies and control spending, legitimize their policy decisions with technical arguments, and provide information for the policymaking process.[34] These preferences and interests change due to external conditions and internal political demands. In some countries and moments, presidents will need planning agencies to advance and legitimize their policies against other social actors or state agencies, while in other circumstances they might not need them, condemning them to irrelevance.[35]

The case of the INP could make us conclude that political incentives explain the whole story: the office gained capacity when Velasco used it as an ally to legitimize its development recipes and to produce documents and plans necessary for his sponsored reforms. Similarly, Alan García used the INP to legitimize his heterodox development plans. The ups (Velasco; García) and downs (Belaúnde I; Morales Bermúdez, Belaúnde II; Fujimori) of the agency's capacity prove how dependent it was on the presidents' preferences and the challenges they faced. This case seems to clearly confirm the predictions of a perspective that finds in politicians' interests and incentives the driving force behind politics in Latin America.

But this is not the full story. A significant problem with political incentives theories is that they are less useful to explain instances of institutional continuity in cases in which incumbents' interests or urgency are no longer

---

[33] Mejía, 2014.

[34] Mejía, 2014, 2015 gives little space for institutional autonomy in his theory. Planning agencies are tools for incumbents, and they will survive if incumbents can use them to advance their interests. In this chapter, I present a more autonomous image of state institutions that could even lead them to become limits to incumbents.

[35] Mejía, 2014: 12–13. As discussed below, Mejía's theory also includes institutional factors to explain why, even if supported by incumbents, some planning offices were not able to adapt to neoliberal times. He proposes that planning offices will be able to gain continuity if two institutional factors are present to allow for their adaptation – first, if fewer veto points to policy reform (such as Congress) were allowed, and secondly, if agencies' rules of creation and functioning made a flexible interpretation of their mandates possible.

aligned with the agency's capacity. A clear sign of state capacity is precisely those agencies which gain autonomy and can limit incumbents' preferences or oppose their short-term interests. Why would self-interested politicians maintain these agencies in the absence of urgency, or when their political incentives are weak to say the least? Certainly, the INP was never one of these agencies, but other cases of continuity in the region (central banks, statistical institutes, ministries of foreign affairs, some regulatory agencies), including other planning agencies, make us wonder what would have contributed to the agency's stability.

So to fully understand this case it is relevant to ask the "why not" question. What other factors help to understand why the INP was unable to gain capacity? As we will see, some of these factors are strongly deterministic, but others offer some space for a different line of action that could have given the INP better chances of gaining capacity. In the next section I turn to this "why not" question. In what remains of this section, I focus on one theory that, even if it does not seem helpful to explain this why-not question, is worth exploring if only to disregard it as the relevant cause of the INP's weakness.

Formal institutional theories find in laws and regulations a relevant source of variation in state capacity. Agencies shielded by the "right" institutional rules are expected to have a higher capacity than agencies that lack adequate institutional protections. The "right" rules will protect some agencies from external pressures and provide them with the necessary tools to advance their work (for example rules that guarantee independent budgets, enhance meritocracy, and foster agency capacity).

No one will deny that there is some truth in formal institutional theories, as there are certainly better rules to protect agencies, such as laws that guarantee independent budgets, enhance meritocracy, and foster agency capacity. Nonetheless, these theories in general face serious shortcomings, and in particular rules and regulations do not explain the case at hand. First, formal rules cannot explain the variation observed in agency capacity in Latin America. Similar laws frequently apply to several state agencies, but are enforced in only some of them, while in others the rules remain ineffective or are manipulated to accommodate political interests. In fact, as Mejía shows, the norms regulating the planning agencies in Latin America were very similar, but only some of them managed to gain capacity and continuity. [36] In the case of Peru, the rules that reinforced the INP during Velasco's government were no longer relevant for other presidents, despite the fact that they remained the same; similar rules did not lead to similar levels of state capacity.

Secondly, the direction of causality that formal institutional theories propose is sometimes the reversed one. Successful agencies frequently develop a positive reputation among political actors, and this helps the agency in persuading (or even pushing) political actors to strengthen the formal rules that protect the

---

[36] Mejía, 2014, 2015.

agency's independence. To a certain extent, therefore, the formal rules protecting an agency from political interference are the result of the agency's (informal) power, and not the cause of it. The INP was never able to achieve such effective institutional protection.

So, until now I have shown that external factors contributed to the creation of the INP but not to its emergence as a strong agency. Political incentives perspectives seem to explain well this capacity enhancement during Velasco's government (and less importantly, its brief resurgence during García's term) and its decline in other instances (Belaúnde I; Morales Bermúdez; Belaúnde II, and Fujimori). Also, institutional rules do not seem to explain this variation in agency capacity levels nor the reasons why incumbents weakened or ignored the INP. In what follows, I propose four other topics that contribute to explain why the INP failed to gain institutional capacity.

WHY DID THE INP FAIL TO GAIN STATE CAPACITY?

I propose four topics that provide us with insights about why the INP failed to achieve continuity and stability after its emergence as a strong institution during Velasco's years. These four topics contribute to our general understanding of the negative and positive conditions for the development of agency capacity in the region. First, previous state weakness, a crucial factor frequently overlooked in studies of institution building, conditioned the later success of the INP when trying to build its capacity from scratch and launch the ambitious state planning program. Secondly, the adoption of this inward-looking development model was simply overwhelming, and so more suitable for a new agency in the process of building its capacity. Thirdly, the political, social, and economic environment in which the office developed was not favorable for its strengthening and continuity, and the agency's isolation strategy did not contribute to build social support. And fourthly, the previous trajectory and strong normative commitments of the INP to the ISI developmental model limited its ability to adapt in years in which this economic model went into crisis.

Previous State Capacity Matters

The INP started from a quite low level in its mission to build state-planning capacity. These start-up costs proved crucial in its effort to ascertain authority and build legitimacy. While new state agencies in developed countries tend to be more uniform in their capabilities, since they enjoy a baseline of resources and capable personnel that allows them to perform their duties, new agencies in weak states, on the contrary, have to overcome their own legacies of state weakness in their efforts to build capacity. That is, they face a structural disadvantage. As the INP case shows, the limits faced to start-up a planning agency from scratch in Peru were considerable: the demands on this office were enormous given the existing capacities of the Peruvian bureaucracy.

De Las Casas precisely highlights, in a highly critical report, how costly for the office were both the lack of human resources who were specialized in planning, and, more crucially, the absence of basic information that could be used to design technical development plans when the INP was created in 1962.[37] Peru lacked censual and statistical information in 1962; universities did not provide courses or career-fostering planning abilities; and the foreign advisors who were supposed to contribute with the implementation of the office failed to train local cadres and mostly focused on designing plans. De Las Casas asks for urgent investment in education for what he refers to as "economic engineers."[38] Simply put, the Peruvian state lacked previous experience and bureaucratic expertise in planning and other technical competences.

This weakness led former INP Deputy Director Otoniel Velasco (1968–1975) to an accelerated effort to reinforce the office.[39] Velasco highlights how foreign aid and linkages with external institutions contributed greatly to this effort. In a very short time the INP was able to attract professional cadres and provide incentives for technical individuals to enter the state.

Nonetheless, the office had to build up its capacity and at the same time design complex development plans that included the supervision of sectorial and regional activities. The strong legacies of state weakness emerged in crucial instances in which new agencies, such as the INP, had to build up their credibility and subordinate competing bureaucratic and social actors who, in turn, distrusted the state and resisted regulation. These start-up costs, in months in which the agency had to build its reputation and enforce its decisions, were a heavy burden for institution building. During the 1980s, the Peruvian state weakness remained a matter of great concern for the INP technocrats. They depicted the state as a "centralized, technically inefficient, economically costly, corrupt and resistant to change machine; perceived by social actors as a constraint and obstacle to their economic and social demands."[40]

It was not just previous weakness that explains the failure. As I highlight in the following section, a more limited set of goals might have been more manageable, but the tasks taken on by this novel agency were enormously demanding and complex; an extraordinary challenge even for a stronger agency.

The Cost of Aiming Too High With Limited Capacity

The content of development plans shows that the office simply overstretched what it (and the Peruvian state) could feasibly accomplish. The INP adopted

---

[37] De Las Casas, 1964.   [38] De Las Casas, 1964.
[39] An army general formally directed the institution, but the technical director making many of the decisions was Velasco.
[40] Instituto Nacional de Planificación, 1986: 42.

structural reform plans that were highly complex and that went beyond the economic realm, an enormously demanding task by itself due to the ISI challenge, to include the social and political. The planning task proved insurmountable for the agency to supervise and enforce and for the state to implement. Therefore, aiming for too much was also a way of weakening the office, as regulations and development plans could not be enforced, adding to the image of the INP as a parchment institution.

In the economic realm, inefficient public enterprises, lagging in the construction of the necessary infrastructure for diversification plans (lack of railroads to transport minerals, for example), or lack of compliance by the private sector, are among many problems mentioned in the INP's *Informes de Coyuntura*, reports produced annually for the president and the Council of Ministers.[41] An example about Pesca Perú, a state enterprise originally created to strengthen the state's position in the fishing industry, shows the distance between original plans and reality:

This company is going through an extremely serious financial situation. It has exhausted its borrowing capacity and its internal resources; thus, it cannot handle the debts incurred. In order to prevent the company's collapse – likely to occur in the short term – we suggest that the Ministry of Fishing implements as soon as possible a Financial Rehabilitation Plan for PESCA–PERU, with the priority support of the Ministry of Economy and Finances and other sectors closely related to it.[42]

Not even in its golden years was the INP able to control state enterprises (sectoral planning), achieve a clear presence in the territory (regional planning), or foster private activities as planned.[43] As mentioned by Cleaves and Schurrah:

Although the proportion of the gross domestic product controlled by the state was significant, the state found that it was enormously difficult to supervise and coordinate all the activities it absorbed. These changes occurred in such a short period of time that in most cases formal state authority was subject to extensive interference by domestic and international economic forces. The state's learning process in the marketing of minerals and fishmeal was painful and costly, leading to management errors that were picked up by groups in the governing elite skeptical of full state control. The INP, despite its power, never succeeded in completely overcoming sectoral competition, reinforced by divisions in the summit of power. The development plans proved difficult to execute, and many of the large public sector enterprises operated without paying much attention to INP directives.[44]

The case shows the cost of lacking the capacity to enforce and implement ambitious plans. Though it was an autonomous agency, it lacked the capacity to implement its own policy goals. In his seminal work on economic planning,

---

[41] Instituto Nacional de Planificación, 1975a, 1975b, 1976.
[42] Instituto Nacional de Planificación, 1976: 5. Own translation.
[43] Instituto Nacional de Planificación, 1972: 2.   [44] Cleaves and Scurrah, 1980: 71–73.

Lewis argues that although development planning was a highly demanding and complex issue for all states, endorsing it was even harder for weak states that did not meet two basic previous requirements: capable bureaucracy and absence of corruption.[45] Pessimistically, he even asserts that "a strong state, competent and honest, is precisely what underdeveloped countries lack."[46] Therefore, by adopting such ambitious commitments the INP was doomed to failure from the outset. Nonetheless, other alternatives were still available: gradual reforms, aiming for simpler objectives, focusing more on public expenditure and infrastructure, and reforming bureaucracy.

Society Matters

But it was not just a problem of state capacity or ambitious plans. There was never a strong social demand to promote and protect a planning institutional in Peru. And on top of that, an isolationist strategy prevented the INP from seeking some available sources of social support in this already negative context.

In recent years social actors have gained more relevance in efforts to understand why state agencies gain capacity. "Bringing society back in" is a fruitful way to explore other determinants of agency capacity. This line of argument builds up on Douglass North's famous dictum, according to which institutions will be stable "only if they are supported by organizations with an interest in their perpetuation."[47] State agencies will only gain continuity if there are social forces interested in their endurance.

There is quite a direct way in which state agencies are of interest to social actors: some actors may be benefited by the activity of the state agency. This is why we observe higher instances of state capacity and continuity in agencies in charge of issues that are functional for the interests of dominant economic actors, such as business coalitions (e.g. finance ministries, central banks). Furthermore, agencies can, through their policies, strengthen actors that become allies of institutional continuity and weaken others that become institutional losers.[48] Agencies can also deliberately form alliances with civil society organizations or even promote the formation of new organizations in an effort to advance their agendas and increase their reputation.[49] Agencies can prove useful for the interests of these social actors, thus involving these actors in their defense, especially (but not only) against political attacks.[50]

---

[45] Lewis, 1957.   [46] Lewis, 1957: 136.   [47] North, 1990: 25.

[48] Pierson, 2000: 251–267; and Dargent, 2015.

[49] Carpenter, 2001. Carpenter shows, in the US context, how bureaucrats can build strong societal support that contributes to their agencies' autonomy.

[50] Evans, 1992, also develops an argument linking state and social actors (in his case, business actors). He finds the keystone for agency capacity in what he calls "embedded autonomy," which means the existence of linkages between autonomous bureaucracies and business actors that these bureaucracies regulate. But Evans' focus is more on how these linkages provide agencies

But there is another, less direct, way in which strong actors, even those affected by the agencies' decisions, can contribute to agency continuity. Agency decisions bring certainty to social actors. Strong agencies, for example, guarantee that agencies affecting powerful interests are not politicized or captured by competing economic or political forces.[51] Social actors may find these new agencies annoying at the beginning, but eventually they become a guarantee of predictability. As highlighted by Levitsky and Murillo, "when institutional arrangements persist (and are enforced) over time, surviving repeated crises and changes of government, actors develop expectations of stability and consequently invest in skills, technologies, and organizations that are appropriate to those institutions."[52] Agencies, as enforcers of formal institutions, provide assurance to social actors that the status quo will not change abruptly. Consequently, they become valuable for these actors.

In a recent work, I theorize how different political and economic "environments" in which agencies operate are more or less favorable for institutional development.[53] The balance of power among important actors (business interests, the incumbent, the political opposition, IFIs) plays a crucial role for enhancing agency capacity and favoring its entrenchment over time. A plural and balanced constellation of powerful actors enhances capacity by providing agencies with more space to adopt their own decisions, and by increasing the possibility that agencies find support to advance their policy preferences. In agencies surrounded by a balanced constellation of powerful social actors, the incumbents are aware that pushing agencies too hard may cause a backlash against them. In contrast, where there is only one powerful actor, usually the incumbent, this actor has an easier time opposing agencies that affect its interests.[54]

The INP faced a negative context to build its autonomy and prestige. To begin with, we do not find in Peru strong regional elites or political actors that could have helped the INP to act as a mediator between the government and these actors, thus gaining autonomy and capacity. This made the INP strongly dependent upon the interests of the current incumbent and thus vulnerable. In Dargent (2015: Chapter IV) I propose that the Departamento Nacional de Planeación (DNP) in Colombia gained capacity not only because it was useful for incumbents, but also because incumbents needed it to negotiate with clientelistic regional leaders. This balance of power contributed to the

---

with better information to achieve their goals. Consequently, agencies that opt for isolation will miss this valuable information for policymaking.

[51] Dargent, 2015; Pierson, 2000; North, 1990; Levitsky and Murillo, 2009: 115–133.

[52] Levitsky and Murillo, 2009: 123.   [53] Dargent, 2015.

[54] Similarly, an unbalanced constellation of social actors, with powerful actors sharing similar interests, may result in agency capture by private actors.

development of institutional capacity in the DNP. The political and economic context was not propitious in Peru.

But although this context was not propitious, there were other sources of social support that could be exploited. An obvious source was business actors who benefited from policies conducted by the INP, more precisely industrialists. These linkages did not develop because of two reasons: (i) the military regime's tense and conflictive relation with business actors, even those who may have gained from the regime's policies, such as industrialists, and (ii) the isolationist style of the INP.

First, the military regime's reformist stance and hermetic character affected economic elites and left little space for a fluid relation between state agencies and private actors. Agro-export traditional interests affected by a substantive land reform were obviously out of the question. But one would expect that a growing industrialist bourgeoisie could become an ally of agencies, such as the INP, which focused on fostering industrialization. This was not the case. The archival research clearly shows that, after some initial enthusiasm, the ISI model in general and the INP in particular did not achieve support from industrialists.

At the beginning of the reforms, industrialists and some other business groups supported the ISI government plans and profited from its incentives. The 1970 Industry Law provided a series of benefits to industrial actors; for instance, tax reliefs to investors in targeted sectors (heavy industry, capital goods, wage goods, and industrial inputs) and state banking-system credits.[55] Some of these measures even included the demands presented by the Sociedad Nacional de Industrias (SNI) in an Industrialization Plan produced in the last years of the Belaúnde government.[56]

Nonetheless, with the passing of time, the state was perceived as an autonomous actor, impenetrable to industrial influence. This autonomy bordering on isolation repealed industrialists, thereby limiting the possibility of building alliances. Durand concludes that this isolation led to the frustration of industrialists and their lack of support for the ISI model.[57] The pyramidal structure of the military government in general, and therefore its lack of contact with social actors, also contributed to this outcome.[58] This was not just a pattern in Peru, the tension was also similar in the authoritarian developmental regimes of Bolivia and Ecuador:

By the mid 1970s, domestic capitalists of the Central Andes found themselves enmeshed in contradictory relationships with their respective military governments. On the one hand, domestic businessmen were the primary beneficiaries of the modernizing and expansionary policies of the period. They were quick to take advantage of the subsidized credit, protectionism, tax breaks, and consumption booms fashioned by the military regimes. Yet, as lucrative as these policies were for individual investors, domestic

---

[55] Conaghan and Malloy, 1994: 59.   [56] Durand, 1982: 48.   [57] Durand, 1982: 49.
[58] Interview with Leceta, 2015; Conaghan and Malloy, 1994: 60.

capitalists soon discovered the political and ideological costs of statism and military authoritarianism.[59]

The radicalization of the Peruvian government ended up completely alienating industrialists. The Industrial Community law, a norm that gave industrial workers considerable power and management responsibilities within the workplace, was the trigger of such alienation as it was further proof of the government disregard of private property rights.[60]

But the INP's isolation was not just a result of the conflicts between the regime and business elites. A second reason explaining why these linkages never formed was the INP's isolationist policy style. The INP lacked the willingness to develop its own agenda of reputation building, being more focused on what it considered its technical duties. As mentioned by one INP official working on industrial policies, the INP did not seem to care what industrialists thought of its policies: industrialists were expected to act according to the new developmental model, but not to be involved in discussions about it or part of its implementation.[61] Furthermore, some official reports suggest that INP technocrats were not only isolated from industrialists, but held a critical view of them for not fulfilling their expected responsibilities.[62] These experts perceived industrialists as lacking compromise with the process of industrialization and ambition to advance to its latter phases, as well as having an incomplete understanding of the challenges involved. INP reports portray Peruvian industrialists as being focused on the production of basic consumption goods, characteristic of the first (an easier) stage of ISI, and not on intermediate or capital goods which were required to advance on the later (and harder) stage of ISI.[63] Consequently they blamed industrialists for not promoting the structural industrial reform embraced by the government. As a 1972 report shows:

Investment intentions by private businessmen in the industry sector do not aim to modify the current industrial structure [...] Thus, new authorized investments, which are those enabling changes in the industrial structure, have been reduced both in terms of the authorized amount, and its relative share [...] New investments, as well as their authorized reinvestments, have focused on industries producing consumption goods, reaching 70.8% of authorized investment. Industries producing intermediate goods and capital industries have only received 19.2% and 9.9% of authorized investment, respectively. Therefore, investment intentions are focused on consumer goods industries, preserving the current industrial structure, in which they prevail.[64]

---

[59] Conaghan and Malloy, 1994: 70.

[60] These divergences included public criticisms to the regime: "Raymundo Duarte, president of the *Sociedad Nacional de Industrias* (SNI), did publicly accuse Velasco of being a communist. He was forced into exile shortly thereafter." (Conaghan and Malloy, 1994: 62n.)

[61] Interview with Guilfo, 2016.   [62] Interview with Velasco, 2015.

[63] See, 1968: 1–32, for a detailed analysis of the different stages of ISI and the political economy of the industrialization attempts in Latin America.

[64] INP 1972b: 38–39.

The INP's isolation did not change substantially with the return to democracy in 1980. Probably by then it was already too late to build linkages with social actors.[65] Due to the nature of Velasco's anti-oligarchic regime and the INP insulation, the links between this agency and social actors that could have supported its continuity were never developed. When the Fujimori government got rid of the INP as part of the neoliberal reforms package in the early 1990s, there was no meaningful opposition.

Normative Commitments Undermine Flexibility

Finally, the commitment of the INP to a quite strong developmental state model made it difficult for the office to adapt to changing economic and political conditions in the early 1990s. In contrast to other planning agencies in the region that endorsed the neoliberal economic model and adapted to perform new duties, the INP was not able to do so and remained quite heterodox. The image of the agency among technocrats with neoliberal ideological commitments and the business community in general was one of an inefficient statism. As a result, when these ideological opponents took over the state in 1990 it was easy to justify the deactivation of the office as simply getting rid of an inefficient institution linked to an out-of-date and failed economic model.

This reputation has been rooted in the INP's actions since the late sixties. As discussed above, the INP aimed to implement quite strong ISI developmental state planning during Velasco's government. This involved the central role of the state as policy planner, entrepreneur, and public services and goods provider. The office committed to the implementation of an inward-looking economic model through industrialization. During the early 1980s, and due to changes in the international economic landscape, the INP stance changed as it became aware of the need to promote the development of market forces, but it kept its programmatic commitment to state interventionism, though to a smaller extent. This programmatic rigidity reinforced the INP's isolation and discredit in the face of business elites. The result was that, according to Conaghan and Malloy:

Domestic capitalists came to view the growing state as a type of Frankenstein, a lumbering uncontrollable force whose expansion threatened the private sector on a number of levels [...] This anti-statist rhetoric remained strong in Peru after the democratic transition: "the state became identified by business organizations as the primary cause of economic stagnation."[66]

---

[65] A similar critical view is held on a 1986 report in which businessman were depicted as having acquired rentier habits caused partially by the economic crisis and previous state policies. The report follows: "the most important consequence is the investors' deep distrust in economic activity and a marked trend to make financial placements in foreign currency." (Instituto Nacional de Planificación, 1986: 40.)

[66] Conaghan and Malloy, 1994: 82.

This image of incompetence and "anti-market" institution only grew during Alan García's government. As mentioned, García involved the INP in the launching of his heterodox plan.[67] The following crisis strengthened the perception that INP's work had no positive results and that planning was fatally associated with inefficient politics.[68] Although the economic reforms had been designed by presidential advisors outside the INP, the agency was part of the effort. Consequently, its reputation as an institution tied to ISI "failed" policies strengthened.

When orthodox reformers were appointed in MEF to adopt market and state reforms, one of their agendas was clear: to dismantle the ISI model in Peru. Planning became highly criticized since it was associated with state inefficiency as well as public enterprises and tariff protections.[69] The task was eased by the lack of support and prestige of the office. From 1990 to 1992 the INP was basically ignored, and suddenly deactivated without previous discussion.

CONCLUSIONS

What is the theoretical relevance of the INP's rise and fall? First, the case shows how existing theories of state capacity inform the adoption and institutional trajectory of the INP. External factors provided incentives for the creation of the INP, but it only gained strength when Velasco and his military advisors saw it was in their interest to reinforce the agency to conduct ISI reforms. Political incentives perspectives seem to explain well this capacity enhancement during this government and, although less relevant, its brief resurgence during García's administration. Also, the lack of these incentives explains its decline in other governments that did not find the agency useful for their interests.

But I also propose that, by trying to answer why the INP failed to maintain its capacity, the case also teaches us about the challenges of building state capacity in the region. First, the case illustrates the difficulties that weak states face when they aim to enhance state capacity. In weak states political support is crucial to advance state capacity, but at the same time this initial political push is largely insufficient to build up enough legitimacy to remain strong under less auspicious rulers. Secondly, this state weakness is also relevant to realizing the cost of adopting ambitious plans of reforms that highly surpass the state capabilities. Thirdly, as pointed out by a considerable literature, the case also shows the importance of social actors for building up state capacity, providing the incentives for governments to strengthen state institutions, and assuring continuity. The INP failed to build these linkages with social actors or to enhance its reputation among these actors. Finally, the case shows how ideological commitments can also become a source of stagnation, limiting adaptation to new environments. These lessons are not only of theoretical

---

[67] Instituto Nacional de Planificación: 1986.   [68] Leceta, 2003.
[69] Interview with DuBois, 2008.

interest; they are important for reformers interested in strengthening the state, a challenge that remains as elusive today as five decades ago.

Lastly, it is worth mentioning that there were consequences for not having a planning institution in Peru. As mentioned, the weakness of the INP allowed for its easy dismantling by market reformers in the 1990s. Since then, planning became almost a forbidden word in the Peruvian state, linked to old and failed *desarrollismo*. The cost of such ideological commitments is perceived two decades after the dismantling of the INP, when a commodity boom provided the country with millionaire resources. The country lacked planning instances with the capacity and power to coordinate and prioritize public investment. The MEF has been quite good at limiting superfluous spending, a "negative planner," but no state agency took a more positive and propositional role. It has taken the country a decade to react and develop a better spending capacity, with clear priorities and proper coordination across decentralized and sectorial levels, all issues that an effective planning office could have helped to prevent.

INTERVIEWS

DuBois, Fritz. 2008. Author interview. Chief of Cabinet in MEF (1991–1997). Lima: June 18.

Giuilfo, Luis. 2016. Author interview. Official in INP during Velasco's government. Lima: December 9.

Leceta, Humberto. 2015. Author interview. Official of the INP (1970–1992). Lima: August 14.

Velasco, Otoniel. 2015. Author interview. Director of the INP (1968–1975). Lima: June 17.

REFERENCES

Bersch, Katherine, Sergio Praca, and Michael Taylor. "Bureaucratic Capacity and Political Autonomy Within National States: Mapping the Archipelago of Excellence in Brazil." In *States in the Developing World*, ed. M. Centeno, A. Kohli, and D. Yashar, with D. Mistree. Cambridge University Press, 2016.

Blass, Abby and Daniel Brinks. "The Institutional Roots of Judicial Power in Latin America from 1975–2009." *Annual Meeting of the American Political Science Association*, Seattle: Washington, 2011.

Boylan, Delia. "Preemptive Strike: Central Bank Reform in Chile's Transition from Authoritarian Rule." *Comparative Politics* 30:4, 1998: 443–462.

Carpenter, Daniel *The Forging of Bureaucratic Autonomy: Reputations, Networks and Policy Innovation in Executive Agencies*. Princeton University Press, 2001.

CIEPA. *La planificación en el Perú: antecedentes, desarrollo y técnicas*. CIEPA: Lima, 1984.

Cleaves, Peter and Henry Pease. "State Autonomy and Military Policy Making." In _The Peruvian Experiment_, eds. C. McClintock and A. Lowenthal, Princeton University Press, 1983.

Cleaves, Peter and Martin Scurrah _Agriculture, Bureaucracy and the Military Government in Peru_. New York: Cornell University Press, 1980.

Conaghan, Catherine and James Malloy. _Unsettling Statecraft: Democracy and Neoliberalism in the Central Andes_. University of Pittsburgh Press, 1994.

Dargent, Eduardo. "Determinantes Internacionales de la Capacidad de las Agencias Estatales," _Apuntes_ 41, 74, 2014: 9–40.

Technocracy and Democracy in Latin America, New York: Cambridge University Press, 2015.

De Las Casas, Luis Felipe. _Los problemas de la planificación en un país subdesarrollado_. Lima: INP, 1964.

Durand, Francisco, _La década frustrada: los industriales y el poder, 1970–1980_. Lima: DESCO, 1982.

Evans, Peter "The State as Problem and Solution: Predation, Embedded Autonomy, and Structural Change." In _The Politics of Adjustment_, eds. S. Haggard, and R. Kaufman, Princeton University Press, 1992.

Geddes, Barbara. "Building 'State' Autonomy in Brazil. 1930-1964." _Comparative Politics_ 22, 2, 1990: 217–235.

Politician's Dilemma: Building State Capacity in Latin America.Berkeley: University of California Press, 1994.

Grindle, Merilee and John Thomas. _Public Choice and Policy Change: The Political Economy of Reform in Developing Countries_. Baltimore and London: The Johns Hopkins University Press, 1991.

Grzymala-Busse, Anna. "The Discreet Charm of Formal Institutions. Postcommunist Party Competition and State Oversight." _Comparative Political Studies_, 39, 10, 2006: 1–30.

Hirschman, Albert. "The Political Economy of Import-Substituting Industrialization in Latin America." _The Quarterly Journal of Economics_, 82, 1, 1968: 1–32.

ILPES, ECLA and ONU, _Los fundamentos de la planificación del desarrollo en América Latina y el Caribe: Textos seleccionados del ILPES (1962–1972)_. Santiago de Chile: Naciones Unidas, 2012.

Instituto Nacional de Planificación. _Plan Económico Anual 1970_. Lima: INP, 1970.

Informe Trimestral Enero-Marzo 1972. Lima: INP, 1972a.

Síntesis de la Evaluación del Plan 1971–1972.Lima: INP, 1972b.

Informe Trimestral. Lima: INP, 1974.

Informe de Coyuntura No 8. Lima: INP, 1975a.

Informe de Coyuntura No 7. Lima: INP, 1975b.

Informe de Coyuntura No 4. Lima: INP, 1976.

Plan Nacional de Desarrollo 1986–1990. Lima: INP, 1986.

Johnson, Matthew. "The Political Logic of Renters' Insurance." Unpublished article, forthcoming.

Kurtz, Markus. _Latin American State Building in Comparative Perspective: Social Foundations of Institutional Order_. New York: Cambridge University Press, 2013.

Leceta, Humberto. "Planificación del desarrollo: a 41 años de su institucionalización en el Perú." *Apuntes* 1, 52/53, 2003: 155–179.

Leiva, Jorge. *Instituciones e instrumentos para el planeamiento gubernamental en América Latina*. Santiago de Chile: CEPAL, IPEA., 2010.

Pensamiento y práctica de la planificación en América Latina. Santiago de Chile: CEPAL, ILPES, 2012a.

Planeamiento gubernamental en América Latina. Santiago de Chile: CEPAL, ILPES, 2012b.

Levitsky, Steven and María Victoria Murillo. "Variation in Institutional Strength." *The Annual Review of Political Science* 12, 2009: 115–133.

Lewis, Arthur. *La planeación económica*, México D.F.: FCE, 1957.

Malpica, Carlos and Ernesto Alayza. *Aspectos administrativos de la planificación en el Perú*, Lima: INP, 1971.

Mann, Michael. "The Autonomous Power of the State: Its Origins, Mechanism and Results." *European Journal of Sociology* 25, 2, 1984: 185–213.

The Sources of Political Power. Volume I: A History of Power from the Beginning to 1760 AD. Cambridge University Press, 1986.

Mejía, Luis Bernardo. *The Changing Role of the Central Planning Offices in Latin America: A Comparative Historical Analysis Perspective (1950–2013)*. PhD thesis, Maastricht University (2014).

"The Changing Role of the Central Planning Offices in Latin America."*Public Organization Review* [Online], 2015. Available at: http://link.springer.com /article/10.1007%2Fs11115-015-0319-x (accessed October 10, 2015).

Migdal, Joel, Atul Kohli and Vivienne Shue. *State Power and Social Forces*. Cambridge University Press, 1994.

North, Douglass. *Institutions, Institutional Change and Economic Performance*, New York: Cambridge University Press, 1990.

Pierson, Paul. "Increasing Returns, Path Dependence, and the Study of Politics." *The American Political Science Review* 94, 2, 2000: 251–267.

Ríos Figueroa, Julio. "Fragmentation of Power and the Emergence of an Effective Judiciary in Mexico, 1994-2002." *Latin American Politics and Society* 49, 1, 2007: 31–57.

Saberbein, Gustavo. *La planificación en el Perú: antecedentes, desarrollo y técnicas*. Lima: CIEPA, 1984.

Skocpol, Theda. *States and Social Revolutions: A Comparative Analysis of Franche, Russia and China*. Cambridge University Press, 1979.

"Bringing the State Back In: Strategies of Analysis in Current Research." In *Bringing the State Back*, eds. Peter Evans, Dietrich Rueschemeyer, and Theda Skocpol, Cambridge University Press, 1985.

Soifer, Hillel. "State Infrastructural Power: Approaches to Conceptualization and Measurement." *Studies in Comparative International Development*. 43, 3/4, 2008: 231–251.

"The Sources of Infrastructural Power: Evidence from Nineteenth-Century Chilean Education." *Latin American Research Review*, 44, 2, 2009: 158–180.

Soifer, Hillel and Matthias vom Hau. "Unpacking the Strength of the State: The Utility of State Infrastructural Power." *Studies in Comparative International Development* 43, 3/4, 2008: 219–230.

Tilly, Charles. *The Formation of the National State in Western Europe.* Princeton University Press, 1975.

Velasco, Otoniel. "La Planificación en Perú." In *Experiencias y Problemas de la Planificación en América Latina,* eds. ILPES-OEA-BID, México D.F.: Siglo XXI, 1974.

Vom Hau, Matthias. "Unpacking the Strength of the State: The Utility of State Infrastructural Power." *Studies in Comparative International Development* 43, 3/4, 2008.

Weyland, Kurt. *Bounded Rationality and Policy Diffusion: Social Sector Reform in Latin America.* Princeton University Press, 2006.

Ziblatt, Daniel. "Why Some Cities Provide More Public Goods Than Others: A Subnational Comparison of German Cities in 1912." *Studies in Comparative International Development* 43, 3/4, 2008: 273–289.

7

A Double-Edged Sword: The Institutional Foundations of the Brazilian Developmental State, 1930–1985

Luciana de Souza Leão

INTRODUCTION

In the aftermath of the 1980s' severe debt crisis that affected many Latin American countries, the general consensus was that the days of developmental states in the region were over and that state interventionism was outdated and ineffective.[1] Similarly to many countries in the region, in the late 1980s, Brazil underwent many structural reforms that were intended to reduce the size of what was considered an inefficient state, governed by rent-seeking bureaucracies that were not equipped to lead the country efficiently into the twenty-first century.[2] With the hindsight of thirty years, nevertheless, it is clear that the diagnosis of complete state failure in the 1980s obfuscated important achievements that the Brazilian state had made until that decade. The same state that was then considered the main villain of the country's economic crisis had also accomplished many important developmental goals, leading the transformation of Brazil from a rural society in the 1930s into an industrialized and urban one by the 1980s.[3]

In the present chapter, I argue that to understand the achievements, failures and breakdown of the developmental state in Brazil we need to investigate how the institutional foundations created in the Vargas era (1930–1945), that allowed the state to lead and shape the modernization of Brazil, were reproduced through time; and the dynamics of change involved in this historical process. I have two main goals: first, I am interested in highlighting the mechanisms through which the Brazilian state developed capacities to lead the socioeconomic modernization of the country. Although many analyses have shown how the developmental project in Brazil was in many senses incomplete, I am interested in tracing the institutions that allowed a developmental state to emerge in the first place, even if this state has never fulfilled all the goals that it had set to itself.[4] Secondly, I aim to highlight how the same institutional

---

[1] Diniz, 2004. [2] Reis, 2009. [3] Schneider, 2014: 32–56. [4] Kohli, 2005; Evans, 1995.

configuration that allowed for many achievements of the Brazilian developmental state also helps to explain its demise – hence the allusion in the title of this chapter to the double-edged nature of Brazil's state during the developmental period. I provide a macrohistorical perspective of these processes, but whenever possible I also provide more specific examples to support my argument.

The chapter is divided into three sections corresponding to the three different political regimes that Brazil experienced during its developmental phase: 1930–1945, 1945–1964 and 1964–1985. I use secondary sources and different economic and political longitudinal indicators to highlight the main political, administrative, and economic characteristics of each period that allowed state authority to shape the development of a modern economy in Brazil, even in the face of major socio-economic and political changes.

THE VARGAS ERA (1930–1945): THE BEGINNING OF A NEW ORDER IN BRAZIL

During the fifteen years of the first Vargas government (1930–1945), important political and institutional mechanisms were implemented that ushered in a new period of state building and a new pattern of interaction between state, society, and market in Brazil, which was characterized by state intervention in the economy, and by the centralization of political and administrative institutions.[5]

The changes that the Brazilian state underwent during this period initiated a process of modernization from above that would be reproduced until the 1980s. Although this specific type of social change (from top down) involves an increase in political and economic differentiation, it does not imply a real break with the past. In this scenario, a strong state becomes the leading agent of modernization because it is the only actor able to conciliate the old and the new orders. The usual dynamics associated with this type of national modernization are the denial of class conflict, the co-optation of social groups, the promotion of economic development, and the rationalization of government administration.[6] In Brazil, this process was initiated in 1930, and strengthened under the Estado Novo (1937–1945) dictatorial regime.

In the political sphere, the changes that the state underwent during the Vargas period were reflected in the processes of political centralization and concentration of power. While in the Old Republic (1889–1930), political power was distributed among four main poles – the regional oligarchies of São Paulo, Minas Gerais, Rio Grande do Sul, and the army – from the 1930s onwards, these diffused sources of power started to be incorporated into what would become the main political center: the national state.[7] The first legislative measure adopted by Vargas in 1930, the Special Powers Law (Lei de Poderes

---

[5] Nunes, 1997; Sola, 1998.   [6] Reis, 1979.   [7] Schwartzman, 1982.

Especiais no. 19398/30), already signaled this new orientation, by securing important federal control over regional economic and political resources, such as the ability that states had to independently negotiate international loans or to have local militias. The fact that this measure was not intended to intervene directly in the regulation of rural labor relations, or in land tenure distribution, made the opportune accommodation of old and new political interests easier to reach.[8]

Moreover, the early provision of social policies and the implementation of the corporatist system allowed the public authority to act as a centralized agent of social control. Although corporatism is a concept with an extense intellectual history, for the purposes of this chapter, I borrow Phillipe Schmitter's conceptualization of corporatism as a system of interest representation, in order to study the institutional arrangements that allowed the Brazilian state to shape class relations, as well as to determine the ways that labor and business organizations had access to decisional structures of the state.[9] To this end, the creation of the Ministry of Labor, Industry and Commerce (MTIC) just one month after Vargas came to power, gave the new regime an institutional and political base through which the state could control the political incorporation of new political actors created by industrialization (mainly urban workers), and it also guaranteed that the representation of interests would be conducted under state tutelage, and as such also served as an instrument of economic regulation.[10]

Moreover, in 1931, the first of a series of labor and union laws was decreed, which replaced the liberal pluralist legislation of 1907, and set the major lines of Brazil's corporatist policy by determining that labor representation would be based on singular, compulsory, non-competitive unions (*sindicalismo único*). The Labor Code of 1943 (the CLT, Consolidação das Leis do Trabalho), institutionalized this initial decree, and also added a provision that the system would be governed by a comprehensive system of labor courts with compulsory jurisdiction, which in practice meant that all disputes between employers and employees would have to be administered through official state channels.[11] The CLT also guaranteed multiple social rights to workers whose occupation was recognized by law, and served as another important mechanism of social control of new groups that were important for the industrialization of the

---

[8] Camargo, 1982; Fausto, 2008. For this reason, the literature that analyzes the 1930 Revolution commonly refers to it as the "revolution that did not exist," as an allusion to the continuity of local oligarchies' power in rural areas. This does not mean, however, that the transfer of political power to the federal government was achieved without conflict. On the contrary, the Vargas administration had to negotiate extensively with local oligarchies and faced strong resistance in some cases, such as in São Paulo, where the discontent with the political changes culminated in the Constitutionalist Revolution of 1932. See CPDOC, 1982.

[9] Schmitter, 1974: 85–131; Schmitter, 1971.   [10] Santos, 1979; Diniz and Boschi, 2004.

[11] Vianna, 1978.

country, while not disturbing the interests of powerful rural oligarchies, since the new Labor Code did not regulate rural and domestic labor.[12]

The multiple functions resulting from the strategy of labor incorporation into the system were an important part of the authoritarian path to modernization initiated during the Vargas era. By acting as the workers' "benefactor," the state secured a source of support independent of the dominant economic interests, which would prove to be of fundamental importance in future years. The corporatist system also served to promote the strategy of modernization from above. By placing the national will above class interests and justifying the need for a strong government to implement social harmony, corporatist doctrine was central to legitimize the strengthening of the state observed in this period.[13]

The new role expected from the state required the creation of a set of legal norms governing the corporatist system and the policy of pre-emptive co-optation, and demanded that state institutions be created to perform these tasks.[14] Therefore, the process of political centralization was accompanied by a fast-paced and segmented process of bureaucratic expansion, which was reinforced during the fifty-five years analyzed in this chapter. On the one hand, the quick spread of the administrative structure of the state was impressive. In the 1930s, the Ministry of Education and Public Health was created, and the first social security and pension institutes were established, allowing the state to strengthen its infrastructural capacity to cover increasingly larger socio-political arenas and territorial regions.[15]

On the other hand, the state seldom had control of the quality and direction of this quick administrative expansion. In fact, the great majority of state agencies and public jobs created during these years were permeated by clientelistic practices. Although the DASP (Departmento de Administração do Serviço Público) was created in 1938, reflecting the first attempt of the state to eliminate clientelistic practices and to modernize its administrative structure, the achievements of DASP were very limited and concentrated in very few federal agencies.[16,17] The fact that DASP was never fully successful in its

---

[12] For these reasons, the system of social policy provisions implemented by Vargas has been described by Santos (1979) as *cidadania regulada* (regulated citizenship), in reference to the fact that access to important gains that workers secured in this period – such as minimum wage, sick leaves, paid vacations, and a social security system – was conditional on having a *carteira de trabalho* (formal employment contract), effectively excluding millions of informal workers from the system. The consequences of this exclusion are examined in the chapter by Brodwyn Fischer in Chapter 15 of this volume. See also Schmitter, 1971.

[13] Reis, 1998; Cardoso, 2007: 109–118.   [14] Schmitter, 1971.   [15] Draibe, 1985.

[16] DASP was officially created by Decree-Law 579 in 1938, but its existence had already been included in the 1937 Constitution. See Gaetani, 2008: 104, for a detailed explanation of the policy process leading to the creation of DASP, especially for the key political support given by Vargas for the creation of a "super central administrative agency – a Department with ministerial status, located at the Presidency, with multiple coordinative functions such as budgeting, personnel, modernization, procurement and control."

[17] Graham, 1968; Gaetani, 2008; Geddes, 1994.

mission to impose a comprehensive civil-service reform signals a characteristic of the Brazilian state apparatus that would be reproduced until the 1980s: the coexistence of a few merit-based bureaucracies with a multiplicity of state agencies dominated by political appointees, since the state became the main source of jobs for those political groups that had lost power in the new regime.[18] The fragmentary character of the modernization of the state apparatus in Brazil was similar to that experienced by other Latin American countries, even if national combinations between autonomous and patrimonial bureaucracies varied greatly across the region (see Chapter 5, by Orihuela, in this volume).

The expansion of the state administrative machine resulted in an increase in size of the public sector, and was also decisive in the formulation and implementation of decisions at the economic level. The role of the state as a catalyst for economic growth stemmed from indirect and direct action. Indirect action involved the creation of several government agencies designed to regulate, control, and supervise many productive sectors that were considered necessary for Brazil's economic development.[19] Direct state action resulted in the creation of many national state companies, including two that would become future players in Brazil's industrial development, Companhia Siderúrgica Nacional (CSN) and Companhia Vale do Rio Doce.[20] These measures contributed significantly to the state's gradual move towards greater control of the economic decision-making process.[21]

By the end of the Vargas era, in 1945, the Brazilian state was quite different from the one that had existed in the Old Republic (1889–1930). A centralized state administrative machine had substituted the former federalist and liberal government arrangement, a corporatist system had been institutionalized, and greater control of the economy had been achieved. In short, a modern state with

---

[18] Nunes and Geddes, 1987: 81–90; Camargo, 2007.

[19] The creation of the following all date from this period: i) regulatory regimes, such as the Código de Águas (1934) that gave the state the capacity to control electricity tariffs; ii) international trade institutes and commissions, such as Instituto Nacional do Café, Conselho Nacional do Petróleo and Conselho Federal de Comércio Exterior, meant to protect the development of certain products and incipient industries from international competition; and iii) official state knowledge institutions, such as the Brazilian Institute of Geography and Statistics (IBGE) that allowed the state to implement censuses and national household surveys, and improve its infrastructural power throughout the Brazilian territory. See Abreu, 1990.

[20] Diniz, 1978.

[21] It is important to highlight that, although the state developed considerable capacity to influence the economic sphere during this period, the dominant idea was that the private sector should lead the industrialization of the country – as John Wirth has convincingly shown, even the creation of CSN was adopted as a last resource, after failed attempts to attract international or national private capital for a leading role in creating a steel-producing corporation (Wirth, 1970). Although a steady industrial growth could be observed in the 1930s, the literature tends to agree that this growth resulted from positive externalities of the federal government's monetary policies, especially in maintaining favorable exchange rates for Brazilian main export products, such as coffee (Suzigan, 1996: 5–20; and Suzigan, 1998: 5–16). A *stricto sensu* coordinated industrial policy was to be first pursued by the Brazilian state in the 1950s (see Diniz, 1978).

centralized control over the Brazilian territory and with institutionalized means of action had been established for the first time in the country's history.

However, when compared to other states in late-developing countries of that time, or to what the Brazilian state would eventually become, the state in 1945 still had very limited capabilities. Kohli points to the fact that the state formed by Vargas still had limited powers to direct Brazil's development, because it was present mainly in urban areas and failed to penetrate and incorporate the vast agrarian periphery; moreover, the state remained dependent on foreign resources and technology, and the economy was based primarily on agricultural commodities.[22] Finally, the prevalence of clientelistic practices in its administrative structure made the Brazilian state considerably different from the ideal type of advanced bureaucratic states.

Even so, if we consider historical processes of change, we should expect to identify new and old elements interacting simultaneously in the Brazilian state, especially in the initial stages of social change.[23] The Vargas era represents the beginning of the transformation of the state, as part of a continuous historical process. If we consider a "fully modern and rational" state, without any traditional traces, as an abstraction without real sociological meaning, then the focus of our analysis should be the study of the dynamics and direction that state transformation took in different periods. Hence, the choice of using the Vargas era as the starting point (or critical juncture) of a period when the state was the main modernizing agent is justified by the fact that political actors, in later periods, used the institutional foundations created by Vargas to shape their own strategies, designed to reinforce the preference of state authority over market or societal mechanisms.

The historical importance of the institutions created in 1930 lies in the role they played in shaping the economic and political development of Brazil in the process of modernization from above.[24] The permanence of these institutions, even in the face of major political and social change, is a testimony to their resistance and flexibility. I will now consider how these dynamics proceeded in the democratic period between 1946 and 1964.

RETURN TO DEMOCRACY AND CONTINUITY OF STATE LEADERSHIP: 1945–1964

In 1945, Vargas was overthrown by the military, and democracy was reestablished in Brazil. However, contrary to what one would expect, the state, as institutionalized during the Vargas era, was not dismantled with the return of a democratic regime. On the contrary, the role of state authority as the leading agent of national modernization was reinforced, even if different mechanisms were adopted, and the main institutions and legislation from the

---

[22] Kohli, 2005.   [23] Bendix, 2007; Mahoney, 2000: 507–548.
[24] Sola, 1998; Boschi, 2010: 1–34.

previous period were left untouched. The only real change was that certain Estado Novo measures, limiting civil rights, were eliminated.[25]

In terms of the political arrangement, it was the maintenance of the corporatist structure that guaranteed the continuity of state leadership, and thus there was a high level of state control over social and political groups, even with the return to democracy. To this end, the fact that the Constitution of 1946 did not eliminate the federal government's right to intervene in labor unions, and did not regulate a labor strike legislation, were key instruments for the state to maintain its autonomy and dominance over economic and political decision-making processes in the same way that it had done during the Vargas era.[26] More problematic for the implementation of a pluralistic system of representation, however, was the fact that the corporatist structure continued to serve as the basis for any new political parties created, thus eliminating any chance of establishing a strong parliamentary system.[27] Finally, the clearly populist character of the new regime, which concentrated power in the office and figure of the president, allowed the state to continue to act as the main agent of social control and centralized power, limiting the independent political participation of a number of political actors in the process of national modernization.[28]

Similarly, in the administrative sphere, the proliferation of government agencies subordinated directly to the Executive, together with the process of bureaucratic insulation of key state agencies, allowed the central government to maintain a sufficient level of autonomy in the economic decision-making process so as to avoid the possible pitfalls and delays associated with democratic decision-making.[29] However, this process was accompanied by a steady expansion of the state machine at the municipal and state levels, resulting in the creation of agencies with overlapping jurisdictions and interests, that served mainly to consolidate a pattern initiated in the Vargas period in which public authority became the major employer outside of the agrarian sector, favoring the state's co-optation of social interests.[30] The fact that recruitment to these state agencies was seldom based on merit or technical expertise also helped to institutionalize clientelistic practices in the public sector that would prove extremely resistant to change.[31]

---

[25] Nunes, 1997; Diniz, 1978; Diniz and Boschi, 2004.   [26] Oliveira, 1973; Vianna, 1978.

[27] Members and resources for the creation of the three main political parties in 1945 came mostly from the corporatist system implemented by the Vargas regime. First, and most obviously, the PTB (Partido Trabalhista Brasileiro) was derived from Vargas' syndical base and state apparatus, recruiting former members from the Ministry of Labor, which helped to institutionalize populist control over workers' representation. Secondly, the PSD (Partido Social Democrático) was composed mostly of state and municipal *interventores* – state officers who had been appointed by Vargas to control state and local opposition to the new regime in the 1930s. Finally, the UDN (União Democratica Nacional) came from a different political base than Vargas' political machine, and would theoretically represent opposition interests, but proved to adopt practices as clientelistic and patrimonial as the other two parties. See Nunes and Geddes, 1987, and Campello de Souza, 1990.

[28] Weffort, 2003.   [29] Nunes, 1997.   [30] Draibe, 1985; Pessoa, 2010.

[31] Nunes and Geddes, 1987.

It is important to note that the main mechanism used to guarantee bureaucratic insulation in this period was the creation of state agencies directly subordinated to the Federal Executive, such as the Technical Councils in Vargas' second government (Assessorias Técnicas, 1951–1954) and the Executive Groups and Council for Development under Juscelino Kubitschek (Grupos Executivos e Conselho do Desenvolvimento, 1956–1961). Even if these insulated agencies were never fully shielded from particularistic and partisan pressures to be characterized as completely "autonomous,"[32] and even if their achievements were characterized by major discontinuities, to a surprising degree they were able to promote several successful developmental projects.[33]

It is worth highlighting that insulated agencies in Brazil were not at all like *independent agencies* in the United States, because American independent agencies are public organizations defined, precisely, for being "insulated from presidential control in one or more ways."[34] The flagship developmental agency in the United States, the Tennessee Valley Authority (TVA), was an independent agency in this sense; its decisions could not be manipulated either by the president or by Congress.[35] In Latin America, the institutional design of the TVA was only followed consistently by the national developmental agency CORFO in Chile (see Chapter 5 and Chapter 12 in this volume). In Brazil, developmental agencies did achieve a high degree of autonomy from Congress, but were always politically subordinated to the Federal Executive Power.[36]

The intermittent, relative success in formulating and implementing economic policies by insulated agencies in Brazil happened in spite of both multiple instances of direct political intervention from the Executive, and their permeability to some industrial groups' interests.[37] And even when these agencies achieved a high level of insulation, it did not mean that politics was excluded from the policymaking process. The fact that insulated agencies

---

[32] Schneider, 2000: 276–305; Schneider, 1991.

[33] According to Geddes, 1994: 67–68 and Appendix A, during the *Plano de Metas* in Kubistchek years (1956–1961), insulated agencies achieved 102 percent of targeted goals involving direct production with BNDES funding (such as installed electrical capacity, petroleum production, refining capacity, and production of chemical fertilizers, steel, alkalis, and synthetic rubber), while funding and subsidies distributed by traditional, uninsulated agencies achieved only 60 percent of their targeted goals, even when they had considerably lower targets as compared to insulated agencies.

[34] Davis and Pierce, 1994: 46; see also the Conclusion by Ferraro and Centeno in this volume.

[35] Hargrove, 1994.

[36] Diniz and Lima, 1986 provide data that corroborates the literature that emphasizes the success of the strategy of bureaucratic insulation from Congress to guarantee state-led development in Brazil. These authors show that between 1946 and 1963, the Brazilian Congress presented a higher number of bills compared to the Executive. However, the Executive had much higher approval rates for its proposed bills, especially its economic bills, while the Congress saw a sharp decline of approval for economic bills in this period.

[37] Nunes and Geddes, 1987.

differed in their specific economic ideology and expertise, and that there were often diverse economic orientations inside the same agencies, meant that it was mostly inside such agencies that the majority of political and economic battles regarding the future direction of the country happened during this historical phase.[38]

During the democratic period 1945–1964, the contours of a strong developmental state could already be observed, resulting from the maturity of the institutional foundation created in the 1930s, and direct intervention of the state in the economy increased significantly.[39] Throughout the 1950s, many state enterprises were created in a number of infrastructure areas to avoid possible bottlenecks in Brazil's industrialization process (including petroleum, electricity, public transportation, and telecommunications, with big players such as Petrobrás, Furnas, and Eletrobrás), giving the federal government experience in organizing massive, technologically difficult projects – a know-how that would improve state capacities in future years. The Brazilian National Development Bank (BNDE) was established in 1952 to provide financial support for these new state enterprises, and to fund the development of national private companies. This process allowed the state to control and influence the majority of long-term credit to industry, and it also secured the state with resources to finance its own public investments.[40] These diverse initiatives gave the state a powerful lever with which to shape and direct the process of capital accumulation.

It is important to stress that the nationalist ideology, and the increase in the state's general involvement in the economy during this period, did not mean that international capital and private companies were excluded from the developmental project. On the contrary, the industrialization model was based on import substitution (ISI) and aimed to encourage the growth of private national firms, initially in the non-durable consumption-goods sector, but then in durable goods too. Nevertheless, the model was dependent on international capital to finance the necessary investments and import the essential technologies.[41] This interaction between state, local capital, and multinationals – the Triple Alliance – although fundamental for rapid industrial and economic growth, was also responsible for the high inflation and the balance-of-payment difficulties that characterized this period.[42]

The implementation of economic planning and price-control policies also enabled the state to maintain its leadership during this period and was key to securing the success of the ISI model of development by artificially maintaining national products' competitiveness.[43] A number of ambitious development projects (President Kubitschek's *Plano de Metas* in particular) were

---

[38] Sola, 1998; Diniz, 1978.   [39] Evans, 1995; Schneider, 2000.

[40] Baer, Kerstenetzky, and Villela, 1973: 23–34; Giambiagi, Villela, de Castro, and Hermann, 2005.

[41] Evans, 1979; Schneider, 2000.   [42] Kohli, 2005.   [43] Abreu, 1990.

significant, because they allowed the state to choose the sectors that were key for Brazil's industrial growth and to invest heavily in them, employing for this purpose the increasing state capacities consolidated since the 1930s.[44]

Moreover, by the late 1940s, the state began to expand its scope of action and influence beyond the South–Central regions, and to take its modernizing project to remote regions of the country.[45] Several regional development agencies were created, beginning with CVSF (Comissão do Vale do São Francisco) in 1948, and continuing with others such as SPVEA (Superintendência do Plano de Valorização Econômica da Amazônia) in 1953, and SUDENE (Superintendência do Desenvolvimento do Nordeste) in 1959. Some of these state agencies, the CVSF in particular, had their organizational design, as well as the blueprints for their first development projects, carefully modeled after the successful experience of the Tennessee Valley Authority (TVA) in the United States.[46] Nevertheless, these agencies tended to have much more ambitious scopes than the TVA model. As Hirschman was to remark a few years later, the designers of CVSF, for example, claimed that this institution had to be "more multi-purposeful than the TVA; since large stretches of the São Francisco Valley lacked roads, schools, health facilities, agricultural credit, industry, and even people, they felt that their project should cover all these facets."[47]

Finally, the transfer of the national capital from Rio de Janeiro to Brasilia in 1960 – with its huge constructions, population displacement, and visual communication strategies – was also a strong symbolic commitment of the state to be present throughout the national territory, and it can be read as an attempt of the state to demonstrate its newly acquired capacities and developmental ambitions. Yet, these great ambitions were never fully materialized, and the North and Northeast regions of the country did not benefit extensively from the more inclusive developmental plans from this period.

In sum, during the period of democracy, 1945–1964, the process of modernization from above was continued and extended. In the span of these twenty years, Brazil underwent impressive structural transformations, almost doubling its population from 47 million in 1946 to 78 million in 1964, while keeping an average GDP growth of 6.9 percent and an industrial growth rate of 9.1 percent.[48] The development process remained state-centered, however, and other social and market forces did not play a significant role in defining the goals of the country's development project. To a great extent, the state-led developmental model was not essentially changed by the democratic regime

---

[44] Suzigan, 1998: 5–16; Vianna and Villela, 2005.   [45] Cohn, 1978.

[46] Less than a year after the creation of CVSF, during his official visit to the United States in May of 1949, President Enrico Dutra made an inspection tour of the Tennessee Valley, and of TVA's regional development initiatives. (See TVA Technical Library, 1952.)

[47] Hirschman, 1971: 53. See also Furtado, 2009.   [48] Abreu, 1990.

due to (i) the maintenance of the corporatist political structure, (ii) the segmented process of bureaucratic development combining insulation of key economic state agencies with an expanding clientelistic administrative machine, and (iii) the increase in state interventionism in the economic arena. These mechanisms of continuity were based on the institutional foundations created during the Vargas era and were used by political actors to reinforce their preference for state leadership vis-à-vis other market and societal forces. As we will see in the next section, the same institutional scheme at first strengthened, but then undermined the capacity of the state to lead the economic modernization of the country during the military dictatorship.

MILITARY PERIOD (1964–1985): FROM STRENGTHENING TO BREAKDOWN OF THE DEVELOPMENT MODEL

In 1964, a military dictatorship was established in Brazil. For the first time in the country's history, the armed forces took direct control of all state functions, and suppressed most civil and political rights. During this period, the strategy of maintaining high economic growth rates was used to legitimize the regime, while civil and military bureaucracies were given the responsibility for implementing development programs. Moreover, the normative and entrepreneurial roles of the state were expanded, and there were attempts to increase the state's capacity to raise revenues, and further centralize decision-making.[49]

During the military period, the process of modernization from above, initiated during the Vargas era, reached its peak, and then collapsed. The processes of political and administrative centralization and state interventionism continued to develop, resulting in a high degree of institutional continuity. As in previous periods, enormous power was concentrated in the Executive (with the difference that competitive politics had now been completely eliminated) and the corporatist structure continued to serve the purpose of maintaining state control over urban groups, and of eliminating any form of voluntary organization that might constitute an independent political force.[50]

For the twenty years of the military regime, business associations continued to enjoy access to decision-making structures of the state, mainly through Economic Councils, but they also faced periods when business elites were excluded from formal and informal instances of consultations with the military government.[51] Labor relations, on the other hand, continued to be governed by the Labor Code of 1943, and to benefit from public jobs available through the corporatist structure, but with the important difference that Labor Code provisions and legislation were expanded to include rural workers.[52]

---

[49] Collier, 1982; Martins, 1988.   [50] Diniz and Lima, 1986.
[51] Diniz and Boschi, 2003; Leopoldi, 2000.   [52] Skidmore, 1973: 3–46.

In the administrative and economic spheres, the network of state corporations and regulatory agencies, created by Vargas and expanded during the democratic period, remained firmly in place and bureaucratic insulation of a few key state agencies was reinforced, with highly qualified civilian staff working closely with the military in defining policies. These measures, together with an exponential expansion of the public sector and the state administrative machine, allowed the state to direct all major economic and social activities.

During the military dictatorship, the number of state firms expanded massively through two distinct mechanisms.[53] First, state-owned enterprises created in the 1940s, which had now reached a high level of maturity, were diversified through the creation of holding companies and subsidiaries, like Siderbrás, Eletrobrás, Petroquisa, and Braspetro, among others, which had national and international production and operations. Some of the key state companies were able to gain positions in international markets: one of the most successful cases, Petrobrás, was considered in 1970 one of the 100 largest companies in the world, and the largest in Latin America. Other state companies like Companhia Vale do Rio Doce (CVRD) and CSN developed sophisticated production lines and expanded their economic reach within the country.[54]

Secondly, many firms were created in productive sectors in which the state was still not present, but which were considered important for the purposes of rapid industrialization. The numbers are remarkable: by 1965 there were only forty state companies. Between 1966 and 1975, 231 new state companies were created, of which 175 were designed to provide public services such as electricity, communications, and transportation, and 42 were heavy-industry firms, mostly in the metallurgical and petrochemical sectors, which allowed the state to reach the final stage of the ISI model, and to guide investments towards the export of national production.[55]

Similar to previous periods, the process of state expansion continued without the elimination of overlapping state structures and clientelistic practices, especially at the municipal and state levels.[56] The increase in public jobs that accompanied the expansion of the state structure was very high: while in 1950 there were 1.1 million civil servants in Brazil, in 1970 there were 2.7 million, and in 1980, 4.3 million.[57] By the 1970s, furthermore, these workers were also differently distributed in Brazil's federative structure: while in 1950, 50 percent of civil servants were employed at the federal level, in 1973, only 35 percent worked at this level, while 45 percent were employed at state level, and 20 percent at the municipal level.[58]

Likewise, the state had direct control of the agencies that were considered fundamental to support economic modernization, but at this point the state had

[53] Evans, 1979.   [54] Baer, Kerstenetzky, and Villela, 1973.
[55] Giambiagi, Villela, De Castro, Lavinia, and Hermann, 2005; Martins, 1985.
[56] Pessoa, 2010.   [57] Sanson and Moutinho, 1987: 43–45.   [58] Pessoa, 2010.

little control over the expansion of the complex mix of state companies and autarchic public entities, which had considerable financial autonomy to direct their own investments.[59] Naturally, this amalgamated state structure made the federal government's planning and coordination efforts increasingly harder to achieve.[60]

The strategic aim of the military was to increase the planning and coordination capacity of the state by means of political and economic centralization, and to accomplish this goal a greater role was given to state companies. The same objective was also pursued through a proliferation of price controls, and comprehensive financial, administrative and fiscal reforms (between 1964 and 1967) that would help provide the state with resources for investment and lending, and facilitate the state's access to the international capital market.[61,62] For this purpose, central financial institutions were created in this period, such as Brazil's Central Bank, which was responsible for implementing monetary policies, and the National Monetary Council (Conselho Monetário Nacional), which had a regulatory role.

The conjunction of these economic and political measures, together with a favorable global economic climate, resulted in Brazil experiencing, between 1968 and 1973, a period called the "economic miracle" – an allusion to a combination of high growth rates (an average annual growth rate of 11.1 percent of GDP in real terms), declining inflation, and overall surpluses on the balance of payments.[63] However, the maintenance of this high-growth-rate strategy depended on the capacity of state agencies to borrow, and thus on the availability of foreign credit and favorable international trade and market conditions. Therefore, the strategy of high growth was seriously hit by the first global oil crisis of 1973, which caused an abrupt increase in international interest rates and a contraction in the global economy. Since the Brazilian state was increasing its dependency on oil imports since the late 1960s to

---

[59] Throughout the 1950s and 1960s, state companies and autarchic public entities had the capacity to self-finance their activities and were sources of revenue surplus for the federal government. However, starting in the 1970s, many state enterprises increasingly depended on international borrowing to finance their expansion, and saw their operations costs increase dramatically. By 1979, with changes in international interest rates and devaluation of Brazilian currency, most state enterprises were not sources of revenue for the federal government anymore, and had accumulated very large debts. See Baer, 2001: 111.

[60] Martins, 1985.

[61] In the initial years of the military regime, reforms that fundamentally changed the governance structure of the state were implemented, and allowed the state to heavily invest in its development project. Among the most important were changes in Brazil's tax legislation that allowed the state to increase tax collection from 17 percent of GDP in 1963 to 26.5 percent of GDP by 1985; and the Public Management Reform of 1967, especially Law-Decree 200/67 that set up a dual administrative structure – direct and indirect – allowing the direct administration to focus exclusively on the planning and budgeting of economic modernization projects (see Giambiagi, Villela, De Castro, Lavinia, and Hermann, 2005; Gaetani, 2008).

[62] Hermann, 2005.   [63] Bacha and Malan, 1989: 120–140.

secure the industrialization of the country – oil imports represented 59 per cent of national consumption in 1968, and had reached 81 per cent by 1973 – the federal government's indebtedness increased greatly in the period.[64]

Despite the worsening international economic scenario, there was no attempt by the military government to make any structural reforms or to revise growth targets downward. On the contrary, a new economic plan was launched in 1974 (the II PND), signaling that the state had decided not only to continue with a debt-led growth strategy, but to intensify the program of import-substitution industrialization with respect to capital goods and raw materials. In fact, the most ambitious developmental projects started after the 1973 oil crisis, such as the hydroelectric dams of Itaipu and Tucuruí, the Carajás Mine Project, the Ethanol Fuel Program (Proálcool), and the Brazilian Nuclear Program, among others. Although this strategy was successful in reducing the country's dependency on imports for certain production branches, it resulted in increased vulnerability to external shocks. After another upsurge in oil prices in 1979, the strategy of modernization from above finally became unsustainable.

The military government's decision to keep pursuing the same developmental strategies, even if this meant that the state had to bear almost all of the costs by itself, is a good illustration of the belief that the state should (and could) deal with any market disequilibriums, and an acknowledgment of the principle that it was the state's role to guarantee the economic welfare of different political and economic interests, even if this meant incurring extraordinary indebtedness.[65] For decades, the Brazilian state had adopted policies designed to minimize possible sources of political conflict, by means of the tryad consisting of the corporatist system, the expansion of public employment, and bureaucratic insulation. When the Brazilian economy almost collapsed in the late 1970s, market and society actors expected the state to deal with the economic crisis, as it had done in previous periods.[66] When the state was incapable of doing so, the political alliance that supported the military regime started to show signs of fatigue, especially concerning local industrialists and business associations that began to associate themselves with the democratic forces.[67]

By the beginning of the 1980s, there was a complete breakdown in the developmental model first adopted in 1930, a model which had incorporated both change and the preservation of the old order by promoting industrialization while, at the same time, protecting rural interests. This collapse was a result of the state strategy of trying to both please multiple political interests and maintain high growth rates. Related to this point, the

---

[64] Carneiro, 1990.
[65] In 1980, the public sector was responsible for 80 percent of the Brazilian debt, whereas, in 1974, this value had been only 50 percent. For explanations of mechanisms that made the state take over an important part of the private indebtedness in Brazil, see Werneck, 1986: 551–574, and Bacha and Malan, 1989.
[66] Sallum and Kugelmas, 1993.   [67] Bresser-Pereira, 1978.

segmented character of Brazil's bureaucratic expansion, that combined an ever-increasing offer of public jobs with partisan and particularistic practices, meant that the costs of maintaining the spoils-system escalated rapidly. Such policies provoked a deep financial and fiscal crisis that progressively reduced the state's abilities to direct and coordinate Brazil's development in the way that it had been doing (or attempting to do) since the Vargas era.[68] This economic fragility, together with an increase in the number of popular protests for a more democratic political arrangement, resulted in the state losing its control over national development.

Kohli points to the fact that the choice of continuing with the debt-led growth model needs to be analyzed in the context of the mixed character of the Brazilian state – "developmental, yet limited" – which constrained the choices available for political actors.[69] When viewed from this standpoint, the state's failure to limit external dependence was the result of the state's historical incapacity to say no to various powerful groups when it came to limiting expenditures, and also to the fact that modernization from above was justified by its success as an economic strategy.[70] The incapacity to limit public expenditures, furthermore, cannot be disassociated from the rapid expansion of the administrative machine, both through corporatist and clientelistic means, which had created public jobs for a considerable share of the Brazilian population.[71]

If we consider the contradictory way in which modernization from above came about in Brazil, it becomes clear that the very same factors that contributed to the success of the developmental model were also responsible for its demise. The state created by Vargas and reproduced until the 1980s attempted to pursue a national development strategy, but this strategy was from the beginning highly dependent on international capital and markets, and it did not stimulate the creation of a strong internal market for Brazilian products, being therefore extremely vulnerable to external shocks.[72] The promotion of economic modernization created new social groups (with new demands) that only had access to state structures through the corporatist system – a system that by the late 1970s was incapable of accommodating multiple, diverse interests into the state structure. Finally, the overarching design of economic planning implemented by a few insulated agencies, that coexisted with a multitude of juxtaposing agencies, did implement successful economic projects, but it was extremely inefficient and imposed a serious financial burden to the state.[73] The state was able to maintain the national development strategy while growth rates were high, but when the economy and society became more complex and the global economic scenario worsened, the process of modernization from above broke down. The institutional basis of the state's development strategy was too fragmentary and contradictory, and it could not be sustained as before.

---

[68] Sola, 1993.   [69] Kohli, 2005: 216.   [70] Reis, 1998.   [71] Pessoa, 2010.   [72] Evans, 1979.
[73] Sola,1993; Sola and Paulani, 1995; Nunes, 1997.

CONCLUDING REMARKS

The debt crisis of the 1980s has been described as "the most traumatic economic event in Latin America's economic history".[74] This characterization refers to the fact that the region's per capita GDP fell dramatically in the 1980s, and many countries faced hard years of hyperinflation and capital flight, which led many of them to default on their sovereign debt. Regarding the policies adopted in those years, the "lost decade" is also associated with the implementation of far-reaching structural reforms, economic stagnation, and the adoption of harsh austerity measures. The trauma, moreover, relates to the displacement of Latin America as the "child prodigy" of foreign investors, being substituted by countries such as South Korea, Singapore, Taiwan, and Hong Kong – the Asian Tigers.

In a sense, the academic literature has also dismissed Latin America's developmental states as a "child prodigy," and placed them more as "average": not successful enough like the Southeast Asian cases to attract all the positive attention, but also not complete failures which would demand correctional devotion, such as some predatorial states in Africa. Latin America is usually placed in between, and is constantly compared to the successes of its Asian counterparts. Hence, Latin America is usually portrayed as a "mixed" or "hybrid" case, since many countries in the region have achieved a considerable level of industrialization since the 1930s, but they are still dependent on the agroexport sector; or because the region does have examples of insulated bureaucracies, but they usually interact with a vast administrative structure that is still dominated by clientelistic practices.[75] However, it is still not clear if this characterization as "mixed," "limited," or "incomplete" has helped to advance our understanding of the developmental period in Latin America, or helped us to appreciate the future possibilities and challenges for states in the region.

In this chapter, I discussed the main political, administrative, and economic factors that made possible the creation of a developmental state in Brazil, which was supported by the understanding that only the state could be the architect of economic modernization. From a macro-historical perspective, I argued that the corporatist structure, the coexistence of insulated bureaucracies with an expanding public administration, and the creation of solid institutionalized means of intervention in the economy allowed the state to lead the socioeconomic development of Brazil for fifty-five years. I explored, moreover, how these institutional characteristics also help to explain the collapse of the developmental model in the 1980s, once Brazilian society and its economy became more complex, and once the international scenario changed.

Interpretations of success and failure of socio-political projects will always depend, to a considerable extent, on intellectual concerns as well as on the basic theoretical framework employed by the analyst. In this chapter, I was less

[74] Ocampo, 2014: 87–115.   [75] Evans, 1979; Kohli, 2005.

worried about finding a definite answer to the question of whether the Brazilian state was successful or not, and more concerned with proposing a possible institutional logic that could help us to understand fifty-five years of many achievements and failures of the developmental project in Brazil.

Yet, I wonder to what extent this institutional lens has led me to tell a story of an *imperfect* success of the developmental state in Brazil. On the success side, the institutional foundations implemented during the Vargas era proved to be extremely flexible and resistant to the many economic and political transformations that the country underwent between 1930 and 1985, and they also made the active recreation of modernization from above possible. However, and following an extense literature about this period, I have argued that these same institutions were very limited since their inception, especially in their political capacity to reconcile diverse sectorial interests. This is mostly because throughout the developmental period, the state, concerned in the first instance with economic stability and growth, sacrificed administrative and bureaucratic efficiency to attenuate political conflicts between different societal groups. The same state also sacrificed a more inclusive and politically democratic developmental model, both in social and regional terms, for the same reason. In this sense, the institutional foundations of the Brazilian developmental state were successful in great part because they served the strategic purpose of continuously accommodating diverse political and economic interests into the state. However, the feature that allowed the Brazilian developmental state to achieve a considerable level of success also made it extremely inefficient, undemocratic and not sustainable in the long run.

REFERENCES

Abreu, Marcelo. *A ordem do progresso – Cem anos de política econômica republicana 1889–1989.* São Paulo: Editora Campus, 1990.
Almeida, Maria Hermínia. "O corporativismo em declínio?" In *Anos 90 – Política e Sociedade no Brasil*, ed. Evalina Dagnino, São Paulo: Editora Brasiliense, 1994: 51–57.
Bacha, Edmar and Pedro Malan. "Brazil's Debt: From the Miracle to the Fund." In *Democratizing Brazil: Problems of Transition and Consolidation*, ed. Alfred Stepan. New York: Oxford University Press, 1989: 120–140.
Baer, Werner. *The Brazilian Economy: Growth and Development.* Westport, CT: Praeger Publishers, 2001.
Baer, Werner, Isaac Kerstenetzky, and Annibal Villela. "The Changing Role of the State in the Brazilian Economy." *World Development* 1, 11, 1973: 23–34.
Boschi, Renato. "Estado Desenvolvimentista no Brasil: Continuidades e Incertidumbres." *Ponto de Vista* 2, 2010: 1–34.
Boschi, Renato and Maria Regina Lima. "O Executivo e a construção do Estado no Brasil – do desmonte da Era Vargas ao novo intervencionismo regulatório." In *A Democracia e os Três Poderes no Brasil*, ed. Luiz Werneck Viana. Belo Horizonte: Editora UFMG, 2002.

Bresser-Pereira, Luiz Carlos. *O Colapso de uma Aliança de Classes.* São Paulo: Editora Brasiliense, 1978.

Camargo, Aspásia. "A Revolução das Elites: Conflitos Regionais e Centralização Política." In CPDOC, *A Revolução de 30 – Seminário Internacional.* Brasília: Editora Universidade de Brasília, 1982.

Campello de Souza, Maria do Carmo. *Estado e Partidos Políticos no Brasil (1930–1964).* São Paulo: Editora Alfa-Omega, 1990.

Cardoso, Adalberto. "Estado Novo e Corporativismo." *Locus: Revista de Historia* 13, 2 2007: 109–118.

Carneiro, Dionísio Dias. "Crise e Esperança: 1974–1980." In *A ordem do progresso – Cem anos de política econômica republicana 1889–1989,* ed. Marcelo Abreu. São Paulo: Editora Campus, 1990.

Cohn, Amélia. *Crise Regional e Planejamento – O Processo de Criação da SUDENE.* São Paulo: Editora Perspectivas, 1978.

Collier, David, ed. *O Novo Autoritarismo na América Latina.* Rio de Janeiro: Editora Paz e Terra, 1982.

CPDOC, ed. *A Revolução de 30 – Seminário Internacional.* Brasília: Editora Universidade de Brasília, 1982.

Davis, Kenneth Culp and Richard Pierce. *Administrative Law Treatise. Vol. 1.* Boston: Little Brown, 1994.

Diniz, Eli. *Empresário, Estado e Capitalismo no Brasil: 1930–1945.* Rio de Janeiro: Editora Paz e Terra, 1978.

Globalização, Estado e Desenvolvimento – Dilemas do Brasil no novo milênio. Rio de Janeiro: FGV Editora, 2004.

Diniz, Eli and Renato Boschi. *Empresários, Interesses e Mercado – Dilemas do desenvolvimento no Brasil.* Belo Horizonte: Editora UFMG, 2004.

"Empresariado e Estratégias de Desenvolvimento." *Revista Brasileira de Ciências Sociais* 18,2003: 15–33.

Diniz, Eli and Olavo Brasil Lima. *Modernização Autoritária: o Empresariado e a Intervenção do Estado na Economia.* Brasília: Convênio IPEA/CEPAL, 1986.

Draibe, Sonia. *Rumos e Metamorfoses: um estudo sobre a constituição do Estado e as alternativas da industrialização no Brasil (1930–1960).* Rio de Janeiro: Editora Paz e Terra, 1985.

Evans, Peter. *Dependent Development: The Alliance of Multinational, State and Local Capital in Brazil.* Princeton, NJ: Princeton University Press, 1979.

Embedded Autonomy: States and Industrial Transformation. Princeton University Press, 1995.

Gaetani, Francisco. "Constitutional Public Management Reforms in Modern Brazil." PhD thesis, London School of Economics and Political Science (LSE), 2008.

Geddes, Barbara. *Politician's Dilemma: Building State-Capacity in Latin America.* University of California Press, 1994.

Giambiagi, Fabio, André Villela, Barros De Castro, Lena Lavinia, and Jennifer Hermann, eds. *Economia Brasileira Contemporânea (1945–2004).* Rio de Janeiro: Editora Campus, 2005.

Graham, Lawrence. *Civil Service Reform in Brazil: Principles versus Practice.* Austin: University of Texas Press, 1968.

Hargrove, Erwin C. *Prisoners of Myth. The Leadership of the Tennessee Valley Authority 1933–1990.* Princeton University Press, 1994.

Hermann, Jennifer. "Reformas, Endividamento Externo e o Milagre Econômico (1964–1973)." In *Economia Brasileira Contemporânea (1945–2004)*, eds. Fabio Giambiagi, André Villela, Lavinia Barros de Castro, and Jennifer Hermann. Rio de Janeiro: Editora Campus, 2005.

Hirschman, Albert O. *Journeys Toward Progress. Studies of Economic Policy-Making in Latin America*. 1963. Reprint, Westport: Greenwood Press, 1971.

Kohli, Atul. *State-Directed Development – Political Power and Industrialization in the Global Periphery*. Cambridge University Press, 2005.

Leopoldi, Maria Antonieta. *Política e Interesses na Industrialização Brasileira: As Associações Industriais, Política Econômica e o Estado*. São Paulo: Paz e Terra, 2000.

Mahoney, James. "Path Dependence in Historical Sociology," *Theory and Society* 29, 4, 2000: 507–548.

Martins, Luciano. "A 'liberalização' do regime autoritário no Brasil." In *Transições do Regime Autoritário – América Latina*, eds. Guillermo O'Donnell, Phillipe Schmitter, and Laurance Whitehead. São Paulo: Vértice, 1988.

Estado Capitalista e Burocracia no Brasil pós-64. Rio de Janeiro: Paz e Terra, 1985.

Nunes, Edson. *A Gramática Política do Brasil – clientelismo e insulamento burocrático*. Rio de Janeiro: Jorge Zahar Editor, 1997.

Nunes, Edson and Barbara Geddes. "Dilemmas of State-Led Modernization in Brazil." In *State and Society in Brazil: Continuity and Change*, eds. John D. Wirth, Edson de Oliveira Nunes, and Thomas E. Bogenschild. Boulder: Westview Press, 1987.

Ocampo, José Antonio. "The Latin American Debt Crisis in Historical Perspective." In *Life After Debt*, eds. Joseph Stiglitz and Daniel Heymann.Palgrave Macmillan: London, 2014: 87–115.

Oliveira, Lucia. "O Partido Social Democrático." PhD thesis, Instituto Universitário de Pesquisa do Estado do Rio de Janeiro (IUPERJ), 1973.

Pessoa, Eneuton. "O aparelho administrativo brasileiro: sua gestão e seus servidores – de 1930 aos dias atuais." In *Estado, Instituições e Democracia*, eds. Alexandre dos Santos Cunha, Bernardo Abreu de Medeiros, and Luseni Aquino. Brasília: Ipea, 2010.

Reis, Elisa."The Agrarian Roots of Authoritarian Modernization in Brazil: 1880–1930." PhD thesis, Massachusetts Institute of Technology, 1979.

Processos e Escolhas – Estudos de Sociologia Política. Rio de Janeiro: ContraCapa, 1998.

"O Estado Nacional como desafio teórico e empírico para a sociologia política contemporânea." In *O sociólogo e as políticas públicas*, eds. Felipe Schwartzman, Isabel Schwartzman, Luisa Schwartzman, and Michel Schwartzman. Rio de Janeiro: FGV Editora, 2009.

Sanson, João and Lucia Moutinho. "A evolução do emprego público no Brasil: 1950–80". *Ensaios FEE* 8, 2, 1987: 31–48.

Santos, Wanderley Guilherme. *Cidadania e Justiça – A Polítical Social na Ordem Brasileira*. Rio de Janeiro: Editora Campus, 1979.

Sallum Jr., Brasílio. "Transição Política e Crise do Estado." In *Lições da década de 80*, eds. Lourdes Sola and Lena Paulani. São Paulo: Edusp, 1995.

Sallum Jr., Brasílio and Eduardo Kugelmas. 1993. "O Leviatã acorrentado: a crise brasileira dos anos 80." *Estado, Mercado e Democracia – Política e economia comparadas*, eds. Lourdes Sola. São Paulo: Paz e Terra, 1993.

Schmitter, Philippe. "Still the Century of Corporatism?" *The Review of Politics* 36, 1, 1974: 85–131.

Schmitter, Philippe. *Interest Conflict and Political Change in Brazil.* California: Stanford University Press, 1971.

Schneider, Ben. *Politics Within the State: Elite Bureaucrats and Industrial Policy in Authoritarian Brazil.* Pittsburgh: University of Pittsburgh Press, 1991.

"The Desarrollista State in Brazil and Mexico." In *The Developmental State,* ed. Meredith Woo-Cumings. Ithaca: Cornell University Press, 2000: 276–305.

"O Estado Desenvolvimentista no Brasil: perspectivas históricas e comparadas." In *Capacidades Estatais e Democracia – Arranjos Institucionais de Políticas Públicas,* eds. Alexandre Gomide and Roberto Pires. Brasília: Editora Ipea, 2014: 32–56.

Schwartzman, Simon. *Bases do Autoritarismo Brasileiro.* Rio de Janeiro: Editora Campus, 1982.

Skidmore, Thomas. "Politics and Economic Policy Making in Authoritarian Brazil 1937–1971." In *Authoritarian Brazil: Origins, Policies and Future,* ed. by Alfred Stepan. New Haven: Yale University, 1973: 3–46.

Sola, Lourdes. *Estado, Mercado e Democracia – Política e economia comparadas.* São Paulo: Paz e Terra, 1993.

Ideias econômicas, decisões políticas. São Paulo: Edusp, 1998.

Sola, Lourdes and Paulani, Lena. *Lições da década de 80.* São Paulo: Edusp, 1995.

Stepan, Alfred. *Authoritarian Brazil: Origins, Policies and Future.* New Haven: Yale University Press, 1973.

Democratizing Brazil: Problems of Transition and Consolidation. New York: Oxford University Press, 1989.

Streeck, Wolfgang and Thelen, Kathleen. *Beyond Continuity – Institutional Change in Advanced Political Economies.* Oxford University Press, 2005.

Suzigan, Wilson. "A experiência histórica da política industrial no Brasil." *Revista de Economia Política* 16, 1, 1996: 5–20.

"Estado e industrialização no Brasil." *Revista de Economia Política,* 8, 4, 1998: 5–16.

TVA Technical Library. *TVA As a Symbol of Resource Development in Many Countries.* Knoxville: TVA, 1952.

Vianna, Luiz Werneck. *Liberalismo e Sindicato no Brasil.* Rio de Janeiro: Editora Paz e Terra, 1978.

A Democracia e os Três Poderes no Brasil. Belo Horizonte: Editora UFMG, 2002.

Vianna, Sérgio and André Villela. "O pós-guerra (1945–1955)." In *Economia Brasileira Contemporânea (1945–2004),* eds. Fabio Giambiagi, André Villela, Lavinia Barros de Castro, and Jennifer Hermann. Rio de Janeiro: Editora Campus, 2005.

Werneck, Rogério. "Poupança estatal, divida externa e crise financeira do setor público." *Pesquisa e Planejamento Econômico* 16, 1986: 551–574.

"Public Sector Adjustment to External Shocks and Domestic Pressures in Brazil, 1970–85." Working Paper 163, Economics Department, Puc-Rio, 1987.

Weffort, Francisco. *O populismo na política brasileira.* Rio de Janeiro: Editora Paz e Terra, 2003.

Wirth, John. *The Politics of Brazilian Development 1930–1954,* Stanford University Press, 1970.

8

Life is a Dream: Bureaucracy and Industrial Development in Spain, 1950–1990

Agustin E. Ferraro and Juan José Rastrollo

INTRODUCTION

The publication of "Bureaucracy and Growth" by Evans and Rauch marked a milestone in the field of studies on economic development.[1] In the paper, the authors present the design and application of an empirical-statistical test for one of Max Weber's major theoretical propositions in economics and sociology. The proposition, which Evans and Rauch describe as the "Weberian state hypothesis," maintains that modern capitalist systems can only reach their full potential in those countries where the state is consistently organized as a "rational" bureaucratic institution. The German sociologist classically defined rational bureaucracies – they have been called "Weberian" bureaucracies ever since – as organizations staffed by career civil servants, recruited and promoted by merit, protected from political interference, and operating according to clearly established rules and regulations.[2]

In order to test empirically the connection between bureaucracy and growth, Rauch and Evans compared data on bureaucratic institutions and GDP variation for a sample of thirty-five countries during the period 1970–1990. They found that the Weberian state hypothesis was amply confirmed by the empirical test. The authors corroborated a "strong and significant" statistical correlation between their measurements of the degree of Weberian rationality in state bureaucracies – based on multiple expert evaluations – and the national variation in GDP per capita for the thirty-five countries of the sample.[3] The empirical-statistical test confirmed, in other words, that state institutions staffed by permanent career civil servants, recruited by merit, and protected from political interference, correlate to substantially higher levels of economic growth, compared to other kinds of state organizations. Simply put, the data

We thank Francisco Javier Braña Pino for comments and suggestions. The mistakes are our responsibility.
[1] Evans and Rauch. 1999: 748–765.   [2] Weber, 1978: 1399.   [3] Evans and Rauch, 1999: 755.

revealed that Weberian bureaucracies contribute decisively to economic development.

Spain represents an interesting case among the thirty-five countries chosen by Evans and Rauch for their sample. The sample does not include fully developed nations in 1970, at the beginning of the period under scrutiny. Most of the countries selected were already advanced on the path to development or "semi-industrialized" at the time – except for five low-income economies added to adjust geographical representation.[4] Remarkably, from all the Western countries in the sample, Spain scored the highest level in the measurement of bureaucratic rationality for its state structures. Only Asian countries such as South Korea or Singapore showed higher measurements in this regard. During the time-span under study, Spain's degree of bureaucratic rationality leaves Latin American countries such as Brazil, Chile, Mexico and Argentina well behind, and also other semi-industrialized countries such as Egypt, Turkey, or even Israel.[5] Such a high measure of bureaucratic rationality is interesting, because Spain had only embarked on a consistent civil service reform since the early 1960s, a few years before the beginning of the period under analysis.[6] Previous to that reform, public employment in Spain had been completely politicized by the Franco dictatorship, candidates for public service were selected on the basis of their loyalty to the regime, and they were generally incompetent as a result.[7]

Both the period and the sample chosen by Evans and Rauch are relevant and useful for their research purposes, but the period does not take into account a further significant circumstance about the Spanish developmental state. At the end of the 1950s, Spain remained one of the poorest countries in Western Europe, with a traditionally agrarian economy. During the sixties, however, Spain experienced rates of GDP growth that surpassed other nations such as Germany, the United States, France, or Italy, and that were only slightly below the growth rates of Japan.[8] Moreover, a substantial component of the fast economic growth in Spain was industrial production; the rate of growth of industrial output for the period 1960–1973 was the highest of any Western country, and more than double the average for Western Europe.[9]

During this time of fast growth, Spain's economy was strongly regulated and state-managed, including high protective tariffs, industrial subsidies, regional poles for domestic industrial production, and other policies promoting economic development, which will be further considered below.[10] In order to attract foreign investment and promote exports, after 1959 the government introduced a cautious opening of the national economy, which had been almost completely closed for the previous two decades. Being internationally isolated after 1945 in any case, the dictatorship had tried, with scant success, to run

[4] Evans and Rauch, 1999: 753.   [5] Evans and Rauch, 1999: 756.   [6] Reñón, 1987: 46.
[7] Nieto, 1986: 338.   [8] Lieberman, 1995: 97.   [9] Lieberman, 1995: 104.
[10] Catalan, 2010: 215.

a nationally self-sufficient, "autarchic" economy. Nevertheless, as Lieberman has pointed out, after the relative opening of 1959 the government "continued to practice a strong *dirigiste* policy," and the government's "*dirigisme* grew stronger in the latter part of the 1960s."[11] In fact, the government introduced comprehensive economic planning beginning in 1964, and three very detailed four-year national plans were implemented until 1975, the period of fastest economic growth.[12]

In view of the relative success of developmental strategies in Spain, the country could represent a useful comparative reference for the discussion of policies that made it possible for a poor, agrarian country, to move towards the goal of becoming an industrialized nation. With all possible criticisms and deficiencies, which will be also examined below, that kind of transformation was quite effectively promoted in Spain during the period of state-led economic development.

However, although such a reading of the process of development in Spain seems obvious, it has been surprisingly controversial among local economists. González stated early that the economic growth of the 1960s was not the result of the development programs put in practice by the government: by interfering with free markets, those development plans actually obstructed economic growth, according to the author, "although some of it can be attributed to them."[13] At the time, Ros, for whom the government's policies only made sense during the short period of relative "economic liberalism" between 1959 and 1963, was even more negative regarding Spanish development policies.[14] Afterwards, during the period of state-led development, the state's impact on the economy lost "consistency and strength," and any kind of reform "stagnated," since structural reforms can only consist of deregulation of markets, according to this author.[15] Carreras was also very skeptical of development policies in Spain, considering in particular the application of protective tariffs for industrial promotion.[16] The relationship between industrial growth and protective tariffs could not be considered positive, according to Carreras; he maintained that any relationship in this regard "should rather be the opposite."[17] Tortella was similarly very critical of any kind of state intervention in the economy; in his opinion it was "very doubtful" that the policies of industrial promotion had a significant role in Spanish economic development.[18] For Tortella, policies such as protective tariffs rather hindered or delayed growth by suppressing market competition.[19]

In sum, for the past four decades, strong critical views on the developmental state have been relatively standard in Spain; they were strengthened with the triumph of neoclassical economics in international academia by the early 1990s,

[11] Lieberman, 1995: 63, 115.   [12] Zaratiegui, 2015: 33–43.   [13] González, 1979: 321.
[14] Ros Hombravella, 1979.   [15] Ros Hombravella, 1979: 31, 57.
[16] Carreras, 1984: 127–157.   [17] Carreras: 146–147.   [18] Tortella Casares, 1994: 257.
[19] Tortella Casares, 1994: 256.

and the ensuing weakness of Keynesian or developmentalist perspectives in scholarly and public policy debates. Moreover, during the transition to democracy and afterwards, many Spanish scholars were logically eager to take distance from the Franco dictatorship, and there was a corresponding trend to repudiate vehemently any positive results of government programs connected to the military regime.[20] Even to this day, a resolute denial of the effectiveness of any kind of state intervention in the economy, and the retrospective application of this thesis to the period of fast economic growth in Spain, remains a common point of view among certain Spanish economists. For Prados, Rosés and Sanz, for example, the relative opening of the Spanish economy in 1959 was the only set of policies that successfully promoted growth during the whole developmental era in Spain.[21] And these measures were effective, precisely, because they can be seen as a "historical precedent" or even as a "forerunner" of the neoliberal prescriptions of the Washington Consensus.[22]

Confronted with often acrimonious debates among Spanish scholars, international economic historians have been understandably reluctant to take sides in the issue of state-led development in the country. Standard works on Spanish economic history remain curiously guarded on the topic of causes and determinants of the fast economic growth during the 1960s and 1970s. Wright displays typical impartiality by stating that if "development plans cannot be deemed to have provided sufficient impulse to account for the scale of industrial development after 1959, this does not mean that the government's role in the industrial sector has been negligible."[23] For his part, Harrison confirms that there is a forceful debate on the subject among Spanish scholars, and that therefore "it is a matter of opinion whether the so-called 'Spanish miracle' can be attributed to indicative planning."[24] Lieberman also observes that there are strongly conflicting viewpoints on this matter in Spain, and salomonically pronounces both wrong.[25]

As a result of the fierce controversy on developmental policies among Spanish economists, together with other factors, the country is almost never considered, in international literature, as a possible model or blueprint for successful – even for partially successful – developmental institutions. Prominent comparative treatments of economic development during the

---

[20] That some scholars denied the economic results of the dictatorship, for understandable political reasons, was pointed out early by Braña, Buesa and Molero, 1984: 200. De la Torre and García-Zúñiga have also observed that anti-Francoism, during the transition, impacted on economic analysis, and all developmental policies of the 1960s and 1970s were declared perverse and useless, regardless of evidence. De la Torre and García-Zúñiga, 2013: 44.

[21] Prados de la Escosura, Rosés and Sanz-Villaroya, 2011: 45–89. Prados de la Escosura, Rosés and Sanz Villarroya, 2010.

[22] Prados de la Escosura, Rosés, and Sanz-Villaroya, 2010: 46n.   [23] Wright, 1977: 60.

[24] Harrison, 1978: 156.   [25] Lieberman, 1995: 113.

twentieth century either barely consider the Spanish developmental state, or they do not mention the Spanish case at all.[26] Even discussions of the developmental state in Latin American countries, otherwise so similar to Spain as regards cultural history and institutions, ignore the Spanish case as a comparative reference, and rather put forward as institutional models or blueprints East Asian developmental states such as Japan or South Korea.[27] Asian economies were exceptionally effective in terms of state-directed development during the twentieth century, but from a Latin American point of view, there are nonetheless interesting points of comparison with Spain.

A comparative perspective between Latin America and Spain can be useful, for example, in order to discuss civil service reform, and its relationship to economic development in the context of Ibero-American institutional cultures. As mentioned earlier, Spain began a civil service reform in the early 1960s, and the partial consolidation of a professional civil service was a major factor for the fast economic growth of the 1960s and 1970s: this was one of the most clear-cut cases of direct correlation between civil service reform and economic development analyzed by Evans and Rauch.[28] In contrast, political practices such as patronage and clientelism have often been described as an obstacle to economic development, a point which has been recently made by Grindle, although this author only compares the extent of patronage in Latin America to the spoils-system in US American experience. For Grindle, at "the outset of the twenty-first century, nowhere in the world, except perhaps in mid-nineteenth century US experience, was patronage more fully embedded in political reality than in Latin America [...] and nowhere had it been more fully decried as a hindrance to development [...]."[29] As outlined above, the Spanish case is usually overlooked in discussions on Latin American state institutions and development, but the fact of the matter is that a Spanish spoils-system, including massive clientelism in public employment, was no less embedded in political reality than the US spoils-system during the nineteenth century.[30]

The mid-nineteenth-century US experience was definitely not the only instance of extended political patronage that can be compared to present-day Latin American practices. Max Weber described the correspondence in patronage and clientelistic practices between Spain and Latin American countries during the nineteenth century. Writing as early as 1919, Weber remarked upon the similarity between the US American spoils-system, and the systems of massive political patronage both in Spain, and in the Latin American "former colonies" of Spain. Only in the case of the United States could Weber observe a trend to civil service reform at that moment – as we will discuss below, the first successful civil service reform in Spain had just begun at the time of

[26] Woo-Cumings 1999. Kohli, 2004. Haggard and Kaufman, 2008. Williams 2014.
[27] Evans, 1995. Ross Schneider, 2015.   [28] Evans and Rauch, 1999.   [29] Grindle, 2012: 141.
[30] Parrado Diez, 2000: 253. Centeno and Ferraro, 2013: 15.

Weber writing this particular essay.[31] The cultural and institutional similarities between political patronage in Latin America and Spain remain strong to this day, as can be shown, among other factors, by the fact that even many terms of exactly the same vocabulary are used to refer to such practices – or decry them – in ordinary political conversation in both regions.[32]

When all is said and done, however, sometimes it can appear as doubtful that something like a developmental state ever existed in Spain. The impact of development policies on the economy has been vehemently denied by many local scholars, and more often than not ignored by the international literature. Maybe everything that was done to promote economic growth was only seemingly effective, but it was not just insufficient, it was also immaterial – practically a dream. Then again, serious doubts about the reality of past public events and occurrences are nothing out of the ordinary in Spain. As portrayed in the classic play by Calderón de la Barca, life is a dream, and as the poet further declared, "even dreams themselves are dreams" in this country.

In order to analyze developmental policies and their impact on economic growth in Spain between 1950 and 1990, we will discuss below industrial promotion as a general growth strategy, and its specific results in Spain. As discussed above, however, development policies cannot succeed if a Weberian bureaucracy has not been consolidated in the first place. In the chapter's second section, we will analyze the political factors that made possible the partial creation of a Weberian national bureaucracy in Spain, between 1918 and 1936, and the reasons that compelled the Franco dictatorship to reestablish a professional civil service, protected from political interference in certain areas, beginning in the early 1960s. In the conclusion, finally, we will summarize the results of the chapter.

DEVELOPMENT AND INDUSTRIAL PROMOTION

In his groundbreaking work *The National System of Political Economy*, Friedrich List introduced the idea that state institutions should promote economic growth, and that initiatives towards this goal should be organized into an overall national strategy.[33] According to List, national economies have stages of development, and the transformation from an "agrarian stage" (*Agrikulturzustand*) to a "manufacturing stage" (*Manufakturstand*) cannot ever take place under a system of free trade, if a given country has to compete with already industrialized nations. As soon as one or more foreign economies have already reached the industrial stage, there is no other path to economic development but for the state institutions of the disadvantaged nations to establish systems of protective tariffs in order to shield and promote local "infant industry" (*junge Industrie*).[34] List drew inspiration for his thesis

---

[31] Weber, 1994: 321.   [32] Centeno and Ferraro, 2013: 20.   [33] List, 1910.
[34] List, 1910: 64–65.

about the shielding of "infant industry" from the US American experience with protective industrial tariffs. He studied the American tariff system during his political exile in the country from 1825 to 1830, where he first conceived of the idea to systematize the promotion of economic production into long-term national strategies.[35]

The ideas and the publicistic work of Friedrich List were instrumental in the adoption of protective tariffs by German state institutions, both before and after unification in 1871, as well as other extensive development projects, such as the nationalization and accelerated expansion of railways after 1879.[36] The German experience of state-led development was very successful, and by the end of the century, the country had clearly overtaken Great Britain as an industrial power.[37] The ideas of Friedrich List became also influential in Japan after the Meiji restoration in 1868, and by the twentieth century, the doctrine of "Japanese developmentalism" was based to a considerable extent on the inspiration of List and other economists of the so-called "German historical school."[38] The Japanese developmental strategies were extremely effective after World War II, and during the 1960s Japan achieved annual growth rates as high as 12 percent, the fastest expansion of any national economy at the time.[39]

Both in Germany and Japan, the policies of state-led development took for granted the previous consolidation of strong professional civil services including positions of the highest authority in government, that is to say, Weberian bureaucracies. As Johnson described in his study of the Japanese developmental state after World War II, career civil servants were entirely in charge of public policy decisions; he compared the role of politicians in Japan to the symbolic role of constitutional monarchs, who "reign but do not rule," since all relevant government decisions were taken by career civil servants.[40] In his classical analysis of "rational" or modern bureaucracies, Weber described an even stronger dominance of the professional civil service over public policy decisions in Germany: all ministers in German governments from the time of Bismarck were career civil servants, with few exceptions.[41] That a developmental state has to be run basically by career civil servants in order to be effective was further corroborated by Evans and Rauch with their empirical-statistical test of the "Weberian state-hypothesis," discussed above in the introduction to this chapter.[42] For Spain and Latin American countries, the consolidation of career civil services, protected from political interference, has been the Achilles heel of every developmental project. Therefore, the previous reform of the civil service has to be kept in mind as a necessary condition for the growth strategies implemented in Spain during the developmental era, which we are going to discuss in what follows.

[35] Chan, 2003: 61. [36] Henderson, 1975: 207. [37] Shin, 1996: 70.
[38] Fallows, 1994: 182. Gao, 1997: 40. [39] Kohama, 2007: 185. [40] Johnson, 1982: 322.
[41] Weber, 1978: 1409. [42] Evans and Rauch, 1999.

The first policy measures conceived to support certain areas of the economy were applied in Spain at the end of the nineteenth century. Protective tariffs were introduced in 1891 to support agricultural production, as well as specific industries, particularly textiles, and they were raised across the board in 1906.[43] Import duties were again substantially increased in 1922 under Finance Minister Francesc Cambó.[44] After 1922, furthermore, protective tariffs were more precisely targeted towards industrial promotion, and they began to be considered as components of an overall national economic plan. Cambó, for example, was a strong supporter of extensive public investment in railways.[45]

From 1913 to 1935, the development of the Spanish industry was moderately succesful, with annual average growth rates of 2 percent.[46] Industrial growth was considerably higher in Spain than in most European countries during this period, although these results were certainly associated with the fact that Spain remained neutral during World War I, and suffered less from the war's consequences as a result. In contrast, during the period from 1935 to 1950, Spanish industrial growth only reached 0.6 percent annual average, a very poor performance that resulted from the catastrophe of the Civil War 1936–1939, from the negative consequences of World War II, even though Spain remained neutral, and from the period of economic isolation after the war.[47]

Spanish development strategies only began to achieve consistent results after 1950. In the rest of the present section, we will illustrate the impact of development policies on a particular branch of the Spanish economy, the motor industry, which was by far the fastest-growing area of production in the country until the 1990s. For the following analysis, we will specifically consider the connection between the development policies applied during this period, the bureaucratic structures in charge of public policy formulation and implementation, and the substantial changes in bureaucratic management styles – and results – that were the consequence of the civil service reform of the early 1960s.

The development of the Spanish motor industry represents an interesting case in the context of any discussion on public policy implementation. As García Ruiz has observed, Spain began "practically from nothing" in this area: during the whole year of 1953, the production of automobiles in Spain was fewer than 600 units.[48] The first period of state-led development of the motor industry went until 1962, and the diverse strategies applied were quite effective, total production reaching more than 100,000 units in the latter year.[49] However, it was only after the civil service reforms of the early 1960s, that is to say, after a professional bureaucracy took charge of public policy decisions, that the development plans for the Spanish motor industry became much more sophisticated and ambitious, as we will see, and much better coordinated.

---

[43] Harrison, 1978: 34.   [44] Lieberman, 1982: 129.   [45] Pabón, 1999: 507.
[46] Carreras, 2005: 364.   [47] Carreras, 2005: 365.   [48] García Ruiz, 2001: 137.
[49] Catalan, 2010: 216.

The results improved dramatically during the second period, and automobile production in Spain, between 1963 and 1973, rose steadily at a rate of 20 percent per year. By 1973, the country had climbed to the tenth position in the world-ranking of automobile manufacturers, with the production of 822,000 units between passenger and utility vehicles.[50] Exports also grew very fast during the second period, 1963–1973, and by the end of this time Spain had reached the position of eleventh in the list of world car-exporters.[51] The automobile industry had become the most successful economic branch in the history of the Spanish economy, and the mainstay of the country's transformation into a relatively advanced industrial nation.

The production of cars in Spain by public, or public–private corporations, began in 1950 with the creation of the firm SEAT (Sociedad Española de Automóbiles de Turismo). The firm was a partnership between the public holding INI (Instituto Nacional de Industria), with 51 percent of the capital, the Italian car manufacturer FIAT, with 7 percent of the capital, and a consortium of six Spanish private banks holding the remainder 42 percent of the capital in equal parts. The initiative and the contacts for the cooperation agreement with FIAT were originally established by one of the private banks, Banco Urquijo.[52]

The public holding INI had been created by the military dictatorship in 1941, two years after the end of the Spanish Civil War, in order to promote the national industry. The creation of INI was mainly based on strategic and military considerations. As Harrison observes, its institutional goals were, first of all, the industrialization of the country "so as to increase its military strength," and secondly, the promotion of resource exploitation and production, in order to diminish dependence on imported raw materials.[53] As Aceña and Comín also remark, economic considerations were subordinate at INI for several years after its creation; the overriding goal of the institution was to increase industrial production, without regard for cost-effectiveness or profitability.[54] San Román has shown that military personnel, such as engineer officers from the naval and artillery branches, were predominant at INI, both in top management and technical roles, including the area related to automobile production.[55] Civilians closely connected with and loyal to the military served at INI, but only in subordinate positions.[56]

The military orientation of INI shaped its management style. The takeover of negotiations with FIAT from Banco Urquijo was a case in point. A private bank, Banco Urquijo had developed a network of contacts with Italian managers at FIAT, and the negotiations were practically completed for the creation of a car-manufacturing business in Spain, with the support of a consortium of other private banks to provide funding. Now, instead of respecting and strengthening

[50] García Ruiz, 2001: 158.   [51] Catalan, 2010: 221.   [52] San Román, 1995: 151.
[53] Harrison, 1985: 130.   [54] Aceña and Comín, 1991: 31.   [55] San Román, 1995: 171.
[56] Aceña and Comín, 1991: 132–133.

those horizontal networks established by Banco Urquijo, thus consolidating the crucial capacity that Evans characterized as "embeddedness" of developmental institutions, INI just took over the whole business project in a heavy-handed way.[57] [58] It is certainly true, as Comín has observed, that Banco Urquijo was generously compensated, and that the project to create a car-manufacturing business in Spain could only succeed with public support.[59] Nevertheless, the vertical and heavy-handed management style of INI, under military direction, was clearly shown by this episode.

The first SEAT plant was located in Barcelona. The firm was declared of "national interest," and therefore, imports of auto-parts and industrial machinery for its use were declared exempt from tariffs.[60] SEAT was supported by what has been defined as a "national champion" strategy, including strict restriction of car imports, cautious licensing of possible rivals, and regulations mandating a high proportion of nationally produced components to be employed for car manufacturing.[61] [62] Production at SEAT began in 1953, and by 1958 SEAT manufactured 22,157 cars in two models, although the whole production was sold nationally, without exporting a single unit.[63]

Added to the founding of the national champion SEAT, the government approved in 1951 the creation of a private firm for the production of automobiles in Valladolid, under the name FASA (Fabricación de Automóbiles Sociedad Anónima). The initiative for the creation of FASA came from a group of individuals closely connected to the government, and to the public holding INI. This group decided to approach France RENAULT in 1950 with a proposal for the manufacture in Spain of cars designed by the French firm.[64] The original investment for the creation of the Spanish FASA was underwritten by more than a hundred small and medium businesses located in the area of Valladolid. RENAULT contributed no share of capital at first, as was part of the agreement, but the next year the French firm acquired a share of 26 percent through its local Spanish subsidiary.[65] The Spanish FASA began producing cars in 1953 with pieces imported from France, but the firm was given a period of grace of four years, by the end of which it had to employ 100 percent of parts manufactured in Spain for its production.[66]

During the 1950s, the passenger-car market in Spain was almost completely dominated by SEAT and FASA. As mentioned above, by 1962 total production in Spain was more than 100,000 units between passenger cars and utility vehicles.[67] The regulations requiring the motor industry to use parts and components produced in Spain were effectively applied during this period, and since the late 1950s SEAT had been employing more than 90 percent of

[57] Evans, *Embedded Autonomy.*   [58] San Román, 1995: 150.   [59] Comín, 2001: 184.
[60] Tappi, 2010: 57–58.   [61] Chiang, 1990.   [62] Catalan, 2010: 211.   [63] Catalan, 2010: 209.
[64] Sánchez, 2004: 150.   [65] Fernández de Sevilla, 2007: 124.   [66] Catalan, 2010: 211.
[67] García Ruiz, 2001: 158.

locally made parts for car production.[68] FASA reached more than 95 percent of locally made parts in 1963.[69] The enforcement of regulations requiring parts and components made in Spain had a strong positive impact on diverse branches of the national economy. However, it was clear by then that the future development of the motor industry had to rely on a substantial increase of exports, and this second phase was going to be difficult for the military management at INI. A general economic measure to promote exports was a drastic (43 percent) devaluation of the peseta in 1959.[70] Currency devaluation made Spanish exports more price-competitive, but this measure could be effective only in the short term.

The new policies of export promotion for the motor industry were naturally focused on the national champion SEAT. The original agreement with the Italian car manufacturer FIAT did not allow the Spanish firm to export any of its production, a requirement which the Italians had imposed against the reluctance of the Spanish partners.[71] The public holding INI, which had a majoritarian share in SEAT's capital, had been requesting the Italian firm to authorize exports since 1956, to no avail.[72]

The failed negotiations with FIAT during the late 1950s and early 1960s were one of the last business plans that the "old school" military top management of INI attempted to carry out. During the years 1963–1964, INI was one of the key state institutions completely reorganized by the process of consolidation of a professional "Weberian" bureaucracy, which was put in charge of public policy decisions in Spain.[73] As shown by Evans and Rauch, the reform of the civil service had a strong impact on bureaucratic structures in Spain, and just a few years later the measurement of bureaucratic rationality of the country's state structures was the highest among Western nations in their sample.[74]

In the years after the reform of INI in 1963–1964, public policy decisions taken by its management became much more technically sophisticated, and therefore much more effective. Among other policy areas, the key strategic goal of increasing industrial exports, which had failed under military management at INI, was to be realized beyond expectations by the new "Weberian" bureaucratic leadership.

The new management at INI took advantage of the opportunity offered by the introduction in 1964 of a new car model by the Italian partners, the legendary Fiat 850, to renegotiate the issue of exporting cars produced in Spain. INI offered to have the government authorize FIAT to import to Spain any number of units of the new model 850, manufactured in Italy, as long as SEAT was not able to produce enough units in Spain to cover the local demand. The Italian firm was committed to the model 850, anticipating a huge sales success, and they made concessions regarding exports, in exchange for the

---

[68] Catalan, 2006: 153.   [69] Fernández de Sevilla, 2014: 143.   [70] López-Claros, 1988: 3.
[71] Catalan, 2006: 145.   [72] Catalan, 2006: 155.   [73] Aceña and Comín, 1991: 329.
[74] Evans and Rauch, 1999: 756.

authorization to import Italian cars to Spain. SEAT was thus authorized by FIAT to export cars to Latin American markets.[75] The sales to Latin America were not very relevant in themselves, but this first authorization of exports became a crucial breakthrough for SEAT.

The government's authorization to import Italian cars to Spain only benefited FIAT for a very short time. Less than two years later, during 1966, the plant of SEAT in Barcelona was able to produce 30,000 units of the new model 850, and more than 100,000 units in total. There was no demand left whatsoever to justify imports from Italy. The Italian partners could have considered themselves tricked, and yet, the new professional civilian bureaucracy in charge of industrial policy in Spain had, by the end of 1966, a completely new offer for FIAT. Actually, it was more than a new offer;the Spanish policymakers went on to propose a redefinition of the whole car business for foreign firms operating in Spain.

The redefinition of the car business was going to take place under a new pattern of coordination between the diverse public agencies with public policy roles in Spain. Under the old military management, conflicts among areas of the Spanish government were relatively common. In fact, an atmosphere of constant in-fighting with the Ministry of Industry had existed since the creation of INI in 1941.[76] The civil service reform of 1963–1964 consolidated a professional civil service that took charge of public policy decisions in Spain, that is to say, a Weberian bureaucracy. However, as Vivek Chibber has shown, bureaucratic rationality is a necessary condition for the success of developmental strategies, but it is not sufficient.[77] A successful development state requires, in addition, disciplinary coordination to forestall interagency rivalry, and strengthen the cohesiveness of state institutions. Without such coordination, even a Weberian bureaucracy will probably fail in promoting economic development, according to Chibber. As an example of successful disciplinary coordination, provided by a "nodal" state agency, Chibber mentions the Ministry for International Trade and Industry (MITI) in Japan, which was assigned coordinating powers over the rest of the administrative apparatus.[78]

In Spain, after the reorganization of INI in 1963–1964, the management of industrial policy showed the end of inter-agency in-fighting that was characteristic of the previous era.[79] The new cohesiveness of state institutions was a contributing factor for the successful reformulation of development strategies for the motor industry. The advancement of negotiations with FIAT are a case in point.

As a first step in the negotiations with FIAT, during 1966 representatives of the Spanish Ministry for Industry informally contacted top managers at the Italian firm to discuss a new framework for the motor business. Once the

---

[75] Catalan, 2006: 159.   [76] San Román, 1995: 147.   [77] Chibber, 2002.
[78] Chibber, 2002: 985.   [79] San Román, 1995: 147.

informal discussions were advanced, the ministry opened a series of meetings between representatives from all partners involved: FIAT, INI, SEAT, and the Spanish private banks that owned shares in SEAT's capital. The Spanish organizations were now acting in coordination, with the ministry operating in its new role as "nodal" state agency. The meetings were not a mere formality, the previous informal contacts between FIAT and the ministry were not intended to decide in advance the issues on the table, as shown by the fact that, once the rest of the partners joined, negotiations went on for another six months.[80] The coordination provided by the ministry was not a vertical imposition of decisions, as often happened under the old military management, it was rather a horizontal coordination of agreements between actors in the industry.

A new settlement was signed by all partners in 1967. The share of FIAT in the Spanish car manufacturer SEAT was increased to 36 percent, and the share of the public holding INI was accordingly reduced to 36 percent. The rest of the capital was distributed among the six Spanish private banks that had participated as investors from the beginning. In this manner, management of the company was effectively divided between FIAT and INI, with the Spanish private banks acting as final arbiters. The arrangement confirmed the new horizontal style for conducting industrial policy in Spain, which the old school military management could never have accepted – or probably even imagined. Under the new agreement, FIAT not only authorized SEAT to export cars, the Italian firm provided its vast international network of car dealerships as infrastructure for the sale of cars manufactured in Spain.[81] As a result of the agreement with FIAT, and agreements with other international car manufacturers that we will describe below, the whole of Spanish car production was transformed into an export-oriented business.

Added to the new cohesiveness and horizontal approach of industrial policy, a further factor was decisive for FIAT's willingness not only to accept, but moreover to support actively the export of cars manufactured in Spain. The representatives of the Italian firm were eager to participate in the new strategic vision projected by the Ministry for Industry. With the government's active sponsorship, the plan was for SEAT's production to increase dramatically, and the resulting massive exports of cars licensed by the Italian firm were going to strengthen FIAT in its longstanding strategic ambition of dominating the European car market. SEAT was going to benefit from a new policy framework aimed at promoting exports in all key industrial branches, including subsidies for industrial firms to support their reconversion to export production, exemption of indirect taxes on foreign sales, exemption of tariffs on all kinds of imported industrial inputs, such as raw materials, parts, or capital equipment, and other, specific measures of financial and credit assistance to exporters.[82]

[80] Catalan, 2006: 160.   [81] Catalan, 2006.   [82] Carreras and Estapé-Triay, 2002: 138.

The ministry's new strategic vision was very successful. A year after the agreement between the Italian and Spanish partners, under the new policy framework introduced in 1967, SEAT was producing slightly over 180,000 vehicles, but only exporting less than 1,000 units. Five years after the agreement, in 1972, the production was close to 340,000 vehicles, and more than 55,000 units were exported. The figure for exports by SEAT amounted to 53 per cent of all Spanish car exports in 1972; the national champion was clearly leading the export market at that time.[83] Less than ten years after the agreement, in 1976, SEAT was producing more than 360,000 cars, and exports had increased to almost 77,000 units – growth in production was almost entirely based on export sales.[84] At the same time, however, SEAT's share of total Spanish automobile exports was down to 42 percent in 1976, and it kept diminishing from there.[85] This reduction of SEAT's share in export sales reflected a changing situation, since exports of automobiles produced in Spain were now open to a new kind of competition, which the Italian partners probably had not foreseen.

In the agreement with FIAT of 1967, the Spanish policymakers had never offered any guarantee that exports by SEAT were going to obtain the same kind of protection that the firm received for the domestic market. Therefore, other international car producers were invited to manufacture their products under license in Spain, with the understanding that this production was going to be sold in export markets, while the domestic market remained protected for the firms already operating in Spain. Rather soon, therefore, FIAT and SEAT were going to have to compete for export markets with the main international producers in the motor industry. FIAT was not pleased by the new situation.

The strategy of industrial growth aimed at export markets, first tried successfully with SEAT, became a general policy framework in 1972. With the previous understanding that both General Motors and Ford Motor Company were eager to install car-manufacturing plants in Spain, the Ministry for Industry designed a new regulation framework for the installation in Spain of international firms willing to produce for sales to export markets. First of all, the regulatory framework established the requirement to employ parts and components produced in Spain at 50 percent, while it remained at 90 percent for car manufacturers producing for the national market. Secondly, the regulations required a minimum investment in fixed assets – such as land, buildings, and equipment – of over 150 million US dollars, or the equivalent of 10 billion pesetas in 1972, which amounts to around 880 million US dollars in inflation-adjusted terms today. The regulatory framework, in the third place, limited domestic sales for firms operating under the new agreements by means of a rather sophisticated system based on two measurements: exports in any given year had to amount at least to two-thirds of the firm's whole car production, and sales in the domestic market could only

---

[83] Catalan, 2006: 169.   [84] Catalan, 2000:150.   [85] Tappi, 2010: 183.

reach up to 10 percent of total sales, including exports, that were completed in the previous year – the second stipulation made it impossible to dodge the first by simply accumulating stock from one year to the next.[86]

Ford began production in 1976. Negotiations with General Motors took slightly longer, and the Detroit firm signed the agreement to install a car-manufacturing plant near Saragossa in 1979, production beginning in 1983.[87] In view of the fierce competition that was developing under the new regulations for the car-export market, and considering the relatively bad results of SEAT in the previous two years, FIAT decided to leave the country altogether in 1981. The SEAT shares of the Italian firm were transferred to the public holding INI, which now became the majoritarian owner. Almost immediately after FIAT's departure, however, the German car manufacturer Volkswagen offered to produce cars in Spain in partnership with SEAT, and the agreement was signed the following year. The government implemented a financial recovery plan for SEAT, and by 1986 the firm was again leading the motor industry in Spain in terms of overall production. As a result, Volkswagen decided to consolidate its involvement in the Spanish car market, and the German firm acquired a participation of 51 percent of the capital of SEAT in the same year.[88]

By the end of the 1980s, the Spanish car industry had become so succesful in exporting most of its production – more on this below – that FIAT decided to return to the Spanish car market in 1990, acquiring 60 percent of ENASA, a firm that manufactured utility vehicles, previously owned by INI. Also in the area of utility vehicles, Japanese firms had entered relatively early into agreements with the Ministry for Industry, Nissan in 1979, and Suzuki in 1982. Following the redefinition of Spanish industrial policy in the early 1970s, the commercial strategy in all these cases was to install car manufacturing plants oriented towards export markets.[89]

The development strategy and the regulatory framework created in the early 1970s for the Spanish motor industry were consistently applied for the next three decades, and the cohesiveness of state organizations remained strong. Long-term results were very positive. By 1996, Spain had reached the sixth position in the world ranking of automobile manufacturers, leaving Italy and the United Kingdom well behind.[90] From a total production close to 2.5 million units in that year, around 80 percent of the vehicles produced were exported.[91]

However, it is important to observe also that, by the end of this period, the Spanish development strategies for the car industry revealed two main weaknesses. The first weakness was caused by the decision to abandon the strategy of protection and support for the national champion in the motor industry, a public policy decision sealed in 1986 with the sale of a majoritarian share in SEAT's capital to Volkswagen. In contrast, as Catalan remarks, a key for South Korea's current dominant position in the international

---

[86] Fernández de Sevilla, 2014: 302.   [87] Catalan, 2010: 221.   [88] Catalan, 2010: 222.
[89] García Ruiz 2001: 150.   [90] Catalan, 2010: 115.   [91] García Ruiz, 2001: 158.

car market has been the longstanding public policy support for the national champion, Hyundai.[92] Significantly, South Korea went from not even appearing among the twenty top car manufacturers in 1973, to the position of fourth in the same ranking by 1996, with a total production close to 3 million vehicles.

The second weakness affecting Spanish development strategies for the automobile industry is partly related to the first. In both the cases of Spain and South Korea, the national champions, SEAT and Hyundai respectively, made the strongest contribution to technological innovation in their industrial areas. Since 1970, SEAT operated its own research and development (R&D) center, and by 1974, it was the single Spanish firm with the highest expenditure on technological innovation from all the national industry. Hyundai created its own R&D center in 1974, and this area of the company expanded continuously afterwards.[93]

The unwillingness of Spanish firms to invest in R&D has been well documented.[94] The deficiencies of Spanish public policy in support of technological innovation have been compounded as a result, and this remains one of the weakest components of the Spanish economy to this day.

Nothwithstanding the overall deficiencies considered, Spanish industrial policies were certainly successful from 1950 to 1996. As outlined in this section, a first phase under the leadership of military officers and engineers could reach the production of more than 100,000 automobile units for the domestic market in 1962. The second phase, from 1963 to 1973, ended with Spain in the tenth position of the world ranking of automobile manufacturers, with the production of 822,000 units. The second phase was under the control of a new professional and autonomous "Weberian" bureaucy, protected from political interference, and this change was reflected in policies, styles of management, overall coordination of state agencies, and other characteristics. After 1973 began a third phase, with a sophisticated and ambitious strategic vision focused on increasing exports, designed and implemented by the professional bureaucracy in charge of public policy decisions since the early 1960s. By 1996, Spain had reached the sixth position in the world ranking of automobile manufacturers, with a total production close to 2.5 million units.

In sum, as shown by the case of the motor industry, one of the keys for the success of developmental policy in Spain was the previous consolidation of a professional bureaucracy in charge of public policy decisions, protected from political interference. Nevertheless, it is important to realize that the Franco dictatorship could not have created such a professional bureaucracy in a few years, just by a top-down act of political will. In fact, compelled to change its style of governance in the early 1960s, the dictatorship decided to reestablish the professional state structures that had been consolidated during the

---

[92] Catalan, 2010: 226.   [93] Catalan, 2010: 215.
[94] Griffith, Huergo, Mairesse, and Peters, 2006.

fundamental period of social and political modernization of Spain between 1914 and 1936. As we will discuss in the next section, in Spain and other countries, civil service reform is always a long and difficult political struggle, never just a technical decision imposed from above.

CIVIL SERVICE REFORM AS A POLITICAL PROCESS

After the end of the Spanish civil war in 1939, the Franco dictatorship carried out massive purges of all those civil servants whose loyalty to the authoritarian regime was suspect. For the two following decades, recruitment to the civil service was based on political commitment to the dictatorship, without much regard to qualifications or experience. The civil service laws and regulations established during the previous democratic period, between 1914 and 1936, remained theoretically in force, but they were entirely disregarded in practice. As a result, after twenty years of authoritarian government, at the end of the 1950s, the professional quality of the Spanish public bureaucracy was extremely deficient.[95]

At the same time, the United States decided during the late 1950s to change the policy of isolation of the Franco dictatorship, and invite Spain to join the Western Coalition in the Cold War. The Western democracies had maintained for almost two decades a rather cold or hostile relationship to the Spanish military government, and the dictatorship seized the offer with alacrity. The visit of President Eisenhower to Spain sealed the agreement in 1959.

In the new situation, the Franco regime realized that it had to change its style of governance. The model of an authoritarian state, staffed by committed fascists, had to be discarded without much delay. The dictatorship chose to bury its inconvenient past by launching a modernizing effort. As part of this process, the professionalization of the public bureaucracy was carried out on the basis of the civil service laws and regulations of the previous democratic period, particularly on the basis of the major civil service reform of 1918. The professionalization of the structures of government and public policy in the 1950s and 1960s was followed by fast economic growth, and both changes pointed the way to the democratic transition. The profound social and political modernization of Spain, which had taken place between 1914 and 1936, was repressed brutally for two decades by the military dictatorship. Nevertheless, the same era of modernization remained the basis for the successful transition to democracy beginning in the 1970s.

The professionalization of state structures during the period 1914–1936 was built around the major civil service reform of 1918, also known as the "Maura Act" (*Estatuto Maura*) in Spain. Considered as a crucial breakthrough in the literature, the reform of 1918 established two central principles for the management of state institutions. [96] Those same principles were reintroduced

---

[95] Nieto, 1986: 338.   [96] Morrell Ocaña, 2005; Jordana and Ramió, 2005.

during the early 1960s, and they were consolidated by a new Civil Service Act in 1964.[97] The first principle was the merit rule, a central component of modern state building since the eighteenth century in Europe. Following the merit rule, the Spanish legislation of 1918 declared that recruitment to the civil service had to be based on merit, that is to say, public examination of qualifications and experience, not on political loyalty – as was the case until then – and that civil servants were to be protected from dismissal for political reasons by security of tenure. Several reforms had already tried to establish the merit principle during the nineteenth century in Spain, but they had always failed in practice, and political patronage remained the standard procedure for the recruitment and promotion of most public employees.

The second principle introduced by the civil service reform of 1918 declared that career civil servants could reach top management positions, in other words, that senior career civil servants were expected to take public policy decisions, not just obey orders as mere subordinates. For this purpose, the act created a new civil service category, *technical staff*, which was meant to provide top management positions, as well as medium-level expert positions, for senior civil servants. This second principle is not as obvious as the first, but it represented an essential component of civil service reform, both in the cases of the United States and Spain. The creation of a career civil service remains only a fragmentary, at best frail improvement in public governance if civil servants are kept only in subordinate positions.[98] In the case of development institutions, as described in the introduction to this chapter, their success is only possible if career civil servants take major public policy decisions without interference from politicians, as has been clearly confirmed by such cases of national development as Germany, Japan, and others.

Nevertheless, considering the civil service reform of 1918 in Spain, or any other civil service reform, it is important to observe that the creation of a career civil service cannot be performed just by the passing of legislation. The civil service reform of 1918 was the result of a long political struggle in Spain. Previous attempts at creating a civil service by a legal decision from above had always failed, and new civil service regulations were disregarded almost from the day they became law. This has been also a common experience in Latin America, where governments have often passed civil service acts or regulations, but where in many cases they have hardly ever been implemented.[99] Therefore, for the cases of both Spain and the United States, one of the most interesting features of a successful civil service reform represents the political process behind the reform, the set of political and other circumstances that resulted in real institutional change. In what follows, we will describe the civil service reform movement in Spain, which began at the end of the nineteenth century, and we will briefly consider some of its similarities to the civil service reform movement in the United States.

[97] Reñón, 1987: 47–49.   [98] Ferraro, 2011.   [99] Centeno and Ferraro, 2013: 16.

There were several attempts to create a career civil service in Spain during the nineteenth century. Curiously enough, however, some of the most renowned legal scholars in the country did not actually condemn the spoils-system. Oliván, perhaps the most influential scholar of public law in Spain during the nineteenth century, considered that the power to dismiss public employees for political reasons was necessary as an "incentive for the subordinates."[100,101] Another prestigious scholar, Posada, considered that public employees had to enjoy their minister's trust, and thus that the minister should have the power to hire or dismiss all of them.[102] Of course, this notion led in practice to the potential replacement of all public employees with each change of government, as happened regularly in Spain, with the result that all employees "from the minister to the doorman of the ministry's building" were dismissed and replaced by political loyalists after each national election, as the King of Spain himself was to complain a few years later.[103]

The tolerance or outright support for political clientelism in scholarly opinion was complemented by the low regard for public employees in the popular press in Spain. Under the name of *empleomanía* (employment-mania), journalists and writers condemned the aspiration to enter public service, assuming that all Spanish civil servants were self-interested and lazy. The celebrated journalist and social critic Larra wrote in 1832 that public employees earned a salary without working, and that those Spaniards "who really love their country must begin by taking their minds off public employment..."[104]

Popular opinion began to change during the second half of the nineteenth century. A new perception of *empleomanía* began to develop, which condemned the practice as an abuse of power by politicians, not as the result of the laziness of public employees. A very interesting early denunciation of the political uses of *empleomanía* appeared as an anonymous pamphlet of seventy-five pages in 1875. Anonymous pamphlets were becoming frequent in those years, they were evidently written by public employees, and kept anonymous to avoid reprisals; the pamphlet of 1875 has been considered one of the most relevant in the genre.[105] Increasing activism in the publication of such pamphlets, and other actions, showed a growing political awareness among civil servants, which would play a crucial role in later years.

The anonymous pamphlet of 1875 criticizes political patronage as the source for bureaucratic incompetence and waste in Spain. Moreover, the pamphlet denounces patronage for its corrupting influence on the press, and on citizens in

---

[100] García de Enterría, 1954.   [101] Oliván, 1843.   [102] Posada de Herrera, 1988: 215.
[103] Alfonso XII, King of Spain, during a conversation with the British Ambassador in 1875, complained about the fact that every political change in Spain implied the wholesale replacement of public employees "from the minister to the doorman of the ministry's building." Quoted in Varela Ortega, 2001: 422.
[104] Larra, 1832: 21.   [105] Carrasco Canals, 1975: 296.

general: patronage promotes servility and obsequiousness towards the powerful.[106] Thus, the pamphlet does not only consider patronage as detrimental for the quality of the state bureaucracy, it goes on to analyze its destructive impact on the ethical foundations of democracy, the dignity and agency of citizens.[107] This is an interesting change of perspective, since patronage had been justified – and it is still very much justified in our day – as a "democratic" instrument. According to such "democratic" vindication of patronage, a newly elected government needs to appoint many political supporters for public jobs, so that these will implement its policy proposals "loyally," and thus the electoral mandate is realized. However, following the pamphlet's change of perspective, career professionals would not only implement the government's policies much more competently than political appointees, patronage actually damages the democratic form of government, by promoting servility among citizens.

In the following decades, the activism of career civil servants increased in Spain, demanding both the outlawing of political patronage, and the end of massive political dismissals after each change of government. The first general association of career civil servants was created in 1895; two years later, the association initiated a public campaign to demand fundamental rights for all public employees.[108]

After 1898, the Spanish defeat in the Cuban War led to widespread denunciations of national decadence. A movement of cultural and political reform emerged under the name of *Regeneracionismo*, launching a public debate over the Spanish predicament. One of the movement's leaders, Joaquín Costa, published in 1901 a report on the government in Spain, where he condemned political patronage and electoral corruption as the sources of bad administration, and of national backwardness as a result. Costa and other members of the movement deplored the isolation of Spain from the rest of Europe, and they advocated taking advanced European nations as the model for reforms. This proposal was further developed by José Ortega y Gasset a few years later. Ortega was the main intellectual leader of a wide progressive movement, known as Generation of 1914, which represented the continuation of *Regeneracionismo*.[109] These two influential cultural and political movements joined with the increasing activism of civil servants in demanding civil service reform. The press began to echo these demands, and national newspapers launched a campaign rejecting the dominance of politicians over civil service matters, as well as also calling for the outlawing of patronage.[110]

The first success in the struggle for civil service reform was reached in 1904. By Act of Parliament, a career civil service was created for the Ministry of the Treasury.[111] The reform established legal guarantees for meritocratic

---

[106] *La cuestion de los empleos públicos en España*, 1875.   [107] Villacorta Baños, 1989: 58.
[108] Villacorta Baños: 153.   [109] Torregrosa, 1996: 112.   [110] Villacorta Baños, 1989: 154.
[111] Morrell Ocaña, 2005: 133.

recruitment and security of tenure, which civil servants had been demanding for more than a quarter century. However, the new regulations were only applied to that specific ministry, and the movement continued to struggle for an extension of civil service reform to other areas of government. New political and professional magazines of civil servants, such as *Revista de Hacienda*, were created in the following years, employing a new open – not anonymous anymore – and "combative" tone to demand further reforms.[112]

A second significant success of the movement was reached in 1908, with the passing of three separate Acts of Parliament establishing civil service regulations for the Ministries of Government, Public Works, and Justice.[113] The movement continued to demand the extension of reform to all administrative areas, and its flagship political magazine, *Revista de Hacienda*, addressed Congress in 1910 with a series of such demands supported by a national plebiscite carried out by the magazine itself.[114] However, during the following years, the reform was only extended to the Ministry of the Presidency, in 1914.[115] The movement's progress seemed to slow down.

In the same year of 1914, however, crucial support for civil service reform was finally won among scholarly opinion. As previously discussed, legal scholars during the nineteenth century were sympathetic, or at least tolerant, regarding the issue of massive political patronage in Spain. With a lecture delivered at the University of Valladolid, Antonio Royo, a prestigious expert on public law, declared his support not only for the professionalization of the civil service, but also for the reform movement as an expression of the political association of civil servants.[116] The lecture presented scholarly and political arguments calling for a consolidation of the modern state in Spain by means of the creation of autonomous bureaucratic institutions. Expert civil servants, affirmed Royo, had to be in charge of running public services without political interference.[117] Royo's arguments were not just introduced in the lecture; they became an important part of his main published work, *Elements of Administrative Law*, a celebrated comprehensive treatment of the field, with fourteen editions by 1934.[118]

In the book, Royo underlines the technical superiority of public institutions run by career experts, compared to amateur political appointees. He also emphasizes the democratic character of a career civil service that manages public institutions without political interference. By not being subordinate to political power, the civil servants can develop a commitment to public service, with independence of partisan loyalties.[119]

The widespread impact of Royo's work in academic circles provided the reform movement with a fundamental endorsement, not only from a technical point of view, but also in terms of constitutional and democratic legitimacy, as

---

[112] Villacorta Baños, 1989: 157.   [113] Morrell Ocaña, 2005: 139.
[114] Villacorta Baños, 1989: 164.   [115] Morrell Ocaña, 2005: 139.   [116] Royo Villanova, 1914.
[117] Royo Villanova, 1930: 30.   [118] Royo Villanova, 1934.   [119] Royo Villanova, 1934: 262.

pronounced by one of the foremost scholars in the field. Added to the previous factors contributing to the advancement of civil service reform, the whole situation was to reach a breaking point after three more years.

The activism of public employees in demand of civil service reform escalated during 1917, including strikes and massive demonstrations.[120] By June of that year, protests and strikes by civil servants were one of the factors contributing to the fall of the country's government.[121] A decisive role in the protests was played by rank-and-file civil servants, the so called "low bureaucracy." The social composition of the protest movement made it easier to form a coalition with the Socialist Party, which took the lead in championing civil service reform during the following parliamentary debates on the issue.[122] In July of 1918, the Civil Service Act was passed by Congress. According to a wide consensus in contemporary scholarship, the reform of 1918 "established the fundament of a modern system of public administration" in Spain.[123]

As previously mentioned, some similarities can be observed between the civil service reform movements in Spain and in the United States. A comparison between the two national cases is interesting, because both countries experienced massive political patronage during the nineteenth century, and therefore, civil service reform involved a long and difficult political struggle. Already Max Weber, as early as 1919, had remarked upon the fact that the United States and Spain were, from among Western nations, the two cases where political patronage was most widely extended, affecting a majority of public employment positions.[124] For Weber, moreover, patronage practices in Spain and Latin America were very similar.[125] We will conclude this section by briefly pointing out three similar elements or components of the process of civil service reform in Spain and in the United States, which seemed to be instrumental for the final success of reforms in both cases.

First of all, an influential factor for the consolidation of a civil service reform movement was the presence, in both national cases, of a wider political orientation demanding improvements in governance, and the elevation of public morality. Such a general political and cultural movement represented in the United States the "Progressive Movement," whose support was crucial for the increasing echo found by demands for civil service reform in public and elite opinion.[126] In Spain, two wide cultural and political orientations had supported civil service reform since the end of the nineteenth century, *Regeneracionismo*, and the movement known as *Generación del 14*.

The endorsement of scholarly opinion was a second significant factor for the reform process. Scholarly endorsement did not involve just the public suppport for reform by prestigious members of the academic community, although this

---

[120] Nieto, 1986: 315, 326.   [121] Gutiérrez Reñón, 1987: 35.   [122] Nieto, 1986: 315.
[123] Jordana and Ramió, 2005: 981.   [124] Weber, 1994: 321.   [125] Weber, 1994.
[126] Cook, 2014.

was of course significant. Scholars also proposed institutional blueprints aimed at strengthening the role of career civil servants vis-à-vis the previous dominance of politicians. In the case of the United States, a classical scholarly endorsement of civil service reform was the work of Woodrow Wilson.[127] Wilson contributed to the design of a key institutional blueprint for the consolidation of a professional public administration in the United States, the independent government agency.[128] In Spain, Antonio Royo similarly proposed the creation of autonomous bureaucratic institutions run by career civil servants, following the French model, in order to protect those institutions from political interference.[129] Furthermore, Royo provided fundamental continuity between the ideas and blueprints for civil service reform that consolidated during the period of social and political modernization in Spain between 1914 and 1936, and the period of state modernization and (controlled) transition to democracy in the country between 1960 and 1978. Royo's comprehensive treatment of administrative law, with fourteen editions published by 1934, had reached twenty-five editions by 1960, thus becoming one of the main scholarly resources for teaching administrative law at Spanish universities. His son, Segismundo Royo, became not only a prestigious administrative law expert in his own right, and a co-author with his father, he was the president (Rector) of the most prestigious Spanish university in Madrid (*Complutense*) between 1956 and 1964. The training of the elite of administrative law experts, which came to be in charge of the modernization of state structures during the early 1960s, was thus based to a considerable extent on the ideas and proposals of Antonio Royo. [130]

Finally, the third factor that contributed to the consolidation of civil service reform in the United States and Spain was perhaps the most decisive: the awareness and engagement displayed by civil servants themselves in fighting for their sense of public mission, and for their reputation as defenders of the public interest. This important dimension of civil service reform has been traditionally overlooked by the literature, which has tended to consider the creation of a professional civil service as a "technical," top-down decision to be taken by public powers. However, the work of Skowronek, Skocpol and particularly Carpenter has shown that among the central actors for the advancement of institutional change during the US Progressive Era were the civil servants themselves, who actively sought the support of citizens' associations, and of public opinion at large, for the consolidation of reform.[131] The case of Spain amply confirms this historical fact. As in the United States, the activism of civil servants was essential for

---

[127] Wilson, 1887: 197–222.   [128] Breger and Edles, 2000: 1111–1294.
[129] Royo Villanova, 1934: 262.   [130] Casanova, 1983: 27–50.
[131] Skowronek, 1982; Skocpol, 1992; Carpenter, 2001; Carpenter, 2010.

consolidating a positive social perception of public service careers, for keeping the issue on the political agenda by means of a growing protest movement, and for building coalitions with other political actors in order to secure the passing of reform.

CONCLUSIONS

The results of the present chapter can be summarized in three points. First of all, the study of a specific industrial area, the automobile industry, has shown that developmental policies in Spain were very effective during the period 1950–1996. Among local economists, the opinions that vehemently deny any positive impact of industrial promotion on economic development seem to be mostly based on orthodox neoliberal ideology. Another motivation to deny the effectiveness of developmental policy in Spain, during and after the transition, was the understandable impulse to repudiate any positive public policy results of the Franco dictatorship, even against all evidence.

Secondly, the effectiveness of industrial policy in Spain was clearly connected to the professionalization of the public bureaucracy. This was shown in general terms by Evans and Rauch with their empirical-statistical test of the Weberian state hypothesis, which included Spain among their sample of thirty-five national cases.[132] The present chapter's first section has provided a much more detailed analysis of the same connection between bureaucratization and growth in Spain, pointing out how the bureaucratic reforms of the early 1960s resulted in much better quality of public management, markedly improved coordination of state agencies, and more sophisticated and ambitious long-term public policies.

The third point corresponds to the understanding of civil service reform as a political struggle spawning several decades, both in the cases of Spain and of the United States, until a professional state bureaucracy could be consolidated. The chapter's discussion underlined the crucial role played by civil servants themselves in advancing the cause of reform from below, but also the role of wide cultural and political movements demanding better, and more democratic public governance, as well as the significant contribution of scholarship. It has been shown, finally, that the legal and institutional blueprints for civil service reform in Spain, which were implemented during the period of state modernization and (controlled) transition to democracy between 1960 and 1978, were originally established during the period of profound social and political modernization of the country from 1914 to 1936.

---

[132] Evans and Rauch, 1999.

REFERENCES

Aceña, Pablo Martín and Francisco Comín. *INI: 50 años de industrialización en España*. Madrid: Espasa-Calpe, 1991.

Braña, Javier, Mikel Buesa, and José Molero. *El Estado y el cambio tecnológico en la industrialización tardía. Un análisis del caso español*. Madrid: Fondo de Cultura Económica: 1984.

Breger, Marshall J. and Gary J. Edles. "Established by Practice: The Theory and Operation of Independent Federal Agencies." *Administrative Law Review* 52, 4, 2000: 1111–1294.

Carpenter, Daniel P. *The Forging of Bureaucratic Autonomy. Reputations, Networks, and Policy Innovation in Executive Agencies, 1862–1928*. Princeton University Press, 2001.

Reputation and Power: Organizational Image and Pharmaceutical Regulation at the FDA. Princeton University Press, 2010.

Carrasco Canals, Carlos. *La burocracia en la España del siglo XIX*. Madrid: Instituto de Estudios de Administración Local, 1975.

Carreras, Albert. "La producción industrial española 1842–1981: construcción de un índice annual." *Revista de Historia Económica* 2, 1, 1984: 127–157.

"Industria." In *Estadísticas Históricas de España. Siglos XIX – XX*. 2nd. edn., eds. Albert Carreras and Xavier Tafunell. Bilbao: Fundación BBVA, 2005, 357–454.

Carreras, Albert and Salvador Estapé-Triay. "The Spanish Motor Industry 1930–1975." In *Entrepreneurship and Organization. The Role of the Entrepreneur in Organizational Innovation*, eds. Michael J. Lynskey and Seeichiro Yonekura. Oxford University Press, 2002: 123–152.

Casanova, José V. "The Opus Dei Ethic, the Technocrats, and the Modernization of Spain." *Social Science Information* 22, 1, 1983: 27–50.

Catalan, Jordi. "La creación de la ventaja comparativa en la industria automovilística española1898–1996." *Revista de Historia Industrial* 18, 2000: 113–155.

"La SEAT del Desarrollo, 1948–1972." *Revista de Historia Industrial* 15, 30, 2006: 143–192.

"Strategic Policy Revisited: The Origins of Mass Production in the Motor Industry of Argentina, Korea and Spain, 1945–87." *Business History* 52, 2, 2010: 207–230.

Centeno, Miguel A. and Agustin E. Ferraro. "Republics of the Possible: State Building in Latin America and Spain." In *State and Nation Making in Latin America and Spain: Republics of the Possible*, eds. Miguel A. Centeno and Agustin E. Ferraro. Cambridge University Press, 2013: 3–24.

Chan, Ha-Joong. *Kicking Away the Ladder: Development Strategy in Historical Perspective*. London: Anthem Press, 2003.

Chiang, Jong-Tsong. "Producing 'National Champions' in Technology Through Deliberate Strategic Decisions." *Technology in Society* 12, 1990: 235–254.

Chibber, Vivek. "Bureaucratic Rationality and the Developmental State." *American Journal of Sociology* 107, 4, 2002: 951–989.

Comín, Francisco. "El triunfo de la política sobre la economía en el INI de Suanzes." *Revista de Economía Aplicada* 9, 26, 2001: 177–211.

Cook, Brian J. *Bureaucracy and Self-Government: Reconsidering the Role of Public Administration in American Politics.* 2nd edn., Baltimore: Johns Hopkins University Press, 2014.

De la Torre, Joseba and Mario García-Zúñiga. "El impacto a largo plazo de la política industrial del desarrollismo español." *Investigaciones de Historia Económica – Economic History Research* 9, 2013: 43–53.

Evans, Peter. *Embedded Autonomy: States and Industrial Transformation.* Princeton University Press, 1995.

Evans, Peter and James Rauch. "Bureaucracy and Growth: A Cross-National Analysis of the Effects of 'Weberian' State Structures on Economic Growth." *American Sociological Review* 64, 5, 1999: 748–765.

Fallows, James M. *Looking at the Sun: The Rise of the New East Asian Economic and Political System.* New York: Pantheon, 1994.

Fernández de Sevilla, Tomàs. "FASA en l'arrencada de la indústria de l'automòbil a l'Estat espanyol, 1951–1965." *Recerques* 54, 2007: 115–144.

"Inside the Dynamics of Industrial Capitalism. The Mass Production of Cars in Spain, 1950–1985." *Revista de Historia Económica* 32, 2014: 287–315.

Ferraro, Agustin E. "A Splendid Ruined Reform: The Creation and Destruction of a Civil Service in Argentina." In *International Handbook on Civil Service Systems*, ed. Andrew Massey. Cheltenham: Edward Elgar, 2011, 152–177.

Gao, Bai. *Economic Ideology and Japanese Industrial Policy: Developmentalism from 1931 to 1965.* Cambridge University Press, 1997.

García de Enterría, Eduardo. "Prólogo" (Foreword to) *De la Administración Pública con relación a España* by Alejandro Oliván, 1843. Reprint, Madrid: Instituto de Estudios Políticos, 1954: 3–23.

García Ruiz, José Luis. "La evolución de la industria automovilística española, 1946–1999: una perspectiva comparada." *Revista de Historia Industrial* 19–20, 2001: 133–163.

González, Manuel-Jesús. *La economía política del franquismo 1940–1970. Dirigismo, mercado y planificación.* Madrid: Tecnos, 1979: 321.

Griffith, Rachel, Elena Huergo, Jacques Mairesse, and Bettina Peters. "Innovation and Productivity Across Four European Countries." *Oxford Review of Economic Policy* 22, 4, 2006: 483–498.

Grindle, Merilee S. *Jobs for the Boys. Patronage and the State in Comparative Perspective.* Cambridge and London: Harvard University Press, 2012.

Gutiérrez Reñón, Alberto. "La carrera administrativa en España: evolución histórica y perspectivas." *Documentación Administrativa* 210–211, May–September 1987: 29–70.

Haggard, Stephan and Robert R. Kaufman. *Development, Democracy, and Welfare States: Latin America, East Asia, and Eastern Europe.* Princeton University Press, 2008.

Harrison, Joseph. *An Economic History of Modern Spain.* New York: Holmes & Meier, 1978.

The Spanish Economy in the Twentieth Century, London and Sydney: Croom Helm, 1985: 130.

Henderson, William Otto. *The Rise of German Industrial Power, 1834–1914.* Berkeley and Los Angeles: University of California Press, 1975.

Johnson, Chalmers. *MITI and the Japanese Miracle. The Growth of Industrial Policy, 1925–1975.* Stanford University Press, 1982.

Jordana, Jacint and Carles Ramió. "Gobierno y Administración." In *Estadísticas Históricas de España. Siglos XIX – XX.* 2nd. edn., eds. Albert Carreras and Xavier Tafunell. Bilbao: Fundación BBVA, 2005, 973–1027.

Kohama, Hirohisa. *Industrial Development in Postwar Japan.* Abingdon: Routledge, 2007.

Kohli, Atul. *State-Directed Development. Political Power and Industrialization in the Global Periphery.* Cambridge University Press, 2004.

La cuestion de los empleos públicos en España, por un político con ganas de dejar de serlo. Madrid: Aribau y Ca., 1875.

Larra, Mariano José de. "Carta de Andrés Niporesas al Bachiller." *El pobrecito hablador. Revista satírica de costumbres, &c. &c.,* 10, December 1832: 5–24. Madrid: Imprenta de Repullés.

Lieberman, Sima. *The Contemporary Spanish Economy. A Historical Perspective.* London: George Allen & Unwin, 1982.

Growth and Crisis in the Spanish Economy 1940–1993. London and New York: Routledge, 1995.

List, Friedrich. *Das Nationale System der Politischen Oekonomie.* 1st edn Stuttgart and Tübingen: Cotta, 1841. Quoted from the reprint of the 7th edn, Jena: Gustav Fischer, 1910.

López-Claros, Augusto. *The Search for Efficiency in the Adjustment Process. Spain in the 1980s.* Washington, DC: International Monetary Fund, 1988.

Morrell Ocaña, Luis. "Las reformas administrativas de Maura." In *Reformistas y Reformas en la Administración Española. III Seminario de Historia de la Administración 2004,* ed. Instituto Nacional de Administración Pública. Madrid: Instituto Nacional de Administración Pública, 2005: 125–141.

Nieto, Alejandro. *Estudios históricos sobre administración y derecho administrativo.* Madrid: Instituto Nacional de Administración Pública, 1986.

Oliván, Alejandro. *De la Administración Pública con relación a España.* Madrid: Boix, 1843.

Pabón, Jesús. *Cambó: 1876–1947.* Barcelona: Alpha, 1999.

Parrado Diez, Salvador. "The Development and Current Features of the Spanish Civil Service System." In *Civil Service Systems in Western Europe,* eds. Hans Bekke and Frits van der Meer. Cheltenham: Edward Elgar, 2000, 247–274.

Posada de Herrera, José de. *Lecciones de Administración.* 1843. Reprint, Madrid: Instituto Nacional de Administración Pública, 1988.

Prados de la Escosura, Leandro, Joan R. Rosés and Isabel Sanz-Villaroya. "Stabilization and Growth under Dictatorship: The Experience of Franco's Spain." Universidad Carlos III de Madrid – Working Papers in Economic History, e-archivo.uc3 m.es /bitstream/10016/6987/1/wp_10–02.pdf (accessed December 2, 2016).

"Economic Reforms and Growth in Franco's Spain." *Revista de Historia Económica / Journal of Iberian and Latin American Economic History* 30, 1, 2011: 45–89.

Ros Hombravella, Jacint. *Política económica española, 1959–1973.* Barcelona: Blume, 1979.

Royo Villanova, Antonio. *La nueva descentralización.* Valladolid: Imprenta Castellana, 1914.

Elementos de Derecho Administrativo. 14ª edicion corregida y aumentada, 14th corrected and revised edn. Valladolid: Imprenta Castellana, 1934.

San Román, Elena. "El nacimiento de la SEAT: autarquía e intervención del INI." *Revista de Historia Industrial* 7, 1995: 141–165.

Sánchez, Esther M. "La implantación industrial de Renault en España: los Orígenes de FASA-Renault, 1950–1970." *Revista de Historia Económica / Journal of Iberian and Latin American Economic History* 22: 1, 2004: 147–175.

Schneider, Ben Ross. *Designing Industrial Policy in Latin America: Business-State Relations and the New Developmentalism*. New York: Palgrave, 2015.

Shin, Jang-Sup. *The Economics of the Latecomers: Catching-up, Technology Transfer, and Institutions in Germany, Japan, and South Korea*. London: Routledge, 1996.

Skocpol, Theda. *Protecting Soldiers and Mothers. The Political Origins of Social Policy in the United States*. Cambridge, MA: Harvard University Press, 1992.

Skowronek, Stephen. *Building a New American State. The Expansion of National Administrative Capacities 1877–1920*. Cambridge University Press, 1982.

Tappi, Andrea. *SEAT, modelo para armar. Fordismo y franquismo (1950–1980)*. Alzira: Editorial Germania, 2010.

Torregrosa, José R. "Spanish International Orientations: Between Europe and Iberoamerica." In *Changing European Identities: Social Psychological Analyses of Social Change*, eds. Glynis Marie Breakwell and Evanthia Lyons. Oxford: Butterworth-Heinemann, 1996: 111–122.

Tortella Casares, Gabriel. *El desarrollo de la España contemporánea. Historia económica de los siglos XIX y XX*. Madrid: Alianza, 1994.

Varela Ortega, José. *Los amigos políticos: partidos, elecciones y caciquismo en la Restauración, 1875–1900*. Madrid: Marcial Pons, 2001.

Villacorta Baños, Francisco. *Profesionales y burócratas. Estado y poder corporativo en la España del siglo XX, 1890–1923*. Madrid: Siglo XXI, 1989.

Weber, Max. "The Profession and Vocation of Politics" (first edition in German published in Munich and Leipzig, 1919). Quoted from the English translation in *Weber Political Writings*, eds. Peter Lassman and Ronald Speirs. Cambridge University Press, 1994: 309–369.

    Economy and Society. An Outline of Interpretive Sociology. Berkeley: University of California Press, 1978.

Williams, Michelle, ed. *The End of the Developmental State?* New York and Abingdon: Routledge, 2014.

Woo-Cumings, Meredith, ed. 1999. *The Developmental State*. Ithaca and London: Cornell University Press.

Woodrow Wilson, "The Study of Administration." *Political Science Quarterly* 2, 2, 1887.

Wright, Alison. *The Spanish Economy 1959–1976*. London and Basingstoke: Macmillan, 1977.

Zaratiegui, Jesús M. "Indicative Planning in Spain (1964–1975)." *International Journal of Business, Humanities and Technology* 5, 2, 2015: 33–43.

PART IV

INDUSTRY, TRADE, AND GROWTH: ECONOMIC POWER

9

Emergence and Maturity of the Developmental State in Argentina, Brazil, and Spain, 1930–1990: an Economic History Approach

Jordi Catalan and Tomàs Fernández-de-Sevilla

INTRODUCTION

The present chapter addresses the question of the degree of success that developmental states were able to achieve in three medium-to-large-sized Latin economies during the period 1930–1990.[1] The work employs the comparative method in economic history, and the cases of study are Argentina, Brazil and Spain.

The notion of the developmental state began to be explored by authors from countries that were lagging behind in real income since the late eighteenth century. They supported the application of state-led economic policies in order to bridge the gap with leading nations. Alexander Hamilton argued that protectionist policies were needed to develop the industry of the recently independent United States.[2] Friedrich List declared it necessary to build a national economy for German states, in order to catch up with the leader of the first industrial revolution, Great Britain.[3] Also in Germany, Max Weber supported the consolidation of a modern state bureaucracy, capable of

The authors wish to express their gratitude to the Spanish Ministry of Economy (MINECO) and to the European Regional Development Fund (ERDF) for their financial support for this research through project HAR2015-64769-P (Industrial crisis and productive recovery in the history of Spain), and to the Kurgan-van Hentenryk Chair in Business History of the Solvay Brussels School of Economics and Management.

[1] We use the terms "Latin" or also "Iberoamerican" to refer to countries in Latin America, and to the two major countries of the Iberian Peninsula, Spain and Portugal. All these nations share a cultural and institutional past with partly common historical origins. Moreover, during the developmental era, the political and technocratic elites of Iberoamerican countries were often closely following the experiences of other nations in the area, as models or benchmarks. This applied particularly to Argentina, Brazil, and Spain, the case studies in the present chapter. Regarding the adoption of relatively similar institutional and economic policy frameworks during the 1960s in the three countries, see Jaguaribe, 1973: 532–533. For more details on the similarities between technocratic authoritarian regimes in Latin countries, see the Conclusion by Ferraro and Centeno in this volume.

[2] Hamilton, 1791.   [3] List, 1841.

promoting social rationality and economic growth.[4] The Meiji Restoration, in Japan, endorsed similar objectives of modernization and industrialization led by state institutions.

In more recent times, a leading economic historian, Alexander Gerschenkron, declared industrial development policies to be necessary in order for national economies to cross the threshold that Great Britain had achieved spontaneously with the main thrust of market forces.[5] For Gerschenkron, the Meiji Restoration suggested that the state can play a decisive role in the promotion of industrialization. It was precisely the analysis of the Japanese success that led to the concept of the developmental state, as defined by Chalmers Johnson.[6] This author described planning in Japan, in charge of the Ministry for Trade and Industry (MITI), and run by a professional bureaucracy, as the key to the Japanese "economic miracle." The strategy of macroeconomic planning guided by the state was also applied in South Korea. Authors such as Alice Amsden and Ha-Joon Chang have focused on the central role of industrial policies adopted by the government as the basis for the economic take-off of the country.[7] The case of South Korea is particularly interesting, because it was the national economy with the biggest growth in GDP per capita during the second half of the twentieth century.[8] Finally, China reaching the industrial podium of the twenty-first century, thanks to the reforms initiated by Deng Xiaoping is another paradigmatic case of the success of the developmental state and of "Confucian capitalism."[9]

The boost to development with a strong state component was not, however, limited to Asia or just to industry.[10] We have already mentioned that some of the pioneers in defending the direct involvement of governments in the promotion of national growth were German, such as List and Weber. Germany had indeed been clearing the way in other key aspects for long-term development. The Lutheran church and compulsory primary education led to high levels of literacy in the German states. Prussia explicitly promoted research and development by creating university chairs and public libraries. In the final stretch of the nineteenth century, Bismarck also paved the way for redistributive policies supporting workers, thus promoting the creation of the welfare state. Authors such as Peter Flora and Michel Albert have underlined these aspects, giving rise to the thesis of the emergence of "Rhine capitalism," as an alternative to the Anglo-Saxon "liberal capitalism."[11] Economic historians such as David Landes and Werner Abelshauser have insisted on this path of modernization,

---

[4] Weber, 1922.   [5] Gerschenkron, 1962.   [6] Johnson, 1982.

[7] Amsden, 1989; Chang, 1993: 131–157; Woo-Cumings, 1999; Chang, 2002; Lin and Chang, 2009: 483–502; and Andreoni and Chang, 2017: 173–187.

[8] For more details on economic development and state bureaucracies in Germany, Japan, and South Korea, see Chapter 8 in this volume. See also Catalan, 2010: 207–230.

[9] Catalan, 2017: 4–34.   [10] See, for instance, Evans, 1995; and Mazzucato, 2013.

[11] Flora and Heidenheimer, 1981; Albert, 1993.

close to the approaches of the developmental state.[12] Indeed, redistributive policies in favor of workers, such as public education, regulation of the labor market, and progressive tax reforms, constituted a mainstay of the developmental state, complementing macroeconomic policy with the promotion of industrial growth.

The aim of the present chapter is to assess to what extent intervention to promote industrial development was adopted by the governments of three Latin countries, Argentina, Brazil, and Spain, and to evaluate their results.

BETWEEN FASCISM AND THE DEVELOPMENTAL STATE, 1930–1953

Spain, Argentina, and Brazil were, in 1930, economies that mainly exported primary products and that showed highly concentrated agricultural land ownership. In the three Latin countries, governments were traditionally dominated by big landowning elites, interested in promoting agricultural exports without establishing too many obstacles to the free operation of the market. However, the hegemony of agrarian interests began to be eroded at the end of the nineteenth century and, above all, as a result of the shock represented by the Great War. During the 1930s and early 1940s, the success of Italian, German, and Japanese fascism exerted an irresistible magnetism over the Latin world.

In Spain, the dominance of free trade was shattered by the agricultural crisis of the turn of the century, which led to the approval of a first protective tariff in 1891, followed by another two in 1906 and 1922. Moreover, after the First World War, the Ministry of Public Works and the *Mancomunitat* of Catalonia supported the modernization of railways and the construction of roads, hydraulic works, and telephone networks. After coming to power by a *coup d'état* in 1923, General Miguel Primo de Rivera adopted similar developmental objectives as part of his policy program, and his administration made significant public investments, but at the expense of increasing the debt. Although Primo de Rivera's goals were for Spain to enter the gold standard and achieve a balanced budget, unequivocal symbols of the liberal order prior to 1914, his administration was very far from achieving those results, and he resigned at the beginning of 1930, leaving the peseta in free fall. In April 1931, after the triumph of the anti-monarchical forces in municipal elections, King Alfonso XIII left for exile in Italy and the Second Republic was proclaimed.

In Argentina, the impact of the First World War on exports of agricultural products and imports of capital was dramatic, and it favored the electoral victory of the Radical Civic Union (Unión Cívica Radical, UCR) in 1916. The administration of President Hipólito Yrigoyen applied redistributive policies in favor of workers, such as the regulation of the 48-hour week, the creation of the minimum wage, and substantial expansion of public employment. He also promoted the creation of Yacimientos Petrolíferos

---

[12] Landes, 1998; Abelshauser, 2005.

Fiscales (YPF) in order to exploit a decisive strategic resource, oil, the company being one of the first international experiences of public intervention in this sphere. In 1927, the peso returned to the gold standard, and fiscal policies became more restrictive. The Wall Street crash of October 1929 led to the collapse of exports of agricultural products, and Yrigoyen was forced to close the *Caja de Conversión* (currency board) in December. The drop in foreign exchange, and the corresponding collapse of the peso, facilitated a military coup, supported by the big meat- and cereal-exporting interests, and the second administration of Yrigoyen came to a violent end in 1930. General Uriburu became the new occupant of the Casa Rosada.

In Brazil, the power of the landowners was, if possible, even greater than in Spain and Argentina, given that the country was the last in the Americas to abolish slavery in 1888. Coffee-export interests continued to control the government of Rio de Janeiro until the end of the 1920s. Like in Argentina and Spain, the tendencies of the military towards *coups d'état* could be felt in republican Brazil, with failed episodes in 1922 and 1927. However, on the eve of the outbreak of the Great Depression, the democratic government continued to be in the hands of the owners of the São Paulo coffee plantations, under the presidency of Washington Luiz, who had also managed to return Brazil to the gold standard in 1927, adopting restrictive fiscal and monetary measures. However, Brazilian stabilization did not last long, and the gold convertibility of the national currency had to be suspended as a result of the shock resulting from the collapse of coffee exports. In October 1930, gold reserves were depleted, and the gold standard had to be abandoned. A new uprising by army lieutenants, initially triumphant in Pernambuco, ended up offering power to Getúlio Vargas, who assumed the presidency in November.

In Spain, the Second Republic abandoned some of the expansionist policies of General Primo de Rivera, and cut back the subsidies to railway companies, as well as the road and hydraulic work programs.[13] Moreover, the Spanish Republic stabilized the peseta in relation to the French franc, at a time when the majority of European currencies began to imitate England, after it abandoned gold convertibility in September 1931. The restrictive Spanish monetary policy contributed to hinder full economic recovery.

Nevertheless, the republican governments attempted to implement developmental policies in other areas, investing in the fight against illiteracy, and in public schools and libraries. Agrarian reform was passed, including the expropriation of large estates and the consolidation of *jurados mixtos*

---

[13] Basic references on the economic history of the Great Depression in Spain and Early Francoism are the following: Fontana and Nadal, 1976: 95–163; Carreras, 1984: 127–157; García-Delgado, 1985: 135–145; Fontana, 1986; Palafox, 1991; Martín-Aceña and Comín, 1991; Catalan, 1995; Comín, 1996; San Román, 1999; Gómez-Mendoza, 2000; Barciela, 2003; Vilar, 2009; Catalan, 2011: 55–114; Catalan, 2012: 229–265; and Comín, 2013: 133–164.

(arbitration boards) to improve labor conditions in agriculture and industry. Wages tended to go up, which avoided deflation, and the minister of finance, Jaume Carner, created a new income tax in order to increase fiscal resources. The lack of foreign reserves made it necessary to adopt exchange controls, and to increase protections for national production. This policy also favored state intervention in industries such as the automobile sector, including tariff reductions for the import of components destined for use in national production.

A group of generals rose against the republican government in July 1936, when the Spanish economy had not yet fully overcome the Great Depression. What was expected to be a quick *coup d'état* became a ferocious class war, which lasted for nearly three years, and which General Francisco Franco eventually won as a result of vast military support from Italy and Germany. As early as 1937, the military insurgents began to implement a plan to promote war-related industrial activities, strongly influenced by the policies of their allies, in particular by the experiences of the *Vier Jahre Plan* of the Third Reich, and by Mussolini's Instituto per la Ricostruzione Industriale. These industrial policies, which were consolidated at the end of the war, in April 1939, included the rationing of inputs, price controls, the adoption of a system of investment licenses, the establishment of a limit to the share of foreign investment of 25 percent of the capital of local firms, the granting of benefits to industries of national interest, and the creation of a state-owned holding company, Instituto Nacional de Industria (INI). Although some of these measures could be considered to be developmental, it should be taken into account that they responded above all to the objective of promoting wartime autarky, a significant priority of Franco himself, and of his first minister of industry and future president of INI, Juan Antonio Suanzes. The great majority of the activities promoted with these policies were therefore directly related to war: synthesis of liquid fuels, communications networks in colonial Morocco, shipbuilding, aircraft construction, mining, aluminum, trucks, and nitrogen.

The type of investments promoted by Early Francoism consumed a great deal of resources and delayed economic recovery. The recovery was further obstructed by the need to service the Civil War debt, which Germany wanted to recover during the Second World War, and by an aggressive foreign policy with the Allies, which ended up cutting off the supplies of strategic inputs to Spain, such as oil and fertilizers, and excluding the country from the 1947 Marshall Plan. Moreover, the banishment of unions and strikes, and the centralized establishment of wages by the Ministry of Labor, led to a dramatic fall in real income during 1939. The inflationary financing of the public budget eroded real wages again during the Second World War, and prevented their recovery when the war ended. Thus, between 1936 and 1952, Spain experienced a permanent reduction in real wages, which ended up affecting workers' efficiency and labor productivity. The high inflation combined with an immovable fixed exchange rate also affected exports very negatively until 1948, when a multiple exchange rate system was adopted – a hidden devaluation.

TABLE 9.1 _Annual Growth Rates of GDP per Capita in 1990 GK Dollars (%)_

	Argentina	Brazil	Spain
1929–53	0.47	2.01	−0.18
1953–73	2.48	4.01	5.82
1973–90	−1.12	1.22	1.97

Note: 1990 Geary-Kamis dollars.
Source: Own calculation with Maddison, 1995.

In the industrial sphere, the regime also began to shift policies, promoting other investments not strictly related to the war, such as electricity production (ENDESA and EN Hidroeléctrica Ribagorzana) and passenger-car production (SEAT). At the beginning of the 1950s, rationing was eased, and some economic controls were eliminated. Nevertheless, Spain's GDP per capita of 1929 was not recovered until 1954, that is to say, fifteen years after the end of the Civil War. Spain lost two decades in terms of development (Table 9.1).

In Argentina, the military coup led by Uriburu also showed a clear anti-urban bias.[14] Uriburu, until 1932, and the governments of the Concordancia, until 1943, promoted a stricter economic orthodoxy than the Spanish insurgents of 1936. During the biennium 1930–1932, the Casa Rosada announced cuts in wages and salaries, brought new public works to a standstill, and endeavored to restore a balanced budget. It also undertook to continue to service the foreign debt in gold. The presidents of the Concordancia regime from 1932 to 1943, especially Agustín Pedro Justo, tried to restore the previous liberal order. In 1933 the Roca–Runciman Treaty was signed, according to which Argentina undertook to continue to service the debt with Great Britain, and offered numerous reductions on customs duties for British manufactures, in exchange for the British commitment to import at least the average amount of meat production acquired in 1931–1932.

However, despite the preference for economic orthodoxy, the Argentine presidents of the 1930s suffered from a drastic scarcity of foreign reserves, and they had to increase custom duties, tighten exchange controls, and renegotiate the servicing of the foreign debt, while trying to compensate for the fall in customs revenue by increasing direct taxation. The Banco Central de

---

[14] The impact of the Great Depression on the Argentinian economy, the economic policy of the Concordancia governments, and the early strategy of Peron are analyzed in Díaz-Alejandro, 1970; Furtado, 1974; Maddison, 1988; Abreu, 1988: 171–190; Taylor, 1994: 649–683; Thorp, 1998; Rock, 2001: 167–222; Barbero and Rocchi, 2003: 261–294; Paolera and Gallo, 2003: 365–375; Cortés-Conde, 2005; Rapoport, 2005; Belini, 2009; Belini and Rougier, 2008; Catalan, 2010: 207–230; Belini and Korol, 2012; Belini, 2014; Catalan, 2014: 15–45; and Belini, 2017.

la República Argentina was established in 1935, as part of a broader package of reform and banking laws. The gradual adoption of not very orthodox economic policies was in line with the regulatory shift that began in the United States with the devaluation of the dollar, the approval of the Glass-Steagall Act, and Roosevelt's New Deal beginning in 1933. Argentina also adopted a multiple-exchange-rate system, which had first been applied in Germany.

The most substantial change of direction toward economic interventionism occurred, however, as a result of a new military putsch led by the United Officers' Group (GOU) in 1943. This new round of military administrations gave greater value to the interventionist policies which had favored the rapid recovery of Nazi Germany and Fascist Italy from the Great Depression. Thus, between 1943 and 1946, the first Industrial Promotion Act was approved, in addition to the creation of the Banco de Crédito Industrial Argentino and a new Secretary of Labor to promote workers' welfare. The position of Labor Secretary was given to Juan Domingo Perón, who had spent a large part of the conflict as military attaché in the Rome embassy. There, he had become an admirer of Mussolini, and especially of his workers' mobilization model, with a vertical union system based on the *Corporazioni*. On his return to Buenos Aires, Perón endeavored to forge a comparable alliance between the government and the workers on the basis of adopting policies which favored the working class through generous wage increases, paid holidays, collective-bargaining agreements, and the inclusion of many groups of workers in the pension system. When the war ended, Perón founded the Justicialist Party (which he initially intended to designate as the Labor Party).

Peron's 1946 electoral victory consolidated the trend toward labor-oriented social policies, and economic planning. The Peronist decade included two consecutive five-year plans, nationalizations, the creation of several public corporations, and a considerable regulation of foreign trade coordinated by the newly established Instituto Argentino para la Promoción y el Intercambio (IAPI). The economic policy of the first Peronism can be considered as an attempt to promote a developmental state in the Southern Cone, although the nationalizations sometimes responded to the interest of the former owners in disassociating themselves from obsolete activities.

Together with the nationalizations of the railways, gas, water, telephones, merchant navy, airlines, and the Central Bank, Perón encouraged initiatives to promote import-substitution industrialization. Some public corporations had already been created before his administration, such as the oil corporation YPF, and military industries. Perón created a new public holding company with firms expropriated from German owners during the war, and tried to favor the establishment of public–private partnerships to support domestic production. Some of the main projects experienced considerable delays or failed due to the growing lack of foreign currency, with the notable case of the steelworks company SOMISA, and the projects run by the Directorate for Military Industries to manufacture basic chemicals, non-ferrous metals, and trucks.

Other projects were more successful: the joint venture ATANOR, with technical support from Monsanto, began the manufacture of synthetic tires and plastic resins. Industrias Aeronáuticas y Mecánicas del Estado (IAME), created in 1952, succeeded in producing four-wheel-drive vehicles and passenger cars.

The developmental policies during the first Peronist era had a high financial cost, which could initially be afforded thanks to the foreign exchange accumulated during the Second World War. The reserves were, however, consumed fast during the second half of the 1940s, and they were almost depleted at the end of the decade. From then onwards, exchange controls were strengthened, but creation of liquidity remained high. Inflation shot up, and Perón was forced to adjust his policies at the beginning of the 1950s. However, in relation to the Spain of the early Franco regime, the policies of Perón's Argentina correspond better to the characterization of a developmental state, and its long-term results were more successful. Argentina grew at an average rate per capita of 0.5 percent from 1929 to 1953 (see Table 9.1).

Brazil maintained the strongest continuity in developmental policies between 1930 and 1953.[15] Getúlio Vargas led the country from 1930 until his suicide in 1954, with a slight parenthesis during the second half of the 1940s. A military junta handed over the presidency to Vargas in November 1930. Until 1933, the former governor of Rio Grande do Sul had to face a civil war, resulting from an uprising in São Paulo. Vargas, however, remained firm at the head of the provisional government until 1934, when he won national elections and became president. In 1937, he demonstrated his authoritarian leanings by proclaiming a form of corporatist state, Estado Novo, which would remain in force until the end of the Second World War. He abandoned the presidency in 1945, but returned with a further electoral triumph in 1951.

Three elements of public policy continuity during the administrations of Vargas are significant. First of all, he adopted interventionist policies that benefited industrial workers: reduction of the working day, introduction of paid leave, minimum wage, social security provisions, protections for women and children, and the creation of new ministries of Labor, Industry and Trade, and Education and Public Health. Although Vargas' fascist temptation led him to repress autonomous trade unionism, and to force the vertical integration of unions, overall his social and labor policies led to a sustained improvement in the living conditions of the Brazilian working class. At the end of the Second World War, Vargas abandoned his more authoritarian orientation, and promoted the foundation of the *Partido Trabalhista*.

---

[15] The Brazilian process of industrialization and the economy of the corporatist state created by Vargas, from its origins during the Great Depression to his suicide, have been characterized in Furtado, 1959; Dean, 1969; Peláez, 1972; Furtado,1974; Cano, 1981; Suzigan, 1986; Peláez, 1987; Dean, 1988: 23–54; Abreu, 1988; Fonseca, 1989; Abreu, 1990; Maddison, 1992; Negri, 1996; Ramalho, 1997: 159–179; Thorp,1998; Fausto, 2006; Wolfe, 2010; Bresser-Pereira, 2014; Catalan, 2014: 15–45; Fonseca and Salomão, 2016: Chapter 3; Schwarcz and Starling, 2016.

Secondly, Vargas adopted developmental policies in the face of demands for budget orthodoxy and the servicing of the foreign debt. Unlike President Uriburu in Argentina, he declared a moratorium on public debt in 1931 and, during the Great Depression, Brazil did not record the levels of deflation that affected the southern republic. The administration of Vargas decisively undertook roadbuilding works and, starting in 1937, directly supported industrial growth. At that time, the Banco do Brasil established its portfolio of industrial financing, and started to give long-term credit for manufacturing projects. Vargas also sponsored the establishment of public or public–private corporations to produce steel (Companhia Siderúrgica Nacional, 1941), to build combustion engines (Fábrica Nacional de Motores, 1942), to extract iron ore (Companhia Vale do Rio Doce, 1942), to produce caustic soda (Companhia Nacional de Álcalis, 1943), and to generate electricity (Companhia Hidroelétrica do São Francisco, 1945). After the presidency of Eugénio Gaspar Dutra 1945–1951, Vargas strengthened the developmental state project, creating the Banco Nacional de Desenvolvimento Economico e Social or BNDE (1952), and the oil and electricity public corporations Petrobras (1953) and Eletrobras (1954). Moreover, during his last administration, Vargas restricted imports of automotive components in order to promote the domestic industry. Beginning in the 1930s, Vargas also attempted to fight illiteracy, which affected almost 50 percent of the population, and had dramatic rates among the descendants of slaves (Table 9.2), making primary education compulsory in 1934. The tax reform approved in that same year increased fiscal resources by expanding the direct tax base and thus mitigating the fall experienced in customs revenues.

Finally, the third axis of public policy continuity during the era of Vargas was the sustained support for agricultural producers, through intervention in markets such as coffee or cotton, the purchase and destruction of surpluses during the Great Depression, and the introduction of a policy of minimum prices since 1943. During the Estado Novo, the Bank of Brazil likewise created a specific portfolio for agricultural credit.

TABLE 9.2 *Proportion of Illiterates among the 15-year-old Population (%)*

Argentina	Brazil	Spain
1947	1950	1950
13.6	50.6	17.6
1970	1976	1970
7.4	24.3	9.8
1980	1991	1986
6.1	20.3	4.2

Source: UNESCO, various years.

Unlike in Spain or Argentina, the developmental policies in Brazil were maintained throughout the period from the early 1930s to the 1950s. Brazil therefore experienced an accelerated expansion of the industrial production of consumer goods, and achieved growth per capita rates much higher than the other two countries. According to Maddison's estimates, its annual rate of growth per inhabitant during 1929–1953 reached 2 per cent (Table 9.1).

THE GOLDEN AGE OF THE DEVELOPMENTAL STATE, 1953–1973.

During the two decades following the Korean War, the three Latin economies consolidated their industrialization policies. Their developmental states reached their peak.

In Spain, the Franco regime reformed its public policy framework to achieve more stable growth.[16] The reforms came in two rounds, which coincided with the two changes of decade. Between 1948 and 1953, the peseta was de facto devalued using the multiple-exchange-rate system, price controls were relaxed, the Industry and Trade portfolios were separated, food rationing was abolished, the centralized distribution of inputs was reduced, and the public holding INI channeled its resources toward activities not strictly focused on war such as electricity production (ENDESA and ENHER), oil-refining (REPESA), passenger-car production (SEAT) and steel manufacturing (ENSIDESA). These policies, together with other exogenous changes, such as the Korean War, United States support, the arrival of foreign tourism, and the increase in reserves sent by Spanish emigrants, favored the achievement of record growth rates during the Second Francoism period, which culminated around 1959.

However, the acceleration of the industrialization process during the 1950s caused some imbalances, which required a new round of reforms. In particular, inflation shot up again during the second half of the 1950s, and foreign reserves ran out at the beginning of 1959. The multiple exchange rate, and the import-license system, tended to benefit businesspeople well connected with the regime, and distortions in the intervention of some markets, such as wheat, cement, and steel, continued to impact negatively on growth. A second round of reforms began slowly in 1957, and consolidated with the 1959 stabilization plan.

The Spanish stabilization plan was designed by a university professor, Joan Sardá, who had worked in his youth for the authorities of Republican Catalonia during the Civil War, and who ended up as the head of the Research Service of the Bank of Spain. The plan was a key element of bureaucratic rationalization of Spanish growth, and it opened the way for the period of Developmental

---

[16] The Francoist economy during the golden age of capitalism has been studied in the following works: Fontana and Nadal, 1976: 95–163; Carreras, 1984: 127–157; Muns, 1986; García-Delgado, 1990: 137–160; Martín-Aceña and Comín, 1991; Comín, 1996; Carreras and Tafunell, 2003; Catalan, 2010; Catalan, 2011; Catalan and Fernández-de-Sevilla, 2013: 254–284; Fernández-de-Sevilla, 2014: 287–315; and Catalan, 2015.

Francoism. It combined strict adjustment measures to curb the unsustainable growth of demand, with structural reforms aimed at consolidating development. The latter included the reunification of the exchange rate, the external convertibility of the peseta, and a sharp devaluation. The limit to the share of foreign investment in local firms was increased from 25 to 50 percent. Tariffs recovered their strategic role in the promotion of industrial development, to the detriment of import quotas and contingents, and a new protective tariff was approved in 1960. The range of products exempted from quotas was gradually expanded until 1962. However, the import of articles such as passenger cars and their components, whose domestic production was considered strategic, continued to be restricted with high tariffs, quotas, and licensing. Central allocation agencies were also dismantled in industries such as cement and steelmaking.

During the biennium 1962–1963, the financial system was reformed. The Bank of Spain and the Banco de Crédito Industrial were nationalized, and the creation of new private banks was authorized, but with a regulation framework separating between commercial or investment banks, along the lines of the system introduced in the United States by the Glass-Steagall Act during the 1930s. Finally, five-year development plans, with indicative orientation following the French model, established objectives which were compulsory for state-owned companies, and voluntary for private companies. Beginning in 1964, concerted actions were established with private capital in order to reach specific development goals. The sectors promoted by the industrial policy of the 1960s were similar to those of the previous decade: steel, automobiles, electricity, shipbuilding, and petrochemical. The new Minister of Industry, Gregorio López Bravo, also gave high priority to exports. As a result of state-led investments, new learning processes with state support, and direct public subsidies, Spain achieved its highest growth rates for industrial production until then. GDP per capita grew fast, recording an average of 5.8 percent from 1953 to 1973 (Table 9.1). Moreover, by 1973, Spain had become an exporter of industrial products with the prominence of state-supported industries, such as automobiles and ships, and some less-subsidized activities, such as footwear and books (Table 9.3).[17]

In Argentina, Perón also tried to reform his original policies, and moderated the redistributive and intervening impetus after his first presidential term of office.[18] During Perón's second administration 1952–1955, the weight of

---

[17] For an analysis of public agencies in charge of development policies for the motor industry in Spain, see Chapter 8 in this volume. See also Catalan and Fernández-de-Sevilla, 2013: 254–284.
[18] The economic development of Argentina between the first presidency of Perón and his return in 1973 has been analyzed in the following works: Díaz-Alejandro, 1970; Sourrouille, 1980; Taylor, 1994: 649–683; Thorp, 1998; Katz, 2000: 307–334; Torre and De Riz, 2001: 223–316; Palma, 2003: 125–151; Barbero and Rochi, 2003: 261–294; Paolera and Gallo, 2003: 369–375; Rougier, 2004; Cortés-Conde, 2005; Rapoport, 2005; Rougier and Schwarzer, 2006; Rougier, 2007; Belini, 2009; Belini and Rougier, 2008; Catalan, 2010; Artopoulos, 2012; Belini and Korol, 2012; Rougier, 2012; Belini, 2014; and Belini, 2017.

TABLE 9.3 *The Fifteen Main Automobile Producers from 1928 to 1991 (Thousands of Units)*

	1928				1950	
1	USA	4539		1	USA	8003
2	Canada	242		2	United Kingdom	784
3	United Kingdom	212		3	Canada	390
4	France	210		4	USSR	359
5	Germany	90		5	France	358
6	Italy	55		6	FRG	305
7	Czechoslovakia	13		7	Italy	129
8	Austria	9		8	Belgium	49
9	Belgium	7		9	Australia	38
10	Switzerland	2		10	Japan	32
11	Sweden	1		11	Czechoslovakia	31
12	Russia	0.8		12	Sweden	17
13	Japan	0.5		13	GDR	9
14	Hungary	0.5		14	Hungary	3
15	*Spain*	0.3		15	Netherlands	1
	1973				**1991**	
1	USA	12638		1	Japan	13245
2	Japan	7088		2	USA	8790
3	FRG	3949		3	FRG	5035
4	France	3242		4	France	3611
5	United Kingdom	2164		5	Russia	2052
6	Italy	1960		6	*Spain*	2082
7	USSR	1604		7	Canada	1889
8	Canada	1575		8	Italy	1878
9	Belgium	1016		9	South Korea	1498
10	*Spain*	823		10	United Kingdom	1454
11	*Brazil*	733		11	Mexico	989
12	Australia	410		12	*Brazil*	960
13	Sweden	383		13	China	709
14	Mexico	283		14	Taiwan	382
15	*Argentina*	282		15	India	355

Sources: Catalan, 2000: 113–154 and "WardsAuto," motor vehicles, facts and figures," wardsauto .com/data-center (accessed November 19, 2017).

salaries in the national income, which had increased from 40 to 50 percent between 1946 and 1952, went down to 47 percent in 1955, as a result of the introduction of wage and price controls. Inflation also moderated. Official reticence towards foreign investment decreased, although without disappearing: Standard Oil of California was authorized to exploit oil fields in Patagonia, and the owner of American Motors, Henry Kaiser, was authorized to create a joint venture based in the province of Córdoba. In addition to American capital, Argentinean public and private shareholders also had a stake in this motor company, baptized as Industrias Kaiser Argentina (IKA). Kaiser Motors transferred technology and accepted to use 90 percent of components of Argentine origin. IKA was devoted to manufacturing jeeps, passenger cars, and vans, and it became the first manufacturer to cross the threshold of mass production in Argentina. It likewise played a decisive role in promoting the local production of components. It was a true national champion of the Argentine automotive industry until the mid 1960s. As a result, Argentina was able to appear among the fifteen main automobile producers at the beginning of the 1970s (see Table 9.3).

Perón did not, however, see this success from the *Casa Rosada*, since he was removed by the *coup d'état* of the *Revolución Libertadora* in September 1955. Between this date and the election of Arturo Frondizi in 1958, the military regime abruptly broke with the Justicialist policies. The application of the Second Development Plan was paralyzed, and the institution created in 1946 to regulate foreign trade (IAPI) was dissolved. Price and wage controls were lifted. However, although Argentina became a member of the International Monetary Fund, and devalued considerably the peso, the policies of the *Revolución Libertadora* resulted in a new upsurge of inflation, which required subsequent adjustment measures. Argentina fully entered stop-and-go cycles afterwards, which meant that the economic growth of the golden age of development was less substantial in the country than in most developing economies.

Frondizi, the leader of the center-left Unión Cívica Radical, won the 1958 election with the promise of legalizing the Justicialist Party, which had been banned by the military, although he never went through with his commitment. His administration applied a stabilization plan, which was not as successful as Sardá's plan in Spain, and tried to continue to support industrial growth, with a high level of tariff protection, but allowing foreign capital to play a greater, sometimes excessive, role. Frondizi's administration signed agreements with ten foreign companies for the extraction of crude oil as early as the summer of 1958. He established the public steelmaking firm SOMISA, and supported investments to manufacture cellulose, pulp, and petrochemical products. He authorized the establishment of a total of twenty-three vehicle-assembly companies, which represented the arrival in Argentina of the sector's biggest international manufacturers. Finally, Frondizi's administration privatized fifteen public corporations of the holding created with firms confiscated from

German owners during the war (DINIE), as well as the public shipyards, and closed down 3,000 km of railway network. In sum, Frondizi's policy framework was half-way between Perón's developmentalism, and the more orthodox liberalism of the *Revolución Libertadora*. However, like the former, he continued to support industrialization.

The administrations of José María Guido 1962–1963, and Arturo Illía 1963–1966, attempted to continue the public support for industrialization, but the former was burdened by the need to apply adjustment and austerity policies to fight inflation. Illía was actually removed from office by disgruntled elements of the military following a fast increase in the inflation rate. The *Revolución Argentina*, which took power in June 1966, was led by Juan Carlos Onganía, who occupied the *Casa Rosada* until June 1970. This general was an avowed admirer of Franco, and shared the latter's interest in industrialization, and especially in the construction of reservoirs and electric and nuclear power stations. His administration built the system of dams and hydroelectricity generation facilities at El Chocón-Cerros Colorados, and expanded the generating capacity of electric plants in the industrial area of Buenos Aires (SEGBA). Onganía also promoted the construction of the *Atucha* nuclear power station. His administration introduced again prices and wage controls in order to curb the progressive acceleration of inflation, and managed to reduce the rate from 32 percent in 1966 to 8 percent in 1969. Industrial production continued to grow at record rates but some sectors, which depended on increasing mass production to remain profitable, suffered from the competition arising from a careless policy of authorizations of new firms. This was the case of the automobile industry, where IKA, despite launching an Argentine prototype – the famous *Torino* – ended up retreating in the face of giants such as Ford and Fiat. The escalating workers' discontent in one of the main industrial areas of the country led to a concentrated social upheaval in March 1969, known as the *Cordobazo*.

Successive short-lived administrations, led by top military officials, replaced Onganía, until the democratic transition resulted in Peronist Héctor Cámpora being elected president in May 1973, and followed by the return of Perón from exile in October. New presidential elections were called, which the old nationalist leader won in a landslide. Perón planned the creation of a new public holding corporation, the Corporación Nacional de Empresas del Estado, and a return to sound economic planning. However, he came back from exile with a new and more tolerant political disposition, and he declared himself to be in favor of promoting a vast social agreement, which was going to include wage moderation in order to tackle inflationary expectations. Unfortunately, the sudden death of Perón in July 1974 marked the end of an era. Overall, the administrations from 1953 to 1973 – with an interruption during the *Revolución Libertadora* of 1955–1958 – agreed on the need to the implement developmental policies, and to promote industrial growth. Some administrations were burdened by the need to apply restrictive measures due to the excessive expansionist policies of their predecessors. Others allowed too much competition for industries where scale of production was the key for profitability, and the presence of too many firms resulted in harm overall. However, when all is said and done, industrialization had progressed, and Argentina achieved a significant annual growth rate (2.5 per cent) during this period, although lower than those of the two other Iberoamerican economies in comparison (Table 9.1).

Brazil never experienced swings in its economic policy comparable with those recorded south of the River Plate.[19] However, the public spending necessary to finance an expansionist industrial policy caused a foreign debt crisis during the last Vargas administration in 1953. The response of Vargas' government was a hidden devaluation of the national currency through the creation of five different exchange rates, assigned depending on commercial priorities. This system contradicted the Bretton Woods Agreements, which required a single exchange rate. After Vargas committed suicide in 1954, he was replaced by a less developmentally oriented president, João Café Filho. However, although Café Filho moderated the growth-oriented enthusiasm of Vargas, his administration authorized only extremely restricted automobile imports, in order to continue the support of the national car industry. The system of discriminatory exchange rates was maintained.

The administration of Juscelino Kubitschek between 1956 and 1961 increased the strength of industrial policies, although granting a greater role to foreign investment than during the governments of Vargas. A few weeks after taking office, Kubitschek presented the *Plano de Metas*, in which the strategic activities to be promoted were identified: energy, basic chemistry, pulp, steel, automobiles, shipbuilding, and consumer durables. The priorities were almost the same as those that Vargas followed with his policy of creating public–private corporations, restricted import authorizations, and high tariffs. But the instruments employed were different. Kubitschek preferred to encourage the investment of foreign capital in the development of these sectors, and granted foreign investors favorable exchange rates to import technology and equipment. He also granted tax exemptions and public credit for industrial projects. Kubitschek's administration likewise mandated for firms with foreign capital to employ 90 percent of locally produced components for automobile production, a measure that had also been adopted by the Spanish administration under Franco and in Perón's Argentina.

---

[19] The economic development of Brazil during the developmental era has been discussed in Furtado, 1959, 1974; Orozco, 1961; Peláez, 1972; Nascimento, 1976; Wells, 1977: 259–279; Cardoso de Mello, 1981; Nunes, 1983; Suzigan, 1986; Tavares, 1986; Peláez, 1987; Abreu, 1990; Shapiro, 1991: 876–947; Sikkink, 1991; Maddison, 1992; Negri, 1996; Shapiro, 1994; Thorp, 1998; Katz, 2000: 307–334; Palma, 2003: 125–151; Arend, 2009; Wolfe, 2010; Artopoulos, 2012; Baer, 2014; Fonseca and Salomão, 2016: Chapter 3.

Kubitschek's industrial policy was to a certain extent mortgaged by the vast and financially very onerous project of creating a new national capital in Brasilia. The project resulted in high public expenditure and contributed to accelerated inflation. The consumer price index grew approximately 50 percent during the last year of Kubitschek's term of office, 1961. Such a high inflation rate was more than double the maximum rates recorded in previous years, with the greatest increases in 1947 of 22 percent, and in 1955 of 23 percent.

The administrations after Kubitschek continued the implementation of developmental policies, but they placed more emphasis on the redistribution of income in favor of the workers. In particular, under the presidency of João Goulart, a significant rise in the minimum wage was approved, and agrarian reform was announced. The remittance of profits by transnational corporations was restricted. Goulart's administration wanted to extend public ownership in the oil sector, and attempted to promote trade unionism in the army. However, inflation shot up again, reaching almost 100 percent in 1964, which the military used as an excuse to overthrow the president.

The first military administration under Humberto Castelo Branco withdrew the most radical measures of Goulart, and stabilized the economy, but the policies of support for industrialization initiated during the Vargas era were not abandoned. Among other measures taken by the military administration, were public spending reduction, restriction of the public credit system, wage reductions, the end of the multiple-exchange-rate system, and the diminishing of the average tariff protection. The military managed to gradually reduce inflation, which went down to 13 percent in 1973, during the presidency of Emilio Medici.

Nevertheless, the military maintained high levels of public investment in activities such as steel, electricity, and the petrochemical sector, which were dominated by state companies. The regulations mandating the employment of 90 percent of national components in automobile production remained in force. In 1969, Empresa Brasileira de Aeronáutica (Embraer) was created, with the aim of manufacturing a small multipurpose aircraft. The state owned 51 percent of the firm's capital, and tariff exemptions were granted for the import of components for production, as well as for acquisitions of its output by public agencies. In 1973, the first Embraer aircraft built on the assembly line was delivered.

In short, from the beginning of the 1950s until the beginning of the 1970s, Spain and Brazil maintained relatively stable developmental policies intended to promote industrial growth although, on occasions, specific imbalances made it necessary to moderate expansionist excesses, and apply adjustment policies. The notion of an "economic miracle" was mentioned for both countries, with Brazil achieving an average annual growth rate of GDP per capita of around 4 percent during the period 1953–1973. In Argentina, although the majority of the governments of this twenty-year period also

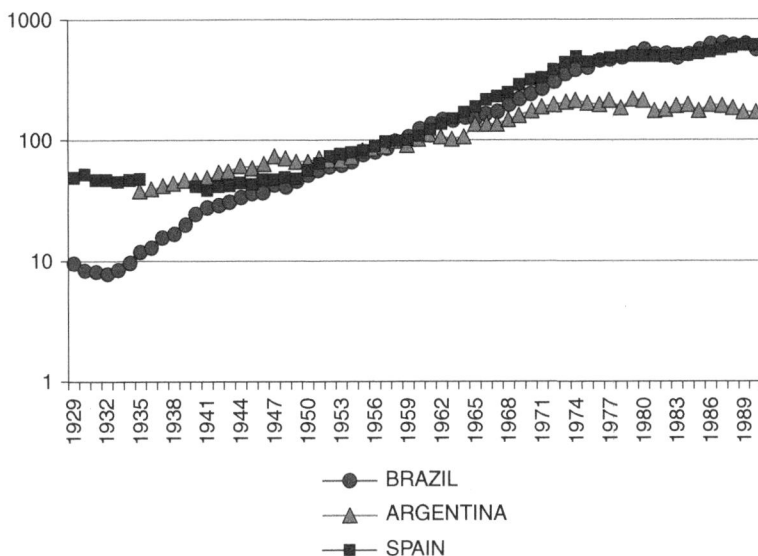

FIGURE 9.1 Patterns of the Industrial Production Index (1958=1000).
Source: Own elaboration with Mitchell, 2003, 2007.

endeavored to promote state-led industrialization, there was not as much continuity in the macroeconomic policy framework.

The promotion by the developmental state of the leading sectors characteristic of the second industrial revolution allowed these three economies to improve their positions on the international manufacturing production rankings (see Table 9.3). Sustained industrialization favored the long-term improvement of productivity and, at the same time, the increase of real wages. Consequently, Spain and Brazil achieved record growth rates in their industrial output, and in their GDP per capita. Argentina also experienced an intense process of industrialization, but without achieving the same sound performance of Brazil and Spain (see Table 9.1, Table 9.3, and Figure 9.1).

EROSION OF THE DEVELOPMENTAL STATE AND DIVERGENCE, 1973–90

While the developmental state in Asian countries such as South Korea became strengthened and consolidated in the 1970s and 1980s, in the Iberoamerican economies under study, it experienced a significant process of erosion. The developmental state was re-scaled downwards in Brazil and Spain, but in Argentina it was completely dismantled.

In Spain, the beginning of the shift occurred during Late Francoism, before the outbreak of the stagflation crisis, which in many countries called into question the developmental and demand side policies.[20] The success of automobile production by SEAT and FASA led the US-based multinationals, which had left Spain because of the policies of Early Francoism, to consider the possibility of setting up again in the peninsula. It was a question of taking advantage of Spain as an export platform toward the EEC, which had granted a Preferential Agreement quite favorable to the Spanish side in 1970. Henry Ford II travelled to Spain in 1972, and he obtained a radical shift in automobile policy: the proportion of national components required for firms producing in the country was reduced from 90 percent to 60 percent for new manufacturers whose production was going to be oriented towards export markets. The return to Spain of the firm from Dearborn was authorized, and a new Ford motor and vehicle plant was built in the vicinity of Valencia. Franco died in 1975, and there were relatively free elections in 1977. The administrations during the transition continued with the liberalizing policy. In 1979, during the presidency of the centrist Adolfo Suárez, the process was completed and, despite the fact that a veto of General Motors had been agreed with SEAT and FIAT four years earlier, Opel, a subsidiary of General Motors, was authorized to set up close to Zaragoza. The models manufactured in Valencia and Zaragoza by Ford and General Motors, the Fiesta, and the Corsa, competed with the main segment of the national champion SEAT, whose blockbuster at the time was the 127. The Americans took a substantial market share from this model, causing severe losses for SEAT, which led FIAT to transfer its part in the capital of SEAT back to the public holding INI in 1981. With all of its shares in public hands, SEAT made an effort to renew its product range, and managed to launch what would be its most successful product over the next thirty years, the Ibiza. However, the socialist government of Felipe González ended up transferring SEAT to Volkswagen in 1986.

Shipbuilding was another strategic sector of Developmental Francoism, which recorded dramatic losses during the stagflation crisis, and ended up being mainly privatized. In 1972, the companies of the public holding INI contributed 94 percent of Spanish ship production. The centrist governments during the democratic transition began to close shipyards and reduce the workforce. By the end of the Leopoldo Calvo Sotelo presidency, in 1982, the weight of the companies of the INI in ship production had diminished to 82 percent. During the González administration, the emphasis on industrial reconversion increased, and the proportion of ships built in publicly owned shipyards went down to 32 percent in 1989. A similar process, although less

[20] The performance of the Spanish economy during Late Francoism and the democratic transition has been discussed in Carreras, 1984: 127–157; Muns, 1986; Cuervo, 1987; García-Delgado, 1990; González-Calvet, 1991: 133–175; Martín-Aceña and Comín, 1991; Argandoña and García-Durán, 1992; Trullen, 1993; Tamames, 1995; Comín, 1996; Juan, Roca, and Toharia, 1996; Recio and Roca, 1998 : 139–158; Carreras and Tafunell, 2003; Catalan, 1999: 324–342, 2011: 55–114; Sudrià, 2013: 193–219; Catalan, 2015; and Fernández-de-Sevilla, 2017: 121–140.

pronounced, occurred with steel production. In 1972, the subsidiaries of the public holding INI, led by ENSIDESA, contributed 46 percent of the steel manufactured in Spain. Ten years later, the proportion of steel production by public firms had diminished to 40 percent, and continued to fall until it reached 32 percent in 1989. The steelworks Altos Hornos del Mediterráneo, located in Sagunto, was one of the most important plants closed.

It was not only unprofitable state-owned corporations in diverse manufacturing industries which were privatized before 1990. Oil and gas exploration, production, and refining had become very profitable in Spain during the developmental era. In 1981, President Calvo Sotelo's administration integrated all public shares of capital in oil and gas corporations under the umbrella of a new independent public holding, Instituto Nacional de Hidrocarburos (INH). The INH was created with firms operating in connected areas: oil and gas exploration and production, refining, distribution and marketing of refined oil products, and natural gas. At the end of 1986, the public holding company INH was restructured, creating a subsidiary focused on oil production and refining. The company was named Repsol, which until then had been the commercial name for a brand of lubricants manufactured by one of the public corporations. Repsol took part in oil exploration, extraction, refining, production, distribution and marketing of petrochemical products, and liquefied natural gas. The socialist government began to privatize Repsol in 1989. The main shareholders in the new private company included the Spanish banks BBV and La Caixa, and the Mexican public oil company Pemex.

In the financial sphere, the administrations during the democratic transition also began to embrace deregulation. Interest rates, which had been subject to considerable intervention throughout the Franco regime, were liberalized. The divide between commercial and investment banking became blurred. Compulsory investment coefficients, which channeled resources toward the companies of the industrial public holding INI, were canceled. Spain's membership of the EEC in 1986, moreover, marked the end of public control on capital flows. In 1989, Spain joined the European Monetary System, which implied the adoption of fixed exchange rates, although with a broad exchange-rate band.

The scope of state intervention in the industrial and financial areas was reduced during Late Francoism and the democratic transition. However, in three public policy areas, state initiatives were actually strengthened. The first one corresponded to the fiscal sphere. The 1977 fiscal reform modernized income tax, allowing enough ordinary tax income to be collected. As a result, the government did not resort too much to the creation of liquidity in order to finance public expenditure, as continued to occur in Latin America. The increase in tax resources also facilitated a substantial increase of public spending on education and health care, which had been comparatively low throughout Francoism. Finally, the tax reform made it possible to increase public spending on Research and Development, which at the beginning of the 1970s was far lower than in democracies with similar levels of per capita income.

The Unión de Centro Democrático administration of President Suárez during the transition was able to reach an agreement with political and social actors, and the pact was instrumental in reducing inflationary expectations. From 1973 to 1976, inflation had been experiencing acceleration, and the forecasts for the end of 1977 placed it at 30 percent. However, the Moncloa Pacts, signed in October 1977, had a strong stabilizing impact. By this agreement, the main anti-Francoist opposition force, the Spanish Communist Party led by Santiago Carrillo, accepted wage moderation. The prior legalization of the party by the Suárez administration paved the way for the agreement. The potential erosion of the purchasing power of wages was offset by the expansion of public education and health care. The increase of employment in these sectors acted as a compensatory mechanism, together with the gradual devaluation of the peseta during the severe industrial recession that Spain experienced until 1985. The fall in the price of oil, and Spain joining the EEC, helped to boost economic recovery during the second half of the decade.

The annual growth rate of Spanish GDP per capita during the period 1973–1990 went down to almost 2 percent (see Table 9.1). The industrialization process slowed down (see Figure 9.1). Domestic capital shrank in the economic struggle with transnational companies. However, the exposure of some key sectors to open markets tended to improve their long-term competitiveness (see Table 9.3).

If the results of the developmental state were ambivalent in the Spain of the 1970s and 1980s, Argentina chose to completely do away with it.[21] Perón returned to the government in 1974 with the plan to seek for a wide social agreement on wage moderation. After his death, however, the administration of his widow, María Estela Martínez, adopted a very erratic economic policy, abusing devaluation of the peso, and dictating indexing prices to wages. In less than two years under the new administration, the cost of living shot up, increasing from a rate of 5 percent in 1974, to an extraordinary 400 percent in 1976. In March, the military took power, and appointed General Jorge Videla as president.

The Minister of Economy of the military government, José Alfredo Martínez de Hoz, remained in office for a relatively long period of five years, until 1981,

---

[21] The issue of the reasons for the long-term economic decline experienced by Argentina represents a traditional debate among historians and economists. Some of the most significant interpretations are Díaz-Alejandro, 1970; Taylor, 1994: 649–683; Thorp, 1998; Katz, 2000: 307–334; Torre and Riz, 2001: 223–316; Barbero and Rochi, 2003: 261–294; Palma, 2003: 125–151; Paolera and Gallo, 2003: 369–375; Rougier, 2004; Cortés-Conde, 2005; Rapoport, 2005; Rougier and Schwarzer, 2006; Rougier and Fiszbein, 2006; Rougier, 2007; Belini and Rougier, 2008; Catalan, 2010; Belini and Korol, 2012; Belini, 2017; and Herrera, 2017: 159–192.

when the presidency passed to General Roberto Viola. Martínez de Hoz applied some of the same neoliberal policies that were being promoted by economists of the University of Chicago, and that had been already applied in Chile. It would certainly have been difficult to reduce the dramatic levels of inflation without applying restrictive fiscal and monetary measures. However, Videla's administration did not only reduce public spending, increase taxes, and reduce the growth of the money supply. The diagnosis was also that public support for import-substitution industrialization had created significant "distortions" in the economy, and that national production needed to focus on areas where it had a comparative advantage. Consequently, Martínez de Hoz liberalized prices, froze wages, significantly cut tariffs protecting industry, liberalized interest rates, opened up the country to foreign investment, and announced a policy of crawling-peg or scheduled gradual depreciation of the peso, known as the *Tablita*. A violent campaign of repression against the democratic opposition and trade union leaders was unleashed, including the disappearance of thousands of activists.

Martínez de Hoz succeeded in reducing the public deficit from 14 percent of GDP in 1975 to 7 percent in 1981 and, in the same year, he brought inflation down to around 100 percent. However, the industrial sector underwent a severe depression, as a combined result of the significant contraction of internal demand, the flooding of the market with imports, and the meteoric rise in interest rates. Argentina's industrial production index declined by 11 percent between 1975 and 1981. Real wages lost over a third of their purchasing power. The *Tablita* system, moreover, favored a continuous drainage of capital from the country, and the relentless purchasing of dollars for speculative operations, since the loss of value of the peso was fully anticipated.

The next military administrations after Videla's could not stop either the rising inflation, or manage the recovery of real wages. Faced with mounting opposition and political protests, President Leopoldo Galtieri decided to invade the Falkland/Malvinas Islands in April 1982. Not only did the country suffer a humiliating defeat, but the public deficit increased substantially again, and inflation accelerated. The Argentine industrial production index went dramatically down again, dropping more than 15 percent below the historical maximum of 1974. The debt crisis of Mexico, in August 1982, spread to the whole region, and it added to the difficulty that Argentine private companies already experienced to service their debts in foreign currency. The administration took the unprecedented decision to offer public guarantees for private debts in foreign currency. After years of private operators buying dollars to benefit from the gradual depreciation of the peso, this decision represented a vast socialization of losses. Annual inflation again rose above 400 percent at the end of 1983, when the new administration of the Radical Civic Union, presided by Raúl Alfonsín, was inaugurated.

Alfonsín's democratic administration initially applied an expansive macroeconomic policy to promote economic recovery. But annual inflation

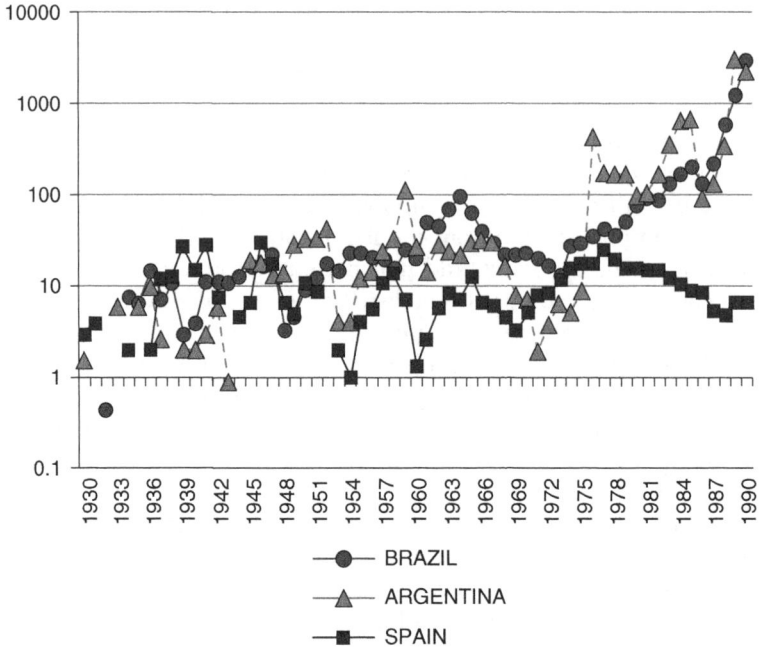

FIGURE 9.2 Annual Rate of Increase of the Consumer Prices Index (%)
Source: Own elaboration with Mitchell, 2003, 2007

went over 600 percent again at the end of 1984. A new minister of economy, Juan Sourrouille, adopted fiscal and monetary adjustment policies, and created a new currency, the Austral, converted at a rate of 1000 pesos per unit. He succeeded in reducing inflation to 90 percent, and brought the public deficit down from 10 percent of GDP reached in 1983, to around 4 percent in 1986. The partial privatization of major public companies such as Aerolíneas Argentinas and Empresa Nacional de Telecomunicaciones began to be prepared. However, the economic situation deteriorated again in the following two years, and the government had to suspend the service of foreign debt in 1988. When Alfonsín left the *Casa Rosada* in 1989, annual inflation was around 3000 percent (see Figure 9.2). Argentina's industrial production index dropped even lower, reaching a historical minimum more than a third below the index of 1974 (see Figure 9.1).

To the surprise of many of his voters, the next president, Peronist Carlos Menem, decided to dramatically extend the policy of privatizations of state-owned corporations, including traditional public companies in areas such as communications, iron and steel industries, hydroelectric power production, and even the "crown jewel" of Argentina's public sector, the petrochemical corporation YPF. This unexpected decision consolidated the abandonment of the developmental state model, which had begun under the military. Menem and his minister of economy, Domingo Cavallo, succeeded in defeating inflation, with a new monetary reform, which reestablished the peso and made it legally convertible into dollars, at the rate of 1 peso to 1 dollar. However, the weight of industry fell again from 36 percent of GDP in the period 1970–1974, to 31 percent in the period 1989–1993, and the real income per capita in 1990 had gone down to around 17 percent below the 1973 level.

In Brazil, the military remained in power from 1964 to 1985. They did not, however, abandon developmental strategies.[22] The military maintained a policy of *Planejamento* that was generally run by economists with sound technocratic training. General Ernesto Geisel, president from 1974 to 1979, responded to the first oil crisis by launching *Pró-Álcool*, a national program to promote sugarcane as an alternative fuel source. His administration initiated also a nuclear-energy program. The motor industry, although mostly foreign-owned, benefited from tariff exemptions on the imports of inputs and equipment, financial and tax support, and subsidies to promote exports. The state maintained its participation in the corporation Embraer, which consolidated its position as a leading producer of aircraft with turbo ventilation engines. The public program of support for exports succeeded in facilitating growing sales of Brazilian aircraft in very competitive markets such as France, the United Kingdom, and the United States. In 1979, the subsidiary Embraer Aircraft Corporation was created, with headquarters in the State of Florida.

In the context of the first oil crisis, and of the international oversupply of credit, Brazilian developmental policies resulted in the increase of foreign debt, especially that of the public sector.[23] In 1973, 40 percent of loans contracted in Brazil corresponded to the government and public companies, but the proportion increased to 77 percent by 1979. The expansive public programs also induced a significant upsurge of inflation. The rise in the cost of living went from around 12 percent in 1973 to 50 percent in 1979. However, although these rates were higher than the Spanish rates of Late Francoism and the transition, they cannot be compared with the dramatic increases of the administration of President Martínez (1974–1976) in Argentina, and with the three-figure inflation rates during the neoliberal dictatorship. Also in contrast to Argentina, industrial production continued to grow during this period in Brazil.

---

[22] Significant studies on the rise and decline of the Brazilian industrialization process can be found in Cardoso, 1981; Castro and de Souza, 1984; Davidoff, 1984; Peláez, 1972; Tavares, 1986; Suzigan, 1986; Abreu, 1990; Sikkink, 1991; Maddison, 1992; Negri, 1996; Thorp, 1998; Katz, 2000: 307–334; Palma, 2003: 125–151; Bresser-Pereira, 2008: 47–71; Nassif, 2008: 72–96; Arend, 2009; Wolfe, 2010; Artopoulos, 2012; Baer, 2014; Schwarcz and Starling, 2016; Bresser-Pereira, 2014; Bresser-Pereira, Nassif and Feijó, 2016: 493–513; Fonseca and Salomão, 2016: Chapter 3.

[23] For a complementary analysis of politics, developmental structures, and the problem of increasing foreign debt in Brazil, see Chapter 7 in this volume.

During the administration of General João Baptista Figuereido (1979–1985), developmental priorities continued, but economic imbalances became more acute as a result of the second oil crisis, and the policy change of the US Federal Reserve, which contributed to the tightening of international credit. The Secretary of Planning, Antônio Delfim Netto, responded to the second oil shock by indexing wages to current inflation. This decision contributed to a faster increase in the cost of living, which almost doubled in less than two years: from 51 percent in 1979 to 96 percent in 1981. Foreign reserves fell from 12 billion US dollars in 1978 to around 7 billion in 1981.

The administration's response to the fall in reserves and the rising inflation was to take adjustment measures, which were intensified after the Mexican debt crisis of 1982. To correct the increasingly negative balance-of-payments performance, incentives for the export of manufactures were strengthened, reaching up to 15 percent of the value of the products exported, and the national currency was devaluated repeatedly. After applying stabilizing measures in 1982, the administration reached an agreement with the IMF in 1983 for further loans, but this meant the adoption of even tighter austerity policies, both fiscal and monetary. Consequently, industrial production recorded the worst fall of the post-war period in 1983, with a drop of 15 percent below the level of 1980. Nevertheless, and again in stark contrast to Argentina, in 1983 the industrial output of Brazil was almost a third higher than ten years earlier (Figure 9.1).

The end of the military regime in 1984 left the country with a three-digit inflation rate, of 172 percent. Tancredo Neves was democratically elected president in 1985, but his illness and death led to Vice-President José Sarney assuming the office for the term 1985–1990. The administration's first stabilization plan, the Cruzado Plan of 1986, eliminated indexing, attempted to freeze wages, prices and public service tariffs, and promoted a monetary reform, creating a new currency, the cruzado, with an exchange rate of 1000 cruceiros. Inflation moderated, going from 202 percent to 129 percent at the end of the year. However, the continuation of price controls led to the disappearance of basic goods from the shops, and it boosted an extensive black market. A new Cruzado II Plan endeavored to change the course, increasing the tariffs of public services, and liberalizing prices. But this caused a new inflationary spiral, which it was not possible to stop during Sarney's administration.

Sarney transferred power to President Fernando Collor in March 1990. The year ended with an Argentine-type inflation rate of 3,000 percent (Figure 9.2). During the period 1987–1990, industrial production fell by around 10 percent. Brazil arrived at the end of the developmental era approaching hyperinflation as was the case in Argentina. However, unlike Argentina, Brazil had not completely renounced the public sector as an economic actor, or abandoned industrializing policies. Despite all the difficulties, Brazil's industrial output in 1990 was more than 50 percent

TABLE 9.4 *Convergence and Divergence of GDP per Capita in Relation to the USA (% of GDP per capita of the United States of America)*

	Argentina	Brazil	Spain
1929	63.2	16.0	42.7
1953	45.2	16.5	26.1
1973	48.0	23.6	52.6
1990	30.1	22.0	55.7

Notes: Original in figures in 1990 Geary-Khamis dollars
Source: Own calculation with Maddison 1995

higher than in 1973, while Argentina's industrial production, as mentioned above, was in 1989 a third lower than in 1974 (Figure 9.1). Also in contrast to Argentina, growth rates of GDP remained positive in Brazil during the period of erosion of the developmental state 1973–1990, and GDP per capita was at the end of this era 20 percent higher than at the beginning.

If we compare the long-term evolution of GDP per capita in relation to the United States, Spain and Brazil tended to converge in relation to the worldwide leader of the second technological revolution during the whole period under study in the present chapter, although Brazil started from a much lower point of departure. Spain went from having a GDP per capita equivalent to 43 percent of the United States in 1929, to around 56 percent in 1990. Brazil started from a GDP per capita of only 16 percent of the US value, and managed to rise to 22 percent at the end of this long-time cycle. On the other hand, Argentina went down from a GDP per capita equivalent to 63 percent of the United States in 1929, to just 30 percent in 1990. It should be stressed, nevertheless, that while Argentina's GDP continued to converge gradually with the US between 1953 and 1973, it experienced a dramatic divergence in the era of the erosion of the developmental state (see Table 9.4).

CONCLUSION

The Latin countries under study adopted developmental strategies in the 1930s and 1940s. In Spain and Argentina, during this initial phase, public policy continuity was fragmentary, with conflicting interests and visions represented by the governments of the Second Republic against Early Francoism in Spain, and the orthodox Concordancia regime against Early Peronism in Argentina. In contrast, the Brazil of Vargas showed more consistency in the implementation of developing strategies, focusing on industrialization and redistribution of income in favor of the working class. Consequently, both in terms of GDP growth and of industrialization, Brazil achieved better results than Spain or Argentina during the period 1929–1953 (see Table 9.1; Figure 9.1).

During the golden age of economic growth, 1953–1973, in all three countries under study, a wide consensus was reached to support industrialization policies, and to improve the real income of workers, despite the fact that all three experienced long periods of military dictatorships. A developmental state was consolidated in the three countries, although in Argentina the consensus was not as unanimous, and a remarkable episode of reversal occurred, the Revolución Libertadora, 1955–1958. Public policy programs such as long-term industrial promotion, growth of public corporations, indicative planning, improvement of real wages, and consolidation of welfare systems, made it possible for the three economies to industrialize fast, and to converge in terms of income per capita in relation to the economic leader of the period, the United States.

During the third period considered, 1973–1990, the developmental state was scaled down in all three countries. Only in Argentina was it fundamentally dismantled, and erratic policies, from excesses in expansive programs to indiscriminate liberalization, caused the collapse of industrial production, and a dramatic drop in levels of real income, which tended to diverge strongly from the US standard reference (see Table 9.4). Brazil was able to continue the industrialization policies, but the abuse of public debt, and the inability to prevent the acceleration of inflation, generated moderate deindustrialization, and a slight increase of the divergence in per capita income to the US benchmark. In Spain, the abandonment of the protection of local industry, and the reduction in the size of the public corporations sector, contributed to weaken the developmental state. However, the agreements among social and political actors during the democratic transition curbed inflationary expectations, and the increase in international competition contributed to industrial restructuring, and to a moderate convergence in terms of per capita income with the United States.

REFERENCES

Abelshauser, Werner. *The Dynamics of German Industry*. New York: Berghahn Books, 2005.
Abreu, Marcelo. "La Argentina y Brasil en los años treinta. Efectos de la política económica internacional británica y estadounidense." In *América Latina en los años treinta. El papel de la periferia en la crisis mundial*, compiled by Rosemary Thorp, México: Fondo de Cultura Económica, 1988: 171–190.
    A ordem do progresso - Cem anos de política econômica republicana 1889–1989. São Paulo: Editora Campos, 1990.
Albert, Michel. *Capitalism Against Capitalism*. London: Whurr, 1993.
Amsden, Alice. *Asia's Next Giant. South Korea and Late Industrialization*. Oxford University Press, 1989.

Andreoni, Antonio and Ha-Joon Chang. "Bringing Production and Employment Back into Development: Alice Amsden's Legacy for a New Developmentalist Agenda." *Cambridge Journal of Regions, Economy and Society* 10, 2017: 173–187.

Arend, Marcelo. "50 anos de industrialização do Brasil (1955–2005): uma análise evolucionária." Unpublished PhD thesis, Universidade Federal do Rio Grande do Sul, 2009.

Argandoña, Antonio and José A. García-Duran. *Macroeconomía española. Hechos e ideas.* Madrid: McGraw-Hill, 1992.

Artopoulos, Alejandro. *Tecnología e innovación en países emergentes.* Buenos Aires: Lenguaje claro, 2012.

Baer, Werner. *The Brazilian Economy. Growth and Development.* Boulder CO: Rienner, 2014.

Barciela, Carlos, ed. *Autarquía y mercado negro. El fracaso económico del primer franquismo, 1939–1959.* Barcelona: Crítica, 2003.

Barbero, M. Inés and Fernando Rocchi. "Industry." In *A New Economic History of Argentina*, eds. Gerardo della Paolera and Alan M. Taylor, Cambridge University Press, 2003: 261–294.

Belini, Claudio. *La industria peronista. Políticas públicas y cambio estructural, 1946–1955.* Buenos Aires: EDHASA, 2009.

Convenciendo al capital. Peronismo, burocracia, empresarios y política industrial, 1943–1955. Buenos Aires: Imago Mundi, 2014.

Historia de la industria en la Argentina. Buenos Aires: Sudamericana, 2017.

Belini, Claudio and Juan C. Korol. *Historia económica de la Argentina en el siglo XX.* Buenos Aires: Siglo XXI, 2012.

Belini, Claudio and Marcelo Rougier. *El estado empresario en la industria argentina.* Buenos Aires: Manantial, 2008.

Bresser-Pereira, Luiz C. "The Dutch Disease and its Neutralization: a Ricardian Approach." *Revista de Economia Política* 28, 2008: 47–71.

A Construção Política do Brasil: Sociedade, Economia e Estado desde a Independência. São Paulo: Editora 34, 2014.

Bresser-Pereira, Luiz C., André Nassif and Carmen Feijó. "A reconstrução da indústria brasileira: a conexão entre o regime macroeconômico e a política industrial." *Revista de Economia Política* 36, 2016: 493–513.

Cano, Wilson. *Raízes da concentração industrial em São Paulo.* São Paulo: T.A. Queiroz, 1981.

Cardoso de Mello, João M. *O capitalismo tardio.* São Paulo: Brasiliense, 1981.

Carreras, Albert. "La producción industrial española, 1842–1981: construcción de un índice annual." *Revista de Historia Económica* 2, 1984: 127–157.

Carreras, Albert and Xavier Tafunell. *Historia económica de la España contemporánea.* Barcelona: Crítica, 2003.

Castro, Antonio and Francisco E. P. de Souza. *A economia brasileira em marcha forçada.* Rio de Janeiro: Paz e Terra, 1984.

Catalan, Jordi. *La economía española y la Segunda Guerra Mundial.* Barcelona: Ariel, 1995.

"Spain, 1939–1996." In *Western Europe, Economic and Social Change Since 1945*, ed. Max-Stephane Schulze, London: Longman, 1999: 324–342.

"La creación de la ventaja comparativa en la industria automovilística española, 1898–1996." *Revista de Historia Industrial* 18, 2000: 113–154.

"Strategic Policy Revisited: The Origins of Mass Production in the Motor Industry of Argentina, Korea and Spain, 1945–87." *Business History* 52, 2010: 207–230.

"Los cuatro franquismos económicos, 1939–77: de la involución autárquica a la conquista de las libertades." In *El mundo del trabajo en la conquista de las libertades*, eds. Salvador Cruz and Julio Ponce, Jaén: Universidad de Jaén, 2011: 55–114.

"Francoist Spain under Nazi Economic Hegemony, 1936–1945." In *Europäische Volkswirtschaften unter deutscher Hegemonie 1938–1945*, eds. Cristoph Buccheim and Marcel Boldorf. Munich: Oldenbourg, 2012: 229–265.

"From the Great Depression to the Euro Crisis." *Revista de Historia Industrial* 56, 2014: 15–45.

El Gran Viaje. Sesenta Años de Industria en España 1955–2015. Madrid: Escuela de Organización Industrial, 2015.

"The Stagflation Crisis and the European Automotive Industry, 1973–85." *Business History*, 59, 2017: 4–34.

Catalan, Jordi and Tomàs Fernández-de-Sevilla. "Die Staatliche Industriepolitik und die Entwicklung der Automobilindustrie in Spanien 1948–1985." In *Automobilindustrie 1945–2000*, eds. Stephanie Tilly and Florian Triebel. Munich: Oldenbourg, 2013: 254–284.

Chang, Ha-Joon. "The Political Economy of Industrial Policy in Korea." *Cambridge Journal of Economics* 17, 1993: 131–157.

Kicking Away the Ladder. Development Strategy in Historical Perspective. London: Anthem, 2002.

Comín, Francisco. *Historia de la Hacienda Pública. España (1808–1995).* Barcelona: Crítica, 1996.

"La gran depresión internacional y la Segunda República." In *España en crisis*, eds. Enrique Llopis and Jordi Maluquer de Motes. Barcelona: *Pasado y Presente*, 2013: 133–164.

Cortés-Conde, Roberto. *La economía política de la Argentina en el siglo XX.* Buenos Aires: Edhasa, 2005.

Cuervo, Álvaro. *La crisis bancaria en España 1977–1985.* Barcelona: Ariel, 1987.

Davidoff, Paulo. *Dívida externa e política econômica.* São Paulo: Brasilense, 1984.

Dean, Warren. *The Industrialization of São Paulo, 1880–1945.* Austin: The University of Texas Press, 1969.

"Industriales y oligarquía en el desarrollo de São Paulo." In *Burguesías e industria en América Latina y Europa Meridional*, eds. Mario Cerutti and Menno Vellinga, Madrid: Alianza, 1988: 23–54.

Díaz-Alejandro, Carlos F. *Essays on the Economic History of the Argentinean Republic.* New Haven: Yale University Press, 1970.

Evans, Peter. *Embedded Autonomy: States and Industrial Transformation.* Princeton University Press, 1995.

Fausto, Boris. *Getúlio Vargas: o poder e o sorriso.* São Paulo: Companhia das Letras, 2006.

Fernández-de-Sevilla, Tomàs. "Inside the Dynamics of Industrial Capitalism: The Mass-Production of Cars in Spain." *Revista de Historia Económica* 32, 2014: 287–315.

"Growth Amid a Storm: Renault in Spain During the Stagflation Crisis, 1974–1985." *Business History* 59, 2017: 121–140.

Flora, Peter and Arnold J. Heidenheimer, eds. *The Development of Welfare States in Europe and America*. New Brunswick: Transaction Books, 1981.

Fonseca, Pedro C. D. *Vargas: o Capitalismo em Construção*. São Paulo: Nacional, 1989.

Fonseca, Pedro C. D. and Ivan Salomão. "Industrialização brasileira: notas sobre o debate historiográfico." In *Estudios sobre la industria en América Latina. Interpretaciones y debates*, ed. Marcelo Rougier, Buenos Aires: Lenguaje Claro, 2016: Chapter 3.

Fontana, Josep, ed. *España bajo el franquismo*. Barcelona: Crítica, 1986.

Fontana, Josep and Jordi Nadal. "España 1914–1970." In *Historia económica de Europa (6). Economías contemporáneas* 2, ed. Carlo M. Cipolla, Barcelona: Ariel, 1976: 95–163.

Furtado, Celso. *Formação econômica do Brasil*. São Paulo: Nacional, 1959.

La economía latino-americana desde la conquista ibérica hasta la revolución cubana. México: Siglo XXI, 1974.

García-Delgado, José L. "Notas sobre el intervencionismo económico del primer franquismo." *Revista de Historia Económica* 3, 1985: 135–145.

"Crecimiento económico y cambio estructural (1951–1975)." In *Empresa pública e industrialización en España*, eds. Pablo Martín-Aceña and Francisco Comín, Madrid: Alianza, 1990: 137–160.

ed. *Economía española de la transición y la democracia*. Madrid: CIS, 1990.

Gerschenkron, Alexander. *Economic Backwardness in Historical Perspective*. Cambridge MA: Harvard University Press, 1962.

Gómez-Mendoza, Antonio, ed. *De Mitos y Milagros. El Instituto Nacional de Autarquía (1941–1963)*. Barcelona: Monografías de Historia Industrial, 2000.

González-Calvet, Josep. "Crisis, Transición y Estancamiento. La Política Económica Española, 1973–82." In *La reestructuración del capitalismo en España, 1970–1990*, ed. Miren Etxezarreta, Barcelona: FUHEM-Icaria, 1991, 133–175.

Hamilton, Alexander. *Report on Manufactures*. Communicated to the House of Representatives, 1791, www.constitution.org/ah/rpt_manufactures.pdf (accessed November 21, 2017).

Herrera, Germán. "El ciclo de desindustrialización en Argentina y sus consecuencias estructurales. Un análisis de la etapa 1976–2010." *Revista de Historia Industrial* 67, 2017: 159–192.

Jaguaribe, Helio. *Political Development. A General Theory and a Latin American Case Study*. New York: Harper & Row, 1973.

Johnson, Chalmers. *MITI and the Japanese Miracle: The Growth of Industrial Policy 1925–1975*. Stanford University Press, 1982.

Juan, Oscar, Jordi Roca, and Luis Toharia. *El desempleo en España. Tres ensayos críticos*. Cuenca: Ediciones de Castilla-La Mancha, 1996.

Katz, Jorge. "The Dynamics of Technological Learning During the Import-Substitution Period and Recent Structural Changes in the Industrial Sector of Argentina, Brazil and Mexico." In *Technology, Learning and Innovation*, eds. Linsu Kim and Richard R. Nelson, Cambridge University Press, 2000: 307–334.

Landes, David. *The Wealth and Poverty of Nations: Why Some Are So Rich and Some So Poor*. New York: W.W. Norton, 1998.

Lin, Justin and Ha-Joon Chang. "Should Industrial Policy in Developing Countries Conform to Comparative Advantage or Defy it? A Debate Between Just Lin and Ha-Joon Chang." *Development Policy Review* 27, 2009: 483–502.

List, Friedrich. *The National System of Political Economy*. London: Longmans, Green and Co, 1841.

Maddison, Angus. *Dos crisis: América y Asia 1929–1938 y 1973–1983*. México: Fondo de Cultura Económica, 1988.

The Political Economy of Poverty, Equity and Growth, Brazil and Mexico. New York: Oxford University Press, 1992.

Monitoring the World Economy 1820–1992. Paris: OECD, 1995.

Martín-Aceña, Pablo and Francisco Comín. *50 años de industrialización española*. Madrid: Espasa Calpe, 1991.

Mazzucato, Mariana. *The Entrepreneurial State: Debunking Public vs. Private Sector Myth*. London: Anthem Press, 2013.

Mitchell, Brian R. *International Historical Statistics. The Americas 1750–2000*. Basingstoke: Palgrave-Macmillan, 2003.

International Historical Statistics. Europe 1750–2005. Basingstoke: Palgrave-Macmillan, 2007.

Muns, Joaquim. *Historia de las relaciones entre España y el Fondo Monetario Internacional 1958–1982*. Madrid: Alianza, 1986.

Nascimento, Benedicto. *Formaçao da indústria automobilística brasileira. Política de desenvolvimento industrial em uma economia dependente*. São Paulo: IGEOG-USP, 1976.

Nassif, André. "Há evidências de desindustrialização no Brasil." *Revista de Economia Política*, 28, 2008: 72–96.

Negri, Barjas. *Concentração e desconcentração industrial em São Paulo (1880–1990)*. Campinas: Unicamp, 1996.

Nunes, António J. A. *Industrialização e desenvolvimento. A economia política de 'modelo brasileiro de desenvolvimento'*. Coimbra: Universidade de Coimbra, 1983.

Orozco, Eros. *A Indústria automobilística brasileira*. Rio de Janeiro: Consultec, 1961.

Palafox, Jordi. *Atraso económico y democracia*. Barcelona: Crítica, 1991.

Palma, J. Gabriel. "Latin America During the Second Half of the Twentieth Century. From the 'Age of the Extremes' to the Age of 'End-of-History' uniformity." In *Rethinking Development Economics*, ed. Ha-Joon Chang, London: Anthem, 2003: 125–151.

Paolera, Gerardo della and Ezequiel Gallo. "Epilogue: The Argentine Puzzle." In *A New Economic History of Argentina*, eds. Gerardo della Paolera and Alan M. Taylor, Cambridge University Press, 2003: 369–375.

Peláez, Carlos M. *História da industrialização no Brasil*. São Paulo: ANPEC, 1972.

Economia Brasileira Contemporânea. São Paulo: Atlas, 1987.

Ramalho, José. "O Estado produtor e a Fábrica Nacional de Motores." In *De JK a FHC. A reinvenção dos carros*, eds. Glauco Arbix and Mauro Zilbovicius, São Paulo: Scritta, 1997: 159–179.

Rapoport, Mauro. *Historia económica, política y social de la Argentina (1880–2003)*. Buenos Aires: Emecé, 2005.

Recio, Abert and Jordi Roca. "The Spanish Socialists in Power: Thirteen Years of Economic Policy." *Oxford Review of Economic Policy* 14, 1998: 139–158.

Roca, Jordi. *Pacte social i política de rendes*. Capellades: Eumo, 1991.

Rock, David. "Argentina 1930–1946." In *Historia de la Argentina*, ed. John Lynch, Barcelona: Crítica, 2001: 167–222.

Rougier, Marcelo. *Industria, finanzas e instituciones en la Argentina. La experiencia del Banco Nacional de Desarrollo 1967–1976*. Buenos Aires: UN Quilmes, 2004.

  ed. *Políticas de promoción y estrategias empresariales en la industria argentina 1950–1980*. Buenos Aires: Ediciones Cooperativas, 2007.

  La economía del peronismo. Buenos Aires: Sudamericana, 2012.

Rougier, Marcelo and Martín Fiszbein. *La frustración de un proyecto económico. El gobierno peronista de 1973–1976*. Buenos Aires: Manantial, 2006.

Rougier, Marcelo and Jorge Schwarzer. *Las grandes empresas no mueren de pie. El (o) caso de SIAM*. Buenos Aires: Norma, 2006.

San Román, Elena. *Ejército e industria: El nacimiento del INI*. Barcelona: Crítica, 1999.

Schwarcz, Lilia and Eloisa Starling. *Brasil. Una biografía*. Barcelona: Penguin-Random House, 2016.

Shapiro, Helen. "Determinants of Firm Entry into the Brazilian Automobile Manufacturing Industry, 1956–1968." *Business History Review* 65, 1991: 876–947.

  Engines of Growth. The State and Transnational Auto Companies in Brazil. Cambridge University Press, 1994.

Sikkink, Kathryn. *Ideas and Institutions: Developmentalism in Brazil and Argentina*. Ithaca NY: Cornell University Press, 1991.

Sourrouille, Juan V. *Transnacionales en América Latina. El complejo automotor en Argentina*, México: Nueva Imagen, 1980.

Sudrià, Carles. "Atraso económico y transición política (1975–1985)." In *España en crisis*, eds. Enrique Llopis and Jordi Maluquer de Motes, Barcelona: Pasado y Presente, 2013: 193–219.

Suzigan, Wilson. *Industrialização Brasileira. Origem e Desenvolvimento*. São Paulo, 1986.

Tamames, Ramón. *La economía española 1975–1995*. Madrid: Temas de Hoy, 1995.

Tavares, Maria da C. *Acumulação de capital e industrialização no Brasil*. São Paulo: Brasilense, 1986.

Taylor, Alan M. "Tres fases del crecimiento económico argentino." *Revista de Historia Económica* 12, 1994: 649–683.

Thorp, Rose M. *Progress, Poverty and Exclusion: An Economic History of Latin America in the 20th Century*. Washington: IADB, 1998.

Torre, Juan and Liliana De Riz. "Argentina desde 1946." In *Historia de la Argentina*, ed. John Lynch, Barcelona: Crítica, 2001: 223–316.

Trullen, Joan. *Fundamentos económicos de la transición política española. La política de los Acuerdos de la Moncloa*. Madrid: MTYSS, 1993.

UNESCO. *Statistical Yearbook*. Paris: UNESCO, various years.

Vilar, Margarita. *Los salarios del miedo*. Santiago de Compostela: Fundación 10 de Marzo, 2009.

Weber, Max. *Wirtschaft und Gesellschaft*. Tübingen: Mohr, 1922.

Wells, John. "The Diffusion of Durables in Brazil and Its Implications for Recent Controversies Concerning Brazilian Development." *Cambridge Journal of Economics* 1, 1977: 259–279.

Wolfe, Joel. *Autos and Progress. The Brazilian Search for Modernity*. New York: Oxford University Press, 2010.

Woo-Cumings, Meredith, ed. *The Developmental State*. Ithaca N.Y.: Cornell University Press, 1999.

10

The Mexican Developmental State, *c.*1920–*c.*1980

Alan Knight

In addressing the – putative – Mexican developmental state, the analyst has to juggle two very different sets of data: the history of Mexico and the concept of the developmental state. The first presents obvious problems of both data and interpretation: basically, the statistical series are deficient, especially for the earlier years; and there are large lacunae – for example, the relations between business and government. These problems, however, are grist to the ingenious historian's mill.

Regarding the "developmental state" (or, indeed, any other big "organizing concept"), the problems are of a different order. While there is a substantial literature dealing with the "developmental state" (so we are not using some vacuous neologism), that literature presents problems, in that (i) it is by no means consensual and unambiguous and (ii) much of it is lodged firmly within the orbit of East Asia, from which it may not easily be pried and deployed elsewhere. In other words, it is certainly a 'contested' concept (like most big concepts, of course) and it may also be a "bounded" concept (one that does not travel well).

Regarding East Asia – a "far-off region of which I know little" – experts point to the substantial differences exhibited by Japan (the ur-developmental state?), South Korea and Taiwan; they also stress the historical specificity of the East Asian context – including the experience of Japanese imperialism, the impact of the Second World War, and the umbrella of postwar US hegemony.[1] [2] Not surprisingly, when it comes to teasing out the 'essence' – or, better, the key criteria – of the East Asian developmental state, experts come up with different checklists, which are at times somewhat contradictory.[3]

---

[1] A "far-off region" is a gloss on the celebrated comment of British prime minister Neville Chamberlain regarding Czechoslovakia at the time of the 1938 Munich crisis.

[2] Pempel, 1999: 149–154, which also notes that particular "developmental states" evolve over time, hence are not static models with which comparisons can be easily drawn.

[3] Pempel, 1999: 160, offers eight criteria; other models tend to be somewhat simpler, which is not to say better.

However, four principal criteria are salient: (i) a strong, effective, Weberian bureaucracy; (ii) a close working relationship between that bureaucracy and big business, a relationship which does not, however, involve business "capturing" the state (since, if it did, the bureaucracy would lose its claim to Weberian status); (iii) a commitment to planning (alias "industrial policy") which falls well short of the socialist/command economy, but also goes beyond mere regulation of the free market (in simple terms, neither Stalin nor Roosevelt); and, finally, (iv) a collective commitment – an "ethos," perhaps – which marries nationalism and development (hence the name). [4] [5] [6]

This marriage is, as successful marriages tend to be, a mutually supportive process: nationalism – an ethic of collective national effort – promotes development, since it encourages people to work and save; and development is genuinely conceived in national, collective terms – it is a project which serves the whole nation, not just a privileged minority.[7] In East Asia, a key component of this marriage – or 'ethos', or 'project' – was land reform, which is stressed by some, but not all, commentators: I have not therefore elevated it to the level of

---

[4] However, Schneider, 1999: 278, includes, as one of his "four essential characteristics" of the *desarrollista* state, "a fluid, weakly institutionalised bureaucracy" which dances to the tune of powerful *políticos*. In the same volume, Johnson, 1999: 38, refers to a "small, inexpensive but elite state bureaucracy staffed by the best managerial talent" – which sounds quite Weberian to me. Also, a small but able bureaucracy can be strong and effective (consider the Indian Civil Service under the Raj?) just as a large and costly one might be corrupt, politicized and therefore ineffective, at least when it comes to providing good government (rather than perks and pay-offs).

[5] Thus, the "developmental state" offers a kind of third way, which falls between (roughly) a *laisser-faire* market economy and a planned command economy; according to one view, it rejects "the deified Western concept of 'the market,'" opting instead for active market manipulation," this being labeled "plan rational," as against "plan market" and "plan ideological": Pempel, 1999: 140, 160. Schneider, 1999: 276, seems to concur, offering three types: "command, developmental and market economies." However, a fellow-author in the same book, Cumings, 1999: 64, refers to the free-market end of this "trichotomy" as "the regulatory state," giving as an example the New Deal, which implies that there must be a fourth – unplanned, non-interventionist, consistently free-market – economic model, loosely presided over by a "nightwatchman" state of the kind which, logically, must have preceded the New Deal in the US. Again, I suspect, we are slicing through continua; but it makes a difference what typology we adopt, how many "types" it includes, thus where the slices are to be made. Since Schneider concludes, p. 278, that the American economy during the two world wars was a "command economy," while today's "OECD countries" are "market" economies, I am tempted to conclude that the typology is causing more trouble than it's worth.

[6] Pempel, 1999: 160, prefers "hegemonic project."

[7] The question arises: is the equation of state policy and collective national interest a matter of reality (the "equation" is real, according to some reasonable notion of the "national interest"), or rather of perception – i.e., people believe in it, perhaps wrongly and naively? A partial answer to this familiar conundrum would be that you can't "fool all of the people all of the time" – i.e., reality eventually determines perception. Another partial answer would be that it is possible to frame objective criteria of "the national interest" against which to judge the performance of the putative "developmental state" (as I shall try to do); then, popular (historical) perceptions become a separate question. Maybe Hoover in 1930 or Hitler in 1939 or Mao in 1958 were seen as serving the national interest; but the reality, viewed objectively and with hindsight, was rather different.

a 'principal criterion' (alias, 'necessary condition'?), but its inclusion makes good sense, given criteria (i) through (iv), and it is relevant not only to the diagnostic East Asian cases, but also to the case I will discuss, Mexico.

A final (negative) typological clarification: I avoid any necessary – or even probabilistic – link to a particular political regime-type. In other words, the 'developmental state' can be democratic or authoritarian or somewhere in between. This seems to be the conclusion regarding East Asia, where countries differed and, again, changed over time.[8] The point is relevant since one study of the "developmental state" in Latin America (Mexico and Brazil, at least), makes "political exclusion" a necessary feature, which seems to me not only questionable from the East Asian perspective, but also open to debate when we consider Mexico.[9]

In deploying these criteria, it is a question of "more or less" along a particular axis (such as bureaucratic strength or nationalist "ethos"); and "more or less" can involve comparisons both with other cases/countries (for example, Mexico compared to Japan) and with the same case/country at different points in its history (e.g., Porfirista Mexico compared to PRIísta Mexico), which involves plotting a "developmental state" trajectory over time (as I will attempt).[10] Deploying multiple criteria may be complicated, but it is much better than setting up an "essential model" and expecting simple binary answers (x is or is not a "developmental state"). And if we find that, across several cases, the four – or more – criteria of "developmentalism" are randomly scattered and failed to display any "elective affinity," this might suggest that the whole notion of the "developmental state" is a conceptual ragbag which disorganizes as much as it organizes.

The conceptual model, of course, may carry policy implications (regarding how development should be promoted). However, as a historian, I am leery of policy debates: they ebb and flow with the capricious tides of the global economy; and, if the model is indeed 'bounded', thus a poor traveller, it may make little sense to tell the Mexicans, Latin Americans, or anyone else, that they should import the East Asian model *tout court*.[11] First, because that model may not work once it is exported; and, secondly, because exporting a historically

[8] Thus, Japan was broadly democratic post-1945, when Taiwan and South Korea were not; but Taiwan and South Korea liberalized and then democratized in the 1980s and 1990s (while remaining "developmental," I assume): Johnson, 1999: 52; Pempel, 1999: 154.

[9] Schneider, 1999: 278, 288, seems to generalize that, in his cases, "political exclusion" is an "essential characteristic" of the state; although he recognizes, p. 278, that the "developmental state" can, as in the case of Japan, adopt a democratic form. Which seems to imply that the (Latin American) *desarrollista* state is, not a subset of, but a rather different category from, the "developmental" state, as exemplified by Japan.

[10] We can, of course, compare a given case against a Weberian ideal type; but since the case will almost certainly fall short in many respects, it then becomes a question of how far it falls short, and we are back to plotting points (or trends) along a continuum.

[11] The rise and fall of the "East Asian" model is a good example: Woo-Cumings, 1999: ix–x; and Krugman, 1996: Chapter 11.

bounded model may be an exercise in unreal historical speculation.[12] If the East Asian developmental state – like the Western European welfare state – is a historical product of the Second World War (i.e., direct participation in the Second World War was a necessary if not sufficient condition of its creation), there may be little point in trying to implement it down in countries – like Mexico – whose experience of the Second World War was radically different.

Similarly, if we believe that ancient ingrained values – such as Confucianism – are key, then the problem of transplanting is even greater, unless, perhaps, Catholicism or some other -ism can functionally substitute for Confucianism.[13] Since I am not much persuaded that, in these grand civilizational terms, "culture matters," I will not pursue this line of inquiry.[14] Nor will I address the role played by "good luck" as a developmental variable.[15]

There is, however, an alternative approach worth pursuing, even though it contains its own deep pitfalls. We could detach "the developmental state" from its East Asian moorings and attempt a working model of – generic, non-specific – "developmental" states. We could call the first, more specific, East Asian model the "narrow" version, and the second variant the "broad" model. The big problem is designing the "broad" model. Whereas the "narrow" model clearly derives from the East Asian experience (thus, requires a reasonably clear and consensual distillation of what that experience was), the "broad" model, being detached from any particular historical/geographical/cultural context, is open-ended and indeterminate.

What goes into this (broad) model and how do we decide what to include or exclude? This is a familiar problem in the social sciences (including history): "fascism," for example, can be specifically derived from supposedly paradigmatic cases (e.g., Italy and Germany), or it can be broadly generalized across time and space on the basis of supposed common features.[16] And such features may comprise both "central" and "radial" features (roughly, those which are necessary and those which are optional,

---

[12] Johnson, 1999: 40.

[13] On the "popular, but intellectually squishy, 'explanations' of Asian economic performance based on notions of national culture like 'Confucianism,'" see Pempel, 1999: 141. In fact, far from acting in a cultural matrix favorable to development, Catholicism has often been blamed for being a perverse obstacle: Veliz, 1980; Landes, 1999: Chapter 20. Advocates of this simplistic view seem to overlook the fact that French industrialization forged ahead in the Catholic northeast of the country, while Bavaria is today an industrial powerhouse in Germany. Either way, Confucianism and Catholicism do not seem to me to be crucial to understanding twentieth-century political economy.

[14] I take this questionable assertion from Harrison and Huntington, 2000.

[15] Johnson, 1999: 47. I omit "good luck" not because it is historically irrelevant, but because it defies comparative analysis.

[16] Although some analysts would favour further "splitting," deeming "Mediterranean," i.e., Italian, fascism to be the "original" version and Nazism, if not a different species, at least a "special form": Sauer, 1967: 421.

not antithetical, but also not essential).[17] Either way, the model is a heuristic device (or, if you prefer, an "organizing concept") which enables us to make sense of "the world," past and present. In other words, models/concepts should be defined and deployed according to a functional logic – how useful are they? – and to be useful they must be both clear and capable of being applied in different contexts.[18]

But "usefulness" is in the eye of the beholder. For an ambitious social scientist – let's say a neoclassical economist – a "useful" concept must travel to the ends of the earth (and even back to the dawn of time), since *homo economicus* is to be found everywhere. While some political scientists restrict their analytical purview to a mere N = 14 (e.g., studies of democratic transition in the modern world), others, perhaps suffering from the common complaint of economics-envy, venture "cross-country analysis, pervaded by almost cosmological convictions," the aim being, not to understand particular cases/countries, but to provide "a source of data to be analyzed for the sake of general theorizing.'[19] [20] In other words, the aim is to perfect the concept/model – and the theory, perhaps the lawlike generalizations – which go with it.[21] In our case, this would mean refining the concept of the "developmental state," thus sharpening a useful weapon in the conceptual armoury of social scientists.

However, while I would agree with Pierre Vilar that history is a social science, I think historians have different priorities.[22] Simply put, they usually operate on the basis of N = 1 (or, if N denotes countries, it may be N = 1/4 or 1/10 or 1/100: that is, they often focus on regions, localities, or sectoral fractions of the national whole). Thus, without getting into the old idiographic versus nomothetic debate, it seems clear that historians typically adopt a narrow focus and are less concerned – indeed, usually are not at all concerned – with refining general concepts, let alone "grand theory."[23] [24] They use such concepts, of course ("state," "nation," "society," "revolution"), but they usually take them

---

[17] Collier and Mahon, 1993: 845–855. Land reform would, therefore, be a "radial" category when it comes to defining the developmental state.

[18] As John Kay puts it: "a good model is like a biblical parable and, like parables, is neither true nor false: only illuminating or unilluminating": Kay, 2003: 11.

[19] Alfred Stepan, *Problems of Democratic Transition and Consolidation: Southern Europe, South America and Post-Communist Europe* (Baltimore, The Johns Hopkins Press, 1996).

[20] Daalder, 2011: 24–25.

[21] I am assuming that, in this as in other cases, concept, model and theory are bound up: the notion of the "developmental state" – like the notion of "capitalism" or "fascism" – embodies not just a static set of criteria, but also, implicitly or explicitly, certain "laws of motion" – or, more modestly, certain behavioural characteristics – of the thing itself.

[22] Vilar, 1980: 9–11.   [23] Berkhofer, 1969: 244–245.

[24] In fact, a feature of recent historiography – often of the know-nothing postmodern variety – has been a blinkered rejection of "grand theory" in general. My point is not that historians should reject "grand theory" (on the contrary, it is worth knowing about), but that they should disabuse themselves of the idea that their job is either to formulate it or to consign it to the garbage heap.

off the shelf and do not claim to be improving the product.[25,26] So, as a historian of Mexico, I am interested in the workings of that country's political economy in the twentieth century, using "the developmental state" as an "organizing concept" or "heuristic device." If my historical analysis helps refine the concept, so much the better. But my aim is to understand a country, not a concept.

So, alongside the narrow (i.e., East Asian) concept of the developmental state, I will also use a more general model, based on the criterion of usefulness.[27] According to this model, the developmental state is committed to – and, if it is successful, promotes – development. (We can assume that this usually means within the nation and not beyond: national *sacro egoismo* is the motor, not global philanthropy.) Development can be conventionally defined in terms of – sustainable? – per capita GDP growth; but that is a somewhat crude metric, which neglects the character and consequences of growth.[28] It is commonly – and, I think, correctly – argued that "development" also carries connotations: of growth that serves broad ("national"?) interests, involving improvements in welfare (health, life expectancy and literacy) and, perhaps, broader social and political outcomes (such as greater equality, more inclusive citizenship, a more socially mobile and "open" society). Indeed, one authoritative overview points out that even the founding fathers of classical economics were concerned with "economic development," defined as "regular progress and rising prosperity" – a process which goes beyond simple per capita GDP growth.[29]

---

[25] Berkhofer, 1969: 246.
[26] Of course, historians can – and should – explain the ("emic") concepts entertained by the historical actors whom they study, but that is a completely different from generating ("etic") "grand theory" or "organizing concepts." The historian of Latin American may need to know about witchcraft, miraculous apparitions and racial league tables; but believing in them is another matter (and is not recommended). Conversely, useful (etic) concepts – like "inflation," "class conflict," "hegemony," "informal empire" and, perhaps, "the developmental state" – can be used even though the historical actors may have been entirely oblivious of them.
[27] I take "usefulness" to subsume some necessary qualities: clarity, intelligibility and, perhaps, originality. (There is no point in deploying a new concept when perfectly serviceable equivalents already exist; unfortunately, the promiscuous spawning of gratuitous neologisms is a feature of modern social science, including history. "Transnational" is one such spawn.)
[28] For growth to be "sustainable," I mean not that it should respect environmental constraints (increasingly relevant though that consideration might be); I mean, rather, that growth is sustained over time and is not the result of short-term stimuli such as wars and commodity booms (whose effects can be swiftly reversed). Apart from simple duration, it is also a question of "linkages": Hirschman, 1970: Chapter 6, remains illuminating.
[29] Bell, 1989 : 1. See also Galbraith, 1975: Chapter 12; Maddison, 1970: 15–16; and Sen, 1999. We should note, however, that Chalmers Johnson, in his original formulation of the "developmental state," did not consider it to be, necessarily, a "welfare state [or] an equality state"; these were optional additional features (i.e., "radial" categories?): Johnson, 1999: 37. Pempel, 1999: 155, observes that the East Asian cases combine conservative politics and a weak left (hence,

These various outcomes are often seen as interdependent; however the nature of that interdependence – which way the causal arrows fly – is much debated: greater equality or social mobility may be positive ends in themselves, but they may also be seen as means to promote economic growth (i.e., "development" in the narrower economic sense).[30] On the other hands, Kuznets famously postulated that sustained growth, in the medium term, was associated with – *ergo*, required? – greater inequality.[31]

The potential list of developmental goals and outcomes is, therefore, long and complicated. But we can offer a schematic summary: (i) a narrow economic formulation (GDP per capita); (ii) a package of welfare indices (life expectancy, infant mortality, literacy); and (iii) indices of equality (GINI coefficients), social mobility and socio-political access.[32] Most of these indices are potentially measurable, which is advantageous when trying to explore change over time (or cross-national comparisons); however, in the case of twentieth-century Mexico the statistical series are, especially for the earlier decades, deficient and unreliable.[33] Some trends – such as social mobility and sociopolitical access (sometimes summed up as "empowerment") – are less amenable to quantitative measurement, so I will throw some "impressionistic" evidence into the pot. After all, the great bulk of the evidence which we historians deploy is "impressionistic."

II

Turning to Mexico, I will first offer a simple chronological framework, into which I will insert the various developmental definitions and indices, in order to derive conclusions about Mexico's putative "developmental state." The chronology relates to political economy, of course, and would not work for all dimensions of Mexican history (a "cultural" periodization, for example, would be quite different). It subsumes presidential *sexenios* but is not shackled by them; the basic unit, as it turns out, is roughly generational, since the chronology involves three periods of about thirty years, interspersed by

---

"none has anything resembling a 'welfare state'"), yet they also enjoy "relatively high levels of social equality."

[30] On the distinction between "intrinsic" and "instrumental" developmental goals, see Sen, 1999: 37. Of course, the argument that growing inequality (within, but not between, nations) inhibits growth is often heard today, in the context of rapid globalization and rising GINIs: Stiglitz, 2013.

[31] Kuznets, 1955: 1–28.

[32] The third category is something of a catch-all, which lumps together both equality of outcome (GINIs) and equality of opportunity (including access to education, employment, and political representation). It could, of course, be broken down, but then the list of developmental goals and outcomes would start to lengthen and the analysis would get overly complicated (for a short essay such as this).

[33] Knight, 2000: 137–141.

shorter transitional decades (more or less).[34] Being generational, this periodization could usefully combine social and personal microhistory with the grand macrohistorical march of the Mexican political economy.[35] It is also a conventional, even consensual, chronology, though I have given it a couple of tweaks. Finally, I admit breaching the chronological boundaries of our inquiry, by including, first, a very short overview of the Porfiriato (1876–1911), then a rather longer analysis of the "revolutionary" political economy which followed, by bracketing the 1920s along with the 1930s. As the discussion should make clear, it is impossible to grasp the novelty, character and impact of the revolutionary – arguably developmental – state without knowing something about the preceding Porfiriato; and, regarding the revolutionary state, 1930 marks a minor shift but not a major watershed. The same, I think, could be said of other Latin America economies; and, indeed, changes in the realm of political economy are usually protracted, thus more usefully calibrated in decades than calendar years.[36]

The backdrop is provided by (i) **the Porfiriato** (1876–1911), which is important, by way of establishing certain ruptures and continuities (the warp and woof of historical analysis). After ten years of violent revolution (1910–*c.*1920), the new regime consolidated through the 1920s and 1930s, giving us (ii) the **Political Economy of the Revolution**. The early 1940s (roughly, the *sexenio* of Avila Camacho, 1940–1946) is another transitional phase, leading to (iii) the **Political Economy of the PRI** (1946–*c.*1982), which I will roughly subdivide into (a) the long period of *desarrollo estabilizador* ("stabilizing development," *c.*1954–*c.*1973) and (b) the shorter phase of PRIísta neopopulism (*c.*1973–*c.*1982) which presaged the (partial) dissolution of the regime and its associated political economy. To complete the sequence – though we are now ranging beyond the scope of this essay – we enter another transitional decade, that of the debt crisis and conversion to neoliberalism (*c.*1982–1988), which was followed by (iv) the **Neo-liberal Period** (1988 to the present). In broad terms, therefore, we have four successive politico-economic generations: Porfirian, Revolutionary, PRIísta and Neo-liberal, the first and last bookending the two in the middle, which are my chief concern.

The Porfiriato, our backdrop, combined unprecedented political stability (of an authoritarian, personalist kind) and economic growth; although, compared to what came after – which is our main concern – growth was respectable rather than spectacular:[37]

---

[34] Mexican presidents serve six-year terms (*sexenios*), though between 1920 and 1928, four-year terms were observed. The peculiar *sexenio* 1928–1934 involved three successive presidents, each to varying degrees beholden to the "*jefe máximo*" – the "big boss" – Plutarco Elías Calles.

[35] On the generational approach to Mexican history, see González, 1984. Space does not allow me to pursue this approach here.

[36] Knight, 2014: 276–339.

[37] Thorp, 1998: 318; Manatou, 1992: 21; and MOXLAD data at http://moxlad.fsc.edu.uy/en.html (accessed June 2015).

TABLE 10.1 *Mexican GDP Growth During the "Long Twentieth Century",* *By [Select] Periods*

	i. GDP growth p.a.	ii. Pop. growth p.a.	iii. Growth p.c.
1. Late Porfiriato (1900–1910)	3.4%	1.1%	2.3%
2. Mature Revolution (1929–1945)	4.2%	1.9%[*]	2.3%
3. PRIísta Period (1945–1972)	6.5%	3.5%[**]	3.0%
4. Early Neoliberalism (1981–1996)	1.5%	1.9%[***]	−0.4%

*1937 figure **1960 figure ***1990 figure

TABLE 10.2 *Government Expenditure, 1910–1940*

	[a] total, pesos of 1950	[b] per capita [1910–11 = 100]
1910–11	0.517 m [100]	34 [100]
1920	0.354 m [70]	26 [76]
1930	0.997 m [193]	60 [176]
1940	1.786 m [345]	91 [268]

Porfirian growth looked good against the mid-nineteenth-century backdrop of war, instability and economic stagnation; furthermore, contrary to what many critics have argued, the Porfirian state undertook a coherent project of national development, including a dose of economic nationalism.[38] In other words, it was not just a corrupt *vendepatrias* state, in hock to foreign interests, a craven creator of its own "dependency." Díaz and the Científicos followed a loosely positivistic prescription: strong government, involving repression where necessary; infrastructural investment (railways, ports, telegraphs), with the state playing a supportive role; a warm but conditional welcome for foreign investment; and a policy of playing off American against European interests.

In this narrow sense, we can say that the Porfiriato had a developmental dimension. But the regime was multidimensional: aside from a fair amount of peculation, rent-seeking and cronyism (what Haber *et al.* grandiloquently call

[38] Interestingly, Maddison, 1970: 63, includes the *Porfiriato* as one of the "isolated cases" of pre-1914 regimes "in which economic development was a major concern of official policy."

"vertical political integration"), it was racist, authoritarian, repressive, exclusionary and lacking in "social penetration."[39,40] In these respects, the old *leyenda negra* of the Porfiriato, the subject of much recent revisionist critique, is far from mistaken. The state waged quasi-colonial wars against dissident Indians, actively promoted the concentration of land (thus, the dispossession of peasant villages), and cracked down on the incipient labour movement (hence the famous massacres at Cananea, 1906, and Río Blanco, 1907).

Apart from these sins of commission, the state also incurred sins of omission: it offered no social safety net (though in this respect it was not so different from most of contemporary Latin America, with the exception of Uruguay); its contribution to mass education was, at best, sketchy; and – most obviously and obtusely – it allowed for no popular representation, no electoral competition,thus no institutionalization of what remained a highly personalist and oligarchic regime.[41] To repeat, it lacked "social penetration," which ultimately made it vulnerable to political mobilization and popular insurrection.

In consequence, respectable GDP growth was not matched by broader developmental advance. From the 1890s, if not before, real wages declined, the death rate rose, and demographic growth slowed (which, of course, made the per capita growth figures look even better); recent biometric research also reveals a telling deterioration in the height of poorer Mexicans during the late Porfiriato.[42] These regressive – "anti-developmental"? – trends were evident across wide swathes of Mexico, although the macro-regional patterns varied: we see extensive peasant dispossession in the populous heartland of central Mexico, harsh conditions of "labour-repressive" production in the deep South (where racism was particularly acute), and serious economic vicissitudes in the North, where "dependence" on the US brought boom-and-bust cycles. Some micro-regions prospered and avoided the growing social polarization of the Porfiriato, but they were exceptions.[43]

The Porfiriato thus witnessed a deterioration in welfare, almost certainly linked to rising inequality (we do not have reliable GINIs, so this is an "impressionistic," but nonetheless confident, assessment).[44] Social mobility

---

[39] Haber, Maurer and Razo. 2003: 29ff.
[40] By "social penetration," I mean, roughly, the state's "engagement" with civil society – its capacity to establish links with its citizens/subjects, including reciprocal links which enable the state to influence opinion (and perhaps promote "hegemony"?), while also granting citizens/ subjects some measure of voice (which is not confined to periodic elections; indeed, "social penetration" can be identified in states which have no claims to electoral democracy).
[41] Vaughan, 1982.   [42] Navarro, 1970: 19, 43, 48; López-Alonso, 2006.
[43] González, 1968 charts the history of one such exception: a *mestizo pueblo*, carved out of a hacienda on the internal frontier of Jalisco during the nineteenth century, the result being a fairly stable, homogeneous and God-fearing community.
[44] Attempts have been made to compile GINI indices for the more distant past (which, for Mexican statistical purposes would probably mean pre-1940); one particularly ambitious attempt, which

probably increased, but much of it was downward, as real wages fell and subsistence peasants lost both land and autonomy. Was this the short- or medium-term price that had be paid for the sake of future (more equitable) development, *à la* Kuznets? Since the Revolution intervened, we cannot say with certainty. But there are reasons for believing that, far from being an example of *reculer pour mieux sauter*, the Porfirian political economy was something of a developmental cul-de-sac: growth depended on the export of primary products, vulnerable to global vicissitudes; industrialization, though it occurred, was constrained by weak, contracting domestic demand; and "human capital" was almost entirely neglected. Indeed, proletarianization depressed real wages, so – in the dominant agrarian sector, at least – the incentive to invest in new technology was reduced.[45] Andean America and Central America – as they developed (or failed to develop) through the 1920s and 1930s – may suggest the path that Mexico would have taken absent the Revolution, under a continued Porfiriato (or, perhaps, "Bernardato").[46]

III

Following the highly destructive hiatus of the armed revolution (1910–1920), a new state, committed to a substantially different sociopolitical project, took power, consolidated, and, over two decades (1920–*c.*1940), embarked on policies of state building and social reform. Though the purposive state project played a part, impersonal circumstances – the Revolution, the two world wars, the Great Depression, and the rise of the United States – created the context in which this project evolved; so, just as global trends made possible the East Asian "developmental state," so the Mexican variant was also a product of its time and

includes Mexico, is Williamson, 2009. The title rather gives the game away. See also Milanovic, Lindert, and Williamson, 2007.

[45] Villaseñor, 1995 is the best study of Porfirian agricultural technology: it shows that, among the most advanced and profitable sectors (Morelos sugar and Chalco wheat) landlords did invest in irrigation, reservoirs, branch railways, steam-powered processing plants (mills and refineries), as well as imported ploughs and harvesters. Thus, the bulk of the investment went into transport and processing; and, when new machines were used for cultivation, they "often served simply to restrain the claims of workers" (p. 357). Given "the low price of labour" (a peon was cheaper than "the worst horse or mule"), landlords "did not seek to make savings in respect of the agricultural labour force" (p. 361); meanwhile, in these (advanced) sectors, as elsewhere in Mexico, landlords relentlessly expanded their holdings at the expense of peasant villages, a policy which also served to expand the labour supply and depress wages. All this was possible, of course, because the Porfirian state was, in large measure, run by landlords in the interests of landlords (and not, it should be added, foreign landlords).

[46] General Bernardo Reyes was widely seen as Porfirio's heir apparent, who would continue his authoritarian "order-and-progress" regime beyond 1910; but Díaz refused to anoint him, and Reyes was too feeble to launch a challenge. The last best (or worst) chance of perpetuating the Porfiriato was therefore lost, and a Revolution happened instead.

place (which means, of course, that policy lessons cannot be simplistically extracted and generalized).

In particular, the Revolution shook up Mexican society, evicting the old Porfirian political elite, weakening the *latifundista* class, empowering common people (including insurgent peasants, newly organized urban workers, and even Indians), while engendering a collective commitment to work and reconstruction.[47] After 1930 , the Depression created additional demands and challenges which, mingling with the still strong currents of revolution, created the flood tide of Cardenismo (1934–1940), the most radical phase of the revolutionary process. After which the tide turned and, we could say, echoing the memorable words of Sellar and Yeatman, the Revolution came to a full.[48]

In terms of per capita growth, the revolutionary period was only slightly more successful (ergo "narrowly developmental") than the late Porfiriato which it followed. This is hardly surprising, since revolutions cannot whistle up growth overnight and the Mexican economy of the 1920s occupied much the same niche in the global economy as it had pre-1910: dependence on the US had, in fact, increased, due to Europe's eclipse; and Mexico's export basket remained more or less unchanged.[49] Some "traditional" foreign "enclaves," such as oil, declined, but foreign investment in manufacturing grew, while mining remained buoyant (till the late 1920s); the "Sonoran" state project never envisaged barring foreign investment, still less did it involve moving towards a command economy.[50] State spending remained relatively low and the Sonorans were happy to welcome – and even to join the ranks of – profitable capitalist businesses.[51]

---

[47] Knight, 1986: vol. II, 518–526.
[48] That is, came to a full-stop: Sellar and Yeatman, *1066 and All That*, 1984: 123.
[49] Ficker, 2010.
[50] Presidents Obregón (1920–1924) and Calles (1924–1928), who both came from the north-western border state of Sonora and Calles, as already mentioned, continued to dominate politics until *c*.1934; thus, the period 1920–1934 is conveniently referred to as that of the "Sonoran dynasty." On 1920s foreign investment, see Riguzzi, 2010: 404. Regarding mining, it should be noted that, although the flow of foreign investment was less in the 1920s than it had been in the 1900s, this was quite compatible with increased mineral exports: Sherwell, 1929: 28–30.
[51] Wilkie, 1967: 22–24. Schneider, 1999: 292–293, sees a "turning point" in the mid 1930s, when "Cárdenas dramatically increased and redirected government spending." The shift towards "social" and "economic" (as against "administrative") expenditure is true, and reflects not only changing political priorities, but also the decline of military spending and default on the foreign debt; however, the overall increase in government spending is not quite so remarkable. Schneider states that Cárdenas "nearly doubled the total budget"; in fact, during Cárdenas' *sexenio*, (1934–1940: not, as Schneider says, 1933–1940) government spending in real terms rose by two-thirds; but, because of population growth, per capita government spending increased by only 50 percent. Perhaps more importantly, government expenditure as a share of GDP rose from 6.7 percent to 8.6 percent: a moderate increase on an initially low share: Wilkie, 1967: 7.

Economic "developmentalism" did not involve systematic state intervention, export-promotion, or industrial policy.[52] *Pace* some critics, there is no evidence of a ballooning bureaucracy (nor, it should be said, was the existing bureaucracy impeccably Weberian in make-up and modus operandi).[53]

While revisionist historians are right to point to this record of continuity, especially as regards Mexico's place in the global economy, they should recognize the profound shifts which took place in the domestic political economy as a result of the Revolution: a marked increase in state regulation of business (but not in state ownership of assets); a qualified empowerment of popular organizations (which provided the revolutionary state with a "mass" base which the Porfiriato had always lacked); greater social mobility, certainly in the realm of politics; and the creation of new institutions – notably the Banco de México – which gradually gave the state greater powers of economic management and which made possible the "protoKeynesian" policies of Alberto Pani in the early 1930s.[54,55,56]

Despite allegations of "Bolshevism," this project – even under Cárdenas – was far removed from state socialism: Cárdenas was no Stalin, nor was the PNR/PRM anything like the CPSU.[57] The state also promoted mass education much more vigorously than had the Porfirian regime; and it pioneered a form of

---

[52] Effective tariff protection fell during the years of the armed revolution, rose in the early 1920s, then flattened out; by 1928 it stood pretty much where it had been twenty years before, at the end of the Porfiriato: Ficker, 2007: 244. Contrary to common wisdom, effective tariffs fell during the 1930s and 1940s, but rose substantially in the 1950s: López Córdova and Zabludovsky, 2010: 706–707. Beyond tariff policy, the only example of clear-cut "industrial policy" was the creation of the state investment bank NAFINSA, in 1933: Story, 1986: 38–39.

[53] A small but suggestive example: when the young anthropologist Manuel Gamio, famed for his excavations at Teotihuacan and possessed of a recent Columbia University doctorate (so, no doubt as to his meritocratic credentials), took up his new role as Under-Secretary of Education in 1925, he soon found himself at loggerheads with his colleagues (both above and below), since he refused to condone the "shameful abuses" (*abusos bochornosos*) prevalent in the ministry; these involved overpaying favored suppliers, signing off fraudulent expenses, failing to maintain inventories (hence two official cars – a Cadillac and a Studebaker – had gone missing) and capricious hiring and firing (for example, the minister of education had sacked an employee "for the pointless reason that he [the employee] had not greeted him [the minister] with sufficient cordiality"): Gamio to President Calles, May 14 and June 3, 1925, Manuel Gamio Archive, INAH, Museo de Antropología, caja 2 expedientes 23 and 27. Finally, having taken to carrying a gun to work, just in case, Gamio tendered his resignation.

[54] PEMEX, set up at the end of the revolutionary period (1938), was a very unusual case; the state's other main commitment to public ownership – the nationalization of the unprofitable National Railways in 1937 – meant that, by the end of the "revolutionary" period, *c.*1940, 16 percent of state spending went to public enterprises (up from 10 percent in 1930), which compares with a whopping 43 percent in 1980: Story, 1986: 42.

[55] Camp, 1980: 27–28.   [56] Knight, 2014: 222–224.

[57] Of course, according to the standard typology mentioned above (see fn. 4), the Soviet economy was not "developmental" in the narrower East Asian sense; but Stalin's commitment to industrialization (ergo, the transformation and rapid growth of the economy) was crucial and, as the Second World War showed, successful. Smith, 2017: 308, has no qualms about referring to the Bolshevik "developmental state."

"cultural nationalism" – most strikingly by means of the muralism of the 1920s, most effectively by expanding primary schooling. The primitive schools which sprang up throughout Mexico – especially rural Mexico – in the 1920s and 1930s thus served to inculcate values of patriotism, secularism, revolutionary solidarity, and, by the 1930s, an eclectic brand of Mexican "socialism."[58]

This project went way beyond eye-catching murals and exalted rhetoric. The land reform – piecemeal in the 1920s, sweeping in the 1930s – transformed the countryside, eliminating the "traditional" *latifundia* and, by means of the *ejido*, reconstituting the peasantry (that is, reversing the Porfirian process of proletarianization), while bringing the 1.5 million *ejidatarios* who had received land under the paternalist wing of the state.[59] Labour reform involved state arbitration of disputes (a costless way of enhancing state power); it clipped the wings of private enterprise, including foreign private enterprise (provoking more denunciations of Callista or Cardenista "Bolshevism"); and, by fostering trade union power, it boosted real wages in major sectors like textiles, oil, electricity, and mining.[60] Indeed, apart from a brief dip caused by the Depression, real wages in general, including the huge agrarian economy, rose, if modestly, through the 1920s and 1930s.[61] This in turn helped boost the domestic market to the advantage of Mexican manufacturing, which, during the 1930s, became the leading sector of the economy in terms of growth.[62]

Improved welfare was also evident in the form of increased life expectancy and falling infant mortality, while the decline in height evident in the late Porfiriato was slowly reversed.[63] Some of these trends were evident elsewhere in Latin America – perhaps because elements of an incipiently "developmental" state, committed to national integration, social welfare, and a measure of *desarrollo hacia adentro*, were already present, especially in the more advanced economies, such as Brazil, Chile, and Cuba, by the 1930s. But other trends, such as land and labour reform, were distinctive consequences of the Revolution, which the Great Depression further promoted, and which had few – or, at best, very feeble – counterparts in the rest of Latin America.[64]

Educational provision, especially for male Mexicans, also improved during the 1920s and 1930s, although this represented less a dramatic U-turn (as, for

---

[58] Vaughan, 1997.
[59] Wilkie, 1967: 194, gives the cumulative total of land recipients, by 1940, as 1,588,567. While this figure includes all who received land since the programme began c.1920 (some of whom would have died), it also refers to family heads, so the total *ejidal* population – in a country of just under 20m. – would have been somewhere nearer 6m. Land reform was, of course, integral to the East Asian developmemtal model, according to several accounts: Pempel, 1999: 160, 164.
[60] "The Revolution has produced a decided betterment in the condition of the workers," concluded Ernest Gruening (a well-informed and perceptive observer): Gruening 1928: 344. Gómez-Galvarriato, 2013: Chapter 7 offers a valuable corroborative case study.
[61] Whetten, 1948: 260–262.   [62] Cárdenas, 1987.   [63] López-Alonso, 2006.
[64] Knight, 2014: 303–304, 307.

example, the agrarian reform did) than a sharp acceleration of prior Porfirian trends.[65] And, closely linked to education, we should mention a key item of the revolutionary project, especially during the Calles presidency and *Maximato* (1924–1934): anticlericalism. Callista anticlericalism, a particularly radical version of an old staple of Mexican politics, was strenuously "developmental": it sought to curtail – even eliminate – the Catholic Church and Catholic beliefs and practices, on the grounds that these promoted superstition, backwardness and obscurantism, while obstructing national integration, economic growth, and the rational ordering of society.[66] As Calles liked to point out, benighted peasants, when faced with drought, paraded wooden icons around their parched fields when they should have been busy drilling wells and digging irrigation ditches.[67]

So, one notable feature of the Callista crusade against the Church was wholesale iconoclasm: the destruction of religious images, which demonstrated that they were the inert artefacts of an irrational cult.[68] In short, the Church blocked "development" (individual, intellectual, social, and economic); or, as the anticlericals usually put it, the Church inhibited "Progress."[69] Like their French Jacobin predecessors, Calles and his cohort placed great faith in the liberating power of secular enlightenment. Anticlericalism, therefore, was closely allied to a broad project of national integration and "progress" (alias "development"); it could be seen as a rough counterpart of Weber's "Protestant Ethic," or the various brands of nationalist "socialism" which flourished in postcolonial Africa. In these cases, political elites deployed eclectic ideologies which combined nationalism, education, science, and statism, all in the service of creating a "workmanlike, rational society."[70] In this, they sought to emulate, wittingly or not, the kind of national "ethos" which legitimated East Asian "developmental" states.

The Mexican variant – which had some pallid Latin American counterparts – was virulently anti-Catholic (even anti-religion) because the Mexican Catholic Church was seen – correctly – as unusually strong and broadly hostile to the revolutionary cause. Anticlericalism – or, to put it more positively, aggressive secularism – was much less apparent in East Asian developmentalism because religion (for example, Japanese Shinto, which offered "the amalgamation of

---

[65] Vaughan, 1994: 107.   [66] Knight, 2007: 21–56.

[67] Ambassador Josephus Daniels to State Dept., November 5, 1934, State Department records, M1370, 812.420/303.

[68] Bantjes, 1997: 87–120.

[69] This was the preferred "emic" term, as it had been in the nineteenth century as well; so far, neither "development" (*desarrollo*) nor modernization (*modernización*) had raised their ugly semantic heads. However, it is fairly clear that "progress" roughly equated to these later neologisms (which are not, it seems to me, much of an improvement).

[70] Apter, 1969: 329.

spiritual authority with political power") was a useful ally, rather than a sworn enemy, of the state's national developmental project.[71]

But whereas Mexican "developmental" policies enjoyed some real success in respect of, say, land and labour reform, as well as nationalist state-building, the anticlerical thrust was soon blunted, not least by the Church's dogged resistance. During the 1930s, as the Depression created fresh economic challenges (to which anticlericalism offered no obvious answers), President Cárdenas changed tack and brokered an informal truce with the Church. Some anticlerical measures remained in force down to the 1990s (and some still persist today); but the ambitious Jacobin project of the 1920s was abandoned, as anticlericalism proved to be a political liability, as well as a developmental cul-de-sac.

In other respects, however, the mass cultural project of the Revolution had some success: nationalism was enhanced (it was by no means created *de novo*), while notions of equality, social solidarity, and a collective ethic were inculcated, at least in some quarters.[72] Apart from simply transferring material resources, the agrarian reform embodied a measure of popular empowerment; endowed with land – and schools – *ejidatarios* acquired a sort of social citizenship which had been denied the peons of the Porfiriato.[73]

Indigenismo – the movement/philosophy dedicated to the emancipation and integration of Mexico's Indian population – became a staple of the regime; and, for all its top-down paternalism and palpable failures, it helped dilute the rampant racism of the past, while legitimating Indian access to political power, at least at the local level.[74] Proof of revolutionary national integration could be seen in the patriotic *ralliement* which greeted the oil nationalization of March 1938; and yet better evidence can be found in the durable

---

[71] Maruyama, 1969: 20. Apter, 1969: 329, generalizes that Third-World developmental "social-ism" has "very little to say about religion." Does that make Mexico a special case (*cómo México no hay dos*, as the Mexicans like to say)? Not necessarily: China would seem to be another – very big – exception, since Mao considered "the system of gods and spirits [religious authority]" to be a source of oppression – especially of gullible women – which should be overthrown, not least by "forbidding superstition and smashing idols"; in which respect he echoed his contemporary Calles, including the latter's anticlerical *machismo*: Chesneaux, Le Barbier, Bergére, 1977: 181–182.

[72] "Quarters" is a deliberately vague term, which could be clarified and analyzed geographically (some regions were more Catholic/clerical, some more "revolutionary") and by gender (women tended to be more Catholic, while anticlericalism was typically a male, macho attribute).

[73] Simpson, 1937: 108.

[74] "Diluting" racist rhetoric could mean sanitizing official discourse, while driving racism down into the local political vernacular (a familiar syndrome in many modern societies): Friedlander, 1975 is a good case study. However, there were also real changes: in Dzitas, Yucatán, for example, while occupational structures remained much the same, "to a considerable and to an ever increasing extent, the indios have 'got out of their place.' The Revolution has taken the municipal government out of the hands of the vecinos and placed it in the control of indios," thus "causing the older vecinos the distress incident to loss of status": Redfield, 1941: 70–71.

commitment to notions of nationalism and social solidarity which are apparent through later decades, not least among teachers.[75]

In short, the revolutionary generation of the 1920s and 1930s, while they neither uprooted the Church nor created a statist Leviathan, did build a stronger state, endowed with greater "penetration" of civil society (by means of schools, unions, *ejidos*, and other mass organizations) as well as enhanced powers of regulation, not least of foreign companies. Despite talk of "socialism" and denunciations of "Bolshevism,", this was more a form of managed capitalism, not radically dissimilar to what was attempted in post-1918 Western Europe, albeit in a very different context.[76] Under this regime, Mexico achieved respectable growth rates, slightly bettering those of the late Porfiriato; but, in broader terms, the state successfully promoted "development" in ways that had eluded – and, indeed, often would have appalled – Porfirian policy makers: land and labour reform, popular and populist education, indigenismo, a measure of economic nationalism, and a vigorous – if often unsuccessful – anticlericalism.

IV

The third and final period of this analysis is the period of the PRI, the party born in 1946 which, it could be said (tersely and arguably), inherited and then cast off the mantle of the Revolution, its somewhat oxymoronic title (Revolutionary Institutional Party) indicating its commitment (in theory) to revolutionary ideals and (in practice) to institutional continuity, which in turn involved the maintenance of order, the circulation of elites, dynamic capitalist growth and a near-monopoly of political power. Compared to their revolutionary predecessors, the PRIístas of the 1940s through 1970s were civilians (none, of course, were veterans of the armed revolution), better educated (some would qualify as *técnicos*), urban in background, and committed to industrialization over agrarianism.[77] During their stable and secure tenure of power (which contrasted with the political upheavals afflicting much of Latin America in those decades), revolutionary myth or discourse remained constant, but became increasingly detached from a Mexican reality, which – as the following analysis will suggest – was politically "semi-authoritarian," economically capitalist (and notably dynamic), and, at least until the 1970s, socially regressive. In other words, much more institutional than revolutionary.

In terms of economic growth (narrow developmentalism), this proved a very successful model: per capita growth rates – 6.5 percent per annum between

---

[75] Levinson, 2001. Regarding the inculcation of national history and nationalism among Mexican schoolchildren, see also Segovia, 1975.

[76] Germany's Weimar Republic provided a model which Mexican revolutionary leaders and intellectuals (many of them traditionally *germanófilos*) admired; some still looked favorably on Germany after 1933. Calles, in particular, visited and drew inspiration from Germany: Buchenau, 2007: 76, 111–112, 185–186.

[77] Vernon, 1963: 136–149.

1945 and 1972 – were sustained and impressive and, if the population had not grown so fast (at 3–3.5 percent per annum), the figures would, of course, have been even better. Inflation remained low, at least from the early 1950s to the early 1970s; and industrialization forged ahead, along with urbanization. The Jeffersonian agrarianism of some old revolutionaries was consigned to the garbage can. Relations with the US improved and US investment – now channeled into manufacturing rather than the old export "enclaves" – benefited from high tariffs and a growing domestic market.[78] But domestic capital formation, both public and private, easily exceeded foreign direct investment; and the motor of growth was clearly endogenous, as exports sunk to a low of 7 percent of GDP in the 1960s.[79] Deliberate efforts to promote industrialization contributed to these trends; it would seem reasonable, therefore, to refer to "industrial policy," which fitted within the broad framework of CEPALista economic thinking.[80]

This was clearly a case of *desarrollo hacia adentro*; it was also the most successful phase of sustained growth in Mexico's long history. Of course, the international context helped: these were decades of post-war reconstruction and growth, of global financial stability under the aegis of the Bretton Woods, and US economic hegemony (being "so far from God and so near the US" was, in this case, not such a bad thing).[81] Of course, Mexico's was not the only "economic miracle" going on at the time: consider Italy, West Germany, Israel and, of course, Japan.

The political economy of the PRI was therefore very successful, especially by its own lights.[82] But was it developmental? Prior to the 1970s the state remained fairly small, in terms of spending, payroll, and public ownership. The Federal budget remained remarkably low – rising from 8.6 percent of GDP in 1940 to 13.7 percent in 1961 – and the PRI gave priority to economic over social and administrative spending.[83] However, the state did assume an ample regulatory role, maintaining high tariffs, import quotas, a paternalistic supervision of

---

[78] Vernon, 1963: 89–90, 196–197.

[79] Vernon, 1963: 22, reckoned that at most 20 percent of Mexican industrial output came from foreign firms; according to Story, foreign investment accounted for 10 percent of capital formation in the 1950s, falling to 3–6 percent in the 1960s and as low as 3 percent in the 1970s: Story, 1986: 56–58.

[80] Story, 1986: 38–41; Babb, 2001.

[81] Which offers a parallel with East Asia, where Japan, Taiwan and South Korea have all been "closely linked both in economic and security policies with the United States": Pempel, 1999: 160. One practical benefit of the American security umbrella was, at least for Japan and Mexico, a very low military budget: Wilkie, 1967: 100–106.

[82] Of course, there were always vocal critics: those on the Right who accused the PRI of statism, authoritarianism and corruption; and those on the Left who alleged that the party had abandoned its revolutionary commitment and ensnared workers and peasants in webs of corporatist control.

[83] Wilkie, 1967: 7, 36. The relative growth of "economic" spending was already evident under Cárdenas but it was continued under his successors: Wilkie gives a breakdown (economic/social/

organized labour, and, in Vernon's words, a "pervasive, selective and particularistic" allocation of credit.[84] Underpinning the model – at least from *c.*1954 onwards – was a commitment to low taxes, sound money, and macroeconomic stability: what Sylvia Maxfield has called the "bankers' alliance."[85] One particular feature of the latter was the stability – and, perhaps, capacity – of qualified personnel in key "meritocratic" ministries, especially Hacienda (Finance) and the Banco de México. Meanwhile, the PRI's cosy relationship with business – which the formal structure of the corporatist party disguised – was underpinned by informal networks from top to bottom, from the metropolitan "centre" out to the provincial periphery, where the hardbitten popular *agrarista* caciques of the 1920s and 1930s now gave way to the new PRIísta power-holders of the 1950s and 1960s: the owners of bus lines, gas stations and Coca-Cola franchises.[86]

In its successful pursuit of sustained growth under the benign aegis of the Pax Americana, the regime of the PRI displays clear similarities with the East Asian developmental state: a dominant, semi-authoritarian party; a working collaboration between the state, including technocratic ministries, and big business; pervasive clientelism; and, perhaps, an ideology of national cohesion and development.[87]

However, it was not notably "developmental" in the broader sense. Despite its incessant revolutionary and nationalist rhetoric, the regime of the 1950s and 1960s presided over increasing inequality.[88] During the 1940s and early 1950s, real wages were seriously squeezed, chiefly by inflation (which, of course, the war stimulated) and by the state's increased control over organized labour, evident in both the Pacto de Unidad Obrera of 1942 and the *charrazos* of the late 1940s.[89] The relative shares of national income accruing to labour and

administrative spending) of 38/18/44 under Cárdenas (1934–1940) and 53/14/33 under Ruiz Cortines (1952–1956), who presided over the onset of *desarrollo estabilizador*.

[84] Vernon, 1963: 23, 25. I opt for "supervision," rather than "control" or "cooptation" (terms which are often bandied about in this context), since, try as it might, the state could never entirely bend Mexico's diverse and historically robust labour movement to its will. The best study is Middlebrook, 1995.

[85] Maxfield, 1990.

[86] Vernon, 1963: 26, speaks of "continual personal contact between government officials and businessmen." For a good regional study of PRIísta "infrapolitics," see Saldana and Mendoza, 1976: 74–76, 117–118, 223–235, 266–267, 269. Not surprisingly, given the Catholic/clerical character of Los Altos, these new PRI bosses cultivated good relations with the Church; however, Church–State *détente*, thus the abandonment of the old (developmental?) anticlericalism of the 1920s and 1930s, was also a national phenomenon.

[87] "Benign," at least, in the eyes of the PRI, whose leaders, for all their nationalist rhetoric, readily cooperated with the American security services: Morley, 2008: 83ff. is suggestive.

[88] Eckstein, 1987.

[89] The *charrazos* – from "charro," a folkloric Mexican horseman – were syndical coups, organized by the Alemán administration in order to replace troublesomely independent union bosses with more pliant collaborators: Niblo, 1999: 4, 121–124, 190–200; Middlebrook, 1995: 111, 141–147. Bortz, 1988, charts the sharp decline in real wages through the 1940s.

capital show a similar pro-business trend. Thereafter, during the thirty or so years of *desarrollo estabilizador*, inequality fluctuated.[90] But, given robust growth and low inflation, overall living standards improved, as did literacy and life expectancy. Compared to the rest of their compatriots, the bottom 10–15 percent of the Mexican population – especially the rural and Indian population of the South – lost out during the "economic miracle"; but even they experienced some improvements, which translated into a decline in absolute poverty and increased literacy and longevity.[91]

Meanwhile, even if *political* mobility declined (compared to the turbulent years of the Revolution), *social* mobility remained relatively high, fuelled by the growth of industry, improved access to education, and rapid migration from countryside to cities (also, to some extent, from Mexico to the US). This pattern explains an ostensible paradox in the Mexican political economy of the time: inequality, measured in terms of real income, increased; however, the structure of the economy was changing fast, with new urban and industrial jobs supplanting "traditional" agricultural and artisanal employment, which meant that many Mexicans and their families benefited. Primary schooling now covered the great majority of the population (even though its quality was patchy) and, for the first time, mass university education became possible, helping to swell the urban middle-class while, of course, making possible the novel mass student

---

[90] Szekely, 1998: 10–11, sees rising inequality up to 1963, then a marked decline until 1984, followed by increasing inequality thereafter. The post-1984 increase is clear-cut; so too, I think, is the evidence of growing inequality through the 1940s and 1950s, as the political economy of the PRI took shape. Falling inequality in the 1970s also makes sense, given the sharp increase in state social spending during Echeverría's "neo-populist" experiment, which was followed by López Portillo's brief oil boom, when state spending reached an all-time high. It is the 1963 point of inflection that is hard to fathom: I am not aware of any sharp shift in government policy under López Mateos (1958–1964), still less under Díaz Ordaz (1964–1970); furthermore, some data suggest mounting inequality right through the 1960s: Smith 1979, following Ifigenía M. de Navarrete, shows GINI coefficients rising consistently through the 1950s and 1960s:

	1950	1958	1963	1969
GINI:	0.50	0.53	0.55	0.58

So, I remain agnostic regarding what happened in the late 1960s; otherwise, the broad trends seem quite clear.

[91] Hence, the "poverty index" charted in Wilkie, 1967: Chapter 9, shows steady improvement from the 1940s through the 1960s, at least in terms of the chosen criteria (which are, arguably, sociocultural as well as material): e.g., literacy, language, footwear, diet, and sewage. In specific cases – such as the Tepalcatepec and Papaloapam Commissions, both set up in the late 1940s – the state launched regional developmental programs designed to improve education, health, and production in poorer southern regions.

mobilization of the 1950s and 1960s.[92] Enhanced social mobility meant that most Mexicans could reasonably expect their children to be better educated and to do better, in terms of employment and income, than they had.

The state's role in all this remained, as I mentioned, quite limited. Contrary to certain common myths, the Mexican state of the 1950s and 1960s, though it grew, was very far from being a massive Leviathan. State ownership of productive assets was limited – PEMEX (1938) and electricity generation (1960) being the big exceptions – and the state payroll was, by Latin American (and European) standards, quite small. State regulation – of labour, foreign investment, and property relations – was extensive, but the PRI exercised its regulative role cautiously, even conservatively. Land reform continued, but without offending commercialized private landowners – at least until Echeverría's last-minute agrarian–populist swansong in 1976.[93] Organized labour remained a dependent ally of the state, benefiting from job protection and political access; but in return, the official unions restrained wage demands and wage inflation – as a result, Mexico did not witness the battles between employers and unions evident in, for example, Argentina. In addition, the PRI now pioneered an extensive social security system which benefited labour in the formal sector, while leaving workers in the informal sector, lacking corporatist representation, to sink or swim. Thanks to the relatively benign economic climate – low inflation, rapid growth, industrial expansion and migration to the US – most Mexicans could make do and even expect modest improvements in welfare, especially for their children. In this, Mexico followed, *mutatis mutandis*, trends also evident in the US and Western Europe.

Finally, it is clear that this benign climate contributed to the long and stable rule of the PRI. Like the Italian Christian Democrats or the Taiwanese GMD, the PRI had the good fortune to govern through some thirty years of post-war growth and stability, which made it possible to maintain a dominant (but not "one-party") regime. Though there were recurrent challenges and even occasional armed protests, the period was one of relative sociopolitical peace, certainly compared to the preceding thirty years. The Pax PRIísta also contributed to Mexicans' toleration of a semi-authoritarian (but "inclusionary") regime: few wanted to go back to the days of revolutionary upheaval.[94] Nor did they wish to emulate the political conflict and regime

---

[92] Szekely, 1998: 10–11, reports a doubling of the middle class, from 24 percent of the population in 1950 to 52 percent in 1977; during the troubled 1980s, however, the increase stalled, reaching only 54 percent in 1992. On student activism (which long antedated 1968), see Pensado, 2013.

[93] Sanderson, 1981.

[94] Understandably, this factor tended to diminish over time: Stevenson and Seligson, 1996: 59–80. However, as late as 1994 – a year of severe economic and political upheaval – the *voto miedo'*("fear vote") supposedly gave a boost to the PRI, which was seen as "safer" than either the PAN or the PRD; and similar concerns may have helped the PRI recover national power in 2012.

instability evident elsewhere in Latin America, from Guatemala down to the Southern Cone. This, the stable, if oddly conservative, regime of the PRI was now the "preferred revolution," and not just in the eyes of its northern neighbor.[95]

Just as we are all dead in the end, so all "economic miracles" eventually cease, all benign climates give way to squalls. The 1970s witnessed global economic turbulence, produced by oil shocks, the devaluation of the dollar and the end of the Bretton Woods system. In Mexico, these challenges were compounded by domestic political problems, as the near-monopoly of the PRI was contested by radical students, regional opposition movements, and insurgent trade unions. In response, the leadership of the PRI opted for statist and populist solutions, clinging to political power (and repressing the opposition), while dramatically expanding the scope of the state: its assets, spending, payroll, regulative role, and social provision.[96] Under presidents Echeverría (1970–1976) and López Portillo (1976–1982), gradual, incremental growth of the state gave way to breakneck expansion, made possible by Mexico's second oil boom, coupled with foreign lending.

We can therefore view the 1970s as the swansong of PRIísta rule, as Echeverría – a quintessential product of the PRI's "political bureaucracy" – and his successor, López Portillo (in his own words, the "last president of the Revolution") ramped up state spending and borrowing, in a desperate attempt to shore up the legitimacy of the party and the political system which it presided over.[97] In the process, they did manage to bring about greater equality in Mexican society, accompanied, for a few short years, by rising real wages. But these "developmental" achievements – premised on oil revenue and foreign loans – were offset by egregious cases of elite consumption and corruption, as well as grandiose public projects.

PRIísta "neo-populism" – to give it its crude label – broke most of the unwritten rules of *desarrollo estabilizador*: it fuelled inflation, ran up the national debt, devalued the peso, offended commercial landowners, and, with the sudden bank nationalization of 1982, alarmed the private sector. The old "bankers' alliance" was thus spectacularly broken. The PRI still ruled and growth rates were impressive, in which respect it was a case of more of the same; but political opposition became more intense, inflation took off, and by the early 1980s, as oil prices fell and debt repayments soared, the scene was set for greater economic upheaval and political

---

[95] Schmidt, 2001: p. 25.
[96] Schneider, 1999: 291, points to the hefty state payroll in 1980s Mexico: 4.4 million employees, or one-fifth of the economically active population. However, this was a fairly recent development; it was not a feature of the "developmental/*desarrollista*" state in Mexico through the 1950s and 1960s. On the growth of public ownership in the 1970s and early 1980s, see also Story, 1986: 39, 41, 155–156.
[97] Schmidt, 1991, offers a good overview.

delegitimization. The neoliberal turn and the PRI's eventual loss of national power loomed on the horizon.

It is important to bear this chronology in mind when it comes to critiques of PRIísta political economy: too often, critics elide the entire period from 1946 (the founding of the PRI) down to 1982, depicting it as a seamless story of statism, nationalism, and economic populism. This would be a fair critique of the later 1970s; but it overlooks the much longer period of sustained economic growth, coupled with stable – if semi-authoritarian – rule, which stretched from the early 1950s to the early 1970s, when Mexico enjoyed the most rapid phase of economic growth in its ("long") twentieth-century history. Of course, it would be ahistorical to claim that the political economy of the PRI (*c.*1950–*c.*1973) could have continued indefinitely – with high levels of protection, heavy state regulation, and, in terms of payroll, taxation and the provision of public goods, a fairly skimpy state. But it is also ahistorical to blame the political economy of *desarrollo estabilizador* (still less the Revolution of 1910–1940) for the debacle of the 1980s. In particular, the charge of "economic populism," though valid for the late 1970s and early 1980s, is unconvincing in respect of the 1950s and 1960s – indeed, of the 1920s and 1930s too.[98] Arguably, phases (ii) and (iii) of Mexico's political economy displayed clear "developmental" characteristics; but only at the end, in phase (iiib), did the commitment to sustained development palpably fail.

V

To conclude: the Mexican case does display some systematic similarities to the East Asian "developmental state," at least for the revolutionary (1920–1940) and PRIísta (1940–*c.*1980) periods, which represented a sharp break with the Porfirian past (and which would end with another, albeit less sharp, break, in the 1980s, with the onset of neoliberalism). The revolutionary regime combined respectable economic growth, radical and innovative social reform (above all, land reform), and successful – more "inclusionary" – state-building, premised on a nationalist/revolutionary ethos. This "project" was "developmental" in both the narrow (East Asian) and the broader senses.

Under the PRI, growth was even more rapid and most Mexicans benefited; but inequality mounted (until the 1970s), which meant that greater benefits accrued to those at the top. However, continued socioeconomic – as well as spatial – mobility (which arguably contrasted with growing political *im*mobility), associated with urbanization, industrialization and better educational access, gave the PRIato (the regime of the PRI) a genuinely "developmental" dimension. Thus it seems reasonable to note comparisons with the contemporaneous "developmental" regimes in East Asia which, like Mexico, took advantage of the Pax Americana and the long postwar economic

[98] Compare Dornbusch and Edwards, 1991.

boom. I would go further and suggest that Mexico was the best, if not the only, case of an East-Asian-style "developmental" regime in Latin America.

It is arguable, too, that in the 1970s PRIísta "neopopulism" implied a stronger commitment to "developmental" goals, involving greater state ownership, investment, and *rectoría* (economic management). Neopopulism also brought a brief reversal in the longstanding postwar trend towards greater inequality. But neopopulism, premised on petroleum income and contaminated by corruption, also proved unsustainable: from the early 1980s, Mexico joined – indeed, within Latin America, arguably led – the rush of the global Gadarene swine into the abyss of neoliberalism. Developmental goals were shelved or sharply demoted; the state's short-lived *rectoría* of the economy was abandoned. Oddly (or perhaps not so oddly) the subsequent economic record was poor: growth rates since the late 1980s have been systematically lower than in previous ("developmental") decades. Predictably, inequality also began to increase. And, when Latin America shifted Left, Mexico remained, at least until 2012, firmly on the neoliberal Centre-Right. The PRI, restored to power in 2012, talked a more "developmental" talk (notably regarding education and fiscal policy); but, given other pressing concerns (such as crime and oil), this tends to remain talk. Thus far – to misquote Mark Twain – reports of the demise of the Mexican "developmental state" do not seem at all exaggerated.

REFERENCES

Ambassador Josephus Daniels to State Dept., November 5, 1934, State Department records, M1370, 812.420/303.
Apter, David E. *The Politics of Modernization*. University of Chicago Press, 1969: 329.
Babb, Sarah. *Managing Mexico. Economists From Nationalism to Neoliberalism*. Princeton University Press, 2001.
Bantjes, Adrian. "Idolatry and Iconoclasm in Revolutionary Mexico: The De-Christianization Campaigns, 1920–40." *Mexican Studies/Estudios Mexicanos* 13, 1, 1997: 87–120.
Bell, Clive. "Development Economics." In *Economic Development*, eds. John Eatwell, Murray Milgate and Peter Newman. London: Palgrave Macmillan, 1989: 1–19.
Berkhofer, Robert F. *A Behavioral Approach to Historical Analysis*. New York: The Free Press, 1969.
Bortz, Jeffrey. *El Salario en México*. México: El Caballito, 1988.
Buchenau, Júrgen. *Plutarco Elías Calles and the Mexican Revolution*. Lanham, MD: Rowman and Littlefield, 2007.
Camp, Roderic A. *Mexico's Leaders. Their Education and Recruitment*. Tucson: University of Arizona Press, 1980.
Cárdenas, Enrique. *La industrialización mexicana durante la Gran Depresión*. Mexico: El Colegio de México, 1987.

Chesneaux, Jean, Françoise Le Barbier, Marie-Claire Bergére. *China From the 1911 Revolution to Liberation*, Hassocks: Harvester Press, 1977.

Collier, David and James E. Mahon, Jr. "Conceptual 'Stretching' Revisited: Adapting Categories to Conceptual Analysis." *American Political Science Review* 87, 4, 1993: 845–855.

Cumings, Bruce. "Webs with No Spiders, Spiders with No Webs." In *The Developmental State*, ed. Meredith Woo-Cumings. Ithaca: Cornell University Press, 1999: 61–92.

Daalder, Hans. *State Formation, Parties and Democracy: Studies in Comparative European Politics*. Colchester: ECPR Press, 2011.

Dornbusch, Rudiger and Sebastian Edwards. *The Macroeconomics of Populism in Latin America*. Chicago University Press, 1991.

Eckstein, Susan. *The Poverty of Revolution. The State and the Urban Poor in Mexico*. Princeton University Press, 1987.

Ficker, Sandra Kuntz. *El comercio exterior de México en la era del capitalismo liberal, 1870–1929*. Mexico: El Colegio de México, 2007.

Las exportaciones mexicanas durante la primera globalización, 1870–1929. Mexico: El Colegio de Mexico, 2010.

Friedlander, Judith. *Being Indian in Hueyapán*. New York: St Martin's Press, 1975.

Galbraith, J.K. *Economics. Peace and Laughter*. Harmondsworth: Penguin, 1975 [1964].

Gamio, Manuel. Letter to President Calles, May 14 and June 3, 1925. Manuel Gamio Archive, INAH, Museo de Antropología, caja 2 expedientes 23 and 27, 1925.

Gómez-Galvarriato, Aurora. *Industry and Revolution. Social and Economic Change in the Orizaba Valley, Mexico*. Cambridge: Harvard University Press, 2013.

González, Luis. *Pueblo en vilo. Microhistoria de San José de Gracia*. México: El Colegio de México, 1968.

La ronda de las generaciones. Mexico: SEP, 1984.

Gruening, Ernest. *Mexico and its Heritage*. London: Stanley Paul, 1928.

Haber, Stephen, Noel Maurer, and Armando Razo. *The Politics of Property Rights: Political Instability, Credible Commitments and Economic Growth in Mexico, 1876–1929*. Cambridge University Press, 2003.

Harrison, Lawrence E. and Samuel P. Huntington. *Culture Matters: How Values Shape Human Progress*. New York: Basic Books, 2000.

Hirschman, Albert O. *The Strategy of Economic Development*. New Haven: Yale University Press, 1970 [1958].

Johnson, Chalmers. "The Developmental State: Odyssey of a Concept." In *The Developmental State*, ed. Meredith Woo-Cumings. Ithaca: Cornell University Press, 1999: 32–60.

Kay, John. *The Truth About Markets*. London: Penguin, 2003.

Knight, Alan. *The Mexican Revolution*. Cambridge: Cambridge University Press, 1986.

"Export-Led Growth in Mexico. 1900–30." In *An Economic History of Twentieth-Century Latin America (vol. 1): The Export Age*, eds. Enrique Cárdenas, Enrique, José Antonio Ocampo, and Rosemary Thorp. London: Palgrave-MacMillan, 2000: 119–151.

"The Mentality and Modus Operandi of Revolutionary Anticlericalism." In *Faith and Impiety in Revolutionary Mexico*, ed. Mathew Butler, 21–56. New York: Palgrave-MacMillan, 2007.

"The Character and Consequences of the Great Depression in Mexico." In *The Great Depression in Latin America*, eds. Paulo Drinot and Alan Knight. Durham: Duke University Press, 2014: 213–245.

"The Great Depression in Latin America: An Overview." In *The Great Depression in Latin America*, eds. Paulo Drinot and Alan Knight. Durham: Duke University Press, 2014: 276–339.

Krugman, Paul. *Pop Internationalism*. Cambridge, MA: MIT Press, 1996.

Kuznets, Simon. "Economic Growth and Income Inequality." *The American Economic Review* 45,1, 1955: 1–28.

Landes, David S. *The Wealth and Poverty of Nations*. New York: W.W. Norton, 1999.

Levinson, Bradley A. U. *We Are All Equal. Student Culture and Identity at a Mexican Secondary School*. Durham: Duke University Press, 2001.

López-Alonso, Moramay. "A History of Poverty and Inequality in Mexico, 1840–1940." Paper given at the XIV International Economic History Congress, Helsinki, 2006.

López Córdova, J. Ernesto and Jaime Zabludovsky K. "Del proteccionismo a la liberalización incompleta: industria y mercados." In *Historia económica general de México*, ed. Sandra Kuntz Ficker. Mexico: El Colegio de Mexico, 2010.

Maddison, Angus. *Economic Progress and Policy in Developing Countries*. London: George Allen and Unwin, 1970.

Manatou, Jorge Martínez. *La revolución demográfica en México, 1970–80*. México: IMSS, 1992.

Maruyama, Masao. *Thought and Behaviour in Modern Japanese Politics*. Oxford University Press, 1969.

Maxfield, Sylvia. *Governing Capital: International Finance and Mexican Politics*. Ithaca: Cornell University Press, 1990.

Middlebrook, Kevin J. *The Paradox of Revolution: Labor, the State and Authoritarianism in Mexico*. Baltimore: Johns Hopkins University Press, 1995.

Milanovic, Branko, Peter H. Lindert and Jeffrey G. Williamson. "Measuring Ancient Inequality." NBER working paper no. 13550, 2007.

Morley, Jefferson. *Our Man in Mexico: Winston Scott and the Hidden History of the CIA*. Lawrence: Kansas University Press, 2008.

Navarro, Moisés González. *Historia moderna de México. El Porfiriato: La vida social*. Mexico: Editorial Hermes, 1970.

Niblo, Stephen R. *Mexico in the 1940s. Modernity, Politics and Corruption*. Wilmington, DE: SR Books, 1999.

Pempel, T.J. "The Developmental Regime in a Changing World Economy." In *The Developmental State*, ed. Meredith Woo-Cumings. Ithaca: Cornell University Press, 1999: 137–181.

Pensado, Jaime M. *Rebel Mexico. Student Unrest and Authoritarian Political Culture during the Long Sixties*. Stanford University Press, 2013.

Redfield, Robert. *The Folk Culture of Yucatán*. Chicago University Press, 1941.

Riguzzi, Paolo. "México y la economía internacional, 1880–1930." In *Historia económica general de México de la Colonia a nuestros días*, coord. Sandra Kuntz Ficker. Mexico: El Colegio de Mexico, 2010.

Saldana, Tomás Martínez and Leticia Gándara Mendoza. *Política y sociedad en México: el caso de los Altos de Jalisco*. Mexico: INAH, 1976.

Sanderson, Steven E. *Agrarian Populism and the Mexican State*. Berkeley: University of California Press, 1981.

Sauer, Wolfgang. "National Socialism: Totalitarianism or Fascism?" *American Historical Review*, 73, 2, 1967: 404–424.

Schneider, Ben Ross. "The Desarrollista State in Brazil and Mexico." In *The Developmental State*, ed. Meredith Woo-Cumings. Ithaca: Cornell University Press, 1999: 276–305.

Schmidt, Arthur. "Making it Real Compared to What? Reconceptualizing Mexican History since 1940." In *Fragments of A Golden Age: The Politics of Culture in Mexico since 1940*, eds. Gilbert M. Joseph, Anne Rubinstein and Eric Zolov. Durham: Duke University Press, 2001: 23–70.

Schmidt, Samuel. *The Deterioration of the Mexican Presidency: The Years of Luis Echeverría*. Tucson: University of Arizona Press, 1991.

Segovia, Rafael. *La politicización del niño mexicano*. Mexico: El Colegio de México, 1975.

Sellar, W.C. and R.J. Yeatman. *1066 and All That*. London, Methuen, 1984 [1930].

Sen, Amartya. *Development as Freedom*. Oxford University Press, 1999.

Sherwell, Guillermo Butler. *Mexico's Capacity to Pay*. New York: 1929.

Simpson, Eyler S. *The Ejido: Mexico's Way Out*. Chicago University Press, 1937.

Smith, Peter H. *Labyrinths of Power*. Princeton University Press, 1979.

Smith, S.A. *Russia in Revolution. An Empire in Crisis, 1890–1928*. Oxford University Press, 2017.

Stepan, Alfred. *Problems of Democratic Transition and Consolidation: Southern Europe, South America and Post-Communist Europe*. Baltimore: The Johns Hopkins Press, 1996.

Stevenson, Linda S. and Mitchell A. Seligson. "Fading Memories of Revolution: Is Stability Eroding in Mexico?" In *Polling for Democracy*, ed. Roderic A. Camp. Wilmington: SR Books, 1996: 59–80.

Stiglitz, Joseph. *The Price of Inequality*. New York: W.W. Norton, 2013.

Story, Dale. *Industry, The State and Public Policy in Mexico*. Austin: University of Texas Press, 1986.

Szekely, Miguel. *The Economics of Poverty, Inequality and Wealth Accumulation in Mexico*. Basingstoke: MacMillan, 1998.

Thorp, Rosemary. *Progress, Poverty and Exclusion. An Economic History of Latin America*. New York: IDB, 1998.

Vaughan, Mary Kay. *The State, Education and Social Class in Mexico, 1880–1928*. DeKalb: Northern Illinois University Press, 1982.

"Rural Women's Literacy and Education during the Mexican Revolution: Subverting a Patriarchal Event." In *Women of the Mexican Countryside, 1850–1950*, eds. Heather Fowler-Salamini and Mary Kay Vaughan. Tucson: University of Arizona Press. 1994: 106–124.

Cultural Politics in Revolution: Teachers, Peasants and Schools in Mexico, 1930–40. Tucson: University of Arizona Press, 1997.

Veliz, Claudio. *The Centralist Tradition of Latin America*. Princeton University Press, 1980.

Vernon, Rayond. *The Dilemma of Mexico's Development*. Cambridge: Harvard University Press, 1963.

Vilar, Pierre. *Iniciación al vocabulario del análisis histórico*. Barcelona: Editorial Crítica, 1980.

Villaseñor, Alejandro Tortalero. *De la coa a la máquina de vapor. Actividad agrícola e innovacción technológica en las haciendas mexicanas, 1880–1914*. Mexico: Siglo XXI, 1995.

Whetten, Nathan. *Rural Mexico*. Chicago University Press, 1948.

Wilkie, J.W. *The Mexican Revolution: Federal Expenditure and Social Change since 1910*. Berkeley: University of California Press, 1967.

Williamson, Jeffrey G. "History Without Evidence: Latin American Inequality since 1491." NBER working paper no. 14766, 2009.

Woo-Cumings, Meredith. "Preface." In *The Developmental State*, ed. Meredith Woo-Cumings. Ithaca: Cornell University Press, 1999: ix–xiii.

The Developmental State and the Agricultural Machinery Industry in Argentina

Yovanna Pineda

INTRODUCTION

In Argentina, the developmental state had many faces during the twentieth and early twenty-first centuries. Many Argentines who lived through the different phases of developmentalism, when asked about that era, evoke memories of politicians calling for economic development, and their own feelings of disappointment about truncated industrialization. This chapter analyzes the sociocultural effects of the developmental state's policies promoting domestic industrialization, specifically farm machinery production, at the regional and national levels. It asks two main questions: First, how did the country's developmental policies influence domestic industry, in particular the farm-machinery sector, during the twentieth century? Secondly, how did populist politics lead to a brief resurgence of the developmental state during the early twenty-first century? Within this chapter, I weave in examples from the agroindustrial town of San Vicente in Santa Fe Province as a significant, but largely understudied, case study to show the intersection of national and regional discourses regarding domestic industry. It draws on national, local, and family archives, invention patents, and more than seventy interviews with the men and women involved in the invention and usage of domestic farm machinery.[1]

In the following section, I discuss the larger historical backdrop of the Argentine developmental state of the twentieth century and its eventual dismantling in the 1990s, and integrate examples from the farm-machine manufacturers of San Vicente, in particular the Senor Harvester Factory, to show how local instances fit within the broader history. The third section briefly examines the country's political and economic transition into the twenty-first

---

[1] University of Central Florida Institutional Review Board has reviewed the interview questions and procedures of this research (Exempt number, IRB ID: SBE-16–12483). To some extent, I followed interview styles similar to those found in Gudeman and Rivera, 1990 and Kotkin, 1997.

century. The fourth and final section concludes with a discussion of President Cristina Fernández de Kirchner's intent to promote domestic farm technology by using Senor family members, descendants of manufacturers of combine-harvesters in San Vicente, to develop a national combine harvester. In this case, both the resurgence of developmentalism and the new combine harvester failed.

RISE AND FALL OF THE DEVELOPMENTAL STATE IN THE TWENTIETH CENTURY

After the First World War, prominent Argentine intellectuals and policymakers perceived industrialization as a way to achieve and sustain progress through development and increase employment.[2] The state created a variety of ad hoc policies to support domestic industry, including protective tariffs, state-supported credit mechanisms, and direct public investment.[3] By 1921, for instance, this helped small-scale companies, such as the Senor Harvester Factory in San Vicente, begin operations and open a factory. At the national level, the Argentine government largely continued policies from previous administrations through the 1930s, including selectively raising tariffs on consumer goods and lowering them for essential raw materials such as iron, steel, and fossil fuels for de facto protection and support.[4] These policies, however, failed to intentionally promote the productivity of the preferred metallurgy and agroindustry. Also, the government was unable to ensure the supply of raw materials during the global depression of the 1930s – though the Senor Factory continued operations and was able to obtain the necessary iron and steel for production.[5]

By November 1940, Finance Minister Federico Pinedo proposed explicit import-substitution programs, especially state support of so-called *natural*, or agroindustry, to sustain employment and economic self-sufficiency.[6] Pinedo's original bill proposal, known as the Economic Reactivation Plan, or Pinedo Plan, died in the Congressional House of Deputies that same year. Historians have argued that regardless of the bill's demise, by the mid 1940s, the military and Peronist (1946–1955) governments had passed the majority of his policies, especially those related to raising productivity in traditional agricultural sectors

---

[2] Beginning in 1914, policymakers, manufacturers, and intellectuals emphasized that industrialization was essential for economic growth and national self-sufficiency. Bunge, 1921; Pantaleón, 2004; Rocchi, 2006.

[3] Barbero and Rocchi, 2003: 261–294; Pineda, 2009.

[4] The result was a cascading tariff structure. Berlinski, 2003: 197–232.

[5] The key was to order and purchase all the anticipated needs at the start of the year in January. Edgardo Botta, personal interview, Santo Tomé, Santa Fe, July, 2016; Danilo Senor, personal interview, San Vicente, Santa Fe, July, 2016.

[6] Llach, 1984: 515–558; Cramer, 1998: 519–550.

through the use of technology and promoting selected manufacturing activities.[7]

Hence, import-substitution policies helped Argentina's industrial production grow during the Second World War and in the early 1950s. At the local level, for instance, it was during this period that the Senor Harvester Factory developed new models of harvesters and under the brand name Industrias Urvig, developed a transmission (powertrain) model specific for harvesters.[8] Overall, by the 1950s, Argentina had developed a relatively solid industrial base that employed urban workers, motivating the administration of President Juan Domingo Perón (1946–1955) to heavily tax agricultural exports to support import substitution, redistribute income, and boost employment.[9,10] Soon after 1952, however, the postwar agricultural boom began to decline. Therefore, economic and political troubles began to increase, characterized by student and labor protests and rising inflation. By 1955, the military removed Perón from power in a September coup owing to the severe political and economic crises that engulfed the country. By 1956, Argentina settled its debts with public creditors in Paris, now known as the Paris Club agreement. From the mid 1950s to the late 1960s, the military leadership initially sought to erase all remnants of Peronism, including persecuting his followers and barring them from all regional and national elections. María Estela Spinelli discusses the irony of this period known as the Revolución Libertadora, wherein the antiperonistas sought to bring in an era of democracy through the exclusion of the Peronist party.[11] This repression helped bring in two opposing party presidents from the divided Radical party into power in 1958 (Arturo Frondizi) and 1963 (Arturo Illia).

Although the military banned the Peronist political party, they still sought to implement economic nationalist policies, and in theory, supported the postwar call for an expansion of state-led industrialization. Beginning in the 1950s, the structuralist economists working in the United Nations Economic Commission

---

[7] Llach, 1984: 515–558; Cramer, 1998: 519–550.

[8] Typically, harvesters had utilized tractor transmissions. Jorge Senor Sr., email interview, May 29, 2017.

[9] For Latin America, "between 1950–1981 ISI delivered a growth rate that was not only higher than in other developing regions, but also—and for the first time ever—higher than that of the OECD (4.2%). Gabriel Palma, "Latin America during the second half of the Twentieth Century: From the 'age of extremes' to the age of 'end-of-history' uniformity," in *Rethinking Development Economics*, ed. Ha-Joon Chang, 125–151 (London: Wimbledon Publishing Company, 2003), 127.

[10] From 1946 to 1955, President Juan Domingo Perón pursued five-year economic plans to raise industrial productivity, while agricultural producers paid the price: "export taxes on agricultural goods to finance the welfare and industrial programs, maintaining relatively low cost of living, price controls on foodstuff imposed, and limiting sales to the domestic market (p. 607)." Luigi Manzetti, "The Evolution of Agricultural Interest Groups in Argentina," *Journal of Latin American Studies* 24, no. 3 (October 1992): 585–616.

[11] Spinelli, 2005.

of Latin America (ECLA) promoted strong state intervention in all Latin American economies. Argentine economist and ECLA Director Raúl Prebisch argued that "core" countries developed at the expense of "peripheral" nations because of unfair international terms of trade between the two regions, thereby leaving the peripheral nations perpetually underdeveloped.[12,13] Prebisch and structuralist theorists had argued that to develop, peripheral governments must promote inward-oriented growth, create national growth strategies and national planning institutions with technocrats capable of implementing policies that expressly supported domestic manufacturing. Consequently, most Latin American nations followed a model of heavy state intervention in the national economy.[14]

In 1958, the newly elected Intransigent Radical Party (UCRI) president, Arturo Frondizi (1958–1962) unveiled a national development plan inspired by Pinedo's, the structuralists' recommendations, and Rogelio Frigerio. When Frondizi assumed the presidency in May 1958, both civilians and the military expected him to present a developmental plan in his inauguration speech. Although he fulfilled this expectation, some audiences were taken aback by announcing his broad plan to support "national development," especially the expansion of oil production and selected heavy machinery industries through foreign direct investment (FDI).[15] Indeed, they viewed FDI in key economic sectors as a betrayal of the principles of economic nationalism, such as self-sufficiency.

Many of the key points in Frondizi's inauguration speech had been developed in 1956 with the creation of UCRI's Integration and Development Movement (Movimiento de Integración y Desarrollo, MID). Although Frondizi anticipated that the MID principles would play a large role in Argentine developmentalism, his messaging remained broad and vague. For instance, MID leader Frigerio had called for strong import-substitution programs, promoting economic development via capital, technology, and heavy industry. But Frigerio never defined how to sustainably obtain these inputs or overcome political obstacles to it.[16] Frondizi failed to do so as well, leaving his opponents, in particular the People's Radical Party (UCRP) and Peronists, suspicious of MID as a development plan.[17] The economic situation was already in decline when

---

[12] After the Second World War, Prebisch was a significant figurehead for economic planning in Latin America. He headed the United Nations Economic Commission on Latin America (ECLA, 1948–1962), created and mentored the Latin American Institute of Economic and Social Planning (ILPES), and played an international role as head of the United Nations Conference on Trade and Development (UNCTAD). Dosman, 2008.

[13] Love, 1996; Prebisch, 1918–1949.

[14] It should be noted that beginning in the 1980s, scholars critiqued the structuralists for conceptualizing development within a limited framework of industrialization and for viewing it solely as a technocratic process: Cyper, 1990; Escobar, 1995.

[15] Szusterman, 1993.   [16] Frigerio, 1965a.

[17] Szusterman, 1993. After his overthrow in 1962, Frondizi continued to defend MID and its plan for agriculture, arguing that more technology was needed to increase rural production and make it globally competitive. Frondizi, 1965b: 13.

Frondizi ascended to power. Within five months of his administration, Frondizi angered the Peronists and UCRP yet again when he negotiated an especially austere aid package with the International Monetary Fund (IMF). The package required implementation of a stabilization program consisting of raising exports, decreasing imports, and increasing foreign direct investment.

It was only by 1961, three years after his inauguration, that Frondizi finally appeared able and determined to put into practice a national development strategy by presidential decree.[18] Like other Latin American countries, a national development council for Argentina was established under the name of CONADE in August of 1961. Although even high-ranking figures inside the administration expressed their disappointment at the long delay in establishing a council, Frondizi had spent a substantial amount of time mollifying political tensions between the presidency and different groups, such as the military, UCRP, and Peronists.[19]

However, in contrast to Chile's national development corporation CORFO (Corporación de Fomento de la Producción) Argentina's council CONADE never became a leading institution in the planning and promotion of economic development in the country. A brief comparison of the two public organizations reveals some of the institutional weaknesses that Argentina's CONADE suffered from the beginning. First of all, as shown in Chapter 12 in the present volume, the creation of the Chilean CORFO was deliberately planned in order to provide the institution with wide political and legal support. CORFO was established, after appropriate – and in part heated – parliamentary debate, by a specific act of Congress.[20] Argentina's CONADE was created by mere presidential decree instead, lacking thus the political and legal support that parliamentary debate and intervention could provide. [21] This contrast was very much a matter of institutional design, and not just an accident due to different political circumstances at the moment the institutions were created. The intervention of Congress in the Chilean CORFO was not only arranged at the moment of its creation, it was a permanent principle, along with the participation of other key social and political actors.

The Chilean corporation CORFO was designed with a directing board that included four permanent representatives of Congress, as well as representatives of other social and political actors with decisive roles in any developmental strategy, such as business associations, banks, the national engineers' association, and unions. As the first development corporation in Latin America, created in 1939, CORFO showed an institutional design that was purposely engineered to increase the political reputation and the network capabilities of the organization. For the next twenty years, among other factors, this strong institutional design enabled CORFO to operate as

---

[18] Love, 1996: 207–274; Szusterman, 1993; Jáuregui, 2013: 243–266.
[19] Szusterman, 1993: 125.   [20] Law 6334 of 1939.   [21] Presidential Decree 7290 of 1961.

a relatively autonomous bureaucracy, and the corporation's policies contributed substantially to industrial development in Chile.[22]

Compared to CORFO, the institutional design of Argentina's development council CONADE was fragile. The design of CONADE did not promote network capabilities, since the directors (or members of the council) were appointed by the president entirely at will. The development council CONADE was just a tool of the president without any kind of bureaucratic autonomy. Other social or political actors had no direct stake in the management of the organization, thus making both networking and reputation-building much more difficult. As a result of such institutional weakness and other factors, Argentina's CONADE was ineffective.[23] Among the interviews of manufacturers and engineers, for instance, none mentioned CONADE. And in one case, the interviewee Jorge Senor of the Senor Harvester Factory, recalled that for a brief period, the Factory had negotiated with Chile's CORFO a few technological exchanges of harvesters and forage choppers.[24] Hence, there is a local recollection of CORFO but not of CONADE.

For the most part, Frondizi's four years of developmentalism (1958–1962) were closely connected to his vision and leadership. He promoted an eclectic program which produced mixed economic outcomes, especially within the agricultural-machine sector. In terms of growth and sheer numbers, it was a success. Between the 1895 national industrial census and 1962, domestic farm-machine producers had outgrown their family-run blacksmith shops and some created small-scale factories with up to 300 hired employees.[25] The number of these factories in the farm-producing regions of the Pampas grew from a few known dozen in 1920 to 447 firms by 1962.[26] Similarly, the combine-harvester sector had grown from approximately three domestic companies in the 1930s with a production of 2–20 machines per year to 23

---

[22] Centeno and Ferraro, 2017.

[23] When the People's Radical Party President (UCRP) Arturo Illia was elected in 1963, he attempted to revive CONADE as a developmental state agency in 1965. He proposed a National Development Plan of 1965, but it never took flight, partly because he was overthrown in a military coup in 1966: Jáuregui, 2013.

[24] Interview with Jorge Senor Senior by author, by email, May 29, 2017.

[25] The numbers are not perfect, but what we know from the census data is: the cost to enter blacksmithing was relatively low, and many artisans or farmers could undertake it. Blacksmith shops increased from 501 in 1895 to 909 by 1935. The Santa Fe provincial census recorded an even higher number of shops. In Santa Fe province, in the heart of the cereal crops region, the number of forge workshops in wheat belt districts rose from 1,876 in the 1887 provincial census to 2,769 by 1895. The discrepancy in the provincial and national figures is likely because national figures recorded commercial shops for profit while the provincial figures represented forges in commercial and non-commercial use. Most small-scale farmers had access to black-smith shops for their daily needs, and some had a blacksmithing area attached to, or near, their homes. Argentina, 1898; Ministerio de Hacienda, 1917; Dirección General de Estadística de la Nación1937); Gallo, 1970: 253; Luciano Prosperi Ramello, videoconference interview, December 2014.

[26] Szusterman, 1993.

factories producing 100–360 harvesters each per year by the mid 1960s.[27] Nevertheless, nine foreign-owned firms accounted for a massive 85.8 percent of production within the country.[28] Several of these domestic company owners benefited from new credit lines offered through the Argentine Industrial Bank and the National Bank as part of an Inter-American Development Bank initiative for the promotion of industrial development during Frondizi's administration.[29] This access to credit helped small-scale producers expand production. In the case of the Senor Harvester Factory, the owners used the credit to help them build a new factory and patent farm machinery during the 1950s and 1960s, including patenting a domestic tractor.[30] They also designed and built unpatented combine models, including the V60 and JE50. By the late 1960s, they adapted the combines for harvesting soy and rice for export abroad to Venezuela and Brazil.[31]

The 1966 military coup terminated the development policies of the Radical Party administrations. Between 1966 and 1972, international negotiations were especially difficult, and previous agreements, such as the one Senor had with CORFO, fell apart.[32] After 1966, two military dictatorships, with a brief and very unstable democratic interval from 1973 to 1976, supported gradual but inconsistent – and often contradictory – economic policies, liberalizing markets and deregulating financial institutions, promoting the service sector, and ineffectually attempting to support export industrialization.[33] Soon after the return to democracy in 1983, remaining developmental programs were shattered by hyperinflation, which drastically decreased investor confidence and encouraged capital flight.

[27] These numbers of machines are estimates. Juan Bergero Senor, personal interview, San Vicente, Santa Fe, July 2, 2016; Botta, personal interview; Osvaldo Savore, interview by Luciano Prosperi, San Vicente, Santa Fe, December 2016; Bil, 2011. The author and aficionado, José María Barrale, has claimed that he found forty-nine different harvester producers across time in Argentina. José María Barrale, personal interview, San Vicente, Santa Fe, June 18, 2017.

[28] Szusterman highlights that foreign firms dominated in seven relevant industrial subgroups by 1962. Szusterman, 1993: 128.

[29] Szusterman, 1993; Banco de la Provincia de Buenos Aires, 1960. Frondizi Archive, Box 03.4.1.8.17, Santa Fe, Special Collections, Biblioteca Nacional, Buenos Aires, Argentina; Danilo Senor, email interview, September 21, 2015; Jorge Senor Sr., personal interview, Roldán, Santa Fe province, June 20, 2017.

[30] "Mejoras en plataformas recolectoras de maíz," Patente de invención 98.117, Juan y Emilio Senor e hijos, Sociedad Anónima, Industrial y Comercial de San Vicente, Provincia de Santa Fe, July 18, 1955; "Mejoras en máquinas cosechadoras-trilladoras de cereales," Patente de invención 126.380, Juan y Emilio Senor e hijos, Sociedad Anónima, Industrial y Comercial de San Vicente, Provincia de Santa Fe, July 7, 1961. "Un nuevo tractor de aplicaciones multiples," Patente de invención no. 130.492, Juan y Emilio Senor e Hijos, Sociedad Anónima, Industrial y Comercial de San Vicente, Provincia de Santa Fe, October 8, 1962. The tractor patent was taken out, but it seems the Senor factory never manufactured it for commercial purposes.

[31] José Luis Prosperi, interview by Damián Bil, San Vicente, Santa Fe, February 11, 2009; Mirando a través de un nombre, n.d.

[32] Jorge Senor Sr., email interview.   [33] Schwartz, 1990: 85–101.

The political and economic crises of the 1970s and 1980s hurt small and medium-sized manufacturers. During this period, the Senor Harvester Factory struggled but remained in business by taking on debt, diversifying production lines, and participating in the export experimentation program. For instance, between 1967 and 1983, they exported harvesters to Brazil (404 units), Paraguay (67 units), Uruguay (19 units), Bolivia (12 units), Venezuela (6 units), and Peru and Chile (1 unit each).[34] Yet export taxes were high (20 percent).[35] The National Bank also extended a special credit in collaboration with the Inter-American Development Bank that helped consumers finance the purchase of heavy farm machinery over five years, and this facilitated sales.[36] The Senor company successfully negotiated an export contract with an assembly factory in southern Brazil, where they sent partially manufactured combines.[37] Despite this small success with exportation, it was insufficient to remain in business as the national economy worsened. Hyperinflation increased production costs, making it difficult to repay loans that the company took out.[38] By April 1987, the Senor Harvester Factory officially went out of business.

After winning the presidential election in 1989, Peronist President Carlos Menem adopted a drastic neoliberal economic program, which defied every tenet of traditional Peronism. The president explained that this surprising policy reversal was justified by the country's bankruptcy. The administration thus began the process of dismantling all Keynesian-style elements in Argentina's economic institutions. Calling it "surgery without anesthetics," Menem implemented a radical privatization plan to denationalize state enterprises, deregulate financial markets, and dismantle the income redistribution and social welfare programs that had been established during the presidency of Juan Peron.[39] In 1991, the new Economic Minister Domingo Cavallo ushered in the Convertibility Law that pegged the US dollar to the Argentine peso and made privatization "no longer an ad hoc policy but [was] incorporated as an integral part of the administration's economic plan."[40] During the 1990s, the economy grew and the era of hyperinflation ended, which prompted neoliberal supporters to rechristen Argentina a "model" state, especially during the East

---

[34] Danilo Senor was a combine salesman for his grandfather's company. Danilo Senor, email interview, September 10, 2015.
[35] Danilo Senor, email interview, September 21, 2015.
[36] The finance negotiation was between the company E. Paquien Limited, the Banco Central de la República Argentina, Banco de la Nación Argentina, and Banco de Brasil to finance the export of Senor machinery to Brazil. Jorge Senor Sr., email interview; Danilo Senor, email interview, September 21, 2015.
[37] Danilo Senor, email interview, September 10, 2015.
[38] Raúl Carletti, personal interview, San Vicente, Santa Fe, July 2, 2016.
[39] Manzetti, 1999: 72–73.
[40] The exchange rate became 1:1 between the US dollar and Argentine peso. The main tenets of the Convertibility Law are listed in Manzetti, 1999: 73.

Asian financial crisis of 1997. Meanwhile, Menem continued with the radical implementation of market-oriented reforms, keeping the fixed exchange rate during the whole decade.

By the late 1990s, a consensus was forged among classical economists close to government circles that import-substitution industrialization policies (ISI) and protectionism had been a failure.[41] Economic historians argued as well that industrial policies were ineffective because they were political compromises or simply ways to maintain employment, rather than genuine attempts to build a strong manufacturing sector.[42] ECLA economist Jorge Katz, for instance, blamed ISI for economic underdevelopment, hyperinflation, and inefficient manufacturing sectors in Argentina and all of Latin America.[43] He characterized the numerous small and medium-sized businesses as having a high degree of vertical integration, poor factory layout, imperfect knowledge and understanding of organization principles, all of which resulted in high unit production costs and low product quality which could not be successfully exported.[44]

In contrast to the views of ECLA and international economists who analyzed macro data, at the micro-level, residents from San Vicente where the Senor Factory was founded, recalled the period of import-substitution, especially the decades of the 1950s and early 1960s, as the "Golden Decades" of the country's industrialization. During the late nineteenth century, the town of San Vicente had been founded through an immigrant colonization program. Some immigrants were allotted land, while latecomers to this program had limited options for land ownership. Some chose to open blacksmith shops and repair farm machinery rather than work as farm hands.[45] Through repair they learned how to adapt and create new machinery. By the mid twentieth century, the three combine-harvester factories and small repair shops in the town employed residents and supplied local farmers with machinery specifically designed for the Santa Fe region, such as a specialized platform design or specialized traction wheels.[46] Hence, residents regarded ISI policies of the past as beneficial to their communities.

TRANSITIONING INTO THE TWENTY-FIRST CENTURY

By 1999, Argentina elected Radical President Fernando de la Rúa and the economy, which had already started to worsen in 1998 under Menem, was

---

[41] "Menem linked hyperinflation to ISI and protectionism while depicting privatization and deregulation as the indispensable antidotes to bring about economic stability." Manzetti, 1999: 88.

[42] Haber, 2006; Barbero and Rocchi, 2003: 261–294.   [43] Katz, 2000.

[44] The quality of these goods, he argued, was well below international standards and could not be exported to more sophisticated markets. Katz, 2000.

[45] Hugo Giovannini, personal interview, San Vicente, Santa Fe, July, 2016; Edna P. de Welschen, personal interview, San Vicente, Santa Fe, July, 2016.

[46] Jorge Senor, email interview, May 29, 2017.

collapsing owing to external shocks, extensive debt, and other factors.[47] Numerous events happened in rapid succession in 2001, the year ending in economic and political crises. In January 2001, the government imposed the Law of Public Emergency and Reform of the Exchange Rate, ending the Convertibility Plan. By March 2001, de la Rúa appointed Domingo Cavallo again as minister of economy to deal with external debt and transitioning out of the convertibility plan. The removal of the plan brought a peso devaluation, decreasing investor confidence. To prevent capital flight, Cavallo imposed a deposit freeze on bank savings accounts, referred to as the *corralito* in early December, leading to mass street protests and looting. By late December 2001, the economy collapsed and the political crisis deepened, resulting in the resignations of de la Rúa and Cavallo. Soon after, four presidents served in hasty succession; each one unable to stabilize the economy. Finally, the fifth interim President Eduardo Duhalde (2002–2003) took power in January 2002 and hurriedly implemented new policies to prevent a government shutdown and halt political chaos.

As the economic and political crises reached a state of near paralysis, new elections were held in 2003. Newly elected Peronist President Nestor Kirchner (2003–2007), who was little known, won the run-off election after Menem stepped down. Kirchner soundly rejected Menem's neoliberal austerity policies of the 1990s which he blamed for the economic collapse and the dismantling of the social welfare state. Once in power, Kirchner focused on implementing policies that boosted economic growth, such as expanding trading partnerships with countries in East Asia and the Middle East, and strengthening Mercosur. He publicly supported mass strikes and protests against private corporations and international organizations, especially against the International Monetary Fund (IMF) and the World Bank. In 2003, he negotiated the refinancing of the huge debt that Argentina owed the IMF, enabling the country to resume its social welfare spending. By 2005, Argentina repaid $10 billion to the IMF to show that it intended to rely less on the agency for credit. Kirchner's actions won him strong popular support, and he ushered in the populist era of the neo-Peronist Kirchnerismo.

RESURGENCE OF THE DEVELOPMENTAL STATE IN THE TWENTY-FIRST CENTURY

By paying back Argentina's external debt with the IMF, Kirchner intended to pave the way for a return to state-sponsored social and economic programs. He did not run for re-election, but instead supported his wife's successful

---

[47] Argentina's debt-service ratio was 75.8 percent in 2000. Comparatively, Mexico had a 23.1 percent ratio, Venezuela 17.4 percent, and Brazil 64.8 percent. Nataraj and Sahoo, 2003: 1641–1644.

presidential campaign.[48] In 2007, Cristina Fernández de Kirchner (often referred to as CFK) became the first woman to be elected president of Argentina.[49] By 2008, CFK's popularity was high partly because she had implemented social welfare programs such as unemployment assistance, distribution of food to the poor, and increased funding for public works projects in the poorer regions of Argentina. After her husband's death in 2010, she deepened her populist and economic agenda, including social welfare reform and state-sponsored manufacturing. She shaped Kirchnerismo, which became known by 2012 as a kind of hyper-populist and interventionist economic agenda. On this agenda was a plan to develop a national industry.

This section analyzes the brief resurgence of the developmental state under the presidency of Cristina Fernández de Kirchner and her evocation of the Senor Family Harvester Company as a model for resurrecting domestic industry. Specifically, it examines her government's attempt to support a national combine-harvester line for domestic and international use. CFK's symbolic support of a state-sponsored, national combine harvester was possible because of three reasons: discourses of industrialization, a historical model of local industrialization, and a collective memory remembering a domestic industrial sector that *was*.

First, there was a longstanding discourse supporting state-sponsored agroindustry since Bartolomé Mitre reunited the country in 1861. As early as the 1870s, National Deputy Carlos Pellegrini had first argued for the importance of supporting agro-industrialization through tariff support.[50] For decades thereafter, many intellectuals and politicians argued for supporting national industry. Economic Minister Federico Pinedo's arguments (1940) supporting an agro-industrial nation, including a farm-machinery sector, had perhaps the strongest impact.[51] Subsequent administrations took Pinedo's argument to support industry in various ways, such as when, in the late 1950s, President Frondizi created a discourse justifying the growth of local industries and expanding developmentalism. Hence, the CFK government could use propaganda from various historical periods to support her interventionist economy.

A second reason was the modernization of domestic industry that began in the late nineteenth century. Although by 1914 domestic industry was relatively small by international standards and could be characterized by the development

---

[48] Rumors circulated that Kirchner would run again for president in 2011. However, he died suddenly of a heart attack on October 27, 2010.

[49] Cristina Fernández has developed a large popular following and is active on various forms of social media. See Cristina Fernández de Kirchner site, www.cfkargentina.com/ (accessed July 17, 2017).

[50] "Los primeros defensores de la producción nacional," 1925: 342.

[51] Similarly, Fernando Coronil in the *Magical State* traces the discourse of the invention of Venezuela as an "oil country" in the 1930s and 1940s and the country's subsequent pursuit of advancing the automobile sector by the 1960s and 1970s. Coronil, 1997: xii.

of a few large-scale modern factories alongside many small-scale, family-owned shops, the country had indeed started its phase of industrialization.[52] Between 1930 and 1960, there was a relatively rapid rise in the number of enterprises and increased investment in diverse manufacturing activities, which continued to grow each year during this period.[53] During a period of relative isolation during the international crises of the 1930s and the Second World War, there were numerous small factories producing farm machinery in agricultural regions. In interviews, people recalled this era positively because of the perception that domestic industry was constantly growing.

Lastly, the CFK government did not need to look far to find nostalgia for domestic industry among those who had lived through the era of domestic industrial growth (1930s–1960s). Although factories grew and thrived through the postwar era, as we have seen, by the 2000s most of the domestic factories in the country had gone bankrupt. Yet the town San Vicente continued to celebrate the legacy of the domestic harvester in an annual National Harvester Festival. In 2003, this festival resurged, and since that year, the festival has nostalgically celebrated the "national harvester" that producers, including the Senor Harvester Factory, once successfully manufactured. Interviewees viewed it as a festival celebrating Argentina's past industrial strength, often recalling President Arturo Frondizi's visit to San Vicente for the first Harvester Festival of 1960. Other interviewees romanticized the domestically produced harvester at the current fairs, mentioning the sounds of the machine or the smell of petroleum and corn stalks, as reasons why they became gleeful or tearful at the festival.[54]

Collective Memory of the Harvester Festival

Several families founded the production of farm machinery in the town, including Boffelli, Senor, and Bernardín. These manufacturers became early supporters of the Radical Civic Union Party (Unión Cívica Radical, UCR).[55] In the early twentieth century, the town's intellectual and political leadership under Dr. Alfredo Grassi had strongly supported the UCR, to the point that some residents recalled San Vicente as a "Radical town." With the election of President Frondizi in 1958, town leader Vicente Boffelli invited the president to attend the first harvester festival organized in San Vicente. He was taken by Frondizi's development ideas, or at least, sought to hold him accountable for

---

[52] Barbero and Rocchi, 2003: 261–294; Rocchi, 2006; Pineda, 2009.
[53] Argentina, 1898; Hacienda, 1917; Estadística, 1935; Dirección Nacional de Estadística y Censos, 1952; Dirección Nacional de Estadística y Censos, 1957; Dirección Nacional de Estadística y Censos, 1950.
[54] Sebastian Forni, personal interview, San Vicente, Santa Fe, June 17, 2017; Various participants, personal interviews, and conversations, San Vicente, Santa Fe, 2016 and 2017.
[55] Some of the town residents recalled that the town's early origins were that "*todos somos Radicales*" (we are all Radicals) and that it was an agroindustrial town focused on the manufacture of combine-harvesters.

them.[56] The harvester festival was initially started as a way to raise funds for a local school and celebrate local industry.[57] But the festival became better known as an important venue for celebrating the country's twenty-three domestic harvester companies to "show off," in the words of Rodolfo Senor, local ingenuity to national and provincial representatives.[58]

Frondizi accepted the invitation, and his presence at the first 1960 Harvester Festival in San Vicente was filmed and covered in numerous local newspapers.[59] Indeed, Frondizi's visits to such festivals organized by small manufacturing towns had a strategic rationale: they were all in targeted regions of productivity, including in Patagonia (coal and oil), Mendoza (oil), and Santa Fe (machine industry) between 1958 and 1961.[60] During the 1960s, San Vicente town leaders also invited his successor, the People's Radical Party President Arturo Illia (1963–1966), who attended the festival in 1964.[61] With each presidential visit, the town rewarded itself with sorely needed infrastructural improvements, including a new airport, paved roads, and a telephone service.[62]

Although San Vicente suspended the festival during the neoliberal era of the late 1980s and the 1990s when the developmental state was dismantled, the festival was revived in 2003 during the previously discussed "economic reactivation" agenda of President Nestor Kirchner.[63,64] Since then, the festival has been held every year and renamed the National Festival of the Combine (Fiesta Nacional de la Cosechadora, FINACO).[65] San Vicente residents who had lived through the 1950s regard FINACO as a way to commemorate the "Golden Era" of farm-machine production in the region. Every year, FINACO features such rituals as the crowning of the harvester queen. Although activities slightly change each year at FINACO, the

---

[56] Boffelli continued to write him through 1976, always discussing the need for government support for national manufacturing.

[57] Lilia Biancotti de Boffelli, personal interview, San Vicente, Santa Fe, July 16, 2016.

[58] Rodolfo Senor, email interview, May 29, 2017.

[59] Letters spanning between 1959 and 1976 between Vicente Boffelli and Arturo Frondizi. Most of the letters in the Boffelli family collection are Frondizi's responses to Boffelli's letters. Courtesy of Lilia Biancotti de Boffelli and Veronica Boffelli Biancotti.

[60] Frondizi Archive, "Visita a San Vicente, Santa Fe, 18 septiembre de 1960"; "19–6 al 20-VI 1961, Visita a Rosario-Día de la Bandera" Box 33.2.12; Special Collections, Biblioteca Nacional, Buenos Aires, Argentina.

[61] Author converted 8mm to HD, receiving permission to view and copy footage from Lilia Biancotti de Boffelli and Veronica Boffelli Biancotti, San Vicente, Santa Fe.

[62] The presidential visits were filmed in black and white and silent on an 8mm film camera. Author converted 8mm to HD, receiving permission to view and copy footage from Veronica Boffelli Biancotti and Lilia Biancotti de Boffelli, San Vicente, Santa Fe.

[63] The festival took place in 1960, 1961, 1964, 1971, and in every year since 2003.

[64] It is interesting to note that the interviewee used a familiar phrase "the reactivation of the economy," which relates to the Pinedo Plan of 1940. Daniel Bianchotti, personal interview, San Vicente, Santa Fe, July 29, 2016.

[65] Daniel Bianchotti, personal interview; "Fiesta Nacional de la Cosechadora," www .finacosanvicente.com.ar/.

descendants of the former and current farm-machine manufacturers are honored in some way or asked to make a speech about their companies. The former Senor Harvester factory is especially revered because of its long business life (1921–1987) in the town.

CFK and Senor

Such nostalgia for the former Senor Harvester Factory likely played a role when CFK's administration contacted descendants of the Senor family, Ricardo Senor Sr., his son, and a third partner to request that they build a national combine line.[66] By 2008, with national and provincial bank loans, they funded a new company, Grandes Máquinas and built a new, sleek combine-harvester under the label Maag Mitos. The government announced that the Maag Mitos machine was now the new national harvester and eighteen of them would be built for export to Angola.

In 2010, CFK held a widely publicized press conference with the enormous combine-harvester parked outside the presidential palace. The press conference resonated with many older Argentines, especially those living in the provinces who fondly recalled the era of industry and perhaps hoped for a return of the golden decades of national industry. Unsurprisingly, the conference was staged, with CFK happily climbing onto the machine, showing the Senor plaque to flashing cameras, and the television narrator confidently asserting that this machine would once again demonstrate the prowess of national industry, implying that this was necessary after the lost decades of neoliberalism.[67]

Suspecting a red herring, several investigative journalists looked into the story behind the new national combine-harvester. In 2012, they broke the story that the combine and export program to Angola was a fraud.[68] In particular, journalist Jorge Lanata led a crusade criticizing CFK's promotion of Maag Mitos as yet another instance of corruption, theft, and cronyism.[69] For their part, some of the engineers working on the project were from San Vicente and they were initially excited about designing a new harvester. After just a few months working on the project, however, it was clear to them that the project had limited vision and direction.[70] The company Grandes Máquinas never accomplished its goals, and declared bankruptcy in April 2014.[71] Nationally, in the meantime, the CFK

---

[66] Lanata, 2012; Cristófalo, 2012.
[67] "C5N-Política," 2012. Rodolfo Senor confirmed that the plaque was owned by all Senor Family Members who were at the factory the day it closed in April 1987. Rodolfo Senor, personal interview, Roldán, Santa Fe, June 21, 2017.
[68] Longoni, 2012.   [69] Lanata, 2012; Cristófalo, 2012.
[70] These engineers and designers were never paid for their labor.
[71] The story of failing before starting the work happened in other developmental programs. Coronil, 1997; "Quebró la fábrica que tenía que hacer las cosechadoras para exportar a Angola," 2014; Huarte, 2014.

administration was confronted with massive protests and strikes over corruption and the ailing economy.

Although the CFK harvester became a story of mismanagement and corruption, her attempt at developmentalism could also be viewed as yet another phase in a long history of the developmental state in Argentina. The case study of the town of San Vicente is weaved into the national history to show the different perspectives among residents, especially their collective memory of the "Golden Decades" of domestic industry, roughly from 1948 to 1962. A romantic vision of domestically produced machinery had permitted residents to initially support projects such as the one that CFK had proposed.

The failure of developmentalism, from Frondizi to CFK, has much to do with the lack of consistent leadership and the inability, or unwillingness, to establish a standing congressional committee or government agency in charge of development, such as the Chilean CORFO. There was also an inconsistent and erratic vision of what "development" should look like. The outcome of these state-sponsored programs has often been negative, with domestic manufacturers going out of business when neoliberalization policies or economic shocks dominated the economy.

REFERENCES ARCHIVES

Frondizi Archive. Biblioteca Nacional, Buenos Aires, Argentina. Special Collections.

INTERVIEWS

Barrale, José María. Personal interview, San Vicente, Santa Fe. June 18, 2017.
Bergero Senor, Juan. Personal interview, San Vicente, Santa Fe. July 2, 2016.
Bianchotti, Daniel. Personal interview, San Vicente, Santa Fe. July 29, 2016.
Boffelli, Lilia Biancotti de. Personal interview, San Vicente, Santa Fe. July 16, 2016.
Botta, Edgardo. Personal interview, Santo Tomé, Santa Fe. July 10, 2016.
Carletti, Raúl. Personal interview, San Vicente, Santa Fe. July 2, 2016.
Forni, Sebastián, Personal interview, San Vicente, Santa Fe. June 17, 2017.
Giovannini, Hugo. Personal interview, San Vicente, Santa Fe. July 16, 2016.
P. de Welschen, Edna. Personal interview, San Vicente, Santa Fe. July 9, 2016.
Prosperi, José Luis. Interview by Damián Bil, San Vicente, Santa Fe. February 11, 2009.
Prosperi Ramello, Luciano. Videoconference interview by author. December 24, 2014.
Savore, Osvaldo. Interview by Luciano Prosperi, San Vicente, Santa Fe. December 26, 2016.
Senor, Danilo. Personal interview, San Vicente, Santa Fe. July 16, 2016.
Senor, Danilo. Email interview. September 10, 2015.
Senor, Danilo. Email interview. September 21, 2015.
Senor, Jorge Jr. Email interview. May 29, 2017.
Senor, Jorge Sr. Personal interview, Roldán, Santa Fe province. June 20, 2017.

Senor, Jorge Sr. Email interview. May 29, 2017.
Senor, Rodolfo. Email interview. May 29, 2017.
Senor, Rodolfo. Personal interview, Roldán, Santa Fe. June 21, 2017.
Various participants. Personal interviews, San Vicente, Santa Fe. 2016 and 2017.

PUBLISHED CENSUS DATA

Argentina, *Segundo censo nacional: Censo de las industrias 1895, Vol. 3.* Buenos Aires: Ministerio de Hacienda, 1898.
Dirección General de Estadística de la Nación. *Censo industrial de 1935.* Buenos Aires: Ministerio de Hacienda, 1937.
Dirección Nacional de Estadística y Censos. *La actividad industrial argentina desde 1937 a 1949.* Buenos Aires: Ministerio de Asuntos Técnicos, 1950.
Censo general de la nación: Censo industrial de 1946, Vol. IV. Buenos Aires: Secretaria de Asuntos Técnicos, 1952.
Censo industrial de 1950. Buenos Aires: Secretaria de Asuntos Técnicos, 1957.
Ministerio de Hacienda.*Tercer censo nacional: Censo de las industrias 1914, Vol. 7.* Buenos Aires: Talleres Gráficos de L. J. Rosso y Compañía, 1917.

SECONDARY SOURCES

Banco de la Provincia de Buenos Aires. *Reseña Anual Informativa*, Buenos Aires: BPBA, December, 1960.
Barbero, María Inés and Fernando Rocchi. "Industry." In *A New Economic History of Argentina*, eds. Gerardo della Paolera and Alan M. Taylor, Cambridge University Press, 2003: 261–294.
Berlinski, Julio. "International Trade and Commercial Policy." In *A New Economic History*, eds. Gerardo della Paolera and Alan M. Taylor, Cambridge University Press, 2003: 197–232.
Bil, Damián. "Acumulación y proceso productivo en la fabricación de maquinaria agrícola en la Argentina (1870–1975). Elementos de su competitividad en el marco del mercado internacional." Unpublished PhD thesis, University of Buenos Aires, 2011.
Bunge, Alejandro E. *La nueva política económica argentina: Introducción al estudio de la industria nacional.* Buenos Aires: Unión Industrial Argentina, 1921.
"C5N-Política: Cristina Kirchner presenta una cosechadora argentina." YouTube video, 5:58. Posted by "c5n", March 12, 2012. https://youtube/NBAA58DwH9E (accessed July 20, 2017).
Centeno, Miguel A. and Agustin E. Ferraro. "With the Best of Intentions. Types of Developmental Failure in Latin America." In *Why Latin American Nations Fail. Development Strategies in the Twenty-First Century*, eds. Esteban Pérez Caldentey and Matías Vernengo, Oakland: University of California Press, 2017: 65–89.
Coronil, Fernando. *The Magical State: Nature, Money, and Modernity in Venezuela.* University of Chicago Press, 1997.

Cramer, Gisela. "Argentine Riddle: The Pinedo Plan of 1940 and the Political Economy of the Early War Years." *Journal of Latin American Studies* 30, 3, October 1998: 519–550.

Cristófalo, Carlos. "Maag Mitos: cómo diseñar una cosechadora en la Argentina." *AutoBlog* Weblog. Entry posted March 30, 2012. http://autoblog .com.ar/2012/03/30/maag-mitos-como-disenar-una-cosechadora-en-la-argentina/ (accessed November 23, 2017).

Cyper, James M. "Latin American Structuralist Economics: An Evaluation, Critique, and Reformulation." In *Progress Toward Development in Latin America: From Prebisch to Technological Autonomy*, eds. James L. Dietz and Dilmus D. James, Boulder, Colorado: Lynne Rienner Publishers, 1990: 41–65.

Dosman, Edgar. *The Life and Times of Raúl Prebisch, 1901–1986*. Montreal: McGill-Queen's University Press, 2008.

Escobar, Arturo. *Encountering Development: The Making and Unmaking of the Third World*. Princeton University Press, 1995.

"Fiesta Nacional de la Cosechadora." www.finacosanvicente.com.ar/.

Frigerio, Rogelio. *El problema agrario argentino*, ed. Arturo Frondizi, Buenos Aires: Editorial Desarrollo, 1965a: 137–157.

"La reforma agraria." In *El problema agrario argentino*, ed. Arturo Frondizi, Buenos Aires: Editorial Desarrollo, 1965b: 137–157.

Gallo, Ezequiel. "Agricultural Colonization and Society in Argentina." Unpublished PhD thesis, Oxford University, 1970.

Gudeman, Stephen and Alberto Rivera. *Conversations in Colombia: The Domestic Economy in Life and Text*. Cambridge University Press, 1990.

Haber, Stephen. "The Political Economy of Industrialization." In *The Cambridge Economic History of Latin America: Volume II. The Long Twentieth Century*, eds. Victor Bulmer-Thomas, John H. Coatsworth, and Roberto Corté Conde, Cambridge University Press, 2006: 537–584.

Huarte, Daniel (interviewee). "La gran estafa las cosechadoras de @CFKArgentina." YouTube video, 8:05. Posted by "Diario Meridonal," April 3, 2014. https:// youtube/VpU4fux6VmU (accessed July 21, 2017).

Jáuregui, Aníbal. "La planificación en la Argentina: el CONADE y el PND (1960–1966)." *Anuario del Centro de Estudios Históricos "Prof. Carlos S. A. Segreti"* 13, 13 (2013): 243–266.

Katz, Jorge. "The Dynamics of Technological Learning during the Import-Substitution Period and Recent Structural Changes in the Industrial Sector of Argentina, Brazil, and Mexico." In *Technology, Learning, and Innovation: Experiences of Newly Industrializing Economies*, eds. Kim Linsu and Richard R. Nelson, Cambridge University Press, 2000: 307–334.

Kotkin, Stephen. *Magnetic Mountain: Stalinism as a Civilization*. Berkeley: UC Press, 1997.

Lanata, Jorge. "Lanata y las cosechadoras para Angola." YouTube video, 11:15. Posted by "Nacionalismo Criollo," El Trece TV, May 9, 2012. www.youtube.com/watch? v=S7DaKqJ6dOw.

Llach, Juan José. "El plan pinedo de 1940, su significado histórico y los orígenes de la economía política del peronismo." *Desarrollo Económico* 23, 92 (January–March 1984): 515–558.

Longoni, Matías. "La otra cara de las cosechadoras que buscan venderle a Angola." *Clarín*, March 20, 2012. Clarin.com. www.clarin.com/politica/cara-cosechadoras-buscan-venderle-Angola_0_rJXX7m82DQe.html (accessed July 21, 2017).

"Los primeros defensores de la producción nacional." *Revista de Economía Argentina* 14, January–June 1925.

Love, Joseph L. "Economic Ideas and Ideologies in Latin America since 1930." In *Ideas and Ideologies in Twentieth-Century Latin America*, ed. Leslie Bethell. Cambridge University Press, 1996: 207–274.

Manzetti, Luigi. "The Evolution of Agricultural Interest Groups in Argentina." *Journal of Latin American Studies* 24, 3, October 1992: 585–616.

Privatization South American Style. Oxford University Press, 1999.

Mirando a través de un nombre, Senor: Evolución del producto. Pamphlet for Senor Family Factory, n.d.

Nataraj, Geethanjali and Pravakar Sahoo. "Argentina's Crisis: Causes and Consequences." *Economic and Political Weekly* 38, 17, April 26–May 2, 2003): 1641–1644.

Palma, Gabriel. "Latin America during the Second Half of the Twentieth Century: From the 'Age of Extremes' to the Age of 'End-of-History' Uniformity." In *Rethinking Development Economics*, ed. Ha-Joon Chang, London: Wimbledon Publishing Company, 2003: 125–151.

Pantaleón, Jorge. "El surgimiento de la nueva economía argentina: el caso Bunge." In *Intelectuales y expertos. La constitución del conocimiento social en la Argentina*, eds. Federico Neiburg and Mariano Plotkin. Buenos Aires: Paidós, 2004: 175–201.

Pineda, Yovanna. *Industrial Development in a Frontier Economy*. Stanford University Press, 2009.

Prebisch, Raúl. "El desarrollo económico de la América Latina y algunos de sus principales problemas." Biblioteca Prebisch del Banco Central, CD-Colección de los ensayos de Raúl Prebisch, 1918–1949.

"Quebró la fábrica que tenía que hacer las cosechadoras para exportar a Angola." *La Nación*, April 3, 2014. www.lanacion.com.ar/1677720-quebro-la-fabrica-que-hacia-las-cosechadoras-para-exportar-a-angola.

Rocchi, Fernando. *Chimneys in the Desert: Industrialization in Argentina during the Export Boom Years, 1870–1930*. Palo Alto: Stanford University Press, 2006.

Schwartz, Hugo. "The Evolution of Argentina's Policies Toward Manufacturing Exports." In *Progress Toward Development in Latin America: From Prebisch to Technological Autonomy*, eds. James L. Dietz and Dilmus D. James, Boulder, Colorado: Lynne Rienner Publishers, 1990: 85–101.

Spinelli, María Estela. *Los vencedores vencidos: el antiperonismo y la "revolución libertadora."* Buenos Aires: Editorial Biblos, 2005.

Szusterman, Celia. *Frondizi and the Politics of Developmentalism in Argentina, 1955–1962*. University of Pittsburgh Press, 1993.

The Chilean Developmental State: Political Balance, Economic Accommodation, and Technocratic Insulation, 1924–1973

Patricio Silva

INTRODUCTION

The establishment of the National Development Corporation (CORFO) in 1939 marked a milestone in the consolidation of the Chilean entrepreneurial state. Since its creation, CORFO became the main engine in the country's efforts to promote a national industry, and the figurehead of the developmental state. The founding of CORFO, however, did not represent the beginning of industrialization in Chile. It was rather the culmination of a process of increasing state involvement in the general development of the country.

The Chilean developmental state finds its origins in the mid 1920s, and becomes consolidated in the late 1930s. It will represent the dominant pattern of development in Chile until the military coup of September 1973, which marked its abrupt end. Therefore, the emergence of the Chilean developmental state was not mainly the result of the 1929 world depression, as was the case in other Latin American countries.

The Chilean developmental state was the outcome of a historical process that went beyond the economic realm. The rise of the country's particular pattern of development was a response to strong political and social demands. Such demands resulted from the widespread discontent with the so-called "Parliamentary Republic" (1881–1924) that was considered by many as an ignominious chapter in Chilean history. During those years, the Chilean aristocracy had adopted a quite sumptuous lifestyle, becoming increasingly detached from the main national problems. This behavioral and cultural change among the elite was mainly the outcome of the new wealth obtained from the nitrite industry, following Chile's victory in the War of the Pacific (1879–1883). The aristocratic regime suffered a profound crisis of social and political legitimacy, leading eventually to its demise in 1924.

The origins of the Chilean developmental state are also closely related to the ascent of the middle classes to the center of the political scene, and their increasing concern with the so-called "social question" among the poor. From the mid 1920s onwards, middle-class political forces took control of the government, and launched a nationalistic developmental project. This was directed towards both achieving economic development, and towards the improvement of the working and living conditions of the popular masses, in order to avoid social upheaval.

The developmental project received a remarkable impulse during the Ibáñez government (1927–1931). He decisively translated the economic and social goals of the middle classes into a package of concrete governmental policies that were directed towards the expansion and modernization of state institutions, including an increasing role of the state in fostering economic and social development.

It can be stated that, until the late 1940s, the performance of the Chilean developmental state was quite successful. From then on, however, the readiness among the main political and economic actors to reach political agreements, and to find the required economic accommodations, began to erode. From the late 1950s until the early 1970s, first the right- and later the left-wing forces attempted to radically transform the structure of the Chilean economy, without reaching any kind of previous consensus with opposing actors. Such a new level of political conflict resulted in the decline and eventual collapse of the Chilean democracy, and the end of the developmental state.

The aim of the present chapter is threefold. To begin with, it aims to establish the main political, economic, and institutional factors that led to the emergence of the Chilean developmental state in the 1920s. Many of these factors will prove to be determinant for both the achievements as well as the limitations of the Chilean developmental model in the period 1924–1973. My second objective is to analyze the creation and development of CORFO during the period 1939–1960. Special attention is given to the particular balance of power existing in the country during the late 1930s, producing a political tie between conservative and reformist forces. Instead of producing paralysis, the stalemate forced both sectors to reach fundamental agreements. The presence of a large group of independent public policy experts in charge of key public agencies would prove to be decisive for the efficient implementation of developmental policies, preventing the politicization of the decision-making process. However, the basis for the political compromises that supported the developmental institutions was rather fragile: it would endure as long as the tie between both camps was not broken in favor of one of the contending political orientations. The final goal of the chapter is to assess the factors that led to the decline of the developmental state in Chile during the 1950s and 1960s. The demise of developmentalism will be the combined outcome of mounting economic problems, and increasing political polarization, which finally destroyed the democratic fabric of the country, and the consensus around the state-led pattern of development.

THE ORIGINS OF THE DEVELOPMENTAL STATE

Although the developmental state only became fully operational from the mid 1940s onwards, a series of significant economic, political, and institutional factors paved the road to increasing state interventionism in the Chilean economy during the period 1880–1920. Among these factors were the extreme dependence of the economy on nitrate exports, and the foreign control of the country's main natural resources. At the turn of the century, the idea that the aristocratic ruling elite was not capable of defending the national interest and modernizing the country began to gain wide currency. This climate of opinion led to a generalized quest for the regeneration of the political class, and for a more decisive involvement of the state in the country's overall development.

Since the beginning of the Republican era in the early 19th century, Chile had been able to establish a relatively strong state and robust political institution. As Jaksic has shown in his study on state building in Chile, the country experienced a brief period of political turmoil during 1823–1830, but afterwards began a long era of political stability. Since the adoption of the 1833 Constitution, the Chilean state imposed its authority in the country. In a period in which most Latin American newly created nations were confronting political chaos and internal armed struggles, the Chilean oligarchy managed to develop a highly centralized state under a strong presidential power.[1] The Chilean state was able to successfully carry out long-term policies in fields such as primary education, defense, communication, infrastructure, mining, and finance. An important factor contributing to the satisfactory performance of the Chilean state was the relatively high degree of probity generally showed by the ruling class and the public employees.[2] This not only allowed a good use of the fiscal resources, but it also proved to be critical for maintaining the political legitimacy of the aristocratic regime.

As a result of the War of the Pacific 1879–1883, vast territories were annexed by Chile with substantial reserves of nitrate, copper and other minerals. Although this new obtained wealth came to be controlled by foreign companies, the Chilean state managed to obtain via taxation considerable revenues, allowing the further expansion of state activities in several fields. In 1883 the Society for Industrial Development (SOFOFA) was created by representatives of Chile's infant manufacture sector in order to defend their collective interests and demand support from the state.

During the administration of José Manuel Balmaceda (1886–1891), a plan of public works was launched, including the expansion of the railway network, and the building of schools, roads, hospitals, and other public infrastructures. President Balmaceda also proclaimed his intention to put an end to the monopolistic position obtained by British companies in the nitrate industry,

---

[1] Jaksic, 2013: 183–186.   [2] Silva, 2016: 178–203.

and to foster a plan to industrialize the country. As Jobet put it, "Balmaceda supported state intervention in the economy in order to achieve industrialization and to diversify the country's economic structure ... He understood the country could not be subordinated to the dominance of the saltpeter-based extractive industry. The latter has only to function as the starting point to make possible Chile's own industrial development."[3] However, Balmaceda faced increased opposition among aristocratic circles, allied to the British nitrate interests, and the conflict led to a short but bloody civil war. The victorious aristocratic forces put an end to Balmaceda's early attempt to give a leading role to the state in fostering economic development. Aristocratic dominance marked the beginning of the so-called Parliamentary Republic (1891–1924) which was characterized by political instability and notorious administrative incompetence. In his classic study of the Chilean political system, Gil described some such flaws of the parliamentary republic. As he indicated, "for the sake of prestige, seats in Congress were bought by wealthy aristocrats in the same way that their ancestors had purchased titles of nobility. Civic spirit and patriotism seemed to be lost ... The prosperity brought by nitrate and copper replaced its frugal and orderly manner of living and habits with luxury and idleness, and moved by the desire for wealth, the aristocracy lost its patriotic sense of social and civil responsibility."[4]

The increasing discontent with the parliamentary republic became quite open after the turn of the century, and particularly around 1910, the year Chile celebrated its first centenary as an independent nation. A series of books and essays appeared in those years stressing the decline of the nation and criticizing the inability of the aristocratic elite to face the challenges of the new century.

In 1900, the influential politician Enrique MacIver delivered a famous lecture on "The Moral Crisis of the Republic" at the Ateneo of Santiago. In the lecture, he stressed the disenchantment and uncertainty which, in his opinion, were invading the soul of the nation. He accused the political elite of having abandoned the path of public probity and patriotism which had characterized the Chilean ruling class since the beginning of the republic. Other authors such as Nicolás Palacios (1904) and Tancredo Pinochet (1909) also denounced the existence of a "moral crisis" in the country. They both proposed to strengthen the sense of nationality among Chileans, by counteracting the economic and cultural influence coming from Europe and from the United States. A call for economic nationalism was expressed by Francisco Encina in his book *Nuestra Inferioridad Económica* (1912).[5] Encina criticized the indifference shown so far by the Chilean state in actively stimulating the national industry. Following World War I, the Chilean nitrate industry began to decay as a result of cheaper synthetic substitutes manufactured in Germany. Previous to the war, the export of nitrate represented 80 per cent of Chile's total exports, and the taxes paid by this industry constituted half of the public revenues. In 1919, the export of

---

[3] Jobet, 1955: 77.   [4] Gil, 1966: 51–52.   [5] Encina, 1912.

nitrate only represented 25 per cent in volume and 20 per cent in value in comparison to the year before.[6] This worrying new scenario represented for many the final evidence that Chile had to end fast its extreme dependency on the export of raw materials.

At the beginning of the twentieth century, a new actor suddenly appeared on the political scene: the popular masses. Supported by left-wing parties, the popular sectors demanded better working conditions and social legislation. Soon the "social question" reached the central stage of public debates. Moderate political sectors pressed the ruling elite to carry out substantial reforms in order to avoid social unrest, and even a possible revolution.

What all expressions of dissatisfaction by intellectuals had in common was the rejection of the parliamentary republic, of party politics and of clientelism, as well as the condemnation of the foreign control of Chilean natural resources. They all demanded a solid defense of Chilean culture and economy, and the consolidation of a modern and strong state. They demanded further for state institutions to acquire political authority and technical capacity to foster the development of the nation. For the intellectuals since the turn of the century, it was clear that the old aristocratic elite in power was neither willing to carry on those transformations nor capable of it. A substantial political change was required, and that eventually came to happen at the 1920 presidential elections. During that historical electoral contest Arturo Alessandri successfully staged an anti-establishment campaign, mobilizing the middle classes and broad sectors of the popular masses. His victory was seen as the triumph of a rebellious middle class. Edwards Vives put it in the following way: "a real class struggle broke out between the petit bourgeoisie educated at the Liceos and the traditional society . . . The rebel middle class rejected domination by an oligarchy which they regarded as incapable, de-nationalized, devoid of morality and patriotism."[7]

The victory of Alessandri led to the strengthening of presidential rule in the country and the adoption of a pro-middle-class agenda demanding profound social, economic, and political changes. This agenda included the adoption of modern social legislation, the creation of new state agencies, and the expansion of state intervention in key public policy fields, including the economy, health, education, and infrastructure.

Alessandri's major competitor during the 1920 elections, José Santos Salas, also presented an ambitious program announcing profound socio-economic and institutional transformations. Salas, who was unofficially the candidate supported by the army, proposed the creation of a National Economic Council which, in corporatist fashion, would have the authority to guide national efforts to promote economic development. He concluded in a long manifesto that "all the living forces of society will be represented at the National Economic Council: the capital, the banking, the technicians, the workers, all of them

---

[6] Palma, 1984: 63–65.   [7] Edwards Vives, 1952: 234–235.

members of the noble productive function. The Council has to be the informed technical voice in the governmental policies, a great heart in which the economic interests of the country will be refunded."[8]

Following Alessandri's inauguration, the conservative forces made use of all means at their disposition to obstruct or at least to delay the realization of his government program. At Congress, they contested most of the initiatives proposed by the executive, particularly the introduction of social legislation and administrative reforms. If the adoption of new legislation was further obstructed, military officers began to threaten military intervention, as finally occurred in September of 1924. General Altamirano took power and forced Congress to vote in favor of the social and administrative reforms promoted by Alessandri: in a matter of hours a series of statutes were passed which had been obstructed for years. During the military government (1924–1925) policies were adopted which strengthened the role of the state in diverse social fields, such as the creation of the Ministry of Public Works, and the Ministry of Hygiene and Social Provision. As Silva Vargas observes, "without a Congress, and by ruling on the basis of law-decrees, the transformations advanced at great speed. Between August and November 1925 four important laws were adopted; a law regulating monetary policies, a law creating a Central Bank, a general law regulating banking activities, and a budget law."[9]

The military finally decided to restore Alessandri to power. Alessandri called for a plebiscite to vote on a new constitution, which was approved in August 1925. The new legal charter strengthened presidential power and simplified the procedures to adopt new legislation by the parliament. Military involvement in the political sphere did not end, however. During the government of Emiliano Figueroa (1925–1927), Colonel Carlos Ibáñez, his minister of the interior, became the new military strongman. He eventually forced Figueroa to resign, assuming the vice-presidency until general elections took place and Ibáñez became president. From 1927 until his fall in 1931, Ibáñez carried out significant transformations in the Chilean state. He began with a reform of the public bureaucracy, firing many public employees hired during the parliamentary republic on the basis of political patronage.

Ibáñez considered that a new generation of civil engineers were going to be the ideal organizers and directors of his ambitious plans to modernize and depoliticize the state apparatus. As Loveman states, during his government "technicians and middle-class professionals staffed growing ministries and public agencies previously manned overwhelmingly through political patronage by the traditional parties."[10] Ibáñez valued the young engineers' know-how and expertise, and their relative detachment from particular social and political interests, stating that "in the government I have surrounded myself with people of good will, open to everything, carrying the ability to achieve victory in the accomplishment of their tasks by their own hands; they are

---

[8] Ibáñez Santa María, 1983: 76.   [9] Silva Vargas, 2013: 764–765.   [10] Loveman, 249.

capable young men, with a fresh mentality for the search of solutions."[11] The recruitment of young engineers was overseen by Ibáñez' right-hand, Minister of Finance Pablo Ramírez, who directly contacted the *Instituto de Ingenieros de Chile*, and asked for their collaboration in modernizing the state. One of the young engineers, Raúl Simon, became Ramírez' closest adviser, and he was behind the most important decisions in the fields of financial reforms, public works, and the modernization and creation of new state agencies.[12]

The involvement of engineers in state agencies was not new. As Crowther indicates, at the turn of the century, a group of civil engineers working for the state railways had already expressed the idea that Chile required state protection for its infant industries. The incorporation of civil engineers into top management positions during the Ibáñez administration was not the initiation but the culmination of a long process of increasing awareness among Chilean civil engineers about the strategic role they were called to play in Chile's developmental strategies.[13]

During the Ibáñez years, the Chilean state carried out profound and fast reforms. Beginning in 1927, state institutions offered a broad line of credits to support productive sectors. Specialized state agencies were created to administer public financial support for mining (Caja de Crédito Minero) and for agricultural (Caja Agraria) and industrial activities (Instituto de Crédito Industrial). In the period 1924–1932, the number of ministries increased from six to eleven. As Bravo Lira stresses, the expansion of the Chilean state has not only to be seen in terms of the number of new state institutions and the increase in the number of public employees. The number of fields in which the state began to exert influence also expanded. This was particularly the case in those areas connected to the welfare of the popular masses such as labor, social provision, public health, and education.[14] Pinto (1985) describes the broad spectrum of policy fields in which a new generation of public officials became involved: "Ibáñez opened the doors allowing the access to the center stage to an administrative and engineering technocracy ... coming from the higher echelons of the middle classes. This phenomenon covered the entire bureaucratic spectrum (education system, judicial power, armed forces, etc.), enhancing their social and economic status and strengthening by this the state apparatus."[15]

At the same time, the ministries expanded the network of new agencies operating under each ministry's authority, reaching the number of seventy in 1933. In the economic area, for instance, a series of entities (called *superintendencias*) were established for the fields of banking, stock corporations, and insurance companies, among others. The new agencies were provided with administrative, technical, and financial autonomy. In the

---

[11] *La Nación*, March 29, 1927: 3.   [12] Silva, 2008: 77.   [13] Crowther, 1973.
[14] Bravo Lira, 2016: 331.   [15] Pinto, 1985: 13.

social field, a General Labor Inspection, and Committees of Popular Housing were created, in order to ensure that both employers and private landlords observed the rights of workers and tenants.

Especially important for the Chilean case was the expansion of parastatal entities. This represented an intricate spectrum of institutions, going from semi-fiscal entities with autonomous administration to state enterprises not under the authority of ministries. In contrast to traditional state institutions, parastatal entities generally had their own managing board, conformed by representatives of the state, entrepreneurs, and employees. They also usually had their own legal personality, assets, and budget, separated from the rest of the state. By 1933, Chile had twenty-seven parastatal institutions.[16]

In 1927 the Ministry for Development (Ministerio de Fomento) was created as the key public institution for the management of public policy programs in this area. Several agencies and programs established since the early 1920s were incorporated into the new ministry. As was the case with other public agencies during the Ibáñez administration, civil engineers were often appointed to high-level management positions. In fact, the list of top management positions assigned to engineers in diverse areas of the administration was impressive. The positions included, among others, Comptroller General of the Republic, Director of the Budget Office, Superintendent of the Customs Office, Director of Inland Revenue, Superintendent of the Nitrate Industry, Director of Administration of State Supplies, and the Heads of the Industry and Commerce Divisions at the Ministry for Development.[17] Many of these positions corresponded to extremely vulnerable areas for possible corruption and the influence of special interests. The reputation for probity of civil engineers helped Ibáñez launch a veritable moral crusade in the public administration. As he put it himself, "we will eradicate the ills and the rottenness, accumulated after so many years of administrative disorder and political *compadrazgo*."[18]

The worldwide depression beginning in 1929 struck the Chilean economy particularly hard. According to a report by the League of Nations, Chile was among the most affected countries in the world, as a result of the collapse of its export-oriented economy. Of a list of thirty-nine nations, Chile presented the highest decline in the value of both exports and imports between 1929 and 1932. Between those years, world trade fell by 25 per cent. In the same period, Chilean exports dropped 68 percent in average, and imports 75 per cent.[19] The crisis generated social and political unrest in the country. Ibáñez was not able to control the situation, leading to the fall of his regime in July 1931, followed by a short period of severe political instability. Political order was reestablished in 1932 after a series of short-lived governments that unsuccessfully tried to counteract the economic depression. Despite their

---

[16] Bravo Lira, 2016: 314–315.   [17] Ibáñez Santa María, 2003: 118–120.
[18] *La Nación*, March 13, 1927:17.   [19] Ellsworth, 1945: 8–9.

different ideological orientations, however, they all shared the conviction that the crisis announced the end of liberalism and of *laisser-faire* economics in Chile. They also shared the view that the Chilean state had to assume a bigger role in order to restore economic, social and political stability in the country.[20]

The increasing state intervention was also legitimated by the new global scenario which emerged from the collapse of the international economic system. In many countries, political regimes and governments of all sorts began to adopt protective policies towards their own industries. While Chilean Communists and Socialists searched for inspiration in the planned economy of Soviet Russia, important segments of the Chilean right looked with great interest towards the corporatist formulas applied in Spain, Portugal, Italy, and later in Germany. Also the American New Deal initiated by President Franklin D. Roosevelt was followed in Chile with great attention.

In October 1932, general elections brought Arturo Alessandri back to power. He inherited a politically convulsed nation with a devastated economy. The internal and foreign debt had dramatically increased since 1929 and a large mass of workers was unemployed. Alessandri's Minister of Finance, Gustavo Ross, became the architect of a successful economic program aimed at the reactivation of the economy, and characterized by its moderate pragmatism. As Pinto points out, Ross maintained the protectionist policies introduced by previous administrations, and he also applied Keynesian-like policies *avant la lettre* oriented towards the strengthening of internal markets. The nitrate industry was restructured following the creation of the Nitrate and Iodine Sale Corporation (Covensa) in 1934, with the result that production and state revenues increased. That same year Arturo Alessandri created the National Economic Council. His first director was Pedro Aguirre Cerda, later president of Chile and founder of CORFO. Although the Council did not win the expected influence on national affairs at that time, it certainly constituted a good training ground for representatives of sectorial interests and state officials to get to know each other and begin to discuss policies that could address economic and developmental issues.

The payments of foreign debt, which had been interrupted during the years 1933–1934, were restarted in 1935. In that same year, the Ministry of Finance was able to drastically reduce the unemployment caused in the mining and related sectors by the collapse of the world economy. Workers were hired for vast programs of public works, such as the construction of the so-called *Barrio Cívico* in downtown Santiago to house new ministries and other public agencies, and further building programs including a national stadium, schools, roads, bridges, and railway tracks. The number of unemployed was reduced from 129,000 in 1932 to 8,000 in 1935.[21] New social programs were also initiated. The health-care system was expanded to cover popular sectors, including a broad plan of preventive medicine beginning in 1937.

---

[20] Góngora, 1988: 217.   [21] Pinto, 1985: 16.

Economic policy was considered so successful, that conservative forces chose the Minister of Finance, Gustavo Ross, as presidential candidate for the 1938 elections. Left-wing forces, organized in the Popular Front, supported the candidature of Pedro Aguirre Cerda, leader of the moderate Radical Party. Chilean Radicals, Socialists, and Communists had established the Popular Front coalition in 1936, following the French experience.[22] Although Aguirre Cerda won the elections, the difference with the conservatives was less than 1 percent of the total vote (50.45 percent against 49.52 percent). Furthermore, the conservative forces had a slight majority of Senate seats and they were determined to carry on with a tough opposition of the new left-wing administration.

The situation reflected a complicated "political tie" between the conservative and reformist forces, which would become evident during the creation of CORFO, and its further development.

THE CORFO PROJECT AND THE "STATE OF COMPROMISE"

The Popular Front planned to strengthen substantially the presence of the state in all policy areas, from industrial development to social security and education. In its electoral program, this center-left coalition had announced the intention to radically transform the economy and the social relations in the country. It also stressed the need for "planning of the national economy in order to increment the mining, industrial and agricultural production, as a mechanism of regulation." In addition, the Popular Front announced its plan to eliminate monopolies, and to revise the tax system. With respect to foreign capital, the program stated that "legislation addressed to imperialistic companies will be passed in defense of the national patrimony and the interests of the state, the employees and the workers." Regarding rural areas, the program promised to carry out an "agrarian reform, providing support to middle and small landowners." Finally, the program contained a plan to expand existing social legislation, and to regulate "reasonable salaries" for blue- and white-collar workers.[23] The Popular Front's electoral victory alarmed the political right, which regarded the Aguirre Cerda government as a potential Communist threat for the country. Powerful business associations such as SOFOFA, the National Society for Agriculture (SNA), The Chamber of Commerce, and the National Mining Society (SNM), prepared for a tough struggle.

President Aguirre Cerda himself always had shown a personal interest in industrial development. He was the author of an influential book on the topic (Aguirre Cerda, 1933). Together with his long political career as a Member of Congress and Minister of State, he also had a solid academic formation. He studied pedagogy and law at the Universidad de Chile, and pursued postgraduate specializations in administrative law, political economy, and

---

[22] Milos, 2008.   [23] Ortega, Norambuena, Pinto, and Bravo, 1989.

social legislation at the Sorbonne University and the College of France in Paris. His book *El Problema Industrial* shows an impressive knowledge of contemporary academic and political debates regarding industrial development. He was well aware of specific industrial policies being applied at that moment in countries such as the Soviet Union, France, Germany, Italy, Spain, and the United States. Furthermore, he makes clear that following the Great War and particularly since the Depression, the new times were marked by economic nationalism and state interventionism. The book, in sum, represents a veritable road map for Chilean industrialization. After an exhaustive and detailed analysis of the country's industrial needs, potentials, and hazards, the author offers a series of concrete policy measures to protect and to strengthen the national industry. When Aguirre Cerda became president, he was fully prepared to give a big boost to the developmental state.

In January 1939, barely a month after inauguration, a devastating earthquake hit several southern provinces. More than 5,000 persons lost their lives, while the infrastructure and the regional economy were severely damaged. This dramatic event immediately triggered the idea to create a state agency in charge of both the reconstruction of the affected provinces, and the fostering of economic development in general. The plan was not new, as there are indications that an influential engineer, Desiderio García, who had worked at the Ministry for Development under Ibáñez, had later in the mid 1930s promoted the idea to create an agency very similar to what finally became CORFO.[24]

The administration sent to Congress an urgent law proposal for the creation of CORFO. The executive's original idea was to finance CORFO through a tax increase on the wealthy. However, the tax increase was successfully opposed by right-wing parties and business associations. The Popular Front had to compromise and accept the financing of CORFO by foreign loans. This resulted in the signing of an agreement between the Chilean government and the US Export-Import Bank (Eximbank). Chile obtained access to a broad line of credits. The loans were given under the condition that they had to be expended in the acquisition of US industrial equipment, however. CORFO industrial activities thus became directly dependent on the import of capital goods from the United States. This allowed the US government to exercise direct influence on the industrialization process in Chile, and to protect American investments in the mining and energy sectors. The establishment of this credit line was also part of the US strategy to avoid further radicalization of the Popular Front government, and to keep Chile on the side of the Allies during World War II. The CORFO–US relations became from the very beginning so close and intensive that CORFO decided in 1940 to open a permanent office in New York to coordinate ongoing commercial operations with the US government and private suppliers. Since 1944, many CORFO projects

---

[24] Ibáñez Santa María, 2003: 136–137.

became financed by the International Bank for Reconstruction and Development (IBRD).

As a result of this increasing dependency on US loans, the left-wing sectors within the Popular Front administration began to adopt a pragmatic stance towards the United States. The initial anti-imperialistic discourse became much more moderated, and the previous calls to harm American interests in the country, like the US copper corporations operating in Chile, soon vanished. To illustrate this new pragmatic attitude among left-wing leaders, Drake refers to the figure of Oscar Schnake, minister of development, who played a key role in the creation of CORFO. This prominent leader of the Socialist Party (PS) actively sought to strengthen Chile–US relations. As Drake points out, "Schnake led the PS into the vanguard of Chileans eager for better political and economic relations with the United States ... His transformation ... personified the Socialist Party's shift to emphasizing economic growth in partnership with the Western allies."[25] The Chilean Communist party also moderated its discourse towards the United States, following the Nazi invasion of the Soviet Union. The Communists embraced the idea that the United States and Great Britain had become allies in the worldwide struggle against fascism, and that the party was called to support the "progressive national bourgeoisie" to fight against German influence.

The fact that the creation of CORFO was part of the relief efforts for victims of the earthquake awakened Chilean patriotism. To be against CORFO was tantamount to opposing help for suffering fellow citizens. Therefore, the conservative forces were eager to declare that they did not oppose the creation of a temporal relief agency to help the victims of the earthquake. They rather criticized the idea to make from the same agency a permanent state instrument in charge of the industrialization efforts. In their view, CORFO should have to restrict itself to the function of provider of state loans and technical support to the private sector, and not become a creator and administrator of new state enterprises. This should lead, in their view, to "unfair competition" as CORFO had access to attractive foreign loans while the Chilean private sector was not allowed to contract debts abroad.

The Chilean right also had deep fears that the parties of the Popular Front coalition would attempt to colonize with their own political appointees CORFO, as well as the future enterprises created under its authority. As a result, the conservative forces demanded to put CORFO under strict parliamentary supervision. The administration argued that the new public corporation, due to the need for urgent action, required to be under the direct command of the president. The stalemate was finally solved as both political orientations agreed on the strict technical nature of CORFO. The new powerful agency was going to be almost exclusively managed in day-to-day affairs by highly trained technocrats, most of them being civil engineers. They would also

[25] Drake, 1978: 245.

enjoy a high degree of autonomy in their daily decision-making vis-à-vis the administration, the political opposition, and business interests. Stevenson suggests that the empowerment of technocrats within CORFO was due to pressure exerted by the Eximbank.[26] Ellswoth argues that it was the minister of finance and president of the corporation, the engineer Roberto Wachholtz, who insisted that the staff had to be chosen on the basis of technical merit and efficiency.[27] Finally, Ibáñez Santa María indicates that the key role given to technicians was also a fundamental condition posed to the government by the engineers Guillermo del Pedregal and Desiderio García, in order for them to accept the positions of Executive Vice-President and General Manager of CORFO, respectively.[28] Be that as it may, since the Ibáñez regime the demand for technocrats to assume the highest echelons of state institutions had become generalized among Chileans who profoundly distrusted political parties and politicians.

It is remarkable that the administration, the opposition, and the business organizations could agree on the need to protect the technical character of CORFO, and its autonomy. But even more impressive is the fact that in the years ahead they indeed kept their word on this point. As Cavarozzi established in his study on CORFO, the key actors involved in CORFO activities in the period 1939–1969 recognized that the relative autonomy of CORFO and their technocrats was to be respected. Many of his interviewees were unable to mention a single case, and sometimes only one, in which the government had attempted to politically influence a decision made by technicians.[29] The CORFO technocrats however, did not take their decisions without regard to other actors. These technocrats had fluid relations with representatives of the industrial sector, and from other state agencies. But at the end of the day, they decided on the basis of rational arguments on a line of action. In this manner, it can be stated that the CORFO technical staff was able to consolidate what Evans called "embedded autonomy."[30] In addition, the existence and maintenance of the CORFO autonomy was not only a concession given by the external actors. As Ibáñez Santa María stresses, the technical staff deployed an institutional culture in which the assertive custody of their autonomy was central. With time, they became themselves a powerful pressure group who protected their professional and working interests within the state institutions.[31]

As a result of the huge amount of financial resources managed by CORFO, both political forces and economic interest groups tried to exert their influence in the definition of its objectives, managerial structure, and in the daily decision-making process. The struggle between the Popular Front government and the business groups around the mentioned issues was substantial, although it was always canalized through institutional mechanisms. This led to compromises

---

[26] Stevenson, 1942: 124.   [27] Ellsworth, 1945: 88.   [28] Ibáñez Santa María, 2003: 141.
[29] Cavarozzi, 1975: 125–126.   [30] Evans, 1995.   [31] Ibáñez Santa María, 2003: 162.

from both sides to avoid a paralysis of the economy, and a further political radicalization in the country. The civil engineers in charge of CORFO played a pivotal role in designing and implementing the state-led industrialization policies and in strengthening the relative autonomy of this mega institution vis-à-vis the administrations and the business associations. The presence of civil engineers at CORFO and other important state companies did also facilitate the establishment and functioning of the so-called "state of compromise," and hence of Chilean democracy until the late 1950s.

The autonomy of the CORFO technical staff was – at least formally – counterbalanced with the creation of a board of directors of twenty-four members which was conceived with a corporatist design. It included the ministers of finance (Chairman), development, and agriculture. The board also included members of both houses of Congress, state agencies, financial institutions, and representatives of the most important business associations. The labor movement was also symbolically represented at the board with a single member. The board reproduced the design of the National Economic Council by including representatives of all the relevant stakeholders. This corporatist type of institutional governance gave both the right-wing opposition and the business groups the guarantee that within CORFO their voice was going to be heard. The SNA, for instance, enthusiastically welcomed in their official journal *El Campesino* the introduction of corporatist representation. The SNA stated that "the reasonable aspiration we kept for long years that a National Economic Council with representation of the producers will be created, has now been almost completely realized in the structure adopted by CORFO. Within this agency the problems affecting the agricultural sector are now discussed without the use of political criteria."[32]

The degree of influence that international models had on the institutional design adopted by CORFO cannot be established with certainty. Chilean authorities were in any case well informed about several international experiences in state intervention, and about the structure of foreign public agencies supporting economic development. Time and again references were made to foreign experiences during discussions on state intervention in the economy. Remarks such as the following, made by Guillermo Azócar, a Socialist senator, during a discussion in the Senate about the establishment of CORFO, were very common at that time: "today there is almost not a single country which has not adopted a general developmental plan, because at the present the New Economy is synonymous of a planned economy. Hence both democratic countries such as France and the United States as well as totalitarian countries such as Italy and Germany, have their own plans."[33] Pinto refers explicitly to the Soviet experience in planning which was particularly popular among the Chilean left. On the other hand, the state-led policies deployed by President Franklin D. Roosevelt and his New Deal in the United States, took the

---

[32] *El Campesino*, March 1939: 695.   [33] Quoted in Muñoz and Arriagada, 1977: 27–28.

attention of many Chilean technocrats who admired US technological innovation and managerialism.[34] The creation in 1933 of the Tennessee Valley Authority (TVA) as a federal initiative to generate electricity on a large scale, attracted the attention of Chilean engineers preoccupied with the lack of enough sources of electric energy in the country. In the years 1935–1939 Chilean civil engineers worked hard to formulate a general plan for electrification, which resulted in a series of path-breaking documents being published by the Instituto de Ingenieros de Chile, such as the documents on "Chilean Electric Policy" (1936) and "The Energy Problem in Chile: Plan for National Electrification" (1939), which later became the foundation for the electricity plans implemented by the Popular Front government. To what extent the TVA initiative served as a blueprint for CORFO is hard to say, as no hard evidence in that direction is available. Nevertheless, it can be established that both institutions were characterized by their great deal of managerial and financial autonomy. TVA was assigned the legal capacity to collect revenues, in the form of tariffs for services such as, among others, the provision of electricity, and to spend those funds based on its own management decisions.[35] In the case of CORFO, financial autonomy seemed to have been even stronger, as the act creating this state corporation in 1939 established also earmarked taxes assigned to a "production development fund" that was to be administered by CORFO. Together with this financial independence, both TVA and CORFO enjoyed political independence, as they had the capacity to take their own decisions on public policy, without interference from the executive. This kind of institutional autonomy is exceptional in Latin America. As chapters 5 and 7 in the present volume show, developmental agencies in Brazil, Colombia, and Peru were constantly exposed to all kinds of political interference from the very beginning.

Finally, the degree of formal representation given to several social, political, and economic stakeholders at CORFO's Board of Directors seems also to have been unique in comparison with other development agencies worldwide. For instance, while the CORFO Board was composed of twenty-four members who represented a broad pallet of interests, the TVA Board had only three members, appointed by the president of the United States with advice and consent by the Senate. The type of corporatist representation incorporated at CORFO provided this state agency with a high degree of legitimacy and support from the actors involved.

In the day-to-day practice, the Board delegated most of the decisions to the technocrats working at the commissions for agriculture, commerce and transport, energy and combustibles, and industry and mining. These commissions were in charge of the formulation and application of so-called "plans of immediate action" for each of those economic sectors.[36] The plans

[34] Pinto, 1985: 23.   [35] Selznick, 1949: 33–36.
[36] Ortega, Norambuena, Pinto, and Bravo, 1989: 78–80.

were created in order to begin immediately with the reconstruction of the areas affected by the earthquake, but also planning for new infrastructure and state enterprises in those areas. CORFO was tasked with the elaboration of a General Plan for Economic Development as a road map for the coming decades. However, due to the inexistence at that time of reliable statistical data about the entire Chilean economy, and the lack of experts in general planning, the plan was postponed for a long time, and it was only presented in 1961.

The negotiations that took place between the Popular Front administration, the right-wing opposition, and the business groups, regarding the goals and attributions to be given to CORFO, were not only decisive for the final institutional design adopted by this giant state agency, it was also crucial for the working of Chilean democracy as such until the early 1960s. The final acceptance by the political right and business organizations of the state-led CORFO project seems to have been also related to an issue not directly connected with the industrial sector as such. Namely, the right and the entrepreneurial groups were extremely concerned with the great political and social agitation generated in the countryside as a result of the Popular Front's victory. Left-wing urban activists went to rural areas to recruit peasants for their political organizations, and to provide support for their demands for land reform and better working conditions. Authors such as Mamalakis, Kaufman, and Loveman have suggested that the Popular Front government had reached a back-door agreement with the right-wing parties and the entrepreneurial organization on this issue.[37] [38] [39] While the latter retired their objections about the final institutional design of CORFO, the government subtly retired from the political agenda both land reform and rural unionization.

The search for accommodation and compromises between the center-left and right-wing forces was going to characterize Chilean democracy until the early 1960s. A basic consensus emerged, regarding both the support for state-led industrialization, and the containment of popular sectors to avoid social and political instability in the country. This so-called "State of Compromise" (Estado de Compromiso) was the result of the existing political tie between the center-left and the right-wing forces, making it impossible for any of the two political sectors to impose its will on the other.[40] At the same time, however, both sectors continuously tried to change the political balance in their favor, attempting to improve their electoral results in order to implement their own agenda without compromises. Therefore, at the eve of each presidential election, such as in 1952, 1958, 1964, and 1970, political polarization reached extremely high levels. In other words, the preservation of the State of Compromise was not guaranteed, and it depended on the maintenance of the equilibrium of forces between both blocs. Cavarozzi is right in concluding that "the consensus that Chilean elites reached during the 1930s and the 1940s was

[37] Mamalakis, 1965: 17.   [38] Kaufman, 1972: 26.   [39] Loveman, 1976: 118.
[40] See Valenzuela, 1978. See also Scully, 1992.

quite tenuous … The fragility of the Chilean political consensus became progressively more obvious beginning in the early 1950s."[41] Boeninger for his part argues that this fragility became particularly visible when economic problems emerged in the early 1950s, such as, among others, high inflation, fall in foreign demand for Chilean products, and weak economic growth. According to this author "it is paradoxical that the State of Compromise existed in a climate of strong political instability and discontinuity. This produced an increasing loss of prestige by political parties, politics, and the practices of negotiation to achieve agreements between party leaders and members of Parliament. This became even more evident as the economic malaise became more accentuated. To put it in present-day terms, the State of Compromise was characterized by its unsatisfactory conditions of governability."[42]

Since the late 1940s the developmental state received academic and intellectual support from the UN Economic Commission for Latin America (ECLA), inaugurated in 1948 at Santiago de Chile. Economists such as Raúl Prebisch justified with a series of studies the adoption by the Latin American states of import-substitutions strategies and defended the protection of the national industry.[43]

Since its creation CORFO was the originator of a large number of industrial initiatives, from big enterprises to medium- and small-sized firms. It also provided credit and technical assistance to countless industrial projects from the private sector. Among the most important enterprises created by CORFO are the National Electricity Company (ENDESA) in 1943, the Pacific Steel Company (CAP) in 1946, the National Oil Company (ENAP) in 1950, and both the Banco del Estado and the National Sugar Company (IANSA) in 1953. The CORFO initiatives led to a substantial increase of the country's industrial output. From 1940 until the mid 1950s, industrial production increased at an annual rate of 7.5 percent, while in the same period the industrial sector's share in the GDP grew from 13.4 to 23 percent.[44]

THE DECLINE OF THE DEVELOPMENTAL STATE

Most Chileans were proud of the national corporations created by the state. Moreover, the good management of these public companies contributed to the positive reputation of their technical staff. This good reputation was however by no means shared by political parties and politicians. At the beginning of the 1950s, the political class had lost a great deal of its legitimacy. Public opinion was hostile to the ongoing expansion of the state bureaucracy as accusations emerged of alleged party favoritism in the recruitment of public employees. Politicians were also held responsible for the mounting inflation which began to affect the Chilean economy from the mid 1940s, and their inability to provide

---

[41] Cavarozzi, 1992: 214.   [42] Boeninger, 1997: 114.   [43] Kay, 1989.   [44] Vergara, 1982: 39.

for effective solutions. The inflation spiral unleashed an open struggle among entrepreneurial groups, public employees, and organized labor about their respective share of the national income.[45]

A clear expression of the existing discontent with the political class was the comeback of Carlos Ibáñez, who won the 1952 presidential elections in a landslide. The symbol during his campaign was a broom, with which he promised to clean up the state apparatus from useless bureaucrats and to put an end to inflation in the country. As Scully put it, his victory "was the expression of an open and generalized sense of disenchantment with party politics. Ibáñez contrasted his managerial style with the inefficiency and corruption of traditional parties."[46]

During this second Ibáñez administration (1952–1958), the government was focused on finding a solution for the macroeconomic and financial difficulties. Plans for further strengthening the developmental state in the economic and social areas were put on hold. In order to control inflation, Ibáñez followed the recommendations made by the American Klein-Saks Mission, which proposed the adoption of a monetarist anti-inflationary program. However, the adopted tough policies did not provide the expected results and generated a broad rejection from both the entrepreneurial groups and the labor movement. This situation forced Ibáñez to abandon his stabilization program.[47]

At the 1958 presidential contest Jorge Alessandri, an engineer, an industrialist, and a son of Arturo Alessandri, won the elections as an independent candidate. At the moment of his presidential victory, Alessandri was the acting president of the Confederation of Production and Commerce (COPROCO), one of the main business organizations. Although most Chilean entrepreneurs had profited from the CORFO credits and technical support, they had actually never accepted the very idea of state interventionism in the industrial sector. After two decades of state support, many private industrialists considered that they were strong enough to play a more decisive and autonomous role in Chilean development. Thus, Alessandri attempted to introduce a fundamental change in the state-led pattern of development followed since the late 1930s. His goal was to place the private entrepreneurs at the central stage of the developmental process and to significantly reduce the role of the state in the Chilean economy. In order to break the power of the public technocracy entrenched in CORFO, the Central Bank and other state agencies, Alessandri replaced the management and the middle-level technical staff with managers and technocrats coming from the private sector.[48] Following what has been a historical demand among entrepreneurial groups, Alessandri also decided to restrict CORFO activities to simply providing credits for the private sector. He appointed businessman Pierre Lehmann as the new executive vice president of CORFO, who dismissed the general manager and the

---

[45] Silva Vargas, 2013: 769.   [46] Scully, 1992: 126.
[47] See Sunkel, 1963: 123–141. See also Sierra, 1969.   [48] Stallings, 1978: 86.

heads of departments, putting an end to the relative autonomy which this state agency had enjoyed since its creation in 1939. Alessandri extended his cleansing operation to the entire bureaucratic system, including ministries and other state agencies. As Cavarozzi points out, "the large cohort of party politicians, who, albeit of different party origins, had almost monopolized the top echelons of the state apparatus since the 1920s, were partially replaced by entrepreneurs, and by former officials of the entrepreneurial associations."[49] This penetration of the state apparatus by members of the dominant social sectors and their corporative representatives produced a situation which Cavarozzi called the "relative de-autonomization of the state."[50] It is significant to see how the entrepreneurial associations rapidly put an end to their traditional attitude of praising the traditional state technocracy, by now openly welcoming their replacement by managers coming from the private sector.

Alessandri also attempted to liberalize the economy by eliminating a series of regulations on prices and tariffs and by introducing market mechanisms to stimulate the influx of foreign investment. However, Alessandri's appeal to the "Schumpeterian spirit" among Chilean entrepreneurs did not receive resolute support from that sector. At the end of the day, Chilean entrepreneurs experienced the reduction of the protectionist tariffs as too risky. As Moulian put it, "state protection (import restrictions, high tariffs, tax exceptions, and credit advantages) made any attempt at modernization unnecessary because it artificially preserved the national industry. Because of this, modernization as proposed by Alessandri did not represent for the entrepreneurs an immediate class interest, being rather a project which could affect their position in the short term."[51]

The austerity measures introduced by Alessandri were strongly resisted by the unions, left-wing political parties, and, at the end, even the industrialists themselves. As had happened to the Ibáñez government in the early 1950s, Alessandri was forced to abandon his pro-business strategy halfway through his administration. In addition, he required the parliamentary backing of the Conservative, Liberal, and Radical parties in order to strengthen his weak political basis to finish the last part of his administration.[52] This change of course led to a rapid politicization of the government and its economic policies, which in turn led to a growing alienation of the business sector from the Alessandri project. They began to abandon many positions within the state agencies they occupied at the beginning of his government, to be replaced by appointees coming largely from the Radical Party.

At the end, Alessandri not only failed to successfully replace the traditional developmental state with his modernization project based in market-oriented policies. He was also responsible for initiating the disruption and politicization of the state apparatus, leaving the state administration in disarray. This also

[49] Cavarozzi, 1975: 361.   [50] Cavarozzi, 1975: 395.   [51] Moulian, 1983: 128.
[52] Scully, 1992: 139.

resulted in the irremediable loss of the relative autonomy that state agencies like CORFO had enjoyed in previous decades.

In the final phase of the Alessandri administration the state of compromise began to show severe signs of fatigue. It became clear that the major political and social forces in the country were not any longer willing or able to reach "agreements on fundamentals" about democracy and the developmental state. The new scenario became characterized by growing ideological polarization and the adoption by most political forces of an explosive confrontational stance. Sectors of the Chilean elite began to regard democracy and popular participation as real threats to their strategic interests. The left-wing parties, being notoriously influenced by the Cuban Revolution, adopted a more radical course of action by announcing their explicit goal to put an end to the capitalist pattern of development and to replace it with socialism.

The victory of the moderate Christian Democrat Eduardo Frei in the 1964 presidential election was seen by some as Chile's last chance to put an end to the further deterioration of the democratic institutions.[53] The United States supported the Frei project, which they saw as a moderate, acceptable alternative to the Cuban revolution.

President Frei and the Christian Democratic Party (PDC) had promised "a revolution in liberty," but they showed no disposition to make compromises with other political forces regarding the government program.[54] Frei had won the 1964 elections by a crushing victory with 55 percent of the vote. This represented an unprecedented electoral result in Chilean politics. Moreover, in the following year the PDC achieved another huge victory by obtaining 43 percent of votes and electing 82 of 147 members of the parliament.[55] This extremely strong starting position convinced the Christian Democrats to fully implement their ambitious plan of economic and social reforms without any concessions. The program included a land reform, the nationalization of part of the copper industry, and a broad package of social policies directed to popular sectors. This followed the recommendations of a series of intellectuals and economists sympathizing with the PDC, who had concluded that since the mid 1950s Chile was in an "integral crisis" which could only be successfully tackled by adopting profound socio-economic reforms.[56]

During the Frei administration, the Chilean developmental state experienced a strong expansion. Under his administration, important state enterprises and agencies were created, such as the National Enterprise for Telecommunication (ENTEL), and the Chilean National Television (TVN). Also, CORFO became strongly reactivated, being at the center of a series of new industrial initiatives in the fields of agriculture, forestry, fishing, energy, and others.[57] Agencies such as the Land Reform Corporation (CORA) and the Institute of Agriculture and

[53] Gross, 1967. [54] Valenzuela, 1978. [55] Fleet, 1985.
[56] See Ahumada, 1958. See also Pinto, 1958.
[57] Ortega, Norambuena, Pinto, and Bravo, 1989: 179–215.

Livestock Development (INDAP) became key institutions in the implementation of the land reform. The Christian Democratic government was also very active in deploying social policies and improving labor legislation.

Frei believed strongly in economic and social planning. In his State of the Nation speech of May 1970, he stated that, "democracy requires the existence of efficient and responsible political leadership which has to make use of planning to reach its goals. Once a plan or program has been approved by general consensus, it can neither be terminated nor distorted in spirit and basic guidelines."[58] Frei had no intention of seeking agreements with other political and social actors: in his view, the administration's program had been endorsed by the Chilean electorate in electing him president, and again in giving his party a majority of parliamentary seats.

In 1967, the National Planning Office (ODEPLAN) was established, with the mission to formulate plans for economic and social development, giving its director the rank of minister. Frei trusted the advice of economists, particularly those associated with ECLA in its headquarters at Santiago de Chile. The ECLA economists, for their part, enthusiastically endorsed most of Frei's plans for economic and social modernization.[59] A young generation of Christian Democratic technocrats, most of them economists and civil engineers, were appointed to direct several state agencies. Although they were without doubt technically competent, they were more ideologically oriented than the traditional technocrats that served before Alessandri launched his attack on the state bureaucracy in the late 1950s. Again, the PDC technocrats did not deem it necessary to achieve consensus for their policies among other actors, including the right- and left-wing opposition, and the business associations. As Ascher indicates, "the technocrats of the party and the administration, themselves satisfied with the progressive merits of the program, attempted to impose it without permitting input – or political credit – to others."[60]

While ODEPLAN functioned as the operational center of the developmental state under the Frei administration, the political decision-making was concentrated in the so-called "Economic Committee." This was chaired by the president himself or his deputy, the minister of finance. The committee held weekly sessions and included the ministers of economy, labor, and agriculture, the director of ODEPLAN, the chairman of the Central Bank, the vice president of CORFO, the chairman of the Banco del Estado, the president's economic adviser, and the director of the Budget Office.[61] Representatives of the business associations were kept outside the decision-making process. As Cleaves indicates, the Economic Committee maintained its bureaucratic insulation vis-à-vis the social and ideological forces in society. Moreover, the central role given to ODEPLAN created a continuous rivalry between this agency and CORFO.[62]

[58] Quoted in Cardemil, 1997: 160.   [59] Moulian and Guerra, 2000: 29.
[60] Ascher, 1984: 125.   [61] Molina, 1972: 161–162.   [62] Cleaves, 1974: 94–95.

The Christian Democratic members of Parliament supported most of the policies proposed by the Economic Committee. However, after 1967 the economic situation deteriorated, and rising political and social tensions began to dominate the scenario. Landowners' organizations protested openly against the radicalization produced by the land reform in the countryside, while in the major cities workers' unions and squatter movements demanded radical political changes. In this new scenario, an increasing number of PDC politicians asked the government to pay more attention to political equilibriums, and to abandon the strictly technocratic insulation in policy making. As Stallings notes, "the Frei government sought a much greater measure of relative autonomy than was the norm in class-dominated Chilean politics. During the 1965–66 period, this approach achieved substantial success ... But at the end of the biennium, however, opposition to the 'neutral state' was beginning to build up on all sides."[63]

The large share of power obtained by the young PDC technocrats led to mounting communication problems with the public administration, political parties, entrepreneurs, and eventually, public opinion. Menges stressed the rapid deterioration of the relations between important state agencies such as CORFO and CORA, and the country's main business associations such as SNA and SOFOFA. While these entrepreneurial organizations were used to employ informal mechanisms to influence policy making, they found in the PDC technocracy a group not disposed to talk or to negotiate about sectorial policies. As he points out, "the Christian Democratic government brought its own complement of economists and technicians to government service, and there has hardly been any collaboration between government ministries and the business groups in the drafting of economic policies legislation."[64] The technocrats' attitude of avoiding consultation with the business organizations forced the latter to strengthen their contacts with members of Parliament, who also felt ignored by these technocratic newcomers.

The insulation of the decision-making process regarding economic and social policies resulted in a rapid deterioration of the political climate in the country. Valenzuela and Wilde go as far as to relate the later collapse of Chilean democracy to the ascent of technocrats and planning ideologies in the 1960s.[65] According to these authors, the extreme rigidity shown by the PDC technocrats collided severely with the traditional Chilean political culture of accommodation and compromise.

At the end of the Frei administration, the government had become dangerously alienated from important social and political actors such as the business associations, trade unions, and the opposition parties. Despite the expansion of the developmental state during the Frei years, a fundamental component of the state of compromise had rapidly evaporated: the negotiation and accommodation between conflicting interests.

[63] Stallings, 1978: 100.   [64] Menges, 1966: 353–354.   [65] Valenzuela and Wilde, 1979: 211.

Following the victory of the Unidad Popular left-wing coalition in the 1970 presidential elections, the state of compromise entered into terminal decline. The Allende government aimed to implement a radical program of profound social and economic reforms, which represented a complete break with the historical path of industrial relations followed by the country since the mid 1920s. The program stated that the Unidad Popular main objective was "to put an end to the domination of the imperialists, monopolists, and the land-owned oligarchy, and to initiate the construction of socialism in Chile."[66] In this way, the Allende government became engaged from the very beginning in a struggle against numerous and powerful adversaries. They included US interests, particularly in mining and industry, the landowners, the industrialists, and the banking sector. In the political arena, the Unidad Popular confronted a broad and powerful coalition of right-wing sectors and the Christian Democratic Party, which held a majority in Parliament.[67]

The initial positioning of the Allende government with respect to economic planning showed many similarities with the Frei administration. The fundamental difference, however, was that while Frei hoped to modernize capitalism in Chile, the Popular Unity government attempted to replace it with socialism. The government program stated that "in the new economy, planning shall play an important role ... The economic policy of the state shall be carried out through the national system for economic planning and such mechanisms as control, guidance, credit to production, technical, political, tax and foreign trade assistance, as well as management of the state sector of the economy."[68] The Popular Unity government assigned to ODEPLAN the responsibility for the national planning system. In 1971, ODEPLAN published its "Six Year Plan, 1971–1976," including an elaborated strategy for economic and social development for the entire period of the Allende administration. The plan announced for the years ahead a huge expansion of state services and coverage in areas such as public health, housing, and social security.[69]

As a result of the nationalization of a large number of private firms in all productive areas, the state soon came to control the most significant part of the country's economic activities. CORFO played a key role in the administration of the nationalized enterprises. The Allende administration appointed an increasing number of managers (*interventores*) in charge of their day-to-day supervision. As a result of the extreme degree of political polarization in those years, radical political militants constantly clashed with state technocrats about the control and administration of nationalized enterprises.[70]

At the beginning of his administration, Allende attempted to protect his technical team from direct pressures by the political parties conforming the Unidad Popular coalition. For instance, he personally selected well-known economists for the position of minister of finance, directors and chief-executives

---

[66] UP (Unidad Popular), 1969: 19.   [67] De Vylder, 1976.
[68] UP (Unidad Popular), 1969: 19, 23.   [69] Zammit, 1973: 287–316.   [70] Falcoff, 1989: 139.

of ODEPLAN, of the National Copper Corporation (CODELCO), and other important state agencies and companies. However, his initial attempts were useless as the ongoing process of radicalization led to the rapid politicization of state institutions (see Sigmund, 1980). Control of state agencies came to be distributed according to political quota among members of the different parties of the governmental coalition, so that no central coordination was possible for developmental plans. Sergio Bitar, minister for mining under Allende, remembered years later the administrative chaos existing at state agencies in the following terms: "since ... each one acted autonomously there existed no single focus of authority, no body or person responsible for the direction or economic policy as a whole. This was a major failure in the conduct of the economy."[71]

The increasing politicization of the state agencies was particularly visible at CORFO, which had a leading role in the administration of many expropriated industries. During the Allende years CORFO lost most of the relative autonomy and strong technical nature which had characterized it since its creation. As Ortega *et al.* conclude: "From November 1970 on, [CORFO] was made to play an entirely different role: that of the instrument for the application of a program of revolutionary transformation in the country. For the first time in its history, the political function became central, with its classical activities or research and development being subordinated to it."[72]

From the beginning of 1972 to the military coup of September 1973, all the efforts and energies of the Allende government were mainly consumed by the struggle for political survival, amidst mounting economic problems. The opposition adopted a seditious strategy exploring all the ways available to put an end to the Unidad Popular administration, including a military coup. The extreme polarization in the country made almost impossible any compromise between the Allende government and the opposition, while the moderate sectors of both sides lost any influence whatsoever.[73]

The military coup of September 1973 put an end to the Allende government amidst a profound political and economic crisis. This represented not only the end of the longstanding Chilean democracy, but also the culmination of the developmental state. The military regime decided to radically break with the traditional path of state-led developmentalism, and to put in its place a neoliberal model. All the key components of the developmental state were systematically eliminated in the next few years.

CONCLUSION

Following the crisis of the parliamentary republic and the collapse of the nitrate-based economy in the early twentieth century, Chile managed in the period 1924–1973 to build up a relatively successful developmental state.

---

[71] Bitar, 1986: 221.   [72] Ortega, Norambuena, Pinto, and Bravo, 1989: 224.
[73] Valenzuela, 1978.

The dramatic downfall experienced by the nitrate industry had convinced many that the extreme dependency of the Chilean economy on export of raw materials had to end. Since the mid 1920s a series of reformist governments actively supported state-led industrialization, based on the ideas of economic nationalism and state protectionism.

However, the decision to build up a developmental state was not only the result of economic considerations. The middle classes and the labor movement demanded an active role for the Chilean state in economic and social development. The aristocratic elite, however, showed no disposition to accept the new social and political reality emerging after World War I. The army eventually unlocked this potential stalemate by forcing the adoption of a series of legal and administrative measures which permitted the establishment of a developmental state in the country. The military leaders correctly understood that, in this extremely unstable scenario, the establishment of a developmental state was necessary to avoid severe social and political conflicts. The government of Colonel Carlos Ibáñez (1927–1931), particularly, created the institutional structures upon which the developmental state was going to rest for the following decades.

Several governments managed to keep those state agencies that were in charge of economic and social policies protected from political interference by party politics and politicians. The reputation and authority of politicians was very low at the beginning of the developmental era, and their influence on those institutions would have been damaging to the public trust in the developmental state. Instead, a conscious effort was made to provide those state agencies with high technical and professional standards. Developmental agencies were staffed with civil engineers and other experts. This fundamental decision resulted not only from the belief that they represented the group in society most prepared to carry out the complex tasks ahead. The decision to place these state agencies in the hands of technocrats, and to give them a high degree of relative autonomy, was also the direct result of the specific balance of political forces existing in the country.

Although the social and economic dominant groups had lost their control of the executive power since the mid 1920s, they still possessed sufficient political and economic resources to defend their interests. For a long time, this created a situation of political tie between the reformist governments and the representation of private interests that resisted state policies in different areas. This political stalemate, however, produced a positive outcome: it forced both sides to reach compromises about the type and degree of state intervention to be applied on the Chilean economy.

The need to reach political compromises between reformist and conservative forces was manifest during the creation of the National Development Corporation (CORFO). The corporation became the central piece in the institutional design of the Chilean developmental state. The high degree of technocratic insulation characterizing this agency was the result of the existing equilibrium of forces between government and opposition, including business groups. The high-ranking experts in charge of running state agencies enjoyed the trust and respect of all involved parties. Hence, their high degree of relative autonomy and institutional insulation was an important safety measure to prevent the infiltration of party politics and private interests in these public institutions.

The search for political agreements and the readiness to find accommodation between contesting economic interests was the essence of the State of Compromise, and the basis of Chilean democracy, until the collapse of 1973.

The State of Compromise and the developmental state did adequately function as long as the equilibrium of forces was not altered and the involved parties did respect their agreement on fundamentals. As we have seen in this chapter, Chilean democracy and the developmental state entered into turbulent waters during the 1950s, as the increasing economic and financial problems resulted in strong social and political agitation. In this scenario, the governments of Carlos Ibáñez and Jorge Alessandri adopted hard economic measures, and more market-oriented policies that attempted to deal with inflation and increasing public debt. In both cases, however, the left-wing parties and the union movement forced the governments to stop such policies. The point to stress here is that neither of those two governments followed the golden principle of reaching compromises and accommodation with the opposition forces before pursuing their policy agenda. In addition, by trying to introduce market-oriented policies and enhance the role of private initiative, they were undermining a key aspect of the developmental state, i.e. the supremacy of the state in conducting national economic and social policy strategies. However, the major attack against the state of compromise was the massive dismissal by Alessandri of high-ranking career civil servants from public agencies, and their replacement with appointees coming from the private sector. And so ended the traditional technocratic insulation enjoyed by top managers of key state agencies.

The 1960s and early 1970s show that the key component of the Chilean developmental state was not the degree of state control of the economy, but the existence of fundamental political agreements. Both the Frei and Allende administration increased radically both the scope and the impact of the developmental state on the country's economic and social development. However, they did it without balancing and accommodating their programs with the interests represented by the political opposition and the business associations. Under the Allende administration, the result was a zero-sum confrontation between left-wing forces, which stubbornly attempted the construction of socialism, and a broad opposition, which deployed all the means at their disposition to bring down the Allende government.

In short, the Chilean developmental state suffered a gradual agony from the mid 1950s, as the political requirements which made its working possible were, in one way or the other, neglected or rejected by both the right- and the left-wing forces. The close interconnection existing between the State of Compromise and the developmental state became fully evident following the military coup of September 1973, as this dramatic event led to their parallel destruction.

REFERENCES

Aguirre Cerda, Pedro. *El Problema Industrial*. Santiago: Prensas de la Universidad de Chile, 1933.

Ahumada, Jorge. *En vez de la miseria*. Santiago: Editorial del Pacífico, 1958.

Ascher, William. *Scheming for the Poor: The Politics of Redistribution in Latin America*. Cambridge, MA: Harvard University Press, 1984.

Bitar, Sergio. *Chile: Experiments in Democracy*. Philadelphia: Institute for the Study of Human Issues, 1986.

Boeninger, Edgardo. *Democracia en Chile: Lecciones para la Gobernabilidad*. Santiago: Editorial Andrés Bello, 1997.

Bravo Lira, Bernardino. *Una historia jamás contada: Chile 1811–2011: desde la modernización desde arriba al despegue desde abajo*. Santiago: Origo Ediciones, 2016.

Cardemil, Alberto. *El camino de la utopía, Alessandri, Frei, Allende: Pensamiento y obra*. Santiago: Editorial Andrés Bello, 1997.

Cavarozzi, Marcelo. "The Government and the Industrial Bourgeoisie in Chile, 1938–1964." Unpublished PhD thesis, University of California at Berkeley, 1975.

"Patterns of Elite Negotiation and Confrontation in Argentina and Chile." In *Elites and Democratic Consolidation in Latin America and Southern Europe*, eds. John Higley and Richard Gunther, New York: Cambridge University Press, 1992: 208–236.

Los sótanos de la democracia: Las esferas de "protección" de los empresarios industriales: la CORFO, represión a los obreros y la inflación. Santiago: LOM Ediciones, 2017.

Centeno, Miguel A. and Agustin E. Ferraro, eds. *State and Nation Making in Latin America and Spain: Republics of the Possible*. New York: Cambridge University Press, 2013.

Cleaves, Peter. *Bureaucratic Politics and Administration in Chile*. Berkeley: University of California Press, 1974.

Correa Prieto, *Luis. El presidente Ibáñez, la política y los políticos: Apuntes para la historia*. Santiago: Editorial del Pacífico, 1962.

Crowther, Warren W. "Technological Change as Political Choice: The Civil Engineers and the Modernization of the Chilean State Railways." Unpublished PhD thesis, University of California at Berkeley, 1973.

De Vylder, Stefan. *Allende's Chile: The Political Economy of the Rise and Fall of the Unidad Popular*. Cambridge University Press, 1976.

Drake, Paul W. *Socialism and Populism in Chile, 1932–52*. Urbana: University of Illinois Press, 1978.

Edwards Vives, Alberto. *La fronda aristocrática: Historia política de Chile*. Santiago: Editorial del Pacífico, 1952 [originally published in 1928].

Ellsworth, P.T. *Chile: An Economy in Transition*. New York: The Macmillan Company, 1945.

Encina, Francisco. *Nuestra inferioridad económica: sus causas, sus consecuencias.* Santiago: Imprenta Universitaria, 1912.

Evans, Peter. *Embedded Autonomy: States and Industrial Transformation.* Princeton University Press, 1995.

Falcoff, Mark. *Modern Chile, 1970–1989: A Critical History.* New Brunswick, NJ: Transaction Publishers, 1989.

Fleet, Michael. *The Rise and Fall of Chilean Christian Democracy.* Princeton University Press, 1985.

Gil, Federico G. *The Political System of Chile.* Boston: Houghton Mifflin, 1966.

Góngora, Mario. *Ensayo histórico sobre la noción de Estado en Chile en los siglos XIX y XX.* Santiago: Editorial Universitaria, 1988.

Gross, Leonard. *The Last, Best Hope: Eduardo Frei and Chilean Democracy.* New York: Random House, 1967.

Ibáñez Santa María, Adolfo. "Los ingenieros, el Estado y la política en Chile: Del Ministerio de Fomento a la Corporación de Fomento, 1927–1939." *Historia* 18, 1983: 45–102.

Herido en el Ala: Estado, Oligarquías y Subdesarrollo, Chile 1924–1960. Santiago: Editorial Biblioteca Americana, 2003.

Historia de Chile, 1860–1973, two vols. Santiago: Centro de Estudios Bicentenario, 2013.

Jaksic, Iván. "Ideological Pragmatism and Nonpartisan Expertise in Nineteenth-Century Chile: Andrés Bello's Contribution to State and Nation Building." In *State and Nation Making in Latin America and Spain: Republics of the Possible,* eds. Miguel A. Centeno and Agustin E. Ferraro, New York: Cambridge University Press, 2013: 183–202.

Jobet, Julio César. *Ensayo crítico del desarrollo económico-social de Chile.* Santiago: Editorial Universitaria, 1955.

Kaufman, Robert. *The Politics of Land Reform in Chile, 1950–1970: Public Policy, Political Institutions, and Social Change.* Cambridge, MA: Harvard University Press, 1972.

Kay, Cristóbal. *Latin American Theories of Development and Underdevelopment.* New York: Routledge, 1989.

Larroulet, Cristián. "Reflexiones en torno al Estado empresarial en Chile." *Estudios Públicos* 24, March 1984: 129–151.

Loveman, Brian. *Struggle in the Countryside: Politics and Rural Labor in Chile, 1919–1973.* Bloomington: Indiana University Press, 1976.

Chile: The Legacy of Hispanic Capitalism. New York: Oxford University Press, 1979.

Mamalakis, Markus. "Public Policy and Sectorial Development: A Case Study of Chile, 1940–1958." In *Essays in the Chilean Economy,* eds. Markus Mamalakis and Clarck W. Reynolds, Chicago: Richard D. Irwin, 1965: 1–100.

Menges, Constantine C. "Public Policy and Organized Business in Chile: A Preliminary Analysis." *Journal of International Affairs* 20, 2, 1966: 343–365.

Milos, Pedro. *Frente Popular en Chile: su Configuración, 1935–1938.* Santiago: LOM Ediciones, 2008.

Molina, Sergio. *El proceso de cambio en Chile.* Santiago: Editorial Universitaria, 1972.

Montero, Cecilia. "El actor empresarial en transición." *Estudios Cieplan* 37, June 1993: 37–68.

Moulian, Tomás. "Desarrollo político y estado de compromiso: desajustes y crisis estatal en Chile." *Estudios Cieplan* 64, July 1982: 105–158.

"Los frentes populares y el desarrollo político de la década del sesenta." *Documento de Trabajo* 191. Santiago: FLACSO, 1983.

Moulian, Luis and Gloria Guerra. *Eduardo Frei: biografía de un estadista utópico.* Santiago: Editorial Sudamericana, 2000.

Muñoz, Oscar, ed. *Proceso a la industrialización chilena.* Santiago: Ediciones Nueva Universidad, 1972.

"La CORFO y el desarrollo nacional." In *Modelo Económico chileno: trayectoria de una crítica*, eds. José Pablo Arellano, René Cortázar, Ramón Downey, et al., Santiago: Editorial Aconcagua, 1982: 205–207.

Chile y su industrialización: pasado, crisis y opciones. Santiago: CIEPLAN, 1986.

ed. *Historias personales, políticas públicas.* Santiago: Editorial los Andes, 1993.

Muñoz, Oscar, and Ana María Arriagada. "Orígenes políticos y económicos del Estado Empresarial en Chile." *Estudios Cieplan* 16, September 1977: 1–53.

Ortega, Luis. "Políticas de 'fomento' en una sociedad en transición: desafíos y obstáculos. Chile en la primera mitad del siglo XX." *Atenea* 514, August 2016: 13–29.

Ortega, Luis, Carmen Norambuena, Julio Pinto, and Guillermo Bravo. *Corporación de Fomento de la Producción: 50 años de realizaciones, 1929–1989.* Santiago: CORFO, 1989.

Palma, Gabriel. "Chile, *1914–1935: de economía exportadora a sustitutiva de importaciones.*" *Estudios Cieplan* 12, March 1984: 61–88.

Pinto, Aníbal. *Chile, un caso de desarrollo frustrado.* Santiago: Editorial Universitaria, 1958.

"Estado y la Gran Empresa: de la precrisis hasta el gobierno de Jorge Alessandri." *Estudios Cieplan* 16, June 1985: 5–40.

Scully, Timothy R. *Rethinking the Center: Party Politics in Nineteenth- and Twentieth-Century Chile.* Stanford University Press, 1992.

Selznick, Philip. *TVA and the Grass Roots: A Study in the Sociology of Formal Organization.* Berkeley: University of California Press, 1949.

Sierra, Enrique. *Tres Ensayos de Estabilización en Chile.* Santiago: Editorial Universitaria, 1969.

Sigmund, Paul. *The Overthrow of Allende and the Politics of Chile, 1964–1976.* University of Pittsburgh Press, 1980.

Silva, Eduardo. "The Import-Substitution Model: Chile in Comparative Perspective." *Latin American Perspectives* 34, 3, May 2007: 67–90.

Silva Vargas, Fernando. "Un contrapunto de medio siglo: democracia liberal y estatismo burocrático, 1924–1970." In *Historia de Chile*, ed. Sergio Villalobos et al., 751–869. Santiago: Editorial Universitaria, 2013 [1974].

Silva, Patricio. "State, Public Technocracy and Politics in Chile, 1927–1941." *Bulletin of Latin American Research* 13, 3, September 1984: 281–297.

In the Name of Reason: Technocrats and Politics in Chile. University Park: Penn State University Press, 2008.

Silva, Patricio. "'A Poor But Honest Country': Corruption and Probity in Chile." *Journal of Developing Societies* 32, 2, April 2016: 178–203.

Stallings, Barbara. *Class Conflict and Economic Development in Chile, 1958–1973.* Stanford University Press, 1978.

Stevenson, John R. *The Chilean Popular Front*. University Park: The University of Pennsylvania Press, 1942.

Sunkel, Osvaldo. "El fracaso de las políticas de estabilización en el contexto del desarrollo latinoamericano." *El Trimestre Económico* 120, 4, October-December 1963: 123–141.

UP (Unidad Popular). *Programa básico de gobierno de la Unidad Popular*. Santiago: Comando de la Unidad Popular, 1969.

Valenzuela, Arturo. *The Breakdown of Democratic Regimes: Chile*. Baltimore: Johns Hopkins University Press, 1978.

Valenzuela, Arturo and Alexander Wilde. "Presidential Politics and the Decline of the Chilean Congress." In *Legislatures in Development: Dynamics of Change in New and Old States*, eds. Joel Smith and Lloyd D. Musolf. Durham: Duke University Press, 1979: 189–215.

Vergara, Pilar. "Pasado y presente de la industria chilena." *Mensaje* 306, 1982: 39–47.

Zammit, J. Ann, ed. *The Chilean Road to Socialism*. Sussex: Institute of Development Studies, University of Sussex, 1973.

PART V

NATIONAL AND CIVIC IDENTITIES: SYMBOLIC
POWER

13

The Developmental State and the Rise of Popular Nationalism: Cause, Coincidence, or Elective Affinity?

Matthias vom Hau

This chapter's starting point is the correspondence between major changes in the institutional development of states and the ideological transformation of nationalism in mid twentieth-century Latin America. The departure from agricultural export-oriented economies and the rise of developmental states were temporally coincident with the departure from liberal-elitist understandings of nationhood, and the rise of popular nationalism as official national ideology. Between 1930 and 1970 most, if not all states in the region adopted class-based and assimilationist conceptions of the nation that celebrated "the people" as the authentic representatives of the national community. Obviously, the timing and extent of this ideological change varied, but nonetheless, it represented the main overall trend in Latin America.

What is the relationship between the rise of developmental states and the emergence of popular nationalism in Latin America? Trying to answer this question, the present chapter explores a variety of plausible explanations. At one extreme stands the argument that treats the developmental state as a direct cause of this ideological transformation, echoing Ernest Gellner's famous contention that nationalism is best understood as a functional prerequisite for urban industrialism.[1] When Latin American state leaders moved away from agro-export oriented economies, and embraced import-substitution industrialization (ISI) as a new economic development strategy, then popular nationalism might have provided them with a convenient tool to legitimate this policy shift, especially because ISI involved redistributing income towards the urban working class to amplify the national consumer base. Seen in this light, representing subordinate sectors as "true" nationals while portraying the old oligarchic order as an obstacle to national progress would help to secure support for potentially divisive measures across politically diverse constituencies. Popular nationalism was therefore actively promoted by vast

---

[1] Gellner, 1983.

public policy programs in areas such as education, culture, mass military service, and others.

Yet, for many authors correlation cannot be understood to imply causation. At this other extreme stands the contention that the temporal congruence between the rise of developmental states in the region and popular nationalism is just a historical coincidence. Following John W. Meyer's world polity approach, one line of reasoning suggests that the emergence of popular nationalism had more to do with world-cultural changes in how the nation was conceived at a global scale.[2] Latin American state leaders adopted popular nationalism because this was what state leaders (and their wider epistemic communities) around the world did. Another body of work implies that the rise of popular nationalism was primarily driven by the commercialization of culture, the expansion of consumer society, and the spread of mass-cultural products such as tabloid newspapers, radio broadcasts and films.[3] In this perspective, corporate mass media and the formation of nationally bounded "imagined communities" around shared consumption habits and tastes were at the root of the growing prevalence of popular nationalism in everyday life and its eventual adoption as official ideology. Either way, according to these arguments the developmental state had little to do with the rise of popular nationalism.

Based on a comparative-historical analysis of Mexico, Argentina, and Peru, this chapter challenges both strands of argument. I argue that popular nationalism was neither a mere legitimation tool of the developmental state, nor completely unrelated to it. Instead, I suggest that the concept of "elective affinity" works better to describe the relationship. The concept of elective affinity was initially employed to describe the preferential combination of chemical substances, then made its way into nineteenth-century romantic literature, most prominently Johann Wolfgang von Goethe's novel *Elective Affinities* (1809) about marriage and erotic attraction. Its use in the social sciences goes back to Max Weber, whose *The Protestant Ethic and the Spirit of Capitalism* (1905) famously postulated a selective affinity between Protestantism and capitalism – that the this-worldly ascetic outlook of many protestant sects was associated with and in many ways facilitated the rise of the specific ethos underpinning modern capitalism. More generally, then, selective affinity describes a close association between two social facts that is neither causal nor merely coincidental. The two appear to go together and sometimes even gravitate towards each other, yet without having a direct causal relationship.[4]

---

[2] Meyer, 1999: 123–146.
[3] Anderson, 1991; Elena, 2011; Karush, 2012; Moreno, 2003; Pilcher, 1998.
[4] On the genealogy of selective affinity and its use in the social sciences since Weber see García, 1992 and Howe, 1978: 366–385.

This is precisely how I use the concept in this chapter. I suggest that the relationship between developmental states and popular nationalism cannot be reduced to one of immediate causality, but is instead filtered, reconfigured, and transformed by political context. Specifically, I suggest that the emergence of anti-oligarchic ruling coalitions led to the adoption of popular nationalism as a new official ideology. Where state leaders sought to distinguish themselves from the old regime and establish political support among previously excluded sectors (e.g., middle and working classes), they came to see popular nationalism as a compelling device to legitimate their agenda and foster political support. And the emergence of these anti-oligarchic ruling coalitions did not necessarily coincide with the rise of developmental states and the implementation of ISI. Rather, the link is best understood as an elective affinity. Developmental states, and the economic development strategies associated with them, enhanced the power of subordinate sectors vis-à-vis established oligarchic elites, but they did not by themselves determine the dynamics of political conflict and the nature of alliance structures in mid twentieth-century Latin America.

Similarly, the connection between the developmental state and differences in the wider resonance of popular nationalism among ordinary citizens is best treated as one of elective affinity. It is certainly true that the implementation of ISI was associated with a substantial increase in state power. Even when taking important exceptions and variations into account, mid twentieth-century Latin American states witnessed a substantial expansion of their administrative and regulatory capacities as well as their territorial reach.[5] Yet, as this chapter will show, the increase in state power associated with the transition from liberal "night-watchman" to developmental states itself did not facilitate broad-based ideological change. Rather, it was the temporal sequence of state expansion and intrastate power relationships that affected the wider resonance of popular nationalism among ordinary citizens. Where state leaders had significant leverage over the construction of the state cultural machinery, and where local state officials tasked with citizen socialization were largely supportive of the new national ideology, popular nationalism likely became a hegemonic discourse. By contrast, where state leaders confronted a cultural machinery already established with fixed organizational routines, and where they were exposed to widespread ideological opposition from local state officials such as teachers, popular nationalism remained a fiercely contested official national ideology. In other words, it was the pre-existing strength of the state, rather than its weakness, that limited the ability of state leaders to institutionalize popular nationalism as an everyday frame of reference.

The chapter organization flows from this argument. The first section traces the transition from liberal-elitist to popular nationalism in Mexico, Argentina,

---

[5] Soifer, 2015; see also the chapter by de Souza in this volume.

and Peru. The three countries are revealing case studies, because they show the full range of such transitions in Latin America. The second section establishes the correlation between this ideological change and the rise of developmental states in the region, while also discussing the limitations of perspectives that suggest either a direct causal relationship or mere historical coincidence. The third and fourth sections develop the chapter's selective affinity approach, both theoretically and empirically. The final section concludes and situates this chapter in relationship to other contributions in the present volume and explores the implications of the main argument for the contemporary study of nationalism and state formation.

THE RISE OF POPULAR NATIONALISM IN MID TWENTIETH-CENTURY LATIN AMERICA

Nationalism constitutes a particular way of framing and experiencing the social world in terms of national identifications and communalities.[6] Its distinctive feature is the notion that the world is first and foremost divided into distinct nations, that states are the political expression of national sovereignty, and that the territorial boundaries of states are or ought to be congruent with the national community.[7] This chapter is primarily concerned with nationalism as an adaptable but explicit and consciously articulated *official ideology* invoked by states to legitimate authority and achieve social control.[8] Specifically, I focus on variations in both the *content* and the wider *resonance* of official national ideologies.

Liberal Nationalism

Even though Mexico, Peru, and Argentina varied dramatically with respect to their colonial history, struggles for national independence, and their postcolonial political development, in all three of them state leaders embraced "liberal nationalism" as official national ideology during the late nineteenth century.[9] An analysis of school textbooks reveals that this form of nationalism fused Enlightment ideals of political citizenship with highly exclusionary and

---

[6] Brubaker, 2004; Calhoun, 1997.   [7] Gellner, 1983.   [8] Hobsbawm, 1990; Smith, 1986.

[9] The term "liberal nationalism" has a specific meaning in the Latin American context and is widely used in the historiography (e.g., Brading, 1991; Halperín Donghi, 1987: 141–165). It fuses the nationalist principle of popular sovereignty with a peculiar blend of liberalism. Distinct from the contemporary use of the word in the United States, and also distinct from the classical liberalism associated with Adam Smith, John Locke, and John Stuart Mill, the form of liberalism present in nineteenth-century Latin America was strongly influenced by the philosophical positivism of Auguste Comte and its emphasis on natural social hierarchies (e.g., Eastwood, 2004: 331–357; Mahoney, 2001). Latin American liberalism thus supported the idea that all people are equally capable of reason and progress, while also portraying the lower classes as biologically incapable of governing themselves.

hierarchical visions of the national community.[10] Liberal national discourses emphasized the political underpinnings of nationhood and celebrated the respective constitutional framework in each country as a major source of attachment and pride. For instance, Mexican textbooks depicted the 1857 Constitution as a central unifying force and teleological ending point of national history. In all three countries, official history was organized around the emergence of a binding legal and political order, while the conflicts between central state elites and regional strongmen that characterized Mexico, Argentina, and Peru during the early nineteenth century were largely absent from these accounts.

Another central feature of liberal nationalism was its emphasis on creating a "civilized nation."[11] During the late nineteenth century in Latin America, official national ideologies were deeply enmeshed in positivism and advanced Comtean ideas about biologically determined social hierarchies and the efficient management of society from above. The spread of "civilization" – a category associated with whiteness, economic modernization, and an urban and cosmopolitan European culture – appeared as the ideal path for achieving national unity and progress. In Mexico, Argentina, and Peru textbooks represented the indigenous population as the main manifestation of "barbarism," to be overcome through education, European migration, or even outright extermination campaigns. Accordingly, national history represented an evolution through different stages, moving toward greater degrees of civilization. Benevolent elites were at the center stage of this process, and accounts of national history focused on major political leaders, whether Aztec or Inca rulers, colonial viceroys, or postcolonial presidents.

Liberal nationalism was not just official rhetoric. In all three countries mundane interactions between state agencies and ordinary citizens intensified. At least in the urban areas public schooling expanded and schoolteachers emerged as major promoters of the nationalizing state. In their majority these new recruits embraced the official project of creating a "civilized nation" and countered regionalisms with the vision of a unified national history.[12] State-sponsored civic festivals gained in public importance and often attracted crowds of several tens or even hundreds of thousands of visitors.[13] Outside the

---

[10] If not indicated otherwise, the school textbook analysis referenced in this section draws on previously published work that also provides a more thorough methodological discussion of coding and sampling strategies (vom Hau, 2009: 127–154, 2013: 146–166). Textbooks are a feasible source to trace official national ideologies because states put major efforts into regulating school textbooks, for instance through special approval commissions. The actual textbook analysis draws upon evidence from sixty to seventy textbooks for each country, examining officially approved texts on national history, civic education, and language instruction used in public primary schools.

[11] For the distinction between *civilized nation* and *homogenous nation* see Quijada, 2000.

[12] Portocarrero and Oliart, 1989; Spalding, 1972: 31–61; Vaughan, 1982.

[13] Beezley, 2008; Bertoni, 2001.

sphere of direct state control, widely available calendars and almanacs celebrated particular heroes and the respective national constitutions.[14] Studies also show that contents of liberal nationalism found entry into public events such as puppeteer performances or street festivals, and informed everyday categories and consumption habits, especially among the emerging urban middle sectors.[15] These examples illustrate that liberal nationalism gradually became a regular product of state organizations and gained salience in the lifeworld of ordinary citizens in late nineteenth-century Mexico, Argentina, and Peru.

Popular Nationalism

The concept of "popular nationalism" is grounded in common characterizations of modern Latin American history. This type of nationalism emerged in the context of broader economic and sociopolitical change during the early and mid twentieth century, precisely when previously marginalized sectors mobilized for their political and symbolic inclusion, and when both fascism and communism gained increasing prominence as global ideological models. Scholars often describe this epoch as "populism" or the "populist period," defined by political and ideological projects evoking the idea of a national people in opposition to an elite.[16]

During well-defined periods, popular nationalism came to replace liberal nationalism as official national ideology in each of the three countries. In Mexico, this ideological transformation unfolded during the 1930s, when ideas of Mexico as a *mestizo* nation of peasants, workers, and smallholders gained prominence as official national ideology. For example, school textbook accounts of national history described Spanish colonialism as a foreign invasion and emphasized the critical role of popular sectors in Mexican independence. A comparable ideological change took place in Peronist Argentina during the 1940s and 1950s – in the absence of revolutionary transformation. Under Perón, official national ideology began to portray the "New Argentina" as a Hispanic and Catholic nation composed of the dispossessed masses of *descamisados* ("shirtless ones"). Textbooks depicted the Peronist movement as destined to complete the unfinished historical task of overcoming the legacies of colonialism and achieving complete economic independence. In Peru, it was during the 1960s that the contents of official national ideology changed, celebrating the precolonial roots of Peruvian identity and portraying popular classes as historical protagonists. Under the left-wing dictatorship of Juan Velasco (1968–1975), Túpac Amaru – the leader of an indigenous uprising during the 1780s – gained status as the original initiator of national independence, and official national discourses celebrated peasants and workers as "true" national subjects.

---

[14] vom Hau, 2017.　　[15] Beezley, *Mexican National Identity*. 2008; Parker, 1998; Pilcher, 1998.
[16] Jansen, 2011: 75–96; Stein, 1980.

Yet the wider resonance of this ideological transformation varied across the three countries.[17] In Mexico, popular nationalism was routinized as a regular product of the state cultural machinery, which in turn contributed to its growing resonance in the lives of ordinary citizens. For example, the majority of Mexican teachers active during the 1930s had no issues using educational materials infused with popular nationalism. The new history textbooks published under the government of Lázaro Cárdenas (1934–1940) received broad teacher appraisal and were rapidly incorporated into classroom practices. Similarly, calendars and almanacs published during this period embraced the masses as authentic Mexicans and drew an intrinsic linkage between the Aztec empire and the modern nation.[18] Cultural tastes and consumption patterns also changed during this period. For instance, the corn tortilla became an encompassing symbol of Mexican identity.[19] Thus, in Mexico popular national discourses translated into everyday forms of nationhood.

By contrast, in Argentina under Perón the institutionalization of popular nationalism stalled. The practices of schoolteachers active during the Peronist era reveal that they rejected popular forms of nationhood found in the new textbooks. Consequently, they employed a variety of strategies to circumvent the transmission of these official national discourses.[20] Public celebrations of peasants and workers were largely confined to official poster and billboard campaigns and did not enter commercial production to the same extent as in Mexico.[21] Popular tastes and consumption patterns remained politically charged. For instance, the association of tango with an authentic Argentinean national culture was fiercely contested among Peronists and anti-Peronists.[22] More generally, conflicts over public policy and public office often morphed into conflicts over national belonging and identity.

Peru falls in between the other two cases. During the 1960s and 1970s popular nationalism gained hold both in national politics and everyday life. The majority of schoolteachers embraced the contents of the new educational materials issued under the Velasco military government.[23] Similarly, patriotic rituals came to celebrate the Andean roots of national culture and began to display indigenous dances, food, and handicrafts.[24] At the same time, popular nationalism did not fully replace the previously dominant liberal nationalism.

---

[17] The larger study this article draws upon combined two sorts of primary sources with relevant secondary literature to investigate the wider resonance of official national ideologies in everyday forms of nationhood. One is teachers as the first transmission belt of textbooks. The others are widely used calendars and postcards as sources outside the sphere of the state (vom Hau, 2017).

[18] vom Hau, 2017.   [19] Pilcher, 1998.

[20] For instance, Argentinean teachers frequently used history textbooks exclusively for grammar exercises and often refused to take part in official training institutes. See vom Hau, 2009.

[21] Gené, 2005.   [22] Azzi, 2002: 25–40.

[23] vom Hau and Biffi, 2014: 191–216; Wilson, 2007: 719–746.

[24] Sánchez, 2002; Wood, 2005.

For example, a significant minority of teachers continued to use textbooks that promoted the creation of Peru as a "civilized nation," while the statue of the Spanish conqueror Francisco Pizarro continued to dominate the central square in the Peruvian capital.[25] Thus, popular nationalism in Peru was significantly less contested than in Argentina, yet did not achieve the same extent of hegemonic acceptance as in Mexico.

THE DEVELOPMENTAL STATE AND POPULAR NATIONALISM – CAUSE OR COINCIDENCE?

How to account for these distinct transformations of nationalism in Mexico, Peru, and Argentina? There are certainly a number of plausible explanations that could and should be explored in response to this puzzle. As I develop elsewhere in greater detail, the different patterns of ideological change that unfolded in the three countries cannot be accounted for by focusing on ethnic demographics or geopolitics alone.[26] Specifically, the transformations of nationalism in Mexico, Peru, and Argentina are not reducible to the respective demographic composition of the national population. If the introduction of popular-assimilationist nationalism was first and foremost meant to deal with the problem of how to nationalize an ethnoracially diverse polity, then Peru, holding the proportionally largest indigenous population among the three, should have undergone the most dramatic transition. And if, on the other hand, homogeneity facilitated the installation of a new national ideology, then Argentina should have undergone a hegemonic transformation. Similarly, international threats to territorial integrity, whether the Mexican-American War (1846–1848) and the French Invasion (1861–1866) in Mexico or the War of the Pacific (1878–1884) in Peru, did not instigate the adoption of popular nationalism in the two countries.[27]

What other macrohistorical changes might then help to explain the puzzle at hand? Given the overall thrust of the volume, this chapter is primarily concerned with unpacking the role played by the rise of developmental states in shaping the distinct transformations of nationalism that unfolded in Mexico, Peru, and Argentina. The historical record certainly reveals a close correlation between the liberal-elitist nationalism and the dominant development model that prevailed in the three countries during the late nineteenth century. The idea that economic growth and collective well-being would be achieved through the export of primary commodities informed much of economic policy making and state building more generally. Subsequent decades witnessed the surge, even

---

[25] Varón Gabai, 2006: 217–236.   [26] vom Hau, 2017.

[27] The larger book project (vom Hau, 2017) also details why rival explanations that emphasize changes in global models of nationhood, democratization, social revolution, political incorporation, and distinct legacies of national independence ultimately remain incomplete or inadequate to explain the puzzle at hand.

though with substantial variation across the three countries, of a radically different development model.

The Developmental State as a Cause of Popular Nationalism?

For one thing, the rise of developmental states implied that state leaders embraced ISI as the economic development strategy of their choice. Closely related but not reducible to it, they pursued the construction of a more interventionist state apparatus that would be actively involved in the transformation of the economy, most importantly by breaking down resistance against market exchange, managing human capital formation, and protecting citizens against the harshest consequences of capitalism.[28] Seen in this light, it is possible to conceive of a number of plausible causal linkages between the emergence of developmental states, and the adoption and institutionalization of popular nationalism.

ISI and Popular Nationalism

ISI involved redistributing income towards the urban working class in order to amplify the national consumer base, while investments in human capital and class transformation required substantial public investments. Seen in this light, popular nationalism provided state elites with a convenient tool to legitimate and dignify this policy shift. Representing subordinate sectors as "true" nationals, while portraying the old oligarchic order as an obstacle to national progress, would help to secure support for potentially divisive measures across politically diverse constituencies.

It is also possible to conceive of a causal link between ISI and the wider resonance of popular nationalism. Mexico, Argentina, and Peru differed in the extent to which ISI became the dominant economic and social policy paradigm. And this variation closely maps onto the distinct transformations of nationalism. Mexico saw a significant break with the previous export-oriented development model, whereas in Argentina and Peru the policy shift was more muted, and the oligarchy remained a dominant force in the country's economy.[29] Accordingly, established agricultural elites had greater political and organizational powers to support the persistence of liberal nationalism.

While being theoretically and empirically plausible, such a focus on developmental states ultimately cannot account for the puzzle at hand. Most importantly, in Argentina, the rise of the developmental state model did not coincide with the ascendance of Perón; ISI, together with a more professionally run, interventionist state had already become a dominant model during the 1920s and 1930s.[30] Similarly, in Peru the governments of the 1950s and 1960s

---

[28] Gereffi, and Wyman, eds. 1990; Hirschman, 1968: 1–32; Thorp, 1992: 181–195.
[29] Villarreal, 1990: 292–320; Jenkins, 1991: 202–208; Thorp, 1992: 182–186.
[30] Kaufman, 1990: 110–138.

already pursued economic policies that broadly followed the ISI framework and implemented social policy concerned with class transformation and human capital creation, without changing the established liberal nationalism. In Mexico, by contrast, the rise of a more interventionist state took off during the 1930s, when state leaders had already adopted popular nationalism as an official national ideology. An explanation concerned with the rise of the developmental state, and the economic and social development strategies associated with it, thus has difficulties in accounting for the timing of when state leaders adopted popular nationalism as a new official national ideology.

Upon closer scrutiny, the causal connection between the rise of the developmental state and the wider resonance of popular nationalism is equally problematic. When treating the relative contribution of export agriculture vis-à-vis manufacturing as an – arguably crude – indicator for the organizational power and ideological influence of these economic sectors, then the empirical record does not consistently support the proposed explanation. Argentina witnessed the most dramatic upsurge in industrial manufacturing during the mid twentieth century, while export-oriented agriculture remained surprisingly extensive in Mexico.[31]

Interventionist States and Popular Nationalism

Similarly, the substantial increase in state strength, commonly associated with the rise of developmental states, cannot account for the distinct transformations of nationalism found in Mexico, Argentina, and Peru. Among the three countries mid twentieth-century Argentina was by far the strongest state. In order to facilitate public-sector intervention in the economy, Argentine state leaders modified the internal functioning of the state apparatus, improved the professional training of civil servants, fostered the specialization of state agencies, and installed more centralized control mechanisms during the 1910s and 1920s.[32] Consequently, by 1930 representatives of the central state, whether police officers, tax officials, or social workers, could even be found in many of the most remote parts of the country.[33] The development of the state cultural machinery followed this overall trend. During the 1910s and 1920s state authorities invested substantial resources into public schooling and teacher training.[34] They also managed to centralize administrative control over education by expanding the federal school network, enhancing private-school supervision, and streamlining the curricula of state and municipal schools.[35]

---

[31] Thorp, 1992.   [32] Campione and Mazzeo, 1999: 87, 95–99, 110.   [33] Romero, 2001.

[34] The Argentinean government earmarked 3 percent of the national budget for education in 1900, and 13 percent in 1914 (Spalding, 1972: 52). The number of public-school teachers increased from around 8,600 to 21,500. By 1932 around 69 percent of the relevant population was enrolled in primary schools. (Gandulfo, 1991: 314–315).

[35] Puiggrós, 1992: 17–64.

In Mexico, and especially in Peru during the same time period, the growth of state power was much lower. The armed phase of the Mexican Revolution (1910–1920) decreased the already limited reach of the central state. Especially between 1913 and 1915, revolutionary factions interrupted and destroyed much of the physical presence of state organizations across the national territory.[36] Similarly, outside the major urban areas, most of the primary schools closed down, and many of the teachers turned their backs on the old regime and became involved in the revolutionary struggles.[37] During the 1920s the rebuilding of railway and road networks was slow. And while the newly formed Secretaria de Educación Pública (SEP) under José Vasconcelos engaged in a number of ambitious projects to transform a conflict-ridden society into a cohesive nation, its actual institution-building record remained limited.[38] State power was even more limited in early and mid twentieth-century Peru. The presence of police stations, courts, health clinics, and schools remained largely confined to coastal cities and major economic centers in the highlands, while in many Andean and Amazonian communities any organizational representation of the central state continued to be absent.[39] These variations in state power thus would predict Argentina to have experienced the most extensive institutionalization of popular nationalism. By contrast, the relative weakness of the Mexican state would constitute an obstacle to the wider resonance of popular nationalism.

Developmental States and Popular Nationalism: Mere Historical Coincidence?

Does this mean that the rise of developmental states and popular nationalism in Mexico, Argentina, and Peru was just a historical coincidence? A variety of theoretical perspectives would answer this question with a resounding "yes," especially those that are generally skeptical about the central role of states in transformations of nationalism.

World Culture and Popular Nationalism

Most prominently, when applying world polity theory and its focus on a supranational "world culture" to the puzzle posed by mid twentieth-century Mexico, Argentina, and Peru, the transformations of nationalism in the three countries were first and foremost motivated by changes in global models of nationhood that provided local actors with a template for legitimate action.[40] State leaders

---

[36] Knight, 2002: 212–253.   [37] Cockcroft, 1968.

[38] In 1922, 8.9 percent of the Mexican federal budget was spent on education; in 1928 it was 8.0 percent. The number of primary schools decreased from 12,271 in 1907 to 9,222 in 1920, and reached 16,692 in 1928 (Vaughan, 1982: 149–153).

[39] Nugent, 1994: 333–369; Soifer, 2015.

[40] Lechner and Boli, 2005; Meyer, Boli, Thomas, and Ramirez, 1997: 144–181. This world culture exerts pressure toward cultural and institutional convergence, by establishing normative and cognitive scripts that designate particular ways of understanding and experiencing the social

in Mexico, Argentina, and Peru drew on global models of nationhood when reformulating official national ideologies.[41] During the late nineteenth and early twentieth centuries, in the context of the decline of the Habsburg and Ottoman empires, European states tended to evoke particularistic and organic conceptions of national identity.[42] And after World War I, when organized labor emerged as a major political force in the core of the world economy, European states embraced national discourses that emphasized "the people" as bearers of sovereignty and national culture.[43] These variants gradually became global models when states in the periphery emulated the new currents of nationhood found in the core countries to legitimize their political projects.[44]

In my estimation, world polity theory is particularly strong when establishing the wider context for the transition from liberal to popular nationalism in Mexico, Argentina, and Peru during the mid twentieth century. No scholar would seriously question that the global diffusion of popular conceptions of nationhood had enormous implications for local manifestations of nationalism. In Argentina, for instance, Peronist imageries of national identity closely resembled the aesthetic language found in the United States during the New Deal era.[45]

Yet, local transformations are not simply reflections of global trends. A narrow emphasis on the global diffusion of new understandings of nationhood directs attention away from major local differences and overlooks important variations in paths of ideological change across the three countries. States did not just copy or replicate global models of popular nationalism. Instead, state leaders reshaped global templates and infused them with different meanings when advancing particular visions of national history and identity.[46] Moreover, an emphasis on global diffusion cannot account for variations in the resonance of popular nationalism among ordinary citizens in Mexico, Argentina, and Peru. If we take seriously the differences in the wider resonance of popular nationalism, it is necessary to analytically differentiate between the adoption and the institutionalization of a new national ideology, and the distinct causal factors driving each process.

Cultural Industries, Mass Consumption, and Popular Nationalism

Another body of work that supports the historical coincidence between the rise of developmental states and popular nationalism is primarily concerned with

world as rational, efficient, and legitimate. The lack of exclusive control over world culture provides ample room for change. Moreover, the inconsistencies and contradictions of world culture itself are responsible for variants among global cultural models: Tensions between principles of cultural autonomy, homogenization, and sovereign authority inherent in nationalism license the emergence of distinct global templates of nationhood (Meyer, Boli, Thomas, and Ramirez, 1997).

[41] Meyer, 1999.   [42] Brubaker, 1996.   [43] Silver, 2003; Goswami, 2002: 770–799.
[44] Wimmer, 2012.   [45] Gené, 2005.   [46] Goswami, 2002.

market-driven processes of ideological change. In this perspective, transformations of nationalism in Latin America were primarily shaped by capitalist development and the commercialization of culture. The basic intuition is that the expansion of cultural industries and mass consumer society facilitated both the adoption and wider resonance of popular nationalism.

Why should that have been the case? One variant of this argument draws inspiration from Benedict Anderson's emphasis on the critical role of "print capitalism" in the spread of nationalism: The relentless capitalist pursuit of profit might have driven cultural industries such as publishing houses, radio broadcasters, and film companies to cater their products to broader audiences by advancing class-based understandings of nationhood and celebrating subordinate sectors as protagonists of national history.[47] This line of argument also assumes that the consumption of the same tabloid newspapers, radio programs, and films fostered unified spaces of communication in everyday life and ultimately propelled ordinary citizens to embrace popular nationalism and conceive of themselves as an integral part of the national community.

In the recent historiography on mid twentieth-century Latin America, another variant of this argument can be detected that puts greater emphasis on transnational processes.[48] In this perspective, the growing dominance of the United States in domains such as film, radio-broadcasting, and music, but also in the consumption of food and clothing, led to counter-movements. Mexican, Argentine, and Peruvian capitalists responded to the real or perceived threat of cultural imperialism by promoting "authentically national" cultural products and practices that were distinct from US-dominated culture but at the same time still compatible with mass consumption. Seen in this light, the celebration of the masses in Mexican commercial radio or Argentine cinema and the elevation of traditional cooking to a national popular cuisine by Mexican food producers was thus the (indirect) result of US dominance in cultural production.[49] More specifically, this perspective suggests that differences in the exposure to and negotiation of US-dominated mass culture were at the root of distinct transitions from liberal to popular nationalism in Mexico, Argentina, and Peru.

The focus on cultural industries and mass consumer society provides important complementary insights, but it ultimately cannot account for the different transformations of nationalism in the three countries. Most importantly, this line of reasoning has difficulties in explaining why popular nationalism gained hegemonic status in mid twentieth-century Mexico, but not in Argentina. The latter probably had the most powerful cultural industry among the three countries. Argentina had a larger number of periodicals than Mexico, and among the most prominent dailies and weeklies, the Argentine ones enjoyed a wider circulation than their Mexican counterparts.[50] Similarly,

---

[47] Anderson, 1991.   [48] Elena, 2011; Karush, 2012; Moreno, 2003; Pilcher, 1998.
[49] Hayes, 2000; Karush, 2012; Pilcher, 1998.   [50] Plotkin, 2002; Cósio Villegas, 1973.

during the 1930s and 1940s, a larger percentage of Argentines had access to radio broadcasting and went to the movies, when compared to Mexico.[51] Finally, Argentina was more integrated into US-dominated circuits of cultural production than Mexico, as for example is indicated by the market share of Hollywood-produced films in mid twentieth-century Argentina.[52]

More generally, the emphasis on cultural industries ignores the state as a key actor involved in the expansion of mass consumption. States provided the legal and regulatory underpinnings and contributed the necessary infrastructure. States were also crucial nationalizing actors in their own right, with varying capacities to engage the public sphere with their own understandings of nationhood. A comprehensive explanation of popular nationalism in Mexico, Argentina, and Peru therefore needs to incorporate the state when seeking to account for the diverse transformations of the phenomenon.

THE ANALYTICAL FRAMEWORK: RULING COALITIONS, INTRASTATE RELATIONS, AND TRANSFORMATIONS OF NATIONALISM

As discussed in the previous section, the rise of popular nationalism as an influential ideology in Mexico, Argentina, and Peru was neither a direct consequence of the rise of developmental states nor a mere historical coincidence. The remainder of the chapter focuses on developing an explanation that moves beyond these two contrasting perspectives. My theoretical perspective remains state-centered. I argue that a focus on state–society relations, the sequence of state formation, and the inner workings of the state can account for the distinct transformations of nationalism found in the three countries.

The Adoption of Popular Nationalism as an Official Ideology

To explain why the contents of official nationalisms changed in Mexico, Argentina, and Peru, I draw on arguments that see state action as fundamentally shaped by power configurations and alliance structures between state authorities and different social groups.[53,54] In this theoretical perspective, changes in ruling coalitions are likely to instigate the adoption of a different national ideology.[55]

---

[51] Hayes, 2000;
[52] Plotkin, 2002.During the 1940s and 1950s, the United States held a market share of up to 80 percent in the Argentine film market, whereas in Mexico during the same period Hollywood films enjoyed a 50 to 60 percent market share. See Falicov, 2007: 6; Fein, 2004: 103–135.
[53] See Collier and Collier, 1991; Rueschemeyer, Stephens, and Stephens, 1992; Slater, 2010; Waldner, 1999.
[54] Alliances are usually conceptualized as regularized patterns of interaction and cooperation among distinct political actors, and are structured by shared principles and norms. Burgess, 1999: 105–134.
[55] Hechter, 2000; Wimmer, 2002.

The decline of established ruling coalitions composed of state elites and entrenched economic elites may initiate the refashioning of official understandings of nationhood. Such a context, usually marked by high levels of intra-elite conflict and changes in political leadership, makes state leaders more likely to draw on a different ideological orientation for consolidating power and attaining legitimacy. By embracing new conceptions of nationhood, state elites represent themselves as distinct from the old regime and seek to reinforce new political alignments. Moreover, changes in alliance structures may also lead to the adoption of a new national ideology because social groups that were previously excluded from state power have gained in political weight. When empowered as members of the ruling coalition, subordinate sectors are better able to pressure for redefining the boundaries of the national political community, while state leaders are bound to consider those new conceptions of nationhood in their quest for representing themselves as acting in the interest of "the people."[56]

Seen in this light, my explanatory framework includes the possibility that the rise of developmental states in Mexico, Argentina, and Peru was connected to the ascendance of popular nationalism. Yet it was most likely an elective affinity: The institutional and policy changes associated with the developmental state model might have led to the rise of new political alliance structures. For example, ISI's programmatic support for the urban working class, whether by enhancing its human capital base or increasing its bargaining power vis-à-vis capital, might have had the (unintended) consequence of constituting organized labor as a new collective actor to be taken seriously in the political arena. But new ruling coalitions might have also been the consequence of a host of other factors, including revolutionary transformations, the demographic reorganization of a country, or splits within the state, for example between the military and civilian governments. Put differently, a focus on power configurations and ruling coalitions provides a mid-range theoretical account for why states adopt new national ideologies. This approach treats the rise of developmental states, not as a direct, but as an indirect and partial cause – one of the plausible causal factors involved in bringing about new political alliance structures and thus a factor that is at least one more step removed in the causal chain.

The Wider Resonance of Popular Nationalism

In order to account for variations in the extent to which popular nationalism achieved wider resonance among ordinary citizens, I put the analytical spotlight on the inner workings of the state and the temporal order of state formation.[57]

---

[56] Wimmer, 2008: 970–1022.
[57] I conceptualize states as composed of differentiated networks of institutions and personnel that reach out from the center to control the territory they claim to govern (Soifer, 2015; see also Tilly, 1994: 131–146; Weber, 1976).

Drawing on Michael Mann's conception of state strength as both infrastructural and relational, I argue that the institutionalization of a new national ideology as a hegemonic frame of reference requires organizational resources and territorial reach, but it also requires support and active collaboration from the rank-and-file state servants.[58] Strained relationships with local state officials who are tasked with socializing citizens or otherwise disseminating official ideological projects undermine the ability to institutionalize different understandings of nationhood. Moreover, a firmly established state apparatus itself constitutes a double-edged sword for the consolidation of a new national ideology. In a state infrastructure already established, ideological production is deeply routinized in organizational practices and often carried out by professional cadres with substantial autonomy from the center of command.[59] Newly adopted national ideologies thus only become hegemonic if state leaders have significant leverage over the construction of the state cultural machinery, and if they can also rely on support from local state actors. By contrast, a new national ideology remains fiercely contested when state leaders confront an already established cultural machinery with fixed routines and local radiating actors that oppose the new official nationalism.

This novel emphasis on the temporal sequence of state development and intrastate relations to explain transformations of nationalism departs from existing scholarship that associates state strength with dominant ideologies, and state weakness with ideological conflict. In fact, the elective affinities approach introduced in this chapter highlights the irony that it is the strength of the state, rather than its weakness, that constrains state leaders in their ability to easily implement a newly adopted national ideology.

A SELECTIVE AFFINITY BETWEEN THE DEVELOPMENTAL STATE AND THE RISE OF POPULAR NATIONALISM IN LATIN AMERICA

Equipped with this analytical framework I return to the cases of mid-twentieth-century Mexico, Argentina, and Peru. In contrast to arguments that either highlight the rise of developmental states as the principal cause, or a mere historical coincidence to explain the installation of popular nationalism, my comparative historical analysis argues for a selective affinity between developmental states and popular nationalism. As will be discussed in the present section, developmental states played only an indirect and partial role in the transformations of nationalism in the three countries. The strengthening of popular nationalism was certainly one of the goals pursued by the

---

[58] Mann, 1993. See also Soifer, 2015, and Soifer and vom Hau, 2008: 213. I use state power and state strength interchangeably.
[59] For related arguments on state-building see Ertman, 1997 and López-Alves, 2000. For a more general treatment of timing and sequence see Pierson, 2004.

developmental states in Mexico, Peru, and Argentina, but the strategies applied to pursue this goal were fragmentary, and they changed and diversified in the conflict with several other social actors pursuing their own ideological projects around nationalism.

Changing Ruling Coalitions and the Adoption of Popular Nationalism

Liberal nationalism, the official state ideology in late nineteenth-century Mexico, Argentina, and Peru, was contested. Growing and increasingly politicized middle and popular sectors demanded political and symbolic inclusion.[60] Similarly, regional elites felt threatened by the rising power of the central state, and politically mobilized Catholics protested the expanding "ideological work" of state organizations that upset the established balance of church and state.[61] Specific social forces varied in their framing strategies, organizational infrastructure, and constituencies, yet they contested established notions about national history and identity and infused them with different political meanings. Their challenge to liberal nationalism also drew inspiration from transnational trends. From the late nineteenth century onwards, nationalist mobilization intensified around the globe, while national claims increasingly built on the ideal of a culturally homogeneous nation and stressed the principle of popular sovereignty and self-determination.[62]

Yet, it was changes in ruling coalitions that led to the adoption of popular nationalism as official national ideology. In Mexico revolutionary struggles led to the ascendance of a new state elite during the 1910s and 1920s, composed of provincial elites and middle sectors.[63] Confronted with a highly mobilized society and eager to distinguish themselves from the Porfirian era, these new state authorities envisioned Mexicans as a transcendental "cosmic race" of *mestizos* and celebrated the Aztec past as the critical epoch of national history. During the same time period, labor unrest intensified in Argentina, against the backdrop of the almost complete demographic reorganization of the country. The Radical Party, representing middle sectors and elite dissidents, came to power and adopted a different political language.[64] Reformulated understandings of nationhood depicted Argentina as a *crisol de razas* ("fusion of races," the local version of the melting pot) and celebrated the *gaucho* as the most authentic national figure. In early twentieth-century Peru, subordinate mobilization was more limited, and the government of Augusto Leguía (1919–1930) continued to embrace liberal nationalism as the official national ideology, even though this modernizing regime at least initially sought to differentiate itself from the oligarchic establishment.[65]

---

[60] Córdova, 1981; Cotler, 2005; Horowitz, 1990; Meyer, 2000: 823–880; Quijano, 1981.
[61] de la Cadena, 2000; Florescano, 1999; Klaiber, 1996; Meyer, 1974; Rock, 1993.
[62] Goswami, 2002; Wimmer, 2012.   [63] Meyer, 2000.   [64] Rock, 1975.   [65] Klarén, 2000.

The most dramatic changes in the contents of official national ideologies unfolded when subordinate movements gained in political weight – linked but not reducible to the rise of developmental states in the three countries – and new ruling coalitions with those societal forces formed. In Mexico under Cárdenas an alliance consolidated between organized labor, peasants, and postrevolutionary state elites.[66] Even though this alliance entailed their domestication, popular sectors obtained substantial material and symbolic concessions, and executive authorities made subaltern interests an integral part of their political calculations.[67] This new ruling coalition pursued ideological change. Postrevolutionary state elites coopted producers of popular nationalism into the state cultural machinery and adopted a different official national ideology. For example, artists associated with the labour movement, most prominently the Mexican muralist Diego Rivera, found themselves on the government's payroll, while activists of the Communist Party were appointed to posts in the SEP.[68] Subsequently, school textbooks approved by the SEP emphasized peasant and worker opposition against colonial authorities as the logical precursor to the Revolution, which marked the endpoint of subordinate struggles for a more egalitarian, industrialized, and economically independent Mexico. Ideas about Mexico as a "Catholic nation" did not enter state-sponsored national discourses.

Peronist Argentina witnessed a comparable adoption of popular nationalism, even in the absence of revolutionary change. When Perón ascended to power, he built a highly personalistic political movement based on the support from organized labor and political Catholics. Similar to Mexico under Cárdenas, this new ruling coalition combined increased state control over subordinate sectors with far-reaching concessions.[69] In contrast to Mexico, this alliance also included political Catholics, at least during the initial phase of Peronism. This group, along with labor leaders and associated cultural entrepreneurs, obtained top-level positions within the state cultural machinery. Following the directives of these new educational authorities, a new generation of textbooks portrayed subordinate classes as protagonists of national history, and the historical actions of the "oligarchy" as antithetical to national progress. The new Peronist texts also fused the idea of Argentina as a *crisol de razas* with an increased emphasis on the Catholic roots of the nation.[70]

Peru during the 1930s and 1940s constituted a sharp contrast to Mexico and Argentina: Popular nationalism was not adopted as state-sponsored national ideology. Under the government of José Bustamante y Rivero (1945–1948) the country experienced a brief democratic opening.[71] Alliances with oligarchic elites crumbled, and state authorities sought to build a multi-class coalition. As a matter of fact, the Bustamante government appointed a number of

[66] Hamilton, 1982.   [67] Knight, 2002.   [68] Azuela, 2005; Vaughan, 1997.
[69] Sigal, 2002, 481–522; Torre, 1990.   [70] Plotkin, 2002.   [71] Cotler, 2005.

indigenista intellectuals and Catholic activists to leading positions within the state cultural machinery.[72] Yet, their impact was limited. The new alliance structures, suffering from massive internal conflicts, proved to be highly volatile and ultimately too short-lived for the adoption of popular nationalism. Only three years later, in 1948, a coup ended this brief experiment and state power remained grounded in oligarchic arrangements and *indigenista* and labor leaders were ousted from government positions.

The main adoption of popular nationalism unfolded under Velasco during the 1960s and 1970s, a period often described as a "revolution from above."[73] More than any previous government in modern Peruvian history, the military government marshalled full autonomy from the traditional oligarchy.[74] Concerned about the intensity of subordinate militancy and eager to distinguish itself from the old established elite, Velasco embraced popular nationalism as official national ideology. An integral part of this ideological change was an encompassing educational reform with the aim to create the "new Peruvian man" able to "shed the bonds of internal and external domination."[75] Velasco recruited political leaders and public intellectuals affiliated with the Communist Party of Peru (PCP – Unidad), the Movement of Social Progressives (MSP), and the Catholic movement into important administrative positions. Together with the help of these civilian elites, military officers worked on the design of new textbooks, the training of teachers, and the formation of radio programs, artisan fairs, and other state initiatives focused on the dissemination of the new national ideology.[76]

State Development and the Wider Resonance of Popular Nationalism

Popular nationalism eventually replaced liberal nationalism as the state-sponsored national ideology in Mexico, Peru, and Argentina. Yet, the extent to which this new national discourse consolidated as a regular product of state organizations, and achieved resonance as the dominant conception of nationhood, depended on the temporal sequence of state formation, and on intrastate relations between the center of command and actors embedded in state-radiating institutions.

In postrevolutionary Mexico during the 1930s, temporal congruence between state infrastructural development and the adoption of popular nationalism, as well as support from within the state, facilitated the resonance of the new adopted ideology. The dramatic expansion of state organizations helped to form new routines for ideological production. During the 1930s Mexico overcame the revolutionary decline of state power. Especially during

---

[72] Contreras, 2004; Portocarrero and Oliart, 1989.   [73] Palmer, 1973; Trimberger, 1978.
[74] Cotler, 2005.   [75] Salazar Bondy, 1975: 29.   [76] Stepan, 1978; Wood, 2005.

the *sexenio* of Cárdenas (1934–1940) state authorities managed to expand the reach of the central state apparatus.[77] The agrarian reform helped to establish a continued presence of various state agencies even in remote rural areas. Similar patterns can be observed for education. The SEP gained control over many municipal and state schools, engaged in the construction of new federal schools, and invested in the training of a new teacher generation.[78] The revolutionary state elites also became increasingly invested in the control and funding of radio broadcasting and cinema, and introduced a number of new national holidays, such as the public commemoration of the revolutionary hero Emiliano Zapata.[79] While the specificities of state formation need to be treated with some caution and there were important subnational variations, the overall expansion of the state apparatus helped to turn the new national ideology into a regular product of state organizations.[80]

Another facilitator was the ideological consensus between the center of command and the state's radiating institutions. The support from actors embedded within the state cultural machinery greatly contributed to the hegemonic status of popular nationalism. Most prominently, the majority of teachers active during the 1930s largely followed suit and embraced class-based understandings of national identity and history.[81] A self-styled revolutionary vanguard, teachers were mostly young and inexperienced. As recent recruits into the profession, they largely welcomed the highly ideological teacher training initiated by the SEP. And even if they had wanted to, during the 1930s Mexican teachers did not exhibit the sense of professional identity and autonomy to effectively challenge the ideological project pursued by the post-revolutionary regime.[82]

Not surprisingly, once institutionalized as a regular product of state organizations under Cárdenas, popular nationalism remained both an official project and an everyday frame of reference, at least up to the late 1960s.[83] One of the consequences of its hegemony was that political confrontations between state elites and various social forces became "uncoupled" from contestations

---

[77] Knight, 2002.

[78] During the 1930s between 12 and 14 percent of the Mexican national budget was dedicated to public education (Knight, 1994b: 393–444, 424). The percentage of children between six and ten years old attending primary schools increased from 30 percent in 1910 to 70 percent in 1940 (Vaughan, 1997: 25).

[79] Hayes, 2000; Knight, 1994b; O'Malley, 1986.

[80] For instance, data on education spending during the 1930s tend to overshadow the fact that many schools suffered from shortages in resources and organization (Knight, 1994b). Similarly, and to an important extent depending on prior state–society relations established during Porfiriato, in some Mexican states the new rural teachers were able to gain the trust of local communities, while in other states their relationship was highly conflictual (Vaughan, 1997).

[81] vom Hau, 2009.   [82] Rockwell, 2007; Vaughan, 1997.

[83] An indication for this ideological stability is school textbooks. The single textbook introduced in the early 1960s for use in all public primary schools remained deeply infused with popular nationalism (Vázquez, 1970).

over national belonging. As a matter of fact, during the 1950s and 1960s, when the postrevolutionary state became characterized by an increasingly authoritarian outlook, popular nationalism contributed to the stability and cohesion of a one-party regime.[84]

In Argentina, state development happened earlier and, due to fierce intrastate opposition, the strength of the state blocked the wider resonance of popular nationalism. When Perón won the presidential elections of 1946, he encountered a cultural machinery that had already been established under the previous ideological regime.[85] Moreover, radiating actors mounted a substantial challenge against their task of disseminating the new national discourses. A prominent example are schoolteachers. In their own understandings of national identity and history, Argentinean teachers tended to follow cultural and highly elitist projections of nationhood.[86] The majority of teachers opposed the contents of the new educational materials as ideologically charged and saw teacher-training institutes as a challenge to their professional autonomy. Their career path and their salary put teachers squarely within the middle class, and they marshaled a high level of collective organization. As a matter of fact, Perón's attempts to replace established independent teacher unions with an association more closely aligned to the central government did not materialize.[87] Thus, while Peronist state leaders could rely on a broad ruling coalition, actors embedded within a cultural machinery that was already established were able to resist the new national ideology.

As a result, the institutionalization of popular nationalism stalled. Popular national discourses existed in a stalemate with the previously dominant liberal nationalism. Public celebrations of peasants and workers were largely confined to state-sponsored poster and billboard campaigns and did not enter the commercial production of calendars and postcards to the same extent as in Mexico.[88] Popular tastes and consumption patterns remained politically charged, as is powerfully illustrated by contestations over what kind of national culture was represented by tango. After the fall of Perón in 1955 political confrontations over policy and office often remained entwined with conflicts over national belonging and identity. Both Peronists and anti-Peronists conceived of themselves as the "true" representatives of the Argentinean nation, and these struggles became increasingly polarized, especially during the 1960s and 1970s.[89]

Peru falls in between the other two cases. State infrastructural power was very limited during the early twentieth century, but the 1950s and 1960s saw a substantial expansion. New responsibilities in steering economic development and social policy went hand-in-hand with a greater territorial reach. Road-building and electrification projects made the rugged national geography more

[84] Collier and Collier, 1991; Hamilton, 1982.   [85] Ciria, 1983; Plotkin, 2002.
[86] Bernetti and Puiggrós, 1993; vom Hau, 2009.   [87] Artieda, 1993: 299–342.
[88] vom Hau, 2017.   [89] Plotkin, 2002; Torre, 1990.

accessible, and central state representatives became a common sight, even in the most remote hamlets in the country.[90]

The state cultural machinery witnessed a similar expansion. During the 1950s and 1960s educational expenditures increased dramatically, a major part going into the construction of schools and teacher training.[91] An expanding network of *escuelas normales* or teacher-training schools socialized new recruits into the profession and provided members of Peru's subordinate race-class groups with a path for social ascendance.[92] During the same time period, state authorities also made the first efforts to regulate previously neglected areas. For example, radio broadcasters were encouraged to play Peruvian music and give more airtime to educational programs about national culture and history.[93] Thus, when Velasco seized power in 1968, he found a state cultural machinery with established routines for reproducing and disseminating liberal nationalism.

At the same time, the military government could build on the ideological support from actors situated within the state. Most prominently, during the 1960s a new generation of school teachers, often highly politicized and with close ties to labor and peasant movements, were already promoting class-based understandings of nationhood.[94] Popular nationalism also found its way into radio broadcasts, archeological excavations, and public festivals. Prominent radio broadcasters and archeologists fully identified Peru with the Inca Empire, and associated Spanish colonialism with oppression and exploitation.[95]

In Peru, therefore, popular nationalism became a regular product of the state cultural machinery and continued enjoying substantial acceptance in everyday life, even after Velasco's removal from power in 1975. At the same time, it was less hegemonic and more politically divisive than in Mexico, especially when class-based understandings of nationhood were adopted by the Shining Path, a Maoist guerrilla group whose violent tactics, together with the violent response of the state, became responsible for upheaval and civil war during the 1980s and 1990s.[96]

CONCLUSION

This chapter has investigated the link between state and nation in mid-twentieth-century Latin America. Specifically, I have explored possible connections between the emergence of developmental states and major transformations of nationalism

[90] Cleaves and Pease, 1983: 209–244; Contreras, 2004.
[91] Between 1940 and 1968 educational expenditures increased from 10.8 percent to 24.5 percent of the Peruvian national budget. By 1966, the Ministry of Education oversaw around 19,600 public schools and 62,400 teachers, compared to 4,900 schools and 12,400 teachers in 1940 (Contreras, 2004: 256, 264).
[92] Wilson, 2007.   [93] Ansión, 1986; Valderrama, 1987.
[94] Portocarrero and Oliart, 1989; Wilson, 2007.
[95] Tantaleàn, 2008: 35–52; Valderrama, 1987.   [96] Degregori, 1989; Klarén, 2000.

in the region. Based on a comparative-historical analysis of Mexico, Argentina, and Peru I have shown that the contents of official national ideologies in these three Latin American countries underwent a major change over the course of the mid twentieth century. State leaders substituted the previously dominant liberal nationalism, characterized by political-territorial yet highly exclusionary understandings of nationhood, with popular nationalism, set apart by cultural-assimilationist and class-based conceptions of the nation. At the same time, the extent to which this new popular nationalism became a regular product of state organizations and reverberated among ordinary citizens varied dramatically among the three countries.

To explain these distinct transformations of nationalism the chapter presented an analytical framework that emphasizes state–society relations, the temporal sequence of state formation, and intrastate dynamics. I have argued that the rise of new anti-oligarchic ruling coalitions led to the adoption of a new national ideology. I have further argued that the extent to which the new popular nationalism consolidated as a hegemonic frame of reference was affected by the temporal and relational aspects of state formation.

In developing this explanation the chapter reinforces one of the central claims advanced by the overall volume. As powerfully argued by Miguel Centeno and Agustin Ferraro in the Introduction, a major lacuna in the existing scholarship on Latin America is the relative absence of works that systematically bring together the study of the state and the analysis of nationalism. As it currently stands, the scholarship on the institutional foundations of the state in the region tends to pay only scarce attention to the implications which distinct trajectories of state institutional development might have for the conceptions of nationhood held by ordinary citizens. By contrast, the literature on nationalism in Latin America either reifies the state into an undifferentiated, all-powerful leviathan, or quickly discards the influence of the state altogether. Yet, as this chapter has shown, the extent to which new national ideologies gain wider resonance cannot be treated as a function of state strength. Similarly, differences in exposure to world-cultural models of nationalism or the expansion of cultural industries and mass consumption ultimately do not explain the differences between Mexico, Argentina, and Peru. This chapter therefore maintains that states should be treated as the central actor involved in creating and promoting nationalism, yet that a more nuanced and complex understanding of the state is warranted to fully unpack its role.[97]

The explanatory framework developed in this chapter also places the cases of Mexico, Argentina, and Peru within a broader comparative context. The distinct transformations of nationalism found in these three Latin American countries are not unique. For example, in Brazil under Getúlio Vargas (1930–1945) new ruling coalitions with subordinate sectors entailed the adoption of popular nationalism. This national ideology combined a class-based understanding of the nation with

---

[97] Abbott, Soifer, and vom Hau, 2017: 885–916.

the celebration of Brazil as a "racial democracy," projecting a homogeneous national identity based on centuries of racial and cultural mixing.[98] The growing reach of the state apparatus, combined with ideological support from within the cultural machinery, facilitated the consolidation of the new discourse.[99] Another example is Bolivia. During the 1952 Revolution, state power became based on alliances with highly mobilized subordinate sectors, and official national discourses envisioned a nation of the working masses, while emphasizing the indigenous roots of national culture. Yet, powerful opposition from within the state made the institutionalization of popular nationalism difficult during this period.[100] In these cases, a focus on ruling coalitions, the temporal sequence of state building, and intrastate relations offers a plausible account of different transformations of nationalism.

More generally, and returning to the main theme of this edited volume, this chapter suggests a selective affinity between the emergence of developmental states and the rise of popular nationalism as official national ideology in Latin America. The comparison of Mexico, Argentina, and Peru has shown that the developmental state model has not been a direct cause of popular nationalism, but that the relationship should not be treated as a mere historical coincidence either. The analysis presented in this paper instead highlights the indirect and partial influence which the transition from export-oriented "night-watchman" states to developmental states had on patterns of nationalism in the region.

REFERENCES

Abbott, Jared A., Hillel Soifer, and Matthias vom Hau. "Transforming the Nation? The Bolivarian Education Reform in Venezuela in Context." *Journal of Latin American Studies*, 49, 4, 2017: 885–916.

Anderson, Benedict. *Imagined Communities: Reflections on the Origins and Spread of Nationalism*. 2nd edn, New York: Verso, 1991 [1983].

Ansión, Juan. *Anhelos y sinsabores. Dos decadas de politicas culturales del estado peruano*. Lima: Grupo de Estudios para el Desarrollo (GREDES), 1986.

Artieda, Teresa. "El magisterio en los territorios nacionales." In *La educación en las provincias y territorios nacionales (1885–1945)*, ed. Adriana Puiggrós, Buenos Aires: Galerna, 1993: 299–342.

Azuela, Alicia. "Arte Y Poder: Renacimiento artístico y revolución social en México, 1910–1945." Zamora, Michoacan: El Colegio de Michoacan, 2005.

Azzi, Maria Susana. "The Tango, Peronism, and Astor Piazzolla during the 1940s and '50s." In *From Tejano to Tango: Essays on Latin American Popular Music*, ed. Walter Clark, London: Routledge, 2002: 25–40.

Basadre, Jorge. *Historia de la República del Perú*. Lima: Editorial Universitaria, 1968.

Beezley, William H. *Mexican National Identity: Memory, Innuendo, and Popular Culture*. Tucson: University of Arizona Press, 2008.

[98] See Chapter 14 of this volume.   [99] Dávila, 2003; Marx, 1998.
[100] Klein, 2003; Luykx, 1999.

Bernetti, Jorge Luis and Adriana Puiggrós. *Peronismo: Cultura política y educación (1945–1955)*. Buenos Aires: Galerna, 1993.

Bertoni, Lilia Ana. *Patriotas, cosmopolitas y nacionalistas: La construcción de la nacionalidad argentina a fines del siglo XIX*. Buenos Aires: Fondo de Cultura Económica, 2001.

Brading, David A. *The First America: The Spanish Monarchy, Creole Patriots, and the Liberal State, 1492–1867*. Cambridge University Press, 1991.

Brubaker, Rogers. *Nationalism Reframed: Nationhood and the National Question in the New Europe*. Cambridge University Press, 1996.

Ethnicity without Groups. Cambridge, MA: Harvard University Press, 2004.

Burgess, Katrina. "Loyalty Dilemmas and Market Reform: Party-Union Alliances under Stress in Mexico, Spain, and Venezuela." *World Politics* 52, 1, 1999: 105–134.

Calhoun, Craig. *Nationalism*. Minneapolis: University of Minnesota Press, 1997.

Campione, Daniel and Miguel Mazzeo. *Estado y Administración Pública en la Argentina: Análisis de su desarrollo en el período 1880–1916*. Buenos Aires: Ediciones Fisyp, 1999.

Ciria, Alberto. *Politica y cultura popular: La Argentina peronista, 1946–55*. Buenos Aires: Ediciones de la Flor, 1983.

Cleaves, Peter S. and Henry Pease. "State Autonomy and Military Policy Making." In *The Peruvian Experiment Reconsidered*, eds. Cynthia McClintock and Abraham Lowenthal, Princeton University Press, 1983: 209–244.

Cockcroft, James D. *Intellectual Precursors of the Mexican Revolution, 1900–1913*. Austin: University of Texas Press, 1968.

Collier, David and Ruth Berins Collier. *Shaping the Political Arena. Critical Junctures, the Labor Movement, and Regime Dynamics in Latin America*. Princeton University Press, 1991.

Contreras, Carlos. *El aprendizaje del capitalismo. Estudios de historia económica y social del Perú republicano*. Lima: Instituto de Estudios Peruanos, 2004.

Córdova, Arnaldo. *En una época de crisis, 1929–1934*. Vol. 9 of *La clase obrera en la historia de México*. Mexico City: Siglo Veintiuno, 1981.

Cósio Villegas, Daniel. *Historia Moderna de México*. Mexico City: Hermes, 1973.

Cotler, Julio. *Clases, estado y nación en el Perú*. Lima: Instituto de Estudios Peruanos (IEP), 2005 [1978].

Dávila, Jerry. *Diploma of Whiteness: Race and Social Policy in Brazil, 1917–1945*. Durham: Duke University Press, 2003.

de la Cadena, Marisol. *Indigenous Mestizos: Race and the Politics of Representation in Cuzco, 1919–1991*. Durham: Duke University Press, 2000.

Degregori, Carlos Iván. *Qué difícil es ser Dios: Ideología y violencia política en Sendero Luminoso*. Lima: El Zorro de Abajo, 1989.

Eastwood, Jonathan. "Positivism and Nationalism in 19th-Century France and Mexico." *Journal of Historical Sociology* 17, 1, 2004: 331–357.

Elena, Eduardo. *Dignifying Argentina: Peronism, Citizenship, and Mass Consumption*. University of Pittsburgh Press, 2011.

Ertman, Thomas. *Birth of the Leviathan: Building States and Regimes in Medieval and Early Modern Europe*. Cambridge University Press, 1997.

Escudé, Carlos. *El fracaso del proyecto argentino: Educación e ideología*. Buenos Aires: Tesis, 1990.

Falicov, Tamara Leah. *The Cinematic Tango: Contemporary Argentine Film.* Wallflower Press, 2007.

Fein, Seth. "Hollywood, US–Mexican Relations, and the Devolution of the Golden Age of Mexican Cinema." *Filmhistoria online* 4, 2, 2004: 103–135.

Florescano, Enrique. *Memoria indígena.* Mexico City: Taurus, 1999.

Gandulfo, Alberto. "La expansión del sistema escolar argentino: Informe estadístico." In *Sociedad civil y Estado en los orígenes del sistema educativo argentino,* ed. Adriana Puiggrós, Buenos Aires: Galerna, 1991: 309–361.

García, José María González. *Las huellas de Fausto: la herencia de Goethe en la sociología de Max Weber.* Madrid: Tecnos, 1992.

Gellner, Ernest. *Nations and Nationalism.* London: Oxford University Press, 1983.

Gené, Marcela. *Un mundo feliz. Imágenes de los trabajadores en el primer peronismo (1946–1955).* Buenos Aires: Fondo de Cultura Económica, 2005.

Gereffi, Gary and Donald L. Wyman, eds. *Manufacturing Miracles: Paths of Industrialization in Latin America and East Asia.* Princeton University Press, 1990.

Goethe, Johann Wolfgang von. *Elective Affinities.* London: Oxford University Press, 1999 [originally published in 1809].

Goswami, Manu. "Rethinking the Modular Nation Form: Toward a Sociohistorical Conception of Nationalism." *Comparative Studies in Society and History* 44, 4, 2002: 770–799.

Halperín Donghi, Tulio. "Liberalismo Argentino y Liberalismo Mexicano: Dos Destinos Divergentes." In *El Espejo de la Historia: Problemas Argentinos y Perspectivas Latinoamericanas,* ed. Tulio Halperín Donghi, Buenos Aires: Editorial Sudamericana, 1987: 141–165.

Hamilton, Nora. *The Limits of State Autonomy: Post-Revolutionary Mexico.* Princeton University Press, 1982.

Hayes, Joy Elizabeth. *Radio Nation: Communication, Popular Culture, and Nationalism in Mexico,1920–1950.* Tucson: University of Arizona Press, 2000.

Hechter, Michael. *Containing Nationalism.* Oxford University Press, 2000.

Hirschman, Albert O. "The Political Economy of Import-Substituting Industrialization in Latin America." *The Quarterly Journal of Economics* 82, 1, 1968: 1–32.

Hobsbawm, Eric J. *Nations and Nationalism since 1780: Programme, Myth, Reality.* Cambridge University Press, 1990.

Horowitz, Joel. *Argentine Unions, the State and the Rise of Perón.* Berkeley: Institute of International Studies, University of California, 1990.

Howe, Richard Herbert. "Max Weber's Elective Affinities: Sociology within the Bounds of Pure Reason." *American Journal of Sociology* 84, 2, 1978: 366–385.

Jansen, Robert. "Populist Mobilization: A New Theoretical Approach to Populism." *Sociological Theory* 29, 2, 2011: 75–96.

Jenkins, Rhys. "The Political Economy of Industrialization: A Comparison of Latin American and East Asian Newly Industrializing Countries." *Development and Change,* 22 2, 1991: 197–231.

Karush, Matthew B. *Culture of Class: Radio and Cinema in the Making of a Divided Argentina, 1920–1946.* Durham: Duke University Press, 2012.

Kaufman, Robert R. "How Societies Change Developmental Models Or Keep Them: Reflections on the Latin American Experience in the 1930s and the Postwar World." In *Manufacturing Miracles: Paths of Industrialization in Latin America and East*

Asia, eds. Gary Gereffi and Donald L. Wyman, Princeton University Press, 1990: 110–138.

Klaiber, Jeffrey. *La Iglesia en el Perú*. Lima: Pontificia Universidad Católica del Perú (PUCP), 1996.

Klarén, Peter Flindell. *Peru. Society and Nationhood in the Andes*. Oxford University Press, 2000.

Klein, Herbert S. *A Concise History of Bolivia*. New York: Cambridge University Press, 2003.

Knight, Alan. "Popular Culture and the Revolutionary State in Mexico, 1910–1940." *Hispanic American Historical Review* 74, 3, 1994b: 393–444.
"The Weight of the State in Modern Mexico." In *Studies in the Formation of the Nation-State in Latin America*, ed. James Dunkerley, London: Institute of Latin American Studies, 2002: 212–253.

Lechner, Frank and John Boli. *World Culture: Origins and Consequences*. London: Blackwell, 2005.

López-Alves, Fernando. *State Formation and Democracy in Latin America, 1810–1900*. Durham: Duke University Press, 2000.

Luykx, Aurolyn. *The Citizen Factory: Schooling and Cultural Production in Bolivia*. Albany: SUNY Press, 1999.

Mahoney, James. *The Legacies of Liberalism: Path Dependence and Political Regimes in Central America*. Baltimore: The Johns Hopkins University Press, 2001.

Mann, Michael. *The Sources of Social Power. Volume 2: The Rise of Classes and Nation States 1760–1914*. Cambridge University Press, 1993.

Marx, Anthony. *Making Race and Nation: A Comparison of South Africa, the United States, and Brazil*. Cambridge University Press, 1998.

Meyer, Jean. *La Cristiada*. Mexico City: Siglo Veintiuno, 1974.

Meyer, John W. "The Changing Cultural Content of the Nation-State: a World Society Perspective." In *State/Culture: State Formation after the Cultural Turn*, ed. George Steinmetz, Ithaca: Cornell University Press, 1999: 123–146.

Meyer, John W., John Boli, George Thomas, and Francisco O. Ramirez. "World Society and the Nation-State." *American Journal of Sociology* 103, 1, 1997: 144–181.

Meyer, Lorenzo. "La institucionalización del nuevo régimen." In *Historia general de México*, ed. Centro de Estudios Históricos, Mexico City: Colegio de México, 2000: 823–880.

Moreno, Julio. *Yankee Don't Go Home!: Mexican Nationalism, American Business Culture, and the Shaping of Modern Mexico, 1920–1950*. Chapel Hill: UNC Press Books, 2003.

Nugent, David. "Building the State, Making the Nation: The Bases and Limits of State Centralization in 'Modern Peru.'" *American Anthropologist* 96,2, 1994: 333–369.

O'Malley, Ilene. *The Myth of the Revolution: Hero Cults and the Institutionalization of the Mexican State, 1920–1940*. New York: Greenwood Press, 1986.

Palmer, David Scott. *"Revolution from Above": Military Government and Popular Participation in Peru, 1968–1972*. Ithaca, NY: Cornell University Press, 1973.

Parker, David. *The Idea of the Middle Class: White-Collar Workers and Peruvian Society, 1900–1950*. University Park: Penn State University Press, 1998.

Pierson, Paul. *Politics in Time: History, Institutions, and Social Analysis*. Princeton University Press, 2004.

Pilcher, Jeffrey. *Que vivan los tamales!: Food and the Making of Mexican Identity.* Albuquerque: University of New Mexico Press, 1998.

Plotkin, Mariano. *Mañana es San Perón: A Cultural History of Perón's Argentina.* Wilmington: Scholarly Resources, 2002.

Portocarrero, Gonzalo and Patricia Oliart. *El Perú desde la escuela.* Lima, 1989.

Puiggrós, Adriana. "La educación argentina desde la reforma Saavedra-Lamas hasta el fin de la década infame. Hipótesis para la discusión." In *Escuela, democracia y orden (1916–1943),* ed. Adriana Puiggrós, Buenos Aires: Galerna, 1992: 17–64.

Quijada, Mónica. "El Paradigma de la Homogeneidad." In *Homogeneidad y Nación,* eds. Mónica Quijada, Carmen Bernand, and Arnd Schneider. Madrid, Spain: Consejo Superior de Investigaciones Científicas, 2000.

Quijano, Aníbal. *Reencuentro y debate: una introducción a Mariátegui.* Lima: Mosca Azul, 1981.

Rock, David. *Politics in Argentina 1890–1930: The Rise and Fall of Radicalism.* New York: Cambridge University Press, 1975.

Authoritarian Argentina: The Nationalist Movement, Its History and Its Impact. Berkeley: University of California Press, 1993.

Rockwell, Elsie. *Hacer escuela, hacer Estado: la educaciòn posrevolucionaria vista desde Tlaxcala.* Zamora: El Colegio de Michoacàn, 2007.

Romero, Luis Alberto. *Breve historia contemporánea de la Argentina.* Buenos Aires: Fondo de Cultura Económica, 2001.

Rueschemeyer, Dietrich, Evelyne Huber Stephens, and John D. Stephens. *Capitalist Development and Democracy.* University of Chicago Press, 1992.

Salazar Bondy, Augusto. *La educación del hombre nueva: La reforma educativa peruana.* Buenos Aires: Editorial Paidos, 1975.

Sánchez, Juan Martín. *Perú 28 de Julio: discurso y acción política el día de Fiestas Patrias 1969–1999.* Mexico City: Editorial Mora, 2002.

Sigal, Silvia. "Intelectuales y peronismo." In *Los años peronistas,* ed. Joan Carlos Torre, Buenos Aires: Sudamericana, 2002: 481–522.

Silver, Beverly J. *Forces of Labor: Workers' Movements and Globalization Since 1870.* New York: Cambridge University Press, 2003.

Slater, Dan. *Ordering Power: Contentious Politics and Authoritarian Leviathans in Southeast Asia.* New York: Cambridge University Press, 2010.

Smith, Anthony. 1986. *The Ethnic Origins of Nations.* Oxford: Blackwell.

Soifer, Hillel. *State Building in Latin America.* New York: Cambridge University Press, 2015.

Soifer, Hillel and Matthias vom Hau. "Unpacking the Strength of the State: The Utility of State Infrastructural Power." *Studies in Comparative International Development* 43, 3–4, 2008: 213.

Spalding, Hobart. "Education in Argentina, 1890–1914: The Limits of Oligarchical Reform." *Journal of Interdisciplinary History* 3, 1, 1972: 31–61.

Stein, Steve. *Populism in Peru: The Emergence of the Masses and the Politics of Social Control.* Madison, Wisconsin: University of Wisconsin Press, 1980.

Stepan, Alfred. *The State and Society: Peru in Comparative Perspective.* Princeton University Press, 1978.

Tantaleàn, Henry. "Las miradas andinas: Arqueologìas y nacionalismos en el Perù del siglo XX." *Arqueologìa Suramericana* 4, 1, 2008: 35–52.

Thorp, Rosemary. "A Reappraisal of the Origins of Import-Substituting Industrialization 1930–1950." *Journal of Latin American Studies* 24, S1, 1992: 181–195.

"The Latin American Economies in the 1940s." *Latin America in the 1940s: War and Postwar Transitions,* 1994: 41–58.

Tilly, Charles. "States and Nationalism in Europe 1492–1992." *Theory and Society* 23, 1, 1994: 131–146.

Torre, Juan Carlos. *La vieja guardia sindical y Perón.* Buenos Aires: Sudamericana, 1990.

Trimberger, Ellen Kay. Revolution from Above: Military Bureaucrats and Development in Japan, Turkey, Egypt, and Peru. Brunswick, NJ: Transaction Books, 1978.

Valderrama, Mariano. *Radio y comunicación popular en el Perú.* Lima: CEPES, 1987.

Varón Gabai, Rafael. "La estatua de Francisco Pizarro en Lima. Historia e identidad nacional." *Revista de Indias* 66, 236, 2006: 217–236.

Vaughan, Mary Kay. *The State, Education, and Social Class in Mexico, 1880–1928.* DeKalb: Northern Illinois University Press, 1982.

Cultural Politics in Revolution: Teachers, Peasants, and Schools in Mexico, 1930–1940. Tucson: University of Arizona Press, 1997.

Vázquez, Josefina Zoraida. *Nacionalismo y educación en México.* Mexico City: El Colegio de México, 1970.

Villarreal, René. "The Latin American Strategy of Import Substitution: Failure or Paradigm for the Region?". In *Manufacturing Miracles: Paths of Industrialization in Latin America and East Asia,* eds. Gereffi, Gary and Donald L. Wyman, Princeton University Press, 1990: 292–320.

vom Hau, Matthias. "Unpacking the School: Textbooks, Teachers, and the Construction of Nationhood in Mexico, Argentina, and Peru." *Latin American Research Review* 44, 3, 2009: 127–154.

"Nationalism and War Commemoration – A Latin American Exceptionalism?" *Nations and Nationalism* 19, 1, 2013: 146–166.

Transformations of Nationalism: State Power and Ideological Change in Latin America. Book manuscript in progress, 2017.

vom Hau, Matthias, and Valeria Biffi. "Mann in the Andes: State Infrastructural Power and Nationalism in Peru." In *Peru in Theory,* ed. Paulo Drinot, Oxford: Palgrave Macmillan, 2014: 191–216.

Waldner, David. *State Building and Late Development.* Ithaca: Cornell University Press, 1999.

Weber, Eugen. *Peasants into Frenchmen: The Modernization of Rural France, 1870–1914.* Stanford University Press, 1976.

Weber, Max. *The Protestant Ethic and the Spirit of Capitalism.* New York: Routledge, 2001 [1930].

Wilson, Fiona. "Transcending Race? Schoolteachers and Political Militancy in Andean Peru, 1970–2000." *Journal of Latin American Studies* 39, 4, 2007: 719–746.

Wimmer, Andreas. *Nationalist Exclusion and Ethnic Conflict: Shadows of Modernity.* Cambridge University Press, 2002.

"The Making and Unmaking of Ethnic Boundaries: A Multilevel Process Theory." *American Journal of Sociology* 113, 4, 2008: 970–1022.

Waves of War: Nationalism, State Formation, and Ethnic Exclusion in the Modern World. Cambridge University Press, 2012.

Wood, David. *De sabor nacional. El impacto de la cultura popular en el Perú.* Lima: Instituto de Estudios Peruanos (IEP), 2005.

14

State, Nation, and Identity in Brazil, 1930–1990

Marshall C. Eakin

THE ARGUMENT

From the 1930s to the 1990s, Brazilians created and shared one of the most powerful narratives of national identity in Latin America. This narrative of cultural and racial *mestiçagem* (miscegenation) emerged out of a truly national conversation across social groups after 1930, and was embraced by the vast majority of Brazilians by the end of the twentieth century. The main rituals and symbols of this narrative arose out of popular culture. Vibrant intellectual and cultural elites produced its most sophisticated articulations. A developmental state after 1930 adopted and aggressively promoted the narrative as one its most important methods of nation building. This narrative of *mestiçagem* was at the core of the most potent form of cultural nationalism in Brazil and also helped foster a dynamic civic nationalism by the 1980s and 1990s. In this essay, I argue that the developmental state in Brazil after 1930 played a central (but not the determinant) role in the construction and success of this narrative, that the narrative played a critical role in the gradual emergence of Brazil as a robust nation-state by the 1970s, and that the power of the narrative spanned political parties, social movements, classes, and regimes. At the end of the essay, I briefly compare this Brazilian narrative with dominant narratives of race and nation in other Latin American countries.

This myth of *mestiçagem* promoted a cohesion and homogeneity that both contributed to the success of the developmental planners (of various ideologies across the political spectrum), and eventually stimulated substantial resistance to the more authoritarian and statist versions of the developmental model.[1]

---

[1] I use the term "myth" in the anthropological sense – as ordered systems of social thought that embody the fundamental perceptions of a people about their social life. See, for example, Fry, 2005: 164 and 174–5. "Social myths, like religious myths, are not simply falsehoods. They are stories that societies tell and retell themselves, stories that therefore become crucial common ground for debate and negotiation even as the powerful deploy them to parry demands for social change." Alberto, 2011: 301.

The appeal of the narrative continues, but its potency has eroded over the past two decades. With the emergence of the Internet and the digital-communications revolution, the ability of the developmental state, or any state, to foster and successfully promote "a" dominant narrative of national identity has become increasingly problematic. In contrast to the half century before the 1980s, the decades since, and in the near future will likely be more challenging for developmentalism due to a likely increasing erosion of the cohesion produced in earlier decades by the power of the dominant national narrative of *mestiçagem*.

THE NARRATIVE

Brazilian national identity, like many others, was constructed up from local society as well as from the state down. The combined and often conflicting efforts of the powerful and the less powerful forge peoples and nations over decades and centuries. Elites who wish to construct nations consciously seek to create a sense of national identity, solidarity, and allegiance to an articulated set of myths, rituals, and symbols. They pursue progress through order and that order and progress hinge on the success of their attempts to impose homogeneity and uniformity. Despite their best efforts – and their power – often the plans of the nation builders fail, either in part or in whole. The less powerful – especially the so-called masses (*povo*) – quite often without setting out to do so, create and shape their own myths, rituals, and symbols that sometimes reach a wide audience resonating with hundreds of thousands – even millions – of persons they have never met nor seen. A generation ago, Benedict Anderson brilliantly described this process as the creation of "imagined communities" (what Brazilian intellectuals would call an *imaginário nacional*).[2]

Since the 1930s, the most important national myth that has bound people together in Brazil is what the anthropologist Roberto DaMatta has called the "*fábula das três raças*." This fable of the three races – what I call the myth of *mestiçagem* – asserts that Brazilians share a common history of racial *and* cultural mixing of Native Americans, Africans, and Europeans.[3] Although he did not invent this myth, Gilberto Freyre's exuberant and optimistic vision of *mestiçagem* has been its most potent and influential version. As Peter Fry has cogently observed, Freyre declared that all Brazilians "whatever their genealogical affiliation, were *culturally* Africans, Amerindians and Europeans."[4] Even those Brazilians who are not biologically *mestiços* are cultural hybrids. In Freyre's own oft-quoted words, "Every Brazilian, even the light-skinned fair-haired one, carries with him in his soul, when not in body and

---

[2] Anderson, 2006. The Brazilians, like the French envision "the imaginary (*imaginaire*) as a constructed landscape of collection aspirations." Appadurai, 1996: 31.

[3] DaMatta, 1990: 58–87. [4] Fry, 2005: 215.

soul . . . the shadow, or at least the birthmark, of the Indian or the Negro."[5] All Brazilians, regardless of the color of their skin, carry with them shadows in their souls, traces of Europe, Africa, and the Americas in their cultural DNA.[6] This is the essence of the Freyrean vision of Brazil, *brasilidade* (Brazilianness), and national identity in the twentieth century.

Before the publication in 1933 of Freyre's monumental *Casa-grande e senzala: formação da família brasileira sob o regimen de economia patriarchal* (*The Masters and the Slaves* in the 1946 English translation), many Brazilian and foreign intellectuals had recognized this mixing but very few viewed this *mestiçagem* favorably.[7] By the 1970s and 1980s, nearly all Brazilians, at some level, shared this belief – it had become something of a "master narrative of Brazilian culture."[8] When queried about race or ancestry for surveys, most Brazilians tell the questioners they are "Brazilian."[9] Today, when more than 200 million Brazilians enjoy the music of Ivete Sangalo, or participate in *carnaval*, or experience the exhilaration of their national team (*seleção*) winning (or losing) a World Cup, they resonate with some of the fundamental markers of Brazilian national identity – ones that are all profoundly shaped by the Freyrean vision of *mestiçagem*.

Sophisticated social science research has shown that this cultural mixing in Brazil has been widespread and deep.[10] People of all skin colors take part in cultural practices and activities that emerged out of European, Native American, and African societies. Perhaps most visible, are the profound African influences that permeate the cultural lives of Brazilians of all hues –

---

[5] Freyre, 2000: 343; and Freyre, 1970: 278.

[6] Recent genetic testing has shown that 87 percent of Brazilians have in their DNA genes that are at least 10 percent African in origin, and nearly half of this population self-classifies as white (*branco*) on the national census. Pena and M. Bortolini, 2004: 43. In a recent study of the descendants of runaway slave communities (*quilombolas*) in the state of São Paulo, 40 percent of the genetic material was of African origin, 39 percent European, and 21 percent indigenous peoples. Lopes, 2013.

[7] "Gilberto Freyre transformed the negativity of the *mestiço* into positivity, which permits the definitive completion of the contours of an identity that had long been taking shape . . . The myth of the three races then becomes plausible and can be actualized as ritual. The ideology of *mestiçagem*, which was trapped in the ambiguities of racist theories, as it was reworked could be socially disseminated and become common sense, ritually celebrated in everyday relations, or in large events like carnival and football. What was *mestiço* became national." Ortiz, 2006: 41.

[8] "No Brazilian awoke such passions, for and against, as Gilberto Freyre." Chacon, 2001: 14. The reference to "master narrative" comes from Sheriff, 2001: 5.

[9] "The high level of recognition of particularist ancestries seems to speak to the idea of the formation of a Freyrean-type metarace or racial fusion. Ethnic and racial boundaries appear blurred in the popular mindset in favor of a more inclusive nationalist category of Brazilianness." Bailey, 2009: 82–83.

[10] "Like racial democracy had been in previous decades, a belief in the positive value of miscegenation remains relatively uncontested, a sort of commonsense truth that continues to represent beliefs about Brazilian race relations. Ideas about racial hybridity and syncretism continue to predominate in popular culture." Edward E. Telles, 2004: 77.

from *candomblé* to *capoeira* and *carnaval*. In the words of one writer, "some Euro-Brazilians are more culturally Afro-Brazilian than some Afro-Brazilians." African influences pervade all facets of Brazilian culture and society leading one scholar to observe that the dominant narrative in Brazil is that no one is really white![11] As Edward Telles has shown with sophisticated statistical and analytical rigor, miscegenation is not "mere ideology" in Brazil. Race mixture has been taking place for centuries, and continues, and represents a significant reality in the daily lives of Brazilians.[12] The influence of Freyre permeates nearly every nook and corner of contemporary Brazilian culture. Even those who vehemently reject Freyre's ideas must grapple with ways to contend with their power and influence.

Decades of sustained and devastating critiques of Freyre's notion of "racial democracy" offer paradoxical testimony to his continuing power and influence on Brazilian identity.[13] The vast literature attacking racial democracy has rarely been accompanied by a rejection of Freyre's most important assertion – that the essence of Brazil and Brazilians is this mixture of races and cultures.[14] In the decades following the publication of *Casa-grande e senzala*, Freyre gradually made stronger and more sweeping claims that the widespread mixing of races and cultures had provided Brazil with a form of racial democracy, a society without the racial prejudice and discrimination sanctioned by law and custom in the United States and South Africa (for example).[15] Since the 1950s this Freyrean view of racial democracy has been repeatedly attacked by scholars in multiple fields of study. While many have argued that racial democracy is some sort of false consciousness or a smoke screen fabricated by the elite to hide the racism in Brazilian society, I agree with those who have shown that few Brazilians (especially those who are darker and poorer) believe that Brazil is a racial democracy. They are fully aware of the racism they confront in their own lives, but cling to racial democracy as an ideal to aspire to – for all Brazilians.[16] At the same time, the most sophisticated sociological surveys

---

[11] Quote is from Walker, 2002: 20. Bailey, 2009: 80–83; Sovik, 2009.   [12] Telles, 2004: 223.

[13] "The racial democracy thesis ... insists that the disproportionate impoverishment of blacks and their absence among elites is due to class discrimination and the legacy of slavery, and that the absence of state-sponsored segregation, a history of miscegenation, and social recognition of intermediate racial categories have upheld a unique racial order." Htun, 2004: 64.

[14] Sueann Caulfield, drawing on the work of Reid Andrews, Peter Fry, Hebe Castro, and Robin Sheriff (among others) sees the power of the myth of *mestiçagem* as far back as the 1920s and concludes that the myths of racial democracy and *mestiçagem*, of racial ideals and persistent racism, "might have developed through social and intellectual interaction rather than a one-way dissemination of elite ideology." (Caulfield, 2000: 147–153.)

[15] Antonio Sérgio Guimarães traces the emergence and usage of the infamous term "racial democracy" in Guimarães, 2002: 137–68. Ironically, Freyre did not create the term "racial democracy," and it apparently does not even come into use until the late 1940s and the 1950s. Vianna, 2001: 215–221; Alberto, 2012: 261–296.

[16] The most persuasive arguments for this view are Goldstein, 2003: esp. 108; Sheriff, 2001; and Bailey, 2009: esp. 218. "Far from being a legitimizing myth, racial democracy might best be

demonstrate that a majority of Brazilians cling to the Freyrean vision of *mestiçagem*.[17] While Freyre's vision of *mestiçagem* and racial democracy are interconnected, the former does not inevitably lead to the latter (although many, many writers conflate the two in their critiques of Freyre). One may fully embrace the notion of mixing without believing it produces racial democracy.[18]

Mestiçagem, however, is a protean concept. It allows those who wish to emphasize the cultural and racial diversity of Brazilian identity to highlight the contributions of the African and Indian to Brazilian culture. Brazilian music, cuisine, arts, language, and even sports offer for them daily evidence of the importance of non-European peoples and cultures to the formation of Brazilian society. At the same time, *mestiçagem* can also provide a means for those who wish to de-emphasize the African and Indian heritage of Brazilians by highlighting the waves of European immigrants as an even more powerful contributor to the cultural and racial mix that is Brazil today. In this version, mixing becomes the means for whitening (*embranquecimento*) Brazilian culture and biology. This vision of *mestiçagem*, combined with racial democracy, has been a powerful alternative to the blatant expressions of white supremacist ideology that became so potent in other societies such as the United States.[19] In a sense, these two very different visions are two sides of the same coin of *mestiçagem*. Both accept *mestiçagem* as central to the national narrative and are reshaped by different regions of Brazil for their own purposes. In effect, one sees *mestiçagem* as whitening, while the other sees it darkening Brazil.

THE ROLE OF THE STATE AND TECHNOLOGY

The role of the Brazilian state in national development has been one of the most studied themes across many disciplines in the social sciences and humanities over the past half-century. Although much debated, the state has clearly been envisioned by most scholars as central to Brazil's national economic development since at least the 1930s, and for some, as the central player in the processes of economic growth and development. Many scholars, especially in the humanities, have focused on the importance of the state in creating and crafting a powerful sense of nationalism and national identity in Brazil since the 1930s. Since the Vargas regimes of the 1930s, state crafters have often believed

---

understood, then, as a collective predisposition; as a set of values, interests, and experiences embraced by the masses; as a principled idea of a society in opposition to the United States and its formalized racial divides." Bailey, 2009: 115.

[17] For an impressive and sophisticated analysis of the data on attitudes toward race, and racial democracy, see Bailey, 2009: esp. 81, 115, 139, and 218. See also, Turra and Venturi, 1995.

[18] For a recent example of scholars unable to distinguish between Freyre's claims about racial democracy and his thesis on racial mixture, see Reiter and Mitchell, 2010: esp. chapters 1 and 12. Reiter and Mitchell also depict a simplistic view of the State imposing Freyre's views on the Brazilian masses (depriving them of any agency).

[19] I would like to thank my colleague, Celso Castilho, for pointing this out to me.

that a strong, unified cultural nationalism should assist their efforts to promote economic development. Conversely, this economic development has also helped reinforce cultural nationalism. In effect, cultural nationalism forms part of a larger developmental discourse aimed at nation building that moves beyond a language of just economic nationalism. Defining and championing the nation, the imagined community, goes hand-in-hand with a defense of the nation as an economic community.[20]

In the 1970s and 1980s scholars highlighted and overemphasized the role of the state with a very top-down view of both the processes of economic development and the formation of cultural nationalism.[21] Beginning in the 1980s with the so-called cultural and linguistic turns, the emergence of post-modernism, post-structuralism, and other theoretical turns in the humanities, the tendency has been to stress greater agency, multiple actors, and mediated messages along with a more fragmented, multi-causal view of politics, culture, and society.[22] In my view, this has led to an odd disconnect between most of the scholarship of those in the more empirically grounded social sciences and humanities, and the dominant mode of the theoretically driven disciplines in the humanities.

The 1930s have long been seen as a critical turning point in modern Brazilian history with the rise of Getúlio Vargas and the increasing ability of the Brazilian state to extend its power into the vast interior of the country. At the same time, the central government had begun systematically to create school curricula, museums, holidays, and national symbols to overcome the long history of regionalism and fragmentation that had characterized Brazilian society, culture, and politics since (at least) independence.[23] The rise of radio in the 1930s, and then film in the 1940s and 1950s, produced a powerful shift with the emergence of popular culture, especially popular music (samba, in particular), *carnaval*, and soccer (*futebol*) as shared national experiences.[24] Post-1930 Brazil is a fascinating mix of the efforts of the state to impose an increasingly unified vision of *brasilidade* as a diverse set of regional symbols, music, dance, and popular culture is eventually broadcast and spread across more than 8.5 million square kilometers of national territory. The expanding mass media bring the local and the regional into the national arena – and into regular contact with each other. New technologies produced (and continue to produce) an accelerating interactive intensity of people, places, and symbols from the 1920s to the present.

---

[20] Schneider, 1999: 276–305; Loveman, 2013: 329–355; Woo-Cumings, 1999: 1–31.
[21] Gellner, 1983; Hanchard, 1994.
[22] Rodgers, 2011: esp. Chapter 3, "The Search for Power", 77–110; Martín-Barbero, 1987.
[23] Williams, 2001.
[24] The literature on the history of music and dance in this period is rich: Vianna, 1995; McCann, 2004; Hertzman, 2013; Chasteen, 2004.

As new technologies (telegraphy, telephony, radio, television) draw more and more locales into an ever larger community the interplay among the local, regional, national, and international intensify. Earlier generations of writers often portrayed this process as largely uni-directional – the top-down imposition (beginning with Vargas) of the state dominated by elites who sought to force the Freyrean vision of Brazil on the masses. The influence and agency of the majority of Brazilians disappear in many of these accounts.[25] I argue that this process of nation-building was not entirely state directed, nor driven simply by the desires and choices of individuals or groups.[26] The emergence of radio and samba from the 1930s to the 1950s initiated the creation of what has been called a "culture industry" in Brazil creating for the first time a shared national popular culture. The Modernists in the 1920s and 1930s played a central role in this technological and cultural shift. In the 1920s, Brazilian Modernism emerged as a movement that explicitly and loudly proclaimed Brazil's cultural independence from Europe.[27] A "modern" Brazil, for these avant-garde artists and writers was a nation that recognized and celebrated its mixed indigenous, African, and European heritage, but was also technologically, scientifically, and industrially advanced. This modernist movement became the crucible of the emergence of the dominant narrative of Brazilian national identity in the twentieth century. The so-called folkloric, popular culture of pre-twentieth-century Brazil and the supposed erudite, cosmopolitan culture of the elites had never been separate, yet they blended and reconfigured in increasingly creative and powerful ways with the rise of mass-media technologies. "The symbioses between radio and literature, cinema and theater, and theater and television," as Renato Ortiz has argued, "were constants." According to Ortiz, the idea of traditional cultures that defined the "popular classes" gave way to products, images, and festivities associated with cultural industries and the "masses."[28] The intervention of the state into the cultural arena in the same decades, stimulated the creation of a "mass culture" (*cultura de massas*) in Brazil, but it was not until the 1960s and 1970s that a truly national community became possible. The conversation and debate about Brazilian national identity has been a long struggle over the very nature of what is deemed Brazilian culture.[29] First with film, and then more importantly, with the

---

[25] Some examples of this top-down view of the State and its power are such classic works as Faoro, 1976 and Schwartzman, 1982.

[26] I differ here, quite dramatically, from the perspective of those such as Gellner who see nationalism as imposed from above. Gellner, 1983: esp. 57. I agree with Peter Sahlins' analysis: "state formation and nation building were two-way processes … States did not simply impose their values and boundaries on local society. Rather, local society was a motive force in the formation and consolidation of nationhood and the territorial state." Sahlins, 1989: 8.

[27] Gouveia, 2013. The cultural vanguards of Modernism in Europe also rewrote their national histories and identities in the early twentieth century.

[28] Ortiz, 2009: 123, 135.

[29] The debate over identity, is and has been "a struggle about culture, not a struggle between cultures." Cooper, 2005: 87.

emergence of television after 1970, the technology was in place that truly stitched together the pieces of the national territory and Brazilian society to create the quilted mosaic that is Brazil today in the midst of this ongoing and never-ending conversation.[30]

In the 1960s and 1970s this developmental and cultural nationalism reached its limits under an authoritarian, military regime that officially endorsed Freyre's vision of *mestiçagem* and his claims that Brazil was a racial democracy. In the last two decades of the twentieth century, the emergence of the neoliberal economic wave, globalization, and the critiques of the Freyrean vision all converged to mark the end of the developmental nationalism that had emerged in the era of Getúlio Vargas and blossomed in the postwar decades. By the 1990s, an increasingly fragmented intelligentsia, a growing and restive civil society, and a weakened nation-state marked the end of a historical period when the creation of a national identity constructed around a dominant narrative not only seemed possible, but close to realization.[31] The last decade of the twentieth century also marks the emergence of a new technological era – of the Internet and global digital communications – that make the 1990s the logical terminus for my analysis.

The Age of Vargas (1930–1945)

Much has been written about the role of the Vargas regimes in the centralization of power, the consolidation of the state in twentieth-century Brazil, and its role in promoting a sense of Brazilian national identity. The Revolution of 1930 brought down the "coffee and cream" oligarchy dominated by São Paulo and Minas Gerais, and ushered in a new era of "conservative modernization" led by the central political figure in twentieth-century Brazil – Getúlio Vargas. In various guises – first as provisional president (1930–1934), then as indirectly elected president (1934–1937), then as the dictator of the authoritarian Estado Novo (1937–1945) – Vargas played the leading role in the transformation of the state, society, and culture in Brazil.[32] As in many countries in the Western world in the 1930s, the economic crisis led to increasing state intervention in all areas of life. Vargas expanded the role of the state, creating a wide variety of new ministries (e.g., Education and Public Health; Labor, Industry, and Commerce) and new departments and councils (e.g., Departamento Administrativo do Serviço Público; Departamento de Imprensa e Propaganda). The intervention into economic activities led to the emergence of the import-substitution industrialization (ISI) model that would dominate economic development policies until the 1960s and 1970s. From my

---

[30] For an astute analysis of the rise of a *sociedade de massas* in Brazil see Ortiz, 1988.

[31] For a provocative analysis of the Brazilian intelligentsia, the developmental nationalist model, and the end of this era, see Martins, 2002: 305–322.

[32] For the most recent synthesis and overview of the period, see Bethell, 2008: 3–86.

perspective, just as important was the intervention of the state into cultural affairs, a topic that has been well studied.[33]

Vargas wisely and cleverly brought many of the major intellectual figures of the 1930s and 1940s into government in key roles in government agencies from education to propaganda to cultural patrimony. Many of the major figures of the Modernist movement such as Mário de Andrade and Carlos Drummond de Andrade became "public functionaries" (*funcionários públicos*). Vargas sought to unify and integrate the Brazilian archipelago – economically, politically, and culturally.[34] These intellectuals were brought on board to craft cultural unity through the creation of a clear sense of Brazilian identity. As Daryle Williams has shown, they engaged in "culture wars" among themselves over exactly what that identity would be – in school curricula, museums, publications, and public events and rituals. In Williams' words, these intellectuals became "cultural managers."[35]

Vargas embarked upon an ambitious and highly effective cultural policy to promote the centralization of power – and to create a sense of Brazilian national identity.[36] The most notorious display of this drive to central power took place shortly after the coup of November 1937 (that created the Estado Novo) when all of the state flags were burned in an elaborate ceremony in Rio de Janeiro.[37] The message was clear – the national state would eradicate the longstanding power of the states/provinces and subordinate them to central authority. In this drive to create a single national identity Vargas and his cultural managers chose to enshrine the Freyrean vision of *mestiçagem* at the core of this cultural policy.[38] As a number of Brazilian scholars and Brazilianists have shown, the 1930s mark a turning point for the intellectual and cultural elites. Vargas and his successors in the succeeding decades created what Sergio Miceli has called a "central market of public positions" (*mercado central de postos públicos*) that gave Brazilian intellectuals access to the halls of power and influence as opposed to the sinecures offered them by the oligarchs of the Republic. In post-1930 Brazil, intellectuals filled not only the mundane posts of *funcionários públicos* but also had the chance to create and shape national culture via the power of the state.[39]

---

[33] For just a couple of examples with very different perspectives: Miceli, 2001: esp. 69–341; Pécaut, 1990.

[34] Oliveira, 2008: 97–111.   [35] Williams, 2001.

[36] "[T]he network of federal cultural policymaking institutions founded during the first Vargas regime built itself into the bedrock of Brazilian culture and state power. Even when these institutions acted as their own worst enemies, they helped the Vargas regime and all subsequent federal administrations lay claim to managing Brasilidade." Williams, 2001: 53.

[37] Bethell, 2008: 57; Oliven, 2006: 303–320.

[38] "It is only with the Estado Novo that official projects are implemented in the sense of recognizing in *mestiçagem* the true nationality." Schwarcz, 2006: 305–334. The quote is on 314.

[39] Miceli, 2001: esp. "Os intelectuais e o Estado," 195–291. See also, Rolland, 2006:, 95–120; Martins, 1987: 65–87.

As literary scholars have long pointed out, the Modernist movement and the political vision of Vargas were both fraught with competing tensions – between cosmopolitanism and cultural nationalism ("contradictory modernity"), modernization, and tradition.[40] The state expanded its influence, either directly or indirectly, into all areas of cultural production after 1930, and especially after 1937. The newly created Ministry of Education under the strong leadership of Gustavo Capanema, in particular, played a leading role in setting an agenda of cultural nationalism. Capanema proved to be a very resilient and effective operator within the power structure of the Vargas regimes. He envisioned the school curriculum as "the cement of *brasilidade.*"[41] A former small-town school teacher from Minas Gerais, Capanema brought two of his fellow *mineiros* with him to Rio – the great poet Drummond de Andrade served as Capanema's chief of staff (and intellectual alter ego), Rodrigo Mello Franco de Andrade (who had helped Freyre find a publisher for *Casa-grande*) headed the new Serviço de Patrimônio Histórico e Artístico Nacional (SPHAN) and many, many other major intellectuals served in positions that shaped cultural production – from music to art to architecture. The convergence between the Modernist movement, intellectuals, and the state under Vargas were crucial in the official consecration of the Freyrean vision of *mestiço* nationalism.[42]

A Fragile Democracy (1945–1964)

After Vargas was forced from power in 1945, populism and nationalism dominated Brazilian politics for the next two decades as tens of millions of Brazilians experienced mass, democratic politics for the first time. The Constitution of 1946 gave the vote to all Brazilians over the age of eighteen (except illiterates, who were perhaps a third of the population). During a period of rapid population growth (from 40 million in 1940 to 70 million by the mid 1960s) a massive shift of people from the countryside to the cities, and an industrial surge (especially under President Juscelino Kubitschek, 1956–1961), Brazilian politics were vibrant, highly charged, and constantly unstable. At this moment of Cold War politics and revolutionary upheaval across Latin America, Brazil's electoral democracy was on the verge of collapse repeatedly in the 1950s and early 1960s. The culture industries and popular culture also grew dramatically and flourished in the post-war decades. In many ways, the period from 1945–1985 is the moment when Brazil truly emerges as a nation, as an imagined community defined by myths, rituals, and symbols that resonate across the national territory and social classes.

---

[40] Johnson, 1994: 5–22. The term "contradictory modernity" comes from Daniel Pécaut, as cited in Pécaut, 1990: 8. See also, Oliveira, 2006: 78.

[41] Bethell, 2008: 61.

[42] Schwartzman, Bomeny, and Ribeiro Costa, 2000; Oliveira, 2008: 104–105.

In the decade after the fall of Vargas in 1945, industrialization, urbanization, and economic growth continued, but with powerful ideological divergences across the political spectrum. Under President Eurico Dutra (1946–1951) the country moved in the direction of a more market-oriented set of economic policies, and then Vargas (1951–1954) tried to move the country back toward greater state intervention, most prominently in key sectors such as petroleum, electricity, iron, and steel. His dramatic suicide and two years of political uncertainty left the country adrift. The presidency of Kubitschek (1956–1961) renewed the more focused and directed path of national development, albeit with a significant commitment to some market-driven initiatives (e.g., the role of Volkswagen in the automotive industry). The infrastructure that would finally truly stitch together the vast regions of Brazil surged in the 1950s in a process that would effectively cover the entire national territory by the 1990s. Radio and television in the decades after 1950 would make it possible to reach nearly all those in the country simultaneously. Kubitschek's emphasis on road and electrical power initiated the final phase in creating the infrastructure for a truly national community.[43]

For Kubitschek, cultural and economic nationalism went hand-in-hand as they had under Vargas. Not as authoritarian as the earlier Vargas regimes, Kubitschek consciously fostered cultural nationalism, in particular, through venues such as the Instituto Superior de Estudos Brasileiros (ISEB) and the conscious appropriation of the dynamic emerging symbols of Brazilian culture on the world stage: *futebol*, music, and modernist architecture.[44] Kubitschek was fortunate in his timing. Brazil's industry entered into a new and very impressive phase of expansion, bossa nova took the musical world by storm, and the *seleção* won its first World Cup with its explosive new superstar, Pelé.

Brasília is perhaps the greatest monument to and symbol of this convergence of economics, politics, and culture in the late 1950s. The architectural and artistic embodiment of Kubitschek's vision of the development state and his aspirations for *grandeza*, Oscar Niemeyer's buildings and Lucio Costa's design boldly exhibit Brazil's blend of economic and cultural nationalism to achieve global prominence. By the early 1960s, *carnaval* and *futebol* had matured to become Brazil's two most important rituals resonating with the vast majority of Brazilians, and popular music became the most important medium for a national conversation about racial and cultural mixture as the core of Brazilian identity. By the early 1960s, the state continued to play the central role in promoting a nationalistic economic development model, and the

---

[43] The literature on Brazilian development in the 1950s is enormous. Chapter 7 in this volume offers a general perspective on Brazilian national developmental strategies and their institutional foundations. Also in this volume, Chapter 3 discusses the intellectual controversies on development among public policy makers, economists, and sociologists in Brazil after World War Two. For a recent synthesis and revisionist argument of Brazilian development in the 1950s, see Ioris, 2014.

[44] For a discussion of ISEB, see Ioris, 2014: Chapter 4, and Campbell, 2014: 157–181.

narrative of Freyrean *mestiçagem* had become the dominant vision of national identity. Brazil's economic development reinforced Brazilians' sense of their emergence as a nation, and a cohesive sense of identity helped the state in its efforts to promote economic development.

Military Rule (1964–1985)

Tragically, the seeming promise of maturing and converging economic and cultural nationalisms very quickly disintegrated in the early sixties. In the midst of high inflation, economic stagnation, and intense ideological battles, Brazilian democracy collapsed in 1964 when the military deposed President João Goulart (1961–1964). The Brazilian coup was the first in a wave of military coups and dictatorships across Latin America over the next two decades. Much to the surprise of nearly all civilian politicians (especially the right, which had called vociferously for military intervention), the armed forces remained in power and attempted to transform the country through brutal repression of dissent (especially, but not exclusively, on the left) and a massive national economic development project. Hundreds "disappeared" and thousands were jailed and tortured. The generals (and admirals) ruthlessly eradicated any leftist threat, and dramatically accelerated industrialization through massive government intervention. Although never completely shutting down politics, the military "purged" all branches of government and created two political parties, one for the government and one for the "responsible" opposition. The repression did not begin to ease until the late 1970s, and the transition back to civilian democracy spanned nearly the entire 1980s.[45]

The right-wing, anti-communist generals in the 1960s and 1970s (much like Getúlio Vargas in the 1930s and 1940s) saw the state as an instrument for national cohesion and the formation of a hegemonic narrative of nationalism and national identity. For the military, Vargas, Kubitschek, and Goulart were too leftist and socialist. The military high command fully intended to promote capitalist development, albeit one that turned out to be profoundly statist. They would use the state to promote economic development and cultural nationalism, and to make the two mutually reinforcing. One of the great beneficiaries of this vision was the businessman Roberto Marinho, the founder of the most powerful media company in Brazil.[46] Marinho envisioned his Rede Globo as a powerful force for the transformation of Brazil into a modern nation – one integrated by telecommunications and drawing together all the locales and regions of Brazil into a national consumer culture. This vision of modernity aspired to emulate Western Europe and the

---

[45] The classic volume in English on the military regime is Skidmore, 1988. In Portuguese, the multi-volume work by Elio Gaspari (Gaspari: 2002–2016), is fundamental for understanding the nature of the regime.

[46] Kottak, 2009: 37–38.

United States with their capitalist, consumerist, urban, industrial societies. In many ways, this modernizing vision represented the latest version of the eurocentric, elite vision of modernity in the nineteenth century. Marinho's aspirations and vision coincided perfectly with the leadership of the military regime in its pursuit of a modern, industrial Brazil constructed around a clear and coherent nationalism – and anti-communism.[47] Globo and the generals became formidable – if not always harmonious – partners.[48] The generals provided the technological infrastructure for national integration, and Globo the cultural intermediary. In the terminology of information technology, the generals constructed the hardware and Globo the software for facilitating and shaping the national conversation on Brazilian identity.

As Globo worked to integrate the nation through telecommunications it simultaneously strove to forge a sense of national unity and development. Leaving the local reporting to its affiliates, the focus of Globo's hugely influential nightly new program, *Jornal Nacional*, was the national and international. The image that dominated was the forging of modern, urban, industrial, consumerist, capitalist Brazil. Ironically, in stressing the role of Brazilians to be good citizens of the nation, Globo was both serving the military regime and, ultimately, helping prepare the way for all Brazilians to demand the rights of citizenship.[49] As the regime went through a long and slow process of *abertura* (political opening) in the late 1970s and early 1980s, Globo walked a complex path, seeking to remain loyal to the generals who made its very existence and spectacular success possible, and recognizing that the regime would eventually have to return power to civilians. The news editors understood this gradual transformation. As one editor noted, the *Jornal Nacional* could not continue simply to serve as a mouthpiece of the regime, but, "In the train of the political opening, Globo Network is the last car and the *Jornal Nacional* is the last seat. But, even when arriving late, we will also arrive in the same station as the locomotive."[50]

In the 1960s and 1970s the military regime put into place many of the conditions for the consolidation of a shared national culture (extending state power and mass communications effectively across all of the national territory), and the climax of this sense of national belonging came, ironically, with the massive mobilization of millions of Brazilians *against* the military regime in the 1980s. In one of the ironies of Brazilian history, at the very moment that this modernizing project to create a sense of national identity finally experienced its greatest success in the 1970s and 1980s, intellectuals and activists had already begun to deconstruct the meaning of identity, nation, nationalism, and modernity, and they began to proclaim the very *impossibility* of the

---

[47] Marinho, 2011. Wallach, 2011: 72.   [48] Ribke, 2011: 49–61.
[49] Kottak, 2009: 36–37, 91–92.   [50] Quoted in Silva, 1985: 40.

modernizing project and the very notion of this version of *"a"* national identity.[51] Many of them announced the death of the Freyrean vision of Brazil.

Mass Politics (1985–1990s)

The half-century of cultural nationalism constructed around the myth of *mestiçagem* laid much of the groundwork for the full-blown emergence of these citizenship movements. By the 1980s the work of constructing the nation – of creating a sense of loyalty and belonging to something called Brazil – had matured. This notion of belonging to the nation – to a national cultural community – and the repression of political rights under the military regime, combined to help produce movements across all of Brazil of tens of millions of people demanding their rights *as Brazilians.* In many ways, the decades of cultural nationalism, of identity construction, paved the way and made possible the rise of movements dedicated to democratization and citizenship. Tens of millions now saw themselves as Brazilians, with loyalties to the nation, and they now demanded the rights promised to them by the state.

The most spectacular and visible convergence of Brazil's cultural and civic nationalisms can be seen in two moments of massive popular mobilization: the *diretas já* (direct elections now) campaign in 1984 and the impeachment of President Fernando Collor de Mello in 1992. In each of these two movements, millions of people took to the streets in the largest public demonstrations (*manifestações*) in the country's history. The first movement failed to achieve its specific political objective – to compel congress to pass legislation calling for the first direct election of a president since 1960. Despite this failure, the movement sounded the death knell of the authoritarian regime, began the final stage in the transition to civilian rule, and marked the massive emergence of national movements seeking the full rights of citizenship for all Brazilians. The second movement built on the first and helped make possible a specific political objective – the impeachment of President Collor de Mello. Both movements consolidated and solidified cultural nationalism as Brazilians quite literally wrapped themselves in some of the most visible symbols of national loyalty and belonging – the flag and its colors – drawing on the powerful rituals, symbols, and personalities of popular culture. Ironically, at the very moment that nearly all those in Brazil finally saw themselves as Brazilians with common myths, rituals, and symbols, the most powerful myth of national identity had already entered into relative decline, facing sustained challenges made possible by a more open, democratic society and the emergence of a dynamic civil society.[52]

---

[51] For a recent argument against the notion of national identities see Seigel, 2009, esp. the Preface and Introduction.

[52] For a concise description of the *diretas já* movement see Skidmore, 1988: 240–244; and Rodrigues, 2003. For a more detailed analysis, see Bertoncelo, 2007. For a deeply personal

The emergence of a potent civic nationalism in the 1980s generated a fractious debate about cultural identity, in particular, the dominant narrative of national identity – Freyre's vision of *mestiçagem*. The maturing cultural nationalism that had been developing since the 1930s simultaneously helped foster the civic nationalism that grew out of re-democratization in the 1970s and 1980s, and then generated clashes as the newly democratic Brazil grappled with how to define and implement citizenship for all. The 1988 Constitution enshrined the principle of equal rights for all Brazilians. Under presidents Fernando Henrique Cardoso (1995–2003) and Luis Inácio "Lula" da Silva (2003–2011), the government also began to promote initiatives that responded to an emerging black activism (*movimento negro*). President Cardoso made the first tentative efforts to address racism and provide government support to prevent and redress racist practices. In 2003, Lula created a Special Office for the Promotion of Racial Equality (SEPPIR) with cabinet-level status.[53]

While these moves encouraged black consciousness activists, the efforts to construct a legal apparatus for affirmative action seemed to others a path to greater social divisions, special treatment, and the unnecessary racialization of Brazil.[54] Two pieces of legislation, in particular, focused this debate – the Lei de Cotas Raciais (1999) and the Estatuto da Igualdade Racial (2000). In 2006, both these bills became the focal point of contentious debates in the Brazilian congress, media, and among academics. Many intellectuals and social scientists who believe Brazil is a *mestiço* nation, wrote a *Carta pública ao Congresso Nacional: "Todos têm Direitos Iguais na República Democrática"* (Public Letter to the National Congress: "Everyone has Equal Rights in the Democratic Republic") and delivered it to the President of the Brazilian Senate in July 2006. While the supporters of quotas and affirmative action argue for the need to redress past discrimination, and that Brazil is a binary society of blacks and whites, these prominent intellectuals see this legislation as antithetical to the very fabric of Brazilian society – one that is racially and culturally mixed. They wholeheartedly agree that discrimination and prejudice have long existed in Brazilian society, but they do not believe the solution is what they call the "racialization" of Brazil.[55] This public letter generated a second, *"Manifesto em favor da Lei de Cotas e do Estatuto da Igualdade Racial,"* ("Manifesto in favor of the Law of Quotas and the Statute of Racial Equality") signed by an equally illustrious group of intellectuals and academics, criticizing the first letter and calling for support of the legislation.[56]

---

journalistic account, see Kotscho, 1984. Polls in 1983 showed that more than three-quarters of Brazilians wanted direct elections for president. Bertoncelo, 2007: 105.

[53] Johnson, 2008: 209–230; Telles, 2004: 47–77.

[54] For an emphatic rejection of the efforts to describe Brazil as a binary racial structure, see Kamel, 2006.

[55] Fry, Maggie, Maio, Monteiro, and Ventura Santos, 2007; Carvalho, 2004: 7.

[56] Johnson, 2008: 227–228.

Despite several decades of increasing criticism of Freyre, the work of Edward Telles and Stanley Bailey has clearly shown, "a belief in the positive value of miscegenation remains relatively uncontested, a sort of commonsense truth that continues to represent beliefs about Brazilian race relations. Ideas about racial hybridity and syncretism continue to predominate in popular culture."[57] Yet, Gilberto Freyre's narrative of Brazilian identity faces stronger and more strident challenges today than at any time since it began to emerge as the dominant narrative in the mid twentieth century. More than just a debate about social policy, at the heart of this heated conversation is "the country's understanding and portrayal of itself."[58] Is Brazil a multiethnic, multicultural nation or is it a *mestiço* one?[59] The voices that have emerged over the last few decades to challenge the Freyrean vision have also been accompanied by a new technological wave that make the creation, maintenance, and dominance of any narrative of national identity increasingly unlikely. The Internet and the incredible access it has given to millions of voices in Brazil since the mid 1990s have not only produced many challenges to the dominant narratives, it has also created many, many more complex contributions to any conversation about hybridity and *mestiçagem*.

While the greatest focus of the attacks on Freyre over the past generation (or more) has been his notion of racial democracy, the rise of black consciousness movements has also mounted a sustained assault over the last three decades on Freyre's more fundamental contribution to national identity, his writings about *mestiçagem*. Most public opinion polls, and most intellectuals, have buried the argument that Brazil is a racial democracy, and that Brazilians believe Brazil is a racial democracy. The central question for those who believe in the myth of *mestiçagem*, and for those who believe there is such a thing as a dominant narrative of national identity, is the ability of the Freyrean vision of *mestiçagem* to survive these attacks and critiques. If, as I have argued, this narrative of *mestiçagem* has been at the core of the dominant narrative of Brazilian identity in the second half of the twentieth century, and if its hold on the Brazilian collective psyche declines, what will that mean for Brazilian identity in the twenty-first century?

CULTURAL COHESION, STATE, AND DEVELOPMENT

Brazil and Mexico may be the most notable examples in Latin America of a successful and mutually reinforcing convergence of processes (and narratives) of both economic and cultural development. From the 1930s to the 1990s the Brazilian and Mexican states took the lead role in creating and consolidating hard and soft national structures – the infrastructure for national economic development (roads, ports, utilities, industries) and cultural

---

[57] Telles, 2004: 77. See also, Bailey, 2009.   [58] Htun, 2004: 61.
[59] "We are either multi-ethnic or we are mixed." Maggie, 2008: 54.

development (radio, television, schools, museums). In the case of Brazil, despite contending ideologies and political parties the country displayed an impressive continuity across the controlled democracy and authoritarianism of the 1930s and 1940s, the fractious electoral politics of the 1940s to the 1960s, the brutally repressive dictatorship from the 1960s to the 1980s, and the re-democratization of the 1980s and 1990s. Mexico under the Partido Revolucionario Institutional, of course, had a much more authoritarian and controlled politics. Although neoliberalism and the exhaustion of ISI had already presented considerable challenges to the statist developmental model in the 1980s, not until the presidency of Fernando Collor de Mello that opened the decade of the 1990s did the Brazilian project face its first substantial reversals. In both Mexico and Brazil, the narrative of *mestizaje/mestiçagem* had achieved enormous popular acceptance by the 1980s. The dominant cultural narrative in Brazil began to confront important challenges in the 1980s, ones that intensified in the 1990s and at the beginning of the new millennium. The narrative may be even more enduring in its strength in Mexico.[60]

Although Brazil did not take the neoliberal turn as dramatically as some other Latin American countries, and certainly nowhere near as emphatically as Chile, the 1990s marked a turning point in the role of the state in economic development. Under Fernando Henrique Cardoso (1995–2003) dozens of state enterprises were privatized, trade barriers were reduced, and a new currency moved Brazil more into the global economy. Looking back to the neoliberal turn that began under Collor de Mello, after a quarter of a century Brazil stands somewhere in the middle of Latin American countries, between the extremes of Chile and Cuba, on the scale of liberalization. The role of the state in economic development has clearly shifted, and this shift has been paralleled by the declining power of the Freyrean narrative of national identity.

The widespread acceptance of the Freyrean narrative fostered a national cultural cohesion that was perhaps matched in Latin America only in Argentina, Uruguay, and Chile. This powerful consensus facilitated the efforts of the state to promote truly national development projects, but these projects collapsed with military coups in the three Southern Cone nations beginning in the 1970s. The widespread acceptance of the need for state-led economic development (even by the military) both reinforced the cultural cohesion and the efforts of a long line of politicians and technocrats to promote the role of the state in national economic development in Brazil into the 1990s. The dominance of economic developmentalism was intertwined with and reinforced by a potent cultural nationalism. In the 1990s, sustained challenges to the developmental state have taken shape, along with growing challenges to the dominant narrative of national identity and a powerfully cohesive cultural nationalism.

---

[60] See, for example, Sue, 2013 and Martínez Casas, Saldívar, Flores, and Sue, 2014: 36–80.

I do not believe that it is a coincidence that Brazil's emergence on the global cultural stage coincides with its successes in economic development. As Brazil surged economically and industrially in the late 1950s, bossa nova and *futebol* made the country an internationally recognized cultural icon. João Gilberto, Antônio Carlos Jobim, Pelé, and Garrincha provided the cultural images along with Brasília and new industries. The military regime quite consciously exploited these converging processes in 1970 as it celebrated the *tri-campeonato* at the height of their so-called economic miracle. As Brazil emerged economically in the early 1970s, Brazil's *seleção* became the favorite team of many around the world as their own national team was eliminated from contention in the World Cup. Even as the path to economic development seemed to collapse in the 1980s, Brazil's music, *carnaval*, and *futebol* continued to captivate and influence globally.

The roller coaster economic swings since the 1930s have also, I believe, produced a certain schizophrenia among Brazilians about economic development. The development surges in the late 1930s, late 1950s, and late 1960s were followed by stalls and (sometimes) crises in the early 1950s, early 1960s, and 1980s. The massive inflation and economic stagnation of the 1980s and 1990s reinforced the pessimistic side of the Brazilian psyche. Although I have argued elsewhere that Brazil has arrived, and is no longer the "country of the future," the economic surge from 2005–2010 that attracted so much attention in world media, and the subsequent downturn in the last five years have no doubt fortified the pessimistic side of the Brazilian psyche.[61]

BRAZILIAN EXCEPTIONALISM?

Clearly, Brazil was not alone among the nations of Latin America in the twentieth century in its promotion of a narrative of racial and cultural mixture. In the 1920s and 1930s, intellectuals in other regions of Latin America had also begun to proclaim the power of *mestiçagem/mestizaje* as the core of national identities.[62] Drawing on influences across the Atlantic world, they rejected the constraints of the prevailing racist theories and made a cultural turn. Following the lead of Franz Boas at Columbia University, they liberated their peoples from the confines of racialism and turned to culture as their salvation and liberation.[63] In Mexico, José Vasconcelos declared Mexicans the "cosmic race" (*raza cósmica*), a blend of indigenous peoples and Spaniards. In the aftermath of the Mexican Revolution, *mestizaje* became the official ideology of the new regime with the Indian (especially the Aztec) as the

[61] Eakin, 2015: 13–30.
[62] Mignolo argues that even the notion of "Latin" America "is the political project of Creole-Mestizo/a elites." Mignolo, 2005: 59.
[63] Quoting Oswald Spengler, Freyre envisioned "race" as a "mysterious cosmic force that binds together in a single rhythm those who dwell in close proximity." Amador, 2015: 146.

iconic figure of national pride. The great Cuban anthropologist, Fernando Ortiz, developed his theory of transculturation to explain cultural mixture in Cuba and the Caribbean basin. José Martí as early as the last decades of the nineteenth century had anticipated the ethnographic work of Ortiz when he spoke of "our mestizo America" (*nuestra América mestiza*).[64] Ironically, in Mexico, the ongoing and powerful racism toward indigenous peoples and those of darker skin belied the official version of race relations. In Cuba, the official ideology became one of a raceless people in a society marked by pronounced racism. Argentina and Uruguay, both the recipients of massive influxes of southern Europeans after 1880 formulated national narratives that recognized the influence of mixture, but gradually erased the country's Afro-descendant past and emphasized whiteness and Europe as the touchstones of national identity.[65]

Very recent survey data from the Project on Ethnicity and Race in Latin America (PERLA) offer sophisticated evidence on how the Brazilian narrative of national identity and Brazilian nationalism may be exceptional when compared to the rest of Latin America. More than 80 percent of respondents across racial groups "believed that Brazil is a mixed country" and nearly as many (78.8 percent) saw this as positive. At the same time, Brazil differs strikingly from the other three cases in PERLA's study: Mexico, Peru, and Colombia. The convergence between skin color and racial categories (both as self-identified and by the interviewer) was much stronger than in the other countries. Race in Brazil, clearly matters, yet identity and appearance were more important in the survey data than color in predicting racial inequalities (again in contrast to the other three countries). When it comes to color, Brazil has less racial ambiguity than the other countries yet, paradoxically, there is more ambiguity about who is Afro-descendant because of the fluidity of culture and appearance. Finally, when asked to choose between racial and national identity, Brazilians overwhelmingly (90 percent and higher across racial categories) chose national identity.[66] Mexico, it seems, is the closest to Brazil in the power and resonance of a narrative of national identity built on *mestizaje*. Post-revolutionary Mexico has witnessed the creation of a narrative of *mestizaje* that is perhaps even more dominant than the myth of *mestiçagem* in Brazil, especially in suppressing discussions of race. Argentina and Uruguay also have constructed powerful narratives, but ones built on whiteness and the erasure of non-white influences in their histories.[67] (As in Brazil, these narratives in recent decades face increasing challenges from a variety of groups.) Brazil appears strikingly unusual in both the construction of a broadly encompassing racial narrative

[64] Sodré, 1999: 105; Vasconcelos, 1997; Ortiz, 1995[1947]; Martí, 1980 [1891].
[65] Shumway, 1991; Andrews, 2010.
[66] Telles and the Project on Ethnicity and Race in Latin America (PERLA), 2014: esp. 194–196 and 214–217.
[67] Sue, 2013; Andrews,2010; Alberto and Elena, 2016.

of national identity, and one that now continues alongside an official recognition of a history of racism and discrimination.[68]

Clearly, at the beginning of the twenty-first century, the myth of *mestiçagem* retains enormous power, but several decades of sustained criticism have heightened racial awareness in Brazil while at the same time failing to raise the percentage of Brazilians identifying with the *movimento negro* even to a tenth of the population. This conversation about race, identity, and inequality has put Brazil in a position unlike its Latin American counterparts. Brazil has moved quickly over the past few decades from widespread denial of racism to government and public recognition, by blacks and whites, "to endorse structural accounts of racial inequality." Contrastingly, in Mexico, the Project on Ethnicity and Race in Latin America survey respondents "seemed unfamiliar with the notion of race" and the defense of the ideology of *mestizaje* remains a pillar of official discourse.[69] Studies of other Latin American countries have shown ways that national ideologies of *mestizaje* have contributed to the marginalization or silencing of the role of Afrodescendant populations in contrast to official recognition of indigenous peoples in the formation of national identities. While Mexico and Peru (and other nations with large indigenous populations) may have had success in promoting a national narrative of *mestizo* identity, this has been to the exclusion of the role of Afrodescendants. In contrast, the myth of *mestiçagem* has allowed the recognition of all groups, and at the same time, its critics have heightened official and public awareness of racial identities.

The great shift across Latin America, including Brazil, since the last two decades of the twentieth century has been a growing movement to contest the power of myths of *mestiçagem/mestizaje* and to replace them with an emphasis on a new multiculturalism. Once seen as progressive and inclusive, *mestiçagem/mestizaje* is now attacked for erasing difference, promoting homogeneity, and (for some) providing a disguised path to whitening. Multiculturalism, in contrast, promotes an identity politics that celebrates differences, pluralism, and heterogeneity. Again, Brazil stands out over the past generation for the striking support of the state for multiculturalism and the widespread recognition of the need to combat the structures of racism. In Brazil, the myth of *mestiçagem* remains dominant even as multiculturalism has become official government policy. Multiculturalism is, in effect, the insurgent narrative of national identity, but one with state support.[70]

---

[68] The closest parallels seem to be Colombia and Mexico. Both have officially recognized a history of racism but this seems to have had minimal impact in Mexico, and in Colombia the myth of *mestizaje* has been much more complicated and weaker than in Brazil. Telles and the Project on Ethnicity and Race in Latin America (PERLA), 2014: chapters 2 and 3.

[69] Telles and the Project on Ethnicity and Race in Latin America (PERLA) 2014: 209, 222.

[70] See, for example, Rahier, 2012; Hooker, 2005: 285–310.

In all of these cases, governments sought to promote national narratives that would help produce homogeneity and unity in the pursuit of development, in all its facets. As in the case of Brazil, the apparent dominance of a single narrative, be it *mestizaje* or whiteness, contributed to state efforts to create a sense of economic nationalism in support of developmentalism. At the same time, as Argentina, Mexico, Chile, and Uruguay achieved greater economic development this success fostered a stronger sense of pride among Argentines, Mexicans, Chileans, and Uruguayans. As in Brazil, cultural and economic nationalism could be mutually reinforcing. In countries with more conflicted narratives of national identity such as Peru, Ecuador, Bolivia, or the Dominican Republic, cultural nationalism was less focused and cohesive, and could not contribute as much to the drive for economic nationalism. The long (and more open) history of racism directed at indigenous peoples in the Andean republics, or against blacks in the Dominican Republic made the narratives of whiteness and *mestizaje* in Brazil, Mexico, Argentina, Chile, and Uruguay more powerful and, no doubt, more successful.[71]

Brazil stands out as one of the most successful examples of economic development in twentieth-century Latin America. I believe that the forging of a cohesive and widely shared master narrative of national identity and cultural nationalism played a key role in this economic development. The two processes were complementary and cross-fertilizing. When one looks across the rest of Latin America it is probably not coincidental that the most successful developers—Brazil, Mexico, Chile, Argentina—also have had a powerful master narrative of national identity (a narrative of *mestizaje/mestiçagem* in the first two cases, of Chileanness with some non-white components in the third, and of whiteness in the fourth). Other nations such as Colombia and Peru experience moderate economic success, and also more contested national narratives. The state plays a key role in the economic development of Brazil, Mexico, Argentina, and Chile, but it is in Brazil and Mexico that the state also plays such a key role in promoting a national identity narrative at the core of cultural nationalism in close conjunction with the drive for state-led economic development. Brazil has been strikingly successful in promoting a widely shared cultural and economic nationalism at all levels of society. That success up to the 1990s, however, may have been momentary and ephemeral.

REFERENCES

Alberto, Paulina L. *Terms of Inclusion: Black Intellectuals in Twentieth-Century Brazil.* Chapel Hill, NC: University of North Carolina Press, 2011.
  "Of Sentiment, Science and Myth: Shifting Metaphors of Racial Inclusion in Twentieth-Century Brazil." *Social History*, 37:3, August 2012, 261–296.

---

[71] Fuente, 2001; Mayes, 2014; Cadena, 2000; Portocarrero, 2007; Whitten and Whitten, 2011.

Alberto, Paulina L. and Eduardo Elena, eds. *Rethinking Race in Modern Argentina.* Cambridge University Press, 2016.

Amador, José. *Medicine and Nation Building in the Americas, 1890–1940.* Nashville, TN: Vanderbilt University Press, 2015.

Anderson, Benedict. *Imagined Communities: Reflections on the Origin and Spread of Nationalism*, rev. edn. New York: Verso, 2006 [1983].

Andrews, George Reid. *Blackness in the White Nation: A History of Afro-Uruguay.* Chapel Hill: University of North Carolina Press, 2010.

Appadurai, Arjun. *Modernity at Large: Cultural Dimensions of Globalization.* Minneapolis: University of Minnesota Press, 1996.

Bailey, Stanley R. *Legacies of Race: Identities, Attitudes, and Politics in Brazil.* Stanford University Press, 2009.

Bertoncelo, Edison. *A Campanha das Diretas e a democratização.* São Paulo: Associação Editorial Humanitas, FAPESP, 2007.

Bethell, Leslie. "Politics in Brazil under Vargas, 1930–1945." In *Brazil since 1930*, v. IX, *Cambridge History of Latin America,* ed. Leslie Bethell, Cambridge University Press, 2008: 3–86.

Cadena, Marisol de la. *Indigenous Mestizos: The Politics of Race and Culture in Cuzco Peru, 1919–1991.* Durham, NC: Duke University Press, 2000.

Campbell, Courtney J. "From Mimicry to Authenticity: The Instituto de Estudos Superiores Brasileiros on the Possibility of Brazilian Culture (1954–1960)." *Luso-Brazilian Review,* 51:1, 2014: 157–181.

Carvalho, José Murilo de. "Genocídio racial estatístico." *Globo,* December 2004: 7.

Caulfield, Sueann. *In Defense of Honor: Morality, Modernity, and Nation in Early-Twentieth-Century Brazil.* Durham, NC: Duke University Press, 2000.

Chacon, Vamireh. *A construção da brasilidade (Gilberto Freyre e sua geração).* Brasília: Paralelo 15 Editores, 2001.

Chasteen, John Charles. *National Rhythms, African Roots: The Deep History of Latin American Popular Dance.* Albuquerque: University of New Mexico Press, 2004.

Cooper, Frederick. *Colonialism in Question: Theory, Knowledge, History.* Berkeley: University of California Press, 2005.

DaMatta, Roberto. "Digressão: a fábula das três raças, ou o problema do racismo à brasileira." In Roberto DaMatta, *Relativizando, introdução à antropologia social.* Rio de Janeiro: Rocco, 1990: 58–87.

Eakin, Marshall C. "The Country of the Present, or, Leaving the Future in the Past." In *Emergent Brazil*, ed. Jeffrey Needell, University of Florida Press, 2015: 13–30.

Faoro, Raymundo. *Os donos do poder: formação do patronato político brasileiro*, 3a. ed. Porto Alegre: Editora Globo, 1976.

Freyre, Gilberto. *Casa-grande e senzala: introdução à história da sociedade patriarcal no Brasil – 1*, 40th edn. Rio de Janeiro: Editora Record, 2000.

  The Masters and the Slaves [Casa-grande e senzala]: A Study in the Development of Brazilian Civilization, trans. Samuel Putnam, 2nd edn. rev. New York: Alfred A. Knopf, 1970.

Fry, Peter. *A persistência da raça: ensaios antropológicos sobre o Brasil e a África austral.* Rio de Janeiro: Civilização Brasileira, 2005.

Fry, Peter, Yvonne Maggie, Marcos Chor Maio, Simone Monteiro, and Ricardo Ventura Santos, eds. *Divisões perigosas: políticas raciais no Brasil contemporâneo.* Rio de Janeiro: Civilização Brasileira, 2007.

Fuente, Alejandro de la. *A Nation for All: Race, Inequality, and Politics in Twentieth-Century Cuba*. Chapel Hill: University of North Carolina Press, 2001.

Gaspari, Elio. *A ditadura envergonhada; A ditadura escancarada; A ditadura derrotada; A ditadura encurralada*; and *A ditadura acabada*. São Paulo: Companhia das Letras, 2002–2016.

Gellner, Ernest. *Nations and Nationalism*. Ithaca, NY: Cornell University Press, 1983.

Goldstein, Donna M. *Laughter Out of Place: Race, Class, Violence, and Sexuality in a Rio Shantytown*. Berkeley: University of California Press, 2003.

Gouveia, Saulo. *The Triumph of Brazilian Modernism: The Metanarrative of Emancipation and Counter-Narratives*. Chapel Hill: University of North Carolina Press, 2013.

Guimarães, Antonio Sérgio, "Democracia Racial: O Ideal, o Pacto e o Mito." In Antonio Sérgio Guimarães. *Classes raças e democracia*. São Paulo: Editora 34, 2002: 137–168.

Hanchard, Michael George. *Orpheus and Power: The Movimento Negro of Rio de Janeiro and São Paulo, Brazil, 1945–1988*. Princeton University Press, 1994.

Hertzman, Marc. *Making Samba: A New History of Race and Music in Brazil*. Durham, NC: Duke University Press, 2013.

Hooker, Juliet. "Indigenous Inclusion/Black Exclusion: Race, Ethnicity and Multicultural Citizenship in Latin America." *Journal of Latin American Studies*, 37:2, May 2005: 285–310.

Htun, Mala. "From 'Racial Democracy' to Affirmative Action: Changing State Policy on Race in Brazil." *Latin American Research Review*, 39:1, February 2004: 60–98.

Ioris, Rafael R. *Transforming Brazil: A History of National Development in the Postwar Era*. New York: Routledge, 2014.

Johnson, Ollie A., III. "Afro-Brazilian Politics: White Supremacy, Black Struggle, and Affirmative Action." In *Democratic Brazil Revisited*, eds. Peter R. Kingstone and Timothy J. Power. University of Pittsburg Press, 2008: 209–230.

Johnson, Randal. "The Dynamics of the Brazilian Literary Field, 1930–1945."*Luso-Brazilian Review*, 31: 2, 1994: 5-22.

Kamel, Ali. *Não somos racistas: uma reação aos que querem nos transformar numa nação bicolor*. Rio de Janeiro: Nova Fronteira, 2006.

Kotscho, Ricardo. *Explode um novo Brasil: diário da Campanha das Diretas*. São Paulo: Brasiliense, 1984.

Kottak, Conrad Phillip. *Prime-Time Society: An Anthropological Analysis of Television and Culture*, updated edn.Walnut Creek, CA: Left Coast Press, 2009.

Lopes, Reinaldo José. "Quilombola é 40% europeu, mostra DNA." *Folha de São Paulo* September 18, 2013.

Loveman, Mara, "Census Taking and Nation Making in Nineteenth-Century Latin America." In *State and Nation Making in Latin America and Spain: Republics of the Possible*, eds. Miguel A. Centeno and Agustin E. Ferraro, New York: Cambridge University Press, 2013: 329–355.

Maggie, Yvonne. "Does Mário Andrade Live On?: Debating the Brazilian Modernist Ideological Repertory."*Vibrant*, 5:1, 2008: 34–64.

Martí, José. *Nuestra América*. Buenos Aires: Losada, 1980 [1891].

Martín-Barbero, Jesús. *De los medios a las mediaciones: comunicación, cultura y hegemonía*. Barcelona: Gustavo Gili, 1987.

Martínez Casas, Regina, Emiko Saldívar, René D. Flores, and Christina A. Sue. "The Different Faces of Mestizaje: Ethnicity and Race in Mexico." In *Pigmentocracies: Ethnicity, Race and Color in Latin America*, ed. Edward Telles, Durham, NC: Duke University Press, 2014: 36–80.

Martins, Luciano. "A Genese de uma Inteligentsia: Os Intelectuais e a Política no Brasil, 1920–1940." *Revista Brasileira de Ciências Sociais*, 2: 4, 1987: 65–87.

"A Inteligentsia em situação de mudança de referentes (da construção da nação à crise do estado-nação)." In *Brasil: fardo do passado, promessa do futuro: dez ensaios sobre política e sociedade brasileira*, ed. Leslie Bethell, trans. Maria Beatriz de Medina. Rio de Janeiro: Civilização Brasileira, 2002. 305–322.

Mayes, April J. *The Mulatto Republic: Class, Race, and Dominican National Identity* Gainesville: University Press of Florida, 2014.

McCann, Bryan. *Hello, Hello Brazil: Popular Music in the Making of Modern Brazil*, Durham, NC: Duke University Press, 2004.

Miceli, Sergio. *Intelectuais à brasileira*. São Paulo: Companhia das Letras, 2001.

Mignolo, Walter D. *The Idea of Latin America*. Oxford: Blackwell, 2005.

Oliveira, Lúcia Lippi. *Cultura é patrimônio: um guia*. Rio de Janeiro: Editora da FGV, 2008.

Oliven, Ruben George. "National and Regional Identities in Brazil: Rio Grande do Sul and its Peculiarities." *Nations and Nationalism*, 12: 2, 2006: 303–320.

Ortiz, Fernando. *Cuban Counterpoint: Tobacco and Sugar*, trans. Harriet de Onís. Durham, NC: Duke University Press, 1995 [1947].

Ortiz, Renato. *A moderna tradição brasileira: cultura brasileira e indústria cultural*. São Paulo: Editora Brasiliense, 1988.

Cultura brasileira e identidade nacional. São Paulo: Brasiliense, 2006.

"Culture and Society." In *Brazil: A Century of Change*, eds. Ignacy Sachs, Jorge Wilheim, and Sérgio Paulo Pinheiro, trans. Robert N. Anderson. Chapel Hill: University of North Carolina Press, 2009.

Pécaut, Daniel. *Os intelectuais e política no Brasil (entre o povo e a nação)*. São Paulo: Ática, 1990.

Pena, Sérgio D. J. e Maria Cátira Bortolini, "Pode a genética definir quem deve sebeneficiar das cotas universitárias e demais ações afirmativas?" *Estudos Avançados*, 18:50, January–April 2004: 31–50.

Portocarrero, Gonzalo. *Racismo y mestizaje y otros ensayos*. Lima: Fondo Editorial del Congreso del Perú, 2007.

Rahier, Jean Muteba, ed. *Black Social Movements in Latin America: From Monocultural Mestizaje to Multiculturalism*. New York: Palgrave Macmillan, 2012.

Reiter, Bernd and Gladys L. Mitchell, eds. *Brazil's New Racial Politics*. Boulder: Lynne Rienner, 2010.

Ribke, Nahuel. "Decoding Television Censorship during the Last Brazilian Military Regime." *Media History*, 17: 1, 2011: 49–61.

Rodgers, Daniel T. *The Age of Fracture*. Cambridge, MA: Belknap Press of Harvard University Press, 2011.

Rodrigues, Alberto Tosi. *Diretas Já: o grito preso na garganta*. São Paulo: Editora Fundação Perseu Abramo, 2003.

Rolland, Denis. "O Historiador, o Estado e a Fábrica dos Intelectuais." In *Intelectuais e Estado,* eds. Marcelo Ridenti, Elide Rugai Bastos, and Denis Rolland, Belo Horizonte: Editora UFMG, 2006: 95–120.

Sahlins, Peter. *Boundaries: The Making of France and Spain in the Pyrenees.* Berkeley: University of California Press, 1989.

Schneider, Ben Ross, "The Desarrollista State in Brazil and Mexico." In *The Developmental State,* ed. Meredith Woo-Cumings. Ithaca, NY: Cornell University Press, 1999: 276–305.

Schwarcz, Lilia Moritz. "Gilberto Freyre: adaptação, mestiçagem, trópicos e privacidadeem Novo mundo nos trópicos." In *Gilberto Freyre e os estudos latino-americanos,* eds. Joshua Lund and Malcolm McNee, Pittsburgh, PA: International Institute of Iberoamerican Literature, University of Pittsburgh, 2006: 305–334.

Schwartzman, Simon. *Bases do autoritarismo brasileiro.* Rio de Janeiro: Campus, 1982.

Schwartzman, Simon, Helena Maria Bosquet, Vanda Bomeny, and Maria Ribeiro Costa, *Tempos de Capanema,* 2nd edn., São Paulo: Paz e Terra/Fundação Getúlio Vargas, 2000.

Seigel, Micol. *Uneven Encounters: Making Race and Nation in Brazil and the United States.* Durham, NC: Duke University Press, 2009.

Sheriff, Robin E. *Dreaming Equality: Color, Race, and Racism in Urban Brazil.* New Brunswick, NJ: Rutgers University Press, 2001.

Shumway, Nicolas. *Inventing Argentina.* Berkeley: University of California Press, 1991.

Silva, Carlos Eduardo Lins da. *Muito além do Jardim Botânico: um estudo sobre a audiência do Jornal Nacional da Globo entre trabalhadores.* São Paulo: Summus, 1985.

Skidmore, Thomas E. *The Politics of Military Rule in Brazil, 1964–85.* New York: Oxford University Press, 1988.

Sodré, Muniz. *Claros e escuros: identidade, povo e mídia no Brasil.* Petrópolis: Editora Vozes, 1999.

Sovik, Liv Rebecca. *Aqui ninguém é branco.* Rio de Janeiro: Aeroplano, 2009.

Sue, Christina A. *Land of the Cosmic Race: Race Mixture, Racism, and Blackness in Mexico.* New York: Oxford University Press, 2013.

Telles, Edward E. *Race in Another America: The Significance of Skin Color in Brazil.* Princeton University Press, 2004.

Telles, Edward and the Project on Ethnicity and Race in Latin America (PERLA). *Pigmentocracies: Ethnicity, Race and Color in Latin America.* Durham, NC: Duke University Press, 2014.

Turra, Cleusa and Gustavo Venturi. *Racismo cordial: a mais complete análise sobre o preconceito de cor no Brasil,* ed. Folha de São Paulo, São Paulo: Editora Ática, 1995.

Vasconcelos, José. *The Cosmic Race: A Bilingual Edition,* trans. Didier T. Jaén. Baltimore: The Johns Hopkins University Press, 1997.

Vianna, Hermano, *O mistério do samba.* Rio de Janeiro: Zahar, 1995.

"A Meta Mitológica da Democracia Racial." In *O imperador das idéias: Gilberto Freyre em questão,* eds. Joaquim Falcão and Rosa Maria Barboza de Araújo. Rio de Janeiro: Fundação Roberto Marinho/Topbooks, 2001: 215–221.

Walker, Sheila S. "Africanity vs. Blackness: Race, Class and Culture in Brazil." *NACLA Report on the Americas,* 35:6, 2002.

Wallach, Joe. *Meu capítulo na TV Globo,* texto original editado por Randal Johnson. Rio de Janeiro: Topbooks, 2011.

Whitten, Norman E., Jr. and Dorothea Scott Whitten. *Histories of the Present: People and Power in Ecuador*. Urbana: University of Illinois Press, 2011.

Williams, Daryle. *Culture Wars: The First Vargas Regime, 1930–1945*. Durham, NC: Duke University Press, 2001.

Woo-Cumings, Meredith, ed. *The Developmental State*. Ithaca, NY: Cornell University Press, 1999.

15

Urban Informality, Citizenship, and the Paradoxes of Development

Brodwyn Fischer

INTRODUCTION

According to many mid-twentieth-century modernizing crusaders, the destiny of Latin American development hinged precariously on the fate of its distended cities. From the 1940s through the 1970s, long before the millennial urbanization of the global south, Latin America's major metropolises grew astonishingly, at rates as high as 5 to 7 percent annually.[1] Cities showcased development's failures and became visible arenas for political strife and revolution, from the *Bogotazo* of 1948 to Pérez Jiménez's 1958 ouster in Caracas, from the 1953 "strike of 300,000" in São Paulo to Fidel Castro's triumphant entry into Havana in 1959. Legions of laborers raised Brasília from the open *planalto* on the promise that city-building could be the catalyst of economic integration, and planners from Rio to Caracas to Mexico City erected row upon towering row of concrete residential blocks in hopes that orderly, modern apartments might foster an orderly, modern workforce.[2] In July of 1959, in a gesture symbolic of international preoccupation with Latin America's urban surge, Chicago sociologist Philip Hauser convened a pioneering gathering of Latin American urbanists in Santiago.[3] His

---

[1] Merrick and Graham, 1979: 194.

[2] Epstein, 1973; Vidal, 2000; Holston, 1989; Lins Ribeiro, 2008; Benmergui, 2009: 303–326; Velasco, 2015.

[3] Hauser was a prominent demographer and member of Chicago's school of (urban) sociology, and loomed especially large in international circles in the postwar years. Between 1958 and 1964, Hauser headed a working group formed at the Social Science Research Council with the aim of bringing a comparative and international perspective to urban theory and practice. He was appointed by UNESCO to organize seminars on urbanization in sub-Saharan Africa (1956) and Asia (1957), and served as the US representative to the UN Population Commission between 1947 and 1951. The 1959 Santiago conference, "Urbanization in Latin America," was cosponsored by UNESCO, the UN Bureau of Social Affairs, and the Economic Commission for Latin America (ECLA or CEPAL), in cooperation with the ILO and the OAS; it brought together many of Latin America's most prominent urban policymakers, sociologists, and planners. For further discussion of the conference and the trends it represented, see Benmergui, 2013: 35–56.

summary of their findings distilled the generational challenge: "The problems of urbanization are indisseverably linked to those of development, and no intelligent solution of both can be achieved unless their nature and interrelationships are perfectly clear."[4]

Many of Hauser's contemporaries concluded that those interrelationships were on a treacherous trajectory across much of Latin America, where precipitous urbanization had created poor, informal, chaotic cityscapes that hollowed every pillar of the North Atlantic urban ideal. For Cold Warriors, the stakes were existential: would "liberty and free economic development" survive the threat of swollen metropolises where "the teeming poor" were "a ripe field for Castroist and Communist political exploitation?"[5] For economic policymakers, overgrown cities threatened the rational allocation of resources: would precious capital that could fund roads, energy, industrialization, and agricultural modernization instead be squandered on housing, urban services, and welfare for the politicized urban masses?[6] For psychological and sociological theorists of development, an influx of unassimilated rural migrants threatened precisely those aspects of urbanity that made cities the ideal laboratory for economic progress: how could "traditional" peoples – unaccustomed to rational decision-making, resistant to change, bound to family and clan – possibly adapt to an "industrial" mindset, and how could emerging industrial societies prosper amidst the social and political chaos that their anomie would provoke?[7] While cities, in their ideal form, nurtured developmental modernity, "there was no worse combination than urbanism without development."[8]

The unifying thread in all such analysis was that Latin America's poor, informal cities generated overwhelming challenges for Latin America's developmental states. That conclusion has remained mostly uncontested by decades of subsequent scholarship, even as many mid-century falsehoods about the mid-twentieth-century informal city have been relentlessly exposed. Few informed observers would now argue (at least in those terms) that mid-century shantytowns were filled with unemployed, isolated, socially maladjusted individuals, or that rural to urban migration provoked psychotic anomie. Informal cities proved largely reluctant to tie their fates to the forces of radical revolution, and their residents have since often become (willingly or not) standard bearers for neoliberal arguments about the inherent entrepreneurialism of the poor.[9] Amidst such revisionism, however, informal urbanism's supposedly parasitic relationship with state-led development has

---

[4] Hauser, 1961: 34.   [5] Parks, 1961.

[6] Hauser, 1961: 37; Prebisch, 1963; McKee and Leahy, 1970: 86–489.

[7] Hauser, 1961: 47–55; Schulman, 1967: 184–195. For summaries of these objections in Brazil, their evolution over time, and their refutation see Mangin, 1967: 65–98; Leeds and Leeds, 1977; Perlman, 1976; Valladares, 2005; Fischer, 2014: 9–67.

[8] Hauser, 1961: 37   [9] De Soto, 2002.

remained common-sense wisdom. *Favelas* and *villas-miseria* may have insured developmentalists a low-cost labor pool and eased rural tensions. They may even have allowed entrepreneurialism to flourish despite heavy-handed bureaucratic restrictions. But it came at a high cost to development and the states that promoted it: distorted allocational priorities, shortsighted redistributionist concessions, political unrest, social violence, and the graphic projection of developmental failure on a global screen. If the main challenges of Latin America's developmental states involved the scarcity of capital, restricted domestic markets, bloated public deficits, the weakness of specialized and technical education, poor infrastructure, a chaotic and unpredictable regulatory environment, and a perception of political and social chaos, how could the region's informal cities have done anything but accelerate developmentalist failure?

This chapter aims to disrupt this normative logic by using the Brazilian case to pose a series of counter-intuitive questions. What did urban residential informality do *for* Latin America's developmental states? Is there a way of understanding the developmentalist dilemma in which urban informality emerges as necessary as well as parasitic? And can such questions help us to penetrate deeper conundrums about disjunctive state-building, persistent inequality, and their impact on Latin America's economic trajectory?

If the relationship between development and informal city-building is viewed with a wide lens – capable of apprehending a more complete view of Brazil's mid-century political economy – it becomes apparent that Brazil's developmentalist state needed its informal cities, in ways bound with material imperatives but also independent of them. Even after decades of revisionist scholarship, scholars often think of urban informality – residential and economic – in opposition to the formal state: as an expression of desperation, as a variety of legal pluralism, as a stubborn assertion of customary norms, or as a manifestation of grass-roots revolutionary impulses.[10] But in Brazil, across Latin America, and in much of the world, it may be more useful to conceive of the legalized state and its informalities in tandem, as interdependent components of the state-building process in a context of scarce resources and fraught consensus over the basic tenets of liberal democracy. Scholars of economic informality have highlighted similar interdependence between extra-legal economies and formal capitalism across Latin America, and scholars of residential informality have noted for half a century the high levels of social, political, and economic integration that characterize *favelas* and similar

---

[10] For the classic exploration of legal pluralism, see Merry, 1988: 869–896. In Brazil, the first theorist to explicitly link *favelas* to the concept of legal pluralism was Boaventura de Souza Santos, who portrayed the entanglement of official and unofficial authority in the *favela* of Jacarezinho ("Pasargada") in 1978 ("The Law of the Oppressed," *Law and Society Review* 12:1, Fall 1977: 5–125). For an interesting critical perspective on this conception of informality, see Oliveira, 2003: 67–89. For an example of informal economies' oppositional relationship to the state, see (from opposite political perspectives) Goldstein, 2016; and de Soto, 2002.

communities.[11] This chapter extends those insights to the analysis of state-building, documenting how informal urbanization was essential to the developmental state's successes, and also constitutive of its many fragilities.[12]

PARAMETERS

Viewed from afar, the historical interaction of urbanization, industrialization, and the Brazilian state seems at first to follow normative North Atlantic patterns. In the late nineteenth and early twentieth centuries, urban expansion roughly accompanied early industrial growth, though both were sustained by an essentially agrarian economy and neither was effectively regulated in most of the country. After the 1930s, when the Brazilian developmental state began to consolidate, both industrialization and urbanization became full-fledged forces of structural transformation, and national and local governments significantly intervened in both processes.[13] Between 1939 and 1966, industry's share of Brazilian GDP rose by 40 percent and it became the engine of the Brazilian economy; in roughly those same years, Brazil's urban population expanded from less than a third to more than half, and by 1980 75 percent of all Brazilians lived in cities.[14] Simultaneously, in partial reaction to the threat of political mobilization among urban workers, the Brazilian state assumed a strong moderating role, constructing a legal infrastructure for workplace regulation and economic citizenship and sharply suppressing the Communist Party and other advocates of more radical redistribution. Just as in the North Atlantic context, development in Brazil implied tightly entwined processes of urbanization, industrialization, and state intervention.

Yet it would be a mistake to think that similar entwinement yielded similar historical processes. In the idealized (but nonetheless paradigmatic) North Atlantic model and its variations, economic development and urban expansion advanced in a mostly virtuous cycle from the mid nineteenth century to the mid twentieth. Cities became cradles of industrial development because they concentrated the necessary human, financial, political, and technical capital. Crude industrial processing of raw materials in cities such as

[11] Roberts, 1994: 6–23; Portes, Castells, and Benton, 1989; Portes and Schauffler, 1993: 22–60; Itzigsohn, 2000; Fernandez-Kelly and Shefner, 2008; Santos, 1979; Tokman, 1978: 1065–1075; Mangin,1967; Leeds and Leeds, 1972: 268–286; Cornelius, 1975; Perlman,1976; Roy, 2011: 223–238.

[12] For an analysis of informal city-building from a historical perspective, focusing on citizenship and inequality, see Fischer, 2008. For an explanation of similar ideas of interdependence in the modern political realm, see Holland, 2016: 232–246.

[13] One might think of the difference between urbanization and urban growth in the same way in which Warner Baer understands the difference between industrialization and industrial growth. In both cases, mere growth was not sufficient to transform the basic structures of an agrarian and rural society; it was only with intentional structural transformation that industry and urbanity became dominant economic and social modalities. See Baer, 2014: 40–41.

[14] Baer, 2014: 66; Merrick and Graham, 1979: 188.

Chicago gave way relatively seamlessly to more technologically advanced factories, bureaucratic and commercial activity complemented industrial development, and urban markets stoked demand for industrially produced goods. Industry attracted workers who, after suffering a period of exaggerated exploitation, successfully mobilized for decent wages, working conditions, housing, and urban services. Those workers, now socially mobile, expanded markets further and drove both urbanization and urbanism, which took on an essentially progressive character and implied significant economic and political entitlements. Populations demanded that their governments provide core urban services, including adequate schooling and medical care as well as basic infrastructure. Slums persisted, but for the white working class they functioned mainly as starting points for trajectories that ended in apartments or houses in the suburbs. The story was different for African Americans and Mexican migrants in the United States, who suffered artificial restriction to racialized ghettoes; the same would later be true for other migrant groups, and especially those without documentation.[15] But even for those groups, for much of the twentieth century, becoming part of the urban, industrialized world in the United States or Europe implied material, civic, and social mobility – access, however limited, to the promise of development. It was only when industry became more capital intensive and globally mobile, and when it became apparent that racialized inequalities were deeply entrenched in both geographic and civic terms, that cities began to be understood as dead ends on the road to opportunity.

This is an exaggerated ideal even for the United States and Northern Europe. In Brazil and in most of Latin America, such virtuous cycles were part of a more muddled reality, especially if we treat immigrant metropolises such as Buenos Aires and São Paulo as the exceptional cases they proved to be. "Cities," to begin with, were not the same in Brazil as they were in the North Atlantic at the beginning of the industrial age, either in their physical and legal infrastructure or in their relationship with the rural and international economies. By the early twentieth century, most Brazilian cities possessed an urbanized core, with basic sanitation, stately architecture, schools, theaters, police, and reasonably well-regulated property and commercial relations. But even in Rio de Janeiro, Brazil's national capital until 1960, that core fell short of what the eye could see: in Afrânio Peixoto's memorable dictum, the *sertão* (or backlands) began on the edges of the Avenida Central.[16] Beyond Rio's downtown and a few prosperous suburbs stretched a vast *município* where urbanity only weakly

---

[15] Drake and Cayton, 1993; Massey and Denton, 1988; Sánchez, 1993; Sugrue, 2005; Rothstein, 2017.

[16] The Avenida Central was the famously ornate central boulevard constructed as the centerpiece of a draconian belle-époque reform of Rio's central districts. As will be seen below, *sertão* was a charged term in early twentieth-century Brazil, denoting backwardness and later debilitating physical weakness as well as the literal northeastern backlands depicted in Euclides da Cunha's classic depiction of the Canudos war. Peixoto is quoted in Hochman, 1998: 217–235.

shadowed the tentacular lines of passenger rails and tramways; even in the central districts, tangles of *cortiços* (tenements) lacked urban services and embryonic *favelas* regularly interrupted the urbanized fabric. In 1933, as the age of industrialization and urbanization began, only about 32 percent of Rio's buildings had sewer service, only 44 percent had electricity, only 58 percent had running water, and only 34 percent of all officially recognized streets were paved.[17] A quarter of Rio's buildings were wooden or "rustic" dwellings. Though São Paulo had considerably fewer improvised constructions – only about 3 percent of those counted in the 1940 census – service provision probably did not exceed two-thirds even for electricity. In northeastern cities such as Recife and Salvador, rustic dwellings were often the majority and residential neighborhoods were more scarcely serviced still.[18]

The differences between North Atlantic and Brazilian cities also stretched into the legal realm. It wasn't that Brazilian cities lacked laws. By the end of the 1930s, Brazil's major cities had all passed building and sanitary codes that formally bound them to modern ideals of urbanism and public health. The codes banned shacks from urban areas, regulated spacing and construction standards, mandated maximum occupancies, required service provision and sought to limit standing water and other vectors of infectious disease.[19] While Brazilian cities lacked centralized property registries, notarial offices were meant to ensure the orderly regulation of urban lots. But in a context where so many extant homes and neighborhoods could not meet the regulations' minimum requirements, and where so much property was occupied or held outside of the law's boundaries, Brazil's urban legislation took on a different and paradoxical significance. Rather than dictate urban norms, the laws served instead to mark the porous, ever shifting boundaries between an official city – regulated and protected by law, and bound to basic guarantees of urban citizenship – and an extralegal one, where the possession, construction, and occupancy of urban property depended on special favors or exemptions from the letter of the law. Although the boundaries of these two modes of urban occupation were porous and tentacular, they correlated closely to both race and socio-economic status.[20]

Brazilian cities' infrastructural and legal scarcities were closely tied to the nature of urban economies, and to their relation with the rural world. Until the early twentieth century, Brazilian cities are best understood not as dynamic centers of production, but rather as entrepôts and crossroads for rural

[17] Brazil, Ministério do Trabalho, Indústria e Commércio, 1935.
[18] Merrick and Graham, 1979: 211; Brazil, State of Pernambuco, 1924; Brazil, Instituto Brasileiro de Geografia e Estatística, 1956: XVII: 1, 120; Marcus André B.C. de, "A cidade dos mocambos: estado, habitação e luta de classes no Recife (1920/1960)," *Espaço e debates* 14 (1985): 44–66, 54.
[19] Brazil, Rio de Janeiro (Distrito Federal); Brazil, São Paulo, 1929; Brazil, Recife, 1936. See Rolnik, 1997; Peixoto-Mehrtens, 2010; Fischer, 2013.
[20] For more detailed exploration of these issues, see Fischer, 2008: esp. part I.

economies and networks of power, and as the places where rural economies locked into global networks of commerce and finance.[21] Brazil's national economy, fueled first by enslaved labor and then by massive European migration, revolved around primary commodities: sugar, precious minerals, coffee, cotton, cacao, and rice. While some cities (Rio, Recife, and especially São Paulo) invested surplus rural capital in light consumer industry, the proportion of industrial workers remained comparatively small, and industry's importance in driving the overall economy was minimal before the Second World War.[22] Cities rose and fell as centers for agricultural commercialization and export, and as the places where agricultural elites formed their networks and negotiated with central authorities, first colonial and then national. While cities could be sites of relative independence and freedom from rural, patriarchal power structures – especially for individuals at various stages of emancipation from slavery, and especially the few cities large enough to provide some semblance of anonymity – they did not generate large independent middle classes and remained well into the twentieth century tightly linked to the economic and political dynamics of rural Brazil. Because of this, Brazil's urban areas had neither the independent economic base nor the autonomous political networks to assert a strong counterweight to rural dominance of national economic and social welfare policies. Industry grew incrementally, but neither industrialists nor the urban bourgeoisie nor an urban proletariat dictated urban or national policy.

Brazil's urban form – infrastructurally incomplete, legally ambiguous, shaped by rural economies and power relations – did eventually provide fertile ground for industrial development. When the combined forces of the rising political power of industrialists, the cataclysmic contraction of international markets, and global economic experimentation hit with full force in the early 1930s, Brazil's progressive planners turned to cities in search of precisely those urban elements that had fostered industrialization throughout the West: capital, technical know-how, infrastructure, and markets. Getúlio Vargas and his successors built support for developmentalism among urban industrial, intellectual, professional, and bureaucratic classes, and they created a nominally generous welfare state in order to court precisely those elements of Brazil's working population that most closely resembled a North Atlantic working class: formally recognized, organized workers and public employees.[23] In many ways, the policies that promoted industrialization simply ignored the divergences between Brazilian cities and those of the North Atlantic, building an industrialization project on familiar elements of urbanity

[21] This conception is somewhat similar to James Scobie's definition of Latin America's "commercial-bureaucratic" cities, but places greater emphasis on cities' roles as integrating spaces for Brazil's rural elites. See Scobie, 1989: 149–182.

[22] Baer, 2014: 40–42; for Rio in particular, see Fischer, 2008: 131.

[23] Santos, 1979; Gomes, 2005; Cardoso, 2010; Fischer, 2014.

as if the larger urban or national context were residual or immaterial. The ideal city of the incipient developmental state could be pieced together in the swirl of contradictions that was Brazilian urbanity. The question was, what would become of the rest of urban Brazil, and how would its evolution impact the larger projects of industrial development and economic modernization?

DEVELOPMENTALISM AND ITS CHALLENGES

If developmentalism is defined in purely economic and technical terms – and if the developmental state is conceived solely as the one that promotes the economic dimensions of state-led industrial modernization with recourse to both national and international capital – then Brazil's story is well known and often repeated.[24] After the so-called Revolution of 1930, Getúlio Vargas led a fifteen-year regime that, while not precisely developmentalist, re-oriented Brazil's national government toward industrial and urban expansion and strengthened the national state's bureaucratic capacity, coherence in economic policymaking, and capacity to mediate conflicting class, regional and sectoral interests. Particularly under the Estado Novo (1937–1945), Vargas consolidated the ministerial and legal frameworks for state intervention in industrial development and labor relations, negotiated the foundations for the Brazilian steel industry, created an extensive welfare system for urban, formal-sector workers, and increased large-scale investments in energy and transportation.

After World War II, and especially during his final presidential administration (1951–1954), Vargas spearheaded accelerated state involvement in industrial planning and credit, transportation, and energy. In the second half of the 1950s – considered by many to be the high-water mark of Brazilian developmentalism – Juscelino Kubitschek introduced an enormously ambitious *"plano de metas,"* which sought to advance Brazil "fifty years in five," in areas ranging from energy to transportation to food, basic industry, and education. Kubitschek's program enjoyed apparent success, especially in relation to transport, energy and the automobile sector; he also realized the seemingly utopian nineteenth-century goal of building a new national capital of Brasília from nothing on Brazil's central plains. The cost, however, was high: inflation, debt, neglect of agriculture, underdeveloped private capital markets, a chronic shortage of capital to finance deepening industrialization, and frustration from workers and bureaucrats whose earnings were significantly eroded by inflation.[25]

---

[24] Developmentalism, and the developmentalist state are contested notions, but most analysts concur on this core economic definition. See Cardoso and Faletto, 1979; Sikkink, 1991; Schneider, 1999: 276–305.

[25] Baer, 2014; Luna and Klein, 2014.

From a developmentalist perspective (though certainly not a political or social one), some of those dilemmas were solved after the military coup of 1964, which suppressed social demands and facilitated internationalization: agricultural productivity increased, a national financial infrastructure was consolidated, foreign investment accelerated, the scale of geographic reach of industrial and mineral production expanded, and growth rates exceeded 10 percent per year between 1967 and 1973.[26] But the military government's economic policies relied excessively on debt, environmentally unsustainable agriculture, and regressive income distribution; in addition, famously inefficient and corrupt state-led industries occupied a greater and greater share of the national economy. As a result, Brazil suffered deeply in the "lost decade" of the 1980s, and developmentalism lost much of its ideological luster. Despite this, Brazil's developmental state did not recede to nearly the same extent as its Latin American counterparts, and it had undeniably succeeded in its project of industrialization, in the broadest sense of the word. Brazil was by the 1970s the largest industrial economy in Latin America and industry was the country's most dynamic sector, central to an increasingly urbanized consumer society.

This history of the political economy of Brazilian developmentalism is widely accepted, but its interaction with Brazil's broader economy and society – including the urban realm – remains highly contested. At the center of these debates lies a fact with direct relevance for the relation between development and urbanization: Brazilian governments, from Vargas through military rule, mostly pursued development with a studied lack of direct engagement with the country's deepest forms of underdevelopment and poverty. Industrialization and the social pacts that made it politically viable concentrated public resources in Brazil's most prosperous regions, with little direct provision for the economic integration or social welfare of the vast majority of Brazil's inhabitants.

The most obvious category excluded from the developmentalist pact was the rural sector. In part, this was simply the political cost and economic logic of the developmentalist project. The agrarian networks that had dominated Brazilian politics through the 1930s accepted industrial modernization, state expansion, and even disadvantageous currency and trade policies on the condition that the national state would mostly avoid direct intervention in the rural world.[27] Rural landownership remained enormously concentrated, rural workers long lacked access to basic labor protections and rudimentary economic citizenship, illiterates were disenfranchised, and rural life and the governance of mostly rural regions continued to be significantly governed by private, patriarchal

---

[26] Luna and Klein, 2014: 197.
[27] Welch, 1999. See also Schneider, 1999; Sikkink, 1991; Luna and Klein, 2014. This tacit agreement was surprisingly similar to that which accompanied the abolition of Brazilian slavery in the nineteenth century: while slaves were freed, eminent calls for land reform or intervention in patriarchal and often violent social and labor relations remained unheeded.

networks.[28] Public social welfare investments – with the important exception of public health – were overwhelmingly targeted toward cities and toward the Brazilian southeast, leaving rural welfare concerns to the webs of personal patronage that had long been critical to rural social orders.

But the rural world was only the most obvious and categorical of the developmental state's exclusions. A second category was defined geographically. Developmentalism dramatically favored the Brazilian Southeast, and such distorted investment cemented northeastern Brazil's incipient status as Brazil's developmental Achilles' heel.[29] Industry, fostered through protectionism, state-led growth, and multinational investment, became the engine of the Brazilian economy by the mid twentieth century. But it functioned as something of a regional enclave, overwhelmingly concentrated in the Southeast and especially in the cities of São Paulo and Rio de Janeiro.[30] These areas received disproportionate shares of private industrial and infrastructural investment, national and foreign. The Federal government catalyzed those trends, from its early subsidies for immigration, coffee production, and infrastructural improvements through the nurturing of the steel industry and Juscelino Kubitschek's vaunted "metas." Public labor and welfare policies further exacerbated these regional and sectoral inequalities: Brazil's developmental state, in an effort to consolidate working-class support and coopt labor activism, geared everything from the basic social safety net to urban improvements to housing and retirement benefits toward public employees and formal-sector urban workers, who also concentrated overwhelmingly in the Southeast and South.

In the 1950s, economist Celso Furtado articulated a full-throated critique of developmentalism's regionally disparate impacts.[31] Following Raúl Prebisch and the economic logic that would eventually lead to dependency theory, Furtado argued that import substitution industrialization (ISI) policies had transformed the internal dynamics of the Brazilian economy, making of the

---

[28] Gini indices for land ownership ranged between .70 and .85 between 1920 and 1950 for most of Brazil's regions and continued high through the rest of the twentieth century (Luna and Klein, 2014: 123, 172, 203). Interestingly, it was under the military government – a violent opponent of agrarian reform – that rural workers first gained some semblance of legal status and the legal mechanisms were put in place for indigenous land rights.

[29] On the emergence of the Northeast as a "problem," see Albuquerque, 2014; Weinstein, 2015; Blake, 2011.

[30] By 1950, some 57 percent of industrial employment was concentrated in Rio and São Paulo, and the balance mostly took place in just a few other states (Minas Gerais, Rio Grande do Sul, and Pernambuco). In 1960, that concentration had increased to 62.2 percent (Merrick and Graham, 1979: 205). Figures for value added and industrial production are still more extreme: the Southeast's share of value added only dipped below 60 percent after 1980 and is still well over 50 percent; its share of industrial production was 76 percent in 1960 and is currently around 60 percent (Baer, 2014: 251).

[31] Conselho de Desenvolvimento do Nordeste, 1959. For discussion of Furtado's evolving thought, see Mallorquín, 1996: 687–728.

Northeast a kind of internal periphery within Brazil's borders. According to this argument, protection increased the prices of consumer goods throughout the Northeast, forcing Northeasterners to buy expensive and inferior national products. At the same time, ISI economists artificially manipulated exchange rates in order to promote the imports of capital goods, driving up the rates that northeastern importers paid for other types of foreign products and inputs. These phenomena, together with capital outflows from the Northeast to industrial investment opportunities in the Southeast and considerable loss of human capital, resulted in a perverse transfer of resources from the Northeast to the South, which remained undercompensated by public transfers or virtuous economic linkages.

Furtado's critique gained substantial urgency in a context of increasing political unrest in the Northeast.[32] It culminated in 1959 with the creation of the Superintendency for the Development of the Northeast (SUDENE), a federal agency charged with the ambitious task of alleviating the regional distortions of Brazilian developmentalism.[33] In its initial formulation, SUDENE aimed to promote northeastern industrialization (largely through tax incentives), increase the efficiency of northeastern agro-export economies, improve the efficiency and ecological sustainability of northeastern food production, and promote colonization of landless workers on the region's northern and southern frontiers. Land reform within heavily populated regions of the Northeast was not initially understood as a component of SUDENE's development policy.

Furtado initiated the project energetically, and sought especially to free SUDENE from the control of political and regional patronage networks. But the results were paltry, especially after the Military Coup of 1964 forced Furtado into exile and curtailed the agency's independence.[34] While the northeastern economy expanded in the 1960s, its growth rates in the Northeast still lagged behind those of the nation as a whole. Industries grew slowly, concentrated overwhelmingly on Salvador and Recife, and tended to be capital intensive, resulting in few employment opportunities. Most new industry extended southeastern or foreign industrial enterprises to the Northeast rather than promoting new regional entrepreneurship: profits

---

[32] Ianni, 1971: 647–659.

[33] SUDENE became the most celebrated and discussed regional development agency in Brazil, due in part to Furtado's renown as one of the foremost intellectual leaders of Latin American developmentalism. However, SUDENE was not Brazil's first regional development agency. Already in 1948, the federal government created the Comissão do Vale do São Francisco (CVSF), following the model of the Tennessee Valley Authority (TVA), a blueprint for the Brazilian project that was made explicit during parliamentary debates. Hirschman, 1963: 53. Other agencies created in the following years were the Superintendência do Plano da Valorização Econômica da Amazônia (SPVEA) for the Amazon region, established in 1953, and the Superintendência do Plano da Valorização Econômica da Fronteira Sudoeste do País (SPVEFS) for the southwestern borderlands, created in 1956.

[34] Andrade, 1977: 25–28; Borello, 1989: 157–165; Baer, 2014: 265.

flowed back to the South, and price structures remained unchanged. Pernambuco, which received the bulk of SUDENE's industrial benefits, accounted in 1970 for only 1.4 percent of Brazil's industrial production and 1.9 percent of its industrial workforce.[35] SUDENE accomplished little in the agricultural realm, and came later to be plagued with personalism, patronage and corruption; by the time of its extinction in 2001, SUDENE was widely regarded as a failed experiment in utopian developmentalism.[36]

A third category of developmental exclusion was less easily demarcated by geographical space: it involved sinuous "peripheries" that persisted even within most prosperous industrial cities of the Southeast.[37] Throughout Brazil, industry was never as important as a source of employment as it was as an engine of GNP growth.[38] The vast majority of urban working people clustered overwhelmingly in low-paid service or informal occupations, and many hovered on the margins of subsistence well into the developmental age. Though they might benefit indirectly from the industrial economy (through family networks, infrastructure, urban services, and regional linkages), they could never participate fully in industrial society as workers or as recipients of public labor and welfare support.[39] As consumers, they were hurt by the higher prices of national industrial goods and foodstuffs. Even before the military government, which systematically devalued working-class wages and benefits even as it formally extended their reach, the advantages of industrialization circulated in a constricted circuit.

BRASÍLIA AND THE URBAN FACE OF DEVELOPMENTAL EXCLUSION

The construction of Brasília was both symptom and symbol of the urban face of the Brazilian developmental state's many exclusions.[40] A modernist urban experiment, constructed in five years as Juscelino Kubitschek's personal crusade, Brasília was at once the realization of a nineteenth-century nationalist fantasy, the embodiment of a socialist utopia, and a forceful plan to integrate Brazil's sprawling regions and extend development to the vast interior. In theory, Brasília was meant to be a developmentalist idyll and an escape from the chaotic disorder and social injustice of Brazilian urban life. In the new capital, every resident would have a function and a social place. Low-level public employees would live and work in close proximity to their superiors, and employment would be the precondition for urban residence. There would be no room for extreme inequality or exclusion, because

---

[35] Mello, 1978: 189–190.

[36] SUDENE was not in this sense exceptional: the SPVEA, created for the Amazon region, faced myriad structural impediments to success.

[37] On this flexible concept of the urban periphery, see Roy, 2011.

[38] Merrick and Graham, 1979: 19; Katzman, 1989: 99–140, 104.   [39] Fischer, 2014.

[40] See note 2, above.

residence would be predicated on membership. Like Brazil's industrial sphere, Brasília promised modernity and relative equality, but the cost was categorical exclusion.

As many have eloquently documented, both Brasília's utopia and its exclusion were stillborn.[41] The heroic hordes of workers imported to raise a city from the plains in a few short years proved unwilling to abandon their creation. The city's constructors thus became its first squatters, thus undermining the promise that had led them to stay. The same, in a sense, could be said of the developmentalist project. If Brazilian industrialization could have operated as a closed circuit, where flows of capital, labor, consumption, and welfare were restricted to the original inhabitants of the southeastern cities and towns where it most prospered, Brazil might easily have followed the virtuous cycles that characterized early industrialization in much of the rest of the world. But there were no borders between Brazil's rural and informal spheres and its industrializing core, and Brazil was for much of the developmentalist period a nominally democratic republic. Poor rural Brazilians apprehended the promise of industrial modernization and citizenship, and demanded their share through physical mobility. In essence, they became squatters on the terrain of industrial development – sometimes figuratively, as in the case of the precursors of the Brazilian MST (landless movement), but more often literally, in the vast informal reaches of Brazil's burgeoning cities.

The demands of unincorporated urban Brazilians in the age of industrialization are relatively poorly documented. Until the late 1950s, they did not organize like industrial workers, and their political activities (while highly significant) were eclectic and locally rooted, most often geared toward urban permanence rather than social revolution.[42] But their very presence and insistent, incremental demands presented Brazil's developmentalist state with an enormous challenge. Materially, how could already strained state finances stretch to house and service an urban poor that expanded exponentially with rural-to-urban migration? Ideologically, how could unlettered rural peoples be incorporated into a modernizing ideal that presumed linear civilizational progress as a precondition of development? Strategically, how could the national government deny their claims or exclude them without draconian violence or revolutionary upheaval? Politically, how could the unincorporated poor be integrated into urban, populist political networks at a low cost and without provoking conflict with actors who benefitted from their weak access to citizenship? It was in this context that urban residential informality emerged as a fundamental tool in easing the foundational tensions of Brazil's developmental state, offering residents access to the dream of modernizing development without the political and economic cost of full integration.

---

[41] See (especially) Epstein, 1973.
[42] Fischer,2008; Gonçalves, 2013; Silva, 2005; Cézar, 1985: 161–182; Assies, 1991; Bezerra, 1965; Gominho, 1998; Rolnick, 1997.

INFORMALITY AND THE MATERIAL CHALLENGES OF MIGRATION

To understand urban residential informality's importance, it helps to grasp the enormous material costs that North-Atlantic-style urbanism implied for a country like Brazil. To begin with, there was nothing organic about such costs: it was only in the glare of North Atlantic norms, during the first age of the "global city," that many of the most distinctive features of Brazil's urban centers appeared distorted and inadequate. The rusticity and legal ambiguity of Brazilian cities – as in Latin America generally – long predated their definition as a problem requiring public action.[43] Brazil's cities were built deliberately, but that deliberation always involved what would eventually come to be called informality: extra-official arrangements whereby slaves, freedpersons, and the dependent poor lived by wit, grit, favor, and grace in attics, backyard huts, tangled *cortiços*, stilted swamp settlements and hillside communities that their owners and social superiors did not consider fully civilized.

It was only in the nineteenth century, with the rise of belle-époque urban reforms and the gradual elimination of informal urbanity from European and US cities that the existence of this alternate urbanity threatened elite notions of civilized life. In Brazil, calls for public solutions to the problems of overcrowded tenements and visible pockets of informal housing had their origin in the 1840s and 1850s, as public health officials zeroed in on tenements as sources of miasmatic or infectious disease.[44] In subsequent decades, intellectuals influenced by theories of scientific racism fretted about the impact of rustic "African" huts on civilized cities, and students of social realism and social psychology dreaded the significance of "promiscuous" overcrowding on the nation's social health.[45] Such fears deepened in the early twentieth century, as the beginnings of the US Great Migration drove early members of what would become the Chicago School of sociology to re-think nineteenth-century theories about rurality, urbanity, and the noxious mix of the two in conditions of rapid (and racially diverse) population flux.[46] In Brazil, Euclides da Cunha's monumental portrayal of the arid *sertão* (or backlands) provoked a new generation to identify the roots of the nation's ills in rural geography, malnutrition, and illness; for many, the informal city was nothing more than another *sertão* in the midst of hard-won urban civilization.[47]

In partial reaction, during the first decades of the twentieth century officials from Rio to Recife undertook periodic urban reforms and campaigns to

---

[43] For a more extended discussion of the problematization of informality, see Fischer, 2014.
[44] Chalhoub, 1996; Benchimol, 1990; Meade, 1997; Sevcenko, 1993; Rolnick, 1997.
[45] Schwarcz, 1993; Orlando, 1908; Backheuser, 1906; Azevedo, 2000.
[46] The classic starting point for this literature is Park, 1915: 577–612; for Latin America, the most important Chicago theorists after Park were Robert Redfield, Oscar Lewis, and (for Brazil) St. Claire Drake and Horace Cayton (whose *Black Metropolis* heavily influenced Florestan Fernandes), and Donald Pierson.
[47] Lima, 2013.

eliminate slums and shantytowns, everything from violent burnings to the paternalistic private construction of *vilas operarias* in exchange for public tax credits.[48] But even with the relatively low rates of internal migration that prevailed before the 1930s, the task of wholesale North Atlantic urbanization was beyond the grasp of municipal governors. As noted above, in the early 1930s improvised or rustic housing probably comprised 25–50 percent of the housing stock in Rio, Recife, and Salvador. São Paulo followed the North Atlantic model more closely in the area of housing; only about 3 percent of its housing was made of wood in 1940, and the vast majority of poor residents lived in tenements rather than shacks.[49] Service provision ranged from abysmal in the Northeast to passable in São Paulo, where even in 1940 electricity and water reached about two-thirds of all urban buildings and roughly a third had toilets.[50] If we consider that Rio and São Paulo had about 302,000 and 272,000 households respectively in 1940 – and that Recife and Salvador had about 72,000 and 67,000 – it is not difficult to grasp the enormous dimensions of upgrading housing and services for so many.[51]

Authorities felt the full force of the urban challenge in the late 1930s, when Pernambuco's Estado Novo interventor Agamenon Magalhães mounted Brazil's first wholesale campaign against informal housing. The so-called "Liga Social Contra o Mocambo" harnessed social science, authoritarian repression, corporatist organizational logic, and Catholic social theory to mobilize the city of Recife to eliminate the 45,581 *mocambos* (rustic shacks) that populated the city's backyards, tidal floodplains, hills, and canyons, sheltering nearly 64 percent of Recife's households.[52] Citing the *mocambos'* supposedly ruinous effects on social psychology, public health, civic well-being, urban modernization, and even rural out-migration, Magalhães personally called on Recife's elite and professional classes to donate to his "crusade" as if they were reacting to a public calamity: "We have to think ... as if there had been an earthquake and 164,837 people had been left without shelter. We are going to harbor the survivors of a catastrophe."[53] No Brazilian city – not even Rio under Pereira Passos – had mobilized so many citizens, under such authoritarian control, for the cause of wholesale elimination of informal settlements. And yet the result was dismal: authorities razed 12,400 *mocambos*, but only 5.5 thousand small houses were built between 1939 and 1944, and the vast majority of *mocambo* residents simply reassembled their

---

[48] Examples include the *morro* of Santo Antonio (Rio) in 1916 and Recife under Health Department head Amaury Medeiros in the early 1920s.

[49] São Paulo also resembled North American cities more closely in terms of ethnic and racial residential segregation. See Fernandes, 1964; Andrews, 1991; Telles, 2006.

[50] Brazil, Instituto Brasileiro de Geografia e Estatística, 1940: Tomo I: *Censo Demográfico – Habitação*, 130–131.

[51] Brazil, Instituto Brasileiro de Geografia e Estatística, 1940.

[52] Brazil, State of Pernambuco, Comissão Censitária dos Mocambos, 1939.

[53] Magalhães, 1939.

dwellings in more distant reaches.[54] When Rio mounted its own wholesale *favela*-removal commission in the 1940s, it was led by Victor Tavares de Moura, a native of Pernambuco, and had similar results: the lakeside shantytown that prefect Henrique Dodsworth personally set ablaze in 1942 was quickly replaced by others, the "Proletarian Parks" built by the commission never housed more than about 7,500 people, and many of those were public employees who had never lived in the *favelas*.[55] The scale of the informal city – the sheer number of houses that would need to be replaced – was simply too great to be eliminated, even in times of political authoritarianism and mass social mobilization.

As rural to urban migration picked up steam in the 1940s and 1950s, the scale of demand for housing and services became more overwhelming still. At fault, at least in part, was the developmentalist model itself. By concentrating public resources, public welfare, and industrial investment in just a few coastal cities, and ignoring the concentration of land, the misery of wages, and the violent and patriarchal social relations of the Brazilian countryside, Brazil's national government set up a situation where migration to cities was the only chance for Brazil's poorest population to claim the fruits of development and expanded citizenship.[56] And yet, paradoxically, that migration was also a direct and enormous challenge to economic development itself: public capital invested in urbanization yielded few developmental linkages, and the property speculation encouraged by rapid urbanization steered private investment away from more productive agricultural and industrial enterprises. At the same time, food shortages caused by rural depopulation and agrarian technological backwardness increased labor costs and social unrest, and a lack of agricultural productivity impeded Brazil's capacity to finance industrialization through primary exports. This dynamic was abundantly clear to contemporaries, who saw the question of urban migration as one deeply tied to issues of rural latifundia and urban overinvestment.[57]

In capturing the scale of Brazil's migrations, numbers speak more eloquently than words. Between 1940 and 1980, Brazil went from a nation that was two-thirds rural to one that was two-thirds urban.[58] All in all, some 41 million rural

---

[54] Leite, 2010; Lima, Rodrigues da Cruz, da Silva, Ventura, and Montenegro, 1988.

[55] Estimates are as low as 5,000 (Pacheco, 1962 and Valla, 1986); the higher number is from Parisse, 1969.

[56] The diffusion of radio, print media and cinema to smaller towns in the Brazilian interior – and Vargas' own unprecedented travels to Brazil's far reaches – also augmented urban allure, as did the stories of migrants returning to the small towns and plantations where they had been born.

[57] See, for example, Costa Porto, 1953.

[58] This migration had significant regional dimensions: the Northeast and the still mostly rural state of Minas Gerais lost significant population, and so did the rural regions of all but the most dynamic frontier states; gains were felt in the far West, the North, the South, and the Southeast. Merrick and Graham, 1979: 132, 134.

people migrated to urban areas between 1940 and 1980; at the peak of this migration between 1970 and 1980, 42 percent of rural Brazilians migrated within a single decade.[59] Their destinations were, overwhelmingly, Brazil's southeastern cities. São Paulo and Rio alone grew from respective populations of 1,326,261 and 1,764,141 in 1940 to 8,587,665 and 5,183,992 in 1980, an increase of nearly 11 million people in just forty years.[60] In the face of such flux, many analysts found the notion of full urbanization absurd: in 1953, in one of the first articles to posit *favelas* as a solution rather than a problem, Alberto Passos Guimarães scoffed that in Rio alone it would take 605 million bricks, 180 thousand doors and 90,000 windows to replace even a third of the city's 90,000 shacks.[61] That was without even considering the costs of property regularization and formal urbanization; although Rio's municipal government repeatedly began expropriation and urbanization processes in Rio's *favelas* in this period, almost none were fully carried out.[62]

Given the enormity of the challenge, municipal governments in the era of the developmental state were in fact remarkably effective in extending both housing and urban services, in both the populist republic (1945–1964) and the military era. In Rio, where we have the best data over the long term, in 1933 approximately 44 percent of homes had electricity, 58 percent had piped water, and 32 percent had sewers. In 1948, 82 percent of Rio's streets had electric illumination, 84 percent had piped water, and 39 percent had sewage lines. In 1980, 80 percent of Rio's homes had legal electric service, 88 percent had public water, and 78 percent private access to the public sewer system.[63] In those same years, the number of "rustic" homes dropped to less than 2 percent of Rio's total, and residents began to construct more permanent dwellings even in *favelas* and illegal subdivisions.[64]

Yet even such impressive urban development signaled a transformation in the nature of Brazil's informal cities rather than their elimination. Official "favelas" were never less than 12 percent of Rio's homes and tens of thousands more families lived in similarly precarious circumstances, even before the economic crisis of the 1980s intensified urban poverty in Rio and across Brazil. Occupancy remained ambiguous or flat-out illegal in *favelas* and subdivisions across urban Brazil, and both *favelas* and most poor neighborhoods failed to comply in some way with building or sanitary codes.

[59] Martine and McGranahan, 2010: 14.
[60] Brazil, Instituto Brasileiro de Geografia e Estatística, 2010.   [61] Guimarães, 1952.
[62] See Fischer, 2014: Chapter 8.
[63] If unmetered electric service is factored in, the service rate in 1980 jumped to 98 percent. See Brazil, Instituto Brasileiro de Geografia e Estatística, 1980: I tomo 6, no. 18, 116 (electric), 108 (water), 109 (sewer).
[64] For urban Brazil as a whole, the proportion of "permanent" dwellings was 95 percent in 1980; 88 percent of urban residents had access to electricity (officially or not), 75 percent had public water, and 36 percent had a public sewer connection. Brazil, Instituto Brasileiro de Geografia e Estatística, 2003: 125.

Shortages of urban services and the irregular or illegal occupation of land remained persistently correlated with region, class, race, and rural origins; the greatest beneficiaries of public financing for housing were overwhelmingly formal sector workers in industry or public service resident in the Rio–São Paulo corridor. Even at the height of Brazil's economic boom in the 1970s – with economic growth sometimes exceeding 10 percent per year, authoritarian military governments determined to eliminate informal urbanity, and international aid and credit abundantly supportive of urban modernization – Brazil's governors could not marshal the material resources to eliminate urban informality altogether. In this context (and with renewed intensity after the economic crash of the 1980s), informal city-building provided a quiet solution to the scarcity of public resources, both material and administrative. The more urbanization could be relegated to poor migrants and the entrepreneurs that profited from them, the fewer public resources would be diverted from more productive investment in the core components of industrial development. In this way, urban informality was functionally similar to other forms of informal economic activity around the globe, easing the economic contradictions of developmental scarcity or failure.[65]

STRATEGY AND POLITICS

The notion that urban residential informality was a "solution" to the material contradictions of developmentalism explains much about its persistence in mid-century Brazil and Latin America.[66] And yet both informality and developmentalism involved logics beyond economics. They were also political and ideological phenomena, and their interdependence extends to those realms.

At the most obvious political level, residential informality provided an escape hatch for tensions created by the "closed circuit" model of industrialization and urbanization, which were sharply exacerbated by the rapid economic changes, heightened popular expectations, and transnational revolutionary militancy in the postwar period.[67] Brazil's politics of development worked relatively well so long as demands for state mediation and welfare were limited to the relatively limited pool of urban, formal sector workers who were (along with industrialists and the state) considered part of Vargas' tripartite political pact. The entire structure of the *trabalhista* bargain was predicated on what Wanderley Guilherme dos Santos famously dubbed "regulated citizenship," the linkage of economic rights to urban economic activity and worker

---

[65] Centeno and Portes, 2008: 23–48, 33.

[66] In the 1960s, an early version of this argument – and also an important precursor of Hernando de Soto's arguments about the economic entrepreneurialism of the poor and the value of their urban investments – was articulated by Mangin, 1967.

[67] In this sense, too, informal urbanism functionally resembled other types of informality explored by Centeno and Portes, 2008.

submission to state labor mediation. Under Vargas' *trabalhista* legal structure – which incorporated elements of both the New Deal and Italy's Fascist labor code – workers gained access to labor protections, health and welfare benefits, housing and social security by virtue of formal, mostly urban employment, and the political loyalty thus accrued was one of the pillars of developmentalism.[68] The system was highly beneficial to many workers, even with its many deceptions, co-optations, and abuses, and the fact that *trabalhista* benefits were defined as rights had enormous meaning for previously disenfranchised workers.[69] But *trabalhismo* was also deeply unjust, distributing the fruits of industrial modernization to relatively narrow working classes while ignoring the more desperate needs of the rural poor.

Policymakers in Brazil were well aware of the political danger of rural exclusion – they saw, or thought they saw, its fruits in Mexico, Bolivia, and Cuba – and closer to home the issue of rural poverty and land concentration fueled widespread support for radical Communist and Catholic social movements.[70] Successive governments proved politically unwilling or unable to undertake agrarian reform, and at various points – most especially in Pernambuco in the early 1960s – agrarian movements seemed a real revolutionary threat. The same series in *Life Magazine* that raised alarms about urban Brazil's "teeming poor" featured dramatic photographs of northeastern peasants bearing agricultural implements with menacing stares and applauding Peasant League leader Francisco Julião: together, they were "potentially the most explosive revolutionary combination in all Latin America."[71]

What often remains undiscussed is the extent to which rural-to-urban migration, facilitated by the toleration of urban residential informality, diffused these political tensions. Throughout the 1950s and 1960s, policymakers in both Brazil and the US worried frequently about revolutionary organization in Brazil's shantytowns, and with good reason: from the 1930s forward, Brazilian communists rallied loyalty among the urban poor by facilitating mobilization against poor living conditions and unequal rights to the city.[72] But both revolutionaries and their enemies sometimes failed to apprehend the degree to which urban informality often worked as a kind of foothold in the *trabalhista* version of the developmentalist dream.[73] What outsiders regarded as squalid and intolerable living conditions actually represented both an escape from rural domination and a first step

---

[68] Santos,1979; Gomes, 2005; Fischer, 2008; Cardoso, 1979: Chapter 4.

[69] Cardoso makes this point especially powerfully. See also French, 2004; Weinstein, 1997; Ferreira, 2001; Dinius, 2010.

[70] Pereira, 1997; Mayberry-Lewis, 1994; Forman, 1975; Welch, 1999; Rogers, 2010.

[71] "A Fidel Front among Impoverished," *Life*, 2 June 1961.

[72] Fischer, 2014: 1–33; Oliveira, 2012: 100–120.

[73] In this sense, I extend on both my own analysis in *Poverty of Rights* (Fischer, 2014: parts II and IV) and Adalberto Cardoso's emphasis on the attainable nature of trabalhista rights (Cardosa,

toward economic and political citizenship. Once in the city, migrants constructed elaborate webs of connection to the populist bargain; one family member might gain formal employment, others would benefit from liberal toleration of informal economic activity, others would reap the fruits of paternalistic networks. Even illiterates, formally disenfranchised, could exercise some degree of citizenship through corrupt clientelist networks. Children could study and perhaps gain a better life; all could survive and sometimes advance because the cost of living in *favelas* and *mocambos* was relatively low even amidst rabid profiteering. Analysts have often considered both urban informality and the limitations and unfulfilled promises of *trabalhismo* as political liabilities. But in fact they served brilliantly to channel popular discontent toward piecemeal accumulation of economic and political citizenship, speeded mightily by the favor and good grace of political authorities and private patronage. In a context where poor and rural people had never previously enjoyed rights, and where social mobility had always involved the fraught combination of material betterment and embeddedness in networks of intimate inequality, urban informality was a natural terrain of compromise.

IDEOLOGY, CITIZENSHIP, AND THE LIMITS OF PUBLIC POWER

Urban informality's immediate material and political utility for the Brazilian developmentalist state has never passed unnoticed, even amidst the persistent cacophony of alarmism surrounding the *favela* phenomenon.[74] But we still lack – in Brazil or elsewhere – a theoretical and historical framework that explores urban informality's role in easing deeper conundrums, impasses faced by the developmental state but rooted in the foundational ambiguities of Brazilian citizenship and national consolidation since independence. The rise of state-led developmentalism was not only a matter of creating the technical mechanisms and political will for full-fledged industrialization. It also involved significant transformations in the nature of the state and its relationship with the Brazilian populace. The consolidation of a developmentalist state implied a recalibration of longstanding conflicts over the meaning of egalitarian citizenship in a country where most nationals did not enjoy full political, social, or civil rights, and where social and political relationships were predicated on the assumption of inequality. It also required the disruption of uneasy accords over the scope and reach of legally bound public power and its ability to define and regulate private domains. The tensions produced by these disruptions were not exclusive to cities, but until the early 1960s Brazil's cities were the arenas in which they played out most consequentially.

2010: Chapter 4). For an early comparison in the Chilean context, see Portes, 1971: 820–835 and 1972.
[74] Mangin, 1967; Portes, 1972; Valladares, 2005; Fischer, 2014.

There is nothing unique about the "differential" nature of Brazilian citizenship.[75] In liberal democracies in Latin America and the world, the notion of "equal" rights has been initially predicated on restricted definitions of the pool of nationals eligible for equality; democracy is, in this sense, everywhere "disjunctive."[76] But categorical exclusion of nationals from citizenship has played an especially complex role in the long history of Brazilian state-making, serving at once as a marker of deep doubts about the civic capacity of certain kinds of nationals and as a way of preserving private, patriarchal power amidst the legal and bureaucratic trappings of liberal republicanism.[77] The distinctive feature in both cases is not citizenship's differential nature, but rather its incremental and precarious one: Brazilian citizenship has developed not as a fully formed birthright, but rather as a piecemeal accumulation of rights, accessed as often as not with the help of favors. This does not imply that Brazilian citizenship is openly exclusionary; on the contrary, even in the nineteenth century, when Brazil's economy still relied on enslaved labor, citizenship was defined with relatively few inherent restrictions such as race or caste. But the road to citizenship was riddled with onerous incremental requirements – property, literacy, income, documentation – and meeting them was often enormously burdensome. Despite those roadblocks, Brazilians – even enslaved Brazilians – regularly moved across the spectrum of citizenship within their lifetimes. But they frequently did so not by exercising public rights, but rather by calling on private obligations based on grace and unequal reciprocity. One of the keys to the persistence of deep inequality in Brazil was that incremental access to civic rights, often considered symbols of liberal equality, required integration into extraordinarily hierarchical networks of private power. This dynamic proved remarkably resilient in the nineteenth century, as Brazil moved from colony to Empire to Republic, abolished slavery, and embarked on the path that would eventually be labeled development.[78]

One function of incremental citizenship was the reconciliation of liberal democracy with deep social prejudice and the widespread naturalization of social inequality. Brazil's nineteenth-century elites – and many of its European immigrant masses – held deeply racist beliefs about the country's large Afro-descendant population. Some adhered to scientific racism, others believed that slavery itself had created a culture of brutality that had indelibly scarred its victims, still others simply fastened on to racism as a shortcut to competitive advantage. Those prejudices overlapped with increasing doubts about Brazil's rural world, held to be stagnant, sick, violent, and hungry, perhaps Brazil's greatest impediment to modern civilization. Rural public health campaigns in the 1910s and 1920s projected enormous optimism that rural people's failures were transient, rooted in malnutrition and disease rather than inherent

---

[75] Phrase and concept from Holston, 2008.   [76] Caulfield, Chambers, and Putnam, 2005.
[77] Costa, 2000: 53–77.   [78] For the etymology of development, see Arndt, 1981: 457–466.

deficiency.[79] A succession of thinkers – from Joaquim Nabuco to Gilberto Freyre to Florestan Fernandes – replaced essentialist racism with theoretically more transient cultural assumptions. But though both racism and anti-rural prejudice mutated, neither disappeared: anti-rural prejudice even attained new vigor with sociological theories describing the supposed marginality and pathological displacement of rural migrants. Throughout the developmentalist age many Brazilians showed enormous resistance to the idea that Afro-descendant and rural people were civilizationally prepared for full economic, social, or political citizenship.

As the Vargas regime expanded citizenship and the developmentalist project promised access to the fruits of modernity, it proved politically impossible to bar rural or Afro-descendant people from Brazilian cities or the benefits of Brazilian law. In both Rio and Recife there were proposals for border controls and forced return to the countryside, but even during the authoritarian Estado Novo, Brazilians had little stomach for categorical civic exclusion: explicit racial bans likewise never prospered beyond a few corners of raw prejudice. But there were many ways to make urban citizenship a favor as well as a right, and thus both to limit the citizenship of rural and Afro-descendant people and to maintain the reach of private, patriarchal power. Municipal codes declared urban informality illegal, and set the bar for legality far beyond the capacity of most poor residents (and even many in the middle classes). Criminal law defined infractions such as vagrancy and arms possession in such a way that virtually anyone could be hauled away at police discretion. Voting was tied to literacy, which was closely correlated with race and rural origin. Charity was tied to good behavior, and *trabalhista* benefits were tied to work status and civic agility. At every step of the way – from exiting a state of outright illegality to attaining full rights to the city – private considerations of reciprocity, power, and prejudice mediated poor urban residents' access to the rights of citizenship. Just as freedom had been a conditional state for black Brazilians in the nineteenth century, so in the twentieth was urban citizenship a state of precarious grace for Afro-descendants, rural migrants, and the poor.[80]

Informal cities thus proved essential terrains of compromise in conflicts involving citizenship in Brazil's developmentalist project. As a corollary, urban informality also helped to ease another deep tension surrounding the notion that rights and laws could supplant private networks of authority in mediating social and economic relations, especially among members of distinct social classes. Succinctly stated, personalistic power relations and private domination of public institutions long coexisted with the structures of Brazil's liberal First Republic, and the imposition of public power on private social relations was one of the greatest (and least explored) challenges faced by Vargas and his developmentalist successors. Both *trabalhismo* and developmentalism required an enormous extension of state

---

[79] Hochman, 1998; Lima, 2013.   [80] On the precariousness of freedom, see Chalhoub, 2012.

authority into previously "private" realms, involving everything from labor norms to price controls to social welfare to gender relations.[81] Among elites and employers, rural and urban, there was open resistance to interference in private labor or commercial relationships and considerable tacit resentment of any attempt to give subordinates (including women) direct recourse to public authority. There was also deep worry about how to control the radical impulses of democracy without the channeling mechanisms of private clientelistic networks. At the same time, while workers, women, and the poor often welcomed the chance to directly engage the state and to use laws as tools, they proved extremely reluctant to entirely give up recourse to private favors and tolerated illegalities in a context where the rule of law was far from being a totalizing system and access to political participation depended on literacy and bureaucratic agility.

Urbanization sharply exacerbated such disruptions, but urban residential informality once again eased them. For the privileged and powerful, informal urban residents' most useful characteristic was their inherent vulnerability: unlike entitled citizens, they depended on extralegal tolerance for land tenure and on politicians' favors for access to vital urban services. Residents' vulnerabilities facilitated the construction of legendary networks of private power from Rio de Recife and everywhere between, involving everyone from personal patrons and petty profiteers to wealthy land developers and politicians. By allowing the proliferation of these networks, state authorities became themselves enmeshed in a reciprocal exchange of private favors, wherein tolerance for private power was traded for personal political support or even (though not explicitly) the rise of "public" governance and developmentalism itself. In this way, informality became an asset, an essential currency in the exchange of private favors that valorized "public" authority and eased its widespread acceptance.

Informality's roles in mediating citizenship and public power are not anomalous. Both are linked to a deeper capacity in Brazilian public life to resolve social conflict through moderating practices that allow the coexistence of seemingly incongruent legal, political, and economic orders. Some of these moderating practices operate by injecting incremental porousness into otherwise draconian categories of inequality (slave/free, rural/urban, black/white, national/citizen, property owner/squatter). Such porousness allows the maintenance of categorical inequalities, because those on the bottom rungs can sustain the hope of incremental mobility, and it also re-enforces patriarchal power networks, which often act as mediators of mobility across the spectra of inequality. Others of these moderating practices operate by allowing systematic exceptions to wildly idealized legal, economic, or urbanistic orders. This serves to sustain the illusion of otherwise unattainable institutional forms and (again) to allow the continual reassertion of aleatory and patriarchal power, as

---

[81] On Gender and Vargas-era law, see Caulfield, 2000.

individuals (and not institutions) hold the power to grant tolerance of lifeways and relationships that fall outside of restrictive legal orders.

For Brazil's developmental state, faced as it was not simply with the material challenges of economic modernization, but also with resistance to changes in the reach of public power and the expansion of citizenship, urban informality was a moderating practice par excellence. Informal urban formations were technically illegal: they offered no rights to the city, required no mandatory investment, and did not force any compromises in either the draconian nature of urban regulation or the impossibly generous promise of urban citizenship. But in the mid twentieth century, *favelas* were often understood by their residents not as spaces of exclusion, but rather as porous sites, places where it was possible to pass incrementally from one end of the spectrum of inequality toward another. Such passage, moreover, depended mainly not only on the impersonal mediation of the state, but also on the private grace of public authorities and the vigorous politicking of speculators and politicians (often one and the same). Ironically, if rural migrants wanted to claim a place in the developmentalist dream – and if *favela* residents wanted to overcome the worst consequences of urban inequality and claim some access to the benefits of urban citizenship – they had to embed themselves deeply into hierarchical networks of private, patriarchal power. In this way, urban ideals could coexist with widespread urban destitution, expanded state authority and access to citizenship could reinforce private power, and a developmental model that disproportionately benefitted a tiny urban minority of the national population could gain widespread popular support.

CONCLUDING SPECULATIONS

Claims of Brazilian developmentalism's late-twentieth-century demise are sometimes exaggerated. The crisis of the 1980s certainly severely tested state-led development's legitimacy, along with informality's capacity to sustain it. The bankrupt Federal government contracted, industrial production and employment plummeted, inflation eroded much of the value of public benefits and services, and state-led industries and utilities flailed. Before the 1980s, developmentalism – even in all of its exclusions and failures – had succeeded in expanding the virtuous circles of industrial modernization over nearly half a century. The hope generated by that expansion – the promise of eventual inclusion and mobility – largely explains informality's capacity to diffuse the tensions of exclusive developmentalism. But in the 1980s, the informal labor market was saturated with unemployed workers, and the children of migrants found that personal networks and populist structures were no longer enough to get them a toehold in the path to urban social mobility. Overcrowded and underserviced *favelas* stagnated, urban services and schools deteriorated, and the chimera of developmentalist progress seemed to dissolve. Illegal drug and arms economies grew in importance; as they effectively rooted themselves in *favelas'* economic and political structures, communities experienced new levels of violence and increasingly complex and corrupt relationships with state security forces. By the early 1990s, the political pact that had supported state-led development seemed to have dissolved, leaving the door open for any solution capable of controlling inflation and imposing some degree of stability and predictability. In Brazil as elsewhere, neoliberalism stepped into that void, often with broad popular support.

Yet Brazil never went so far as Chile or Mexico in implementing neoliberal reforms. In the 1990s, governed by a centrist president who had contributed greatly to the development of dependency theory, the Brazilian state retained both direct and indirect roles in industrial development, and did less than other Latin American countries to dismantle the populist welfare state.[82] After 2002, the era of the Workers' Party was marked by neo-developmentalism, especially under Dilma Rousseff.[83] This tendency was perhaps most evident in relation to energy and agribusiness, but it also infused the urban arena. Particularly in terms of housing and urban planning, the years after 1988 were arguably the most interventionist in Brazil's urban history, with a bewildering swirl of constitutional guarantees, legal dictates, ministerial structures, security measures, housing programs, urbanization plans, and full-scale evictions and expropriations in anticipation of the 2014 World Cup and the 2016 Olympic Games.[84] While the crisis of the mid 2010s has seemingly marked a sharp reversal in course, Brazil is still notable for its tendency to adhere to developmentalist principles across radically divergent political regimes.

Conversely, however, one might argue that Brazil's developmental state survived precisely because it never entirely dominated Brazilian power relations, particularly in the urban arena. Long before de Soto called for his "other path" – and long even before William Mangin anticipated some of his claims in the 1960s – informal cities across Brazil and Latin America were expanding as urban spaces that operated outside of legally mandated norms, free of both the burdens and the benefits of formal rights to the city. Brazil's informal cities were not, as de Soto would have it, liberal bastions of freewheeling entrepreneurship in the midst of "mercantile" bureaucratic domination.[85] They were, rather, spaces that allowed

---

[82] Thorp, 1998.

[83] If we work specifically with Ben Ross Schneider's notion of a "desarrollista state," which specifies the "political exclusion of the majority of the adult population" and a "fluid, weakly institutionalized bureaucracy" in addition to the presence of developmental discourse and political capitalism, then the continuity is a bit harder to sustain. Suffrage is now not only possible but mandatory for all competent adults, and Brazil's bureaucratic class has in some respects been greatly professionalized. Schneider, 1999: 278.

[84] For a summary of urban policies as they relate to *favelas* in Rio, see McCann, 2014; for titling programs, see Fernandes, 2011 and Gonçalves, 2009: 237–250; for "rights to the city" since the 1988 constitution, see Rolnick, 2013: 54–64; Fernandes, 2007: 201–219; 2007: 177–189; Maricato, 2010: 5–22.

[85] Among many critiques, see Mitchell, 2008: 244–275; Gilbert, 2012: v–xvii.

developmentalism – with all of its ambitions and limitations – to move forward less impeded by the material demands of urbanization, the political discontent of those excluded from industrialism's closed circuit, and deep uneasiness about Brazilians' preparedness for full citizenship and the state's reach into previously private realms of economic and social life. In this conception, Brazil's developmental state evolved in open and dependent entanglement with urban and other informalities; it could exist as an exclusive sphere because informality offered viable pathways around it. The question, as this new age of neo-developmentalism fades, is whether it is possible to imagine a less entangled future, in which poverties of rights do not have to be the cost of expanded citizenship and the instruments of equality do not have to be obtained at the cost of unequal reciprocities.

REFERENCES

Albuquerque, Durval Muniz de. *The Invention of the Brazilian Northeast*. Durham, NC: Duke University Press, 2014.
Andrade, Manuel Correia de. "The Process of Industrialization in Recife." *Geojournal* 1:4, July 1977: 25–28.
André, Marcus, B.C. de. "A cidade dos mocambos: estado, habitação e luta de classes no Recife (1920/1960)." *Espaço e debates*, 14, 1985: 44–66, 54.
Andrews, George Reid. *Blacks and Whites in São Paulo*. Madison: University of Wisconsin Press, 1991.
Arndt, H.W. "Economic Development: A Semantic History." *Economic Development and Cultural Change*, 29:3, April 1981.
Assies, Willem. *To Get out of the Mud: Neighborhood Associativism in Recife, 1964–1988*. Amsterdam: CEDLA, 1991.
Azevedo, Aluísio. *The Slum: A Novel*. Oxford and New York: Oxford University Press, 2000.
Backheuser, Everardo. "Habitações populares: relatório apresentado ao Exm. Senhor Doutor J. J. Seabra, Ministro de Justiça e Negócios Interiores." Rio de Janeiro: Imprensa Nacional, 1906.
Baer, Wener. *The Brazilian Economy*, 7th edn. Boulder, CO: Lynne Rienner, 2014.
Benchimol, Jaime Larry. *Pereira Passos: Um Haussmann Tropical*. Rio: Biblioteca Carioca, 1990.
Benmergui, Leandro. "The Alliance for Progress and Housing Policy in Rio de Janeiro and Buenos Aires in the 1960s." *Urban History* 36:2, 2009: 303–326.
  "The Transnationalization of the 'Housing Problem:' Social Sciences and Developmentalism in Postwar Argentina." In *The Housing Question: Tensions, Continuities and Contingencies in the Modern City*, eds. Edward Murphy and Najib B. Hourani. New York: Routledge, 2013: 35–56.
Bezerra, Daniel Uchoa Cavalcanti. *Alagados, Mocambos e mocambeiros*. Recife: Instituto Joaquim Nabuco, 1965.
Blake, Stanley. *The Vigorous Core of our Nationality*. University of Pittsburgh Press, 2011.

Borello, José Antonio. "Una evaluación del programa de industrialización de la SUDENE." *Revista Geográfica* 109, January–June 1989: 157–165.

Brazil, Instituto Brasileiro de Geografia e Estatística. *Recenseamento Geral do Brasil*, 1940, Série Regional, Parte XVII, Tomo I: Censo Demográfico – Habitação (São Paulo). Rio de Janeiro: IBGE, 1940.

VI Recenseamento Geral do Brasil. Rio: IBGE, 1956, XVII: 1.

IX Recenseamento Geral, Rio de Janeiro: IBGE, 1980.

Estatisticas do século XX. Rio de Janeiro: IBGE, 2003.

"Sinopse do Censo Demográfico 2010: Tabela 1.6, População nos censos demográficos, segundo os municípios das capitais – 1872/2010," www.censo2010 .ibge.gov.br/sinopse/index.php?dados=6&uf=oo (accessed January 3, 2018).

Brazil, Ministério do Trabalho, Indústria e Commércio. Serviço de Estatística da Previdência e Trabalho. *Estatistica predial do Districto Federal, 1933.* Rio de Janeiro: Departamento de Estatística e Publicidade, 1935.

Brazil, State of Pernambuco, Departamento de Saúde e Assistência, Inspectoria de Estatística Propaganda e Educação Sanitaria. *Recenseamento do Recife, 1923.* Recife: Secção Téchnica da Repartição de Publicações Officiaes, 1924.

Brazil, State of Pernambuco. Comissão Censitária dos Mocambos. *Observações estatísticas sobre os mucambos do Recife.* Recife: Imprensa Oficial, 1939.

Brazil, Prefeitura da cidade do Recife. Lei 1051, September 11, 1919; and Decreto 374, August 12, 1936.

Brazil, Rio de Janeiro Prefeitura da cidade do (Distrito Federal). Decreto 6000, *Código de Obras de 1937*, July 1, 1937.

Brazil, Prefeito do Municipio de São Paulo. *Código Arthur Saboya*, November 19, 1929.

Cardoso, Adalberto. *A construção da sociedade do trabalho no Brasil.* Rio de Janeiro: FGV, 2010.

Cardoso, Fernando Henrique and Enzo Faletto. *Dependency and Development in Latin America.* Berkeley: University of California Press, 1979.

Caulfield, Sueann. *In Defense of Honor.* Durham: Duke University Press, 2000.

Caulfield, Sueann, Sarah Chambers, and Lara Putnam, eds. *Honor Status and the Law in Modern Latin America.* Durham: Duke University Press, 2005.

Centeno, Miguel Angel and Alejandro Portes. "The Informal Economy in the Shadow of the State." In Patricia Fernández-Kelly and Jon Shefner, *Out of the Shadows*, University Park, PA: Penn State University Press, 2008: 23–48.

Cézar, Maria do Céu. "As organizações populares do Recife: trajetoria e articulação política (1955–1964)." *Caderno de estudos sociais* 1:2, 1985: 161–182.

Chalhoub, Sidney. *Cidade febril.* São Paulo: Cia. das Letras, 1996.

A força da escravidão. São Paulo: Cia. das Letras, 2012.

Conselho de Desenvolvimento do Nordeste. *A Policy for the Economic Development of the Northeast.* Recife, 1959.

Cornelius, Wayne. *Politics and the Migrant Poor in Mexico City.* Stanford University Press, 1975.

Costa, Emilia Viotti da. "Liberalism." In Viotti da Costa, *The Brazilian Empire: Myths and Histories*, Chapel Hill: University of North Carolina Press, 2000: 53–77.

Costa Porto. "Causas do Êxodo e da Fixação." *Diário de Pernambuco*, January 4, 1953: Section 2, p. 1.

De Soto, Hernando. *The Other Path*. New York: Basic Books, 2002.

Dinius, Oliver. *Steel City*. Stanford University Press, 2010.

Drake, St. Clair and Horace Cayton. *Black Metropolis*. University of Chicago Press, 1993.

Epstein, David. *Brasília: Plan and Reality*. Berkeley: University of California Press, 1973.

Fernandes, Edésio. "Constructing the 'Right to the City' in Brazil." *Socio Legal Studies* 16, 2007: 201–219.

"Implementing the Urban Reform Agenda in Brazil."*Environment and Urbanization*, 19:1, 2007: 177–189.

The Regularization of Informal Settlements in Latin America. Cambridge: Lincoln Land Institute, 2011.

Fernandes, Florestan. *A integração do negro na sociedade de classes*. São Paulo: FFCL/ USP, 1964.

Fernandez-Kelly, Patricia and Jon Shefner. *Out of the Shadows*. University Park, PA: Penn State University Press, 2008.

Ferreira, Jorge. *O populismo e sua história*. Rio de Janeiro: Civilização Brasileira, 2001.

Fischer, Brodwyn. *A Poverty of Rights*. Stanford University Press, 2008.

"The Red Menace Reconsidered." *Hispanic American Historical Review* 94:1, 2014: 1–33.

Fischer, Brodwyn, "A Century in the Present Tense." In *Cities from Scratch*, eds. Fischer, and Javier Auyero. Durham, NC: Duke University Press, 2014: 9–67.

Forman, Shepard. *The Brazilian Peasantry*. New York: Columbia University Press, 1975.

French, John. *Drowning in Laws*. Chapel Hill: UNC Press, 2004.

Gilbert, Alan. "De Soto's *The Mystery of Capital*: Reflections on the Book's Public Impact." *International Development Planning Review*, 34:3, 2012: v–xvii.

Goldstein, Daniel. *Owners of the Sidewalk*. Durham: Duke University Press, 2016.

Gomes, Angela de Castro. *A invenção do trabalhismo*. Rio de Janeiro: FGV, 2005.

Gominho, Zélia de Oliveira. *Veneza Americana x Mucambópolis*. Recife: CEPE 1998.

Gonçalves, Rafael. "Repensar a regularização fundiária como política de integração socioespacial." *Estudos Avançados* 23:66, 2009: 237–250.

Favelas do Rio de Janeiro. Rio de Janeiro: PUC, 2013.

Guimarães, Alberto Passos. "As favelas do Distrito Federal e o censo demográfico de 1950." Rio de Janeiro: IBGE, 1952.

Hauser, Philip. *Urbanization in Latin America*. New York: UNESCO, 1961.

Hirschman, Albert O. *Journeys Toward Progress*. New York: The Twentieth Century Fund, 1963.

Hochman, Gilberto. "Logo ali, no final da avenida: os sertões redefinidos pelo movimento sanitarista da Primeira República." *Historia, Ciências, Saúde – Manguinhos*, 5 sup., July 1998: 217–235.

A era do saneamento. São Paulo: Hucitec/ANPOCS, 1998.

Holland, Alisha. "Forbearance." *American Political Science Review*, 110:2, May 2016: 232–246.

Holston, James. *The Modernist City*. University of Chicago Press, 1989.

Insurgent Citizenship. Princeton University Press, 2008.

Ianni, Octavio. "A origem política da SUDENE." *Revista Mexicana de Sociologia* 33:4, 1971: 647–659.

Itzigsohn, José. *Developing Poverty*. University Park, PA: Penn State University Press, 2000.

Katzman, Martin. "Urbanization since 1945." In *Social Change in Brazil 1945–1985*, eds. Edmar Bacha and Herbert Klein, Albuquerque: University of New Mexico Press, 1989: 99–140.

Leeds, Anthony and Elizabeth Leeds. *A sociologia do Brasil urbano*. Rio: Zahar, 1977.

Leite, Ricardo. "O Recife dos morros e córregos." Unpublished paper presented at the Encontro National de História Oral X, Universidade Federal de Pernambuco, Recife, 26–30 April 2010.

Life Magazine, "A Fidel Front among Impoverished," 2 June 1961.

Lima, Antonio Vidal de, Arnaldo Rodrigues da Cruz, João Lopes da Silva, Iêda Ventura, and Antonio Torres Montenegro. *Casa Amarela: memórias, lutas, sonhos*. Recife: Departamento de Memória de Casa Amarela/FEACA, 1988.

Lima, Nísia Trindade. *Um sertão chamado Brasil*. São Paulo: Hucitec 2013.

Lins Ribeiro, Gustavo. *O capital da esperança*. Brasília: UnB, 2008.

Luna, Francisco Vidal and Herbert Klein. *The Economic and Social History of Brazil since 1889*. Cambridge University Press, 2014.

Magalhães, Agamenon. "Na cruzada contra o mocambo." *Folha da Manhã*, November 11, 1939.

Mallorquín, Carlos. "Celso Furtado y la problematica regional: el caso del nordeste brasileño." *Estudios sociológicos* 14:42, 1996: 687–728.

Mangin,William. "Latin American Squatter Settlements: A Problem and a Solution." *Latin American Research Review* 2:3, Summer 1967: 65–98.

Maricato, Erminia. "The Statute of the Peripheral City." In *The City Statute in Brazil: A Commentary*, eds. C.S. Carvalho and A Rossbach, São Paulo: Ministry of Cities, 2010: 5–22.

Martine, George and Gordon McGranahan. "Brazil's Early Urban Transition: What Can it Teach Urbanizing Countries?" International Institute for Environment and Development and United Nations Population Fund, 2010. www.citiesalliance .org/sites/citiesalliance.org/files/IIED_Brazil'sEarlyUrbanTransition.pdf (accessed January 3, 2018).

Massey, Douglas and Nancy Denton. *American Apartheid*. Cambridge: Harvard University Press, 1988.

Mayberry-Lewis, Bjorn. *The Politics of the Possible*. Philadelphia: Temple University Press, 1994.

McCann, Bryan. *Hard Times in the Marvelous City*. Durham: Duke University Press, 2014.

McKee, David and William Leahy. "Intra-Urban Dualism in Developing Economies." *Land Economics* 46:4, November 1970: 86–489.

Meade,Teresa. *Civilizing Rio de Janeiro*. University Park, PA: Penn State University Press, 1997.

Melo, Marcus André B.C. de. "A cidade dos mocambos: estado, habitação e luta de classes no Recife (1920/1960)." *Espaço e debates* 14, 1985: 44–66.

Mello, Mario Lacerda de. *Metropolização e subdesenvolvimento: o caso do Recife*. Recife: UFPE, 1978.

Merrick, Thomas and Douglas Graham. *Population and Economic Development in Brazil*. Baltimore: Johns Hopkins University Press, 1979.

Merry, Sally Engle. "Legal Pluralism." *Law and Society Review* 22:5, 1988: 869–896.

Mitchell, Timothy. "The Properties of Markets." In *Do Economists Make Markets?*, edited by Donald MacKenzie and Fabian Muniesa, Princeton, NJ: Princeton University Press, 2008: 244–275.

Oliveira, Luciano. "Legal Pluralism and Alternative Law in Brazil: Notes for a Balance." *Beyond Law*, 9:26, January 2003: 67–89.

Oliveira, Samuel Silva Rodrigues de. "O movimento de favelas de Belo Horizonte." *Revista Mundos do Trabalho* 4:7, January–June 2012: 100–120.

Orlando, Artur. *Porto e cidade do Recife*. Pernambuco: Typ. do Jornal do Recife, 1908.

Pacheco, Maria Stella Bezerra. "Uma experiencia de desenvolvimento e organização de comunidade no Parque Proletário Provisório no. 3." Undergraduate thesis, Pontifícia Universidade Católica do Rio de Janeiro, 1962.

Parisse, Luciano. *Favelas do Rio de Janeiro: evolução-sentido*. Rio de Janeiro: Centro Nacional de Pesquisas Habitacionais, Pontifícia Universidade Católica do Rio de Janeiro, 1969.

Park, Robert E. "The City: Suggestions for the Investigation of Human Behavior in the City Environment." *American Journal of Sociology* 20:5, March, 1915: 577–612.

Parks, Gordon. "Latin America Part II: Freedom's Fearful Foe: Poverty." *Life Magazine*, June 23, 1961.

Peixoto-Mehrtens, Cristina. *Urban Space and National Identity*. New York: Palgrave Macmillan, 2010.

Pereira,Anthony. *The End of the Peasantry*. University of Pittsburgh Press, 1997.

Perlman, Janice. *The Myth of Marginality*. Berkeley: University of California Press, 1976.

Portes, Alejandro. "Political Primitivism, Differential Socialization, and Lower-Class Leftist Radicalism." *American Sociological Review*, 36:5 (Oct. 1971): 820–835. "Rationality in the Slum." *Comparative Studies in Society and History* 14:3, 1972: 268–286.

Portes, Alejandro, Manuel Castells, and Lauren Benton. *The Informal Economy*. Baltimore: Johns Hopkins University Press, 1989.

Portes, Alejandro and Richard Schauffler. "Competing Perspectives on the Latin American Informal Sector." *Population and Development Review* 19:1, March 1993: 22–60.

Prebisch, Raúl. *Toward a Dynamic Policy for Latin America*. New York: United Nations, 1963.

Roberts, Bryan. "The Informal Economy and Family Strategies." *International Journal of Urban and Regional Research* 18:1, March 1994: 6–23.

Rogers, Thomas. *The Deepest Wounds*. Chapel Hill: UNC Press, 2010.

Rolnik, Raquel. *A cidade e a lei*. São Paulo: Studio Nobel/FAPESP, 1997. "Ten Years of the City Statute in Brazil: From the Struggle for Urban Reform to the World Cup Cities." *International Journal of Urban Sustainable Development* 5:1, 2013: 54–64.

Rothstein, Richard. *The Color of Law*. New York: Liveright, 2017.

Roy, Ananya. "Slumdog Cities: Rethinking Subaltern Urbanism." *International Journal of Urban and Regional Research* 35:2, March 2011: 223–238.

Sánchez, George. *Becoming Mexican American*. New York: Oxford University Press, 1993.

Santos, Milton. *O espaço dividido*. Rio de Janeiro: F. Alves, 1979.

Santos, Wanderley Guilherme dos. *Cidadania e justiça*. Rio de Janeiro: Campus, 1979.

Schneider, Ben Ross. "The Desarrollista State." In *The Developmental State*, ed. Meredith Woo-Cumings. Ithaca: Cornell University Press 1999: 276–305.

Schulman, Sam. "Family Life in a Colombian 'Tugurio." *Sociological Analysis* 28:4, Winter 1967: 184–195.

Schwarcz, Lilia. *O espetáculo das raças*. São Paulo: Cia. das Letras, 1993.

Scobie, James. "The Growth of Cities." In *Latin America: Economy and Society, 1870–1939*, ed. Leslie Bethell, Cambridge University Press, 1989: 149–182.

Sevcenko, Nicolau. *A Revolta da Vacina*. São Paulo: Scipione, 1993.

Sikkink, Kathryn. *Ideas and Institutions*. Ithaca: Cornell University Press, 1991.

Silva, Maria Lais Pereira da. *Favelas Cariocas*. Rio de Janeiro: Contrapunto, 2005.

Souza Santos, Boaventura de. "The Law of the Oppressed." *Law and Society Review* 12:1, Fall 1977: 5–125.

Sugrue, Thomas. *Origins of the Urban Crisis*. Princeton University Press, 2005.

Telles, Edward. *Race in Another America*. Princeton University Press, 2006.

Thorp, Rosemary. *Progress, Poverty and Exclusion*. New York: Inter-American Development Bank, 1998.

Tokman, Victor. "An Exploration into the Nature of Informal-Formal Sector Relationships." *World Development* 6:9–10, September 1978: 1065–1075.

Valla, Vitor. *Educação e favela*. Rio de Janeiro: Vozes, 1986.

Valladares, Lícia. *A invenção da favela*. Rio de Janeiro: FGV, 2005.

Velasco, Alejandro. *Barrio Rising*. Berkeley: University of California Press, 2015.

Vidal, Laurent. *De nova Lisboa a Brasília*. Brasilia: UnB Press, 2000.

Weinstein, Barbara. *For Social Peace in Brazil*. Chapel Hill: UNC Press, 1997.

The Color of Modernity. Durham: Duke University Press, 2015.

Welch, Cliff. *The Seed was Planted*. University Park, PA: Penn State University Press, 1999.

PART VI

CONCLUSION

16

Authoritarianism, Democracy, and Development in Latin America and Spain, 1930–1990

Agustin E. Ferraro and Miguel A. Centeno

THE END OF AN ERA

In the serene atmosphere of Princeton University, a group of prominent experts on Latin America held a series of meetings in 1976 and early 1977. Events occurring at the time in Latin America infused the talks with a certain anxiety and distress. Some of the participants had recently escaped from military dictatorships that were displaying a new kind of vicious political violence in their countries. Friends and former students were in harm's way; terrible things seemed to be happening. The mood of the gatherings at Princeton was probably not very different from the one prevailing at meetings of the Frankfurt School in the 1930s, after the Nazis had risen to power in Germany, and the survivors began to reunite in New York as political exiles.

In one respect, however, the meetings at Princeton were less about the present, and more about how it came to be. All the social scientists at the meetings had been enthusiastic supporters of economic development for the countries in the southern hemisphere. The suspicion was now that the promotion of development could have inadvertently contributed to the chain of events that ended in ruthless military dictatorships. Did the social scientists partially have themselves to blame for the political catastrophe?

The cordial host of the group at Princeton was Albert O. Hirschman, one of the foremost experts on economic development in Latin America, and a well-known scholar and intellectual in the United States. In the paper he presented for discussion, Hirschman expressed his profound dismay at the suspicion mentioned above. He conceded that there was a general feeling of disenchantment with development as a political and intellectual project, because, after twenty-five years of efforts, the countries of the South remained comparatively "underdeveloped" and poor. However, the worst reason for the disenchantment was the particular suspicion that "the effort to achieve growth, whether or not successful, brings with it calamitous side effects in the political realm, from the loss of democratic liberties at the hand of authoritarian, repressive regimes to the wholesale violation of elementary human rights."[1]

The wave of military takeovers in Latin America was depressing enough. But the source for Hirschman's anxiety, regarding the unintended consequences of the social scientists' own work, was a research paper written by Guillermo O'Donnell, one of the participants of the Princeton meetings.[2]

O'Donnell claimed in his paper that industrial development in Latin America was associated with the establishment, during the 1960s, of a new type of military dictatorship in the region: the "bureaucratic–authoritarian state." One of O'Donnell's best-known theoretical contributions, the bureaucratic–authoritarian state corresponded to a high level of modernization, and it was characterized, among other factors, by the "pivotal role" played by large bureaucracies, led by technocrats with specific "career-patterns and power-bases."[3] The role of "technocratic civilians" was so significant that the fact that the military "appear[ed]" to hold power could be considered "typologically inconsequential" for this kind of regime.[4] In Latin America, the clearest instances of bureaucratic–authoritarian states were implanted in Brazil and Argentina during the 1960s.

The research paper by O'Donnell connected a specific stage of economic development with the emergence of bureaucratic–authoritarian states. The author affirmed that the instauration of such regimes corresponded to the "deepening" (*profundización*) of capitalism in countries that were already partially industrialized. The deepening of capitalism was a second, advanced phase of industrial development. During the first, or import-substitution phase, the national industry had been focused on producing consumer goods for the internal market.[5] The first phase was characterized by a modest expansion of the elements of industrial production such as physical infrastructure and sources of energy; it was supplemented by moderate manufacture of industrial inputs such as steel and chemical components. Most of the industrial inputs, equipment, and technology required for national production during the first phase of industrialization had to be imported. The process of industrialization, therefore, resulted in increasing imports for an industrial output sold in the internal market, and this caused a structural imbalance of payments, that is to say, chronic trade deficits that led to an "increasingly serious crisis."[6]

In order for the economy to regain stability and grow further, continued O'Donnell, a second phase or deepening of capitalism became indispensable.

---

[1] Hirschman, 1979: 61,62.   [2] O'Donnell, 1975.   [3] O'Donnell, 1973: 95.

[4] O'Donnell, 1973: 112.   [5] O'Donnell, 1972: 11.

[6] O'Donnell, 1973: 14. The issue of "persistent external disequilibrium," that is, balance-of-payments problems, had been defined since the early years of the UN commission CEPAL as one of the main structural factors that hindered development in Latin America. See Chapter 2 in this volume. The issue had been extensively discussed again by economists and social scientists associated with CEPAL during the years inmediately previous to O'Donnell's paper. See Chapter 3 in this volume.

The second phase was aimed at the development of national industries that could begin "without delay a significant current of industrial exports," and thus solve the critical difficulties associated with the imbalance of payments.[7] To achieve this result, these countries had to substantially increase the production of manufactures that could be sold in export markets, as well as undertake extensive national production of capital goods – such as buildings, machinery, equipment, vehicles, and tools – to replace imports. The second phase of capitalism required massive investments, much more advanced technology, and sophisticated business organizations. For this reason, the second phase of industrial development could only be launched with active support and involvement by state institutions, and with considerable financial commitment by international investors.[8]

From the perspective of the social groups that were in the position to take control of the process, the bureaucratic–authoritarian state could substantially improve the chances of success for the costly and complex economic transformation involved with the deepening of capitalism. At times, O'Donnell designated those social groups that called for the imposition of the bureaucratic–authoritarian state "dominant classes," following the terminology of the Marxist tradition in sociology but, as we will see, there was nothing "deterministic" in his analysis, which was indebted to diverse sociological traditions.[9]

The bureaucratic–authoritarian state was assumed to provide two main guarantees for the process of industrial deepening. First of all, since the goal of deepening was to begin massive industrial production for export markets, the bureaucratic–authoritarian state had to provide a solid continuity of public policy decisions, especially regarding key economic areas such as the promotion of industrial exports, and exchange rates.[10] In fact, high previsibility was necessary in all areas of the macroeconomic and public policy framework, in order to make calculations on the return of long-term investments possible.[11] However, in Latin America, public institutions had been very erratic in their economic decisions. Due to the dominance of high-ranking technocrats, the new bureaucratic–authoritarian model was supposed to provide the necessary public policy continuity. O'Donnell theorized that the bureaucratic–authoritarian state could provide *insulation* to expert bureaucracies. Such insulation would protect the decisions of expert bureaucracies from political interference, including the interference of military officers in high-ranking government positions.[12] As mentioned above,

---

[7] O'Donnell, 1975: 15.   [8] O'Donnell, 1975: 16.   [9] O'Donnell, 1975: 18.
[10] O'Donnell, 1975: 17.   [11] O'Donnell, 1975: 18.
[12] Regarding the fragile bureaucratic insulation of key development agencies in Brazil, Colombia, and Peru, see Chapter 7 and Chapter 5 in this volume. For a description of the comparatively better performance of insulated bureaucratic agencies in Chile, under democratic governments, see Chapter 5 and Chapter 12 in this volume.

O'Donnell made clear that the military only "appeared" to hold power in the bureaucratic–authoritarian state, under this institutional model the key decisions were supposed to be made by "technocratic civilians."[13]

The bureaucratic–authoritarian state was assumed to provide a second guarantee for the process of industrial deepening. This second guarantee, according to O'Donnell, consisted of economic and political "peace and order," and it was based on the violent repression of the workers' movement, which had made significant social and political conquests during the first phase of industrialization in Latin America.[14] The repression of the workers' movement included the exclusion of ample groups of citizens from political participation, the targeting of individual leaders for repressive measures including clandestine detention, torture and murder, and the "restoration" of workers' discipline in industrial firms.

In sum, O'Donnell's analysis brilliantly showed that the process of industrial development had reached a stage, in Latin America, where the imposition of bureaucratic–authoritarian states became an "optimal" political solution from the perspective of certain political actors. Such actors expressed the social interests that had acquired vast economic and political power during the first stage of industrialization: business owners and top managers, experts with technocratic roles, high-ranking military officers, and international investors. As Hirschman sadly corroborated, when all was said and done, a necessary relation seemed to have established itself between industrialization and authoritarianism. Did the process of industrialization, that is to say the development process, have to end in political catastrophe?

Although certainly anxious about the mere possibility of these connections, Hirschman was not willing to accept outright O'Donnell's analysis. In his own paper for the discussions at Princeton, as well as in personal correspondence, Hirschman tried to articulate two main counterarguments.[15] The same counterarguments were further elaborated during the Princeton discussions by Serra and Kaufman.[16]

The first counterargument affirmed that O'Donnell's thesis was excessively "deterministic." In his contribution, Hirschman criticized any explanation that appealed to economic causes for political processes because of the influence of Marxism on the social sciences, which conferred to such explanations "an excessive aura of a priori plausibility."[17] Serra developed this same criticism in more detail. He admitted that there was a connection between industrial deepening and the bureaucratic–authoritarian state regarding, for example, the repression of the workers' movement. He warned, however, that such processes were only "trends" happening in Latin America, and that social theory had to avoid exaggerating those trends, and "elevating them to the status of rigid, iron-clad 'laws.'"[18]

---

[13] O'Donnell, 1973: 112.   [14] O'Donnell, 1975: 18.   [15] Adelman and Fajardo, 2016: 16.
[16] Serra, 1979; Kaufman, 1979.   [17] Hirschman, 1979: 71.   [18] Serra, 1979: 105.

The first criticism was potentially strong, but unfair, because O'Donnell had made very clear that his thesis did not involve any kind of determinism. Nothing about the industrial deepening of capitalism was "necessary," he stated, and there was, moreover, no real guarantee that the process was going to succeed. O'Donnell rather mocked in advance the Marxist impulse to postulate any kind of historical determinism about industrialization, stating that, certainly, "there was no metaphysical necessity for deepening as has been defined above, and neither was to be found, at the end of the process, the entry door to the club of central countries of world capitalism."[19]

The bureaucratic–authoritarian state was not necessary for the industrial deepening of capitalism, it just happened to be attractive, as an institutional design, for certain "social classes and sectors that consolidated their power by means" of this authoritarian model in Latin America, and expected to benefit substantially from its implantation.[20] The similarity of bureaucratic–authoritarian institutions in diverse Latin American countries was not the result of any "historical necessity," it was simply the result of the general appeal of this institutional design across the region, based on the fact that the model had already been tried in Spain, and had been very successful. In his paper, O'Donnell mentioned several times that the bureaucratic–authoritarian state had been consolidated as an institutional model in Spain, well before it was tried in Brazil, Argentina, and other Latin American countries.[21]

Instead of a historical necessity, the diffusion of the bureaucratic–authoritarian state in Latin America was rather a clear-cut case of the phenomenon we define, nowadays, as institutional transfer or isomorphism.[22] Simply put, military dictatorships in Latin America were deliberately adopting the economic and political model of the Spanish military dictatorship under Franco.[23]

The so-called "economic miracle" in Spain was obviously the model for the kind of process that O'Donnell described, in his research paper, as the strategy for industrial deepening. The process involved the reconversion of the national industry so that a substantial part of its production was oriented towards export markets, thus preventing the chronic trade deficits that affected developing economies for structural reasons. As an example, under the management of a group of "technocratic civilians" protected from political interference in Spain, the automobile industry grew considerably, with strong public support and guidance. From the production of 79,432 vehicles in 1962, with exports of only 1 percent of units produced, the Spanish automobile industry went on to produce 988,964 vehicles in 1977, with exports of more than 30 percent of units

---

[19] O'Donnell, 1975: 15.   [20] O'Donnell, 1975: 15.   [21] O'Donnell, 1975: 6, 45, 47.

[22] For a general overview of theories on institutional isomorphism and institutional convergence, see Chapter 5 in this volume.

[23] For specific discussions of the Spanish developmental state under the Franco dictatorship, see Chapter 9 and Chapter 8 in this volume.

produced.[24] As described by O'Donnell, this process was made possible in Spain by carefully controlled state regulation, and massive investments by international firms.

That the military dictatorships implanted during the 1960s in Argentina and Brazil took inspiration from Franco's Spain was a well-known fact. There was a strong affinity between those military groups in terms of mentalities, organization, religious orientation, fierce anti-communism, and other elements. The concept of "authoritarianism," originally coined by Linz to define the characteristics of the Spanish military regime under Franco, was soon applied to military dictatorships in Brazil and Argentina by O'Donnell and other scholars.[25] O'Donnell was the first to apply the concept of authoritarianism to Latin America, since this had been the subject of his graduate work at Yale in the late 1960s – with Linz himself as thesis advisor. However, the characterization of Latin American dictatorships as authoritarian regimes, following Linz, soon became commonplace.

In both Argentina and Brazil, there was a very deliberate attempt to transfer the Spanish blueprint of state management consolidated under the late Franco dictatorship since the early 1960s, which was designed in order for certain public policy areas to be entirely run by "technocratic civilians" without outside political interference. This institutional design was particularly evident in the areas of development planning and industrial policy, and here the Franco dictatorship had reached its best public policy results. Already in 1973, Jaguaribe had discussed such type of authoritarian regime as "Opus Dei technocratic neoliberalism," pointing out that this political and institutional design was first tried successfully in Spain, and later on emulated by the Medici dictatorship in Brazil, 1969–1974, and the Ongania dictatorship in Argentina, 1966–1970.[26] Jaguaribe mentioned the Opus Dei, because all three military regimes were eager to hire, for top management positions, experts from this right-wing, technocratically-oriented Catholic organization.[27]

In sum, the first counterargument introduced by Hirschman and Serra, against the thesis by O'Donnell, was certainly unfair. There was no determinism in the latter's thesis, it was instead a case of the phenomenon we would call today institutional convergence or isomorphism. The misunderstanding probably resulted, in part, from Hirschman's and Serra's lack of attention to the Spanish case, which they did not mention at all in their contributions to the Princeton discussions.[28]

The second criticism of Donnell's thesis was introduced by Hirschman during the Princeton meetings, and it was further developed by Kaufman.[29] This second criticism was certainly much more accurate than the first. It pointed

[24] García Ruiz, 2001: 158.
[25] Linz, 1964: 251–283; see also O'Donnell, 1973 and Germani, 1978.
[26] Jaguaribe, 1973: 532–533.   [27] Casanova, 1983: 27–50; Rock, 1993: 201.
[28] Hirschman, 1979; Serra, 1979.   [29] Kaufman, 1979: 165–167.

out something that O'Donnell actually seemed to have missed in his analysis of the bureaucratic–authoritarian state in Latin America or, to be entirely fair, that could not be perceived clearly when he created the concept. The Latin American instances of this institutional design were not behaving as the model predicted. By the time of the Princeton discussions in 1976 and 1977, bureaucratic–authoritarian states were not applying developmental policies consistently, or with much stability. According to O'Donnell, this type of regime had been established to promote a second phase of industrialization but, as Hirschman observed, some of its instances were applying the exact opposite of developmental policies. Authoritarian regimes in Latin America were implementing a kind of orthodox, laissez-faire economic liberalism, and they were hiring for top public policy positions, instead of development experts, members of a new generation of "Latin American economists who had received graduate training at the University of Chicago."[30]

Hirschman did not discuss specific national cases in his contribution, he only referred in general terms to "authoritarian regimes" in Latin America. But the phenomenon he described was already well known. The Pinochet dictatorship, as the foremost example, was infamous at the time for its rigid adherence to neoliberal prescriptions, which had plunged the country into a severe recession.[31] Other bureaucratic–authoritarian states, such as Argentina or even Brazil, were also introducing neoliberal measures into their previously developmental policy framework, sometimes in erratic fashion, with predictably negative results. As early as 1964, the Castelo Branco dictatorship in Brazil was applying an economic plan that Skidmore defined as "quasi orthodox," and which included sharp reductions in the level of public spending, and in the rate of growth of the money supply.[32] The result was a recession in the industrial heartland of São Paulo, and a decline in industrial output of 5 percent for 1965.[33]

After the military coup of March 1976, the Videla dictatorship in Argentina adopted an economic policy framework of "orthodox inspiration," based on a "neoliberal agenda."[34,35] The dictatorship's economic plan included a series of austerity measures, cuts in wages, strict monetary policy, and a radical strategy of trade liberalization; but the plan failed to take control of inflation, and devastated the national industry.[36] As a percentage of GDP, the manufacturing sector in Argentina went from over 29 percent in 1974 to 22.1 percent in 1981; industrial production as a whole dropped 17 percent from 1975 to 1981.[37] The dictatorship's economic plan was ill-conceived, but perhaps even worse was the fact that policy measures were applied in a very erratic, and sometimes contradictory fashion. Lack of public policy consistency was the result of constant pressures and interference on the Ministry of

---

[30] Hirschman, 1963: 76.   [31] Edwards and Edwards, 1991: 34.   [32] Skidmore, 1988: 29.
[33] Skidmore, 1988: 44.   [34] Torre and de Riz, 1991: 160.   [35] Arceneaux, 2001: 132.
[36] Riggirozzi, 2009: 92.   [37] Smith, 1989: 253.

Economy, coming from different political sectors inside the military. Economic actors became increasingly alarmed by erratic public policy decisions. In August of 1979, a group of business representatives went as far as meeting with President Videla to demand "the need for a coherent policy in the economic sphere," and in the following year, an association of industrial firms issued a strong statement declaring that "more than four years after assuming power, the economic team still owes industry its opinion on the industrial plan towards which it wishes to arrive."[38]

Meanwhile, in Brazil, the Figueiredo administration began to implement in 1979 similar orthodox policies to those applied by the neoliberal military regimes in Chile and Argentina, with the declared goals of achieving financial stability, and reducing inflation.[39] The policies of financial and monetary adjustment, described at the time as "shock therapy," were notoriously unsuccessful, and in the year 1980 inflation reached 110 percent in Brazil, a (then) record for the century; while industrial output dropped by 5.5 percent in 1981, and, for the first time since 1942, GDP as a whole showed a decline in Brazil, of 1.6 percent.[40] Macroeconomic policy was again erratic, the administration of Figueiredo "alternated between recessionist and growth policies," and such lack of consistency was one of the main factors that resulted in two further years of depression until 1983, with an overall decline in GDP per capita more severe than during the Great Depression in the 1930s.[41]

Arbitrary and erratic public policy decisions were applied even to areas which, until then, had grown very successfully in Brazil, such as the computer industry. Public policy in the field of computer electronics had been established since 1972 by an independent commission, led by experts in the field, and protected from political interference, under the name of CAPRE (Comissão de Coordenação das Atividades de Processamento Eletrônico). As a result of long-term "greenhouse" development strategies, by 1982 more than a hundred domestic firms manufactured 67 percent of the computers installed in Brazil, providing 18,000 jobs, and including initiatives of hardware and software innovation that were competing successfully with international firms.[42] Nevertheless, shortly after assuming power, the Figueiredo's administration decided to reassert presidential authority, and to put an end to the bureaucratic autonomy of CAPRE. The commission was simply dissolved, and replaced by a new Secretary of State under the name SEI (Secretaria Especial de Informatica), directly under the authority of the president. Most of the top and medium-level managers and experts of CAPRE were fired, and replaced by political appointees. The SEI took erratic policy decisions from the beginning, showing support for the greenhouse strategy and then contradicting itself, sometimes reversing decisions after sudden interventions from

---

[38] Arceneux, 2001: 134.   [39] Skidmore, 1988: 217, fn. 21.   [40] Skidmore, 1988: 230–231.
[41] Fernandes, 1996: 99.   [42] Centeno and Ferraro, 2017: 75–76.

Figueiredo's office. After a few years, erratic policies and bad public governance decimated the Brazilian computer industry.

Of the three contributions critical of O'Donnell that were presented at the Princeton discussions, the paper by Kaufman focused specifically on the phenomenon we just described above, that is to say, the lack of policy consistency of bureaucratic–authoritarian states in Latin America. The paper analyzed economic policy under the military dictatorships in four countries: Brazil, Argentina, Chile, and Uruguay. Kaufman willingly conceded that O'Donnell's model of bureaucratic–authoritarian regimes was fundamentally accurate.[43] Nevertheless, he had to observe that, against the commitment to industrial deepening of bureaucratic–authoritarian states assumed by O'Donnell, it was visible some years later that "there was often little consensus within these regimes about any specific developmental strategy."[44] The dictatorships of Chile and Uruguay, in particular, seemed to be focused on "economic stabilization," with the result that they applied orthodox austerity measures, and abandoned developmental policies – Kaufman's paper was written before the Argentinean and Brazilian dictatorships began to apply the same kind of neoliberal policies, in the usual erratic way.

O'Donnell had been proven wrong in expecting for bureaucratic–authoritarian states, in Latin America, to provide a solid continuity of public policy decisions in economic or other matters.[45] The bureaucratic–authoritarian model was supposed to protect the decisions of expert bureaucracies from political interference – including the interference of military officers in high-ranking government positions. This was the blueprint that the Latin American military were deliberately trying to imitate. It had been very effective in Spain, where the military dictatorship had delegated decisions on developmental policies to high-ranking "technocrats," with great success in the area of industrial promotion, and in other public policy fields. O'Donnell had simply expected for the Latin American military to be able to establish bureaucratic–authoritarian states in a consistent, orderly fashion. But the military failed badly at this task in Latin America, since top officers in government could not restrain themselves from interfering constantly with public policy decisions for political reasons, changing or reversing course, dissolving successful public agencies to reassert the "authority" of the commander-in-chief, or other similar arbitrary interventions.

Of course, as Arceneaux has observed regarding economic policy under the Argentinean dictatorship after 1976, even if the neoliberal economic program had been consistently implemented as "originally envisioned," nothing indicates it was going to be successful – the opposite would have been the most likely case.[46] But the "inconsistency of what was implemented eventually disadvantaged nearly every sector" and destroyed any confidence

---

[43] Kaufman, 1979: 248.   [44] Kaufman, 1979: 248.   [45] O'Donnell, 1975: 17.
[46] Arceneaux, 2001: 141.

in the economy.[47] The Argentinean model showed a combination of badly conceived public policy with constant political interference, which resulted in erratic implementation. In other cases, however, as shown by the decimation of the Brazilian computer industry under Figueiredo, the military were also prone to interfere and wreck well-conceived and successful developmental policies.

Hirschman was right in stating that, by 1976–1977, the concept of the bureaucratic–authoritarian state did not seem to apply very well to the realities on the ground, because this model, as actually implemented in Latin America, was entirely authoritarian, but not really bureaucratic. High-ranking experts were not insulated from the short-term politicization of public policy decisions by the government. For the implementation of developmental policy, those authoritarian regimes could never be successful. And this demonstrated conclusively that the bureaucratic–authoritarian state was not "necessary" in any way for the further development of the industrial sector, or any other area of the economy in Latin America – the opposite was rather the case. O'Donnell had never affirmed that any such necessity existed, but the issue had to be discussed at Princeton. O'Donnell's mistake was the belief that the Latin American military were going to be able to imitate the blueprint of technocratic authoritarianism in late Francoism, and thus successfully promote industrial development – eventually gaining political legitimacy for a negotiated transition to democracy. It happened that the Latin American military were much more incompetent at governing than he anticipated.

Hirschman was without question one of the best-trained observers of development in Latin America for detecting precisely that problem with O'Donnell's theoretical conceptualization. For Hirschman, the erratic implementation of development policies, as a result of the lack of bureaucratic autonomy of developmental agencies, was not a new phenomenon. Analyzing developmental projects since the 1950s in the region, he had realized early on that constant pressures and interference on public policy decisions, for short-term political considerations, was an ingrained problem. Therefore, the influence of developmental and planning agencies on public policy fluctuated wildly, as Hirschman confirmed in his contribution for the Princeton discussions: "Strangely, the planning agencies which had been set up to impart greater stability to governmental action in the economic field were themselves subject to considerable instability."[48]

The building of developmental states began during the 1920s and 1930s, in Latin America and Spain, with the creation of specific institutions for the planning and implementation of public policy strategies, and those institutions were supposed to take public policy decisions with a substantial degree of autonomy from partisan political considerations.

The bureaucratic–authoritarian state, as defined by O'Donnell, was certainly not the first case of institutional transfer or isomorphism in the region. The issue

---

[47] Arceneaux, 2001: 141.   [48] Hirschman, 1979: 84.

of institutional design, and the attention paid to successful models and blueprints already applied elsewhere, had been a serious concern from the beginning. But which blueprints should Latin America have adopted? We noted in the first volume of this series how the region had been searching for institutional models since independence. But it failed to find any that would make the right transition to stable, inclusive liberal democracies. Similarly, in the second third of the twentieth century, Latin American military dictatorships looked for institutional models and thought they had found the right one in Franco's Spain. However, as we have seen in the first section above, the military drew the wrong lessons, focusing on authoritarianism rather than on the consolidation of independent, professional bureaucracies. Latin America's experience indicates that the Spanish developmental achievements may have had less to do with Franco as a dictator, and more with his regime's decision to reconstruct and strengthen the capacities of the Spanish state bureaucracy, which had originally been developed during the era of social and political modernization in the country, between 1914 and 1936. State modernization under the Spanish bureaucratic–authoritarian regime since the early 1960s was intended only as a first step towards a (controlled) transition to democracy, but it happened to also be a foundation for the extraordinary developmental achievement of the next three decades.[49]

Other institutional models that had been tried previously in Latin America also held much promise, until quashed by the same ideological rigidities that characterized the 1960s in the continent. In the next and last section of this conclusion, we will go back to the origins of the developmental era, and reconsider the promise for a better and more democratic governance than those original models contained.

DEMOCRATIC DEVELOPMENT ABANDONED

Ten years before the Princeton discussions, Hirschman finished the last volume of his trilogy of studies on economic development.[50] Somewhat neglected at the time of publication, the studies became classics in the field. Among other subjects, Hirschman examined institutional and policy models, and he conceded, somewhat grudgingly, that no development project seemed acceptable in Latin America, unless its blueprint was the Tennessee Valley Authority (TVA), and if possible, the project was certified expressly by David Lilienthal himself.[51]

Created in 1933, TVA was one of the most emblematic among the public agencies that carried out the New Deal's strategies for economic and social modernization in the United States. Its long-time director until 1946, Lilienthal

---

[49] See Chapter 8 in this volume for a detailed discussion of state modernization in Spain during the early 1960s.
[50] Hirschman, 2015.   [51] Hirschman, 2015: 19.

has been described as one of the leaders of the New Deal that better articulated the movement's confidence and optimism. His best-seller book *TVA: Democracy on the March*, published in 1944, was considered as a "manifesto that expressed the scale and scope of New Deal liberalism."[52,53]

TVA promoted effectively the economic and social development of a vast geographical area in the United States, which was afflicted at the time by dismal poverty, even for Great Depression standards. The programs of TVA not only reduced poverty drastically, they came to redefine working-class living conditions in the whole country. The mass consumption of electric appliances was originally conceived by TVA as an industrial and commercial strategy, in order to encourage the use of the energy produced by its growing network of hydroelectric dams along the Tennessee Valley. This strategy had to be pushed through against the resistance of the industry, which until then had mostly targeted upper-class residences for the sale of electric products.[54] The working-class home kitchen, amply provided with electric appliances, became one of the global icons for the American way of life. Furthermore, TVA was one of the first federal agencies that applied community organization methods as a technique for the implementation of public policy programs, that is to say, citizens' participation in public policy. Lilienthal discussed in his book the notion of participatory public policy as a principle connecting public management, economic and social development, and democratic values and practices.[55] TVA's contribution to democratic practices was another reason for its widely positive reputation, both in the United States and abroad.

The creation in 1944 of the International Bank for Reconstruction and Development (the World Bank), and Truman's "Four Point Program," announced with his inaugural address in 1949, led to the widespread diffusion of the concept of economic development. Truman's address was the first time on record that development was defined as a dynamic process and contrasted to "underdevelopment."[56] Truman's notion of development was explicitly based on the TVA experience; his proposals for vast programs of foreign assistance were oriented towards the creation of similar developmental agencies in poor regions of the world.[57]

The influence of TVA in Latin America began in the late 1930s.[58] According to the prestigious Chilean economist Pinto, the central development agency of Chile, Corporación de Fomento de la Producción (CORFO), created in 1939, was "particularly" inspired by the "great energy and global project of the Tennessee Valley."[59] Additionally, TVA sources reported that "a number of engineers and technicians" of CORFO visited TVA "during the first years" after

---

[52] Lilienthal, 1944.   [53] Smith, 2006: 255.   [54] Tobey, 1996: 12, 19.
[55] Hargrove and Conkin, 1983.   [56] Rist, 2008: 73.   [57] Ekblad, 2010: 99.
[58] The adoption of TVA as a blueprint for development agencies in Latin America is considered in chapters 4, 5, 7, 11, and 12 in the present volume.
[59] Pinto Santa Cruz, 1985: 23.

the creation of the Chilean corporation, and some of them remained at TVA for periods of six to twelve months.[60] Chile's President Gabriel González Videla visited the United States in 1950, and he spent two days at TVA's headquarters in Knoxville, Tennessee.[61]

President Miguel Alemán of Mexico was the first Latin American chief of state to visit TVA, in 1947. He met Lilienthal, and inspected operations of TVA in the Tennessee Valley.[62] In the next years, four regional commissions were created in Mexico according to the institutional blueprint of TVA: the Papaloapan, Tepalcatepec, Fuerte, and Grijalva River Commissions.[63]

Brazil's Comissão do Vale do São Francisco (CVSF), created in 1948, also followed the institutional and public policy models of the TVA, as was pointed out during the parliamentary debates leading to the creation of the Brazilian agency.[64] In what was already becoming something of an official ritual, President Eurico Dutra of Brazil visited TVA's hydroelectric dams in 1949.[65]

Even considering the general interest for the TVA model in Latin America, Colombia represented a special case.[66] During 1954 and 1955, Lilienthal traveled several times to Bogotá for consultations on the design of a regional developmental agency, the Cauca Valley Corporation, which was created in 1955 closely following his proposals.[67] The initiative to work in Colombia came originally from Lilienthal's friend and associate Lauchlin Currie.[68] One of the main architects of the New Deal in the United States, Currie was chief economic advisor to President Roosevelt from 1939 to 1945.[69] A member of the team that drafted the charter of the World Bank at Bretton Woods, in 1944, Currie became a leading intellectual supporting the transformation of the Bank, from a traditional financial organization – as it was originally conceived – into a developmental credit institution for relatively poor regions of the world.[70] The first international mission of the World Bank was sent to Colombia in 1949, with the task of preparing a general development strategy for the country, and helping with its implementation. Currie was head of this mission.

The three leading American development experts, Lauchlin Currie, David Lilienthal, and Albert Hirschman, were to meet and work together in Bogotá during the early 1950s. As it happened, Hirschman and Currie never much liked each other.[71] By association, Hirschman didn't much like Lilienthal either – Currie and Lilienthal were friends.[72] This is all purely anecdotal, however.

[60] TVA Technical Library, 1952: 29.   [61] Watson, 1951; González Videla, 1975: 884–885.
[62] *The Times Recorder*, 1947.
[63] Barkin and King, 1970: 93; Cole and Mogab, 1987: 311; Robinson, 2007: 80.
[64] Hirschman, 1963: 53.   [65] TVA Technical Library, 1952: 16.
[66] Due to the rigorous application of the TVA model, and other factors, Colombia was seen as a "showcase" of development, as discussed by Karl in Chapter 4 in this volume.
[67] Neuse, 1996: 261–262.   [68] Schwarz, 1993: 338.   [69] Sandilands, 1990: 96.
[70] Alacevich, 2009.   [71] Sandilands, 1990: 175.   [72] Neuse, 1996: xvii.

Much more serious was the actual reason for the three of them working together in Colombia at the time. With all their personal commitment to international development, the fact of the matter is that they had to leave the United States in the wake of a campaign of vicious personal attacks, whose target were all those liberal experts and intellectuals who had planned and directed New Deal programs and policies.[73] The campaign was supposedly a hunt for Communists. In truth, the three leading American development experts were political exiles in Colombia.[74] The attacks on these men reflected a changing political climate in the United States. After the end of World War II, southern members of the Democratic Party in Congress became increasingly willing to vote together with Republicans in order to support an aggressive, militaristic foreign policy orientation.[75] Southern support had been politically necessary for the New Deal to have any chance of implementation in the 1930s, but by the end of the war liberal Democrats found themselves with only a minority of votes in Congress, against a new conservative bloc formed by Republicans and southern Democrats. As Katznelson observes, the ultimate reason for this historic political shift was the fact that southern members of the Democratic Party came to perceive the New Deal's economic and social progress as a potential threat for the system of white racial hegemony in the South.[76]

The idea that all liberal New Dealers, such as Currie, Lilienthal, or Hirschman, concealed a deep affinity to Communism, has an interesting intellectual history, which found its parallel in much of the anti-intellectualism of the Latin American dictatorships of the 1960s and 1970s.

---

[73] Schrecker, 1998: 110.

[74] Both Currie and Lilienthal were publicly accused of being Communists, or outright Soviet spies. Lilienthal was a powerful public speaker, and he made his opponents in the Senate look ridiculous, confronting head-on their accusations of being a Communist sympathizer during the hearings for his confirmation as head of the Atomic Energy Commission in 1947. See Neuse, 1996: 186–187. Currie was not as gifted as a public speaker, and he had the added weakness of being a naturalized American citizen, born in Canada. Although no charges were ever brought against him, innuendo propagated by associates of Senator McCarthy was enough to have Currie deprived of American citizenship in 1954. See Boughton and Sandilands, 2003: 73–99. As with many other thousands of government employees, Hirschman's political opinions were secretly investigated by the FBI while he was working for the Federal Reserve Board from 1946. See Adelman, 2013: 284. The professional career of Hirschman began to suffer mysterious obstructions, and by the end of 1951 he realized that it was better for him to leave government service altogether, and even to leave the country. A few months later, he and his family had moved to Colombia. See Adelman, 2013: 281. Meanwhile, the attacks on Lilienthal continued relentlessly during his tenure as head of the Atomic Energy Commission (AEC). Congressional investigations and hearings targeted at Lilienthal, and at the staff of AEC, based on secret political investigations about their loyalty, resulted in day-to-day operations at AEC being practically paralyzed by 1949. Feeling "tired, disheartened, and burned out," Lilienthal decided to resign the AEC chairmanship, retire from public life in the United States, and seek employment and business opportunities abroad. See Wang, 1999: 235–236.

[75] Katznelson, 2013: 16.   [76] Katznelson, 2013: 474.

The insinuation was originally made by James Burnham in his classic book of 1941, *The Managerial Revolution.*[77]

The suspicion of hidden Communist sympathies, or also "creeping socialism," became a powerful weapon against the New Deal, and against public strategies for economic and social development in other countries, and especially in Latin America. Burnham provided a strong rhetorical weapon against developmental programs: his redefinition of the concept of "technocracy" as a hidden authoritarian trend shared by the New Deal and Soviet Communism.[78] Until then, the word "technocracy" had been associated in the United States with a benevolent, paternalistic political orientation, which called for a system of national planning for industry and infrastructure, to be coordinated by engineers.[79] With Thorstein Veblen as its best-known leader, the aim of the technocratic movement was to combine scientific planning with democratic ideals, although engineers were expected to be in charge of technical decisions.[80] By the early 1940s, the movement had lost all influence. Burham redefined the concept of technocracy as a subtle form of authoritarianism, and as part of a global conspiracy against capitalist democracies.

However, as Lilienthal and Currie had shown during the New Deal, and they were to make clear again with their work in Colombia, there was nothing remotely "technocratic" with their public policy styles and proposals. The New Deal, and more specifically TVA as its flagship agency, were firmly opposed to the paternalistic orientation of the old technocratic movement. The New Deal, for example, did not grant engineers a particularly eminent position.[81] Lilienthal was a lawyer and public intellectual, who not only opposed any kind of technocratic "superiority" for experts, he promoted at TVA a whole new approach to encourage citizens' participation in public policy decisions, which he characterized as "grass-roots" administration.[82] He advocated for such participatory practices in his book *TVA: Democracy on the March*, where he also described many experiences of citizens' participation in the implementation of public policy programs initiated by TVA.[83] For Lilienthal, grass-roots administration was not only more democratic, it led to better results: "results depend chiefly upon the people's participation. Getting that participation was to be almost wholly on a voluntary basis. To get a job done in this way ... required the invention of new devices and new methods."[84]

Both Lilienthal and Currie would follow in Colombia the same democratic, grass-roots inspiration of the New Deal. Under the encouragement and leadership of Lilienthal, the Cauca Valley Corporation (CVC) developed a model of administration based on citizens' participation and horizontal

---

[77] Burnham presented the connection between Communism and the New Deal as a profound sociological process, part of an underground revolutionary trend towards the imposition of "technocracy" by a new ruling class, the managers. James Burnham, 1941.

[78] Burnham, 1941.   [79] Akin, 1971: 184.   [80] Burris, 1993: 28.   [81] Ndiaye, 2007: 228.

[82] Selznick, 1949: 28.   [83] Lilienthal, 1944.   [84] Lilienthal, 1944: 199.

public policy implementation. The full deployment of this design had to wait, however, until after the end of the dictatorship of Rojas Pinilla (1953–1957). The World Bank mission to Colombia, led by Currie, had begun in 1949 under a democratic administration in the country. The military coup of 1954 was an unfortunate setback for liberal development experts, and Currie immediately ceased any kind of collaboration with the government, retiring to live and work on his dairy farm thirty miles west of Bogotá.[85] Lilienthal tried to keep development projects going, but he got into increasing trouble with the dictatorship, and he resigned as CVC consultant in 1956, the whole board of CVC following suit with their own collective resignation in 1957.[86] After the democratic transition, CVC was legally reestablished in 1960.[87] The goals of the corporation included now the promotion of *acción comunal* (community participation), and the corporation's board was integrated by representatives of diverse social and political actors, such as business and civic associations. The design of the board encouraged the creation of a coalition of political support for CVC, and it followed the horizontal approach to public policy that Lilienthal had defined as "the very essence of TVA's method."[88]

Lilienthal and Currie have been considered as the early architects of the wide *acción comunal* or community participation programs that represented a fundamental organizational mechanism for rural and urban development in Colombia.[89] In their early study of CVC, Posada and Posada described *acción comunal* simply as the "translation" to Colombia of the grass-roots practices that were one of the main institutional features of the Tennessee Valley Authority.[90] The same authors observed that CVC had been quite successful at promoting community participation in the Cauca Valley, and they further underlined the fact that CVC agronomists always worked in systematic consultation with diverse local actors, such as civic boards, government officials, priests, and directors of public health.[91]

One of the most significant contributions of Currie to developmental theory and practice was the focus on urban planning as a key component for any general strategy for economic and social development.[92] In Colombia, following the guidance of Currie, the Centro Interamericano de la Vivienda y Planeamiento (CINVA) was created in 1951 under the auspices of the OEA. This center has been described as "the most influential institution for urban planning in Latin America," and it promoted from the beginning techniques of community organization and advocacy planning in urban development, on the basis of New Deal experiences, and in particular of the TVA model.[93]

---

[85] Adelman, 2013: 309; Sandilands, 1990: 176.   [86] Neuse, 1992: 262.

[87] Ministerio de Agricultura (Colombia), 1985: 14.   [88] Lilenthal, 1941: 37.

[89] Valencia, 2009: 37.   [90] Posada and Posada, 1966: 12.   [91] Posada and Posada, 1966: 216.

[92] As shown by Fischer in Chapter 15 of the present volume, the phenomenon of urban informality had a very negative impact on the consolidation of egalitarian citizenship regimes in Latin America during the developmental era.

[93] Peña Rodriguez, 2008: 187–188.

Currie stayed in Colombia for the rest of his life, working as an economist, university teacher, and government consultant. After the return to democracy in 1958, he was awarded Colombian citizenship by newly elected liberal President Lleras Camargo. López has described Currie as simply one of the "most important economists" in the nation's history, and Vélez remarked that Currie was the "definitive" economics professor for the training of a whole generation of economists in the country.[94] As mentioned above, after resigning from the Atomic Energy Commission chairmanship in 1950, Lilienthal never worked again in public service in the United States. In 1954, he created a consulting firm, Development and Resources Corporation (R&D), which worked almost exclusively with projects abroad. The projects of R&D were located "in more Latin American nations than in any other world region."[95] As regards Hirschman, after spending more than four years in Colombia, the worst of McCarthyism had passed, and he was able to return to the United States with his family in 1956, although he never worked for the American government again. He became a prestigious scholar of development, teaching at several US American Universities for relatively short periods of time, until he was hired by Princeton in 1974, where he remained until the end of his career.

The work of Currie, Lilienthal and Hirschman had a strong positive influence in Colombia. However, some characteristics of public governance in the country, which are not unusual in Latin American and Spanish institutional contexts, resulted in it going relatively soon from "showcase" to "failure" of international development.[96] As head of the World Bank mission to Colombia, Currie recommended the creation of a National Planning Council, which was established in 1952 as the main public agency coordinating national development strategies – Currie and Hirschman served on the council together.[97] In 1958, a Planning Department was also created, as an administrative division of the executive power. However, the 1962 election of President Valencia created serious problems for this institutional structure. According to the "National Front" agreement of 1958 between the Conservatives and the Liberals, the two parties were to rotate in power every four years, and 1962 was the turn of a Conservative to assume office. The expectation of the Conservatives was to benefit from massive political appointments, extending the rotation in office to the bulk of public employment. As a result, just in the first 100 days of the Conservative administration, 80 percent of professional employees at the National Planning Council and the Planning Department quit their jobs – or were fired.[98] Deprived of professional advice and planning competence, during the following years the

---

[94] López Acero, 2011: 24; Vélez Álvarez, 2013: 233.   [95] Neuse, 1996: 1298.
[96] In Chapter 4 of the present volume, Karl describes this process in detail.
[97] Alacevich, 2009: 52; Sandilands, 1990: 174.
[98] As stated by Karl in his chapter, Colombia's planning capacity simply "disintegrated" as a consequence of the bureaucratic purges.

administration took key public policy decisions in a predictably erratic manner. The Colombian agreement to rotate in office between the two main parties was not unheard of, a very similar agreement had existed between Conservatives and Liberals in Spain, at the end of the nineteenth century, known as *turno pacífico* (peaceful turn). Both agreements stipulated not only that each political orientation would be assigned the presidency in advance, after a stated period, but also that spoils of office were to be shared by turns, so that the party in power would appoint its members to public jobs en masse, firing the other party's at will.[99] Public policy planning, or even the most basic stability of public policy decisions, were almost impossible under such kinds of arrangements. The case of Colombia during the developmental era, or Spain at the end of the nineteenth century, show that the willingness to compromise and reach political agreements is not always good for public governance.

When all is said and done, probably the most effective public agency in Latin America during the whole developmental era, and certainly the most stable, was the Chilean Corporación de Fomento de la Producción (CORFO) created in 1939. The creation of CORFO was the result of a national political compromise.[100] But instead of an agreement on sharing the spoils of office, the two main political orientations in Chile reached an agreement on keeping this key developmental agency out of partisan politics. Therefore, the agency was staffed and run by career civil servants, instead of amateur political appointees. The agreement was finally broken by President Alessandri in 1958, and management positions in the public bureaucracy – not only in CORFO – began to be assigned increasingly on the basis of political loyalty, instead of professional competence.[101] This had a very negative impact on the quality of governance in Chile, and eventually on democratic stability. Nevertheless, a stable run of almost twenty years under professional management was a considerable achievement for CORFO, and it was reflected in the very positive results of developmental policies in the country.

The case of CORFO shows the possibilities, but also the limits of institutional transfer, that is to say, the international translation of institutional blueprints. The TVA institutional model had a considerable influence on CORFO, in particular regarding the managerial and financial autonomy allowed to both public agencies. However, the principle of keeping certain areas of public governance out of short-term partisan conflict, and excluding the institutions in those areas from the spoils-system, was not an innovation in Chile at the time of the creation of CORFO. The practice went

---

[99] Varela Ortega, 2001: 422.
[100] The political compromise that was the basis for the creation of CORFO is analyzed by Silva in Chapter 12 of the present volume. See also Orihuela's Chapter 5.
[101] Centeno and Ferraro, 2017: 79–81.

back to the nineteenth century in the country, when nonpartisan experts began to be hired on a long-term basis for leading public policy roles. In some celebrated cases, those public policy experts were also foreigners, and this reinforced their nonpartisan reliability.[102]

In sum, the institutional blueprint of TVA as a model developmental agency could not work if a new public agency was to be considered part of the spoils, so that, with the next change of administration, most of the agency's management and technical staff were fired, and replaced by political appointees. The model didn't work under military dictatorships, either, because Latin American top military officers in government positions could never restrain themselves from interfering constantly with public policy decisions, and they were certainly very hostile towards citizens' participation in public policy.[103] The TVA blueprint for a succesful developmental agency turned out to be most useful and productive in a democratic political environment that supported a stable framework for professional public governance, such as in Chile. If state institutions were conceived as professional, nonpartisan champions of the public interest, instead of being part and parcel of the spoils of office, the TVA model had the potential to provide a key contribution for institutional design.

FINAL REMARK

Let us briefly summarize the comparison between Spain's developmental success and Latin America's reputed failure. First, as noted in the previous chapters, the Latin American developmental states actually accomplished a great deal. It was only when public institutions stopped being consistently developmentalist, and turned instead to arbitrary, erratic, and authoritarian policy styles, that they completely failed to live up to the promise of the institutional blueprints provided by TVA, CEPAL, and Spanish professional bureaucracies. The problem was not that Latin American states were too involved in the economy, but that they never cohered as stable, democratic institutional actors preserved from partisan conflict. False readings of this legacy would have long-term negative repercussions for the reform of Latin American state institutions in the following decades. Among others, we discuss the issue of recent state reforms, and their results, in the last book of the present three-volume series on state and nation making in Latin America and Spain. The focus of research in the third volume is the neoliberal state and its aftermath, from 1990 to the present.

---

[102] Centeno and Ferraro, 2013.
[103] See the first section above, as well as Chapter 3 and Chapter 7 in this volume.

REFERENCES

Adelman, Jeremy. *Worldly Philosopher. The Odyssey of Albert O. Hirschman.* Princeton and Oxford: Princeton University Press, 2013.
Adelman, Jeremy and Margarita Fajardo. "Between Capitalism and Democracy: A Study in the Political Economy of Ideas in Latin America, 1968–1980." *Latin American Research Review* 51, 3, 2016: 3–22.
Akin, William E. *Technocracy and the American Dream. The Technocrat Movement, 1900–1941.* Berkeley: University of California Press, 1971.
Alacevich, Michele. *The Political Economy of the World Bank. The Early Years* (trans. by IBRD/The World Bank). Palo Alto and Washington: Stanford University Press and The World Bank, 2009.
Arceneaux, Craig L. *Bounded Missions. Military Regimes and Democratization in the Southern Cone and Brazil.* University Park: The Pennsylvania State University Press, 2001.
Barkin, David and Timothy King. *Regional Economic Development: The River Basin Approach in Mexico.* London and New York: Cambridge University Press, 1970.
Boughton, James and Roger Sandilands. "Politics and the Attack on FDR's Economists: from the Grand Alliance to the Cold War." *Intelligence and National Security* 18, 3, 2003: 73–99.
Burnham, James. *The Managerial Revolution. What Is Happening in the World.* New York: John Day, 1941.
Burris, Beverly H. *Technocracy at Work.* Albany: SUNY Press, 1993.
Casanova, José V. "The Opus Dei Ethic, the Technocrats, and the Modernization of Spain." *Social Science Information* 22, 1, 1983: 27–50.
Centeno, Miguel A. and Agustin E. Ferraro. "Paper Leviathans. Historical Legacies and State Strength in Contemporary Latin America and Spain." In *State and Nation Making in Latin America and Spain. Republics of the Possible*, eds. Miguel A. Centeno and Agustin E. Ferraro. Cambridge and New York: Cambridge University Press, 2013: 399–416.
"With the Best of Intentions. Types of Developmental Failure in Latin America." In *Why Latin American Nations Fail. Development Strategies in the Twenty-First Century*, eds. Esteban Pérez Caldentey and Matías Vernengo. Oakland: University of California Press, 2017: 65–89.
Cole, William E. and John W. Mogab. "The Transfer of Soft Technologies to Less-Developed Countries: Some Implications for the Technology/Ceremony Dichotomy." *Journal of Economic Issues* 21, 1, 1987: 309–320.
Edwards, Sebastian and Alexandra Cox Edwards. *Monetarism and Liberalization. The Chilean Experiment.* Chicago and London: The University of Chicago Press, 1991.
Ekblad, David. *The Great American Mission: Modernization and the Construction of an American World Order.* Princeton University Press, 2010.
Fernandes, Ana Maria. "Neoliberalism and Economic Uncertainty in Brazil." In *Liberalization in the Developing World. Institutional and Economic Changes in Latin America, Africa and Asia*, eds. Alex E. Fernández Jilberto and André Mommen. London: Routledge, 1996: 96–121.

García Ruiz, José Luis. "La evolución de la industria automovilistica española, 1946–1999: una perspectiva comparada." *Revista de Historia Industrial*, 19–20, 2001: 133–163.

Germani, Gino. *Autoritarismo, fascismo e classi sociali*. Bologna: Il Mulino, 1975 (quoted from the English version *Authoritarianism, Fascism, and National Populism*. New Brunswick: Transaction Books, 1978).

González Videla, Gabriel. *Memorias, Vol. 2*. Santiago: Gabriela Mistral, 1975.

Hargrove, Erwin C. and Paul C. Conkin. *TVA. Fifty Years of Grass-Roots Bureaucracy*. Urbana and Chicago: University of Illinois Press, 1983.

Hirschman, Albert O. *Journeys Towards Progress. Studies of Economic Policy-Making in Latin America*. New York: The Twentieth Century Fund, 1963.
Development Projects Observed. Washington D.C.: The Brookings Institution, 2015 (first edn, 1967).
"The Turn to Authoritarianism in Latin America and the Search for Its Economic Determinants." In *The New Authoritarianism in Latin America*, ed. David Collier, Princeton University Press, 1979: 61–98.

Jaguaribe, Helio. *Political Development. A General Theory and a Latin American Case Study*. New York et al.: Harper & Row, 1973.

Jaksic, Iván. "Ideological Pragmatism and Non-Partisan Expertise in Nineteenth-Century Chile: Andrés Bello Contribution to State and Nation Building." In *State and Nation Making in Latin America and Spain. Republics of the Possible*, eds. Miguel A. Centeno and Agustin E. Ferraro, Cambridge and New York: Cambridge University Press, 2013: 183–202.

Katznelson, Ira. *Fear Itself: The New Deal and the Origins of Our Time*. New York: Liveright, 2013.

Kaufman, Robert R. "Industrial Change and Authoritarian Rule in Latin America: A Concrete Review of the Bureaucratic-Authoritarian Model." In *The New Authoritarianism in Latin America*, ed. David Collier, Princeton University Press, 1979: 165–244.

Kimball, Roger. "The Power of James Burnham." *The New Criterion*, September 2002, https://www.newcriterion.com/articles.cfm/burnham-kimball-1911 (accessed October 14, 2017).

Lilienthal, David. "Management – Responsible or Dominant?" *Public Administration Review*, 1, 4, 1941: 390–392.
TVA. Democracy on the March. New York and London: Harper & Brothers, 1944.

Linz, Juan J. "An Authoritarian Regime: The Case of Spain." In *Cleavages, Ideologies, and Party Systems: Contributions to Comparative Political Sociology*, eds. Erik Allardt and Yrkö Littunene, Helsinki: The Academic Bookstores, 1964: 251–283.

López Acero, Héctor F. "Lauchlin Currie y el desarrollo colombiano." *Criterio Libre* 9, 14, 2011: 21–42.

Lowndes, Joseph E. *From New Deal to the New Right: Race and the Southern Origins of Modern Conservatism*. New Haven: Yale University Press, 2009.

Ministerio de Agricultura (Colombia). *Creación y funcionamiento de las corporaciones autónomas regionales de desarrollo. Tomo 1*. Bogotá: Ministerio de Agricultura, 1985.

Ndiaye, Pap A. *Nylon and Bombs: DuPont and the March of Modern America* (trans. Elborg Forster). Baltimore: Johns Hopkins University Press, 2007.

Neuse, Steven M. "The TVA Dream. David Lilienthal in Latin America." *International Journal of Public Administration*, 15, 6, 1992: 1291–1324.

David E. *Lilienthal: The Journey of an American Liberal.* Knoxville: The University of Tennessee Press, 1996.

O'Donnell, Guillermo. *Modernización y autoritarismo.* Buenos Aires: Paidós, 1972 (quoted from the English version: *Modernization and Bureaucratic-Authoritarianism.* Berkeley: Institute of International Studies and University of California, 1973).

"Reflexiones sobre las tendencias generales de cambio en el Estado burocrático-autoritario" (Mimeograph). Documento CEDES/G.E. CLACSO/N°1. Buenos Aires: CEDES, 1975.

Peña Rodriguez, Martha Liliana. "El Programa CINVA y la acción comunal." *Bitácora* 12, 1, 2008: 185–192.

Pinto Santa Cruz, Aníbal. "Estado y gran empresa. De la precrisis hasta el gobierno de Jorge Alessandri." Colección Estudios CIEPLAN 16 (June) 1985: 5–40, www.cieplan.org/media/publicaciones/archivos/69/Capitulo_4.pdf (accessed June 2, 2018).

Posada, Antonio and Jeanne Anderson Posada. *The CVC Challenge to Underdevelopment and Traditionalism.* Bogotá: Ediciones Tercer Mundo, 1966.

Prebisch, Raúl. 1949. "El desarrollo económico de la América Latina y algunos de sus principales problemas." Document issued by the United Nations Economic and Social Council, Mimeo, UN Symbol: E/CN.12/89, May 14, 1949, (quoted from the English version, *The Economic Development of Latin America and Its Principal Problems.* Lake Success: United Nations Department of Economic Affairs, 1950).

Riggirozzi, Pia. "After Neoliberalism in Argentina. Reasserting Nationalism in an Open Economy." In *Governance after Neoliberalism in Argentina*, eds. Jean Grugel and Pia Riggirozzi. Houndmills and New York: Palgrave Macmillan, 2009: 89–112.

Rist, Gilbert. *The History of Development. From Western Origins to Global Faith* (3rd edn). London and New York: Zed Books, 2008.

Robinson, Niklas F. "Revolutionizing The River: The Politics of Water Management in Southeastern Mexico, 1951–1974." Unpublished PhD dissertation, Ann Arbor: Tulane University, 2007. (ProQuest document ID 304785437.)

Rock, David. *Authoritarian Argentina. The Nationalist Movement, its History and its Impact.* Berkeley: University of California Press: 1993.

Sandilands, Roger J. *The Life and Political Economy of Lauchlin Currie. New Dealer, Presidential Adviser, and Development Economist.* Durham and London: Duke University Press, 1990.

Saunders, Frances Stonor. *The Cultural Cold War. The CIA and the World of Arts and Letters.* New York and London: The New Press, 2013 (originally published as Saunders, Frances Stonor. *Who Paid the Piper? The CIA and the Cultural Cold War.* London: Granta Books, 1999).

Schrecker, Ellen. *Many Are the Crimes: McCarthyism in America.* Boston: Little Brown, 1998.

Schwarz, Jordan A. *The New Dealers: Power Politics in the Age of Roosevelt.* New York: Knopf, 1993.

Selznick, Philip. *TVA and the Grass Roots. A Study in the Sociology of Formal Organization.* Berkeley and Los Angeles: University of California Press, 1949.

Serra, José. "Three Mistaken Theses Regarding the Connection between Industrialization and Authoritarian Regimes." In *The New Authoritarianism in Latin America*, ed. David Collier, Princeton University Press, 1979: 99–164.

Skidmore, Thomas. *The Politics of Military Rule in Brazil 1964–1985.* Oxford University Press, 1988.

Smith, Jason Scott. *Building New Deal Liberalism: The Political Economy of Public Works, 1933–1956.* Cambridge University Press, 2006.

Smith, William C. *Authoritarianism and the Crisis of the Argentine Political Economy.* Stanford University Press, 1989.

Stepan, Alfred, ed. *Authoritarian Brazil. Origins, Policies, and Future.* New Haven and London: Yale University Press, 1973.

The Times Recorder (Zanesville, Ohio). "Returns Call." April 10, 1947, front page. https://newspaperarchive.com/zanesville-times-recorder-apr-10–1947/.

Tobey, Ronald C. *Technology as Freedom: The New Deal and the Electrical Modernization of the American Home.* University of California Press, 1996.

Torre, Juan Carlos and Liliana de Riz. "Argentina since 1946." In *The Cambridge History of Latin America. Volume III. Latin America Since 1930*, ed. Leslie Bethell, Cambridge University Press, 1991: 73–194.

TVA Technical Library. *TVA as a Symbol of Resource Development in Many Countries.* Mimeograph. Knoxville: TVA, 1952.

Valencia, Luis Emiro. *Historia, realidad y pensamiento de la acción comunal en Colombia 1958–2008.* Bogotá: Escuela Superior de Administración Pública, 2009.

Varela Ortega, José. *Los amigos políticos: partidos, elecciones y caciquismo en la Restauración, 1875–1900.* Madrid: Marcial Pons, 2001.

Vélez Álvarez, Luis Guillermo. "Lauchlin Currie: el maestro de los economistas colombianos." *Lecturas de Economía* 79, July–December 2013: 233–239.

Wang, Jessica. *American Science in an Age of Anxiety. Scientists, Anticommunism, and the Cold War.* Chapell Hill and London: The University of North Carolina Press, 1999.

Watson, Thomas John, ed. *Campeón de la Democracia. Visita del Excelentísimo Señor Don Gabriel González Videla, Presidente de la República de Chile, a los Estados Unidos de América. Documentos Históricos.* N.p.: International Business Machines Corporation, 1951.

Index